Sybex's Quick Tour

Minimize **Maximize** **Close**

Start button   *Documents*   *A folder*   *Taskbar*   *Shortcuts*   *Speaker volume*   *Time & date*

The Desktop *is where your programs, files, and shortcuts reside.*

My Computer *allows you to browse the contents of your computer, open folders, open documents, and run programs.*

Network Neighborhood *gives you direct access to other computers (and shared resources, such as printers).*

The Microsoft Network *dials up your connection to Microsoft's online service.*

The Internet *starts up the Internet Explorer, a World Wide Web browser (available only with Plus!).*

Inbox *starts Microsoft Exchange and opens your inbox, so you can see if you have any new mail.*

My Briefcase *is a new feature for keeping documents consistent as you move them between computers.*

Recycle Bin *makes it easy to delete and undelete files.*

The Start button *pops up the Start menu, from which you can run just about every program.*

The Taskbar *displays a button for every running program.*

Create **shortcuts** *on your Desktop for frequently used programs and documents.*

Every window has a **Minimize, Maximize** *(alternating with Restore), and* **Close** *button. The Close button is new; the others just look different.*

FORMATTING A FLOPPY DISK

To format a floppy disk, first double-click the My Computer icon. Put the floppy in the disk drive. Then right-click the 3½ Floppy icon in the My Computer window and choose Format. The Format dialog box appears.

If you want some density other than the standard 1.44MB, click the Capacity drop-down list box and choose another option. To give the disk a label, click in the Label box and type one. Then click Start.

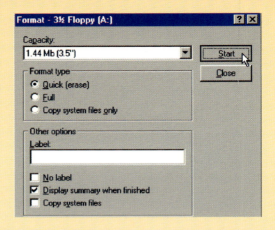

USEFUL KEYBOARD SHORTCUTS

TASK	KEYSTROKE
Get help	F1
Quit a program	Alt+F4
Pop up shortcut menu for selected item	Shift+F10
Pop up the Start menu	Ctrl+Esc
Cut a selection	Ctrl+X
Copy a selection	Ctrl+C
Paste a selection	Ctrl+V
Delete a selection	Delete
Undo the last action	Ctrl+Z
Select all items in window	Ctrl+A
Refresh a window	F5
Open folder one level up from current one	Backspace
Close a folder and all its parents	Shift and click Close button
Rename a selection	F2
Find a file starting with current folder	F3
Delete a selection without putting it in Recycle Bin (be careful!)	Shift+Delete
View a selection's properties	Alt+Enter or Alt+double-click
Copy an icon	Ctrl+click and drag
Create a shortcut from an icon	Ctrl+Shift+click and drag

Sybex Inc.
2021 Challenger Drive
Alameda, CA 94501
Tel: 510-523-8233 · 800-227-2346
Fax: 510-523-2373

© 1995 SYBEX Inc.

Mastering
1-2-3 97 Edition
for Windows 95

Mastering™ 1-2-3® 97 Edition for Windows® 95

Douglas Hergert

SYBEX®

San Francisco • Paris • Düsseldorf • Soest

Associate Publisher: Amy Romanoff
Acquisitions Manager: Kristine Plachy
Acquisitions & Developmental Editor: Richard Mills
Editor: Vivian Perry
Project Editor: Linda Good
Technical Editor: Don Hergert
Book Design Director: Cătălin Dulfu
Book Designer: Suzanne Albertson
Electronic Publishing Specialist: Kate Kaminski
Production Coordinator: Nathan Johanson
Production Assistant: Michael Tom
Indexer: Nancy Guenther
Cover Designer: Design Site
Cover Photographer: Mark Johann
Photo Art Direction: Ingalls & Associates

Screen reproductions produced with Collage Plus.
Collage Plus is a trademark of Inner Media Inc.

SYBEX is a registered trademark of SYBEX Inc.

Mastering is a trademark of SYBEX Inc.

1-2-3 is a registered trademark of Lotus Development Corporation.

TRADEMARKS: SYBEX has attempted throughout this book to distinguish proprietary trademarks from descriptive terms by following the capitalization style used by the manufacturer.

The author and publisher have made their best efforts to prepare this book, and the content is based upon final release software whenever possible. Portions of the manuscript may be based upon pre-release versions supplied by software manufacturer(s). The author and the publisher make no representation or warranties of any kind with regard to the completeness or accuracy of the contents herein and accept no liability of any kind including but not limited to performance, merchantability, fitness for any particular purpose, or any losses or damages of any kind caused or alleged to be caused directly or indirectly from this book.

An earlier version of this book was published under the title *Understanding 1-2-3 Release 5 for Windows* copyright ©1994 SYBEX Inc.

Copyright ©1997 SYBEX Inc., 1151 Marina Village Parkway, Alameda, CA 94501. World rights reserved. No part of this publication may be stored in a retrieval system, transmitted, or reproduced in any way, including but not limited to photocopy, photograph, magnetic or other record, without the prior agreement and written permission of the publisher.

Library of Congress Card Number: 96-71019

ISBN: 0-7821-1771-6

Manufactured in the United States of America

10 9 8 7 6 5 4 3 2

Acknowledgments

This book represents the talents of many able contributors. Guy Hart-Davis originally developed and wrote the eight appendixes, and Don Hergert updated them for 1-2-3 97 Edition. Richard Mills made many helpful suggestions at the outset. Vivian Perry completed a smooth and graceful copy edit. Linda Good guided the book through the various steps of publication. Don Hergert kept an eye on technical accuracy. Nathan Johanson served as the Production Coordinator, and Kate Kaminski was the Electronic Publishing Specialist. Claudette Moore of Moore Literary Agency offered advice and encouragement. In addition, the following people worked on the book's previous editions: Peter Weverka, Val Potter, Adebisi Oladipupo, David Clark, Dianne King, Christian Crumlish, Savitha Varadan, and Sheila Dienes. My sincere thanks to all.

Contents at a Glance

Introduction		xxi
Part One: 1-2-3 on the Windows 95 Desktop		**1**
Chapter 1:	The Elements of 1-2-3	2
Chapter 2:	1-2-3, Windows, and the Web	46
Part Two: The Components of 1-2-3		**87**
Chapter 3:	Worksheet Basics: Entering Data	88
Chapter 4:	Worksheet Basics: Organizing Data and Writing Formulas	120
Chapter 5:	Formatting Data	148
Chapter 6:	Presenting and Printing Data	178
Chapter 7:	Formulas and Functions	212
Chapter 8:	Categories of Functions	242
Chapter 9:	Introduction to Charts	292
Chapter 10:	Chart Types and Maps	314
Chapter 11:	Database Tables	342
Chapter 12:	Database Queries	364
Chapter 13:	Database Calculations	390
Chapter 14:	Scripts	412
Part Three: More 1-2-3 Features		**435**
Chapter 15:	Versions and Team Computing	436
Chapter 16:	Worksheet Tools	460
Chapter 17:	Links between Files	496

Part Four: Appendixes — 517

Appendix A:	An Overview of 1-2-3's Functions	518
Appendix B:	Calendar Functions Reference	542
Appendix C:	Database Functions Reference	566
Appendix D:	Engineering Functions Reference	582
Appendix E:	Financial Functions Reference	594
Appendix F:	Information, Logical, and Lookup Functions Reference	642
Appendix G:	Mathematical and Statistical Functions Reference	688
Appendix H:	Text Functions Reference	784
	Index	811

Table of Contents

	Introduction	xxi
Part One ▶	***1-2-3 on the Windows 95 Desktop***	**1**
Chapter 1	**The Elements of 1-2-3**	**2**
	Lotus 1-2-3: The Basics	5
	The Worksheet	7
	The Menu Bar	11
	Adding Sheets to a Workbook	13
	SmartIcons, Shortcut Menus, and the Status Bar	16
	The 1-2-3 Classic Window	20
	Entering Data	21
	Exiting 1-2-3	23
	Planning and Creating a Worksheet	23
	Developing a Worksheet	25
	Entering the Labels and Data	25
	Writing Formulas	27
	Preparing the Worksheet for Presentation	32
	Making Changes in the Data	34
	Creating Charts	37
	Designing a Chart	37
	Creating a Chart	38
	Performing Database Operations	40
	Defining a Database	41
	Sorting and Querying the Database	42
	Summary	44
Chapter 2	**1-2-3, Windows, and the Web**	**46**
	Exploring the 1-2-3 Window	48
	Title Bar and Control Buttons	49
	The 1-2-3 Menus	54
	Shortcut Menus	56
	Using an InfoBox	58

The Edit Line	63
The SmartIcons	67
Sheet Tabs	73
The Status Bar	75
Getting Help	77
Finding Context-Sensitive Help	79
Help Window Features	80
Using the Help Index	82
1-2-3 and the Internet	84
Finding Information on the Web	84
Summary	85

Part Two ▶ The Components of 1-2-3 — 87

Chapter 3 Worksheet Basics: Entering Data — 88

Developing a Worksheet	92
Entering Labels	92
Entering Values and Computing Totals	97
Selecting Ranges	100
Creating Range Names	107
Copying a Range of Values	110
Saving the Workbook	114
Saving a Workbook File	115
Summary	118

Chapter 4 Worksheet Basics: Organizing Data and Writing Formulas — 120

Changing the Worksheet	123
Moving Ranges of Data	123
Inserting Rows and Columns	127
Working with Formulas	130
Entering Formulas	131
Copying Formulas	134
Controlling the Order of Operations	143
Examining "What-If" Scenarios	145
Summary	147

Chapter 5 Formatting Data — 148

Working on an Existing Sheet	150
Using the Go To Command	150
Changing the Appearance of a Sheet	152
Setting Column Widths	153
Hiding Columns	158

Table of Contents

Aligning Data	160
Freezing Worksheet Titles on the Screen	166
Changing the Workbook Properties	168
Formatting Numeric Values	170
Using Common Numeric Formats	172
Selecting Sheet and Range Formats	173
Summary	176

Chapter 6   Presenting and Printing Data   178

Working with Dates in a Sheet	180
Performing Date Arithmetic	183
Entering Time Values into a Worksheet	187
Performing Time Arithmetic	189
Preventing Accidental Revisions	193
Creating a Finished Document	197
Font Sizes, Type Styles, Shadings, and Borders	198
Defining Style Names	202
Printing a Worksheet	204
Selecting Print Settings	207
Printing the Conference Workbook	210
Summary	211

Chapter 7   Formulas and Functions   212

How Functions Work	214
Filling Ranges with Sample Data	216
Creating a Custom SmartFill List	218
Writing Formulas	220
Documenting Formulas with Cell Comments	222
Understanding the Categories of Formulas	225
Finding Errors in Formulas	233
Using Functions	235
Entering a Function into a Cell	236
Summary	241

Chapter 8   Categories of Functions   242

Statistical Functions	244
Financial Functions	248
Depreciation Functions	248
Other Financial Functions	251
Mathematical Functions	256
Trigonometric Functions	257
Exponential and Logarithmic Functions	259
The @RAND Function	260

	More Mathematical Functions	266
	Date and Time Functions	269
	Working with Date and Time Functions	272
	Logical Functions	277
	The @IF function	277
	Text Functions	280
	Lookup Functions	286
	Summary	289
Chapter 9	**Introduction to Charts**	**292**
	Developing a Chart	296
	Understanding Data Series	297
	Creating the Profits Chart	299
	Moving and Resizing a Chart	301
	Changing the Elements of the Chart	303
	Changing the Data Series and the Chart Type	307
	Performing What-If Experiments with a Chart	310
	Adding Drawn Objects to a Chart	311
	Summary	312
Chapter 10	**Chart Types and Maps**	**314**
	Working with Other Chart Types	316
	Creating Line Charts and Area Charts	316
	Creating Pie Charts	322
	Setting the Default Chart Type	329
	Creating XY Charts	331
	Creating Mixed Charts	332
	Creating HLCO Charts	334
	Creating Radar Charts	336
	Maps	337
	Creating a Map	339
	Summary	341
Chapter 11	**Database Tables**	**342**
	Creating a Database Table	344
	Creating a Database	348
	Creating Calculated Fields	349
	Creating Multiple Tables in a Database	350
	Defining Range Names for Database Tables	352
	Sorting a Database	353
	Using the Sort Command	355
	Sorting by More Than One Key Field	357
	Summary	362

Table of Contents

Chapter 12	**Database Queries**	**364**
	Creating and Using a Query	367
	Copying Selected Data to an Output Range	368
	Finding Records That Match Multiple Criteria	370
	Using a Query to Delete Records	374
	Updating the Linked Database Table	375
	Joining Two Database Tables	378
	Other Database Objects	383
	Using a Form	384
	Creating Mailing Labels	386
	Summary	388
Chapter 13	**Database Calculations**	**390**
	Calculations on Numeric Fields	392
	Understanding the Database Functions	393
	Creating a Report with Groups and Totals	399
	Using the Crosstab Command	403
	Querying an External Database	406
	Summary	409
Chapter 14	**Scripts**	**412**
	Recording Scripts	415
	Examining the Lines of a Recorded Script	417
	Running a Script	419
	Creating an Action Menu and Shortcuts	421
	Using Scripts as Procedures	423
	Creating a SmartIcon for a Script	425
	Designing Scripts for Other Actions	428
	Creating a Random-Number Script	429
	Creating a Button for a Script	430
	Summary	433

Part Three ▶ More 1-2-3 Features   435

Chapter 15	**Versions and Team Computing**	**436**
	Preparing a Sample Worksheet	438
	Understanding Versions	441
	The Range ➤ Version Commands	441
	Defining Versions	444
	Choosing a Version	447
	Displaying Versions	449
	Creating Groups of Versions	451

	Creating a Report from Versions	454
	Developing Versions by Team	456
	Summary	459
Chapter 16	**Worksheet Tools**	**460**
	Using SmartMasters	462
	Creating a Worksheet from a SmartMaster	463
	The Range ➤ Analyze Menu	465
	Using the What-If Table Command	466
	Using the Backsolver Command	474
	Using the Distribution Command	476
	Using the Regression Command	478
	Using the Matrix Commands	481
	Outlining	489
	Summary	494
Chapter 17	**Links between Files**	**496**
	Creating Links between Workbooks	499
	Using File References	500
	Building a "Totals" Workbook	501
	Revising a Source Workbook	504
	Updating Files	506
	Combining Files	508
	Creating Links between Documents	510
	Transferring Data from a Workbook	510
	Summary	515
Part Four ▶	***Appendixes***	***517***
Appendix A	**An Overview of 1-2-3's Functions**	**518**
	Using Functions	519
	Entering Functions into Cells	519
	Getting Help with Functions	520
	The Elements of a Function	520
	1-2-3 Functions Quick Reference	521
Appendix B	**Calendar Functions Reference**	**542**
	Overview of the Calendar Functions	542
	Descriptions of the Calendar Functions	545
	@D360(*start-date,end-date*)	545
	@DATE(*year,month,day*)	547
	@DATEDIF(*start-date,end-date,format*)	548

	@DATEINFO(*date,attribute*)	550
	@DATESTRING(*date-number*)	551
	@DATEVALUE(*text*)	551
	@DAY(*date-number*)	552
	@DAYS(*start-date,end-date,[basis]*)	553
	@DAYS360(*start-date,end-date*)	554
	@HOUR(*time-number*)	555
	@MINUTE(*time-number*)	556
	@MONTH(*date-number*)	556
	@NETWORKDAYS(*start-date,end-date,[holidays-range],[weekends]*)	557
	@NEXTMONTH(*start-date,months,[day-of-month],[basis]*)	558
	@NOW	560
	@SECOND(*time-number*)	560
	@TIME(*hour,minutes,seconds*)	561
	@TIMEVALUE(*text*)	561
	@TODAY	562
	@WEEKDAY(*date-number*)	563
	@WORKDAY(*start-date,days,[holidays-range],[weekends]*)	563
	@YEAR(*date-number*)	565
Appendix C	**Database Functions Reference**	**566**
	Overview of the Database Functions	567
	Arguments for the Database Functions	568
	Descriptions of the Database Functions	569
	@DAVG(*input,field,[criteria]*)	569
	@DCOUNT(*input,field,[criteria]*)	570
	@DGET(*input,field,[criteria]*)	572
	@DMAX(*input,field,[criteria]*)	573
	@DMIN(*input,field,[criteria]*)	574
	@DPURECOUNT(*input,field,[criteria]*)	575
	@DSTD(*input,field,[criteria]*)	577
	@DSTDS(*input,field,[criteria]*)	578
	@DSUM(*input,field,[criteria]*)	578
	@DVAR(*input,field,[criteria]*)	579
	@DVARS(*input,field,[criteria]*)	581
Appendix D	**Engineering Functions Reference**	**582**
	Overview of the Engineering Functions	582
	Descriptions of the Engineering Functions	583
	@BESSELI(*numeric_value,order*)	584
	@BESSELJ(*numeric_value,order*)	585
	@BESSELK(*numeric_value,order*)	585

	@BESSELY(*numeric_value,order*)	585
	@BETA(*numeric_value1,numeric_value2*)	586
	@BETAI(*numeric_value1,numeric_value2,numeric_value3*)	586
	@DECIMAL(*hexadecimal*)	586
	@ERF(*lower-limit,[upper-limit]*)	588
	@ERFC(*numeric_value*)	588
	@ERFD(*numeric_value*)	589
	@GAMMA(*numeric_value*)	590
	@GAMMAI (*numeric_value1,numeric_value2,[complement]*)	590
	@GAMMALN(*numeric_value*)	591
	@HEX(*number*)	591
	@SERIESSUM(*value,power,increment,coefficients*)	592
Appendix E	**Financial Functions Reference**	**594**
	Overview of the Financial Functions	594
	Descriptions of the Financial Functions	598
	@ACCRUED(*settlement,issue,first-interest,coupon,[par], [frequency],[basis]*)	598
	@CTERM(*interest,future-value,present-value*)	600
	@DB(*cost,salvage,life,period*)	601
	@DDB(*cost,salvage,life,period*)	602
	@DURATION(*settlement,maturity,coupon,yield,[frequency],[basis]*)	604
	@FV(*payments,interest,term*)	606
	@FVAL(*payments,interest,term,[type],[present-value]*)	606
	@IPAYMT(*principal,interest,term,start-period,[end-period], [type],[future-value]*)	608
	@IRATE(*term,payment,present-value,[type],[future-value],[guess]*)	610
	@IRR(*guess,range*)	611
	@MDURATION(*settlement,maturity,coupon,yield,[frequency],[basis]*)	614
	@MIRR(*range,finance-rate,reinvest-rate*)	615
	@NPER(*payments,interest,future-value,[type],[present-value]*)	617
	@NPV(*interest,range,[type]*)	619
	@PAYMT(*principal,interest,term,[type],[future-value]*)	620
	@PMT(*principal,interest,term*)	622
	@PMTC(*principal,interest,term*)	623
	@PPAYMT(*principal,interest,term,start-period,[end-period], [type],[future-value]*)	624
	@PRICE (*settlement,maturity,coupon,yield,[redemption], [frequency],[basis]*)	626
	@PV(*payments,interest,term*)	628
	@PVAL(*payments,interest,term,[type],[future-value]*)	629
	@RATE(*future-value,present-value,term*)	630
	@SLN(*cost,salvage,life*)	631

	@SYD(*cost,salvage,life,period*)	632
	@TERM(*payments,interest,future-value*)	634
	@VDB(*cost,salvage,life,start-period,end-period,* [*depreciation-factor*],[*switch*])	636
	@YIELD(*settlement,maturity,coupon,price,*[*redemption*], [*frequency*],[*basis*])	639
Appendix F	**Information, Logical, and Lookup Functions Reference**	**642**
	Overview of the Information Functions	643
	Descriptions of the Information Functions	644
	@CELL(*attribute,location*)	644
	@CELLPOINTER(*attribute*)	647
	@COLS(*range*)	648
	@COORD(*worksheet,column,row,absolute*)	648
	@DATALINK(*app-name,topic-name,item-name,* [*format*],[*max-rows*], [*max-cols*],[*max-sheets*])	649
	@ERR	651
	@INFO(*attribute*)	651
	@NA	654
	@RANGENAME(*cell*)	655
	@REFCONVERT(*reference*)	656
	@ROWS(*range*)	656
	@SCENARIOINFO(*option,name,*[*creator*])	657
	@SCENARIOLAST(*file-name*)	658
	@SHEETS(*range*)	659
	@VERSIONCURRENT(*range*)	659
	@VERSIONDATA(*option,cell,version-range,name,*[*creator*])	660
	@VERSIONINFO(*option,name,*[*creator*])	661
	Overview of the Logical Functions	662
	Descriptions of the Logical Functions	664
	@FALSE	664
	@IF(*condition,true,false*)	664
	@ISAAF(*name*)	666
	@ISAPP(*name*)	667
	@ISBETWEEN(*value;bound1;bound2;*[*inclusion*])	667
	@ISEMPTY(*location*)	667
	@ISERR(*value*)	668
	@ISFILE(*file-name,*[*type*])	668
	@ISMACRO(*name*)	670
	@ISNA(*value*)	670
	@ISNUMBER(*value*)	670
	@ISRANGE(*range*)	671
	@ISSTRING(*value*)	672
	@TRUE	672

Overview of the Lookup Functions 674
Descriptions of the Lookup Functions 675
   @@(*location*) 675
   @CHOOSE(*value,list*) 676
   @HLOOKUP(*key,range,row-offset*) 677
   @INDEX(*range,column,row,[worksheet]*) 678
   @MATCH (*cell-contents,range,[type]*) 681
   @MAXLOOKUP(*range-list*) 682
   @MINLOOKUP(*range-list*) 682
   @N(*range*) 683
   @VLOOKUP(*key,range,row-offset*) 684
   @XINDEX(*range,column,row,[worksheet]*) 686

Appendix G   Mathematical and Statistical Functions Reference   688

Overview of the Mathematical Functions 688
Descriptions of the Mathematical Functions 692
   @ABS(*number*) 692
   @ACOS(*number*) 693
   @ACOSH(*number*) 693
   @ACOT(*number*) 694
   @ACOTH(*number*) 694
   @ACSC(*number*) 694
   @ACSCH(*numeric-value*) 695
   @ASEC(*numeric-value*) 695
   @ASECH(*numeric-value*) 695
   @ASIN(*numeric-value*) 696
   @ASINH(*numeric-value*) 696
   @ATAN(*numeric-value*) 697
   @ATAN2(*numeric-value1,numeric-value2*) 697
   @ATANH(*numeric-value*) 698
   @COS(*numeric-value*) 698
   @COSH(*numeric-value*) 699
   @COT(*numeric-value*) 699
   @COTH(*numeric-value*) 700
   @CSC(*numeric-value*) 701
   @CSCH(*numeric-value*) 701
   @DECILE(*tile;range*) 702
   @DEGTORAD(*degrees*) 703
   @EVEN(*numeric-value*) 703
   @EXP(*numeric-value*) 704
   @EXP2(*numeric-value*) 704
   @FACT(*number*) 705
   @FACTLN(*number*) 705

@INT(*numeric-value*)	705
@LARGE(*range,number*)	706
@LN(*numeric-value*)	707
@LOG(*numeric-value*)	708
@MOD(*number,divisor*),@MODULO(*number,divisor*)	708
@ODD(*numeric-value*)	709
@PI	709
@QUARTILE(*tile;range*)	709
@QUOTIENT(*number,divisor*)	710
@RAND	711
@RADTODEG(*radians*)	712
@REGRESSION(*x-range,y-range,attribute,[compute]*)	712
@ROUND(*numeric-value,number*)	714
@ROUNDDOWN(*numeric-value,[number],[direction]*)	715
@ROUNDM(*numeric-value,multiple,[direction]*)	716
@ROUNDUP(*numeric-value,[number],[direction]*)	718
@SEC(*numeric-value*)	719
@SECH(*numeric-value*)	719
@SIGN(*numeric-value*)	720
@SIN(*numeric-value*)	720
@SINH(*numeric-value*)	721
@SEMEAN(*range*)	721
@SMALL(*range,number*)	721
@SQRT(*numeric-value*)	722
@SQRTPI(*numeric-value*)	723
@SUBTOTAL(*list*)	723
@SUM(*list*)	724
@SUMPRODUCT(*list*)	725
@SUMSQ(*list*)	726
@SUMXMY2	726
@TAN(*numeric-value*)	727
@TANH(*numeric-value*)	727
@TRUNC(*numeric-value,[decimal]*)	728
Overview of the Statistical Functions	729
Descriptions of the Statistical Functions	733
@AVEDEV(*list*)	733
@AVG(*list*)	733
@BINOMIAL(*trials,successes,probability,[type]*)	734
@CHIDIST(*numeric-value,degrees_freedom,[type]*)	736
@CHITEST(*range1,[range2]*)	737
@COMBIN(*number,number_chosen*)	738
@CORREL(*range1,range2*)	739

Function	Page
@COUNT(*list*)	739
@COV(*range1,range2,[type]*)	740
@CRITBINOMIAL(*trials,probability,alpha*)	741
@DEVSQ(*list*)	742
@FDIST(*numeric-value,degrees-freedom1,degrees-freedom2,[type]*)	742
@FORCAST(*a,range1,range2*)	743
@FTEST(*range1,range2*)	744
@GEOMEAN(*list*)	744
@GRANDTOTAL(*list*)	745
@HARMEAN(*list*)	746
@KURTOSIS(*range,[type]*)	747
@MAX(*list*)	748
@MEDIAN(*list*)	749
@MIN(*list*)	749
@NORMAL(*numeric-value,[mean],[std],[type]*)	750
@PERMUT(*number-object,number-chosen*)	751
@PERCENTILE(*numeric-value,range*)	752
@POISSON(*number,mean,[cumulative]*)	753
@PRANK(*numeric-value,range,[places]*)	754
@PRODUCT(*list*)	756
@PUREAVG (*list*)	756
@PURECOUNT(*list*)	757
@PUREMAX(*list*)	757
@PUREMEDIAN(*list*)	758
@PUREMIN(*list*)	759
@PURESTD(*list*)	760
@PURESTDS(*list*)	761
@PUREVAR(*list*)	763
@PUREVARS(*list*)	764
@RANK(*item,range,[order]*)	766
@SKEWNESS(*range,[type]*)	767
@STD(*list*)	768
@STDS(*list*)	770
@SUMNEGATIVE(*list*)	771
@SUMPOSITIVE(*list*)	772
@TDIST(*numeric-value,degrees-freedom,[type],[tails]*)	773
@TTEST(*range1,range2,[type],[tails]*)	774
@VAR(*list*)	776
@VARS(*list*)	778
@WEIGHTAVG(*data-range,weights-range,[type]*)	780
@ZTEST(*range1,mean1,std1,[tails],[range2],[mean2],[std2]*)	781

| Appendix H | **Text Functions Reference** | **784** |

Overview of the Text Functions — 784
Descriptions of the Text Functions — 788
    @CHAR(*code*) — 788
    @CLEAN(*"text"*) — 789
    @CODE(*text*) — 789
    @EXACT(*text1,text2*) — 789
    @FIND(*search-text,text,start-number*) — 790
    @LEFT(*text,number*) — 792
    @LENGTH(*text*) — 793
    @LOWER(*text*) — 795
    @MID(*text,start-number,number*) — 796
    @PROPER — 798
    @REPEAT(*text,number*) — 799
    @REPLACE(*original-text,start-number, number,new-text*) — 800
    @RIGHT(*text,number*) — 802
    @S(*range*) — 803
    @SETSTRING(*text,length,[alignment]*) — 804
    @STRING(*numeric-value,decimal*) — 806
    @TRIM(*text*) — 807
    @UPPER(*text*) — 807
    @VALUE(*text*) — 809

Index — **811**

Introduction

1-2-3 97 Edition is the latest version of the popular and enduring spreadsheet software from Lotus. This book guides you through the stages of mastering this powerful program. In a sequence of tutorial-style chapters you'll master all the essential details of 1-2-3 while you work through complete business examples on your own computer. In these hands-on exercises you'll learn to:

- ▶ Produce clear, accurate, and flexible workbook documents
- ▶ Generate presentation-quality charts from worksheet data
- ▶ Build accessible databases and use Approach—the companion Lotus database management program—to perform varieties of query operations on your worksheet data
- ▶ Record script programs to streamline everyday tasks in 1-2-3

Along the way, you'll discover many features that Lotus has introduced in 1-2-3 97 Edition—including tabbed InfoBoxes that simplify the process of changing the properties of sheets, charts, and databases; effective mouse techniques that make your work faster and easier; Internet support and team computing tools; and many visual and functional improvements in the 1-2-3 user interface.

Each chapter in this book begins with a feature called Fast Track, designed both as a preview of the material to come and a quick-reference guide to essential 1-2-3 procedures. In addition, you'll find hundreds of screen illustrations, showing you exactly what happens in 1-2-3 when you perform the steps of specific operations.

The book is divided into three parts, followed by appendixes. The two chapters of Part One give you an introductory overview.

Chapter 1, "The Elements of 1-2-3," presents illustrations of the spreadsheet, charting, and database components of 1-2-3, previewing the features you'll be studying individually in later chapters. In the hands-on portion of Chapter 1, you'll begin exploring the interface that makes 1-2-3 easier to use than ever before.

Chapter 2, "1-2-3, Windows, and the Web," highlights the elements of 1-2-3 in the Windows 95 environment and introduces 1-2-3's connections to the World Wide Web. In addition, you'll take a first look at the comprehensive Help tools that are included with 1-2-3.

Part Two contains twelve chapters that introduce the basics of 1-2-3—the spreadsheet, the charting and mapping capabilities, the database, and scripts.

Chapter 3, "Worksheet Basics: Entering Data," takes you through the initial steps of building a worksheet for a business application. You'll learn how to enter labels and numeric data into the worksheet; to calculate totals; to perform important range operations, such as assigning range names and moving data; and to save your work to disk.

Chapter 4, "Worksheet Basics: Organizing Data and Writing Formulas," shows you how to write effective formulas and copy them from one location to another in the worksheet. Along the way, you'll master the essential distinctions between absolute, relative, and mixed references in formulas; and you'll learn how to plan a worksheet as an effective what-if tool.

Chapter 5, "Formatting Data," continues your introduction to basic spreadsheet operations. You'll learn to apply formats and type styles to numbers and labels on your worksheet, and to make adjustments in the appearance of the worksheet itself to accommodate your data.

Chapter 6, "Presenting and Printing Data," guides you through the steps of printing your worksheet, producing effective presentations of your data on paper. You'll also begin working with date and time values, and you'll learn the tools and techniques of date and time arithmetic.

Chapter 7, "Formulas and Functions," introduces you to the large library of calculation tools that 1-2-3 provides for your use in worksheets. You'll expand your understanding of numeric, chronological, logical, and text formulas, and of built-in functions you can use to simplify calculations.

Chapter 8, "Categories of Functions," is a survey of 1-2-3's collections of built-in @ functions for uses in specific applications—including statistical, financial, mathematical, chronological, logical, string, and lookup functions. This chapter includes many worksheet exercises for you to examine and work with as you master the use of these important spreadsheet tools.

Chapter 9, "Introduction to Charts," helps you explore the tools and techniques available for creating, editing, and manipulating chart objects. You'll find out how to add drawn objects such as arrows and boxes to a chart. You'll also learn to use a chart as a tool for exploring what-if scenarios.

Chapter 10, "Chart Types and Maps," shows you how to create varieties of charts from numeric data—including line charts, area charts, pie and doughnut charts, XY charts, mixed charts, HLCO charts, and radar charts. Finally, you'll learn to use 1-2-3's map feature to create visual representations of geographical data.

Chapter 11, "Database Tables," takes up the third major component in 1-2-3, the database management tools. This chapter introduces you to essential database concepts, and guides you through a series of hands-on exercises in which you'll create and work with a database. In particular, you'll learn to define fields, enter records, and to create calculated fields.

Chapter 12, "Database Queries," shows you how to use the resources of Lotus Approach to create a query table from a database. You'll learn to extract a subset of records and fields from a single database, and to use the query for a variety of database operations. You'll also see what it means to *join* information from two or more database tables.

Chapter 13, "Database Calculations," teaches you more about database capabilities available from 1-2-3 and Approach. You'll learn to use the special library of statistical functions designed for database queries, including @DCOUNT, @DSUM, @DAVG, @DSTD, and @DGET. You'll also learn the steps for creating reports and crosstab tables from a database, and for performing queries on external databases.

Chapter 14, "Scripts," shows you how to create your own library of 1-2-3 scripts to streamline your work with worksheets, charts, and databases. By recording a script, you can reduce the steps for almost any 1-2-3 procedure to a simple pair of keystrokes. For example, you'll learn to create scripts to enter a company name and address instantly into a range of worksheet cells and to choose options from 1-2-3. You'll also learn to create your own SmartIcons, buttons, and menu commands to represent scripts.

Part Three discusses a variety of advanced worksheet tools. This final part of the book includes three chapters.

Chapter 15, "Versions and Team Computing," introduces 1-2-3's powerful Version Manager, which you can use to maintain multiple versions of data in the context of a single workbook. You'll also review features designed to facilitate worksheet development when a team of people are involved in the process.

Chapter 16, "Worksheet Tools," helps you master some of 1-2-3's most sophisticated features. You'll take a look at the SmartMasters collection—professionally-designed templates for streamlining the production of standard business worksheets. Then you'll examine the powerful features available in the Range ➤ Analyze menu. These include What-If Table, for performing multiple what-if calculations in a single operation; Backsolver, for finding an input value that produces a desired bottom-line calculation; Distribution, for examining the frequency of values on a worksheet; Regression, for exploring the correlation between numeric data sets; and the Matrix commands, for solving simultaneous equations. Finally, you'll learn how to use outlining to view different levels of data in a worksheet.

Chapter 17, "Links between Files," shows you how to work with multiple-file applications in 1-2-3 and Windows 95. Lotus 1-2-3 allows you to write formulas that create links between workbooks. With a link formula, one workbook can read data from another, whether the source file is open or not. In an example presented in this chapter, you'll learn to take advantage of workbook links to create a business summary from data contained in four different files. In addition, 1-2-3 allows you to transfer data and objects between documents in different Windows applications. Chapter 17 helps you explore these links.

Appendixes A through H serve collectively as a reference guide to the entire library of functions available in 1-2-3. They present complete information about all the built-in functions, with syntax descriptions, explanations, tips, notes, warnings, and examples. The reference is organized in useful formats so you can quickly find the information you need.

PART 1

1-2-3 on the Windows 95 Desktop

CHAPTER 1

The Elements of 1-2-3

Fast Track

To move the cell pointer to a new position inside the active worksheet,   9

press an arrow key on the keyboard, or click the target cell with the mouse.

To activate the 1-2-3 menu bar and pull down a menu,   12

press the Alt key plus the letter that represents the menu, or click the menu name with the mouse. In this book, the notation Menu ➤ Command represents a command from a menu list. For example, an instruction to choose File ➤ Save means "pull down the File menu and choose the Save command."

To add a sheet to a workbook,   13

click the New Sheet button, located at the right side of the line that displays sheet tabs.

To divide a workbook into panes,   14

select a cell at the location where you want to divide the panes. Then choose View ➤ Split, select one of the Type options, and click OK.

To return to a single pane,	**20**
choose View ➤ Clear Split.	
To select a sheet in a workbook,	**15**
click the sheet's tab, displayed on the line just above the workbook window.	
To read a brief description of a SmartIcon,	**17**
position the mouse pointer over the target icon. The description appears in a bubble over the icon.	
To choose a command from a shortcut menu,	**17**
position the mouse pointer over the object whose shortcut menu you want to view, and click the right mouse button. Then click the command you want to carry out.	
To choose an option from the live status bar,	**19**
click one of the buttons on the status bar (at the bottom of the screen), and then choose an option from the resulting pop-up menu.	
To view the 1-2-3 Classic window,	**20**
press the slash key (/) on the keyboard.	
To determine whether 1-2-3 is accepting a cell entry as a label or as a value,	**22**
look at the mode indicator (located at the right side of the status bar) after you begin the entry. You will see either the word Label or Value.	
To exit from 1-2-3,	**23**
choose File ➤ Exit.	

Lotus 1-2-3 97 Edition contains three interrelated software components, known as spreadsheet, charting, and database management:

- ▶ The spreadsheet provides efficient tools for working with tables of numbers, labels, and calculations.

- ▶ The charting component lets you create and print visual representations of your data. You can choose among a variety of two- and three-dimensional formats, including bar charts, pie charts, line charts, area charts, and many others.

- ▶ The database management software gives you techniques for storing and managing records of information. In 1-2-3 97 Edition, database operations are performed by a companion program named Lotus Approach. Approach is installed on your computer at the same time as 1-2-3.

Along with these major components, 1-2-3 provides important tools for a variety of other operations, such as creating maps to represent geographically oriented data, producing and maintaining spreadsheets in a team environment, transmitting 1-2-3 documents over the Internet, and customizing 1-2-3 to meet the particular requirements of your own work.

In addition, 1-2-3's Desktop interface has been creatively redesigned to meet important new standards for Windows 95 applications. The new tools in this environment make 1-2-3 easier to use than ever before. If you're upgrading from an older version of the spreadsheet, you'll find many important advantages in the 1-2-3 97 Edition:

- ▶ Like other major Windows 95 programs, Lotus 1-2-3 has pull-down menus, dialog boxes, special-purpose keyboard functions, easy mouse control, elaborate Help features, and a large collection of *SmartIcons* that allow you to perform important tasks at the click of a mouse.

- ▶ 1-2-3 gives you efficient new ways to change the properties of a worksheet, chart, or other object—either by selecting options from a special property InfoBox or by choosing properties from the 1-2-3 Status Bar. You'll learn about these techniques in the chapters ahead.

- On the Windows 95 Desktop you can run 1-2-3 alongside other applications. Switching back and forth from one program to another is as easy as clicking a button on the Windows 95 Taskbar.

- You can exchange data between Lotus 1-2-3 and other programs in a variety of ways. For example, you can use the Clipboard to copy data or charts from 1-2-3 to your word processor. In addition, the Windows protocol known as OLE (Object Linking and Embedding) gives you powerful ways to incorporate the features of one document within another.

- If your system is Internet-ready, you can publish 1-2-3 worksheets on the World Wide Web and you can open related documents from the Internet. In addition, you can look to the Web to find online support for Lotus applications. (You'll learn about these topics in Chapter 2.)

This chapter introduces you to the major components of 1-2-3—spreadsheet, charting, and database—and shows you how they interact with one another. You'll take a first look at what the program can do, and you'll consider ways to use 1-2-3 in your own work. You'll also begin learning how Lotus 1-2-3 operates in Windows 95. Exercises in this chapter will help you explore the features, appearance, and scope of the application.

Lotus 1-2-3: The Basics

A worksheet, also known simply as a sheet, is a large grid of individual cells, ideal for organizing and analyzing tables of information. In 1-2-3 97 Edition, a workbook is a file that may contain as many as 256 sheets, each represented by a tab displayed at the top of the workbook window. This three-dimensional worksheet arrangement gives you the opportunity to arrange many interrelated tables of data in one convenient location.

Figure 1.1 shows the 1-2-3 window as it appears when you first run the program in Windows 95. To view this screen on your own computer, choose Lotus 1-2-3 from the Start menu. When the Welcome to 1-2-3 window appears on the screen (Figure 1.2), click the button labeled Create a Blank Workbook. You'll learn more about the Welcome window later.

Chapter 1   The Elements of 1-2-3

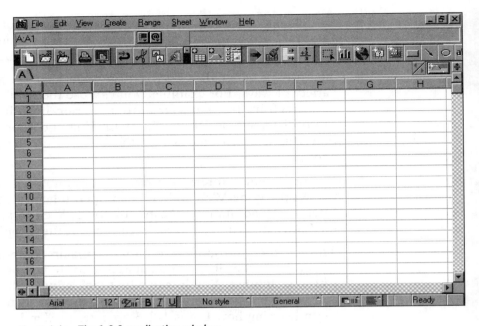

Figure 1.1: **The 1-2-3 application window**

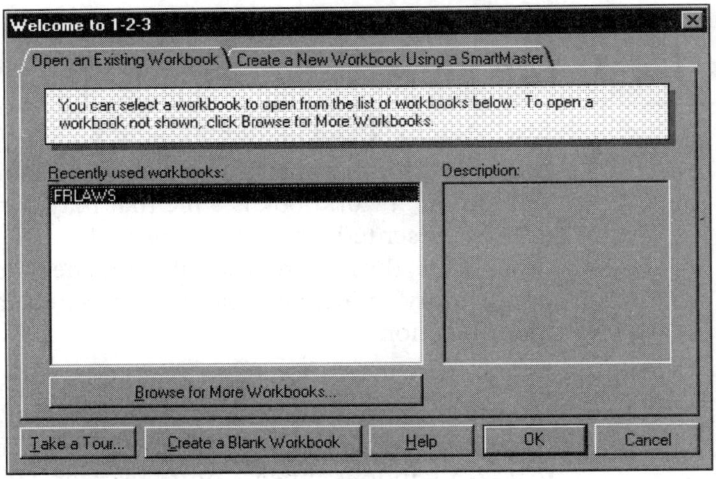

Figure 1.2: **The Welcome window**

At first glance the 1-2-3 application seems to contain a bewildering assortment of elements, but you'll quickly learn to use each category of tools to create efficient and effective workbooks. At the top of the screen you see the menu bar and the edit line. Beneath the edit line is a row of SmartIcons, which provide fast access to important 1-2-3 operations. Beneath the SmartIcons you can see the tab line for the active workbook. Initially a workbook contains only one sheet, identified by a tab labeled A, but you can easily add new sheets to a file and change the label on a tab.

The worksheet itself, organized in rows and columns, takes up most of the screen area. Beneath the sheet you see the status bar, which provides additional techniques for changing the appearance of a worksheet.

The 1-2-3 window and the active workbook contain many of the familiar features of the Windows environment, including Control menus, Maximize and Minimize buttons, scroll bars, and title bars. If you're new to Windows 95, you can learn more about all these features in Chapter 2.

The Worksheet

Worksheets are divided into rows and columns of cells. Each row is identified by a number, and each column by a letter. A cell has an address made up of its column letter and row number. For example, the cell at the intersection of column D and row 9 has the address D9.

To develop a useful collection of data in a worksheet, you simply begin typing numbers and labels into individual cells. The current cell—the cell ready to receive a data entry—is marked by a bold frame called the cell pointer. As you can see in Figure 1.1, cell A1 is the current cell when you begin working in a new sheet. The column and row headings of the current cell—initially A and 1—have a sunken appearance; this visual feature makes it easy to identify the address of the current cell. In addition, the current cell address is displayed—as A:A1, identifying both the sheet name and the cell address—in the first panel of the edit line, near the upper-left corner of the screen.

At the time that you save a workbook file to disk, you assign the workbook a name. When a workbook window is maximized—enlarged to its maximum size within the 1-2-3 application window—the workbook's name appears in the 1-2-3 title bar at the top of screen.

NOTE *Untitled* is the default name of the first workbook you open in 1-2-3. As you begin entering data into this workbook, you'll save it as a file on disk, giving the file a name that you choose yourself. Until then, the default name *Untitled* appears on the title bar.

Arranging the Workbook Window

When a workbook is maximized on the 1-2-3 Desktop, buttons on the 1-2-3 menu bar allow you to control the workbook's appearance. An icon at the left side of the menu bar—just to the left of the File menu—represents the workbook's control menu. Click this icon once with the mouse to view the list of commands in the workbook's control menu, allowing you to change appearance of the window, to activate a different window, or to close the window. (Press Esc on your keyboard to close this menu without choosing one of its commands.) At the right side of the 1-2-3 menu bar you can see the familiar trio of buttons that allow you to minimize, restore the size, or close the current workbook window.

Along the right side of the window is a vertical scroll bar for navigating up and down the rows of the worksheet. Along the lower border of the window you see a horizontal scroll bar for navigating left and right across the columns of the worksheet.

NOTE The mouse pointer initially appears on the screen as a white arrow, pointing up and to the left. You'll see the pointer change temporarily to a variety of other shapes as you start working with 1-2-3. To select a cell or another item in the 1-2-3 window, you move the pointer to an object on the screen and click the left mouse button.

In the following exercise, you'll use the control buttons and scroll bars to explore the dimensions of the worksheet:

1. Click the Restore button—the middle button at the right side of the menu bar—to reduce the size of the active workbook. (Alternatively, press Alt+hyphen from the keyboard to pull down the window's Control menu, and then press R to choose the Restore command.)

As you can see in Figure 1.3, several changes take place in the appearance of the workbook window. The window now has its own title bar, which displays the name *Untitled.123*. The Control menu icon appears at the left side of the title bar, and the Minimize, Maximize, and Close buttons are at the right.

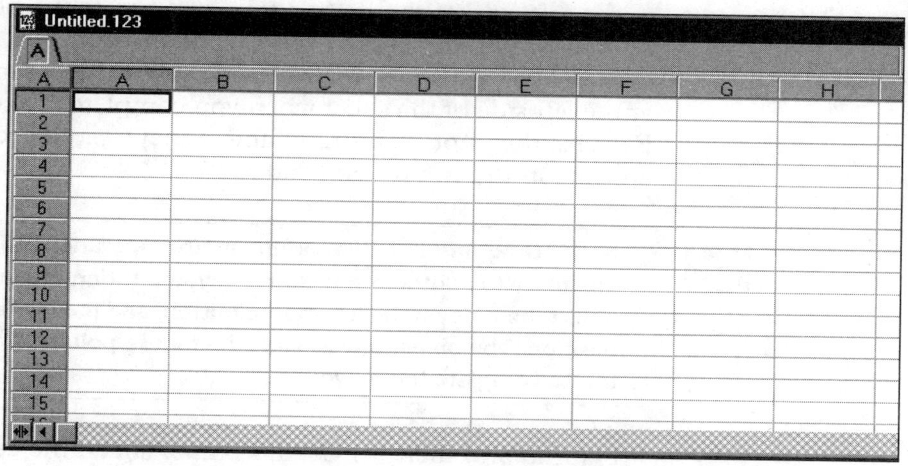

*Figure 1.3: **The result of clicking the Restore button***

2. Restore the window's original appearance by clicking the Maximize button (or by pressing Alt+hyphen and then X).

3. Press → once on your keyboard. The cell pointer moves one cell to the right, to address B1. Repeat this action six times to move the cell pointer to H1. Column H is at the right side of the current workbook window.

4. Now move the cell pointer one more column to the right and watch what happens to the worksheet. Column A disappears from the left side of the window to make room for column I on the right side. As this action demonstrates, a sheet contains many more columns and rows than can be displayed in the window at one time.

5. Press the ↓ key on the keyboard. The cell pointer moves down one position, to cell I2. Press ↓ repeatedly until the cell pointer reaches I17, and then move the pointer down one more cell. Row 1 disappears from the workbook window to make room for row 19.

6. Position the mouse pointer over the small gray *scroll box* that appears at the left side of the horizontal scroll bar at the bottom of the sheet. Hold down the left mouse button and drag the box part way across the bar. (As you do so, a small box identifies the column that will appear at the left side of the sheet when you complete the scrolling operation.) Release the mouse button, and a new sequence of columns now appears in the workbook window.

NOTE Dragging is an important mouse operation. To drag an object from one place to another on the screen, you position the mouse pointer over the object, hold down the left mouse button, and move the pointer to the target position. The object moves with the mouse pointer. Release the mouse button to complete the move.

7. Press End and then →. On this empty sheet, the cell pointer moves to column IV, the last column in the sheet.

   The first 26 columns of a sheet are identified by the letters A through Z, the next 26 by AA though AZ, the next 26 by BA through BZ. IA through IV are the last columns. Under this lettering scheme, a sheet has a total of 256 columns.

8. Press End and then ↓ to move to the final row on the empty sheet, row 8192. The cell at the bottom-right corner of the worksheet has the address IV8192, as shown in Figure 1.4.

9. Press the Home key on the keyboard. Pressing Home moves the cell pointer back to its beginning position, cell A1.

   A sheet is a huge grid of over 2 million cells (256 columns × 8192 rows). The window can show only a small part of the sheet at a time, but you can scroll the sheet to view any group of cells that you want to work with.

   As you've learned, a workbook file can contain many tabbed sheets in which you organize tables of interrelated data. By writing formulas that refer to data values in more than one sheet, you can establish relationships among the multiple sheets of a file. In upcoming exercises, you'll explore the use of multiple sheets in a workbook. Along the way you'll begin working with 1-2-3 menu commands.

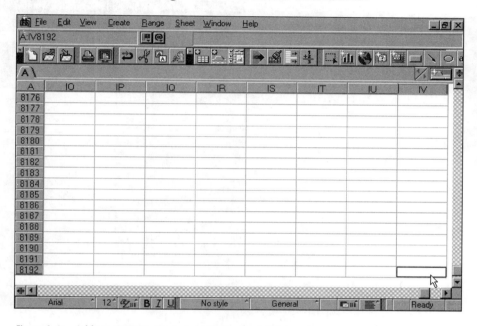

Figure 1.4:   Address IV8192, the last cell in the worksheet

The Menu Bar

As in most Windows applications, the menu bar is the horizontal row of commands at the top of the screen, just below the title bar:

```
File   Edit   View   SCreate   Range   Sheet   Window   Help
```

When you choose one of these commands, a pull-down menu appears with a list of options. For example, Figure 1.5 shows the commands displayed when you click File on the menu bar. When you highlight a menu or a command inside a menu, the 1-2-3 title bar displays a brief description of your selection.

The 1-2-3 menus are context-sensitive; the available menus and commands typically apply to the task you're currently working on. In some cases, you'll find that interrelated operations are grouped together in multipurpose dialog boxes. This arrangement simplifies your work with the menu system and its commands.

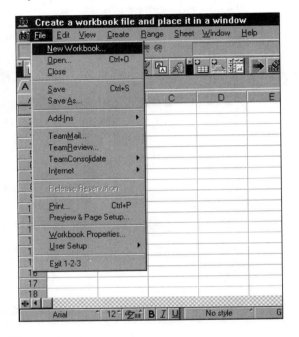

Figure 1.5: **The File menu**

Choosing Menu Commands

Several mouse and keyboard techniques are available for choosing commands from the 1-2-3 menu system:

▶ Press the Alt key or the F10 key to activate the menu bar. With the menu bar active, you can press → or ← to highlight one of the Main menu commands and ↵ to pull down the menu.

▶ To use a keyboard shortcut, press the Alt key followed by the underscored letter in a menu name. For example, pressing Alt+F pulls down the File menu.

▶ With the mouse, pull down a menu by clicking the corresponding command in the menu bar. For example, to pull down the File menu, position the mouse pointer over File in the menu bar and click the left mouse button.

> **NOTE** In this book, the notation Menu ➤ Command represents a command from a menu list. For example, an instruction to choose File ➤ Save means "pull down the File menu and choose the Save command."

> **TIP** To back out of the menu system and return to your work in the worksheet, use the Escape key. Press Escape once if the menu bar is active but no pull-down menu is displayed. Press Escape twice to back out of a pull-down menu. Alternatively, click anywhere inside the worksheet with the mouse.

Adding Sheets to a Workbook

In the following exercise you'll learn to add new sheets to a workbook and to change the way you view multiple sheets on the screen. Along the way, you'll try your hand at choosing menu commands and using dialog boxes.

1. Find the New Sheet button, located at the right side of the line that displays sheet tabs. (Because the workbook currently contains one sheet, A is the only tab displayed.) Click the New Sheet button twice with the mouse.

   With each click, 1-2-3 adds a new sheet to the current workbook. After the second click, you'll see three sheet tabs—labeled A, B, and C—as shown in Figure 1.6. Each tab represents one sheet in the current workbook. Sheet C is currently active, displayed as the front sheet in the workbook.

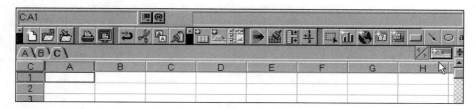

Figure 1.6: **Adding sheets to a workbook**

2. Select cell B1. Then pull down the View menu by pressing Alt+V or clicking View on the menu bar. Choose the Split command. This brings up the Split dialog box, with options for changing the appearance of the workbook window:

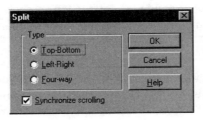

3. Notice that the dialog box offers three ways to split the workbook window: Top-Bottom, Left-Right, and Four-Way. Click Left-Right (or press Alt+L from the keyboard) to select the second of these options.

4. To confirm the new option and close the dialog box, press ↵ or click the OK button with the mouse.

   When you complete these steps, the workbook window appears as shown in Figure 1.7. It's now divided into two panes; in each pane you can view any one of the existing sheets.

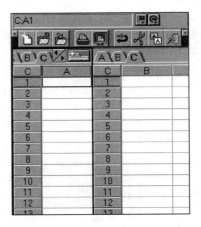

Figure 1.7: **The workbook window divided into panes**

5. Try clicking different sheet tabs in each of the individual panes. For example, click tab A in the first pane and tab B in the second pane.

6. Now return to the original view of the workbook by pulling down the View menu and choosing the Clear Split command.

> TIP Another way to create multiple views of one workbook is to create two or more windows for the same file. First click the restore button to reduce the size of the workbook window. Then pull down the Window menu and choose the New Window command. In response, 1-2-3 creates another window in which you can view the contents of your workbook. Within a given window you can click any tab to view a particular sheet. You can also resize or reposition individual windows to view data in new juxtapositions. To close a window, click the close button at the far right side of the title bar.

Take a moment to review what you've learned in these initial hands-on exercises. A workbook can contain multiple sheets—as many as 256. A new workbook starts out with one sheet. The simplest way to add new sheets is to click the New Sheet button one or more times. Each new sheet is represented by a tab; you activate a sheet by clicking its tab. By dividing the workbook window into panes—or by creating multiple windows for a given workbook—you can view the contents of several sheets at once.

Multiple sheets in a file are identified by letters of the alphabet, from A, B, and C for the first three worksheets, up to IV for worksheet 256. These letters initially appear on the sheet tabs, but you can change the label on any tab, as you'll learn in Chapter 2.

A complete cell address consists of three elements:

▶ The sheet letter, followed by a colon

▶ The column letter

▶ The row number

For example, C:E29 refers to the cell at the intersection of column E and row 29 on sheet C.

You've used menu commands and their resulting dialog boxes to make changes to the appearance and content of a workbook window. To streamline your work, 1-2-3 offers several kinds of alternative tools for accomplishing particular tasks. Depending on how you prefer to work, these alternatives can be quicker and simpler than the standard menu commands. You'll examine some of these tools in the upcoming sections of this chapter.

SmartIcons, Shortcut Menus, and the Status Bar

SmartIcons—the row of buttons displayed above the worksheet area in the 1-2-3 window—are one-step shortcuts for accomplishing common operations, including file storage, printing, copying, charting, formatting, and many other tasks. To perform the action that an icon represents, you simply click a SmartIcon with the mouse. But SmartIcons are not the only alternative techniques available to you in 1-2-3. The application also has special lists of context-sensitive commands known as shortcut menus, along with a variety of "live" tools on the status bar at the bottom of the screen. You can use all these tools to carry out worksheet operations quickly and efficiently. You'll take a first look at these features in this section.

NOTE SmartIcons, shortcut menus, and the live status bar all require the use of the mouse.

SmartIcons

Lotus 1-2-3 initially displays a collection of SmartIcons that you're likely to use most commonly as you develop worksheets. The graphic on each of these buttons gives you a clear idea of what the SmartIcon does. For example, two of the buttons show images of a folder, with arrows pointing out of or into the folder; these are for opening and saving files, respectively. Likewise, the button that contains a small picture of a printer is for printing the active worksheet; the buttons displaying scissors and a pot of glue are for cut-and-paste operations; the button with a bar chart image is for adding a chart to your worksheet; and so on.

Lotus 1-2-3 offers a simple technique for finding out the use of each SmartIcon. Simply position the mouse pointer over the icon you want to learn about. In response, 1-2-3 displays a *bubble* that gives a brief description of the tool. For example, if you position the mouse pointer over the fourth button in the row of SmartIcons, the description "Print" appears in the bubble:

Lotus 1-2-3: The Basics

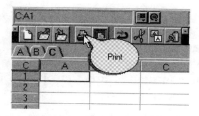

Take a moment to read the description of each button in the row of SmartIcons. This initial row actually shows two of the various SmartIcon "bars" available in 1-2-3. Other bars are just a couple of mouse-clicks away. Notice the small arrow button that appears just to the left of the first SmartIcon. Click this arrow to view a list of other bars. Select a name from this list to view or hide SmartIcon tools:

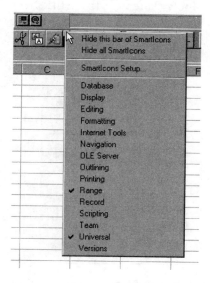

You can also customize each SmartIcon set, using the SmartIcons Setup command. The resulting dialog box gives you simple ways to rearrange, insert, and delete the icons in a selected set. You'll learn more about customizing the SmartIcon sets in Chapter 2.

Shortcut Menus and InfoBoxes

Sometimes you may want to see a short list of menu commands that relate to a specific object on the screen. Like many Windows 95 applications, 1-2-3 offers shortcut menus for just this purpose. A shortcut menu is a list of commands that you can view for a particular item in the 1-2-3 window. To bring up a shortcut menu, you position the mouse pointer over an item and click the *right* mouse button. The resulting selection of commands are the ones you're most likely to want to use on your selection.

For example, try positioning the mouse pointer over any cell in the active sheet, and then click the right mouse button. As you can see in Figure 1.8, the resulting shortcut menu contains commands that relate to the cell selection—for example, cutting and pasting, copying, formatting, and naming the cell that you've selected. To choose a command, you can press arrow keys at the keyboard or click a command with the mouse. (To close the shortcut menu without choosing a command, press Escape or click on the worksheet with the left mouse button.)

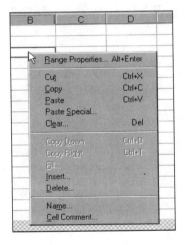

Figure 1.8:   *A shortcut menu. To display a shortcut menu, position the mouse pointer over an item and click the right mouse button.*

Shortcut menus allow you to perform common worksheet operations without having to memorize the menu locations of specific commands. You'll find lots of good uses for shortcut menus as you work through the exercises in this book.

Notice that the first command in the shortcut menu is Range Properties. When you select this command, 1-2-3 displays a tabbed InfoBox containing all the various properties you can apply to a cell or range of cells:

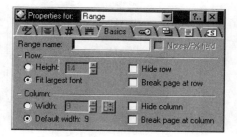

You can use this dialog box to select fonts, alignments, data formats, display colors, data protection schemes, and other properties. Conveniently, you'll see similar InfoBoxes for setting the properties of entire sheets and other objects that you'll work with in 1-2-3. You'll learn much more about properties and InfoBoxes as you continue your work in this book.

The Status Bar

The status bar, located just below the horizontal scroll bar, provides yet another set of shortcuts you can use for worksheet tasks. The 1-2-3 status bar not only *displays* information, but also gives you some simple ways to *change* the settings of your work. Take a first look at the status bar as it initially appears on the screen. For a selected cell, individual buttons on the bar show you the settings that determine how a data entry will be displayed—the font, the point size, the text color, the text properties (bold, italic, underlining), the style, the numeric format, the background color, and the alignment:

You can click any of these buttons with the mouse to view a complete list of the available settings in each category. These lists can save you lots of time when you want to change the appearance of data on your worksheet. For example, Figure 1.9 shows the list that appears when you click the Numeric Format button, which is initially labeled "General."

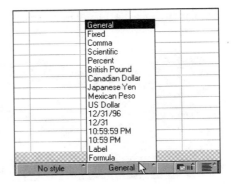

Figure 1.9: **The list of numeric formats from the status bar**

In short, 1-2-3 often gives you several different ways to carry out a given operation on a worksheet. SmartIcons, shortcut menus, InfoBoxes, and the status bar present you with convenient alternatives for completing your work. It's always up to you to decide which technique is the easiest and most efficient.

Another special feature is the 1-2-3 Classic window, the subject of the next section of this chapter.

The 1-2-3 Classic Window

The 1-2-3 Classic window is an alternate menu system for users who are upgrading from a DOS version of this spreadsheet application. By default, this menu system appears on the screen when you press the slash key (/), the key that has traditionally accessed menus in DOS versions of Lotus 1-2-3. Press the slash key now, and you'll see the 1-2-3 Classic window at the top of the screen, as in Figure 1.10. If you've worked with a DOS version, the commands in the Classic window will seem familiar. This alternate menu system is accessible only from the keyboard, not with the mouse. Press Escape to close the Classic menu without choosing a command.

TIP You may want to use the 1-2-3 Classic window while you're first adjusting to the 1-2-3 97 Edition interface, but you should abandon it as quickly as possible. Learn to use the standard menu bar, the SmartIcons, shortcut menus, InfoBoxes, and the status bar to accomplish tasks in this new environment. In the long run, you'll become a much more efficient 1-2-3 user if you adjust yourself to these new features.

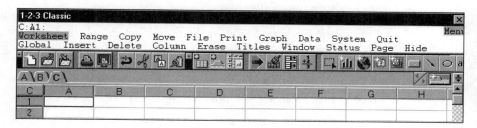

Figure 1.10: The 1-2-3 Classic window

As an exercise with the Classic menu system, try using its commands to split the workbook window into two panes:

1. Select cell A8 on the current sheet. Then press **/** to bring up the 1-2-3 Classic menu.

2. With the menu displayed on the screen, choose the **W**orksheet command.

3. Choose **W**indow.

4. Choose **H**orizontal. The result is the same as choosing View ➤ Split from the standard 1-2-3 menu, and then selecting the Top-Bottom option in the Split dialog box. The current window displays two panes, one above the other. Notice that the 1-2-3 Classic menu disappears after you select the commands.

5. Press the following four keys in sequence: **/WWC**. (This is the traditional notation for representing command selections in DOS versions of 1-2-3. In this case, the notation represents the /**W**orksheet **W**indow **C**lear command from the 1-2-3 Classic menu.) The current window once again displays a single pane.

As a final introductory exercise, you'll enter data values into some of the cells of the worksheet you've been examining.

Entering Data

Lotus 1-2-3 recognizes two general types of data entries in the cells of a sheet—*labels* and *values*:

▶ A label is a non-numeric entry beginning with a letter of the alphabet or with one of several special symbols that 1-2-3 recognizes as the first character in a label.

▶ A value is a number or the numeric result of a formula. (Lotus also recognizes date and time entries, and translates them into numeric values.)

In the following brief exercise, as you enter a label and a value into two cells on the active sheet

1. Press the Home key, if necessary, to select cell A1.

2. From the keyboard, hold down the Shift key and type the letter **P**.

   Notice the mode indicator at the right side of the status bar. It shows the word *Label*, which means that 1-2-3 is accepting your entry as a non-numeric data item:

3. Complete the label by typing the remaining letters of the word *Profit*. If you make a mistake, you can press the Backspace key to erase the last character you typed.

4. Confirm the entry by pressing ↵. Notice that the cell pointer automatically moves one cell down in the sheet, to A2.

   The label you've just entered is left-justified inside the cell. This is the default alignment for labels in 1-2-3. The mode indicator now displays the word *Ready*.

5. Type the four digits **9876** from the keyboard. This time the mode indicator displays the word *Value*, which means that 1-2-3 is accepting your data entry as a numeric value:

   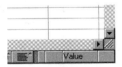

6. Press ↵ to complete the data entry. The pointer moves down to cell A3.

   Notice that the value 9876 is displayed right-justified inside cell A2. Numeric values are right-justified by default. As you'll see later, you can change the alignment of both values and labels.

7. In cell A3, begin the following label entry: **ABC**. (Do not press ↵.) Now cancel the entry by pressing Escape.

TIP You can always check the mode indicator during data entry to make sure that 1-2-3 is accepting your data the way you are expecting it to—that is, as a label or a value.

You can complete an entry by pressing ↵ or by pressing a direction key (↑, ↓, ←, or →). Cancel an entry by pressing the Escape key.

Exiting 1-2-3

This is the end of the hands-on portion of this chapter. If you wish to exit 1-2-3 before you continue reading, here are the steps:

1. Choose File ➤ Exit from the menu bar (or press Alt+F4).
2. In the Exit dialog box, click No to indicate that you wish to exit without saving your current worksheet.

After these steps, you return to the Windows 95 Desktop; the 1-2-3 application window is no longer open.

In the remainder of this chapter, you'll look at examples of the three major 1-2-3 components—spreadsheet, charting, and database management.

Planning and Creating a Worksheet

You can enter labels, numbers, and chronological values (dates and times) as the data values on a worksheet. You can also enter formulas that instruct 1-2-3 to perform arithmetic operations on your data. Given a table of data, a worksheet simplifies all kinds of calculations, from finding bottom-line numeric totals to performing complex statistical and financial formulas.

Perhaps the single most important feature of the spreadsheet is this: 1-2-3 automatically recalculates totals and other formulas whenever you change the data that the formulas work with. This essential characteristic is what distinguishes a computer spreadsheet from manual calculations with paper and pencil. You can change underlying data values at any time without facing the prospect of redoing the rest of your work. If you plan and write your formulas appropriately, 1-2-3 recalculates all the results that depend on the data you've changed.

You can think of automatic recalculation as the spreadsheet's "what-if" feature. A worksheet shows you instantly what happens to a set of calculations when changes occur in the underlying numeric data. "What-if" questions come up in an infinite variety of common business applications. Consider the following examples:

- What is the new break-even point in the projected sales of a product if costs increase by a specific amount per unit?
- What happens to your projected tax rate this year if you purchase a major depreciable asset, such as a new computer?
- What is the new monthly payment on a business loan if the term of the loan is doubled and the interest rate decreased by 1 percent?

In calculations that are done by hand, finding the answers to questions like these can take a lot of time and effort. But in 1-2-3 you simply change the appropriate data entries in your worksheet, and the rest of the work is done for you. As you gain experience with worksheets, you'll quickly learn to organize your work to take full advantage of this important feature.

The worksheet examples you're about to examine are designed to illustrate the "what-if" power of 1-2-3. Here is the context for these examples: A company has invited a nutritionist to conduct a series of on-site lunchtime seminars for its employees. The topic is good eating habits for working people. Some employees have expressed concerns about the fat content of fast-food meals (typical lunchtime fare for many workers), and are interested in the possible benefits of the so-called 30-percent fat diet.

The nutritionist, named Barbara Johnson, is using 1-2-3 to prepare a series of handouts on which to base her discussion of this subject. These handouts will take the form of worksheets, charts, and databases. She begins her preparations by designing some sheets that analyze the caloric and fat content of what she imagines are typical lunches eaten by the employees in her audience.

As you examine Johnson's work, keep in mind your main goals in this chapter: to gain a general understanding of the components of 1-2-3, and to begin imagining uses for the spreadsheet in your own work. For the moment, focus on capabilities and features; you'll master specific techniques in later chapters.

Developing a Worksheet

Many worksheets eventually become tools for presenting information to other people. Whether you're sharing data with the person in the next office or exchanging ideas with a room full of professionals, your data needs to be accurate, clearly organized, attractively presented, and easy to understand. Lotus 1-2-3 includes a great many tools designed to help you meet these requirements.

Creating a successful worksheet typically involves several detailed tasks:

▶ Placing a descriptive title near the top of the worksheet.

▶ Entering column headings and row labels that describe the categories of numeric information that you'll include in the worksheet table.

▶ Entering the numeric data values themselves.

▶ Writing formulas that perform specific calculations on the numeric data. When appropriate, you can copy these formulas to other cells on the worksheet to perform the same calculations on other columns or rows of data.

▶ Improving the presentation by changing display formats and styles in particular cells. For example, you might display certain numbers in a currency or percentage format. Titles, labels, and numbers can also be displayed in special type styles for clarity and emphasis. You can display data in boldface, italic, and underlined styles.

These tasks are illustrated in Barbara Johnson's worksheet examples. Her initial goal is to explain the significance of the 30-percent fat diet, and, in the context of this diet, to analyze typical lunches that employees eat in fast-food restaurants or bring to work themselves.

Entering the Labels and Data

As the starting point for her research, Johnson visits the fast-food restaurant located across the street from the company's offices. She knows that lots of the employees come here to buy quick, inexpensive lunches. She asks for nutritional information about several items on the menu and is given a printed nutritional report. The report lists the calories and fat content of each item on the menu; this is the data she'll need for her presentation.

Back at her office, she imagines the typical lunch served by this restaurant: a hamburger, an order of French fries, some cookies, and a diet soda. She starts up 1-2-3 and begins designing a worksheet on which to present nutritional information about this particular meal.

She begins by entering a title for the worksheet in cells A3 and B3:

Lunch #1   **Fast-Food Restaurant**

Because she's planning to create additional worksheets for other menus, she identifies this one as Lunch #1.

Her purpose in this worksheet is to analyze the fat content of a meal and compare it with the recommended fat intake for a healthy adult. Secondarily, she wants to translate nutritional information into meaningful data that employees will find useful when they choose what to eat for lunch. The two major nutritional facts she'll present in her seminar are the following:

▶ Nutritionists recommend that the daily fat intake of healthy adults be 30 percent or less of their total daily caloric consumption (hence the term "30-percent fat diet").

▶ One gram of fat is equivalent to nine calories.

The nutritional panels on food packages usually list the fat content per serving in grams, but not always as a percentage of total calories. For this reason, the health-conscious consumer needs to do some arithmetic to figure out whether a food item is a reasonable part of a 30-percent fat diet. Johnson will eventually express this arithmetic in formulas that she enters on her worksheet.

She continues her work by entering labels for four columns in rows 5 and 6:

	Total	**Fat**	**% Fat**
Item	**Calories**	**in Grams**	**Calories**

The first column, "Item," is for the name of the food item. The second and third columns, "Total Calories" and "Fat in grams," will list data acquired from the nutritional report she picked up at the restaurant. The final column, "% Fat Calories," is for information that will be calculated from the nutritional data—the percent of total calories represented by the fat content in each food item.

Next, Johnson types rows of information for the four food items she's including in her first sample menu. She enters the name of each food item, the number of calories, and the fat content in grams. For the moment, she leaves the percent fat column blank.

Figure 1.11 shows Johnson's work up to this point. Notice two interesting features of this worksheet: She has widened column A to accommodate the names of the food items, and she has removed the grid lines—the vertical and horizontal lines that separate columns and rows in a worksheet. These are two ways in which Lotus 1-2-3 gives you control over the appearance of a sheet.

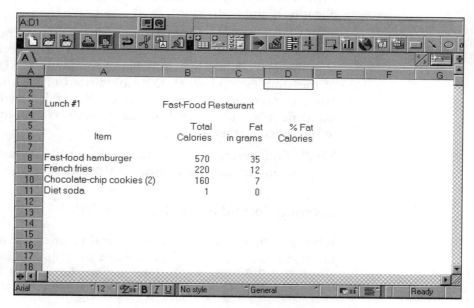

Figure 1.11: **The first stage of the Lunch #1 worksheet**

Now the nutritionist has completed the first few steps of her worksheet design. She has created a title, entered descriptive column headings and row labels to identify the numeric data in the table, and copied the basic numeric data into the table. Her next step is to write formulas to perform calculations.

Writing Formulas

The purpose of a formula in a worksheet is to calculate a value, usually from existing data on the worksheet. When you complete a formula entry, 1-2-3 displays the result of the formula in the cell where the formula is located. To view the formula itself, you can select the cell where the result is displayed and look up at the edit line.

Here are some of the most common elements you'll include in formulas:

- Literal numeric values, such as 9 and 365.
- Cell addresses, such as D5 or B4. In a formula, an address represents the value that is currently stored in the corresponding cell.
- Arithmetic operators, such as + (addition), – (subtraction), * (multiplication), and / (division).
- Tools from 1-2-3's large function library. Each built-in function is designed to perform a specific calculation. The names of functions begin with the @ character in 1-2-3. For example, the @SUM function—one of the simplest and most commonly used of all—finds the sum of a group of numbers. (Chapter 8 surveys the built-in worksheet functions; the appendixes at the end of this book provide complete information in reference format.)

You'll find examples of all these elements in the formulas Barbara Johnson enters into her Lunch #1 worksheet.

Entering Formulas and Values in Cells

Johnson's first task is to find the total calories and the total grams of fat in the meal. In most spreadsheet programs—and in previous versions of 1-2-3—she might have accomplished this by typing the following formula into cell B13:

    @SUM(B8..B11)

But now there's a simpler way. Because @SUM is used so often in worksheets to find totals for columns and rows of numbers, 1-2-3 provides an elegant new technique for entering this function: Simply type the word "Total" at the beginning of the row or the top of the column where you want the @SUM formulas to appear. In response to this one label entry, 1-2-3 examines your worksheet, determines the appropriate locations for the @SUM functions, and enters the formulas for you.

Accordingly, Barbara Johnson moves the cell pointer to A13 and enters the word **Total**. The total calories and total grams of fat for the lunch menu appear instantly in cells B13 and B14, as shown in Figure 1.12.

Planning and Creating a Worksheet

By moving the cell pointer to each of these locations in turn, Johnson can look at the edit line to examine the actual formulas that 1-2-3 has entered into the cells:

```
@SUM(B8..B12)          @SUM(C8..C12)
```

As you might guess, B8..B12 and C8..C12 indicate the locations of data that the @SUM function will use to calculate totals. The result of the @SUM function in cell B13 is 951, the total calories in the meal. Similarly, the value in cell C13 is 54, the total grams of fat. An expression like B8..B12 represents a *range* of cells. The two periods tell 1-2-3 to include all cells between the two listed cells in the calculation. You'll find many contexts in which ranges are important during your work with 1-2-3.

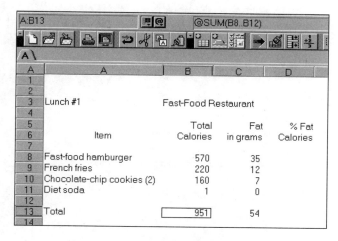

Figure 1.12: **Typing "Total" to enter @SUM functions**

Next, Johnson has to devise a formula to calculate the fat calories in each food item as a percentage of the total calories. Given that there are nine calories in each gram of fat, here is the formula for finding the ratio of fat calories to total calories:

(Fat Grams × 9) ÷ Total Calories

Johnson's task is to translate this into a formula that 1-2-3 can accept and perform. She moves to cell D8 and enters the following:

```
+C8*9/B8
```

Cell C8 contains the number of grams of fat in a hamburger. Multiplying this value by 9 gives the total calories of fat. Dividing the product by the total calories (stored in cell B8) gives the ratio.

> **NOTE** The * symbol represents multiplication in a 1-2-3 formula.

When Johnson first enters this formula into cell D8, 1-2-3 calculates the result as 0.552632. This number is the decimal format of the ratio, but Johnson wants to display the ratio as a percentage. With the cell pointer still in D8, she clicks the Number Format button on the status bar (the button that is currently labeled General). From the resulting pop-up menu list, she chooses the Percent format, as shown in Figure 1.13. She then clicks the adjacent panel in the status bar and chooses 0 for the number of decimal places in her percentage, as shown in Figure 1.14. As a result of her selections, the percentage is displayed simply as 55%.

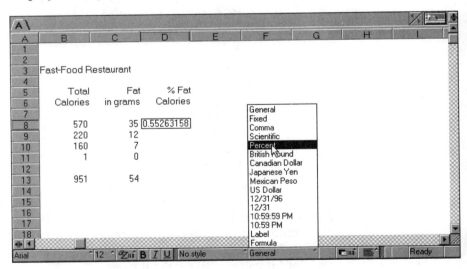

Figure 1.13: **The Number Formats list in the status bar**

Johnson has written a successful formula. The fat calories account for 55 percent of total calories in the hamburger. Now she copies this formula down column D—first to find the percent of fat calories for the other food items on the menu, and then to find the total percent of fat calories for the entire meal. Figure 1.15 shows the results of her work. Notice that fat calories for the meal amount to 51 percent of total calories—far above the recommended 30 percent. Johnson notes that this worksheet will easily prove a point about the nutritional value of fast-food lunches.

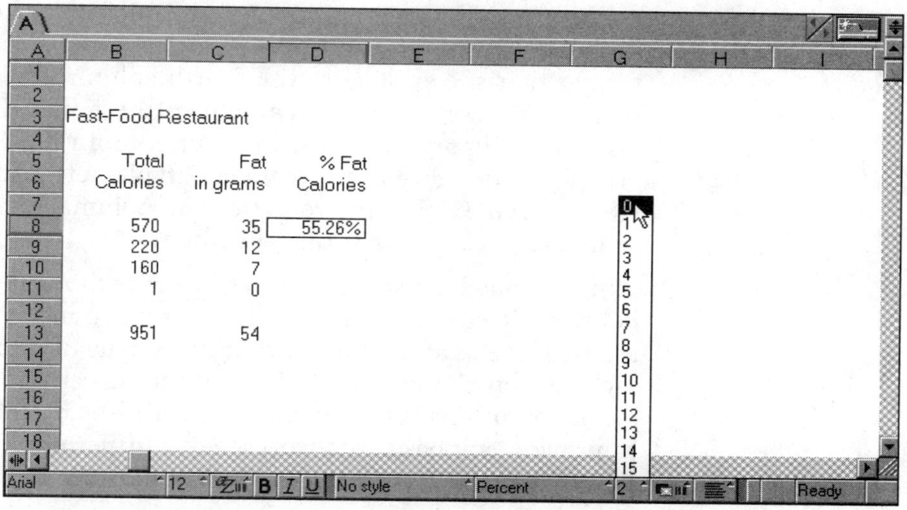

Figure 1.14: **The Decimal Places list in the status bar**

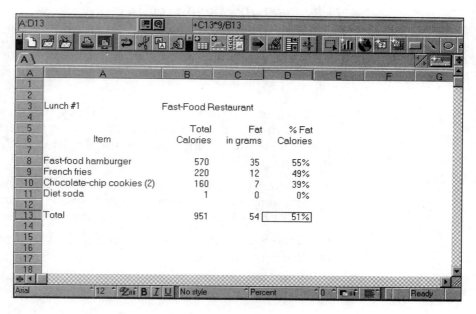

Figure 1.15: **Adding formulas to the worksheet**

Preparing the Worksheet for Presentation

Up to now, Barbara Johnson has concentrated on entering data and writing formulas, without worrying much about the appearance of her worksheet. With two exceptions, she's left data items in their default formats, alignments, and display styles. One exception is the percent format that she applied to the fourth column (column D) in her data table; the second is the alignment of the four column headings. You can see in Figure 1.15 that the four column heading labels in rows 4 and 5 are not displayed in their default, left-justified positions. The label in cell A6 is centered over the column of food items, and the remaining headings are right-justified.

Now the nutritionist is ready to give some thought to the appearance of her worksheet. 1-2-3 offers a rich variety of options for changing appearances. For example, she can change formats of numeric values, displaying them in the currency, decimal, or percentage format. Values and labels can be displayed in different styles—bold, italics, or underlining—to provide emphasis in a worksheet. Furthermore, 1-2-3 offers a selection of fonts and sizes for displaying and printing the information in a worksheet.

Changing Styles and Type Size

Johnson decides to use combinations of bold, italic, and underlined styles—along with larger type sizes for selected data items—to prepare her worksheet for presentation. You can see the result of her work in Figure 1.16.

Changes in style and size can be accomplished with the click of a mouse, thanks to 1-2-3's status bar. For example, here are the steps Johnson takes to change the column of food items (A8 to A11) to bold italic type style:

1. Select the target range of cells—in this case, A8 down to A11—by positioning the mouse pointer at A8 and dragging the mouse down to A11. Lotus 1-2-3 highlights the entire range.

2. Click the Bold button on the status bar. The bold style is applied to all the labels in the range.

3. Click the Italics button on the status bar. The italic style is applied to the labels.

Planning and Creating a Worksheet

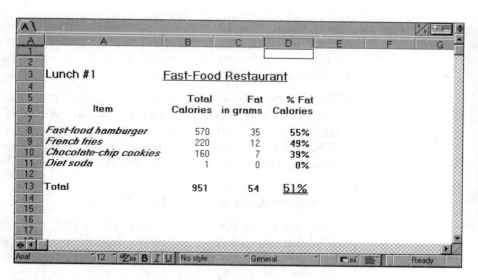

Figure 1.16: New type styles for the worksheet

Notice how these actions are accomplished. First you select a range of cells on which to perform the action, and then you choose an option to apply to the range. This is a typical way of accomplishing many kinds of tasks in a worksheet. Conveniently, Lotus 1-2-3 for Windows often lets you choose between the following two approaches:

▶ Select a range first, and then choose a command that applies to the range.

▶ Choose a command, and then use the command's dialog box to specify the range over which the command will act.

The method you choose is usually a matter of personal preference and convenience. The end result is the same.

The nutritionist has now completed her first version of the lunch worksheet. She saves her work to disk by pulling down the File menu and choosing the Save As command. She supplies the name Lunches for her worksheet, and 1-2-3 saves the file under the name LUNCHES.123.

 NOTE 123 is the default extension name for workbook files.

She's now ready to begin formulating other lunch menus to include in her presentation. Clearly there's nothing particularly healthy about this first menu. She decides to prepare two more menus, the first a combination of items purchased from the fast-food restaurant and food prepared at home, and the second a "brown bag" lunch brought from home.

This is where 1-2-3's "what-if" facility becomes central to her work. As you'll see, the nutritionist can create the two new lunch worksheets simply by changing a few data items in the original worksheet. Whenever she enters new numeric data values to describe a particular food item, 1-2-3 automatically recalculates the applicable formulas.

Making Changes in the Data

For Lunch #2, Johnson decides to make two changes in the menu. She substitutes a turkey sandwich for the fast-food hamburger and a carton of low-fat milk for the diet soda. She begins by entering the names of the two new food items in cells A8 and A11, as follows:

A8	Turkey sandwich (with mayo)
A11	Low-fat milk (1/2 pint)

To change the contents of a cell in a worksheet, you can simply select the cell and enter a new label or value. When you confirm the entry by pressing ↵, the previous data item disappears and the new item takes its place. If you've applied a display style to the cell, it is retained. In this case the two new food items are still displayed in bold italic type.

Next, Johnson determines the approximate caloric and fat contents of these two new menu items. She enters the calories into column B (cell B8 for the turkey sandwich and B11 for the milk). She enters the fat content, in grams, into column C (cell C8 for the sandwich and C11 for the milk).

Automatic Recalculations

Each time Johnson enters a new numeric data value, three changes take place instantly:

▶ A new column total appears in the Total row at the bottom of the worksheet (row 13).

▶ A new fat percentage appears in the final column of the worksheet (column D).

Planning and Creating a Worksheet

▶ The new total fat percentage for the meal appears in cell D13.

In effect, these are the "what-if" factors for her worksheet. What happens to the total calories, the total fat content, and the fat percentages if she changes an item in the menu? Because 1-2-3 recalculates formulas instantly, the answers appear as soon as the nutritionist makes changes to the worksheet data. Figure 1.17 shows the second lunch menu, with the revised nutritional information. (Notice that the title of the worksheet has also been changed.) In terms of fat calories, this meal is an improvement over the first one, but it still does not meet the goal of the 30-percent fat diet.

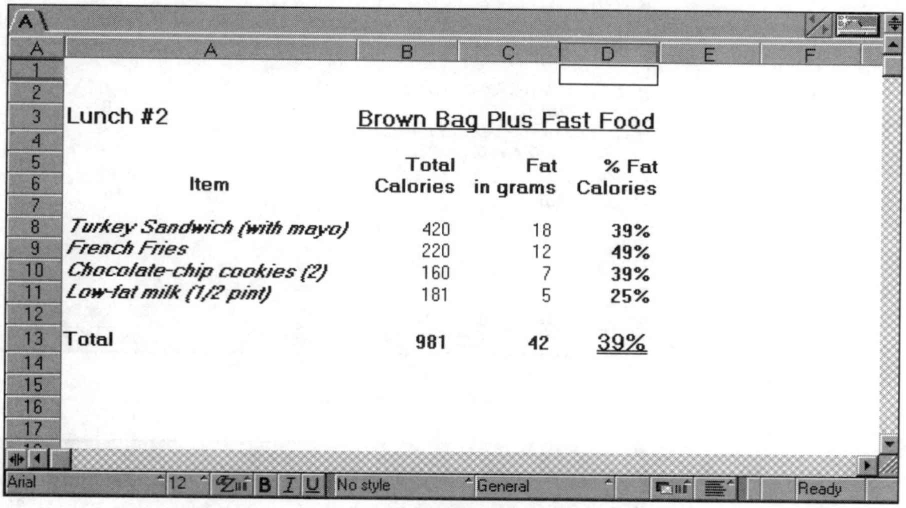

	A	B	C	D
3	Lunch #2		Brown Bag Plus Fast Food	
5		Total	Fat	% Fat
6	Item	Calories	in grams	Calories
8	Turkey Sandwich (with mayo)	420	18	39%
9	French Fries	220	12	49%
10	Chocolate-chip cookies (2)	160	7	39%
11	Low-fat milk (1/2 pint)	181	5	25%
13	Total	981	42	39%

Figure 1.17: Revised data and recalculated formulas

For her third menu, the nutritionist wants to illustrate the importance of making simple but careful dietary decisions. After revising the title again, she makes two more changes to the menu. She removes the mayonnaise from the turkey sandwich and substitutes an apple for the French fries. She enters the new calorie and fat data into columns B and C. Once again, 1-2-3 recalculates her formulas as she changes nutritional data. The final result, shown in Figure 1.18, is a dramatically reduced fat percentage, well below the 30-percent goal.

For convenience, Barbara Johnson decides to save all three of the lunch worksheets in a single file. She clicks the New Sheet button twice to add two sheets to the current workbook, and copies the current version of the lunch menu to each of the two new sheets. She reformulates the first two menus in worksheets A and B, and retains the final menu in worksheet C. When she saves her work to disk, the LUNCHES.123 workbook file contains three sheets, one for each lunch menu she will present in her seminar. Figure 1.19 shows two of these sheets in separate panes.

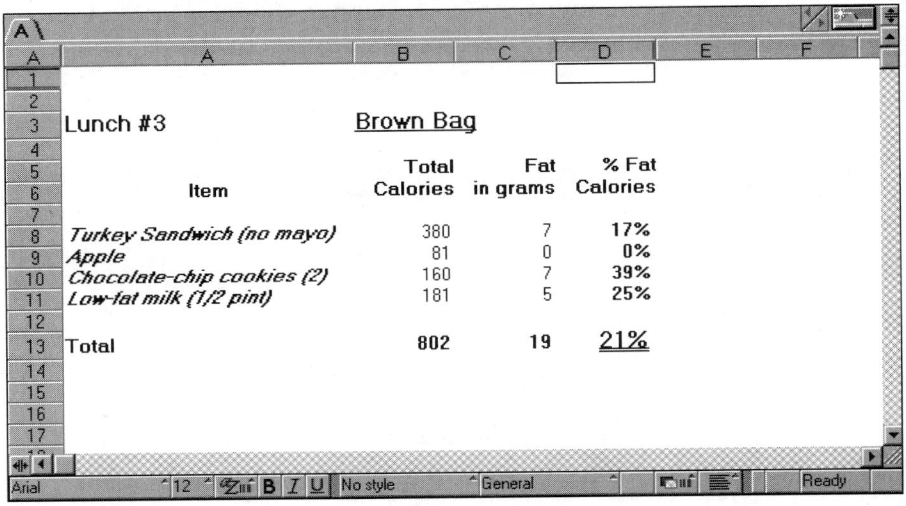

	A	B	C	D
3	Lunch #3		Brown Bag	
5		Total	Fat	% Fat
6	Item	Calories	in grams	Calories
8	Turkey Sandwich (no mayo)	380	7	17%
9	Apple	81	0	0%
10	Chocolate-chip cookies (2)	160	7	39%
11	Low-fat milk (1/2 pint)	181	5	25%
13	Total	802	19	21%

Figure 1.18: *The final lunch menu*

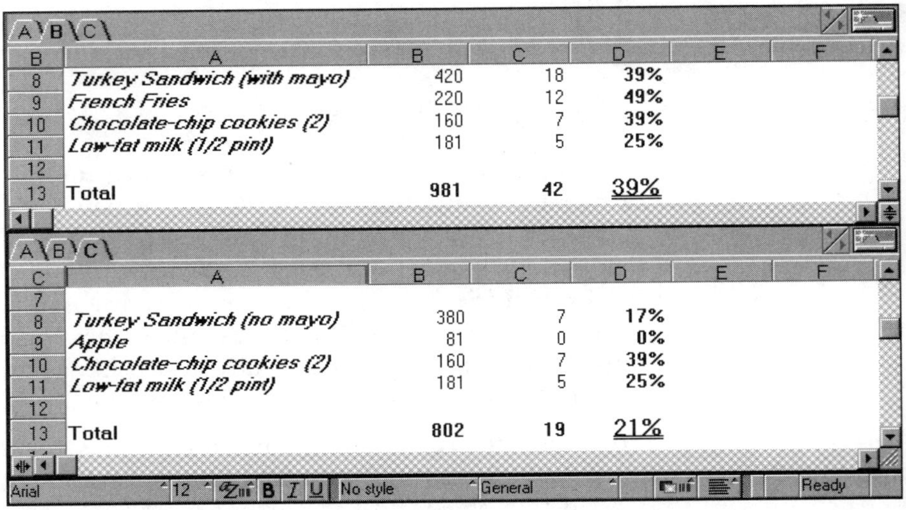

Sheet B:

	A	B	C	D
8	Turkey Sandwich (with mayo)	420	18	39%
9	French Fries	220	12	49%
10	Chocolate-chip cookies (2)	160	7	39%
11	Low-fat milk (1/2 pint)	181	5	25%
13	Total	981	42	39%

Sheet C:

	A	B	C	D
8	Turkey Sandwich (no mayo)	380	7	17%
9	Apple	81	0	0%
10	Chocolate-chip cookies (2)	160	7	39%
11	Low-fat milk (1/2 pint)	181	5	25%
13	Total	802	19	21%

Figure 1.19: *Two of the three lunch sheets, displayed in separate panes.*

Creating Charts

The charting component of 1-2-3 gives you efficient tools for creating graphs and charts from your worksheet data. Lotus 1-2-3 supports an impressive variety of two- and three-dimensional chart types, including line charts, bar charts, and pie charts. The initial steps for creating a chart are simple:

1. Select a worksheet range with the titles, numbers, and labels you want represented in your chart.
2. Click the Chart SmartIcon.
3. Click inside your worksheet at the location where you want the chart to appear.

> **NOTE** For a detailed look at creating charts, see Chapters 9 and 10.

After you have created the initial chart from a table of data, you can change the chart type and revise the chart's titles, labels, and legend if you wish. You can also add other graphic objects, including arrows and frames. Menu commands and SmartIcons offer options for all these features. You can make other revisions directly on the chart itself.

Like the formulas in a worksheet, charts are dependent upon the original data. When you make changes in the data that a chart represents, 1-2-3 automatically redraws the chart.

Designing a Chart

Barbara Johnson now turns her attention to a new topic that she wants to cover in her seminar. She realizes that some consumers have trouble interpreting the nutritional information that appears on food labels. Regarding fat content, Johnson wants a clear way to illustrate the distinction between fat grams and fat calories in a serving of a particular food. For example, Johnson has found the following information on a package of bologna:

Serving size:	1 slice (30 grams)
Calories per serving:	90
Fat per serving:	8 grams

In this example, the fat content (8 grams) is less than a third of the total weight of a serving (30 grams). However, the significant factor is not the weight of the fat, but rather the fat calories in proportion to the total calories. The 8 grams of fat are equivalent to 72 calories, or more than three-quarters of the total caloric content of a serving.

To underscore the importance of this distinction, Johnson decides to create some simple charts and hand them out at the seminar. The charts should illustrate clearly the proportional differences between the weight content and the caloric content of fat in a particular food item.

For this second topic, the nutritionist will take advantage of the charting component of 1-2-3. She begins by creating a small worksheet table with the information about a slice of bologna. As shown in Figure 1.20, the worksheet has two rows of numeric data, giving the weight and the caloric content of the food serving. There are three columns of numbers. The first two columns display the fat content and the total serving data. The final column is a calculation of the percentage of fat. While the fat is only 27 percent of the weight of a serving, it is a full 80 percent of the caloric content.

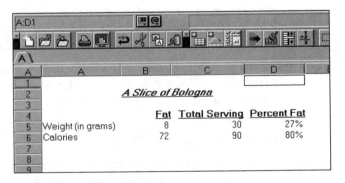

Figure 1.20:   The Bologna worksheet

Creating a Chart

After completing this worksheet, the nutritionist follows a quick and easy sequence of steps to create her charts. She decides to create one chart to represent the relationship between the total weight of a serving and the fat weight in the serving. She'll then create a second chart to represent the relationship between total calories and fat calories.

She bases each chart on a particular range of numeric data: B5..C5 for the weight and B6..C6 for the calories. To create a chart, she clicks the Chart SmartIcon and then clicks the location on the Bologna worksheet where she wants the chart to appear. Then she can make any adjustments she wants in the style and appearance of the chart.

> **NOTE** When a chart is the object currently selected on the screen, the Chart menu option appears in the menu bar in place of the Range menu option.

The entire job of creating the charts takes only a few minutes. The result of Johnson's work appears in Figure 1.21. Each chart contains two bars. The first chart shows the relationship between the fat weight and the total weight of a serving, and the second chart shows the relationship between fat calories and total calories. The contrast between these two relationships is dramatic, and the nutritionist is satisfied that this handout will adequately illustrate her point to the seminar participants.

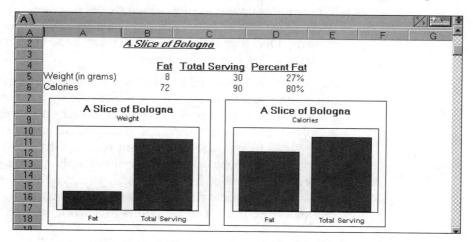

Figure 1.21: **The bologna charts**

For the final topic in her nutrition seminar, Barbara Johnson wants to apply the 30 percent fat diet to a group of people with different nutritional needs. For this purpose, she has created a database of imaginary, but representative, individuals whose daily caloric and fat requirements vary. She wants to compare these individual requirements with the nutritional content of one of the lunch menus she devised earlier. Her goal is to demonstrate the suitability—or inadequacy—of this menu for meeting specific nutritional needs.

Performing Database Operations

A database in 1-2-3 is a collection of records organized in the rows and columns of a worksheet. For example, a database might serve as a business address directory, an employee roster, or an inventory list. Each row in the database contains one record of information—an address, an employee description, an inventory product.

Worksheet columns contain the fields of the database, showing categories of information within each record. The field names appear as column headings in the top row of the database. For example, an employee database might include fields for a worker's name, department, position, salary, supervisor, hiring date, and length of employment. Typically a record in the database includes a data entry for each field. Some entries are labels or numbers that you enter directly from the keyboard. Others may be calculated fields—that is, numeric or chronological items that are calculated from the data in other fields.

The length of a database is equal to the number of records it contains. A database might have a length of a few dozen, or a few thousand, records. Over time, the length of a database changes as you add new records or delete existing records.

After you've developed a database, you can perform a variety of operations on the information it contains. A *query* is an important database operation that finds specific records, based on search criteria that you supply. 1-2-3 uses a companion database management program, Lotus Approach, to manage the query process. But 1-2-3 also offers other important database operations. For example, you can sort the database records in alphabetical, numerical, or chronological order. You can also apply statistical functions to selected records. Lotus 1-2-3 offers a complete set of built-in functions that work on databases.

 NOTE Databases, queries, and database functions are discussed in Chapters 11, 12, and 13.

For the purposes of this introduction, you'll examine the short database that nutritionist Barbara Johnson might develop to describe the nutritional requirements of a representative group of individuals.

Defining a Database

The first step in creating a database is to design the field structure. How many fields should the database contain? What is an appropriate data type and name for each field? The nutritionist wants to include seven fields in her database. On the first row of her database table, she enters seven field names. The first four names—Name, Age, Sex, and Weight—are the headings for personal information about each client. The final three fields—Total Calories, Fat Calories, and Fat Grams—represent nutritional guidelines:

Total Calories	The recommended daily caloric intake needed to maintain a person's current weight. This value is entered directly from the keyboard for each record.
Fat Calories	The recommended maximum daily fat consumption for a person. To find the value of this field, Johnson writes a formula that calculates 30 percent of each entry in the Total Calories column.
Fat Grams	The recommended maximum daily fat consumption in grams. This is also a calculated field, found by dividing the entries in the Fat Calories column by 9. (You'll recall that a gram of fat is equal to nine calories.)

Entering the Records

After creating the field names, Johnson begins entering the individual records of the database. Each client record occupies one row of the table. She begins by entering data in the fields that are not calculated—Name, Age, Sex, Weight, and Total Calories. When these fields are entered for each record, she writes and copies formulas for the two calculated fields, Fat Calories and Fat Grams.

Her completed database appears in Figure 1.22. Notice that the records are in alphabetical order by client name. To work more effectively with the information, she may want to view the database in a different order. 1-2-3 has an efficient Sort command that she can use to rearrange the records quickly. She'll also want to perform other database operations to create a meaningful handout for the seminar participants.

	A	B	C	D	E	F	G
1							
2			Daily Calories and Maximum Fat Consumption				
3							
4	Name	Age	Sex	Weight	Total Calories	Fat Calories	Fat Grams
5	Allen, N.	41	M	135	1650	495	55
6	Barnes, J.	32	F	120	1350	405	45
7	Byron, A.	23	M	185	2250	675	75
8	Everette, Y.	39	F	140	1550	465	52
9	Giles, C.	25	M	225	2700	810	90
10	Hall, N.	52	M	160	1950	585	65
11	Johnson, C.	35	F	155	1700	510	57
12	Lange, G.	27	F	115	1250	375	42
13	Paulson, G.	45	M	145	1750	525	58
14	Ralston, T.	59	F	130	1450	435	48
15							
16							

Figure 1.22: **The database of nutritional guidelines for individual clients**

Sorting and Querying the Database

The Range ➤ Sort command is a simple but versatile tool for rearranging the records of a database. In the Sort dialog box, you select one or more key fields by which the records will be sorted, and you specify whether you want to sort in ascending or descending order. For example, here is what the Sort dialog box looks like for a two-key sort:

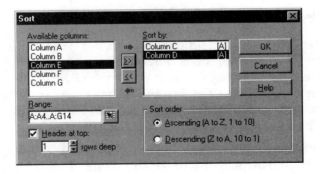

The nutritionist begins her work by sorting the clients from youngest to oldest—in ascending order by the Age field. Figure 1.23 shows the result of this operation. Another useful way to arrange the records is to divide the database into male and female clients, and then sort by weight within the two groups. This sort requires two key fields: The Sex field is the primary key and the Weight field is the secondary key. Figure 1.24 shows the database after this two-key sort has been completed.

	A	B	C	D	E	F	G
1							
2			Daily Calories and Maximum Fat Consumption				
3							
4	Name	Age	Sex	Weight	Total Calories	Fat Calories	Fat Grams
5	Byron, A.	23	M	185	2250	675	75
6	Giles, C.	25	M	225	2700	810	90
7	Lange, G.	27	F	115	1250	375	42
8	Barnes, J.	32	F	120	1350	405	45
9	Johnson, C.	35	F	155	1700	510	57
10	Everette, Y.	39	F	140	1550	465	52
11	Allen, N.	41	M	135	1650	495	55
12	Paulson, G.	45	M	145	1750	525	58
13	Hall, N.	52	M	160	1950	585	65
14	Ralston, T	59	F	130	1450	435	48
15							

Figure 1.23: Sorting the database by the Age field

	A	B	C	D	E	F	G
1							
2			Daily Calories and Maximum Fat Consumption				
3							
4	Name	Age	Sex	Weight	Total Calories	Fat Calories	Fat Grams
5	Lange, G.	27	F	115	1250	375	42
6	Barnes, J.	32	F	120	1350	405	45
7	Ralston, T	59	F	130	1450	435	48
8	Everette, Y.	39	F	140	1550	465	52
9	Johnson, C.	35	F	155	1700	510	57
10	Allen, N.	41	M	135	1650	495	55
11	Paulson, G.	45	M	145	1750	525	58
12	Hall, N.	52	M	160	1950	585	65
13	Byron, A.	23	M	185	2250	675	75
14	Giles, C.	25	M	225	2700	810	90
15							

Figure 1.24: Sorting the database by two key fields, Sex and Weight

Formulating Selection Criteria

Finally, the nutritionist would like to query the database to isolate a specific subset of records from the original table. She wants to find client records that meet a particular condition. Specifically, she'll use data from her Lunches worksheet to answer the following question: Which clients can use the menu from Lunch #3 as a satisfactory way of staying within their maximum fat guidelines?

The nutritionist starts with the assumption that fat consumed at lunch should total no more than one-third of the total daily fat consumption. She chooses the Create ➤ Database ➤ Query Table command to create the initial query, which appears on her worksheet as an object managed by Lotus Approach. Using tools provided by the Lotus Approach application, she defines a criterion for selecting records, and ultimately produces the query shown in Figure 1.25.

Lunch #3 OK			
Name	Age	Sex	Fat Grams
Johnson, C.	35	F	57
Paulson, G.	45	M	58
Hall, N.	52	M	65
Byron, A.	23	M	75
Giles, C.	25	M	90

Figure 1.25: **Querying the database**

As you can see, only half of the clients in the sample database meet this criterion; for the other half, lunch #3 appears to contain too much fat. Barbara Johnson will use this query table to illustrate a final point to her seminar participants: Each client must measure his or her total caloric and fat intake in relation to nutritional requirements and personal weight goals.

Summary

The three components of 1-2-3—spreadsheet, charting, and database management—are designed to work smoothly together in an integrated environment. In many business applications, you'll use these components together to create interrelated tables and documents. Perhaps the single most important characteristic of a 1-2-3 worksheet is its ability to recalculate formulas based on changes that occur in basic data. You'll see examples of this "what-if" capability in many different contexts throughout this book.

In Part Two of this book you'll study the three components in detail. But first, Chapter 2 introduces some additional features of 1-2-3 in the Windows environment.

CHAPTER 2

1-2-3, Windows, and the Web

FAST TRACK

To switch to another application while you're working in 1-2-3,   53

click a button on the Windows 95 taskbar. Or, from the keyboard, press Alt+Tab to step through the open applications, and release the Alt key when you've selected the icon for the program you want to activate.

To view a shortcut menu of commands related to a selected object on the 1-2-3 Desktop,   56

click the object with the right mouse button. Shortcut menus are available for sheets, ranges, charts, graphic objects, database queries, and other objects you'll work with in 1-2-3.

To change the properties of an object,   59

click the object with the right mouse button, and choose the Properties command from the top of the shortcut menu. The resulting InfoBox contains tabbed sections representing categories of properties.

To edit the entry in a cell,   65

double-click the cell itself to switch into Edit mode. 1-2-3 supports in-cell editing.

To change the position and shape of a SmartIcon bar,   **67**

position the mouse pointer over the narrow blue selector at the beginning of the bar, and drag the bar to a new location on the Desktop. Then drag the borders of the bar to change the shape.

To display a different SmartIcon bar,   **68**

click the small down-arrow button at the beginning of any bar, and choose the name of a SmartIcon bar from the resulting pop-up menu.

To change the selection of icons in a SmartIcon bar,   **69**

choose File ➤ User Setup ➤ SmartIcons Setup to open the SmartIcons Setup dialog box. Choose the bar you want to revise from the Bar name list. Remove an icon from the selected bar by dragging the target item out of the Preview box. Add a new icon to the bar by dragging an item from the Available icons list to a target location in the Preview box.

To add a new sheet to a workbook,   **73**

click the New Sheet button at the right side of the tab line. Alternatively choose Create ➤ Sheet and specify the number of sheets you want to add and the location where you want them to appear.

To display a meaningful name on a sheet tab,   **74**

double-click the tab and type the new name directly into the text box that appears on the tab. Press ↵ to confirm the new name.

To get context-sensitive help about almost any command or activity,   **79**

press the F1 function key, or click the Help button on any open dialog box.

To search for a particular help topic by keyword,   **82**

choose the Help ➤ Help Topics command, and click the Index tab. Enter the keyword in the text box at the top of the dialog box, and then select a topic from the index list.

To jump to the Lotus home page on the World Wide Web,   **84**

choose Help ➤ Lotus Internet Support ➤ Lotus Home Page. (Your computer must have a working modem, a Web browser, and an Internet access provider.)

WINDOWS 95 applications work in consistent and predictable ways, regularly providing familiar techniques to carry out everyday tasks. Because Windows programs have many elements in common, you naturally apply much of what you know about one program to all the other applications you learn. For this reason, each new Windows application is easier to master than the previous one.

In this chapter you'll review a variety of features that Windows 95 applications have in common, and you'll see how these features appear in Lotus 1-2-3. In particular, you'll examine:

▶ Menus, shortcut menus, dialog boxes, and icons

▶ Document windows, and the mouse and keyboard techniques for manipulating them

▶ The 1-2-3 Help system

▶ Internet support—including links to online help, and techniques for exchanging documents over the World Wide Web

You took a first look at some of these features in Chapter 1. Now you'll examine them in greater detail in a sequence of hands-on exercises.

> **TIP** If you're a veteran Windows 95 user, you'll move quickly through this chapter, focusing on any details that are new and unfamiliar to you. But if Lotus 1-2-3 is your first major Windows 95 application, you may want to read this chapter from beginning to end and work through each exercise.

Exploring the 1-2-3 Window

As you saw in Chapter 1 (Figure 1.2), the Welcome to 1-2-3 window appears on the screen when you first start the program. If you click the button labeled Create a Blank Workbook to begin your work, two windows fill the Desktop:

▶ The 1-2-3 application window.

▶ A workbook window, displayed inside the application window. This window is initially maximized so that you can see as much of its contents as possible.

You've already worked briefly with both of these windows. Now take another look at the lines located above and below the workbook window, including the title bar, the menu bar, the edit line, the row of SmartIcons, the row of worksheet tabs for the current workbook, and the status bar at the bottom of the screen. The tools on these lines give you a variety of ways to carry out operations on 1-2-3 worksheets. There's an intentional redundancy built into all these tools; you can often choose among two or three different techniques for accomplishing the same task. Accordingly, 1-2-3 also lets you rearrange the application window itself to suit your own work patterns.

For example, you can move the row of SmartIcons to other places on the screen. You can also remove several sets of tools from the screen altogether to make more space for displaying the contents of the worksheet window. The items you can hide from view include the edit line, the row of SmartIcons, the worksheet tabs, and the status bar.

Throughout this chapter you'll examine these tools and the features they represent. In later chapters, you'll focus on what these tools actually do as you create worksheets, graphs, and databases.

Title Bar and Control Buttons

At the beginning of a session with 1-2-3, the caption in the title bar identifies the Lotus software suite, Lotus SmartSuite 97; the current application, 1-2-3; and the temporary name of the active worksheet, Untitled. When you save a worksheet to disk and assign it a name, the title bar gives the name and location of the file, for example:

```
Lotus SmartSuite 97 - 1-2-3: [C:\LUNCHES]
```

Depending on your current activity, the title bar may provide other information. For example, when you choose a menu or highlight a command, the title bar provides a brief description. To review this feature, try this exercise:

1. Press the Alt key to activate the menu bar, and press → a few times. Each time you highlight a new item in the menu bar, the description on the title bar changes accordingly. For example, when you highlight the View menu, the title bar provides a general-purpose description of the tools in the View menu:

    ```
    Control the display settings for the sheet and 1-2-3
    ```

2. With the View menu highlighted, press ↓ several times and notice the descriptions in the title bar. For example, the description of the Split command is

   ```
   Split the window into two or four panes
   ```

3. Press the Escape key twice to close the menu and deactivate the menu bar. Now the application name reappears in the title bar.

Sizing and Moving the Application Window

As you saw in Chapter 1, the minimize, restore, and close buttons for the workbook window are initially displayed at the right side of the menu bar. Likewise, the application window has its own equivalent of these three buttons, at the right side of the 1-2-3 title bar. Experiment with 1-2-3's control buttons in the following exercise:

1. Click Restore, the middle button on the right side of the 1-2-3 title bar. The application window shrinks to a smaller size. The Restore button is replaced by the Maximize button—an icon representing a full-screen application window.

2. Place the mouse pointer over the right border of the 1-2-3 window. The mouse pointer becomes a double arrowhead, pointing left and right. Holding down the left mouse button, drag the border to the left, toward the center of the screen, and release the mouse button.

   You've reduced the 1-2-3 window to about half its full-screen width. Notice how 1-2-3 rearranges the menu bar so that you can still see all of the menu names.

3. Position the mouse pointer over the bottom border of the window, and drag the border up toward the center of the screen. You've now reduced the vertical dimension of the window by about half of the full-screen length.

4. Position the mouse pointer over the 1-2-3 window's title bar, hold down the left mouse button, and drag the window toward the center of the screen. Figure 2.1 shows a partial view of the Desktop after all these actions are complete. (Of course, you'll see your own set of application icons on the Windows 95 Desktop.)

Exploring the 1-2-3 Window

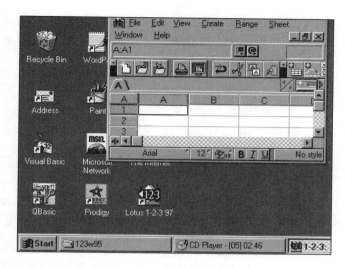

Figure 2.1: **Moving and changing the size of the 1-2-3 window**

> **TIP** Reducing the size of the application window gives you the opportunity to view more than one application at a time in the Windows environment.

5. Click the application window's Maximize button, the middle of the three buttons at the right side of the title bar. The 1-2-3 window returns to its full-screen dimensions.

6. Click the Minimize button. The 1-2-3 window disappears and is represented by a button on the Windows 95 Taskbar.

7. Click the 1-2-3 button on the Taskbar. The 1-2-3 window reappears in its original dimensions.

If you sometimes prefer to use the keyboard rather than the mouse for Desktop operations, an application's Control menu provides convenient alternatives, as you'll learn in the next section.

The 1-2-3 Window Control Menu

The Control-menu icon for the application window is on the left side of the title bar. You can pull down the application's Control menu by clicking the Control-menu icon with the mouse or by pressing

Alt+spacebar at the keyboard. The Control menu contains the following commands:

Restore

Move

Size

Minimize

Maximize

Close

Some of these commands are dimmed in certain contexts; that is, they appear in light gray text. A dimmed entry in any menu means that the command isn't available for use in your current activity. The Restore, Minimize, Maximize, and Close commands are equivalent to buttons that appear on the right side of the title bar. The Move and Size commands are tools you can use to move and size the application window. Try working with these commands in the following exercise:

1. Press Alt+spacebar to pull down the 1-2-3 Control menu, and press **R** to choose the Restore command. The 1-2-3 window returns to the location and size you gave it in the previous exercise (Figure 2.1).

2. Pull down the Control menu again and press **M** to choose the Move command. A four-headed pointer appears over the window.

3. Press ↑ on your keyboard. A shadow border appears above the 1-2-3 window. Keep pressing ↑ until the top of the shadow border is near the top of the Desktop. Then press ← until the left side of the shadow border approaches the left side of the Desktop. Press ↵ to complete the move operation.

4. Pull down the Control menu again and press **S** to choose the Size command. Press → and ↓ repeatedly to extend the right and bottom borders, until the 1-2-3 window border takes up almost the full dimensions of the Desktop. Press ↵ to complete the Size operation.

5. Pull down the Control menu again and press **X** to choose the Maximize command. The window returns to its original, full-screen dimensions.

The Close command in the Control menu—like the Close button on the 1-2-3 title bar—closes the 1-2-3 window and ends your current session with the application. Choosing Close (or pressing Alt+F4) is the same as choosing File ➤ Exit 1-2-3. Before an exit, 1-2-3 checks all open workbooks to see if you've made any changes without saving them to disk. If any unsaved workbooks are found, a dialog box appears on the screen, giving you the options of saving or abandoning your work:

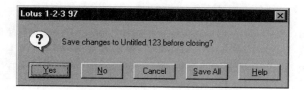

You can click the Cancel button or press Escape at the keyboard to cancel the Exit and return to your worksheet.

As you saw in Chapter 1, workbook windows have their own Control menus with commands similar to the list in the 1-2-3 Control menu. You can use these commands—or the corresponding buttons on the right side of the menu bar—to change the size and shape of the workbook window, or to close the window altogether.

Switching between Applications

To switch to another open application on the Windows Desktop you don't need to close or minimize the 1-2-3 window. Instead, you can simply click the target application's button on the Windows 95 Taskbar. Or, if you prefer to use the keyboard to make the switch, use the shortcut Alt+Tab. When you press these keys concurrently, a box appears over your current work, displaying icons for all the programs you're currently running, for example:

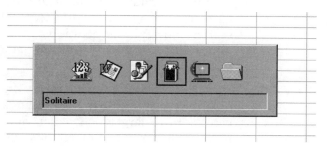

To select another application, press Tab repeatedly (while holding down the Alt key) until the rectangular marker moves to the icon for the program you want to activate. Release the Alt key to make the switch. Repeat this process when you're ready to return to 1-2-3.

The 1-2-3 Menus

Activate the 1-2-3 menu bar by pressing Alt or F10, or by clicking one of the menus with the mouse. When a workbook is active, the menu bar contains eight names, each representing a pull-down menu:

Menu	Description
File	Includes commands for creating a new workbook, opening an existing workbook file from disk, saving workbooks to disk, printing sheets, and previewing your work before you print it. Other useful features include team-computing commands, Internet commands, and access to the Workbook Properties dialog box, which allows you to control the appearance and operations of the current workbook. The User Setup commands are for customizing 1-2-3's appearance and behavior. A list of file names at the end of the File menu gives you a quick way to open files you've recently worked with; simply choose a name from the menu list to open a file.
Edit	Provides an Undo command for reversing an action in 1-2-3. This menu also includes commands for performing cut-and-paste and copy-and-paste operations; for clearing information from a selection of worksheet cells; for creating links between 1-2-3 workbooks and documents from other applications; for copying formulas across ranges of worksheet cells; for performing search-and-replace operations; for checking the spelling in a workbook; and for creating and managing macros and script programs.
View	Provides ways of controlling a workbook's appearance on the screen. With the commands in this menu, you can zoom to larger or smaller views of the workbook; hide or display the SmartIcons, the edit line, and the status bar; freeze rows or columns of titles in view on

the current sheet; split the current workbook window into panes; and open the Workbook Properties dialog box, via the Set View Preferences command.

Create   Gives you direct ways to add new objects to the current workbook file, including sheets, charts, maps, database queries (and other database-related objects), drawn objects and other graphics, and embedded OLE objects from other applications.

Range   The Range Properties command provides a useful dialog box for changing the properties on a selection of worksheet cells. In addition, the Range menu contains individual commands for inserting and deleting rows or columns in a sheet; assigning names to sheet ranges; filling ranges with series of data; sorting records of data; storing comments in worksheet cells; transposing the dimensions of tables; parsing long labels; and copying formats from one part of a sheet to another. The Version commands are designed to expand the power of what-if analysis on a worksheet. Finally, the Analyze commands provide a host of advanced analysis tools.

Sheet   The Sheet Properties command opens the Sheet Properties dialog box, a one-stop location for changing the characteristics of the current sheet. In addition, the Sheet menu contains commands for deleting sheets from a workbook; outlining the information in a sheet; hiding a sheet or restoring it to view; and creating a group of sheets for the purpose of copying properties from one sheet to another.

Windows   As you saw in Chapter 1, the New Window command creates additional windows for viewing the contents of the current workbook. This menu also contains Tile and Cascade commands for arranging multiple open worksheet windows within the 1-2-3 application; and a list of all open files, giving you a convenient way to activate the file you want to work with.

Help   Provides a variety of entry points into the 1-2-3 Help system, as well as an introductory tour and links to Internet support.

Before reading on, take a few minutes to browse through the menu system and examine the brief descriptions that 1-2-3 displays in the title bar for each command in the pull-down menus.

Context-Sensitive Menus

In some contexts, 1-2-3 replaces the Range and Sheet menus with other menus designed to provide commands for specific tasks. Menus you'll see as you continue your work with 1-2-3 include Chart, Drawing, and Map for tasks related to charts and graphics; Query for database operations; Preview for making use of the print preview window; Script and Debug, for developing programs for use in 1-2-3; and menus for managing objects that you embed in a 1-2-3 workbook.

Shortcut Menus

As you've seen, 1-2-3 gives you another convenient way to perform tasks on selected objects: You can click an object with the right mouse button to view a shortcut menu of commands that relate specifically to the object you've selected. In this context, the object you're working with might be a chart, a database query, a sheet, a range of cells on a sheet, or even a single cell.

For example, suppose you have selected a range of cells on the current sheet and you want to view the menu commands that apply to a range. You know that you can find range-related commands in both the Edit menu and the Range menu, but for convenience you'd rather see all the commands in a single list. A shortcut menu is just the tool you need. Try this exercise:

1. In the current sheet, position the mouse pointer over cell A1 and hold down the left mouse button. Move the mouse pointer down to cell D6 and then release the button. In response, 1-2-3 displays the area from A1 to D6 as a black background and white borders. This is a range selection.

2. Now position the mouse pointer anywhere within the range that you've selected, and click the right mouse button once. The resulting menu list contains the most commonly used commands from the Edit and Range menus that apply to a range.

3. Move the mouse pointer down the list of commands in the shortcut menu. As you do so, 1-2-3 highlights each command, one at a time, and displays a brief description of the current command on the title bar, as shown in Figure 2.2.

4. To select a command from the shortcut menu and carry out the action it represents, you could simply click the command with the mouse. But for now, click elsewhere on the sheet, or press the Escape key, to close the shortcut menu.

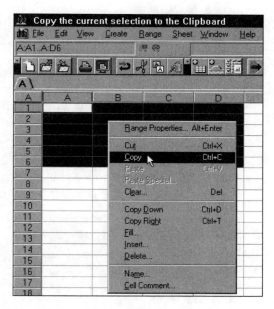

Figure 2.2: **Viewing the shortcut menu for a range. Click a range, or any other object, with the right mouse button to display a shortcut menu of relevant commands.**

As you continue working with the features of 1-2-3, you'll find that shortcut menus are often the the best way to select commands for tasks related to a particular object. You may be surprised at the variety of shortcut menus available in 1-2-3; if you're not sure whether a shortcut menu exists for an object, just point and click the right mouse button to find out.

You can view another example of a shortcut menu by clicking the A tab of the current sheet with the right mouse button. When you do so, you'll see the shortcut menu for a sheet:

This menu contains a combination of commands from the Create and Sheet menus. In particular, you can choose commands for creating a new sheet, deleting the current sheet, hiding a sheet, or restoring a hidden sheet to view.

Notice that the first command in this menu is named Sheet Properties. The Properties command typically appears at the top of each shortcut menu. When you choose this command, 1-2-3 displays an InfoBox, a central location for changing many properties at once:

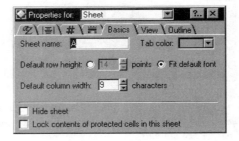

You'll take a look at this important feature next.

Using an InfoBox

In the previous generation of spreadsheet programs, commands for changing the format and appearance of a sheet or a range were typically scattered around several different menus. For example, if you wanted to change the name, column width, colors, font, numeric format, alignment, and other characteristics of a sheet or range, you might find yourself working with a variety of different menus, commands, and dialog boxes. In 1-2-3 97 Edition, you can select settings for all these properties in a single location, called an InfoBox.

The InfoBox for an object is organized into tabbed sections, where each tab represents a particular category of properties. For example, the InfoBox for a sheet contains seven tabs, one each for fonts, alignments, number formats, colors, "basic" properties, display properties, and outlining features. When you position the mouse pointer over a particular tab, 1-2-3 displays an information bubble that identifies the contents of the tabbed section:

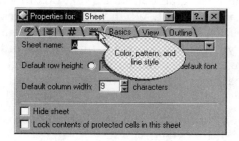

To switch to a different category of properties, you simply click the appropriate tab.

The InfoBox has two important features that make it different from the typical dialog box:

▶ The box stays open until you intentionally close it by clicking the close button at the right side of the title bar. This means that you can change as many properties as you wish—from any sequence of tabbed sections—while the InfoBox remains on the screen. You can also move freely back and forth between the InfoBox and your work on the sheet itself. For example, you can select a cell or range, enter new data, edit existing data, and even choose other menu commands while the InfoBox is open on the Desktop.

▶ Whenever you change a setting in the InfoBox, you can see the result immediately in the range, sheet, or object that you're working with. For example, suppose you increase the default column width in the InfoBox for a sheet. As soon as you make the change, the columns are adjusted on the sheet itself, where you can see the results.

Options in the InfoBox

As you the examine various tabbed sections representing the categories of sheet properties, you'll see that InfoBoxes contain a variety of *controls* to accept choices, settings, or information from you. Text boxes, scrollable lists, option buttons, check boxes, command buttons, color palettes—these are some of the most common controls you'll see in InfoBoxes and other dialog boxes that appear on the screen as you work with 1-2-3. Because these controls are common to most Windows 95 programs, they are both familiar and intuitively easy to use.

For example, the Basics tab contains a text box in which you can enter a name for the current sheet. When you do so, your entry becomes the caption on the sheet's tab. The Basics tab also contains two other text boxes, in which you can enter the default column width and the default row height. You can enter numeric settings into these boxes directly from the keyboard, or you can click the adjacent arrows with your mouse to increase or decrease the current settings.

The Number Format tab displays scrollable list boxes from which you can select a format by category:

This tab also contains check boxes that allow you to turn certain features on or off. Click a check box with the mouse to change its status from checked to unchecked or from unchecked to checked. In a group of check boxes, each option is independent from the others.

By contrast, a group of option buttons requires you to select one among two or more options, as illustrated in the Outline tab:

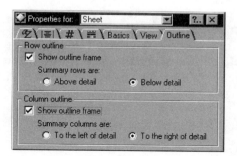

In the first pair of option buttons, you can choose to display summary rows above or below the detail rows in a sheet outline. In the second pair, you can show summary columns to the left or the right of detail columns. When you click an option button to switch it on, any other buttons in the same group are automatically turned off. (You'll learn about 1-2-3's outlining feature in Chapter 16.)

The View tab provides a color box from which you can choose the color of grid lines in your sheet. This box appears when you click the down-arrow button at the right side of the Grid lines option:

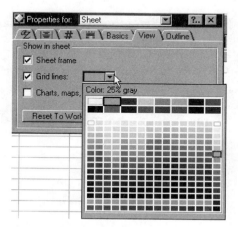

To change the color of the grid lines, you simply click a color in the box. This color appears immediately, on the lines that separate rows and columns of cells in your sheet. Notice that the View tab also contains a command button displaying the caption "Reset to Workbook

Defaults." After you've made changes in the appearance of your sheet, you can click this button if you decide to return to the original settings.

In addition to the shortcut menu, there are two ways to open the InfoBox for a range, sheet, or object. You can choose a command from the menu bar; for example, the Sheet ➤ Sheet Properties command opens the InfoBox for the current sheet. Alternatively, you can click the appropriate SmartIcon. The Sheet Properties SmartIcon opens the sheet InfoBox:

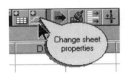

To open the InfoBox for a cell or a range of cells, select the range, and then choose the Range Properties command from the Range menu. Or click the Range Properties SmartIcon:

The Workbook Properties dialog box (shown in Figure 2.3) gives you the opportunity to specify settings for all the sheets in a workbook. (Unlike other property boxes, Workbook Properties requires you to click OK to confirm any changes you've made in the settings; in this sense, it is different from the InfoBoxes for sheet, range, and object properties.) To view this dialog box, choose File ➤ Workbook Properties, or click the Workbook Properties SmartIcon:

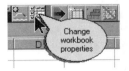

As you begin working with other 1-2-3 objects—such as charts, database queries, maps, drawn objects, and so on—you'll learn that you can typically open InfoBoxes by choosing a command from a shortcut menu or the menu bar, or by clicking a SmartIcon.

Now you'll continue to explore the elements of the 1-2-3 application window, focusing next on the edit line.

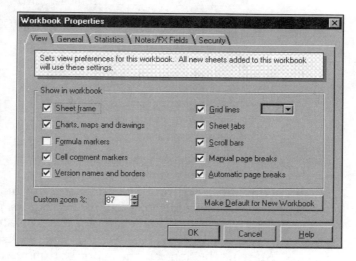

Figure 2.3: The Workbook Properties dialog box allows you to change the settings of all the sheets in a particular workbook.

The Edit Line

The edit line contains two main parts, the *selection indicator* and the *contents box*. In addition, it displays two important buttons, called the Navigator and the Function selector:

▶ **Selection indicator.** On the left side of the edit line, the selection indicator gives the address of the current cell in the active sheet, as shown at the top of Figure 2.4. The complete address includes the letter name of the active sheet followed by a colon and the cell address, as in A:E8. When you select a cell or range for which you've defined a name, the selection indicator displays the name rather than the address.

▶ **Contents box.** The contents box at the right side of the edit line displays the value, label, or formula that is stored in the current cell. The contents box shows what is actually *stored* in the cell, rather than what is *displayed* in the cell. For example, cell E8 in Figure 2.4 contains a formula that finds the sum of the values in row 8. As you can see, the contents box displays the formula @SUM(B8..D8), while the cell itself displays the result of the formula.

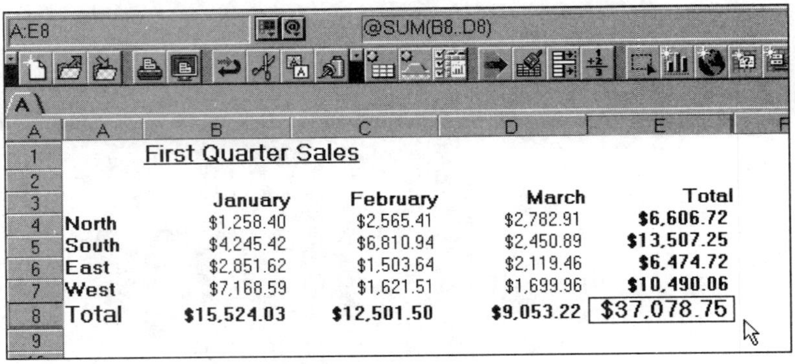

[figure showing edit line with First Quarter Sales spreadsheet]

Figure 2.4: The elements of the edit line

▶ **Navigator button.** The Navigator button, located just to the right of the selection indicator, is a useful tool for jumping to any named area on a worksheet. For example, the worksheet in Figure 2.5 contains ranges named North, South, East, West, January, February, and March. Clicking the Navigator button results in an alphabetized list of all these names. To select a corresponding range on the worksheet, you can simply click one of the names in the list. You'll learn much more about range names in Chapter 3.

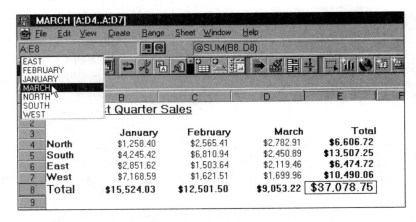

Figure 2.5: A drop-down list of range names from the Navigator

▶ **Function selector.** The Function selector, located to the right of the Navigator button, provides a list of commonly used @ functions, such as @SUM, @AVG, and @ROUND, as shown in Figure 2.6. As you learned in Chapter 1, functions are built-in tools for performing calculations in a 1-2-3 worksheet. Chapters 7 and 8 cover functions in detail, and the appendixes provide a reference guide to the entire function library.

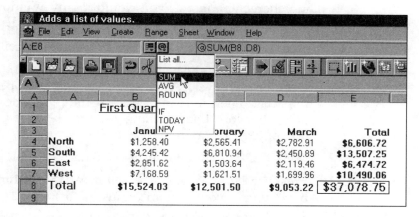

Figure 2.6: *The drop-down list of commonly used @ functions available from the Function selector*

When you activate the Contents box to edit the entry in the current cell, 1-2-3 displays two additional buttons between the Function selector and the contents box; these buttons are known as the Cancel button (a boldface **X**) and the Confirm button (a ✔):

You can click the Cancel button to back out of the current edit without changing the contents of the active cell; or you can click the Confirm button to complete an edit.

In-Cell Editing

Thanks to 1-2-3's in-cell editing feature, you're not likely to use the edit line as frequently as you might have in older versions of the program.

In 1-2-3 97 Edition, you can type and revise a value directly in the cell where you're entering it. While you are first entering a value, you can press the F2 function key to switch into Edit mode; then you can use the Home, End, →, and ← keys to move the cursor to a new position within your entry in the cell. You can insert, delete, or overwrite existing characters, just as you would in any Windows text box. To complete an entry, press ↵; to cancel it, press the Escape key.

Here is a brief exercise that demonstrates in-cell editing:

1. Select cell A1 in the active worksheet, and type the word **Spreadsheet**. (Don't press ↵ yet.) As you type, your entry appears directly in the current cell. The mode indicator, at the right side of the status bar, displays the word Label, telling you that 1-2-3 is accepting your entry as text rather than a numeric value.

2. Press F2. The mode indicator changes to Edit.

3. Press the Home key. In the cell itself, the flashing cursor jumps to the beginning of your text entry, just before the *S*.

4. Now type **Lotus 1-2-3**, followed by a space. This new text is inserted before the existing text.

5. Complete the entry by pressing ↵. 1-2-3 returns to the Ready mode.

When you complete these steps, the label "Lotus 1-2-3 Spreadsheet" appears in cell A1.

You can also edit an *existing* entry in any cell of a worksheet:

1. Position the mouse pointer over the cell you want to edit. (Make sure the pointer has the shape of a white arrow pointing up and to the left; if it has some other shape, move the pointer to the center of the cell.)

2. Double-click the left mouse button. The mode indicator displays Edit.

3. Use the Home, End, ←, or → keys to move the cursor to the position where you want to change the entry. You can also use the Backspace key to delete the character just before the cursor, or Del to delete the character after the cursor.

4. Press the Ins key one or more times to toggle between insert and typeover modes. In the insert mode, any new characters you type at the

keyboard are inserted at the current cursor position; in the typeover mode, each character you type replaces the character at the cursor position.

5. Make any necessary changes in the entry, and press ↵ to confirm.

Before you read on, you might want to practice this technique on the label you've entered in cell A1.

Removing the edit line   Because of the in-cell editing feature, the edit line is likely to become less central to your work than in previous versions of 1-2-3. Accordingly, 1-2-3 allows you to remove the edit line from the screen altogether if you want to. To do so, choose the View ➤ Hide Edit Line command. In response, 1-2-3 removes the edit line from the top of the Desktop, giving you an extra line of space for your workbooks. The disadvantage of removing the edit line, however, is that you no longer have access to the Navigator and Function selector buttons. Decide for yourself whether or not the edit line tools are important to your work. (To restore the Edit line, choose View ➤ Show Edit Line.)

The SmartIcons

Just below the Edit line is the row of SmartIcons, the one-click shortcuts for performing common operations in 1-2-3. The SmartIcons are organized into different sets of tools that are related to specific tasks or objects. Each set is known as a SmartIcon *bar*. The SmartIcon bars can be customized in several interesting ways; for example, you can:

▶ Display or hide a selected bar, depending on your current activity.

▶ Move a SmartIcon bar to a different position on the screen.

▶ Choose between two display sizes for SmartIcons, regular or large.

▶ Change the selection of tools displayed in a particular SmartIcon bar.

▶ Create new SmartIcons and write programs to define the corresponding action.

To view a list of some of the available SmartIcon bars, click the small down-arrow button that appears at the beginning of any bar. By making selections from the resulting menu, you can display or hide particular bars, or open the SmartIcons Setup dialog box:

In many cases, 1-2-3 automatically displays a new SmartIcon bar when you create or select a particular object. For example, when you're working with a chart, a database query, or a graphic object, 1-2-3 displays the icon set that's most likely to prove useful to you with the current selection. By default, the Universal SmartIcon bar is always displayed, because it contains tools that are relevant to almost any activity in 1-2-3. Other bars appear to the right of the Universal bar. For example, try clicking the A tab for the current sheet. In response, 1-2-3 displays the Sheet SmartIcon bar to the right of the Universal bar:

Now click any cell inside the sheet itself; in response, 1-2-3 replaces the Sheet bar with the Range SmartIcon bar:

Using the SmartIcons Setup dialog box, you can change the selection of icons in any bar—producing a set of tools that suits your own work patterns. The following section shows you how to do this, and how to move a SmartIcon bar to new positions on the screen.

Changing the Contents of a SmartIcon Bar

To customize a set of SmartIcons, begin by choosing the SmartIcons Setup command from the SmartIcon menu (the menu that appears when you click the arrow button at the beginning of a SmartIcon bar). Alternatively, choose the File ➤ User Setup ➤ SmartIcons Setup command. The SmartIcons setup dialog box appears, as shown in Figure 2.7. At the left side of this dialog box you see a scrollable list of all the available SmartIcons. At the top of the dialog box is a row of the icons that are part of a selected bar (the Range bar in this illustration). At the right is a drop-down list named Bar Name, from which you can select the bar you want to modify. To remove an icon, you simply drag it out of the current bar. To add a new icon, you select the icon from the Available icons box and drag it into the current bar.

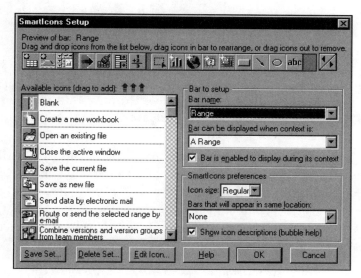

Figure 2.7: **The SmartIcons Setup dialog box**

For example, suppose you want to remove the Undo SmartIcon from the Universal bar, and replace it with the Check Spelling SmartIcon. Here are the steps for making this change:

1. Choose File ➤ User Setup ➤ SmartIcons Setup. The SmartIcons Setup dialog box appears on the screen.

2. Pull down the Bar name list, and choose Universal. In response, 1-2-3 displays the icons of this bar in the Preview box, as shown in Figure 2.8.

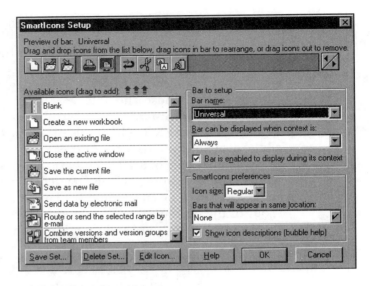

Figure 2.8: Selecting the Universal bar

3. Move the mouse pointer to the Undo SmartIcon in the Preview box. Holding down the left mouse button, drag the Undo icon out of the box. When you release the mouse button, this icon is removed from the Universal bar.

4. Scroll down the Available icons list until you locate the "Check spelling" icon. As you can see in Figure 2.9, this icon contains a picture of a small book labeled ABC.

5. Using your mouse, drag this icon up to the Preview bar and drop it in place at the former location of the Undo icon.

6. Click OK to complete the change.

When you complete these steps, the new SmartIcon appears in the Universal bar:

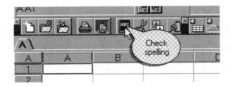

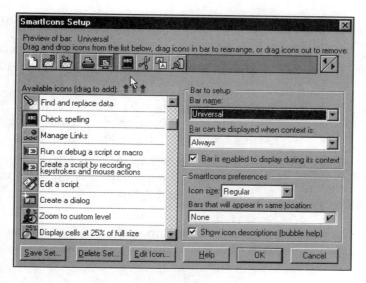

Figure 2.9: Dragging a new SmartIcon to the Universal bar

To restore the original selection of icons in this bar, choose File ➤ User Setup ➤ SmartIcons Setup, drag the Check Spelling SmartIcon out of the Universal set, and drag the Undo icon back in again.

TIP At the top of the Available icons list in the SmartIcons Setup dialog box, you'll see an entry labeled "Blank" (see Figure 2.8). This is not a SmartIcon, but rather a tool that you can use to separate groups of icons in the bar. Drag it to any position along the bar to create a narrow blank space between two icons.

NOTE Several other options in the SmartIcons Setup dialog box may prove useful to you as you customize the SmartIcons in the 1-2-3 environment. The list named "Bar can be displayed when context is" allows you to choose the context in which a particular SmartIcon set will appear on the screen. The Icon size list gives you a choice between Regular or Large icons. You might want to select the Large option to make the SmartIcons easier to see. Finally, the check box labeled "Show icon descriptions (bubble help)" determines whether 1-2-3 displays help bubbles when you place the mouse pointer over a particular SmartIcon. This option is checked by default, but you can uncheck it if you find bubble help unnecessary or inconvenient.

Changing the Position of the SmartIcon Bar

You can use your mouse to drag a SmartIcon bar to a new position on the 1-2-3 Desktop and to display the bar in a new shape. To do so, follow these steps:

1. Move the mouse pointer to the small blue space just at the beginning of a SmartIcon bar. The pointer takes the shape of a hand that looks like it's ready to grab the SmartIcon bar.

2. Hold down the left mouse button and drag the bar to the location where you want to display it. A dotted border marks the place where the bar will ultimately appear.

3. Release the mouse button. The SmartIcon bar moves to the target location. For example, Figure 2.10 shows the Universal bar near the bottom of the application window.

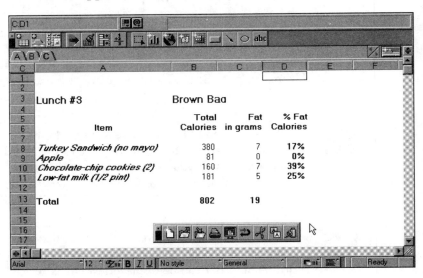

Figure 2.10: **Moving the Universal SmartIcons to a position near the bottom of the 1-2-3 window**

4. To give the SmartIcon bar a new shape, position the mouse pointer along any border of the bar and drag the border to create new dimensions. For example, Figure 2.11 shows the Universal bar in the form of a rectangle.

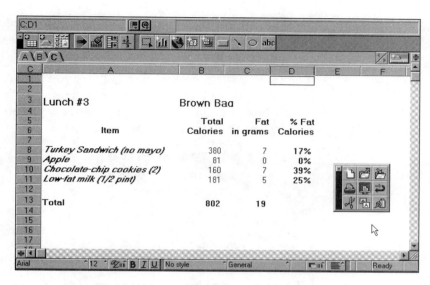

Figure 2.11: Changing the shape of the SmartIcon bar

Sheet Tabs

Just above the workbook window is the tab line. This line displays tabs for all the sheets in a workbook. Each time you click the New Sheet button, an additional tab appears. For example, Figure 2.12 shows a workbook that contains many sheets. As you can see, a pair of tab-scroll arrows appears just to the left of the New Sheet button when a workbook contains too many tabs to display at once.

Figure 2.12: Tabs, tab-scroll arrows, and the New Sheet button

To summarize, here is a review of the tools on the tab line:

▶ **Sheet tabs.** The sheet tabs themselves identify the sheets in a workbook. Tabs are initially labeled with letters of the alphabet, from A to Z, AA to AZ, BA to BZ, and so on. Each new workbook starts out with only one sheet, labeled A; but you can store as many as 256 sheets in a given workbook.

▶ **Tab-scroll arrows.** The tab-scroll arrows are for scrolling through the tabs of a workbook if there are too many tabs to be displayed at once on the tab line.

▶ **New Sheet button.** The New Sheet button adds a new sheet to the active file. Each time you click this button, 1-2-3 adds one new sheet immediately after the active sheet.

The Create ➤ Sheet command allows you to add multiple sheets to the current workbook at a position that you specify. In the Create Sheet dialog box you can specify the number of sheets to be added and the position in relation to the current sheet:

Changing the Name on a Sheet Tab

You can easily change the labels on tabs to assign meaningful names to the sheets of a workbook. For example, Figure 2.13 shows a workbook that contains several sheets for keeping household records. The tab for each sheet has a name that clearly identifies the contents of the sheet itself.

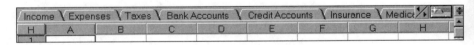

Figure 2.13: Changing the names displayed on tabs

Here are the steps for changing the name displayed on a tab:

1. Double-click the tab belonging to the sheet you want to rename. Inside the tab, 1-2-3 displays a text box in which you can enter the new name.
2. Type a new name for the sheet.
3. Press ↵.

After you change the name of a sheet, you can use either the new name or the original letter name to refer to the sheet. For example, in Figure 2.13 you can use A:A1 or Income:A1 to refer to the upper-left corner cell in the first sheet.

TIP Another way to give each sheet tab a distinctive appearance is to assign different colors to the tabs in a workbook. To change the color of a tab, click the tab with the right mouse button, and choose Sheet Properties from the resulting shortcut menu. Click Basics in the InfoBox for sheet properties and then select a color from the Tab color control.

The Status Bar

As you've seen, the 1-2-3 status bar is more than a source of information about your current work. It's one of several dynamic tools you can use to change the appearance of a worksheet or an object on a sheet. Across the length of the status bar are buttons you can click to view and change options for your current work.

The status bar options vary according to the object that is currently selected. For example, different sets of buttons appear for a chart, a graphic object, a query, and a worksheet range. Figure 2.14 shows the status bar buttons for a range; they give you quick ways to apply fonts, colors, formats, and styles to entries on a worksheet. To use one of these buttons, begin by selecting a target range of cells; then click a button and select an option:

Button	Description
Font	Lists the text fonts available on your system.
Point size	Shows the available point size options.
Text color	Displays a grid of available text colors.
Font attribute	Provides three on/off buttons for boldface, italics, and underlining.
Style	Lists any named styles you've defined for the current sheet. (Named styles are covered in Chapter 6.)
Format	Shows the available numeric formats, including currency, percentage, date, and time formats.
Decimal	Lists options for the number of digits after the decimal point for the current number format.
Background color	Displays a grid of available background colors.
Alignment	Shows the horizontal alignment and justification options for a range of data.

Figure 2.14: **The status bar buttons for a range**

The Mode Indicator

The second-to-last button at the right side of the status bar is the mode indicator, which identifies your current activity. Here's a review of several common modes:

Mode	Meaning
Ready	1-2-3 is ready for your next action—for example, a data entry or a menu selection.
Label	1-2-3 recognizes your current entry as text.
Value	1-2-3 recognizes your current entry as a numeric value.
Point	You are pointing to a range as part of a new formula entry.
Menu	You are in the process of choosing a menu command or selecting options from a 1-2-3 dialog box.
Edit	You are ready to edit the contents of a cell.

TIP Check the mode indicator when you're in doubt about the status of your current activity. Sometimes you'll find that 1-2-3 is in a different mode than you thought. In some cases you can press Escape one or more times to return to the Ready mode.

A Review

You've now examined the title bar, menu bar, edit line, SmartIcon set, sheet tabs, and status bar in some detail. Here's a review of what you've learned:

Feature	Description
Title bar	Displays the application name and the current workbook name, or a brief description of a selected menu command.

Menu bar	Provides access to menu lists and dialog boxes in the 1-2-3 command set.
Edit line	Contains the selection box and contents box, along with the Navigator and Function selector buttons.
SmartIcon bars	Display versatile sets of tools for streamlining your work with worksheets, charts, database queries, and other objects.
Sheet tab line	Identifies the multiple sheets in a workbook, and provides the New Sheet button.
Status bar	Contains buttons you can use to change the appearance of a range or object.

Getting Help

A complete and systematic Help system is a typical part of any Windows 95 application. 1-2-3 meets the standards for providing help, giving you clear and relevant on-screen help for any task you need to perform. While you're working in 1-2-3, you can bring up detailed information about virtually any topic, command, function, procedure, tool, or technique. You can also view multi-step demonstrations of some key tasks.

Information is organized by general topics or by indexed keywords. One good way to begin exploring the help system is by browsing through the general contents. Choose Help ➤ Help Topics and click the Contents tab on the resulting Help window. As shown in Figure 2.15, the Help contents are organized into "books" of general information about the program.

Double-click any book in the Contents tab to view the topics it contains. Some books are further organized into additional books; others contain a list of topics. For example, when you double-click the Top 10 Tasks book, you'll see a list of ten help topics that you can read about (Figure 2.16). Double-click a topic to open a selected Help window. Figure 2.17 shows the window for "Copying, moving, and filling." Like many help topics, it contains cross-references to related topics, displayed in green text with a solid underline. You can jump to a related topic by clicking this cross reference. (The mouse pointer becomes an upward-pointing hand when you select a cross-reference topic in a help window.)

Figure 2.15: **The general topics of the Help system**

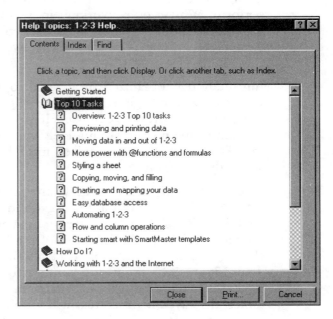

Figure 2.16: **Help topics contained in a book. Open any book in the Contents tab by double-clicking the book icon.**

Finding Context-Sensitive Help

Context-sensitive help is one of the most useful features of any online Help system. You can get help relevant to your current activity by clicking a Help button or pressing the F1 key at almost any time during your work in 1-2-3. For example, imagine that you are selecting options in a dialog box, but you can't recall exactly how to use some aspect of the command in question. To get help you click the Help button on the dialog box. A Help window appears with specific information about the command you're working with.

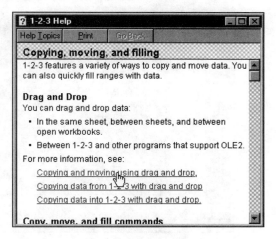

Figure 2.17: *A help topic. You can jump to a cross-referenced topic by clicking the underlined green text.*

TIP Many Help topics contain important terms and essential vocabulary that are displayed in green and underlined with a dotted line. When you click one of these references, 1-2-3 displays a definition box that explains the meaning of the term. After reading the definition, you can return to the original Help topic by clicking inside its window.

Here is a brief exercise to demonstrate this feature:

1. Click the Workbook Properties SmartIcon (or choose File ➤ Workbook Properties) to open the tabbed dialog box in which you can set the properties for the current workbook.

2. When the Workbook Properties box appears on the screen, click the Help button at the lower-right corner. In the resulting Help window you can read briefly about the options of the View tab, and you can select from several cross-referenced topics, displayed in green with solid underlining, as shown in Figure 2.18.

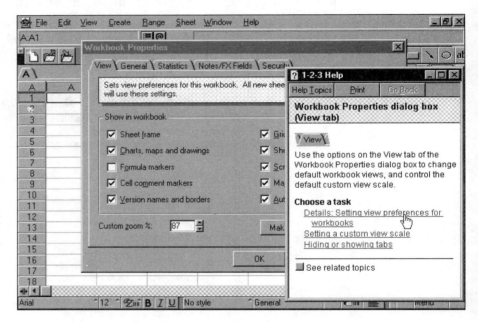

Figure 2.18: **Getting context-sensitive help**

3. Click any of the related topics for detailed information about a specific task.
4. Optionally, read definitions of important terms or special vocabulary by clicking green cross-references with dotted underlining (Figure 2.19).

To close a Help topic, click the Close button at the upper-right corner of the window, or press Escape on the keyboard.

Help Window Features

As you saw in the previous exercise, the Help windows have their own title bars, Control-menu boxes, and Minimize, Maximize, and Close buttons. These features work the same way as in other windows. For example, if you need to enlarge a Help window so you can see more information at once, click the Maximize button.

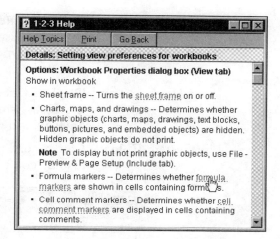

Figure 2.19: Jumping to a cross-referenced topic. Notice the reference to a definition, marked by dotted underlining.

Just beneath the title bar is a row of buttons (see Figure 2.19) that you can use to work within the Help system. Click Help Topics to jump to the original Help window, as shown back in Figure 2.15. Click Print to send the current Help topic to your printer. Click the Go Back button to return to the previous Help topic.

You can also view a shortcut menu for any topic by clicking inside the Help window with the right mouse button. As shown in Figure 2.20, the resulting menu contains several important commands that will help you work with a topic:

Command	Description
Annotate	Opens a window in which you can enter and save your own notes related to a particular Help topic.
Copy	Sends a copy of the current topic to the Windows 95 Clipboard. You can then paste the text of the Help topic to any other document within Windows. (For example, you might want to paste a Help topic to a word-processed document.)
Print Topic	Sends the current topic to your printer.

Font   Displays a menu of three size options. You can choose to display Help topics in small, normal, or large type. (The Normal option is the default.)

Keep Help on Top   Displays three options that determine whether the Help window will always stay on top of other windows on the 1-2-3 Desktop.

Use System Colors Can be checked or unchecked to specify the display colors for the Help window.

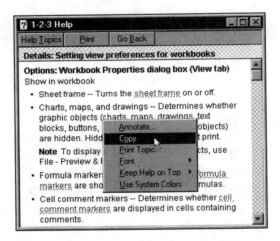

Figure 2.20:   *The shortcut menu for a Help topic. To open this menu, click inside the Help window with the right mouse button.*

Using the Help Index

You can also find information in the Help system by searching for indexed keywords. Here's a brief exercise that will introduce you to the Index:

1. Choose Help ➤ Help Topics.
2. Click the Index tab. The resulting window contains a text box for the target search word and a scrollable list of index entries from which you can select the information you want (Figure 2.21).

3. In the text box at the top of the window, enter the word **InfoBox**. As you do so, the index list beneath the text box automatically scrolls to the InfoBox topic. Beneath InfoBox you'll see a list of indented subtopics.

4. Double-click the **overview** subtopic. A new Help window appears with a general discription of the InfoBox feature.

5. When you've finished reading this help topic, click Help Topics to return to the Index, or press Escape to return to your work.

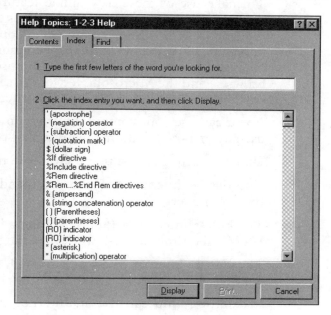

Figure 2.21: **The Index for the Help system**

The 1-2-3 Help menu provides other resources and services that prove helpful in some circumstances. The Help ➤ Tour command starts an animated tour of the 1-2-3 application. This introductory tour is worth taking for both beginners and experienced 1-2-3 users. It provides a good orientation to the major features of the program.

Finally, Help ➤ Lotus Internet Support displays a list of Lotus support sites on the World Wide Web. Internet connections are the final subject of this chapter.

1-2-3 and the Internet

In an effort to catch the current wave of cybermania, most major Windows applications now offer various forms of Internet support. Lotus 1-2-3 and its companion applications in Lotus SmartSuite 97 are no exception. You can use 1-2-3 to publish information on the Web or to open files that are available on the Web. You can also use the Web to find support and help for Lotus applications.

To make use of these new online features, your system needs to be ready to connect to the Internet. This means you need a working modem, a Web browser, and an account with an Internet service provider. In Windows 95, one common software combination for meeting these requirements is the Microsoft Internet Explorer (a Web browser) and the Microsoft Network (a service provider, for which you pay a monthly membership fee). But there are many alternatives.

If you can use your computer to sign on to the Web, you'll be able to use any of 1-2-3's Internet features and connections, including:

- Direct links to Lotus support sites from the Help menu.
- The File ➤ Internet ➤ Open command, for opening a file from an Internet server.
- The File ➤ Internet ➤ Publish command, for creating a Web page (an HTML file) from a 1-2-3 worksheet range.
- The File ➤ Internet ➤ Save command, for saving a 1-2-3 workbook file to an FTP server.

In addition, you can use an Internet connection as a tool in team computing. You can exchange workbook documents with colleagues and receive their feedback via e-mail. You'll explore this topic in Chapter 15.

Finding Information on the Web

As a quick online experiment, try choosing the Help ➤ Lotus Internet Support ➤ Lotus Home Page command now. If all goes well, Lotus activates your Web browser, and the sign-on window for your service provider appears on the Desktop. Once online, you jump directly to the Lotus home page. One version of the page appears in Figure 2.22.

From the home page, you can jump to any topic that interests you by clicking an underlined hyperlink.

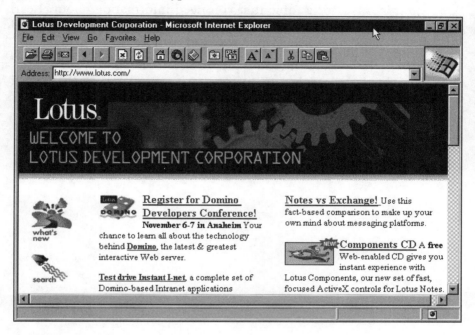

Figure 2.22: **The Lotus home page**

Summary

The 1-2-3 application window displays several lines of important tools—the title bar, menu bar, edit line, SmartIcons, sheet tabs, and the status bar. As you learn to take advantage of these tools, your work in 1-2-3 becomes more efficient and more effective.

In addition, 1-2-3 provides tools like shortcut menus and InfoBoxes to streamline your work. A shortcut menu displays the most important commands related to a selected object on the 1-2-3 Desktop. An InfoBox is a central location for changing the properties of an object. InfoBoxes are organized in tabbed sections, representing categories of properties. An InfoBox stays on the Desktop until you close it, allowing you to change any selection of properties in one operation.

One of the most important resources in 1-2-3 is its Help system. The Help menu and the Help window each give you many ways to search for a topic that you need information about. Learn to take advantage of the 1-2-3 for Windows Help window as a guide to understanding worksheets, charts, and databases.

New Internet support features allow you to exchange data over the Internet, or to connect to resources on the World Wide Web. You'll explore these features further in upcoming chapters.

PART 2

The Components of 1-2-3

CHAPTER 3

Worksheet Basics: Entering Data

FAST TRACK

To delete the contents of a cell or range on the worksheet,   94
select the cell or range and press the Delete key.

To undo the effect of your last command or action,   95
choose Edit ➤ Undo or click the Undo SmartIcon.

To complete an entry in a cell and select a neighboring cell for the next entry,   96
press ↵ to move to the next cell down; or press →, ←, or ↑ to move to a different cell after you complete the entry.

To compute the total of a range of numbers,   97
select a blank cell at the end of the range, then click the Sum SmartIcon; or enter a @SUM function directly into the worksheet. Alternatively, enter **Total** as the label just to the left of a row—or just above a column—where you want to see totals.

To select a range with the mouse,   105
point to one corner of the target range, hold down the left mouse button, and drag the mouse pointer to the opposite corner.

To select or preselect a range with the keyboard,	**106**

press the F4 function key to switch to the Point mode, then use arrow keys to define the range. (Use Ctrl+PgUp or Ctrl+PgDn to define a three-dimensional range over adjacent worksheets in a window.) Press ↵ to complete the range selection and return to the Ready mode.

To assign a name to a range of cells,	**107**

select the range and choose Range ➤ Name; enter the name and click OK. Alternatively, click the range with the right mouse button and choose the Range Properties command from the resulting shortcut menu. Then click the Basics tab and enter a name for the range.

To copy a range using the drag-and-drop operation,	**110**

select the range that you want to copy and position the mouse pointer along the perimeter of the range. The pointer takes the shape of an open hand. Hold down the right mouse button and the Ctrl key on the keyboard, and drag the range to the location where you want to display a copy of the data.

To perform a copy-and-paste operation,	**112**

select a source range and click the Copy SmartIcon; then select the top corner cell of the destination range and click the Paste SmartIcon.

To save a worksheet file for the first time and supply a name for the file,	**115**

click the Save SmartIcon and enter a file name into the Save As dialog box.

To assign a password to a worksheet file,	**116**

click the Protect File button on the Save As dialog box. Enter the password twice into the Set Password dialog box.

To update an existing file after you've made changes in the active worksheet,	**118**

click the Save SmartIcon or choose File ➤ Save.

ONE of the most remarkable qualities of the 1-2-3 spreadsheet is its flexibility. Rather than providing a single set of fixed techniques for performing tasks, 1-2-3 offers you a multitude of tools and options so you can do your work in your own way. As soon as you begin entering data onto a sheet, the results reflect your own requirements, preferences, and style.

In this chapter you'll practice the basic procedures for entering data:

- Entering labels and values
- Selecting ranges on a sheet
- Calculating totals
- Assigning names to ranges
- Copying ranges of data from one place to another
- Saving a worksheet

To work on these skills, you'll begin developing a worksheet for an imaginary company named Computing Conferences, Inc., which plans and conducts computer training conferences for businesses. Your worksheet will compute the projected revenues, expenses, and profits of a one-day conference.

Figure 3.1 shows a sample of the sheet, similar to the way it will appear when you finish the exercises in Chapters 3 through 6. The worksheet is divided into sections. The top section gives general information about a one-day conference: the name, location, date, price of admission, and two attendance estimates (a minimum and a maximum). The next two sections show projected revenues and expenses, based on attendance. The two columns on the right side of the worksheet display financial figures based on the minimum and maximum attendance estimates, respectively. The bottom line gives the anticipated profit, again with projections based on the two different attendance estimates.

This version of the worksheet contains projected data for a particular training conference. But at the same time, the sheet is carefully designed as a general-purpose template for any event that Computing Conferences is planning. It can easily be reused to display the expenses, revenues, and profits of other conferences. The five areas that are shaded in light gray are the input ranges for information about a given conference. All the other numeric values are calculated from the input data. When new values are entered into the input areas, 1-2-3 recalculates the formulas in the worksheet and displays new results in other ranges. You'll see how this works as you proceed.

```
          Computing Conferences, Inc.
       Profit Projection for a One-Day Conference

   Conference: Computing for Video Stores
   Place:      St. Louis
   Date:       15-Oct-97                Expected Attendance
                                        Minimum    Maximum
   Price:      $195.00                     80         150


                              Per Person   Min.Total   Max.Total
   Projected Revenues
       Attendance                          $15,600.00  $29,250.00
       Video Sales            $35.00        $1,400.00   $2,625.00

       Total Revenues                      $17,000.00  $31,875.00

   Projected Expenses -- Fixed
       Conference Room                      $1,500.00   $2,000.00
       Video Production                     $1,000.00   $1,000.00
       Promotion                            $3,500.00   $3,500.00
       Travel                                 $800.00     $800.00
       Total Fixed Expenses                 $6,800.00   $7,300.00

   Projected Expenses -- Variable by Attendance
       Conference Materials   $8.25           $660.00   $1,237.50
       Coffee and Pastries    $3.25           $260.00     $487.50
       Box Lunch              $4.75           $380.00     $712.50
       Total Variable Expenses              $1,300.00   $2,437.50


   Projected Profit                         $8,900.00  $22,137.50
```

Figure 3.1:   The conference worksheet

This example represents an important approach to developing worksheets in 1-2-3. You can simplify and streamline your work if you think of each new worksheet you develop as a template for similar tasks you might need to accomplish in the future. To be sure, not all worksheets lend themselves to this kind of planning. But each time you start a new sheet, you should ask yourself whether you're likely to perform a similar job again, on a daily, weekly, monthly, quarterly, or even yearly basis. If so, you should carefully organize your work so that you can reuse the sheet for future computational tasks.

Start up 1-2-3 now if you haven't already done so. In this chapter's hands-on exercises, you'll enter a variety of labels and values onto the sheet.

Developing a Worksheet

As you begin creating a worksheet, you may sometimes find yourself entering data in a temporary location. Because 1-2-3 gives you simple ways to move blocks of data from one place to another and to insert new blank rows and columns, you're free to perform initial data-entry tasks in any way that's convenient. You can easily reorganize your work later. With this in mind, you'll begin your work in the following exercise by entering the data for fixed expenses at the top of the worksheet. Then, when you're ready to develop other parts of the worksheet, you'll make room by moving the fixed-expense section down to its final position in the sheet.

Entering Labels

You'll recall that a label is a non-numeric data entry in a cell. Labels typically appear on sheets as titles, column headings, and row descriptions. When you begin entering a label, 1-2-3 switches into Label mode. By default, 1-2-3 left-aligns labels, but you can easily use the alignment button on the status bar to change label alignments.

Lotus 1-2-3 has an interesting way of displaying long labels. When a left-aligned label has more characters than will fit in a cell, the display extends across adjacent cells to the right if those cells are empty. But if the cells to the right already contain data, the long label display is cut short within its own cell. To see how this works, enter the two title lines at the top of the conference worksheet:

1. Use the arrow keys or the mouse to select cell B1. Type the company name, **Computing Conferences, Inc.**

   As you type, your entry appears in the cell itself. The mode indicator (at the right side of the status bar) displays the word Label.

2. Press ↵ to complete your entry. The entry extends across row 1, into cells C1 and D1, as shown in Figure 3.2. When you press ↵, 1-2-3 automatically moves the cell pointer down to B2.

3. Enter the worksheet title in this cell: **Profit Projection for a One-Day Conference**.

4. Press ↵ to complete the entry. Again, the long label crosses empty cells C2, D2, and E2.

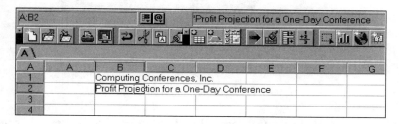

Figure 3.2: *Entering long labels into worksheet cells*

Now press ↑ to move back up to cell B2. By examining the contents box on the edit line (see Figure 3.2), you can see how 1-2-3 identifies the entry in cell B2:

```
'Profit Projection for a One-Day Conference
```

Even though this label is displayed across cells B2 through E2, its actual storage location is cell B2 alone.

> **NOTE** In the contents box, a single-quotation mark (') at the beginning of a label means that the label is left-aligned. Other alignment prefixes include the double-quotation mark (") for right-alignment, and the caret (^) for center-alignment.

What happens to a long label if you enter data in the cell to its immediate right? To answer this question, try the following exercise:

1. Press → to select cell C2. Notice that the contents box shows no entry for this cell. Cell C2 is empty, even though the display of the label in B2 extends into C2.

2. Type **abc** as a temporary label in cell C2.

3. Press ↵ to complete the entry. Notice what happens to the long label display in cell B2. It's cut off within the width of its own cell, and C2 now displays the new label.

4. Press ↑ and ← to select cell B2 again.

As shown in Figure 3.3, the contents box in the edit line displays the entire long label that you originally entered in cell B2, even though the sheet itself displays only the first several letters of the label.

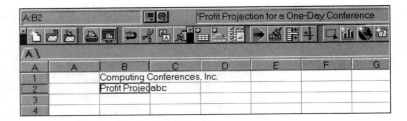

Figure 3.3: **Experimenting with a long label**

In summary, the display of a left-aligned long label extends into the cells to the right if those cells are empty. But the long label display is truncated if a cell to the right contains an entry of its own. As a result of this experiment, you now have an unwanted label entry in cell C2. Deleting this entry is a simple step.

Deleting an Entry

To delete a label or value in a cell, you can simply select the cell and press the Delete key on your keyboard. For example, follow these steps to delete the "abc" label in cell C2:

1. Select C2.
2. Press the Delete key.

When you delete the label in cell C2, the long label in cell B2 is displayed once again across cell C2, D2, and E2. There's no entry in cell C2 to interrupt the display.

Now pull down the Edit menu, shown in Figure 3.4, to look briefly at commands you can use for deleting the contents of a cell or range of cells. The Cut command deletes an entry and copies it to the Windows 95 Clipboard; this is the first step in a cut-and-paste procedure. By contrast, the Clear command gives you the options of clearing the contents, style, and format of a cell—along with other properties and contents—as you can see in the Clear dialog box:

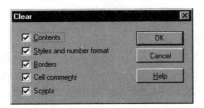

> **TIP** The Cut and Clear commands are also available in the shortcut menu that appears when you click a cell or range with the right mouse button.

Figure 3.4: The Edit menu

Because the Delete key is so readily available for deleting the contents of a cell or range of cells, you might sometimes perform deletions unintentionally. If this happens—or if you make any other mistakes during your work in 1-2-3—you can use the Undo command to restore your worksheet to its state before the last action.

Using the Undo Command

To undo the effect of your last action at the keyboard or with the mouse, you can pull down the Edit menu and choose Undo, the first command on the menu, or use the keyboard shortcut, Ctrl+Z. Or, simplest of all, you can click the Undo SmartIcon, the sixth button on the Universal SmartIcon bar.

Here is an exercise with the Undo command:

1. Press ← to select cell B2. This is the cell that currently contains the second line of the worksheet title "Profit Projection for a One-Day Conference."

2. Press the Delete key. The entry in the cell disappears. Imagine that you've performed this action by mistake. You now want a quick way to correct your error.

3. Click the Undo SmartIcon. The label entry in cell B2 reappears.

> **NOTE** To use Undo successfully, you have to correct a mistake before you perform another action. Undo operates only on an action you perform just previous to choosing the command.

Next you'll continue entering labels into the conference sheet, to produce the work shown in Figure 3.5. As you do so, keep in mind that you can press an arrow key (right, left, or up) instead of the ↵ key to complete an entry. Like ↵ itself, an arrow key performs two actions at once: It completes your entry in the current cell and moves the pointer to a new cell for the next entry.

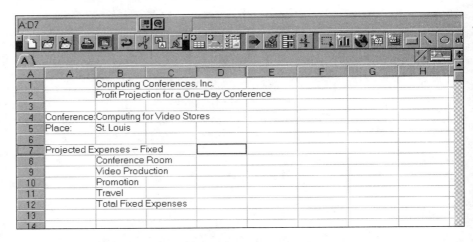

Figure 3.5: **Entering labels into the conference worksheet**

Follow these steps to enter the labels:

1. Enter **Conference:** into cell A4 and **Place:** into A5.

2. At the right of these entries, enter the name and place of the current conference: **Computing for Video Stores** in B4 and **St. Louis** in B5.

3. Enter the subtitle **Projected Expenses—Fixed** into cell A7.

4. Finally, enter these column labels, representing the fixed-expense categories, into the range of cells from B8 to B12:

Cell	Enter
B8	**Conference Room**
B9	**Video Production**
B10	**Promotion**
B11	**Travel**
B12	**Total Fixed Expenses**

These categories represent the expenses that remain unchanged regardless of the number of people who attend the conference—the one-day rental cost of the conference room, the cost of producing a video of the conference, the pre-conference promotion expenses, and the amount spent on travel to the conference site. (Later you'll enter a group of variable expenses that depend directly on attendance.)

The next step is to begin entering numeric values for the fixed expenses.

Entering Values and Computing Totals

As you know, a value is an entry that 1-2-3 accepts as a number. A value can become part of an arithmetic formula in your worksheet.

> **TIP** Whenever you begin an entry with a digit, 1-2-3 assumes you're beginning a numeric value. Accordingly, the mode indicator displays the word Value. But sometimes you may enter a label that happens to begin with a digit—for example, in an address entry such as 456 Flower Street. When you complete a label entry like this one, 1-2-3 automatically recognizes the switch in data type, and accepts your entry as a label rather than a value. In the contents box, a single quote character (') appears just before your entry: '456 Flower Street.

> **NOTE** If you want to enter a sequence of digits as a label, begin the entry with a single quote character. For example, to enter 1997 as a label, type the entry as '1997.

In the following exercise you'll begin entering numeric values into the worksheet:

1. Select cell D8, the top cell of the column range where you'll enter the expense figures.

2. Type **1500** into D8. Notice that the word Value appears in the mode indicator as soon as you type the first digit of this number. To complete the entry and select the next cell down, press ↵.

3. Type **1000** into cell D9 and press ↵.

4. Type **3500** into cell D10 and press ↵.

5. Type **800** into cell D11 and press ↵.

Now that you've entered an entire column of numbers, you'll want to compute the total and display it in cell D12. Calculating the total of a column or row of numbers is a common spreadsheet operation—so common that 1-2-3 provides some convenient tools designed to make the operation almost automatic.

Three Ways to Calculate Totals

One technique is simply to enter the word "Total" in the cell just to the left or just above the location where you want the total to appear. Because of the way the Conference worksheet is organized, this technique doesn't happen to be very convenient in your current work. But in the following exercise, you'll try it out anyway and then delete the results:

1. Select cell C12.

2. Type the word **Total** and press ↵. Two events immediately take place: The sum of the numbers in the range D8..D11 appears in cell D12; and the label you've entered into cell B12 is truncated.

3. Select cell D12 and look up at the Edit line. You can see that 1-2-3 has entered a formula into the cell to produce the total. In response to the **Total** entry, 1-2-3 has automatically determined the correct range of numbers to sum.

4. Now delete the entries in cells C12 and D12. Select the range C12..D12 and press the Delete key. The full label entry in cell B12 ("Total Fixed Expenses") is redisplayed on the sheet.

The Sum SmartIcon is a more convenient tool to use on the Conference worksheet. To use this tool you simply select a cell at the bottom of a column of numbers or to the right of a row of numbers. Then you click the Sum SmartIcon, the seventh button on the Range SmartIcon bar. In response, 1-2-3 enters a @SUM formula. Try it now: Select cell D12 and click the Sum SmartIcon. As you see in Figure 3.6, the result is displayed as 6800. The contents box shows the formula that carries out this calculation:

    @SUM(D8..D11)

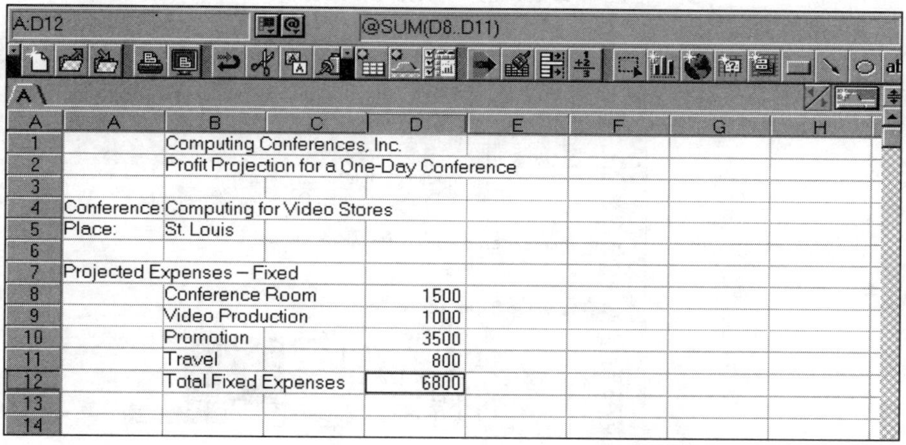

Figure 3.6: Using the Sum SmartIcon

@SUM is one of the tools in 1-2-3's large library of built-in functions. In this case, 1-2-3 has entered a formula that finds the sum of the numeric values stored in the range D8..D11. You'll study this and other functions in Chapters 7 and 8.

Of course, you can enter the @SUM function into cell D12 directly from the keyboard if you prefer. (You may have no other choice in cases where the organization of your worksheet isn't suited to the use of the **Total** technique or the Sum SmartIcon.) To try entering a @SUM formula, begin by selecting D12 and pressing Delete to erase the cell's current contents. Then follow these steps:

1. Start the summation formula by entering **@sum(** from the keyboard. When you do so, 1-2-3 switches into the Value mode.

2. Press ↑ four times, selecting cell D8. 1-2-3 switches into the Point mode and automatically enters the cell address into the summation formula you're building.

3. Press the period key (.) to *anchor* the range. In this case, D8 is the starting point for the range.

4. Press ↓ three times to highlight the range D8..D11. This range notation appears in the summation formula. At this point the screen looks like Figure 3.7.

5. Type the) character to complete the @SUM function.

6. Press ↵ to enter the formula.

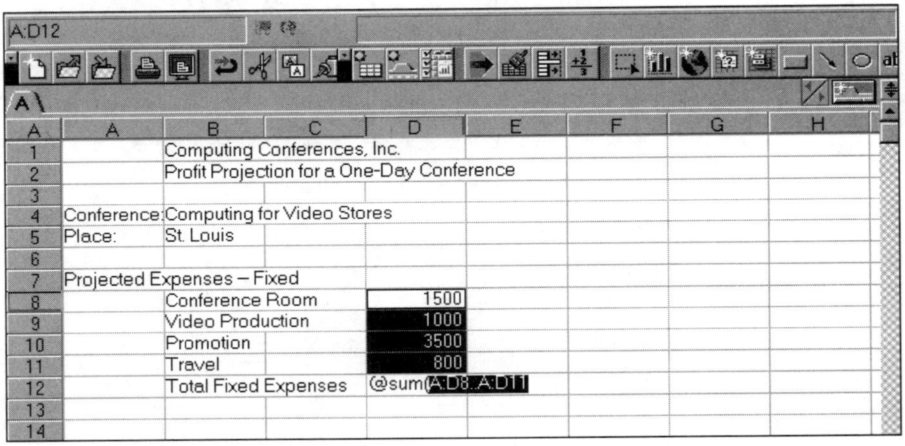

Figure 3.7: Entering the @SUM formula from the keyboard

The calculated result is the same as before. After trying three different techniques, you can see how much time you save by using the **Total** entry or the Sum SmartIcon. All the same, entering the formula manually is an instructive exercise. You've learned to use a pointing technique for incorporating a range in a formula. In the next section you'll expand your understanding of ranges, and you'll learn other ways to select a range.

Selecting Ranges

As you know, a range is a rectangular area of cells that you select for a particular operation. Many of 1-2-3's menu commands and functions work with ranges. A range consists of any of the following arrangements of cells in a sheet:

▶ A single cell

- A group of contiguous cells contained within one row or one column
- A two-dimensional rectangle of cells within multiple rows and columns in a worksheet
- A three-dimensional group of cells, consisting of identically addressed ranges from adjacent sheets in a workbook

> **TIP** 1-2-3 also allows you to select multiple ranges at once, which is known as a *collection*. To do so, hold down the Ctrl key and use the mouse to point to each range that you want to include in the collection.

The notation for a range in 1-2-3 consists of two cell addresses separated by two dots. For a range on a single sheet, this notation can appear with or without the sheet name. For instance, a range of cells on sheet A might be identified either as A:B2..A:F6, or simply as B2..F6 if there is no possibility of confusing this range with the same ranges on other sheets.

Here are some examples of ranges, as illustrated in Figures 3.8 through 3.12:

- **B4..B4** is a range consisting of a single cell on a sheet, at address B4 (see Figure 3.8).
- **C5..C10** is a column range—that is, a range of cells all contained within a single column, C in this case (see Figure 3.9). C5 is the top of the range and C10 is the bottom.
- **A6..E6** is a row range—a range of cells contained within row 6 (see Figure 3.10). A6 at the left is the first cell and E6 at the right is the last cell.

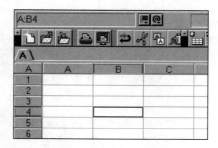

Figure 3.8: A range consisting of a single cell, B4..B4

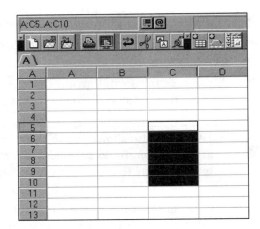

Figure 3.9: *A column range, C5..C10*

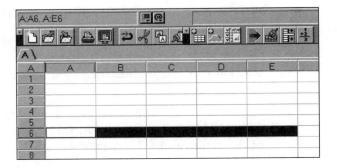

Figure 3.10: *A row range, A6..E6*

▶ **B2..F6** is a two-dimensional range (see Figure 3.11). B2 is the upper-left corner of the range, and F6 is the lower-right corner.

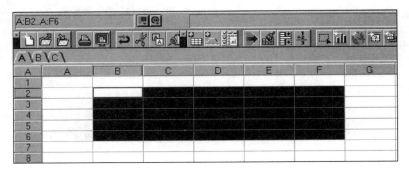

Figure 3.11: *A two-dimensional range, B2..F6*

▶ **A:A1..C:C3** (or **C:A1..A:C3**) is a three-dimensional range, consisting of cells from three different sheets in a workbook—that is, the range A1..C3 in sheets A, B, and C (see Figure 3.12).

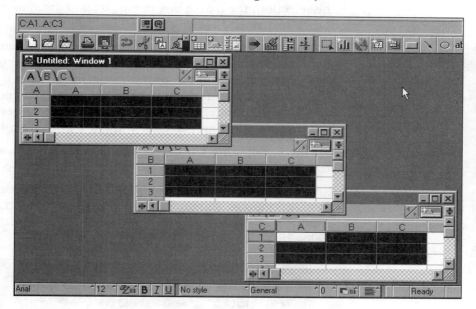

Figure 3.12: A three-dimensional range, A:A1..C:C3

 NOTE Figure 3.12 shows three windows for viewing the contents of the same workbook. In this case, each window displays a different sheet, A, B, or C. The windows have been resized and arranged on the Desktop so that the range selections on all three sheets can be seen at once. The Window ➤ New Window command creates a new window for viewing the contents of the current workbook.

For convenience, 1-2-3 allows you to select a range for a particular operation either before or after you choose a menu command. If a dialog box is already on the screen, a special *range selector button* gives you the opportunity to go back to the sheet and select a range for the task at hand.

Using the Range Selector Button

When you choose a specific command that operates over a range, the resulting dialog box contains a text box in which you specify the target

Chapter 3   Worksheet Basics: Entering Data

range. The range selector button is typically displayed just to the right of the Range text box. When you click this button, the dialog box disappears temporarily so you can select a range. After you complete the selection, the dialog box reappears and the range is displayed in the Range text box.

As an introduction to the range selector button, consider the File ➤ Print command. This command sends the contents of the current workbook or sheet to the printer, or gives you the option of sending a selected range of information to the printer. To specify the range, you can click the range selector button that appears on the Print dialog box. In the following exercise, you'll see how it works:

1. On the Computing Conferences worksheet that you've been developing, press the Home key to move the cell pointer to A1.

2. Choose the File ➤ Print command. The Print dialog box appears on the Desktop, as shown in Figure 3.13. Notice the Selected Range option—and the associated text box—at the lower-left corner of the dialog box.

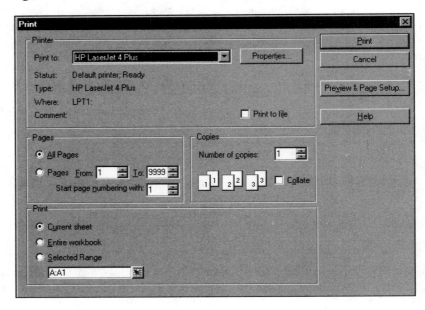

Figure 3.13: **Using the range selector button on the Print dialog box**

3. Click the range selector button, located just to the right of the Selected Range text box. When you do so, the Print dialog box temporarily

disappears from the Desktop. You return to the current sheet, and a small window named Range Selector appears on the Desktop.

4. Use your mouse to select the range A7..D12, which contains the list of fixed expenses for the one-day conference. Position the mouse pointer over cell A7, hold down the left mouse button, and drag the pointer down to D12. As you make the selection, the mouse pointer appears in the shape of a white arrow superimposed over a range-selection icon. The Range Selector box shows the notation for the range you've selected: A:A1..A:D12.

5. Release the mouse button. When you do so, the Print dialog box returns to the Desktop. The Selected Range option is activated, and the text box contains a reference to the range you've highlighted on the sheet:

6. Click the Print button to complete this operation. 1-2-3 prints the selection of data that you've selected. (Alternatively, you can click Cancel or press Escape to cancel the printing operation for now.)

> **NOTE** The InfoBox for range properties allows you to select a range without the use of a range selector button. Open the InfoBox by choosing Range ➤ Range Properties or by clicking the Range Properties SmartIcon. This special dialog box remains on the Desktop until you explicitly close it, and allows you to select—and work with—any number of ranges in sequence. While the InfoBox is displayed, you can use your mouse to select any range on the current sheet and then to select the tab for the properties that you want to change.

Preselecting a Range

Selecting a range before you choose a menu command is sometimes called preselecting. Some of the 1-2-3 SmartIcons and status bar options require a preselected range. You can preselect a range with the mouse or the keyboard. As you carry out the action, 1-2-3 highlights your selection.

You are now familiar with the general steps for preselecting a worksheet range with the mouse:

1. Position the mouse pointer over the first cell in the range.
2. Hold down the left mouse button and drag the pointer down and/or across to the last cell in the range.
3. Release the mouse button when the target range is highlighted.

From the keyboard, the F4 function key switches 1-2-3 from the Ready mode to the Point mode. The Range Selector window appears on the Desktop:

Here are the steps for preselecting a range with the keyboard:

1. Select the cell that is to become the first cell in the range.
2. Press the F4 function key. This anchors the current cell as the starting point of the range, and switches 1-2-3 into the Point mode.
3. Press arrow keys to highlight the target range—for example, the ↓ key for a column range and/or the → key for a row range.
4. To select a three-dimensional range over adjacent worksheets in a file, press Ctrl+PgUp or Ctrl+PgDn while you are in the Point mode. (The current file must already contain two or more sheets.)
5. Press ↵ to complete the range selection. This final step switches you back into the Ready mode, but leaves the selected range highlighted.

Here is a second keyboard technique for preselecting a range:

1. Select the first cell of the range.
2. Hold down the Shift key as you press the →, ←, ↑, or ↓ keys to define a range on the active worksheet.
3. Press Ctrl+Shift+PgUp or Ctrl+Shift+PgDn to select a three-dimensional range over multiple sheets in the active file.
4. Release the Shift key—and the Ctrl key if applicable—to complete the selection.

You'll have the opportunity to practice these techniques as you continue developing the Conference worksheet.

> **TIP** A preselected range can be a convenient shortcut when you're preparing to enter data into specific rows and columns of a worksheet. To streamline the process, select the entire input range first and then simply press ↵ at the end of each data entry. Pressing ↵ moves the cell pointer to the next cell in the range. (Pressing ↵ at the last cell in the range moves you back up to the first cell in the range.) This technique works in a one-row or one-column range, or in a range of multiple rows and columns.

Creating Range Names

Formulas that contain the addresses of cells and ranges are sometimes difficult to read and understand. For example, consider the summation formula you entered into the Conference worksheet. If you return to this worksheet some weeks or months from now, you may not immediately see the significance of this formula:

    @SUM(D8..D11)

But if the range notation D8..D11 were replaced with a meaningful name—such as EXPENSES—you would have an easier time recognizing the purpose of the formula:

    @SUM(EXPENSES)

For this reason, 1-2-3 gives you the option of assigning names to individual cells or to ranges of cells on a worksheet. To do so, you select the range, choose the Range ➤ Name command, and make an entry in the Name dialog box (Figure 3.14).

Figure 3.14: **The Name dialog box**

TIP If you prefer, you can use the InfoBox to assign a name to a range. Select the range and click the Range Properties SmartIcon (or choose Range ➤ Range Properties). In the resulting InfoBox, click the Basics tab, and enter a name into the Range name text box. While the InfoBox is on the Desktop, you can select any number of other ranges and assign names to them.

A range name may contain as many as fifteen characters. 1-2-3 automatically converts a range name entry to all uppercase letters. As a first exercise with range names, try assigning the name EXPENSES to the range of fixed expenses on the conference worksheet:

1. Select the range of expense values, D8..D11.
2. Choose Range ➤ Name.
3. Enter the name **EXPENSES**.
4. Click the OK button or press ↵ to confirm your entry.

This new definition doesn't change the appearance of your sheet. But the next time you need to write a formula involving the column of fixed expenses, you can use the name EXPENSES to represent the range. Notice that the selection indicator on the Edit line now displays the name of the range rather than the address. Furthermore, if you select cell D12, you'll find that 1-2-3 has automatically substituted the range name for the address in the @SUM formula:

    @SUM(EXPENSES)

Using the Navigator Button

Conveniently, 1-2-3 provides a list of all the existing range names defined for the current worksheet. View the list by clicking the Navigator button on the Edit line. You can select from this list while you're in the process of building a formula.

In the following exercise you'll try yet another technique for entering the summation formula into cell D12, this time using the new range name you've defined. This exercise gives you the chance to practice using two important buttons on the Edit line—the Navigator and the Function selector:

1. Select cell D12 and press the Delete key to erase the formula currently in the cell.

2. Click the Function selector, the button labeled with a @ character on the edit line. As shown in Figure 3.15, the resulting list contains a selection of 1-2-3's built-in functions.

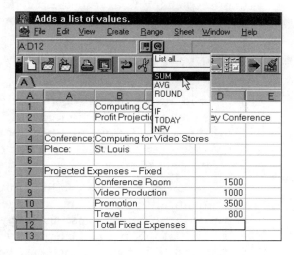

Figure 3.15: **The Function selector list**

3. Click the SUM function near the top of the list. In response, 1-2-3 closes the Function selector list, and enters @SUM(list) in the current cell. The word *list* is highlighted in the formula, ready to be replaced by an actual range. Notice that you're in the Edit mode at this point.

4. Click the Navigator button, located just to the left of the Function selector on the edit line. 1-2-3 displays a drop-down list of the range names defined on the current worksheet. In this case, you've defined only one name, EXPENSES, as shown here:

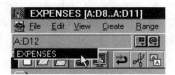

5. In the list, click EXPENSES. The Navigator list disappears, and the name EXPENSES appears in the SUM formula:

    @SUM(EXPENSES)

6. Press ↵ to complete the entry. The calculated result is the same as for the previous entries you've made in cell D12.

Next you'll copy the fixed-expense figures from column D to column E in the conference worksheet. Looking back at Figure 3.1, you can see that the fixed expenses are almost the same in the two columns. Rather than reenter the figures in the second column, you can quickly copy them and then revise the data in column E as necessary.

Copying a Range of Values

There are several ways to copy a range of data from one place to another in a worksheet. Probably the fastest and simplest technique is 1-2-3's drag-and-drop action, in which you use your mouse to drag a copy of a selected range to a new location. Other techniques employ the Windows Clipboard as a temporary storage place for the range of data you want to copy.

In the following exercises you'll try three different techniques that produce identical results on the worksheet itself—drag-and-drop, copy-and-paste with SmartIcons, and copy-and-paste from the keyboard. After each of the first two exercises you'll delete the copy so you can try the next technique. In each case you begin your work by selecting the range of cells that you want to copy. Make this range selection using either the mouse or the keyboard.

The Drag-and-Drop Action

Here's how you use the drag-and-drop operation to copy the range of expense data:

1. Select D8..D12, the range you want to copy. Notice that this range includes the @SUM formula at the bottom of the expense figures.

2. Position the mouse pointer anywhere around the perimeter of the selection (except at the right bottom border) and watch for the pointer to take the shape of an open hand:

6		
7	Projected Expenses – Fixed	
8	Conference Room	1500
9	Video Production	1000
10	Promotion	3500
11	Travel	800
12	Total Fixed Expenses	6800
13		

3. Hold down the left mouse button. The mouse pointer changes to an icon that represents a hand holding a document, and a bold border appears around the perimeter of the range:

6		
7	Projected Expenses – Fixed	
8	Conference Room	1500
9	Video Production	1000
10	Promotion	3500
11	Travel	800
12	Total Fixed Expenses	6800
13		

4. Hold down the Ctrl key on the keyboard. A small plus sign appears beneath the "document" in the mouse pointer. (This sign indicates that you are about to perform a copy operation, rather than a move.) While continuing to hold down both the left mouse button and the Ctrl key, drag the selection one column to the right. The bold border appears around the range E8..E12:

6		
7	Projected Expenses – Fixed	
8	Conference Room	1500
9	Video Production	1000
10	Promotion	3500
11	Travel	800
12	Total Fixed Expenses	6800
13		

5. Release the mouse button and then release the Ctrl key. A copy of the entries in D8..D12 now appears in the new target range:

6			
7	Projected Expenses – Fixed		
8	Conference Room	1500	1500
9	Video Production	1000	1000
10	Promotion	3500	3500
11	Travel	800	800
12	Total Fixed Expenses	6800	6800
13			

Because the source range is a column of values, 1-2-3 assumes you want to copy the same arrangement of values to the destination, starting at E8.

There is another very important point to notice in the result of this copy operation. Move the cell pointer down to E12 and look at the contents box to examine the formula that 1-2-3 has copied to the cell:

@SUM(E8..E11)

This formula was copied from the equivalent formula in cell D12. In the copy, 1-2-3 has adjusted the range of the @SUM function to E8..E11. Thanks to this adjustment, the formula in cell E12 produces the total of the expense figures in column E. Furthermore, this formula will be recalculated if you make any changes in those figures. To see that this is true, move the cell pointer to E8 now and enter 2000 as the cell's new value. In response to this new entry, 1-2-3 instantly recalculates the formula in cell E12, giving a new result of 7300. In Chapter 4 you'll learn much more about the adjustments 1-2-3 makes in formulas that you copy from one location to another in a worksheet.

To prepare for the next copy exercise, delete the copy you've just made. Select the range E8..E12 and press the Delete key at the keyboard. Delete has the same effect on a range of cells as it does on a single cell: All the data is cleared away. In the steps ahead you'll use SmartIcons to perform an operation known as copy and paste.

Performing a Copy-and-Paste Operation

The Copy and Paste commands appear in the Edit menus of most major Windows 95 applications, and they operate in much the same way from one application to the next. The Copy command copies the currently selected data to the Windows 95 Clipboard without deleting or otherwise changing the original version of the data. The Paste command copies the contents of the Clipboard to a specified location in the current document.

Because these operations are used so commonly, 1-2-3 provides shortcuts for them, the last two buttons in the Universal SmartIcon bar. The Copy SmartIcon appears as a pair of overlapping squares, each containing the letter A, and the Paste SmartIcon is depicted as a jar of paste. Here's how to use these SmartIcons to perform a copy-and-paste operation on the Conference worksheet:

1. Select the range D8..D12.
2. Click the Copy SmartIcon.
3. Select cell E8.
4. Click the Paste SmartIcon.

   Once again examine the formula stored in cell E12 after the copy operation is complete. You'll see the same adjustment as before: The @SUM function applies to the data in column E.

Other ways to perform a copy-and-paste operation are to choose the Copy and Paste commands directly from the Edit menu, or to choose the same commands from a shortcut menu. To use a shortcut menu, select the range that you want to copy, click the selection with the right mouse button, and choose the Copy command, as shown in Figure 3.16. Then click the destination with the right mouse button, and choose the Paste command from the shortcut menu.

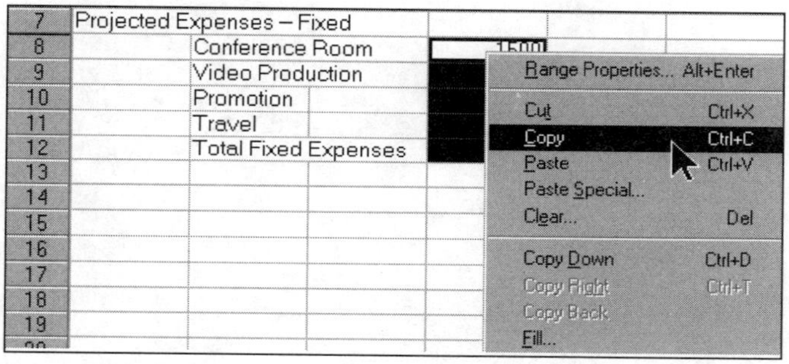

Figure 3.16: Choosing the Copy command from a shortcut menu

Finally, if you prefer to keep your hands on the keyboard as much as possible, you can use keyboard shortcuts to complete a copy-and-paste operation. Before trying the next exercise, you should once again select the range E8..E12 and press the Delete key to erase the data you've just copied.

Using Keyboard Shortcuts to Perform a Copy-and-Paste Operation

The keyboard shortcuts for the Copy and Paste commands are Ctrl+C and Ctrl+V, respectively. (These shortcuts are available almost universally in Windows applications.) Here is the keyboard technique for copying the expense data from column D to column E:

1. Use arrow keys to select cell D8.
2. Hold down the Shift key and press ↓ four times to select the range D8..D12.
3. Press Ctrl+C to copy this range to the Clipboard.
4. Press → once to select cell E8.

5. Press Ctrl+V to paste a new copy of the expense data to the range E8..E12.

   As the final step in this first stage of worksheet development, enter 2000 as the conference room expense in cell E8. Your sheet appears as shown in Figure 3.17. In the next chapter you'll change the sheet in several ways to make room for additional data. But now it's time to save the workbook as a file on disk. At this point, the workbook consists of a single sheet of data.

	A	B	C	D	E
1		Computing Conferences, Inc.			
2		Profit Projection for a One-Day Conference			
3					
4		Conference	Computing for Video Stores		
5		Place:	St. Louis		
6					
7		Projected Expenses – Fixed			
8			Conference Room	1500	2000
9			Video Production	1000	1000
10			Promotion	3500	3500
11			Travel	800	800
12			Total Fixed Expenses	6800	7300
13					
14					

Figure 3.17:   The first stage of development for the conference worksheet

Saving the Workbook

As in any other program, you should perform frequent save operations during your work in 1-2-3. If you experience a hardware or software problem, you may suddenly find that you've lost any data you've entered since the last save. The appropriate length of time between save operations therefore depends upon how much data you are willing to risk losing. Fortunately, 1-2-3 saves your workbook at the click of a SmartIcon—so it's easy to save workbooks at regular intervals.

The first time you save a workbook to disk, the Save As dialog box appears on the screen, eliciting a name for the file. Windows 95 allows long file names with spaces; if you wish, you can take advantage of this feature to create descriptive names for your 1-2-3 files. When you save a workbook, 1-2-3 supplies a default extension name of 123 for the workbook file. The Save As command also has a password option you can select if you want to restrict access to the file.

Saving the Workbook

After the first save operation, you can simply choose the Save command to save new versions of your workbook to disk under the same file name.

Saving a Workbook File

To save a workbook for the first time, you can choose the File ➤ Save As command or you can simply click the Save SmartIcon. Either way, the dialog box shown in Figure 3.18 appears on the screen. You can use the Save in box to select the folder where you want to save your file. (A large box displays a list of any workbook files currently found in the folder you've selected.) Once you've chosen a folder, enter a name for your workbook in the File name text box. Then click the Save button (or press ↵) to complete the save operation.

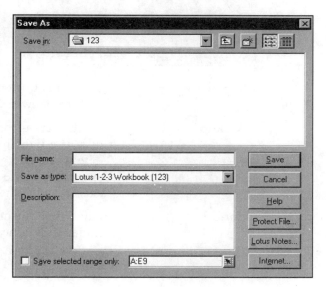

Figure 3.18:   The Save As dialog box

> **TIP**   The Save As dialog box also has a Description box in which you can save a brief description of the workbook you're saving. This description is saved with the file.

Follow these steps to save the Conference worksheet for the first time:

1.   Click the Save SmartIcon. You can save your worksheet file in the current directory, or select another location.

2. For the moment, enter the short file name **CONF** into the File name text box. (You can experiment with longer file names later, when you're ready to save different versions of this workbook to disk.)

3. Click Save or press ↵ to save the file.

   As a result of these steps, the worksheet is saved as CONF.123.

   The Save As dialog box allows you to select an existing file name from the File name list box as the name for the current save operation. If you do so, a second dialog box appears on the screen prompting you for specific instructions. The box displays the message "File already exists" and offers you four choices:

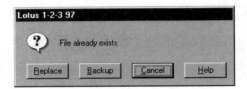

Replace	Click this button to replace the existing file with the new file you are now saving.
Backup	Click this button to retain the existing file on disk as a backup for the current worksheet. The worksheet you are saving receives the extension name 123, and the extension of the existing worksheet on disk is changed to BAK.
Cancel	Click this button to cancel the save operation under the name you have selected.
Help	Click here to open the Help topic for this operation.

Assigning a Password to a File

Finally, you can save a file with password protection to restrict the number of people who are allowed to open it. When you attempt to open a password-protected file, 1-2-3 prompts for the password—and denies access to the file if you can't supply the password correctly.

 WARNING Keep in mind the inevitable liability of password protection: If you forget the password you've created, you won't be able to open your own file.

Here are the general steps for saving a file with a password:

1. Choose File ➤ Save As.

2. After supplying a file name, click the Protect File button at the right side of the Save As dialog box (see Figure 3.18). The Set Password dialog box appears on the screen prompting you for the password that will be assigned to the file:

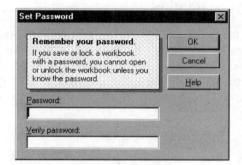

3. Enter the password twice, first in the Password box and then in the Verify password box. Asterisks appear in both boxes as you enter the characters of the password. The password may be up to fifteen characters long. Alphabetic case is significant; whatever combination of uppercase and/or lowercase letters you create in a password, 1-2-3 will require exactly the same combination when you try to open the file.

4. Click OK in the Set Password dialog box to confirm the password, or click Cancel if you change your mind. Click Save in the Save As dialog box.

When you attempt to open a password-protected workbook file, the Password dialog box appears first on the screen, prompting you to enter the file's password:

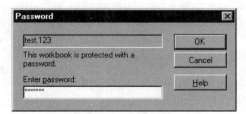

As you type the password, 1-2-3 displays a string of asterisks in the Enter password text box. Click OK; if your password is correct, 1-2-3 opens the file.

You can change a file's password—if you know the original password—by opening the file and selecting the Save As command to resave the file.

Using the Save Command

After you save a file for the first time, you can update the file by choosing File ➤ Save or by clicking the Save SmartIcon. Updating means storing the current version of the worksheet under its existing file name. As you make significant changes in data, formatting, or organization during the development of a worksheet, you should update your file regularly.

Here are the steps for updating a file:

1. Activate the window containing the workbook you want to save.
2. Choose File ➤ Save, or simply click the Save SmartIcon.

For now, exit from 1-2-3 if you wish. In Chapter 4 you'll continue developing the Conference worksheet. You'll begin by reorganizing the sheet to make room for projected revenues. As anticipated at the beginning of this exercise, you'll have to move the range of expense data down several rows below its current position. You'll see how to move a range of data and to insert blank columns and rows at specified locations in the worksheet. Then you'll learn much more about formulas in a 1-2-3 worksheet.

Summary

Although accurate data entry is a always a demanding task, 1-2-3 has many features designed to help you along the way. During an entry, the status bar distinguishes clearly between a numeric entry (a value) and a nonnumeric entry (a label). Given a row or column of numbers, you can quickly produce a sum by clicking the Sum SmartIcon or by entering **Total** as an adjacent label. To copy a block of data from one place to another on your sheet, you can use the drag-and-drop procedure or you can choose the Copy and Paste commands.

When a command operates over a range of data, you often have the choice of preselecting the range before you choose the command, or of pointing to the range after the command's dialog box has appeared on the screen. Either way, you can use the keyboard or the mouse to highlight a range of data for a given operation. By assigning names to specific ranges of data, you can make your sheet easier to develop and formulas easier to understand.

Once you've begun investing your time in a worksheet, you'll want to save your work to disk without much delay. The Save As command in the File menu gives you the opportunity to name your file and to add password protection if you wish. For subsequent updates of your worksheet file you can simply click the Save SmartIcon.

CHAPTER 4

Worksheet Basics: Organizing Data and Writing Formulas

FAST TRACK

To move a range of data from one place to another in a worksheet,   123

select the source range and drag it to its new location. While you drag, the mouse pointer takes the shape of a closed fist.

To insert a blank row or column at a specific position on the worksheet,   127

select a cell at the target position and choose Range ➤ Insert. In the Insert dialog box, select Columns or Rows and click OK.

To create range names from existing labels,   129

select the labels on the sheet and then choose Range ➤ Name. In the Name dialog box, select an option from the For cells list and then click the Use labels button.

To select a name from a list of the range names defined for the current worksheet, 130

click the Navigator button on the edit line and choose a name from the resulting list.

To enter a formula, 131

start the formula with the plus sign (+) if the first element of the formula is an address or range name.

To copy a formula to adjacent cells, 134

select the range containing the formula itself and the cells to which you want to copy the formula. Click the range with the right mouse button and choose Copy Right or Copy Down.

To change the reference type of an address in a formula entry, 136

press the F4 key after you've entered the reference. Each time you press F4, the address changes to the next reference type—from relative to absolute to mixed.

To fill a range with copied formulas, 142

select the cell containing the formula you want to copy. Then move the mouse pointer to the lower-right corner of the cell; the mouse pointer takes on the distinctive shape of the drag-and-fill operation. Hold down the left mouse button and drag across and/or down to designate the range that you want to fill. Release the mouse button to complete the operation.

To override the default precedence rules for operations in a formula, 143

put parentheses around the operations that should be performed first.

OFTEN, after you've begun entering data onto a sheet, you may decide to make changes in the structure and design of your work. Your plans for revision might include moving blocks of data to new places, creating new categories of information, and preparing your sheet for important new formulas. Because the initial data entry is such a time-consuming part of the task at hand, you want to avoid having to type any information a second time. For this reason, you need simple and reliable techniques for reorganizing the existing data on a sheet.

As you continue your work on the profit worksheet for Computing Conferences, Inc., you'll begin this chapter by revising the layout of the data table. You'll learn how to move data from one place to another on a sheet, and how to insert blank rows and columns within an existing range of data.

Then you'll turn your attention to formulas. As you've begun to see already, formulas transform a sheet from a static collection of data to a dynamic calculation tool. You'll create formulas on the Conference worksheet to compute revenues, expenses, and profit figures. Along the way, you'll learn to:

▶ Develop formulas accurately and copy them to new ranges

▶ Select the appropriate reference type—absolute, relative, or mixed—for addresses in formulas

▶ Use parentheses to establish the order of operations

When you complete the formulas on this sheet, you'll begin exploring "what-if" scenarios. What happens to the projected profit if changes occur in the basic data? Thanks to carefully planned formulas, 1-2-3 instantly recalculates the bottom line whenever you change the input numbers.

Reopen the Conference workbook now if necessary. If you're just restarting 1-2-3, choose the CONF file from the Recently used workbooks list in the Welcome to 1-2-3 dialog box. Alternatively, if 1-2-3 is already running, choose File ➤ Open, or click the Open Smart-Icon. Then select the CONF.123 file from the Open dialog box, and click Open.

Changing the Worksheet

You've seen how to use a drag-and-drop operation to copy a range of data. Now you'll learn to use a similar mouse action to move data from one place to another in your sheet. You'll also experiment with alternative techniques for achieving the same effect—using the cut-and-paste operation and inserting blank rows or columns at selected locations.

Moving Ranges of Data

To move a range of data, you simply select it and drag it to its new location. For example, in the following steps you'll move the range of expense data down the worksheet by several rows:

1. Select the range A7..E12.
2. Position the mouse pointer over the border of the selection, and watch for the pointer to take the shape of an open hand.
3. Hold down the left mouse button and drag the top of the selection down to row 15, as shown in Figure 4.1. The mouse pointer changes to a closed fist while you drag.

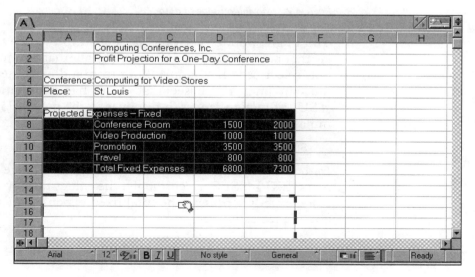

Figure 4.1:   *Performing a drag-and-drop operation*

4. Release the mouse button to complete the move.

Figure 4.2 shows the result of the drag-and-drop operation.

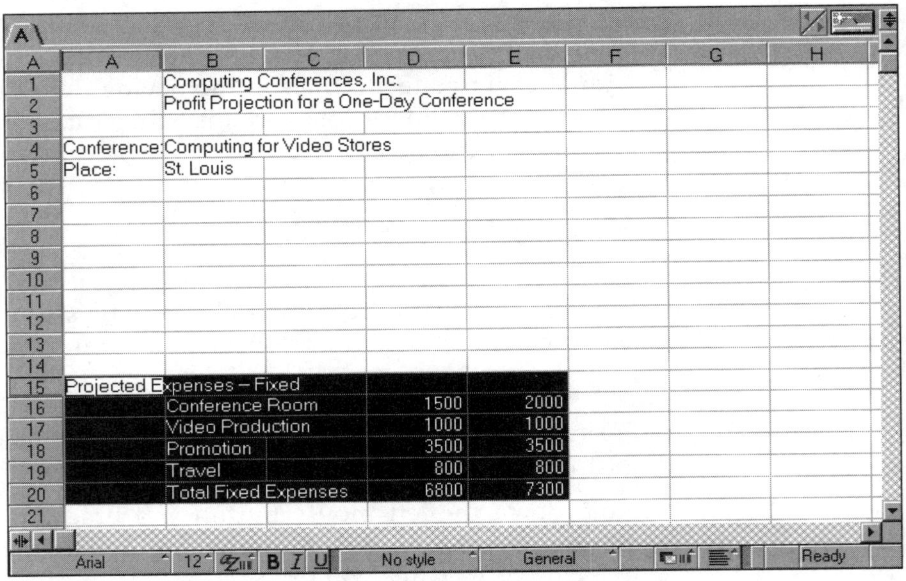

[Figure 4.2 screenshot: spreadsheet showing]

	A	B	C	D	E
1		Computing Conferences, Inc.			
2		Profit Projection for a One-Day Conference			
3					
4	Conference:	Computing for Video Stores			
5	Place:	St. Louis			
15	Projected Expenses — Fixed				
16		Conference Room		1500	2000
17		Video Production		1000	1000
18		Promotion		3500	3500
19		Travel		800	800
20		Total Fixed Expenses		6800	7300

Figure 4.2: **Moving a range of data**

You might wonder what has happened to the two summation formulas that are included in the range of data that you just moved. To find out, select cells D20 and E20 in turn and examine their formulas on the edit line. You'll see that 1-2-3 has automatically adjusted the @SUM function ranges in response to the move. For example, the formula in cell E20 is now

   @SUM(E16..E19)

In the case of cell D20, 1-2-3 has adjusted the range represented by the name EXPENSES. Accordingly, the values displayed in D20 and E20 still correctly represent the total fixed expenses for the low- and high-attendance estimates.

By the way, if you attempt to drag a range of data to a location that already contains other entries, 1-2-3 displays a warning box on the screen:

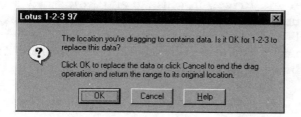

Take a careful look at your worksheet before you proceed. If you click OK, you'll lose the data that was previously entered at the destination of the move.

Using the Cut-and-Paste Operation

The cut-and-paste technique is an alternative to drag and drop. To perform a cut-and-paste operation, you select the range that you want to move and choose the Edit ➤ Cut command; this removes the data from the current range and copies it to the Clipboard. Then you select the destination of the move and choose the Edit ➤ Paste command. You can access the Cut and Paste commands by any of these methods:

▶ Click the Cut and Paste SmartIcons.

▶ Choose Cut and then Paste from the Edit menu.

▶ Click a range selection with the right mouse button and choose Cut or Paste from the resulting shortcut menu.

▶ Use keyboard shortcuts: Ctrl+X for Cut and Ctrl+V for Paste.

If you want to try a cut-and-paste operation, follow these steps:

1. Click the Undo SmartIcon to undo the result of your previous drag-and-drop action.

2. Select the range of expense data, A7..E12.

3. Choose Edit ➤ Cut. The data disappears and is copied to the Clipboard.

4. Select cell A15.

5. Choose Edit ➤ Paste. The data reappears at its new location.

In the area that has been opened up by the move, you can now enter the new labels and values that you see in Figure 4.3. The label entries include two new items of basic information about the conference itself (**Date:** and **Price:**, in cells A6 and A8); a new section for projected revenues (A10..B13); and some headings for the expected attendance (D6..E7). The numeric entries include a per-person attendance fee of **195** in cell B8; and attendance estimates of **80** and **150** in cells D8 and E8. Enter all this information carefully into your own copy of the sheet.

> **NOTE** Notice that the Minimum and Maximum labels in cells D7 and E7 are right-aligned in their cells. For now, you can achieve this effect by beginning each label entry with a double-quotation mark ("). 1-2-3 reads this character as an instruction for right-alignment. You'll learn other ways to control alignment later.

	A	B	C	D	E
1		Computing Conferences, Inc.			
2		Profit Projection for a One-Day Conference			
3					
4	Conference:	Computing for Video Stores			
5	Place:	St. Louis			
6	Date:			Expected Attendance	
7				Minimum	Maximum
8	Price:	195		80	150
9					
10	Projected Revenues				
11		Attendance			
12		Video Sales			
13		Total Revenues			
14					
15	Projected Expenses – Fixed				
16		Conference Room		1500	2000
17		Video Production		1000	1000
18		Promotion		3500	3500
19		Travel		800	800
20		Total Fixed Expenses		6800	7300

Figure 4.3: *Entering new data into the Conference sheet*

Now if you compare Figure 4.3 with your final goal for this sheet (Figure 3.1, shown at the beginning of Chapter 3) you'll notice that you need some additional space on the sheet for information that you haven't entered yet. Specifically, you need a blank row for column headings just above the Projected Revenues label; and you need a blank column for the per-person revenue and expense figures, just to the right of column C. One way to open up these ranges would be to move the appropriate ranges of data, using the drag-and-drop or copy-and-paste operation. But in this case you can accomplish the task more simply by inserting a blank row and a blank column at selected positions on the worksheet. You'll learn how to do this in the next section.

Inserting Rows and Columns

The Range ➤ Insert command contains options for inserting new rows or columns in an active sheet:

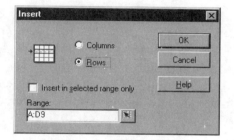

(This command is also available from the shortcut menu for a range.) To add a single new row or column to the active sheet, you can use the Insert command in the following way:

1. Select a cell located in the row or column position where you want to make the insert.
2. Choose Range ➤ Insert.
3. Click either the Columns or Rows option.
4. Click OK or press ↵ to complete the insert operation.

To insert more than one row at a time, select a range of consecutive cells in a single column—one cell for each row that you want to insert. Conversely, to insert multiple columns, preselect a range of adjacent cells in a row—one cell for each column you want to insert. Choose Range ➤ Insert and click the Row or Column option after you've selected the range.

In the current version of the Conference worksheet you can select cell D9 as the insert position for both the new row and the new column. Follow these steps to make the insertions:

1. Select cell D9 on the worksheet.
2. Choose Range ➤ Insert. In the Insert dialog box, keep the default Rows option; click OK.
3. Choose Range ➤ Insert again. This time click the Columns option and then click OK.

After these insertions you might once again want to examine the summation formulas, now located in cells E21 and F21. As before, 1-2-3 has adjusted the ranges in these formulas in response to the changes you have made in the sheet.

Now you're ready to enter additional information onto the sheet. As you can see in Figure 4.4, there are three new right-aligned column headings to enter into cells D10, E10, and F10. Type a double quotation mark at the beginning of each entry to achieve right alignment as you enter these three headings. Then enter a value of **35** in cell D13. This is the price-per-copy of the conference video, a secondary source of revenue for Computing Conferences, Inc.

	A	B	C	D	E	F	G	H
1		Computing Conferences, Inc.						
2		Profit Projection for a One-Day Conference						
3								
4	Conference:	Computing for Video Stores						
5	Place:	St. Louis						
6	Date:				Expected Attendance			
7					Minimum	Maximum		
8	Price:	195			80	150		
9								
10				Per person	Min. Total	Max. Total		
11	Projected Revenues							
12		Attendance						
13		Video Sales		35				
14		Total Revenues						
15								
16	Projected Expenses – Fixed							
17		Conference Room			1500	2000		
18		Video Production			1000	1000		

Figure 4.4: **Reorganizing the Conference worksheet and entering column headings**

Once you complete this second stage of data entry into the worksheet, you should take a moment to assign range names to a few important cells on the sheet:

1. Select cell B8 and choose Range ➤ Name. The Name dialog box appears:

2. Enter **Price** as the name for cell B8 and press ↵.

3. Likewise, select cell D13, choose Range ➤ Name, and enter **Video** as the name for this cell.

4. Select the range E7..F7 (containing the Minimum and Maximum labels) and choose Range ➤ Name. Near the bottom of the Name dialog box, click the down-arrow button next to the For cells box, and select Below from the resulting drop-down list:

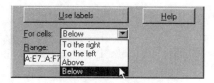

5. Click the Use labels button and click OK to confirm.

This final action instructs 1-2-3 to assign the labels in cells E7 and F7 as the names for cells E8 and F8. Specifically, you've just assigned the name MINIMUM to cell E8, and the name MAXIMUM to cell F8. You can use these two names to represent the two attendance estimates in formulas you write for the worksheet.

Now choose File ➤ Save or click the Save SmartIcon. This saves the latest version of the conference worksheet to disk, still under the file name CONF.123. The next step in the worksheet development is to enter formulas for calculating the minimum and maximum revenue projections, based on expected attendance. When you enter these formulas, you'll use the range names you've created for several individual cells on the worksheet. To review the five names you've defined, click the navigator button on the edit line. You'll see the following list:

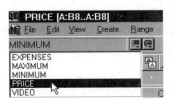

When you highlight an entry in this list, the title bar identifies the cell or range that the name represents.

Working with Formulas

As you first saw in Chapter 1, formulas are made up of a variety of elements, including:

▶ Arithmetic operations, such as +, −, *, and /

▶ Literal numeric values such as 2 or 5280

▶ Cell addresses—or alternatively, range names—that represent the values stored in those cells

▶ Worksheet functions like @SUM

When you enter a formula, 1-2-3 immediately evaluates it and displays its numeric result in the cell. Furthermore, 1-2-3 recalculates a formula whenever you change the value of a cell that is part of the formula. This is what users sometimes refer to as the "what-if" feature of a spreadsheet.

As a quick demonstration of this feature, try this exercise:

1. Click the New Sheet button to add sheet B temporarily to the CONF workbook. (You'll delete this sheet when you've finished with this exercise.)

2. Enter a value of **92** in cell A1 of the new sheet B.

3. Select cell B1 and enter the formula **2*A1**.

   For this exercise, you can simply enter the entire formula directly from the keyboard. (Later you'll use the pointing technique to enter a cell address into a formula.) The formula multiplies the value stored in A1 by 2. The result displayed in B1 is 184.

4. Select A1 again and enter **32** as the cell's new value. In response, 1-2-3 instantly recalculates the value in B1, displaying the result as 64.

5. Try several more new values in A1, one at a time: **5, 3212, 19, 543,** and **27**. Each time you enter a new value into A1, 1-2-3 instantly recalculates the value in B1. The values 10, 6424, 38, 1086, and 54 appear in turn in cell B1.

6. When you are finished experimenting, click the B tab (on the line above the worksheet) with the right mouse button, and choose Delete Sheet from the resulting shortcut menu. Sheet B is removed, leaving the workbook with its original sheet A.

The idea is the same on complex worksheets designed to perform business calculations: Given a formula containing a cell reference, 1-2-3 recalculates the formula whenever you change the value in the cell.

Return now to the Conference sheet for a more interesting illustration of this feature. In an upcoming exercise you'll enter formulas into cells E12 and F12 to calculate the projected attendance revenue from the conference.

Entering Formulas

The attendance revenue is calculated by multiplying the price per person by the number of people attending the conference. The price per person is stored in cell B8 and the first of the two attendance estimates (the minimum attendance) is stored in cell E8. You know that multiplication is represented by the asterisk character (*). Given all this information, you might expect to enter the following formula into cell E12 to calculate the minimum projected revenue from attendance fees:

   B8*E8

But there is a problem here. If you type the first character, **B**, of this formula into the cell, 1-2-3 switches into the Label mode, whereas the correct mode for entering a formula is Value. You need to start the formula with a character that triggers the Value mode.

A general-purpose character for starting a formula in 1-2-3 is the plus sign (+). This character is not needed in all formulas—for example, when a formula begins with a number or with the @ symbol of a function. But when the first element of a formula is a cell address, the plus sign is a good way to begin in the Value mode. Here, then, is a correct format for the projected revenue formula:

```
+B8*E8
```

Using the Pointing Technique

You can enter a formula like this one directly from the keyboard if you want to. But there is an easier way. As you are entering the formula, you can use the mouse or the keyboard to point to cells that you want to include in the formula. You'll review this technique as you enter the first revenue formula into cell E12:

1. Select cell E12 in the conference worksheet.

2. Enter the plus sign (+) to begin the formula. The + appears in the cell, and the mode indicator displays the word Value.

3. To point to the first cell address in the formula, B8, press ↑ four times and ← three times. The mode switches to Point while you are pointing to the cell. Cell E12 now displays the formula as +PRICE, referring to the name you've assigned to cell B8.

4. Enter the asterisk character (*), for multiplication.

5. To point to the second cell address in the formula, E8, press ↑ four times. When the cell is selected, the formula is displayed as +PRICE*MINIMUM.

6. Now press ↵ to complete the formula entry. When you do so, 1-2-3 immediately calculates the result of the formula and displays it in cell E12 as 15600.

Now select cell E12 again and take a look at the contents box on the edit line. Because both of the references in your formula are represented by names, 1-2-3 automatically uses those names to express the formula. This convenient feature makes your formula easy to understand.

Using the Navigator

You now need to enter a similar formula into cell F12 to calculate the revenue projection from the maximum attendance estimate. Recall that cell F8 is named MAXIMUM. You can therefore plan the formula as:

    +PRICE*MAXIMUM

Notice that the formula must still begin with a plus sign to start the entry correctly in the Value mode. You can type this formula directly into cell F12 from the keyboard, or you can click the Navigator button on the edit line and select names from the resulting list. Here are the steps of this second approach:

1. Select cell F12 and type + from the keyboard to start the formula.

2. Click the Navigator button and select PRICE from the list of range names. 1-2-3 enters this name as the first reference in your formula. Type * to continue the formula.

3. Click the Navigator button again and select MAXIMUM from the name list. Then press ↵ to complete the formula entry.

When you have finished these steps, 1-2-3 enters the result of your formula into cell F12. The revenue projection is displayed as 29250.

Now you've seen two distinct ways of entering formulas into the Conference worksheet. You can identify cell references by pointing to them or by selecting them from the navigator list. There are two more formulas to enter into the revenue section of the worksheet before you compute the total revenue. In cells E13 and E14 you need formulas to calculate projected revenues from sales of the conference video. The planners at Computing Conferences, Inc., know from experience that they can count on approximately half of the participants of a given conference to order the video tape. Given this expectation, the estimated revenue is equal to the retail video price times one-half the number of participants.

You'll recall that you assigned the range name VIDEO to cell D13, where the unit retail price of the video is stored. The formula you can enter into cell E13 is therefore +VIDEO*MINIMUM/2. Likewise, the formula for cell F13 is +VIDEO*MAXIMUM/2. Enter these two formulas into their respective cells now, using any entry technique you choose. The result is 1400 for the minimum revenue projection (E13) and 2625 for the maximum (F13).

Finally, you need to enter summation formulas into row 14 to find the two total revenue projections. Using the Sum SmartIcon, you can enter both formulas in a single action. Here are the steps:

1. Select the range E14..F14.
2. Click the Sum SmartIcon.

When you click the SmartIcon, 1-2-3 enters the two summation formulas into cells E14 and F14. The results of the formulas are displayed as 17000 and 31875, respectively. Figure 4.5 shows what the worksheet looks like at this stage of your work. Click the Save SmartIcon now to save your work to disk.

	A	B	C	D	E	F	G	H
4	Conference:	Computing for Video Stores						
5	Place:	St. Louis						
6	Date:				Expected Attendance			
7					Minimum	Maximum		
8	Price:	195			80	150		
9								
10				Per person	Min. Total	Max. Total		
11	Projected Revenues							
12		Attendance			15600	29250		
13		Video Sales		35	1400	2625		
14		Total Revenues			17000	31875		
15								
16	Projected Expenses – Fixed							
17		Conference Room			1500	2000		
18		Video Production			1000	1000		
19		Promotion			3500	3500		
20		Travel			800	800		
21		Total Fixed Expenses			6800	7300		

Figure 4.5: *Entering the formulas for projected revenue*

You still have two sections of information to enter into the Conference worksheet—the variable expenses and the bottom-line profit. As you work on these sections you'll explore another important worksheet topic, the techniques for copying formulas from one range to another.

Copying Formulas

In many worksheets, a formula in one cell may be identical in structure to formulas you need to enter into other cells. Rather than entering these similar formulas one by one, you can copy the original formula to other locations on the sheet. 1-2-3 handles this copy operation in a logical manner, taking care to adjust cell references and range addresses as necessary.

You've already seen an example of this. In Chapter 3 you copied the summation formula for fixed expenses from one column to an adjacent column. At the time of the copy operation, the expense figures were located in column D and the summation formula in cell D12 was @SUM(D8..D11). When you copied this formula to cell E12, 1-2-3 automatically adjusted the range reference, producing the formula @SUM(E8..E11).

The logic that 1-2-3 follows to make this adjustment is simple: In a formula copied from column D to column E, a reference to a range in D becomes a reference to the adjacent range in E. The range address in this copy operation is an example of a *relative reference*. When you copy a formula containing a relative reference, 1-2-3 adjusts the cell or range address relative to the location of the copy.

A similar adjustment occurs when you copy a formula from one row to another. For example, imagine that you have entered the following formula into cell C3:

　+A3+B3

This formula adds the contents of the two cells located to the left of C3 in row 3. If you copy this formula down to cell C4, 1-2-3 adjusts the formula as follows:

　+A4+B4

The logic is the same: A formula copied to row 4 should contain references to the data stored in row 4. Accordingly, 1-2-3 adjusts the address references relative to the row to which the formula is copied.

Unless you specify otherwise, 1-2-3 treats cell and range addresses as relative references whenever you copy a formula from one place to another. In short, relative references are the default in copy operations. But in some contexts you will want to override this default. A formula may contain a reference to a fixed cell address—that is, an address that must remain unchanged when you copy the formula to other locations. In this case, you express the address as an *absolute reference*. You'll learn how to do this in upcoming exercises.

Understanding Reference Types

The distinction between relative and absolute references is perhaps the single most important concept for you to master now as you continue your work in 1-2-3. The concept itself is not difficult or subtle, but it does force you to make a variety of decisions while you're writing a formula. In effect, you must think carefully about two characteristics of each formula you create:

▶ The arithmetic structure of the formula—the specific operations and operands that ultimately produce the correct result in the original formula

▶ The types of address references in the formula—the notations that specify how the formula will be copied to other places in the sheet

Of course, relative and absolute reference types are relevant only in formulas that you intend to copy. If you write a formula that applies to only one location on a worksheet—a formula that will not be copied elsewhere—then you don't have to worry about relative and absolute references. But as you develop your own worksheets you may be surprised at how often you find yourself copying formulas.

Absolute and Relative References

Lotus 1-2-3 has a simple notation that you use to distinguish between relative and absolute references—and a simple technique for changing an address from one reference type to another. The default address format that you've been using in all your work up to now is the relative reference format. For example, the following address is a relative reference:

    B8

To change this address to an absolute reference, you insert a dollar-sign character ($) before each element of the address. Here is the absolute reference to this same address:

    $B$8

You can also form an absolute reference from a range name. Place a $ character just before the name:

    $PRICE

One way to create an absolute reference is simply to type $ characters at the appropriate locations of a cell address as you enter a formula. But 1-2-3 offers an easier technique for transforming a reference from relative to absolute. During formula entry, you can press the F4 function key to toggle a reference between relative and absolute formats.

In the following exercise you'll explore the significance of absolute references, and you'll practice the mechanical details of changing an address from relative to absolute. For the purposes of this exercise, you're going to backtrack a little in the Conference worksheet and redo some work that you completed earlier. Specifically, you'll reenter the formula for projected attendance revenues in cell E12; then you'll copy this formula to cell F12. Keep in mind that the formulas in these cells are both designed to multiply the attendance price per person by the anticipated number of people attending the conference. You'll make no change in the structure of these formulas—and the end result will remain the same. What you'll change is the reference type that allows you to copy the formula successfully from E12 to F12.

To prepare for this exercise begin by deleting the current contents of these two cells. Select the range E12..F12 and press the Delete key. Now you have an empty range in which to perform the following steps:

1. Select cell E12 and enter the reference to the cell that contains the attendance price, **+B8**. This entry switches 1-2-3 into the Value mode.

2. Press the F4 function key once. In response, 1-2-3 changes the cell address to +$PRICE, an absolute reference to the name of cell B8.

3. Now type the * sign, representing multiplication.

4. Press ↑ four times to point to cell E8. The formula now appears as +$PRICE*MINIMUM. Don't change the reference type of this second address. It remains a relative reference for the purposes of copying the formula.

5. Press ↵. The value 15600 appears in cell E12. This is the same as the value produced by the previous version of the formula, but now when you select cell E12 the contents box displays the formula as +$PRICE*MINIMUM. The first name, preceded by a $ sign, is an absolute reference; the second name is a relative reference.

Now you're ready to copy the formula in cell E12 to cell F12. To do so, you can use any of the copying techniques you've already learned, including the drag-and-drop action or the various mouse and keyboard approaches to a copy-and-paste operation. Alternatively, try this new method, using the Copy Right command:

1. Select the range E12..F12.
2. Click the selection with the right mouse button, to view the corresponding shortcut menu.
3. Choose the Copy Right command from the shortcut menu:

The same value as before appears in cell F12—a projected attendance revenue of 29250.

To see exactly what has happened in this exercise, you should now examine the new formulas in cells E12 and F12. At E12 you see the formula you've entered, with an absolute reference to $PRICE (equivalent to $B$8, the address of the attendance price) and a relative reference to MINIMUM (equivalent to E8, the address of the minimum expected attendance level):

    +$PRICE*MINIMUM

Then at F12 you find the copied formula:

    +$PRICE*MAXIMUM

In copying the formula, 1-2-3 has made no change in the absolute reference but has adjusted the relative reference appropriately. This is exactly what you wanted to happen: The original formula in cell E12 calculates the minimum expected attendance revenue and the formula copied to cell F12 gives the maximum revenue.

In summary, you write absolute and relative references to instruct 1-2-3 exactly how to copy a formula:

▶ An absolute reference is copied without change.

▶ A relative reference is adjusted according to the row or column to which it is copied.

But this isn't the complete picture. In some worksheets you might plan to copy a particular formula in *two* directions—both down a column and across a row. To anticipate this double copy operation, you'll find yourself working with a third type of address format—the *mixed reference*. You'll learn about mixed references as you complete the final sections of the Conference worksheet.

To prepare for the remaining exercises of this chapter, you'll need to perform a few more data-entry tasks. As shown in Figure 4.6, the variable expense section goes into rows 23 to 27. Enter the labels for this section into columns A and B, and then enter the three per-person expense figures (**8.25** for conference materials; **3.25** for coffee and pastries; and **4.75** for a box lunch) into the range D24..D26. Finally, enter the label **Projected Profit** into cell A29.

	A	B	C	D	E	F	G	H
9								
10				Per person	Min. Total	Max. Total		
11	Projected Revenues							
12		Attendance			15600	29250		
13		Video Sales		35	1400	2625		
14		Total Revenues			17000	31875		
15								
16	Projected Expenses – Fixed							
17		Conference Room			1500	2000		
18		Video Production			1000	1000		
19		Promotion			3500	3500		
20		Travel			800	800		
21		Total Fixed Expenses			6800	7300		
22								
23	Projected Expenses – Variable by Attendance							
24		Conference Materials		8.25				
25		Coffee and Pastries		3.25				
26		Box Lunch		4.75				
27		Total Variable Expenses						
28								
29	Projected Profit							
30								

Figure 4.6: **Preparing the final sections of the worksheet**

Mixed References

A mixed reference instructs 1-2-3 to adjust one part of an address and leave another part unchanged when the address is copied from one cell to another. In the notation for a mixed reference, a $ character appears to the left of one address element but not the other. For example, in the following reference the column is absolute and the row is relative:

    $D24

When you copy a formula containing this address, 1-2-3 retains a fixed reference to column D but adjusts the row reference to match the row of the copy. Conversely, the following example contains a relative column reference and an absolute row reference:

    E$8

In copies of this address, 1-2-3 adjusts the column reference to match the column location of the copy, but retains a fixed reference to row 8.

To create a mixed reference, you can type the address directly from the keyboard, complete with the $ symbol representing the absolute component. Alternatively, you can use the F4 function key, just as you did to create absolute references. Press F4 multiple times to cycle through the various reference types. As you have seen, the first key press gives an absolute reference. When you press F4 additional times, the address switches between forms of the mixed reference. You'll see how this works shortly.

The variable expense section of the conference worksheet presents an opportunity to experiment with mixed references. In the range E24..F26, you need to enter six instances of essentially the same formula. The formula should calculate the total expense amounts for each variable-expense category—that is, the per-person expense amount times the number of participants. Using mixed references, you can enter this formula once into cell E24. Then you can copy the formula in two directions: down column E and across to rows 24, 25, and 26. Here are the steps:

1. Select cell E24 and enter the first mixed reference directly from the keyboard: **+E$8**. This is a reference to the cell that contains the minimum attendance estimate.

2. Type the * character, representing multiplication.

3. Type the second reference, **D24**, without any $ symbols. This is a reference to the cell that contains one of the per-person variable expense amounts. You'll use this reference to experiment with the F4 function key.

4. Press F4 three times. With each key press, the reference to cell D24 changes in format—from an absolute reference ($A:$D$24) to forms of mixed reference. The third time you press F4, the address appears as $A:$D24. When you later copy the formula to other rows, column D will remain fixed but the row number will change.

5. Press ↵ to complete the formula entry.

The value 660 appears in cell E24. When you select the cell, the formula in the contents box appears as +E$8*$A:$D24. There's nothing arbitrary about this formula. It contains the exact reference formats that allow you to copy the formula successfully in two directions. Here are the steps for copying the formula:

1. Select the range E24..F24.

2. Click the selection with the right mouse button, and choose Copy Right from the resulting shortcut menu. 1-2-3 copies the formula from cell E24 to F24.

3. Select the range E24..F26.

4. Click the selection with the right mouse button, and choose Copy Down from the shortcut menu. 1-2-3 copies the selected formulas from row 24 down to the cells in rows 25 and 26.

Here's what this section of the sheet looks like now:

22				
23	Projected Expenses – Variable by Attendance			
24	Conference Materials	8.25	660	1237.5
25	Coffee and Pastries	3.25	260	487.5
26	Box Lunch	4.75	380	712.5
27	Total Variable Expenses			
28				

The best way to see the effect of mixed references on the copy operations you have just performed is to examine the six formulas in the range E24..F26:

+E$8*$A:$D24   +F$8*$A:$D24

+E$8*$A:$D25   +F$8*$A:$D25

+E$8*$A:$D26   +F$8*$A:$D26

For each row, 1-2-3 has adjusted the row portion of the second reference ($A:$D24, $A:$D25, $A:$D26). Likewise, the first reference has been adjusted appropriately from E$8 in the first column to F$8 in the second column.

Using the Drag-and-Fill Technique to Copy Formulas

Before you move on, you should try your hand at yet another technique available for copying a formula to a range of cells. Using the *drag-and-fill* procedure, you can efficiently copy the formula in cell E24 to all the other cells in the range E24..F26. To prepare for this exercise, begin by deleting the formulas you just copied to this range. Leave the formula in cell E24 in place, but delete formulas from F24, E25, F25, E26, and F26. Then proceed as follows:

1. Select cell E24 and move the mouse pointer to the lower-right corner of the cell. The mouse pointer takes on a distinctive new shape, representing the drag-and-fill operation:

2. Hold down the left mouse button and drag the mouse one cell to the right and two cells down. As a result, 1-2-3 displays a broken bold border around the range E24..F26:

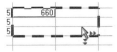

3. Release the mouse button. When you do, 1-2-3 fills the range with copies of the formula in cell E24, adjusting each copy appropriately in relation to its row and column.

4. As a final step, produce the total variable-expense projections. Select the range E27..F27 and then click the Sum SmartIcon. Your worksheet now appears as in Figure 4.7.

	A	B	C	D	E
15					
16	Projected Expenses – Fixed				
17		Conference Room		1500	2000
18		Video Production		1000	1000
19		Promotion		3500	3500
20		Travel		800	800
21		Total Fixed Expenses		6800	7300
22					
23	Projected Expenses – Variable by Attendance				
24		Conference Materials	8.25	660	1237.5
25		Coffee and Pastries	3.25	260	487.5
26		Box Lunch	4.75	380	712.5
27		Total Variable Expenses		1300	2437.5
28					
29	Projected Profit				
30					

Figure 4.7: Copying a formula in two directions

The drag-and-fill operation is perhaps the most efficient copying tool you've seen yet. It also has other uses in a sheet, for filling a range with a numeric series or a sequence of labels. You'll learn more about drag-and-fill in Chapter 7.

Now you're ready to enter the formula for the projected profit. As you do so, you'll learn how to control the order in which operations are performed.

Controlling the Order of Operations

By default, 1-2-3 follows standard mathematical rules for the *order of precedence*—that is, for deciding the order of operations in a formula that contains more than one operation. For example, here are the two rules governing the most common arithmetic operations:

▶ Multiplication and division are performed before addition and subtraction.

▶ Given operations of equal precedence, 1-2-3 performs the operations from left to right.

You can override the precedence rules by inserting pairs of parentheses in a formula. Operations enclosed in parentheses are performed before others. Furthermore, one pair of parentheses can be nested inside another pair; in this case, 1-2-3 begins with the operation inside the innermost parentheses.

The formula for calculating the bottom-line profit in the Conference sheet requires parentheses. The profit is calculated as revenue minus expenses. But in this worksheet there are two groups of expenses, fixed and variable. To make sure that the two expense categories are added together before the subtraction is performed, you must enclose the expense references in parentheses. For example, here is the formula that you'll enter into cell E29 for the first profit projection:

```
+E14-(E21+E27)
```

Cells E21 and E27 contain the two expense subtotals and cell E14 contains the total revenues. If you were to omit the parentheses from this formula, 1-2-3 would perform the operations from left to right, resulting in an incorrect calculation.

Enter this formula into cell E29 now, and then copy the formula over to F29:

1. Select cell E29 and enter the + character to begin the formula.

2. Use the mouse or the arrow keys on the keyboard to point to the total revenue figure in cell E14.

3. Type the minus sign and then the open parenthesis character, (. At this point the formula appears as +A:E14-(.

4. Point to the total fixed expense figure in cell E21.

5. Type the plus sign.

6. Point to the total variable-expense figure in cell E27.

7. Type the close-parenthesis character,). The formula now appears as +A:E14-(A:E21+A:E27). Notice that all the address references are relative. There is no need for absolute or mixed references for the upcoming copy operation.

8. Press ↵ to confirm the formula entry.

9. Use any of the copy techniques you've learned to copy the formula from cell E29 to cell E30.

10. Click the Save SmartIcon to save this version of the worksheet to disk.

The final version of the worksheet for this chapter appears in Figure 4.8.

	A	B	C	D	E	F	G	H
9								
10				Per person	Min. Total	Max. Total		
11	Projected Revenues							
12		Attendance			15600	29250		
13		Video Sales		35	1400	2625		
14		Total Revenues			17000	31875		
15								
16	Projected Expenses – Fixed							
17		Conference Room			1500	2000		
18		Video Production			1000	1000		
19		Promotion			3500	3500		
20		Travel			800	800		
21		Total Fixed Expenses			6800	7300		
22								
23	Projected Expenses – Variable by Attendance							
24		Conference Materials		8.25	660	1237.5		
25		Coffee and Pastries		3.25	260	487.5		
26		Box Lunch		4.75	380	712.5		
27		Total Variable Expenses			1300	2437.5		
28								
29	Projected Profit				8900	22137.5		
30								

Figure 4.8: Calculating the projected profit

Examining "What-If" Scenarios

The Conference sheet presents many opportunities for exploring variations in the plans and projections. For example, imagine that Computing Conferences, Inc. is considering the possibility of increasing the price of attendance from $195 to $225. In so doing, they anticipate a possible 15 percent decrease in attendance. They would like to see what happens to the projected profit under these combined circumstances.

To view the results of this scenario, revise three values in the worksheet:

1. Enter a value of 225, the new fee, in cell B8.
2. Enter a value of 68, the new minimum attendance, in cell E8.
3. Enter a value of 128, the new maximum attendance, in cell F8.

Each time you enter a new value, 1-2-3 instantly recalculates all the formulas that contain references to the revised cell. The split sheet in Figure 4.9 shows the three revised values and the new profit projections.

Comparing this worksheet with Figure 4.8, you can see that the range of profits in this scenario is down from the original projection. The company therefore decides against raising the price at this time.

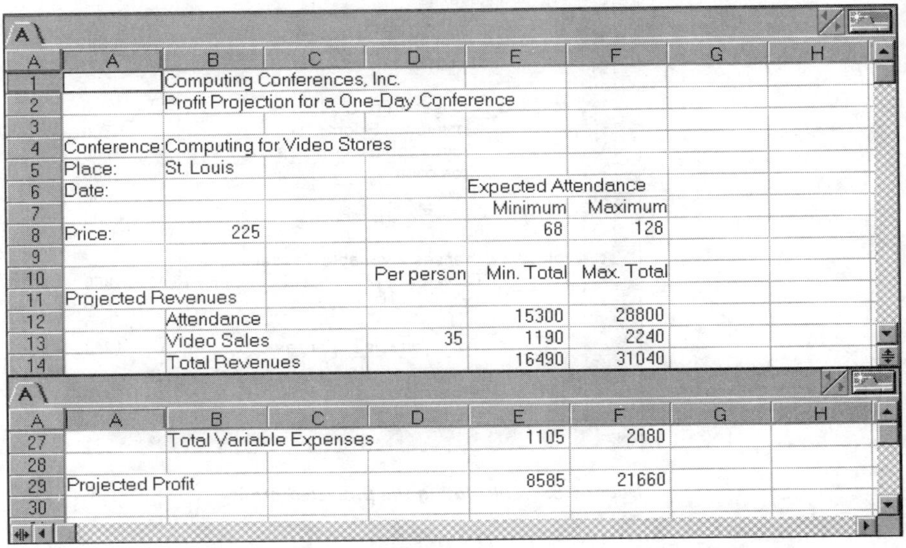

	A	B	C	D	E	F
1		Computing Conferences, Inc.				
2		Profit Projection for a One-Day Conference				
3						
4	Conference:	Computing for Video Stores				
5	Place:	St. Louis				
6	Date:				Expected Attendance	
7					Minimum	Maximum
8	Price:	225			68	128
9						
10				Per person	Min. Total	Max. Total
11	Projected Revenues					
12		Attendance			15300	28800
13		Video Sales		35	1190	2240
14		Total Revenues			16490	31040
...						
27		Total Variable Expenses			1105	2080
28						
29	Projected Profit				8585	21660
30						

Figure 4.9: Experimenting with changes in the initial data

You might want to try other changes in the worksheet to see what happens to profits. For example, make the changes corresponding to each of these situations:

▶ The company is notified of a 10 percent price increase for the use of the conference room.

▶ Due to last-minute revisions in the curriculum, some conference materials have to be redone—increasing the cost of materials by $5 per person.

▶ The company decides to produce a radio commercial promoting the conference. The commercial adds $2,500 to promotion costs, but the company anticipates a possible 25 percent increase in attendance.

These and other experiments demonstrate the flexibility of the worksheet as a tool for exploring the variations and unknowns in any business projection.

When you finish these exercises, exit from 1-2-3 *without* saving the latest revisions to disk. You'll continue working with the Conference worksheet in Chapter 5, using the original data that you've already saved in the CONF.123 file. Specifically, you'll begin exploring the variety of formatting and style options available in 1-2-3, and you'll see the results of these options on the printed worksheet.

Summary

In the first steps of creating a new worksheet you're normally preoccupied with data entry and organization. To help you with these tasks, 1-2-3 has a variety of tools you can use to move and copy data from one location on the worksheet to another, or to delete entries from a cell or a range. You perform these procedures by choosing menu commands, clicking SmartIcons, or performing special mouse actions such as drag and drop.

As you complete sections of numeric data in your worksheet, you can begin adding formulas to display calculated values. The use of range names can often make formulas simpler and clearer. When you write a formula that you intend to copy to other locations on your worksheet, you must choose carefully among relative, absolute, and mixed address references. (While you are entering a formula, pressing the F4 function key cycles you through these reference types.) References determine how 1-2-3 ultimately copies your formula to other cells.

A well-organized worksheet becomes an ideal tool for investigating what-if questions. By making changes in key data items, you can find out what happens to totals and other calculated values under new assumptions.

CHAPTER 5

Formatting Data

Fast Track

To move the cell pointer quickly to a named cell or range,	**150**
click the Navigator button on the edit line and select a name from the list; or press F5 to open the Go To dialog box, and select from the Name list.	
To change the width of a column using mouse techniques,	**153**
in the frame at the top of the worksheet, drag the column's border to the right to increase the width, or to the left to decrease it. Alternatively, double-click the border to find the best fit.	
To change the column width on an entire sheet,	**155**
click the Sheet Properties SmartIcon and click the Basics tab on the resulting InfoSheet. Change the setting in the Default column width box.	
To hide a range of columns on a sheet,	**159**
drag the mouse pointer across column headings to select the columns you want to hide. Then click the selection with the right mouse button and choose Hide Columns from the resulting shortcut menu.	
To restore hidden columns to view,	**160**
select the columns on either side of the hidden columns, click the selection with the right mouse button, and choose Unhide Columns from the resulting shortcut menu.	

To left-align, center, or right-align the data in a range of cells, 160
select the range, click the Alignment button on the status bar, and select an alignment option.

To center a label over a horizontal range of cells, 162
select a range of adjacent cells in a row, where the first cell contains the label that you want to center. Click the Range Properties SmartIcon and click the Alignment tab on the resulting InfoBox. Check the Align across columns option, and click the center button in the Horizontal alignment group.

To wrap a long label within a cell, 164
select the cell and click the Range Properties SmartIcon. In the Basics tab, increase both the column width and the row height to dimensions that will accommodate the long label. Then click the Alignment tab and check the Wrap text in cell option.

To freeze titles so they'll remain in view when you scroll your worksheet, 166
select a cell just below the range of rows you want to freeze, or just to the right of a selected range of columns. Then choose View ➤ Titles, select the Row and/or Column, and click OK.

To remove the display of grid lines from the worksheet window, 169
click the Workbook Properties SmartIcon, uncheck the Grid lines check box, and click OK.

To apply a format globally to the numeric values on a sheet, 171
click the Sheet Properties SmartIcon and click the Number format tab on the resulting InfoBox. Select a category of formats from the Category list and then choose an option from the Current format list.

To apply a format to a selected range on a sheet, 173
select the range, click the Range Properties SmartIcon, and click the Number format tab on the resulting InfoBox. Select a format category and a specific format within the category. Alternatively, select an entry from the Format button on the status bar.

AFTER you create a working table of data and formulas, your next task is to refine the appearance of your worksheet. As in any application, you want to present information as clearly and attractively as possible—for your own benefit as you work with data on the screen, and for the benefit of people who later see your work as a printed document. 1-2-3 has a wealth of options for controlling the appearance of values and labels on a sheet.

In this chapter and the next you'll concentrate primarily on commands that affect the way your sheet looks and functions. First you'll learn to accomplish the following tasks:

- ▶ Change column widths for the entire sheet or for individual columns.
- ▶ Control the alignment of labels on the sheet.
- ▶ Hide columns and ranges of data.
- ▶ Select numeric formats for the sheet and for selected ranges.

Then in Chapter 6 you'll continue to explore the aesthetics of data presentation, as you prepare to print your sheet.

To practice these procedures, you'll return to your work on the Conference worksheet. The sheet is already a functioning tool for projecting the revenues, expenses, and profit of a future business event. Now you'll transform it into a lucid document that places appropriate emphasis on specific parts of the information.

Working on an Existing Sheet

Reopen the Conference worksheet that you saved at the end of the last chapter. Pull down the File menu and choose CONF from the list of file names at the end of the menu. The Conference worksheet reappears on the screen with all the work that you've already completed.

In upcoming exercises you'll be moving back and forth to specific ranges and cells on the Conference worksheet to change formats and styles. A tool that can speed you on your way to a specified location on the worksheet is the Edit ➤ Go To command.

Using the Go To Command

In response to the Go To command, the cell pointer jumps to a cell or range that you specify. To perform the command, choose Edit ➤ Go

To or press the F5 function key. (Another keyboard shortcut for this command is Ctrl+G.) The Go To dialog box appears on the screen:

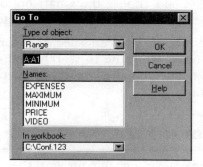

In this box you can enter the address of the cell to which you want to move, or you can select a range name from a list box that the command displays.

The Go To box shows the list of range names you've defined on the Conference sheet. To jump to the cell or range represented by one of these names, highlight the name and press ↵, or double-click the selected name in the list. If you select a name that represents a range of cells, 1-2-3 highlights the range. For example, try the following exercise:

1. Press F5 to choose the command.
2. Highlight the EXPENSES name in the Names list.
3. Click the OK button or press ↵.

   In response, 1-2-3 highlights the range E17..E20, the range you've named EXPENSES.

   As you work through the exercises in this chapter, you'll find that the F5 function key—representing the Go To command—is a good tool for moving quickly to a particular location in the current worksheet window. Of course, the Navigator button on the edit bar is another convenient tool you can use for jumps to a named range in the current workbook. But the Go To command has a few advantages over the navigator for specific situations:

▶ You can use the Go To command to jump to an unnamed cell or range, by entering an address (rather than a name) in the text box just below the Type of object box.

- The Go To command provides a list of objects you can jump to. For example, if you want to select a chart in an open workbook, pull down the Type of object list and choose the Chart option. The Names list then shows the names of all the charts in the selected workbook.

- If more than one file is open, you can select the workbook you want to view by choosing a name from the In workbook list at the bottom of the Go To dialog box. Then choose a range or object you want to jump to in the selected workbook.

Changing the Appearance of a Sheet

While working on the appearance of your worksheet, keep in mind that many properties can be changed in two ways:

- Globally for an entire sheet
- Selectively for one or more ranges on the sheet

Before modifying a given property, decide whether you want to make the change for the whole sheet or for a range on the sheet.

As you know, 1-2-3's InfoBox gives you an easy way to change the properties of a range or a sheet. To open an InfoBox you can click the Range Properties or Sheet Properties SmartIcon, or choose the corresponding menu command (Range ➤ Range Properties or Sheet ➤ Sheet Properties). Furthermore, you can quickly switch from range properties to sheet properties in the same InfoBox. For example, suppose you open the InfoBox for a range and then decide you want to work with the properties of the entire sheet. Simply pull down the Properties for list on the title bar for the InfoBox:

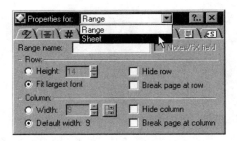

Changing the Appearance of a Sheet

Choose Sheet in the drop-down list, and 1-2-3 displays the tabs representing sheet properties:

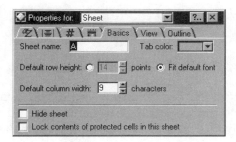

You'll work extensively with these two InfoBoxes—for range properties and sheet properties—in the exercises ahead.

Setting Column Widths

Column width is an example of a visual property that you can change for the whole sheet or individual columns. To increase or decrease the width of all columns, you click the Basics tab on the InfoBox for a sheet. The Default column width box has a default setting of 9 characters:

Under this default, each column in the sheet is wide enough to display a nine-digit number in the default font, 12-point Arial. In the Column width box you can enter any value from 1 to 240 for the worksheet's global column width.

Take the following steps now to increase the global column width of the Conference worksheet to 11:

1. Click the Sheet Properties SmartIcon. If necessary, click the Basic tab on the resulting InfoBox.

2. Change the Default column width setting to 11. You can enter the new value directly from the keyboard, or you can click the up-arrow button twice with the mouse to increase the setting from 9 to 11. As soon as you complete the entry, you'll see the column width increase on the current sheet.

3. Click the Close button (labeled X) at the upper-right corner of the InfoBox.

After you widen the columns, the data on your worksheet spreads out over most of the width of the application window.

Changing the Width of a Range of Columns

In the InfoBox for range properties you'll find controls for changing the width of a column or a range of columns. You can use these controls to set the width numerically, to adjust a width to accommodate the contents of a column, or to restore columns to the sheet's default width setting. These choices are presented as two option buttons, a text box, and a command button:

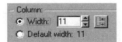

To change the width of a selected range of columns, select the Width option and enter a new numeric setting. To go back to the default sheet width, select the Default width option. If you want 1-2-3 to find the best-fit width for the contents of a column, click the button located to the right of the Width text box; the following help bubble appears when you position the mouse pointer over this button:

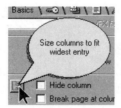

You'll learn more about the best-fit width later.

TIP To designate a range of columns and change their widths, you can select either a row of cells within the columns or the entire columns. To select whole columns, drag the mouse horizontally over the target column letters in the sheet's frame. 1-2-3 highlights the columns you've selected.

As an experiment with the Column Width dialog box, follow these steps to widen columns E and F to a setting of 13 characters:

1. Drag the mouse pointer over column letters E and F along the frame at the top of the sheet. 1-2-3 highlights columns E and F:

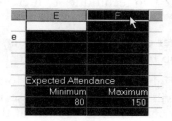

2. Click the Range Properties SmartIcon and click the Basics tab if necessary.
3. Select the Width option button in the Column group, and position the mouse pointer over the small up-arrow button located to the right of the Width text box. Click the button twice. The column width setting changes to 13. (Alternatively, you can enter a value of **13** directly from the keyboard.)
4. Close the InfoBox.

Using the Mouse to Change Column Widths

There are two convenient mouse techniques for changing the width of a column. To use these techniques, you start by positioning the mouse pointer over the border between two column headings in the worksheet's frame. For example, to change the width of column C, you position the pointer between the C and D headings; when you do so, the pointer changes to a double-headed arrow icon:

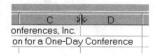

Here are the ways you can use this pointer:

▶ You can drag a column's border to the right to increase the column width, or to the left to decrease it. This technique allows you to change a column visually. While you make the change, a size box appears on the sheet to show you the current numeric width setting.

▶ You can double-click the left mouse button when the pointer is positioned over a border between two columns. In response, 1-2-3 resizes the column to its best fit, the ideal width for the current contents of the column.

Try using the first of these two techniques to increase the width of column C:

1. Position the mouse pointer over the vertical border line between the C and D headings at the top border of the worksheet.

2. Drag the border to the right. As you do so, a dotted-line shows you where the new border will be when you release the mouse button. Move this border to a position just to the left of the D heading. The size box displays the setting as 16 characters:

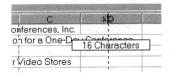

3. Release the mouse button.

Figure 5.1 shows the 1-2-3 window at this point in your work. Column F is now partly out of view because of the increased column widths.

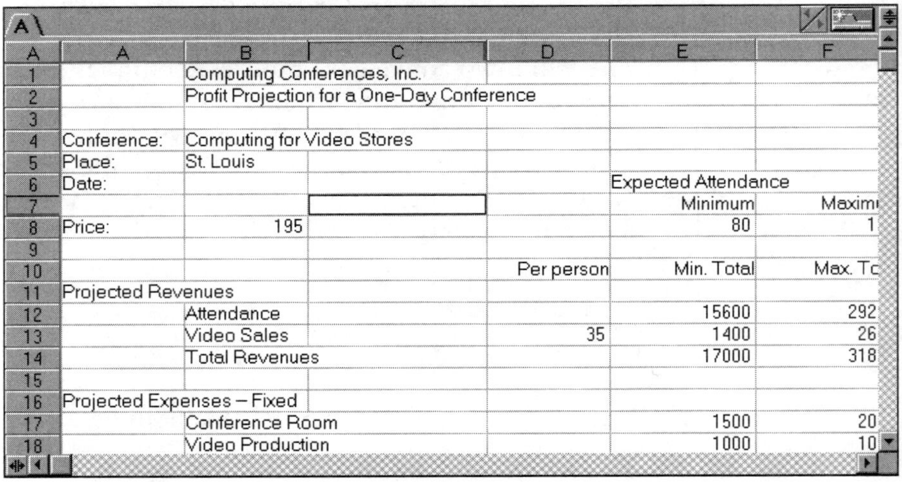

	A	B	C	D	E	F
1		Computing Conferences, Inc.				
2		Profit Projection for a One-Day Conference				
3						
4	Conference:	Computing for Video Stores				
5	Place:	St. Louis				
6	Date:				Expected Attendance	
7					Minimum	Maximi
8	Price:	195			80	1
9						
10				Per person	Min. Total	Max. To
11	Projected Revenues					
12		Attendance			15600	292
13		Video Sales		35	1400	26
14		Total Revenues			17000	318
15						
16	Projected Expenses – Fixed					
17		Conference Room			1500	20
18		Video Production			1000	10

Figure 5.1: *Changing column widths on the worksheet*

Resizing a Column to Its Best Fit

In the Conference sheet, changing the column widths is meant simply to improve the presentation of your data. In other cases, you may need to increase widths for a more essential reason—to enable your worksheet to display all of its numeric data. If a number in a cell is too long to fit in the width of the corresponding column, 1-2-3 replaces the numeric display with a string of asterisks. These asterisks tell you that you have to increase the column width in order to display the number itself.

Experiment with this effect in the following exercise:

1. Click the New Sheet button to add a temporary sheet B to the CONF.123 workbook.

2. Type the value $123456789.00 in cell A1. (Including a dollar sign and decimal places in the entry is one way to apply a dollar format to this numeric value.) When you press ↵, the cell fills with a string of asterisks:

3. Now position the mouse pointer over the border between the A and B column headings, and double-click the left mouse button. 1-2-3 adjusts the column width appropriately, and you now see the number displayed as $123,456,789.00:

4. After you've examined the result of this exercise, click the sheet's B tab with the right mouse button, and choose the Delete Sheet command from the resulting quick menu. The workbook once again has only one sheet, labeled A.

In this experiment, the entry in cell A1 wasn't displayed until you increased the column width appropriately.

There are actually several ways to resize a column to its best fit:

- Double-click the border between the column headings.
- Click the Size columns button in the Basics tab of the InfoBox for range properties.
- Click a column selection with the right mouse button, and choose the Fit Widest Entry or the Fit Widest Number command from the resulting shortcut.
- Click the Size columns button in the Range SmartIcons bar:

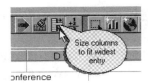

Another interesting adjustment you can make in a worksheet is to hide a column completely.

Hiding Columns

You may want to hide one or more columns temporarily so that you can concentrate on other columns of data on your worksheet. Or you may have other reasons for hiding columns. If you're planning to distribute a particular worksheet to many people, you might decide to hide a column of sensitive or private information.

Whatever your reasons, you can use any of three techniques to hide one or more columns on a sheet:

- Select the columns you want to hide, click the selection with the right mouse button, and choose Hide Columns from the resulting shortcut menu.
- Select a range of cells within the target columns, click the Range Properties SmartIcon, and check the Hide column option in the Basics tab.
- Drag the border of a target column to the left until the size box shows a column width setting of 0.

For example, imagine that you've decided to focus temporarily on the projections for maximum attendance on your Conference worksheet.

You want to hide the column containing the minimum estimate, column E. Here's one way to accomplish this:

1. Click the E column heading in the sheet's frame. 1-2-3 selects all of column E in response.

2. Click the selected column with the right mouse button. The shortcut menu for a selected column appears on the Desktop:

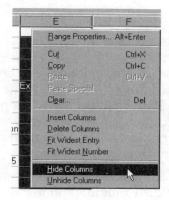

3. Choose the Hide Columns command from the shortcut menu.

After these steps, column E disappears from the worksheet, as you can see in Figure 5.2. You can now concentrate on the data in column F.

Figure 5.2: **Hiding a column**

At some point you'll want to restore the hidden data in column E. There are several ways to do this:

▶ Position the mouse pointer between the D and F column headings on the sheet's frame. When the mouse pointer takes the shape of a gray two-headed arrow, you are ready to restore the size of the hidden column; drag the pointer to the right until the size box displays the width you want for column E:

▶ Drag the mouse pointer horizontally along the D and F column headings to select these two columns. Then click the Range Properties SmartIcon and select the Basics tab on the resulting InfoBox. Notice that the Hide column check box is filled with gray, indicating that part of the current selection is hidden. Click this option once to unhide column E. Then close the InfoBox.

▶ Select columns D and F and click the selection with the right mouse button. Choose the Unhide Columns command from the resulting shortcut menu.

Use any one of these techniques now to redisplay column E. The worksheet is restored to its original state, with all its columns in view. Column E has the column width setting you assigned it before the Hide operation.

Now you're ready to start applying new display properties to the data in the sheet. One property you've already worked with is alignment. When you initially developed the Conference sheet, you used double quotation mark prefixes to right-align the label entries Maximum and Minimum in their cells. Often it's easier to apply alignment properties to a range of entries *after* you enter the data onto the worksheet.

Aligning Data

By default, labels are left-aligned and numbers are right-aligned, but you can change the alignment of either. 1-2-3 offers left-, center-, or right-alignment options for any entry. These formats are available from the Alignment tab in the InfoBox for range properties:

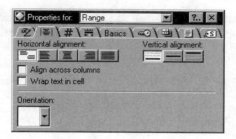

Alternatively, you can choose an option from the Alignment button on the status bar:

The icon at the top of this list represents the default: left alignment for labels and right alignment for values. The next three options represent left-, center-, and right-alignment. The final option is for labels only; it evenly spaces the characters of a label within its cell.

 TIP You can choose an alignment for an entire sheet from the Alignment tab on the InfoBox for sheet properties. Alternatively, click the tab for the sheet (A, for example) and then click the Alignment button on the status bar.

When you set the alignment of a label, 1-2-3 changes the label's prefix in the contents box. A single-quotation mark (') produces left-alignment, the default. A caret symbol (^) centers a label in its cell. A double quotation mark (") produces right-alignment. As a quick experiment with alignments, try changing the alignments of the labels in the range A4..A8 on the Conference worksheet. This range contains the labels Conference:, Place:, Date:, and Price:, all of which are initially left-aligned. Notice that a single quote appears as the prefix for each label in the contents box; for example:

    'Conference:

Here are the steps for examining the other possible alignments:

1. Select the range A4..A8.

2. Click the Alignment button on the status bar, and choose the center-alignment option. Then deselect the range. The four labels are centered in their cells:

4	Conference:	Computing for Video Stores
5	Place:	St. Louis
6	Date:	
7		
8	Price:	195

3. Select A4..A8 again. Click the Alignment button on the status bar and choose the right-alignment option. Deselect the range. The labels are right-aligned:

4	Conference:	Computing for Video Stores
5	Place:	St. Louis
6	Date:	
7		
8	Price:	195

4. As a demonstration of numeric alignment, select cell B8 (which currently contains the value 195) and choose the left-alignment option from the status bar. The numeric entry moves to the left side of the cell.

5. Right-alignment is a good choice for the labels in A4..A8, but a small adjustment is now necessary. Double-click the label in cell A4 to toggle into the Edit mode. Press the spacebar once to append a space to the end of the label, and then press ↵ to complete the edit.

6. Repeat this step for the other three labels, in cells A5, A6, and A8. On the printed worksheet this space will separate the right-aligned labels in column A from the left-aligned data in column B.

> **TIP** The previous exercise served as a reminder that 1-2-3 allows in-cell editing. To edit any entry in a cell, you simply double-click the cell with the mouse, or select the cell and press F2. The contents box on the edit line is also available as a location for editing, but in-cell editing is generally more convenient.

You can change the horizontal alignment of long labels in two different ways—around a single cell or over a range of adjacent cells in a row. For example, consider the two title lines of the Conference worksheet, in cells B1 and B2. If you select B1..B2 and choose the center option, 1-2-3 centers the labels horizontally around the cells that contain them. Each centered label is displayed from column A to column C:

1-2-3 also gives you a simple way to center these titles horizontally over the sheet. To do so, you begin by selecting a horizontal range and then you open the InfoBox for range properties:

1. Select the range B1..E2 on the Conference worksheet.
2. Click the Range Properties SmartIcon, and click the Alignment tab in the resulting InfoBox.
3. Click the Align across columns option, placing a check in the corresponding check box.
4. Click the center-alignment option:

5. Close the InfoBox.

When you complete this procedure, 1-2-3 centers the two title labels horizontally within the width of columns B through E. As you can see in Figure 5.3, this centers the titles approximately over the worksheet area. The titles themselves are still contained in cells B1 and B2. Selecting each of these cells in turn, you see the following labels in the contents box:

^Computing Conferences, Inc.

^Profit Projection for a One-Day Conference

Notice that 1-2-3 uses the caret prefix for centering within either a single cell or a horizontal range of cells.

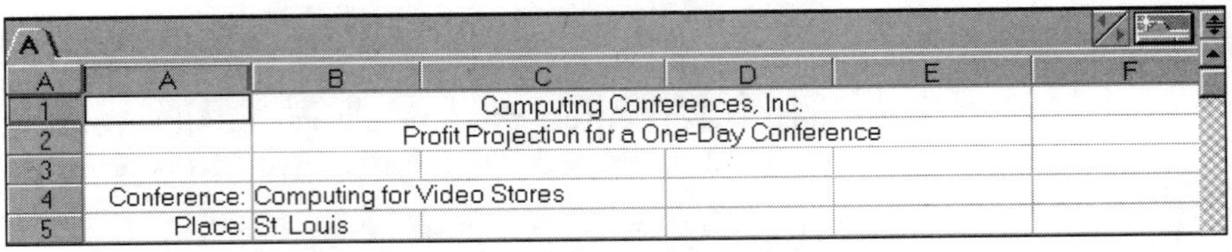

Chapter 5   *Formatting Data*

Figure 5.3: Centering titles over a horizontal range of cells

Wrapping Text in a Cell

Another way to display a long label is to wrap it within the dimensions of a cell. To create this special effect, you can increase both the column width and the row height of the target cell, and then choose the Wrap text in cell option. Try it in the following exercise:

1. Click the New Sheet button to add a temporary sheet B to the CONF .123 workbook.

2. In cell A1 enter the text **Profit Projection for a One-Day Conference**.

3. Select A1 again and click the Range Properties SmartIcon. Begin by selecting the Basics tab in the InfoBox.

4. Select the Width option and increase the column width to a setting of 20.

5. Select the Height option and increase the row height to a setting of 30.

6. Now click the Alignment tab in the InfoBox. Click the Wrap text in cell option, placing a check in the corresponding check box.

7. In the Horizontal alignment options, click the center-alignment button.

As a result of these changes, the label in A1 is now displayed as two lines of text, centered horizontally in the cell:

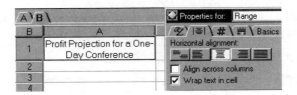

Use the Wrap text in cell option whenever you want to create a multi-line title within the dimensions of a single cell.

You can close the InfoBox for range properties now, but don't delete sheet B yet from the current workbook. You'll use it again for the upcoming exercise.

Repeating Characters

1-2-3 has a fourth label prefix, but it's not related to alignment. The backslash prefix (\) instructs 1-2-3 to fill a cell with a single repeating character or with a pattern of repeating characters. You can use this feature to create division lines or other visual effects in a cell or a row of cells. Try this exercise with the backslash prefix:

1. On sheet B, use the mouse to expand the width of column B to a setting of 50.
2. Enter the following labels, one each into cells B3 through B7:

Cell	Enter
B3	\#
B4	\.
B5	\-
B6	\:
B7	\\

Here's the result of these five entries:

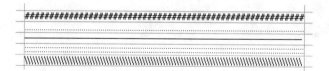

When you've finished examining these visual effects, click the tab of sheet B with the right mouse button and choose Delete Sheet from the resulting shortcut menu. This action removes sheet B from the CONF.123 workbook.

Freezing Worksheet Titles on the Screen

As in other types of Windows documents, you can scroll down a worksheet by pressing the PgDn key on the keyboard or by clicking in the vertical scroll bar. Normally when you scroll down by a window's length, the rows at the top of the worksheet disappear from view. Likewise, when you scroll to the right—by pressing Ctrl+→ or by clicking in the horizontal scroll bar—you normally lose sight of the columns located at the left of your worksheet. Sometimes you might want a way to hold a range of rows or columns on the screen, even when you scroll down or across the worksheet. The View ➤ Titles command "freezes" the top rows and/or left-hand columns on a sheet, so that the information in these ranges always remains in view.

For example, on the Conference sheet it would be convenient to freeze the first ten rows in the worksheet—the rows containing the worksheet title, the general information about the planned conference, and the column headings. In other words, you might like to have all this information stay in view as you scroll down the worksheet. Here are the steps for freezing these rows on the worksheet:

1. Move the cell pointer to cell A11. This is the row just below the range of rows that you want to freeze onto the screen.

2. Choose View ➤ Titles. The Freeze dialog box appears. Check the Rows above current cell option:

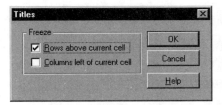

3. Click OK or press ↵ to complete the operation.

   In response, 1-2-3 removes the grid lines from rows 1 through 10 of the sheet; this shows you that these rows contain the titles that will remain in view.

   Now press the PgDn key to scroll down the worksheet. When you do so, the first ten rows remain in view, and scrolling takes place only in the lower half of the worksheet. For example, in Figure 5.4 the worksheet has been scrolled all the way down to the projected profit line, juxtaposing the summary information (in the first ten rows of the sheet) and the bottom-line profit. Notice that rows 11 through 27 do not appear on the sheet.

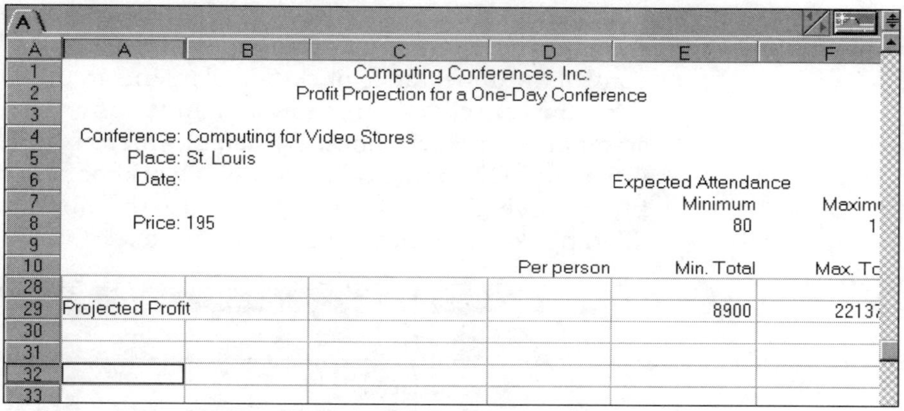

Figure 5.4: A range of frozen rows at the top of the worksheet

You can use the keyboard or the mouse to select cells or ranges inside a frozen range:

▶ With the keyboard, press the Home key and then use the arrow keys to move into the frozen range.

▶ With the mouse, simply click the cell or drag over the range that you want to select.

Using either of these techniques, you can move into the frozen range to edit the data it contains or to change its appearance or format.

To return to the default scrolling mode for a sheet, choose View ➤ Titles again and remove the check or checks from the Row and Column options. When you click OK, the grid lines reappear in the range that had previously been frozen.

Before you read on, you might want to try freezing columns at the left side of the worksheet. For example, try establishing columns A and B as a titles range. Then scroll toward the right side of the worksheet. What happens as you do so? What's the advantage of freezing these columns? When you're finished with this exercise, choose View ➤ Titles again and clear the Column option.

Changing the Workbook Properties

The Workbook Properties dialog box provides options for changing the appearance of all the sheets in a workbook. To open this dialog box, choose File ➤ Workbook Properties. As you can see in Figure 5.5, the View tab contains a group of ten check boxes that you can use to control the appearance of certain elements in the workbook. For example, you can choose to show—or hide—the sheet frame, sheet tabs, scroll bars, and grid lines. By default, these features are all part of the visual and functional definition of a workbook; to hide them, you simply remove the check mark next to the appropriate option in the Workbook Properties dialog box, and click OK.

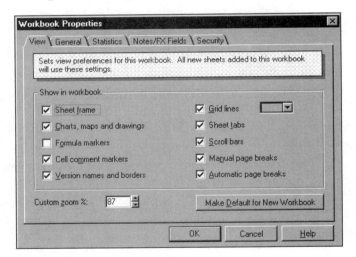

Figure 5.5:   *The Workbook Properties dialog box*

NOTE The View tab in the InfoBox for sheet properties has options for showing or hiding the features of individual sheets. For example, you can use these options to remove the sheet frame and grid lines of a sheet, without changing the appearance of other sheets in the current workbook.

Changing the Appearance of a Sheet

Suppose you want to remove the grid lines from sheets in the current workbook. Working with or without grid lines is a matter of personal preference; this option does not affect any other aspect of operations inside the worksheet. To hide the grid lines, remove the check from the Grid lines option in the Workbook Properties dialog box:

1. Choose File ➤ Workbook Properties.
2. In the View tab of the Workbook Properties dialog box, click the Grid lines option. This removes the check from the corresponding box.
3. Click OK.

1-2-3 removes the grid lines from the workbook window, as shown in Figure 5.6.

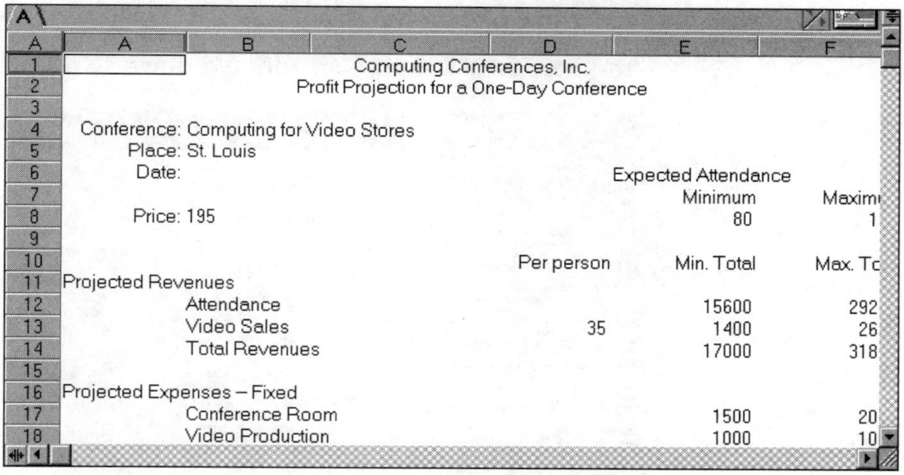

Figure 5.6: **Removing the grid lines from the workbook window**

Restore the grid lines now by opening the Workbook Properties dialog box again and placing a check in the Grid lines option.

Other View options in the Workbook Properties dialog box allow you to hide or show a variety of standard objects; you might want to experiment with these features now, before you read on. Finally, the Custom zoom text box (look back at Figure 5.5) allows you to change the size of cells as they are displayed on the screen—increasing the size by as much as 400 percent or decreasing it by as much as 25 percent. For example, here is a detail of the worksheet, zoomed up to 200 percent:

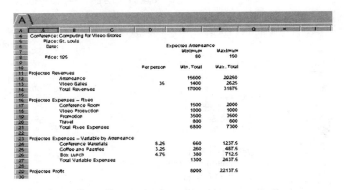

And here is the worksheet zoomed down to 40 percent:

> **TIP** The View ➤ Zoom to command provides an additional method for changing the size of the current worksheet. When you choose this command, a list of preset zoom percentages appears.

Formatting Numeric Values

One way to add meaning to a numeric value on your worksheet is to pair the value with a descriptive label. A number and an adjacent label together form a clearly identified item of information; for example:

```
Price:    195
```

But another important technique for establishing the meaning of numbers—and to improve the general readability of your worksheet—is to apply appropriate formats to numeric values:

    Price: $195.00

1-2-3 provides standard numeric formats that you can assign to the values on a sheet. Like other properties, number formats can apply to an entire sheet or to particular cells or ranges. A format does not change the value of a numeric entry, only the way the number is displayed in the cell.

You can apply formats before or after you enter values onto your worksheet. To establish formats for the entire worksheet, use the Number format tab on the InfoBox for sheet properties:

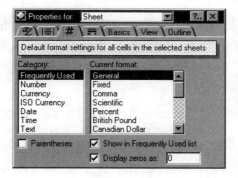

Choose a format category and then a specific format within the category. 1-2-3 applies the selected format to all values in the current sheet.

The InfoBox for range properties supplies a similar arrangement of options, designed for applying formats to a selected range on the worksheet rather than the entire sheet:

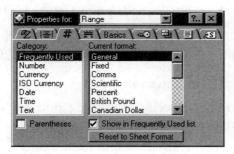

This InfoBox also has a Reset to Sheet Format command button; clicking this button resets the format to the current default for the sheet.

Using Common Numeric Formats

Here are examples of six commonly used formats:

Numeric Formats	
Fixed:	34567.89
Scientific:	3.46E+004
US Dollar:	$34,567.89
Comma:	34,567.89
General:	34567.89
Percent:	3456789.00%

The following list provides a brief description of each of these formats.

Format	Description
Fixed	Displays values with a specified number of decimal places, up to fifteen.
Scientific	Displays numbers in an exponent notation, where the digits after the letter E represent the power of 10 by which the base value is multiplied.
US Dollar	Displays a dollar sign at the beginning of the number, and a comma before every third digit at the left of the decimal point.
Comma	Displays a comma before every third digit at the left of the decimal point.
General	Displays a value without special formatting.
Percent	Multiplies the displayed value by 100 and appends a percent sign.

The Format button of the status bar is a useful shortcut for changing the number formats for a range or for an entire sheet. This list simplifies the process of formatting values:

1. Select a cell or range of cells containing numeric entries, or click a sheet tab to format an entire sheet.

2. Click the Format button on the status bar. The format list pops up on the screen:

3. Select a format from the list.

   You'll have a chance to practice using this technique as you change the numeric formats on the Conference worksheet.

> **TIP** The Number format tab on the InfoBox for sheet or range properties contains a check box labeled Show in Frequently Used List. This check box gives you the opportunity to modify the list of formats available from the Format button on the status bar. To include or exclude a format, select its name in the Current format box, and click the Show in Frequently Used List check box.

Selecting Sheet and Range Formats

Because most of the values on the Conference worksheet are dollar-and-cent figures, it is convenient to assign a US Dollar format to the entire sheet and then go back and change the formats of values that do not represent monetary amounts. Here are the steps:

1. Click the A tab for the Conference sheet. This action selects the sheet, rather than any range on the sheet, and prepares the way for assigning a number format to the entire sheet.

2. Click the Format button on the status bar, and choose the US Dollar format. As a result, all of the values on the worksheet are displayed as

dollar-and-cent values. But the worksheet currently contains two values that should be displayed as simple integers: the minimum and maximum attendance estimates in cells E8 and F8.

3. Select the range E8..F8.

4. Click the Format button on the status bar, and select the General option at the top of the format list.

In Figure 5.7 you can see the changes that take place in your worksheet when you complete these formatting operations. Click the Save SmartIcon now to save all the changes you've made in the CONF.123 workbook.

	E	F
6	Expected Attendance	
7	Minimum	Maximum
8	80	150
9		
10	Min. Total	Max. Total
11		
12	$15,600.00	$29,250.00
13	$1,400.00	$2,625.00
14	$17,000.00	$31,875.00
15		
16		
17	$1,500.00	$2,000.00
18	$1,000.00	$1,000.00
19	$3,500.00	$3,500.00
20	$800.00	$800.00
21	$6,800.00	$7,300.00
22		

Figure 5.7: *Formatting values on the Conference worksheet*

In the InfoBoxes for sheet and range properties, you'll notice that 1-2-3 offers a great variety of international currency formats in addition to the US Dollar:

The Format button on the status bar also includes a selection of these formats.

Automatic Formatting

In automatic formatting, 1-2-3 applies a common numeric format according to the way you initially enter a value into a cell. For example, if you enter a value as a currency, a date, a time, or a percentage—in a format that 1-2-3 can recognize—the corresponding numeric format is automatically applied to the cell. If you subsequently enter a different value into the same cell, the new value is displayed in the established format.

In the following exercise you'll experiment with the effect of automatic formatting. You'll begin by using the File ➤ New Workbook command to create a new workbook file.

1. Choose File ➤ New Workbook, or click the New Workbook SmartIcon (the first button in the Universal SmartIcons bar). In the New Workbook dialog box, click the button labeled Create a Blank Workbook.

2. Type **$1234.56** into cell A1 of the new sheet. You haven't included a comma in your entry, but the initial dollar sign is enough to assign the US Dollar currency format to the cell. Press ↵ and note the results. The cell displays the new entry as $1,234.56. Select cell A1 again; you'll see that the status bar reports the cell's format as US Dollar.

3. Enter a new numeric value, **6543.21**, into the same cell. The US Dollar format is applied to this new entry, which appears as $6,543.21.

4. Now enter **27%** into cell A2. Select A2 again; the status bar identifies the format as Percent, though the edit line displays the value as 0.27.

5. Try entering a new value in A2, such as **.88**. The value is displayed as 88%.

6. Select cell A3 and enter a date: **15-Apr-9**7. 1-2-3 automatically applies a date format to the cell. You'll learn more about date entries in Chapter 6.

7. When you've finished examining the results of this exercise, choose File ➤ Close and click the No button on the resulting dialog box to close the workbook file without saving it.

NOTE In the InfoBoxes for sheet and range properties, 1-2-3 supplies a rather atypical format named Label. You generally apply this format to a sheet or range before you begin entering data. When you do so, 1-2-3 accepts all subsequent entries as labels, even if they begin with digits or other characters that would normally result in the Value mode. 1-2-3 inserts an alignment character in front of each entry (', ", or ^, depending upon the current alignment setting for the sheet or range).

Summary

In this chapter you've worked with commands and options that change the appearance of a worksheet. The InfoBox for sheet properties allows you to establish default characteristics for an entire worksheet, such as column width, alignment, and number format. Alternatively, you can apply these properties selectively to individual cells or ranges on a worksheet, using the InfoBox for range properties. As always, 1-2-3 gives you a variety of ways to accomplish a task. Rather than open an InfoBox, you can select options from the status bar, click the corresponding SmartIcons, or choose commands from shortcut menus.

In Chapter 6 you'll continue to learn about properties that can improve and clarify the appearance of a worksheet.

CHAPTER 6

Presenting and Printing Data

FAST TRACK

To display a date value in a cell,   182
enter the date in a format that 1-2-3 recognizes (such as 10/15/94 or 15-Oct-94). 1-2-3 stores your entry as a date number, but displays it in a date format.

To display a time value in a cell,   187
enter the time in a format that 1-2-3 recognizes (such as 7:00 PM or 19:00). 1-2-3 stores your entry into a decimal fraction, but displays it in a time format.

To establish a protection scheme for a sheet,   193
click the Security tab on the InfoBox for range properties, and establish one or more ranges that you want to remain unprotected. Then click the Basics tab on the InfoBox for sheet properties and check the box labeled "Lock contents of protected cells in this sheet."

To establish protection for an entire workbook,   196
click the Workbook Properties SmartIcon and then click the Security tab on the resulting dialog box. Check the Lock workbook box. Optionally, supply a password to prevent others from unlocking the workbook.

To change the font or type size of a range on the worksheet,   198
select the range and choose new settings in the Font and Size buttons of the status bar.

To see a preview of a printed workbook,   205
click the Preview SmartIcon.

To compress or expand the size of a worksheet on the printed page,   208
click the Margins, orientation, and placement tab on the Preview and Page Setup InfoBox. Then choose an option from the Page fit list.

To create a header or a footer to be included on each page of printed output,   209
click the Print Preview SmartIcon and then click the Headers and footers tab on the resulting InfoBox. Enter the text of the header into any of the three Header boxes, and/or the text of the Footer in the three Footer boxes. Click Insert buttons to include the date, time, page number, total number of pages, file name, or an item of worksheet data in the header or footer.

As you continue to revise the contents and properties of a workbook, you gradually produce a clear and engaging document that is ready for distribution. For example, your final goal in the Conference workbook is to develop an accessible presentation of financial and scheduling data for a particular training event. In this chapter you'll add two new sheets to the workbook, illustrating the use of date and time values. Along the way you'll investigate a variety of important topics:

- Entering date and time values in appropriate display formats, and understanding how 1-2-3 stores these values internally
- Performing arithmetic operations with date and time entries
- Protecting the workbook from accidental revisions
- Selecting styles, fonts, shadings, colors, and borders to enhance the appearance and readability of your work
- Printing a workbook for distribution on paper

If you haven't already done so, start 1-2-3 and open the CONF.123 workbook. Up to now you've adjusted only a few of the visual properties of the sheet—column widths, alignments, and number formats. In this chapter you'll make several dramatic changes in the presentation.

Working with Dates in a Sheet

1-2-3 has a versatile collection of tools designed to help you work with calendar dates. You can enter dates on your worksheet as specially formatted numeric values. Then you can use date entries in operations known as date arithmetic. For example, you can:

- Find the number of days between any two dates.
- Find the date that is a specific number of days forward or backward from another date.

Performing these operations can be a complicated programming task in some software environments, but in 1-2-3 you accomplish them with simple arithmetic formulas.

A date can actually be recorded as either a label or a value in a 1-2-3 worksheet. If you want to display a date, but you have no plans to use the date in arithmetic operations, a label entry is a simple option. 1-2-3 accepts a data entry as a label when you begin the date with the complete name of a month, for example:

    October 15, 1997

But if you anticipate working with the date entry in any calendar-related calculations, you need to enter the date as a value.

To use date values successfully, it's important to understand 1-2-3's date system. The system relies on the ability to convert a date entry into a date number, which in 1-2-3 means the integer equivalent for any date between January 1, 1900 and December 31, 2099. The first of these dates, January 1, 1900, is day 1 in the system, and each date forward is numbered consecutively—that is, 1 greater than the previous date. Here is a sampling of date numbers in this system:

Date	Date Number
January 1, 1900	1
January 2, 1900	2
May 10, 1910	3783
December 1, 1945	16772
March 2, 1976	27821
October 15, 1997	35718
December 31, 2099	73050

When you enter a value in one of the specific formats that 1-2-3 recognizes as a date entry, the value is stored as a date number. You can examine the various date display formats in the InfoBox for sheet or range properties:

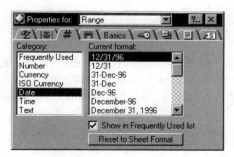

Although all of these formats can be applied to an existing date value, 1-2-3 recognizes only a few of them as appropriate formats for new date entries. For example, you can enter a date numerically, as follows:

06/15/97

Or you can choose a format with a three-character month abbreviation, such as:

15-Jun-97

15-Jun

Jun-97

In short, a date is as easy to enter as a value. You simply type the date in one of the formats that 1-2-3 recognizes. Internally, 1-2-3 converts your entry into the corresponding date number. To practice this technique, return now to the Conference worksheet. Cell B6 is set aside for the date of the conference, but the cell is still empty. Here are the steps for entering this date:

1. Select cell B6 and type the date of the conference as follows:

   15-Oct-97

2. Press ↵ and then ↑ to select cell B6 again. Notice that 1-2-3 initially right-aligns the entry, an indication that the date has been accepted as a value, not a label.

3. Click the Alignment button on the status bar and choose the left-align option.

   The date is displayed just the way you entered it:

4	Conference:	Computing for Video Stores
5	Place:	St. Louis
6	Date:	15-Oct-97
7		
8	Price:	$195.00
9		

At this point you might want to try changing this entry temporarily to a numeric format, in order to learn more about the nature of dates in 1-2-3. With the cell selector still at B6, try the following exercise:

1. Click the Range Properties SmartIcon, and select the Number format tab on the resulting InfoBox. Notice how the date format is represented:

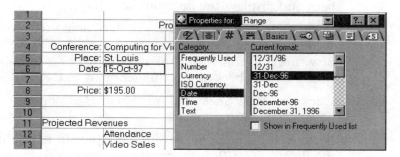

2. Click the Frequently Used option in the Category list, and keep the General selection in the Current format list. In response, 1-2-3 converts your entry to a date number, confirming that the numeric value of the date 15-Oct-97 is 35718:

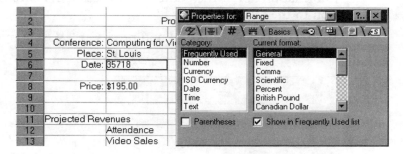

3. Switch back to the date format again. Select Date in the Category list and 31-Dec-96 in the Current format list. Your entry is once again displayed as a date.

4. Close the InfoBox, and then click the Save SmartIcon to save your work to disk.

Now that you've learned how to enter a date value, you can begin experimenting with date arithmetic.

Performing Date Arithmetic

Computing Conferences, Inc., has decided to offer discounts to conference participants who enroll and pay in advance. There will be a 10 percent discount for payments received 45 days in advance, and a

20 percent discount for payments received 90 days in advance. So the conference organizers want to develop a small worksheet that formulates and displays the discount schedule.

In the following steps you begin developing this schedule by adding a second sheet to the Conference workbook. You've temporarily added new sheets to this workbook in previous exercises, but this time you'll save the new sheet as a permanent part of the file:

1. Click the New Sheet button. Sheet B is added to the window, and becomes the current sheet.

2. Select cell A9 and choose View ➤ Split. In the Split dialog box, keep the default Top-Bottom option selection, and click OK. In the lower pane, click the A tab so that you can see both sheets A and B at once.

3. In cell B:A2 enter the title **Discount Schedule for Advance Enrollment**.

4. In worksheet A, select the range A:A4..A:B8, which contains the basic information about the conference. Press Ctrl+C to copy this information to the Clipboard.

5. In sheet B, select cell B:A4 and press Ctrl+V. A copy of the conference information appears in worksheet B:

6. Choose View ➤ Clear Split to toggle back into a view of worksheet B alone.

7. Select cell B:B8, click the Number format button on the status bar, and choose US Dollar from the list of numeric formats.

8. In cells B10, C10, and D10, enter the three headings you see in Figure 6.1. Then select the range B:B10..B:D10, click the Alignment button on the status bar, and choose the right-align option.

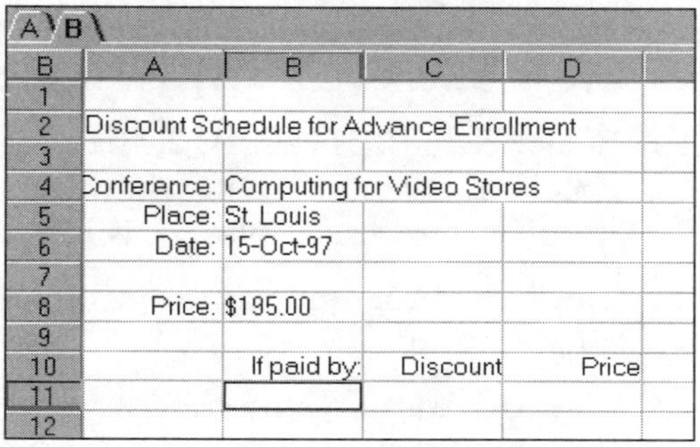

Figure 6.1: Creating a discount schedule on sheet B

At this point in the process, worksheet B appears as shown in Figure 6.1. The next step is to enter formulas in cells B:B11 and B:B12 to display the deadline dates for the two discount rates. Because cell B:B6 contains an entry representing the date of the conference, you'll create formulas that subtract the appropriate number of days from this date.

Enter the following formula in B:B11:

```
+B:B6-90
```

As you can see, this formula subtracts a value of 90 (representing 90 days) from the date number stored in cell B6. The result displayed in cell B6 is 35628. Now enter the following formula into cell B:B12 to subtract 45 days from the conference date:

```
+B:B6-45
```

The result is 35673.

Now you have to format these two cells so they'll appear as dates. You can use the Copy Styles SmartIcon to duplicate the format that is already applied to the date in cell B6. This tool is located on the Range SmartIcons bar:

As you'll see, it provides a quick technique for copying a set of styles from one location to another:

1. Select cell B:B6, which has the format that you want to copy.
2. Click the Copy Styles SmartIcon. When you move the mouse pointer over the worksheet, the pointer takes on the form of a paint brush icon.
3. Select cells B:B11..B:B12, the range over which you want to apply the specified format. When you release the mouse button, the two entries in this range are displayed as left-aligned dates.
4. Click the Alignment button on the status bar and choose the right-align option.

The discount payment dates are now displayed as 17-Jul-97 (90 days before the conference date) and 31-Aug-97 (45 days before the conference).

Now follow these steps to complete the discount schedule worksheet:

1. Enter a value of **20%** in cell B:C11 and a value of **10%** in B:C12.
2. Select cell B:D11 and enter the following formula:

    +$B:$B$8*(1−B:C11)

    (Use the pointing technique to create the formula. Type a plus sign and then click cell B8 with the mouse. Press the F4 function key to change the address to an absolute reference. Then continue the formula. The reference to cell C11 remains as a relative reference.)

3. Use the drag-and-drop technique to copy this formula into cell B:D12. The copied formula—adjusted for its position relative to the original formula—appears as +$B$8*(1−C12).
4. Select the range B:D11..B:D12, click the Number format button on the status bar, and choose the US Dollar format from the resulting list.

Changing the Labels on Worksheet Tabs

Now that the Conference workbook contains two sheets, you should take this opportunity to change the tab labels for each sheet. As you know, the initial names for multiple sheets in a worksheet file are letters of the alphabet (A, B, C, and so on). But you can easily change these names. To do so you simply double-click a tab, type a new name, and press ↵. Try changing the names of sheets A and B now:

1. Double-click tab A, type **Conference** as the new sheet name, and press ↵.

2. Double-click tab B, type **Discounts** as the name, and press ↵.

Figure 6.2 shows the result of your work in sheet B, now called Discounts.

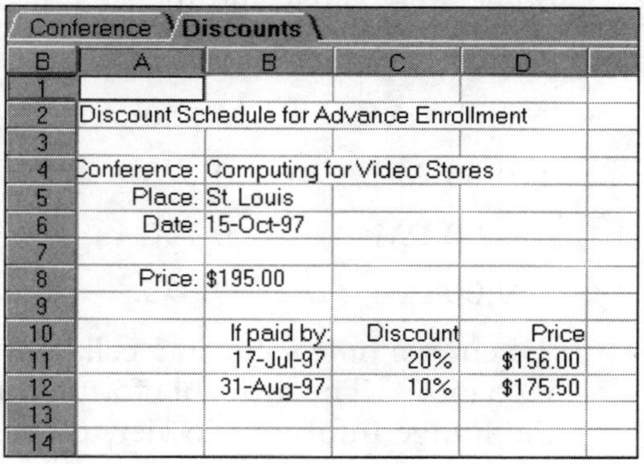

Figure 6.2: **Completing and naming the Discounts sheet**

TIP For another clear way to distinguish between different sheets in a file, you can display sheet tabs in color. Select the sheet tab that you want to change. Then click the Sheet Properties SmartIcon, and click the Basics tab on the resulting InfoSheet. Click the down-arrow button next to the Tab color box. Select a color from the resulting palette. If you wish, you can select other sheets and change their tab colors before you close the InfoBox.

Entering Time Values into a Worksheet

1-2-3 also performs arithmetic operations on chronological values—points in time during a 24-hour day. Like a date, a time value is stored internally as a number but can be displayed in any one of several time formats that 1-2-3 recognizes. The time arithmetic operations include:

▶ Finding the number of hours or minutes between two time values in a 24-hour day

▶ Finding the point in time that is a specified number of minutes forward or backward from another time value

Once again, it's useful to learn how 1-2-3 translates time values into numbers before you try to perform operations like these. A time number is a fractional value, expressed as a decimal. Specifically, the decimal fraction expresses the portion of the 24-hour day that has gone by at a particular time. For example, the time value for 12:00 noon is 0.5, because one-half of the day has elapsed at noon. Here is a sampling of other time values and their equivalent time numbers:

3:00 AM	0.125	One eighth of the day
6:00 AM	0.250	One fourth of the day
9:00 AM	0.375	Three eighths of the day
6:00 PM	0.750	Three fourths of the day
9:00 PM	0.875	Seven eighths of the day

To enter a time value in a cell, you type the value in a format that 1-2-3 recognizes. The available formats appear on the Number format tab of the Range InfoBox. To view them, select Time in the Category list:

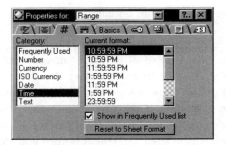

You can choose among a variety of AM/PM and 24-hour formats. When you enter a value in one of these formats, 1-2-3 recognizes your entry as a time and stores the entry as a decimal time number. The format of your entry is applied to the cell.

In a first exercise with time values, you'll add yet another sheet to the Conference workbook—a sheet initially named C. You'll begin by entering one time value onto this worksheet, but then you'll go on to build another document for Computer Conferences, Inc. Here are the beginning steps:

1. Select Discounts as the active sheet, and then click the New Sheet button. 1-2-3 adds sheet C to the file.

2. Select cell C:D8 for the first entry on this new sheet. (You'll see why shortly.) In the cell, enter the value **7:00 AM**. Press ↑ to select the cell again. 1-2-3 has automatically applied a time format to the cell.

3. As an experiment with the value you've entered, click the Number format button on the status bar and select General from the resulting list. In response, 1-2-3 displays the numeric equivalent of the time entry, 0.29166667. This is the fraction of the day that has gone by at 7:00 AM.

4. To restore the entry to its original time format, click the Number format button again and choose the time format represented as 10:59 PM.

   In the next section you'll use this time entry as the starting point for an exercise in time arithmetic.

Performing Time Arithmetic

The conference organizers at Computing Conferences, Inc., are ready to begin planning the schedule for the one-day conference in St. Louis. During the course of the conference day there will be four major presentations, each lasting between one and two hours. In addition, there will be other miscellaneous activities, including an introduction, an hour of hands-on demonstrations, coffee breaks, and lunch. The planners therefore want to develop a worksheet that calculates the day's schedule, given the length of each event. They also want to be able to adjust the length of time allotted to a given activity and immediately see the effect on the whole schedule.

You'll develop this schedule on sheet C of the Conference workbook. Begin with the following formatting and data-entry tasks:

1. Select cell D8 and click the Copy Styles SmartIcon. Then drag the paint brush mouse pointer over the range C:D9..C:D18. Click the Copy Style SmartIcon again to toggle out of the copy mode. 1-2-3 applies the time format to each cell in the range D9..D18. Because the range contains no data yet, no visible change takes place on the sheet.

2. Press the Home key to select cell A1, and enter **Conference Schedule** as the sheet's title.

3. Click the Discounts sheet tab to activate worksheet B. Select the range B:A4..B:B6 and press Ctrl+C to copy this selection to the Clipboard. Then click the C tab, select cell C:A3, and press Ctrl+V to paste a copy of these entries to the new sheet.

Chapter 6 — Presenting and Printing Data

4. Enter the labels and values you see in Figure 6.3. Row 7 contains three column headings, displayed in bold. Column A (A8..A18) displays the list of individual events that make up the conference day, and column E (E8..E18) shows the proposed duration in minutes of each event.

5. When you complete the data entry, select cell C:D9 to prepare for an upcoming formula.

	A	B	C	D	E
1	Conference Schedule				
2					
3	Conference:	Computing for Video Stores			
4	Place:	St. Louis			
5	Date:	15-Oct-97			
6					
7	**Event**			**Start Time**	**Minutes**
8	Coffee and Pastries			07:00 AM	45
9	Introduction				30
10	Managing a Video Database				90
11	Coffee Break				15
12	Managing a Customer Database				120
13	Hands-on Demonstration				60
14	Lunch and Discussion				60
15	Setting up a Computer System				120
16	Coffee Break				30
17	Software Options				60
18	No-Host Cocktail Hour				60

Figure 6.3: Creating a Schedule worksheet

A Quick Check for Spelling

In a worksheet that contains as much text as this one, you may want to check for spelling errors after you've completed the data entry:

1. Choose Edit ➤ Check Spelling. The Check Spelling dialog box appears on the Desktop.

2. Select the Current sheet option in the drop-down list labeled "Look in":

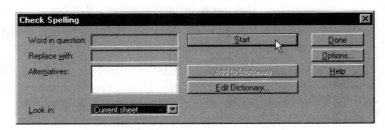

3. Click the Start button, and 1-2-3 begins checking the spelling on the active sheet.

   For any word that 1-2-3 doesn't find in its dictionary, the Check Spelling dialog box displays the unknown word in the Word in question text box and provides possible alternatives. To correct the error, select the appropriate alternative and click Replace. To keep a word in its current spelling, click Skip.

   When the spell check is complete, 1-2-3 displays a final message box. Click OK and then click Done to close the Check Spelling dialog box.

Writing and Copying a Schedule Formula

You now need to write a formula in cell D9 that calculates the starting time of the second event. The algorithm that the formula represents is straightforward: Add the length in minutes of the first event (C:E8) to the starting time of the first event (C:D8). But there is one complication—the worksheet expresses these two values in incompatible terms. The starting time is stored as a decimal time number, and the length of the event is expressed in minutes. To add the two values you must first find a way to convert them into common terms.

In this worksheet, the best approach is to convert the minutes to a decimal time value. The following expression calculates the fraction of a 24-hour day represented by the minutes in cell C:E8:

```
+C:E8/(60*24)
```

Multiplying 60 by 24 gives the number of minutes in a day. Dividing the value in cell E8 by this number results in the appropriate decimal time value. Given this expression, here is the formula that calculates the starting time of the second event:

```
+C:D8+C:E8/(60*24)
```

In the following steps you'll use the pointing technique to enter this formula into cell D9. Then you'll copy the formula down the appropriate range in column D:

1. With the cell pointer positioned at D9, type **+** to start the formula entry.
2. Press ↑ once to point to the starting time in D8. Then type **+** again.

3. Press ↑ and → once each to point to the value in cell E8. Then complete the formula by typing **/(60*24)**. Press ↵ to confirm the formula entry. Cell D9 displays 07:45 AM as the formatted time value.

4. Select D9 again, and press Ctrl+C to copy this formula to the Clipboard. Then select D10..D18 and press Ctrl+V to paste a copy of the formula to each cell in the range.

5. Double-click the C tab and type **Schedule** as the new name for this sheet. Press ↵ to confirm the new name.

Figure 6.4 shows the Schedule sheet. Examine the formulas that 1-2-3 has copied into cells D9 through D18. Do you see why relative references were appropriate for the addresses in this copy operation?

	A	B	C	D	E
1	Conference Schedule				
2					
3	Conference:	Computing for Video Stores			
4	Place:	St. Louis			
5	Date:	15-Oct-97			
6					
7	Event			Start Time	Minutes
8	Coffee and Pastries			07:00 AM	45
9	Introduction			07:45 AM	30
10	Managing a Video Database			08:15 AM	90
11	Coffee Break			09:45 AM	15
12	Managing a Customer Database			10:00 AM	120
13	Hands-on Demonstration			12:00 PM	60
14	Lunch and Discussion			01:00 PM	60
15	Setting up a Computer System			02:00 PM	120
16	Coffee Break			04:00 PM	30
17	Software Options			04:30 PM	60
18	No-Host Cocktail Hour			05:30 PM	60

Figure 6.4: **Entering and copying the formula to calculate the schedule**

Now suppose the conference planners want to adjust the schedule for the morning events. They want lunch to take place one-half hour earlier than its currently scheduled time at 1:00 PM. To accomplish this, they decide to reduce the time for the second presentation—"Managing a Customer Database," in row 12—by thirty minutes.

Enter a new value of 90 in cell C:E12, and watch what happens to the schedule. All the starting times from C:D13 down are adjusted for the half-hour change, as shown in Figure 6.5. The schedule worksheet is working according to design.

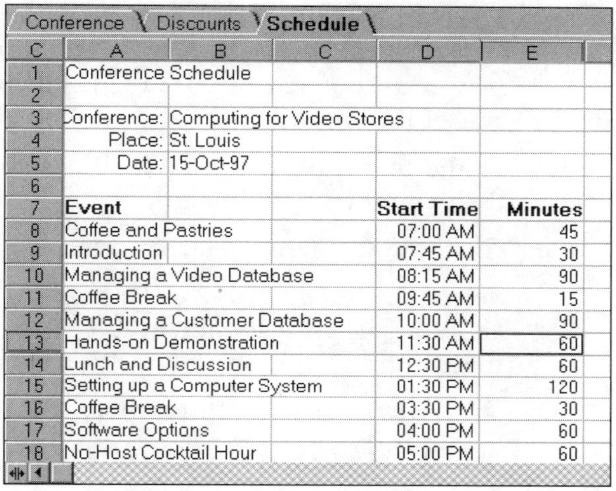

Figure 6.5: **Changing the schedule**

Click the Save SmartIcon now to update the Conference workbook to disk. In the next section you'll learn to protect a sheet from inadvertent revisions or deletions.

Preventing Accidental Revisions

The Conference sheet is designed to be reused for planning other conferences. By entering new data values in the sheet's "input" ranges, the managers at Computer Conferences, Inc., can quickly produce financial projections for any conference in the future. When you create a tool like this one, you may find yourself distributing copies of the workbook file to other people who need to perform similar tasks in 1-2-3. But other users may not be aware of your sheet's carefully designed structure. In particular, a user may fail to distinguish between cells that contain simple data entries and cells that contain formulas. The structure of the sheet can easily be ruined if a user inadvertently enters a new value in a formula cell.

To prevent this from happening, you can establish a protection scheme for a sheet. The purpose of protection is to prohibit new entries in cells that contain formulas, allowing new entries only in appropriate "input" cells. Two steps are involved in establishing this protection scheme.

First you use the InfoBox for range properties to specify the ranges of cells that will *not* be protected—that is, the cells where you want to allow new entries. Then you use the InfoBox for sheet properties to lock the rest of the sheet.

In the following exercise you'll designate the unprotected ranges and then you'll lock the sheet:

1. Click the Conference tab to return to the first sheet in the workbook.

2. Select the range A:B4..A:B8, which contains the basic information about a particular conference. Then hold down the Ctrl key and select these additional ranges:

    ▶ A:E8..A:F8 (the minimum and maximum attendance estimates)

    ▶ A:D13 (the price-per-copy of the conference video)

    ▶ A:E17..A:F20 (the fixed expenses under each attendance estimate)

    ▶ A:D24..A:D26 (the per-person variable expenses)

    1-2-3 highlights all five ranges as you select them. These are the five ranges containing "input" data that you may want to revise for a different conference projection.

3. Click the Range Properties SmartIcon, and select the Security tab on the resulting InfoBox. The Security tab is identified by a key icon:

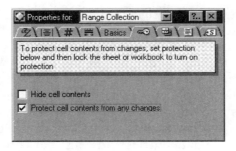

4. Remove the check from the box labeled "Protect cell contents from any changes." By doing so, you designate the current range collection as unprotected cells.

5. On the InfoBox title bar, pull down the Properties for list, and choose Sheet. Click the Basics tab if necessary.

6. Click the check box labeled "Lock contents of protected cells in this sheet." As a result, 1-2-3 locks all cells on the Conference sheet except the ranges that you've designated as unprotected:

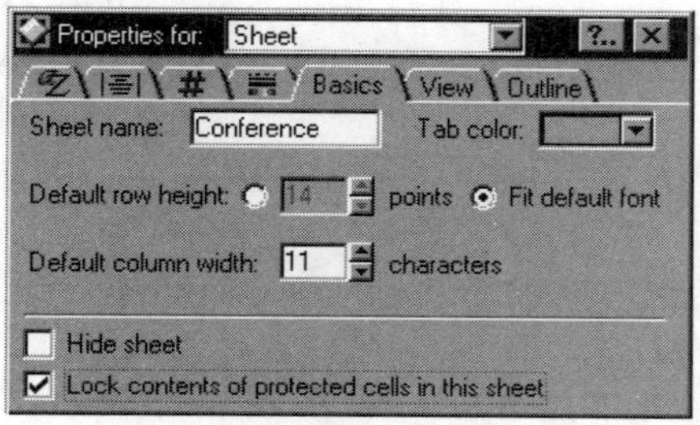

7. Close the InfoBox and press Home to move the cell pointer to A1. 1-2-3 highlights the unprotected ranges by displaying their contents in blue. These ranges are shown in bold in Figure 6.6.

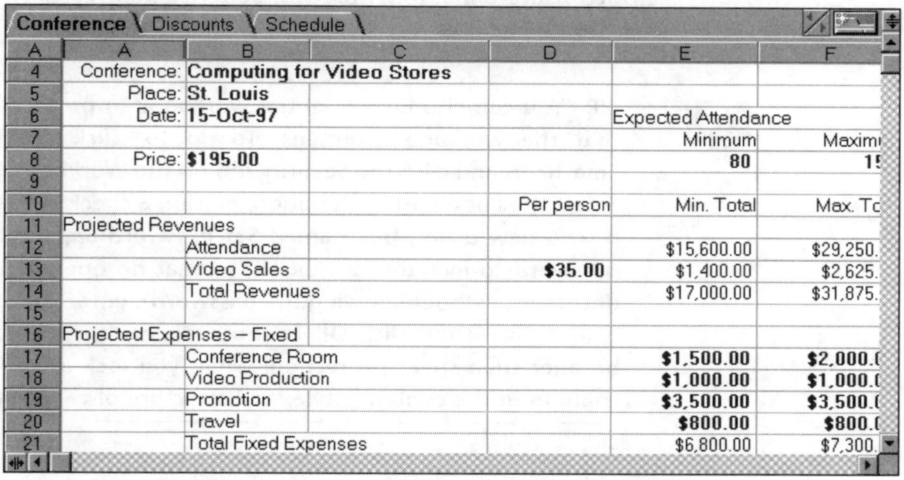

	A	B	C	D	E	F
4	Conference:	**Computing for Video Stores**				
5	Place:	**St. Louis**				
6	Date:	**15-Oct-97**			Expected Attendance	
7					Minimum	Maximı
8	Price:	**$195.00**			**80**	**1!**
9						
10				Per person	Min. Total	Max. Tc
11	Projected Revenues					
12		Attendance			$15,600.00	$29,250.
13		Video Sales		**$35.00**	$1,400.00	$2,625.
14		Total Revenues			$17,000.00	$31,875.
15						
16	Projected Expenses – Fixed					
17		Conference Room			**$1,500.00**	**$2,000.(**
18		Video Production			**$1,000.00**	**$1,000.(**
19		Promotion			**$3,500.00**	**$3,500.(**
20		Travel			**$800.00**	**$800.(**
21		Total Fixed Expenses			$6,800.00	$7,300.

Figure 6.6: ***Designating unprotected ranges on the worksheet***

Now the worksheet is protected from changes, except for the five ranges that you've designated as unprotected. You can try entering a new value into one of the unprotected ranges. For example, select cell B8 and enter a new price of $225.00. When you do so, 1-2-3 accepts your new entry and instantly recalculates all the worksheet formulas that depend on this value, just as it did before you established protection. (Change the value in B8 back to $195.00 before you move on.)

By contrast, 1-2-3 prevents changes in any protected cell. As an experiment, try entering a new value into any cell that's not displayed in blue. The following message pops up on the screen:

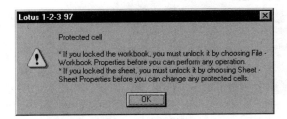

In summary, protection makes your worksheet a safer and more valuable tool for distribution to other users. By restricting new input to appropriate cells, a protection scheme insures the continued reliability of your formulas.

> **TIP** You can also lock an entire workbook to protect data on all the sheets that the workbook contains. To do so, click the Workbook Properties SmartIcon and click the Security tab on the Workbook Properties dialog box. Select the Lock workbook option, placing a check in the corresponding check box. A new dialog box named Set Password appears. If you want to use a password to lock the workbook (so that no one will be able to unlock the document without knowing the password), enter your password twice in this dialog box. Then click OK on both dialog boxes. Workbook protection is broader than sheet protection; when you lock a workbook, 1-2-3 prevents changes in the content, style, and structure of all sheets in the workbook.

Turning Protection Off

For now, deactivate the protection mode so that you can perform some additional tasks on the Conference sheet:

1. Click the Sheet Properties SmartIcon, and click the Basics tab if necessary.
2. Remove the check from the option labeled "Lock contents of protected cells in this sheet."
3. Close the InfoBox.

When you complete these steps, notice that the unprotected ranges are still displayed in blue, even though protection is off. If you later decide to lock the sheet again, these unprotected ranges will resume their role as the sheet's input cells.

Creating a Finished Document

Now it's time to put the finishing touches on the Conference sheet, in preparation for printing the document. In this section you'll examine 1-2-3's options for displaying—and ultimately printing—font sizes, type styles, borders, lines, and shadings on your worksheet. You apply these effects by choosing options from the InfoBox for range properties or by selecting settings from the status bar.

As you work with these options, you may sometimes want to insert new blank rows into your worksheet to improve the overall visual impact. This is the case on the Conference sheet. You can use the Insert Rows command in the Range menu to insert additional blank rows where necessary. The command appears in the Range menu only when you select entire rows on the sheet. For example, here are the general steps for inserting a row at a given location:

1. At the left side of the sheet frame, click the row number that is just below the location where you want to insert a new row.
2. Choose Range ➤ Insert Rows.

Use this technique to insert rows at each of the following five locations; at some of these places there will now be two blank rows:

▶ Above row 4, which identifies the subject of the current conference.

▶ Above row 11, which contains the column headings for revenue and expense projections.

▶ Above row 16, which contains the Total Revenues line.

▶ Above row 19, which contains the Projected Expenses—Fixed label.

▶ Above row 33, the Projected Profit line.

When you complete these five row insertions, your worksheet appears as in Figure 6.7. (Here the Zoom setting has been reduced on the Workbook Properties dialog box to show the entire sheet.) Now you're ready to make several improvements in the appearance of the worksheet.

	A	B	C	D	E	F
1		Computing Conferences, Inc.				
2		Profit Projection for a One-Day Conference				
3						
4						
5		Conference:	Computing for Video Stores			
6		Place:	St. Louis			
7		Date:	15-Oct-97		Expected Attendance	
8					Minimum	Maximum
9		Price:	$195.00		80	150
10						
11						
12				Per person	Min. Total	Max. Total
13		Projected Revenues				
14			Attendance		$15,600.00	$29,250.00
15			Video Sales	$35.00	$1,400.00	$2,625.00
16						
17			Total Revenues		$17,000.00	$31,875.00
18						
19						
20		Projected Expenses -- Fixed				
21			Conference Room		$1,500.00	$2,000.00
22			Video Production		$1,000.00	$1,000.00
23			Promotion		$3,500.00	$3,500.00
24			Travel		$800.00	$800.00
25			Total Fixed Expenses		$6,800.00	$7,300.00
26						
27		Projected Expenses -- Variable by Attendance				
28			Conference Materials	$8.25	$660.00	$1,237.50
29			Coffee and Pastries	$3.25	$260.00	$487.50
30			Box Lunch	$4.75	$380.00	$712.50
31			Total Variable Expenses		$1,300.00	$2,437.50
32						
33						
34		Projected Profit			$8,900.00	$22,137.50
35						
36						
37						

Figure 6.7: Inserting blank rows in the worksheet

Font Sizes, Type Styles, Shadings, and Borders

Begin with the title lines displayed at the top of the worksheet. Keep in mind that these two labels are stored in cells B1 and B2. To place emphasis on the titles, you'll select a larger font size, display the text in combinations of bold and italics, apply a dark gray shading to the range and contrasting white to the text, and add a "designer" frame. Here are the steps:

1. Select B2 alone and click the Italics button on the status bar.
2. Select B1..B2 and click the Bold button on the status bar.
3. Without changing the selection, click the Size button on the status bar and select 18 from the resulting size list:

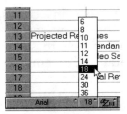

The type size increases accordingly, and the heights of rows 1 and 2 are automatically adjusted to accommodate the new size.

4. Select the range A:B1..A:E2 and click the Range Properties Smart-Icon. Click the Color, pattern, and line style tab on the resulting InfoBox:

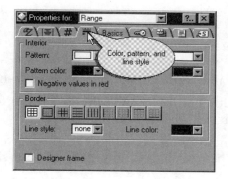

5. Click the down-arrow button at the right side of the Background color box. A color palette appears. Click the dark gray selection on the second line of the palette (just to the right of the black selection). This becomes the background color of the range:

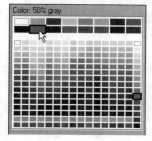

6. Now click the down-arrow button at the right side of the Text color box. On the resulting color palette, click the white selection at the upper-left corner of the palette. This becomes the text color.

7. Select the Designer frame option at the lower-left corner of the Info-Box; a check appears in the corresponding check box, and the Frame style and Frame color options appear.

8. Click the down-arrow button at the right of the Frame style box. A selection of frame options appears:

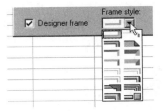

9. Click the third frame from the bottom in the right-hand column.
10. In the InfoBox title bar, pull down the Properties for list and choose Sheet. Then click the View tab on the InfoBox.
11. Click the Grid lines option, removing the check from the corresponding check box. The grid lines disappear from your sheet.

    Close the InfoBox and then deselect the current range by moving the cell pointer to some other part of your worksheet. The titles appear as follows:

TIP You can change the font and size of a worksheet selection either by making selections from the Font and Size buttons on the status bar or by choosing options from the Font tab of the InfoBox for range properties. The Font tab contains a list of the fonts available on your system, and also a group of options for applying bold, italics, underlining, and other style properties to a range of data. You can also choose a text color from this tab.

NOTE As you've seen, 1-2-3 automatically increases the row height when you select a font that is larger than the current size. Alternatively, you can change the row height manually by clicking the Basics tab on the InfoBox for range properties, and entering a new setting in the Height box. The height of a row is measured in points, the same as the measurement for font sizes. You can also change the height of a row by dragging the row's lower border up or down with the mouse.

Continue your work on the Conference sheet by copying the size, shading, and text color from the title lines to the Projected Profit line in row 34:

1. Select cell B2.
2. Click the Copy Styles SmartIcon.
3. Scroll down the sheet and select the range A34..F34. The mouse pointer appears as a small paintbrush. When you release the mouse button, the styles are copied to the information in row 34. Click the Copy Styles SmartIcon again to toggle out of the copy mode. You may now have to adjust the width of column F to accommodate the new text sizes.
4. Select the range A:A5..A:A27 and click the Bold button on the status bar. 1-2-3 applies the boldface style to all the labels in the selected range. Repeat this step for the following cells and ranges: E7, D12..F12, B17..F17, B25..F25, B31..F31.
5. Select cell B5. Click the Bold SmartIcon and then the Italics SmartIcon. Repeat this combination for the following ranges: E8..F8, B14..B15, B21..B24, B28..B30.

Drawing Horizontal Lines

Next you'll use the Color, pattern, and line style tab of the InfoBox for range properties to draw horizontal lines between sections of the worksheet. The Border group in the InfoBox contains a row of buttons representing the variety of border lines that can be drawn within a given range. There are also Line style and Line color options:

Here are the steps for drawing lines on the Conference worksheet:

1. Select the range A:A11..A:F11.
2. Click the Range Properties SmartIcon. In the resulting InfoBox, click the Color, pattern, and line style tab.
3. In the Border group, click the second-to-last button, representing a top border line.
4. Pull down the Line style list and select the bold single-line border.

5. Click the down-arrow button at the right of the Line color box. In the resulting color palette, click the black color selection near the top-left corner of the box.

6. Without closing the InfoBox, select A:A19..A:F19.

7. Make the same selections in the Border group, to draw a bold black single-line border at the top of the selected range.

8. Close the InfoBox.

   Back on the worksheet, horizontal lines now separate the general conference information from the revenue section, and another line separates the revenue and expense sections, as shown in Figure 6.8.

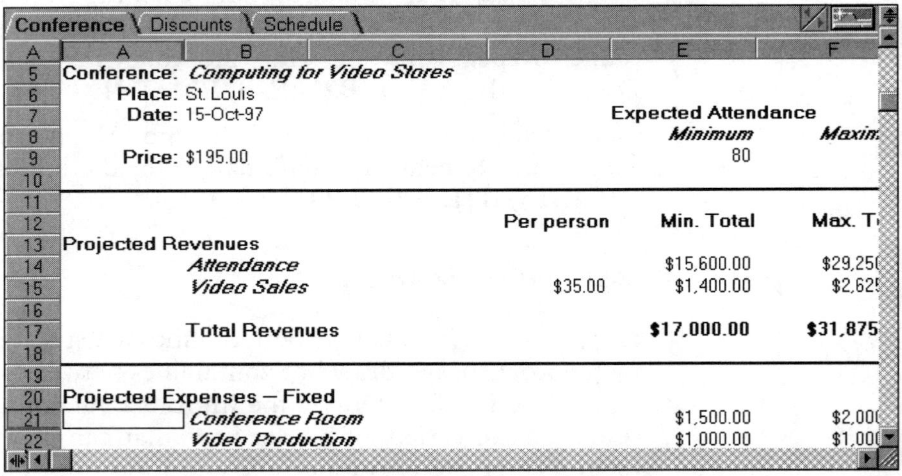

Figure 6.8: Drawing lines to separate sections of the Conference worksheet

Next you'll look at the Named style tab (on the InfoBox for range properties), where you can assign names to your own most frequently used style combinations. This feature gives you a convenient way to apply styles to selected ranges on a sheet.

Defining Style Names

Using the Named style tab, you create styles names that are then available from the Style button on the status bar. Each style name you create can represent a combination of style effects. Here are the general steps for creating a new style name:

1. Apply one or more styles to a range on the worksheet. Keep this range as the current selection.

2. Click the Range Properties SmartIcon and click the Named style tab:

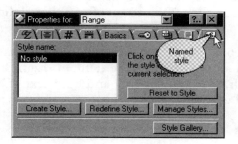

3. Click the Create Style button. In the resulting dialog box, enter a name for the style you're defining:

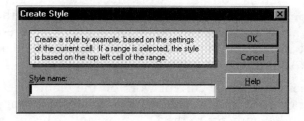

4. Click OK. Back in the InfoBox, the newly defined style is included in the Style name list.

5. Optionally, close the InfoBox.

   When you click the Style button on the status bar, the style name you've defined appears as one of the entries in the pop-up list. Style names are available for all the sheets in a given workbook. To create a simple example of a named style, try the following exercise on the Conference sheet:

1. Select the range A:B5..A:C9.

2. Click the Range Properties SmartIcon. On the InfoBox, click the Color, pattern, and line style tab. Then click the small down-arrow button next to the Background color box. On the resulting color palette, click the second color selection in the top row of colors, a light gray shade.

3. Now select the range A:B6..A:B9 and click the Bold SmartIcon.

4. Select cell B6, which represents the style combinations to which you're about to assign a name—light gray shading and boldface text.

5. Click the Named style tab on the InfoBox.

6. Click the Create Style button. In the Style name box, enter the name **LightShade** and click OK to confirm this definition. Close the InfoBox.

7. Select cell A:D15. Click the Style panel on the status bar. A pop-up list shows the name of the style you've defined, LightShade. Choose this name; as a result, the light shading and bold text effects are applied to the selected cell on the sheet:

8. Now use this same technique to apply the LightShade style to the other "input" areas on the worksheet—the ranges A:E21..A:F24, A:D28..A:D30, and finally A:E9..A:F9. (Because the US Dollar format is also part of your named style, you'll have to reselect the General format for the minimum and maximum attendance estimates in A:E9..A:F9 after you apply the named style.)

This completes your current work on the Conference worksheet. As a further exercise with the style options, you could try applying a variety of styles and alignments to the Discounts and Schedule sheets (B and C). In addition, you may need to adjust some column widths on these sheets before you try printing them. When you complete your work, click the Save SmartIcon to update the Conference workbook on disk.

In the final sections of this chapter you'll learn to print your work.

Printing a Worksheet

All the special visual effects that you've created in this chapter can be printed on paper. But before printing, you can set properties that affect the layout and content of the printed page.

In general, printing a sheet is as simple as choosing File ➤ Print (or clicking the Print SmartIcon) and selecting options from the resulting dialog box. Alternatively, you can open a preview of the printed page by choosing File ➤ Preview and Page Setup (or clicking the Print

Preview SmartIcon). When you take this intermediate step, 1-2-3 displays a Preview window like the one shown in Figure 6.9. This window gives you the chance to examine and modify the document's layout before printing it out on paper.

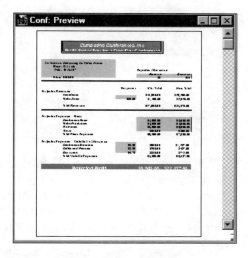

Figure 6.9: *A preview of the printed page*

1-2-3 has several important features related to printing. In the final exercises of this chapter you'll review the use of these tools:

▶ **The InfoBox for Preview & Page Setup Properties.** This InfoBox appears—along with the Preview window itself—when you click the Print Preview SmartIcon. The various tabs of this InfoBox give you ways to arrange information on the printed page, to specify what pages and objects you want to print, to define headers and footers, and to choose other options that change the visual impact of your printed document:

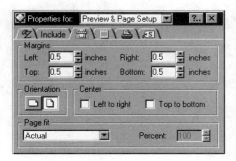

▶ **The Named style tab.** You can use the Named style tab of this same InfoBox to save the current print settings under a style name that you supply. By saving several named print styles, you can define a variety of ways to print a particular workbook:

▶ **The Print dialog box.** This dialog box (Figure 6.10) appears when you choose File ➤ Print or when you click the Print SmartIcon. It identifies—and allows you to change—some of the properties of the upcoming print job, including the pages that will be printed, the number of copies, and the sheets or ranges that will be included.

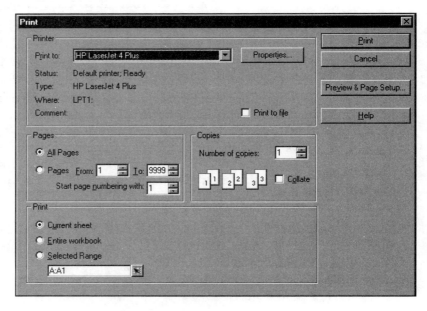

Figure 6.10: **The Print dialog box**

▶ **The Printer dialog box.** This appears when you click the Printer button on the Printer and paper size tab of the Preview and Page Setup InfoBox. The Print to list contains the names of the printers installed on your system, and allows you to choose among them for a particular print job. By clicking the Properties button for a selected printer, you can gain access to the options provided by the corresponding driver software:

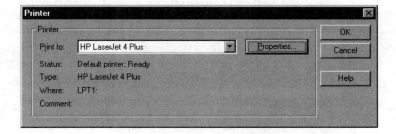

Selecting Print Settings

The options in the Preview and Page Setup InfoBox provide great flexibility for the design of printed documents. You'll find controls for the following tasks:

▶ Selecting a horizontal or vertical orientation for the page layout

▶ Changing the page margins

▶ Selecting horizontal and/or vertical centering options

▶ Compressing or expanding the print size so your data will fit on a page

▶ Creating a header and/or a footer

▶ Selecting ranges, sheets, and objects that will be included in the printing

Take a moment to review these tasks

Selecting a Print Orientation

By default, 1-2-3 prints the rows of a sheet one by one down the length of the page, in portrait orientation. In a table that contains many columns, you might prefer to print the rows of the worksheet sideways, across the length of the paper; this option is called landscape orientation. To select between landscape or portrait printing, click one of the

Orientation buttons on the Margins, orientation, and placement tab of the Preview and Page Setup InfoBox:

Setting Print Margins and Centering Options

The Margins group in the Margins, orientation, and placement tab contains four text boxes, labeled Left, Right, Top, and Bottom. In these boxes you can enter specific numeric measurements, in inches, for the four margins of the printed page:

The Center options are just below the Margin group. By checking one or both of the Center boxes (Left to right, Top to bottom), you can instruct 1-2-3 to center your worksheet lengthwise or widthwise on the page.

Selecting a Page Fit for the Printed Page

The Page fit list contains special options for adjusting the print size to match the available space on a page. In effect, these instruct 1-2-3 to compress the printout to create a single page of output or expand the printout to fill the page:

The Fit all to page option instructs 1-2-3 to contract or expand the worksheet data in two dimensions in an attempt to fit the page. By contrast, the Fit rows to page and Fit columns to page options allow individual vertical or horizontal adjustments in the size of the printed output.

Choose the Custom option if you want to supply a specific percentage for compression or expansion. In this case, you supply a percentage—from 15 to 1000—in a corresponding text box. Finding just the right percentage may take some experimenting.

Creating a Header and Footer

A header is a line of text that 1-2-3 prints at the top of each page of the worksheet. A footer is a line of text printed at the bottom. You enter the text of these elements into the Header and Footer boxes on the Headers and Footers tab of the InfoBox. Both the header and the footer are divided into three areas: left, center, and right. You can supply text for any or all of these areas. In addition, you can click the Insert buttons to insert special information in a header or footer. From left to right, the Insert buttons are the date, the time, the page number, the total number of pages, the file name, and the contents of a particular cell on your worksheet:

Just beneath the Headers and footers group you'll find a pair of options labeled "Print as titles on each page." When you print a long worksheet you might want to include column headings or row labels from your worksheet on each page of the printout. For example, imagine a worksheet that has five hundred rows of data, with column headings displayed in row 1. In the multiple-page printout of this worksheet you would want the column headings from row 1 to appear at the top of each page. Conversely, imagine a worksheet containing dozens of columns, with row labels in column A. You would want the row labels to be repeated on each page of the printed worksheet. To accomplish these effects, enter range references into the Rows and/or Columns boxes.

Printing Objects from a Workbook

Sometimes you may want to print only a particular sheet from a workbook, or even a range of data inside a sheet. Other times you'll want to print an entire workbook, including all its data and any graphic objects it might contain. The Include tab on the Preview and Page Setup InfoBox gives you the opportunity to specify exactly what should be included in a given printout:

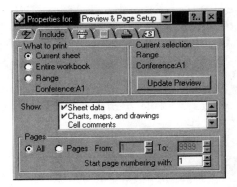

To print a single sheet, a range, or an entire workbook, select the appropriate option button in the What to print group. In addition, the Show list contains a check list of items that you can include or exclude from the printed document. For example, you can choose to print the sheet frame (with column letters and row numbers), the grid lines, cell comments, and so on. 1-2-3 places a check mark next to the items you select from this list.

Printing the Conference Workbook

In this chapter's final exercise, you'll go through the steps of printing the three sheets of the Conference workbook:

1. Move the cell pointer to A:B1, which contains the company name. (You'll see the significance of this cell selection shortly.) Then click the Print Preview SmartIcon.

2. Click the Include tab in the Preview and Page Setup InfoBox. In the What to print group, select the option button labeled Entire workbook.

3. Click the Margins, orientation, and placement tab. In the Page fit list, select the Fit all to page option.

4. Click the Headers and footers tab.

5. Activate the Left header text box and click the first of the Insert buttons to print the date in the left portion of the header line. 1-2-3 inserts @ into the text box to represent the date.

6. Next activate the Right header text box and type the word **Page** followed by a space. Click the third Insert button to print the page number in the right portion of the header. 1-2-3 inserts # to represent the page number.

7. Immediately after the # character, type a space and then the word **of** followed by another space. Click the fourth Insert button to print the total number of pages. 1-2-3 inserts a % character to represent this figure.

8. Activate the Left footer text box and click the last of the Insert buttons to print the contents of a specified cell on the worksheet. 1-2-3 inserts a backslash character \A:B1 into the text box. This notation arranges to print the company name—Computer Conferences, Inc.—at the left side of the footer.

9. Close the InfoBox and the Preview window.

10. Choose File ➤ Print or click the Print SmartIcon. Then click the Print button on the Print dialog box.

Summary

1-2-3 gives you many ways to add a professional appearance to the sheets you create. You can select styles, fonts, shadings, colors, and borders to enhance the presentation of your work. All these properties are conveniently available from the range and sheet InfoBoxes.

When you've designed the look of your sheet, you can turn to the task of printing your work. The Preview feature allows you to view the layout of your worksheet on the screen before you actually send the document to the printer. The Preview and Page Setup InfoBox contains many options for controlling the output to the printer. For example, you can create headers and footers, set margins, arrange to print headings or titles on every page, and compress or expand the worksheet to fit a page.

CHAPTER 7

Formulas and Functions

Fast Track

To fill a worksheet range with a series of numbers,   216

use 1-2-3's drag-and-fill mouse action. Begin by entering one or more values that serve as examples for the series you want to create. Select the range of examples. Then position the mouse pointer over the lower-left corner of the range, hold down the left mouse button, and drag the mouse through the range where you want the series to appear.

To fill a range with a sequence of labels,   217

enter a label from one of 1-2-3's built-in "SmartFill" lists—for example, the days of the week or the months of the year. Then use the drag-and-fill technique to extend the sequence through the target range.

To create a custom SmartFill list,   218

choose File ➤ User Setup ➤ SmartFill Setup. Click New List and enter a name for the list you want to create. Then click Add Item and enter a label for each element of the list.

To start a formula entry in a worksheet cell,   220

enter a plus or minus sign, a digit, a decimal point, an open parenthesis character, or an @ character for the beginning of a function name.

To store a note with a formula,	*222*

type a semicolon at the end of the formula and then enter the note. The note appears in the contents box whenever you select the cell that contains the formula.

To store a comment in a cell,	*223*

click the cell with the right mouse button and choose Cell Comment from the resulting shortcut menu. The InfoBox for range properties opens onto the Desktop. In the Cell comment tab, enter the text of the comment you want to store in the cell. Then close the InfoBox.

To view a cell comment,	*224*

select any cell that displays a cell comment marker—a small red dot at the upper-left corner of the cell. Click the cell with the right mouse button and choose Cell Comment from the shortcut menu.

To find the number of days between two dates,	*227*

enter the dates in two different cells, using one of the date formats that 1-2-3 recognizes. Then write a formula that subtracts one of the date numbers from the other.

To find the number of hours between two time values,	*227*

enter the times in two different cells, using one of the time formats that 1-2-3 recognizes. Then write a formula to subtract one of the values from the other and multiply the difference by 24.

To write a logical formula or expression,	*228*

use the relational operators, =, <>, <, >, <=, and >=, and/or the logical operators, #NOT#, #AND#, and #OR#.

To join two strings or labels in a text formula,	*231*

use the & text operator.

To view a list of 1-2-3 functions,	*236*

click the Function selector button, and then choose the List All option to open the @Function List dialog box.

To view the Help topic for a particular function,	*237*

press the F1 function key after entering the function's name into a cell.

WRITING formulas is the creative part of your work with 1-2-3. Without your precise and detailed instructions—which you express in formulas—a worksheet can do nothing. Formulas are responsible for establishing the relationships among data items, supplying the steps of operations, producing new values and labels, and defining the structure of your worksheet.

Depending on what you want to accomplish on a sheet, the formulas you write can be succinct and straightforward, or painstakingly complex. To simplify the task of writing formulas, Lotus 1-2-3 has a large library of functions that you can use within formulas—or, in many cases, as substitutes for formulas. A function is a predefined calculation or operation, represented by a specific name that denotes the function's role in the worksheet. Function names in 1-2-3 begin with the @ character.

NOTE This chapter is a general introduction to the use of formulas and functions, and Chapter 8 is a review of specific functions by category. For more complete coverage of the 1-2-3 function library, turn to the appendixes at the end of this book.

How Functions Work

You've seen one function example, @SUM, which you entered into the Conference worksheet to find the total of a column of numbers. Like @SUM, many of the 1-2-3 functions are designed to replace formulas that you would otherwise have to write yourself.

For instance, suppose you need to calculate the monthly payment for a fixed-rate bank loan, for which you know the principal, the interest rate as a percent, and the term in years. You've entered these three loan parameters into a column of your worksheet, and you've assigned the range names PRINCIPAL, RATE, and TERM to the three cells containing the data. Next you need to enter the formula for calculating the monthly payment on the loan.

Not many people can produce the formula for this loan calculation from memory. But you could look it up in a business mathematics book, and then carefully enter the formula into a cell of your worksheet. The entry would look something like this:

```
(PRINCIPAL*RATE/12)/(1-(1+RATE/12)^(-TERM*12))
```

Although it successfully calculates the monthly payment, this formula takes time and effort to produce. Fortunately, 1-2-3 offers a much simpler approach for this common calculation. The formula for finding a monthly loan payment is available in one form as the function named @PMT. Using this function, you can calculate the loan payment without having to concern yourself with the details of the formula itself. Here is how you would enter the @PMT function:

```
@PMT(PRINCIPAL,RATE/12,TERM*12)
```

NOTE Other payment functions are available in 1-2-3. Among them are @PAYMT and @PMTC, which you can read about in Appendix E.

Arguments The three loan parameters appear as the arguments of the @PMT function. An argument is a value you supply for a function to work with. In order to calculate the monthly payment amount, you express the rate and the term as monthly values; for this reason, two of the arguments you send to the @PMT function appear as calculated values (RATE/12 and TERM*12). As you can see, this use of the @PMT function is a lot simpler than the equivalent loan payment formula.

TIP Throughout this book you'll see commas used as separators between the arguments of a function. The comma is a commonly used character for this purpose, but the actual character you use on your system may be determined by an option in the Regional Settings Properties dialog box for your installation of Windows 95. You can examine—and change—the setting for the separator character by choosing Settings ➤ Control Panel from the Windows 95 Start menu and double-clicking the Regional Settings icon. In the resulting dialog box click the Number tab. The default separator character for your system appears in the text box labeled "List separator." In 1-2-3, the semicolon (;) is the *standard* argument separator; it always works, regardless of the Windows 95 setting for the list separator.

Other functions are designed to perform specific data operations. The effect of these functions is to give you broader options and greater flexibility for the design of your worksheet. For example, you can use the @HLOOKUP function to select values from a look-up table, a collection of numeric data items organized like an income tax table. Using this function, a formula can read appropriate data items from a two-dimensional data table that you've entered in a worksheet range.

In short, functions simplify your work and expand the range of tasks you can perform on a sheet. This chapter provides a general introduction to the use of functions on a sheet; then in Chapter 8 you'll see examples of functions in several categories.

Filling Ranges with Sample Data

As you proceed through this material, you'll find exercises designed to help you understand specific formulas and functions. As a technique for supplying sample data in some of these exercises, you'll use the efficient mouse action known as drag and fill. This action can quickly produce a sequence of numbers or labels in a selected range on your worksheet, following an example that you enter into the beginning of the range. Here is an exercise with the drag-and-fill action:

1. On a blank worksheet, enter a value of **1** in cell A1. Then press ↑ to move the cell pointer back up to A1.

2. Position the mouse pointer over the lower-right corner of cell A1. Two pairs of arrowheads—pointing down and to the right—appear around the mouse pointer:

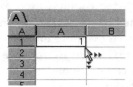

3. Hold down the left mouse button and drag the pointer down to cell A12.

4. Release the mouse button. When you do so, 1-2-3 fills the range A2..A12 with a column of numbers from 2 to 12.

5. Now select cell B1 and enter **January** into the cell. Press ↑ to select B1 again. Using the same technique as before, drag the mouse pointer from B1 to B12, and then release the mouse button. 1-2-3 fills the range B2..B12 with month names from February to December. This is an example of one of 1-2-3's SmartFill lists.

6. Enter **Sunday** into cell B15, and **21** into B16. Then select the two-cell range B15..B16. Position the mouse pointer at the lower-right corner of the selection:

7. Drag the pointer from column B to column H and then release the mouse button. 1-2-3 fills row 15 with labels representing the days of the week, and row 16 with sequential digits from 21 to 27.

8. Enter a value of **5** in cell E1 and a value of **10** in E2. Then select the two-cell range E1..E2 and position the mouse pointer over the lower-right corner of the selection.

9. Drag the pointer down to E12, and then release the mouse button. Following the example of your initial two entries, 1-2-3 fills the range with a sequence of numbers in increments of 5.

10. Finally, enter **0** in F1 and **−0.75** in F2. Then select F1..F2 and use the drag-and-fill operation to fill the range F1..F12.

    As you can see by studying the examples in Figure 7.1, the drag-and-fill operation is a simple but versatile way of entering an evenly incremented or decremented sequence of numbers—or a particular sequence of labels—into a range on your worksheet. You'll use this convenient tool in several exercises in this chapter.

> **TIP** The Range ➤ Fill command is an alternative tool for filling a range with a series of numbers or labels. To use this command, begin by entering the initial value or values into a worksheet and then select the entire range you want to fill. Choose Range ➤ Fill. In the Fill dialog box, select the Fill by Example option in the Fill type list. Then click OK to complete the operation. (The Fill command is also available in the shortcut menu that appears when you click a range with the right mouse button.) Range ➤ Fill can also be used to fill a range with a defined series of numeric, date, or time values. In the Fill dialog box you choose a fill type, and then specify start and stop values and an increment for the sequence that 1-2-3 will enter into the selected range. You can select special interval options for chronological series.

Chapter 7 Formulas and Functions

Figure 7.1: Using drag and fill to create a sequence of numbers or labels

Creating a Custom SmartFill List

As illustrated in the previous exercise, certain labels are defined in 1-2-3 as built-in SmartFill lists—sequences of names that you can use to fill a range on a sheet. In addition to the days of the week and the months of the year, the built-in SmartFill lists include directions (North, South, East, and West) and quarters of the year (Quarter 1, Quarter 2, Quarter 3, and Quarter 4).

You can create your own custom SmartFill lists by choosing the File ➤ User Setup ➤ SmartFill Setup command. The controls on the SmartFill Setup dialog box give you simple techniques for creating a sequence of labels that 1-2-3 will recognize as a SmartFill:

Filling Ranges with Sample Data

For example, suppose you want to create a SmartFill list representing the names of the departments in a company. Here's how you might proceed:

1. Choose the File ➤ User Setup ➤ SmartFill Setup command.
2. Click the New List button on the SmartFill Setup dialog box. In the New SmartFill List dialog box, enter **Department** as the new list name. Click OK or press ↵ to confirm:

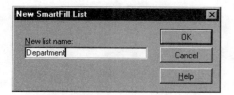

3. Click the Add Item button in the SmartFill Setup dialog box. In the Add Item dialog box, enter **Editorial** as the first name in the new SmartFill list. Click OK or press ↵ to confirm:

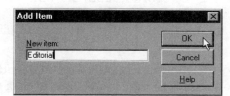

4. Repeat step 3 to add the following additional labels to the list: **Technical**, **Production**, **Sales**, **Customer Service**, **Accounting**, **Support Staff**. The list you are creating is displayed in the box labeled "Items in list":

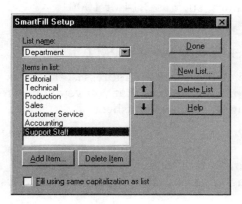

5. Click the Done button to complete this operation.

   Now you can experiment with your new SmartFill list. On a blank sheet, enter the label **Editorial** in cell A1. Move the cell pointer back to A1, and use the drag-and-fill technique to fill the range from A2 to A7. Here's the result:

   A custom SmartFill list is available for use in any workbook that you open. You can create lists for any sequence of labels that you commonly use in your work, for example, employee names, products, procedures, accounting categories, and so on. To delete a custom SmartFill list, choose File ➤ User Setup ➤ SmartFill Setup, choose the name of the list that you want to delete, and click the Delete List button.

   As you return to the topics at hand—formulas and functions—you'll find several opportunities to practice using the drag-and-fill technique.

Writing Formulas

As you've learned, formulas may contain a variety of elements, including:

▶ Literal data values, such as 3.14 or 1000

▶ Operators, such as + or −

▶ Functions, such as @SUM or @PMT

▶ References to cell or range addresses, such as A1, $B:$C$5, or $B$3..$K$7; or range names that you've defined to represent particular cells or ranges on your worksheet

1-2-3 recognizes any one of several characters as the beginning of a formula entry. For example, the plus sign (+) often serves as the starting point of a formula that begins with a reference to a cell address. The following paragraphs describe some common ways to begin formulas in 1-2-3.

Formulas that begin with numbers When the first element of a formula is a number, the formula can begin with a digit, an optional plus sign (+), a minus sign (–), or a decimal point (.). For a positive numeric value, you can begin the formula with the first digit of the number, from 0 to 9. For example, the following formula multiplies a positive number by the value stored in cell A5:

```
365*A5
```

You can begin this same formula with an optional plus sign, but 1-2-3 drops the + from the formula after you press ↵. When a formula begins with a negative number, you type a minus sign to start the formula; for example:

```
-19*C2
```

If the first element is a decimal value, you can begin the formula with a decimal point, but 1-2-3 changes the format of your entry after you press ↵. For example, you can enter a formula as:

```
.123*B1
```

But once you complete the entry, the formula appears in the contents box as:

```
0.123*B1
```

If the decimal value is very small, 1-2-3 converts the number to scientific format. For example, consider this formula:

```
.0000000000123*B1
```

After you press ↵ to complete this entry, 1-2-3 changes the format of this number to:

```
1.23E-11*B1
```

Formulas that begin with an address reference A plus sign or a minus sign is required as the first character of a formula that begins with an address reference. For example, the following formula instructs 1-2-3 to multiply the value in cell E19 by 10:

```
+E19*10
```

This formula multiplies the result by –1:

```
-E19*10
```

After you type either the plus sign or the minus sign, you can type the address reference directly from the keyboard or you can use a pointing technique to enter the address. You can use either the mouse or the arrow keys on the keyboard to point to a cell or range while you're creating a formula.

TIP If you've worked with spreadsheet programs produced by other software publishers, you might be used to beginning a formula with an equal sign (=). 1-2-3 recognizes the equal sign as the start of a formula, but drops it (or converts it to a plus sign) once you complete the formula entry.

Formulas that begin with a function   An initial @ character indicates that a formula begins with one of 1-2-3's built-in functions. A function can appear by itself as the complete entry in a cell, or a function name can be one of several elements in a formula. For example, the following function finds the sum of a range of values:

    @SUM(C5..C10)

The following formula multiplies the sum by 25:

    @SUM(C5..C10)*25

In both cases, the result of the function or the calculation appears in the cell where you enter the formula.

Formulas that begin with an open parenthesis   Any formula can begin with an open parenthesis character. You can use parentheses to enclose operations in a formula when you want to override 1-2-3's default order of operations. For example, the following formula adds two numbers together and then multiplies the sum by 5:

    (A1+A2)*5

Documenting Formulas with Cell Comments

You can include a note or comment at the end of a formula to help you remember what the formula does. To place a note at the end of a formula, type a semicolon (;) immediately after the formula itself and then type your note. For example:

    @PMT(PRINCIPAL,RATE/12,TERM*12); The monthly payment.

When you later examine the formula, your note appears along with the formula in the contents box on the edit line. This is one simple way to document the structure of a sheet, so that you can later review how you've organized your work.

A more versatile way to include notes in a sheet is to write cell comments. Any cell in a sheet may store a comment along with the cell's actual data entry or formula. To create a comment in a particular cell, follow these general steps:

1. Click the target cell with the right mouse button.
2. Choose the Cell Comment command from the resulting shortcut menu:

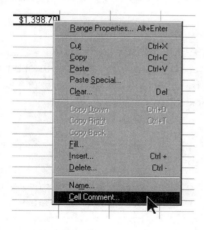

3. In the InfoBox for range properties (the Cell Comments tab), enter the text that you want to store as the comment for the current cell:

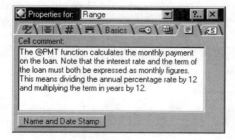

4. Close the InfoBox.

To mark the existence of a cell comment, 1-2-3 displays a small red dot at the upper-left corner of the cell itself. For example, cell B4 contains a comment on the following sheet:

	A	B
1	Principal	$112,000
2	Rate	12.75%
3	Term	15
4	Payment	$1,398.70
5		

You can view the cell comment by clicking the cell with the right mouse button and choosing the Cell Comment command from the shortcut menu.

TIP To delete a cell comment without otherwise changing the content or format of the cell, select the target cell and choose Edit ➤ Clear. In the Clear dialog box, remove the checks from all the boxes except the one labeled "Cell comments." Click OK to confirm.

Viewing Formula Markers

The *formula marker* is another visual tool that gives you general information about the contents of cells. When you activate this feature for a given workbook, a small dot appears in the lower-left corner of any cell that contains a formula. To activate formula markers, follow these steps:

1. Choose File ➤ Workbook Properties.
2. In the View tab of the Workbook Properties dialog box, click the Formula markers option, placing a check in the corresponding box:

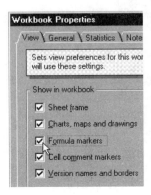

3. Click OK or press ↵ to confirm.

   In the following sheet, cell B4 shows both a cell comment marker and a formula marker:

	A	B
1	Principal	$112,000
2	Rate	12.75%
3	Term	15
4	Payment	$1,398.70
5		

   The formula marker gives you an easy way to distinguish between cells that contain formulas and cells that contain data when you examine a sheet.

> **NOTE** You can turn off both formula markers and cell comment markers by removing the checks from the appropriate options in the View tab of the Workbook Properties dialog box.

Understanding the Categories of Formulas

A formula in 1-2-3 can perform several types of operations:

▶ Calculate a numeric value

▶ Perform date or time arithmetic

▶ Evaluate a logical condition—that is, an expression that is either true or false

▶ Build a label or a text display

You've already written formulas that perform some of these operations. In the upcoming sections you'll further examine each kind of formula.

Numeric Formulas

You've seen examples of the four most common numeric operations (addition, subtraction, multiplication, and division) and the operators that represent them: +, −, *, and /. You've also seen the use of the plus and minus signs to represent positive and negative values or references. 1-2-3 has another numeric operation known as *exponentiation*. Given a base value *x* and an exponent *y*, this operation finds *x* to the power of *y*. In 1-2-3, exponentiation is represented by the caret symbol (^). For example, consider the following formula:

    +A1^3

If A1 contains a value of 5, this formula results in 125—or 5 to the power of 3. The exponent can also be fractional, in which case exponentiation produces a root value; for example:

    +A1^(1/4)

This formula finds the fourth root of the value in A1. To try this formula on your worksheet, enter a value of 2401 in cell A1, then enter +A1^(1/4) in cell A2. The result displayed in A2 is 7.

In the order of operations followed by 1-2-3, exponentiation has the highest precedence—that is, exponentiation is performed before any other numeric operation. Here are the numeric operations in their order of precedence:

1. Exponentiation (^)
2. Positive and negative sign (+ and -)
3. Multiplication and division (* and /)
4. Addition and subtraction (+ and -)

As you know, parentheses can be used in a formula to override this order of precedence. For example, given the formula +A1^(1/4), 1-2-3 performs the division before the exponentiation.

Date and time arithmetic operations are evaluated as numeric formulas, even though the results displayed on a sheet appear to be very different from numbers. You began exploring date and time arithmetic in Chapter 6. In the upcoming section of this chapter you'll see some additional examples.

Date and Time Formulas

In the discount worksheet that you developed in Chapter 6, you subtracted 90 days and 45 days from a conference date to calculate two different payment due dates. Similarly, on the schedule worksheet you added the length in minutes of each conference activity to a starting time, to calculate the schedule for the next activity. As these operations illustrate, a formula can increase or decrease an individual chronological entry by a fixed time value to produce a new value.

You can find the difference between two chronological values by subtracting one from another. For example, given two date entries named DATE1 and DATE2, the following formula subtracts one date from the other:

```
+DATE1—DATE2
```

This formula finds the number of days between the two dates. This result is a positive value if DATE1 is later on the calendar than DATE2, or a negative value if DATE1 is earlier on the calendar.

You might want to find the difference between two dates in a variety of business contexts. For example, on a customer billing worksheet you can calculate the number of days a customer takes to pay your invoices—that is, the difference between the billing date and the payment date. On an employee worksheet, you can find the number of days that have elapsed since an employee's last evaluation, or the number of days since the employee was hired.

You can also subtract one time value from another:

```
+TIME1—TIME2
```

This formula gives the elapsed time, expressed as a decimal fraction. You'll recall that a time number in 1-2-3 is a decimal that represents a portion of a 24-hour day. Again, the result of the subtraction is positive if TIME1 is later than TIME2, or negative if TIME1 is earlier than TIME2. One common use for this operation is in determining the length of time spent on a given task or project.

The following exercise helps you experiment with these two important chronological operations:

1. Enter **15-Apr-97** in cell A1 and **22-Apr-97** in cell A2 of a blank sheet. Select A1..A2, and use the drag-and-fill operation to fill the range A1..A5 with a sequence of dates that are one week apart.

2. Enter today's date in cell B1. Use the 31-Dec-96 date format for the entry. Then select B1..B5, click the range with the right mouse button, and choose Copy Down from the resulting shortcut menu. This action copies today's date into each cell of the range.

3. Enter **+B1-A1** into cell C1. The result displayed in C1 is the number of days between the dates in A1 and B1. Use the Copy Down command

to copy this formula down column C, to the range C1..C5. The upper half of the worksheet in Figure 7.2 shows the result. Of course, the values displayed in column C on your own sheet depend upon the date you enter in column B.

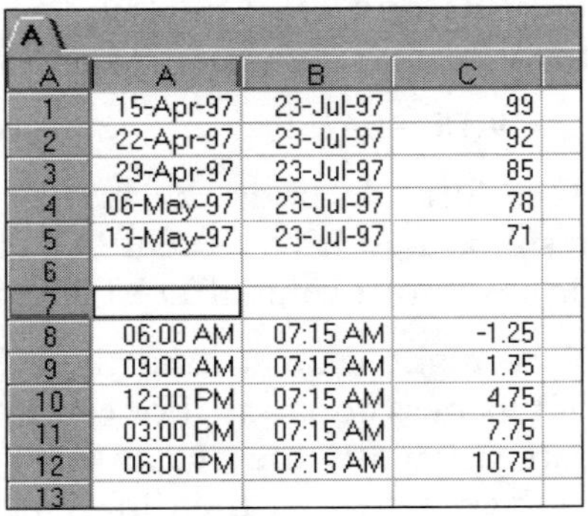

	A	B	C
1	15-Apr-97	23-Jul-97	99
2	22-Apr-97	23-Jul-97	92
3	29-Apr-97	23-Jul-97	85
4	06-May-97	23-Jul-97	78
5	13-May-97	23-Jul-97	71
6			
7			
8	06:00 AM	07:15 AM	-1.25
9	09:00 AM	07:15 AM	1.75
10	12:00 PM	07:15 AM	4.75
11	03:00 PM	07:15 AM	7.75
12	06:00 PM	07:15 AM	10.75
13			

Figure 7.2: **Experimenting with date and time arithmetic**

4. Enter **6:00 AM** in cell A8 and **9:00 AM** in A9. Then select A8..A9 and use the drag-and-fill operation to extend this sequence through the range A8..A12. As a result, time values from 6:00 AM to 6:00 PM appear in the selected range.

5. Enter **7:15 AM** in cell B8, and then use the Copy Down command to copy this time value down column B, to the range B8..B12.

6. Enter **(A8–B8)*24** into cell C8. The result displayed in C8 is the number of hours between the two time values in A8 and B8. (Do you see why the formula multiplies the difference by 24 in order to calculate the elapsed time in hours?) Copy this formula down column C, to the range C9..C12. The lower half of the worksheet in Figure 7.2 shows the result.

Study Figure 7.2 carefully and make sure you understand the two operations represented in the sheet. (Close this sheet without saving it when you're finished with the exercise.) In Chapter 8 you'll examine other chronological operations performed by 1-2-3's built-in date and time functions.

Logical Formulas

The purpose of a logical formula is to determine whether a particular condition is true or false. A condition is typically expressed as a relationship between two or more data values on a worksheet. As the result of a logical formula, 1-2-3 generates a numeric value:

- A value of 1 represents true.
- A value of 0 represents false.

Relational operators   To build logical formulas, you use 1-2-3's relational and logical operators. The six relational operators express relationships of equality or inequality between pairs of numbers. These operators are as follows:

Operator	Description
=	is equal to
<>	is not equal to
<	is less than
>	is greater than
<=	is less than or equal to
>=	is greater than or equal to

Here is an example of a logical formula that compares the values stored in cells A1 and B1:

+A1<B1

This formula results in a value of 1 (true) if the number stored in A1 is less than the number stored in B1; or a value of 0 (false) if the number in A1 is greater than or equal to the number in B1.

Logical operators   The three logical operators available in 1-2-3 are represented as #NOT#, #AND#, and #OR#. Note that these operators are always enclosed within a pair of number signs. The #AND# and #OR# operators are *binary*, meaning that they are each designed to work with two logical values. The #NOT# operator is *unary*: its role is to modify the result of a single logical value.

In the following descriptions, suppose that VAL1 and VAL2 are names of cells containing logical values of true or false:

- The expression #NOT#VAL1 results in the opposite value of VAL1. If VAL1 is true, #NOT#VAL1 is false; if VAL1 is false, #NOT#VAL1 is true. (Note that you can begin the entry of a logical formula with the # character if the formula begins with the #NOT# operator.)

- The expression +VAL1#AND#VAL2 is true if both VAL1 and VAL2 are true. If either VAL1 or VAL2 is false—or if both are false—the #AND# expression is also false.

- +VAL1#OR#VAL2 is true if either VAL1 or VAL2 is true, or if both are true. If both VAL1 and VAL2 are false, the #OR# expression is also false.

Here is an example of a logical formula that uses the #AND# operator:

```
+B1>A1#AND#B2>A2
```

This formula results in a value of 1 (true) if both of the relations are true—that is, if the value in B1 is greater than the value in A1 and the value in B2 is greater than the value in A2. If one or both of the two relations are false, the formula itself results in a value of 0 (false). Notice that 1-2-3 evaluates the relational operations (>) before the logical operation (#AND#). You'll see additional examples in the upcoming exercise.

Logical formulas are sometimes useful as entries in a worksheet. In addition, logical expressions appear as arguments in a 1-2-3 function named @IF. As you'll learn in Chapter 8, the @IF function chooses between two results, depending upon the true-or-false result of a logical expression.

Here's an exercise that demonstrates the results of logical formulas:

1. On a blank worksheet, enter the six integers shown in the range A1..B3 in Figure 7.3. In addition, enter the six labels in column A, from A5 through A10. (You'll right-align these labels in the next step.)

2. Select the range A5..D10. Click the Bold button on the status bar to display the six labels in boldface. Then click the Range Properties SmartIcon and select the Alignment tab. Click the right-align button, and check the Align across columns option. Close the InfoBox.

3. Enter the six logical formulas into column E, from E5 to E10, as shown in Figure 7.3.

Figure 7.4 shows the results of the formulas. You can see that each of these six logical formulas has produced a value of 1 or 0, representing true or false. Study each formula and make sure you understand why it produces the value it does. You'll learn more about logical values in Chapter 8.

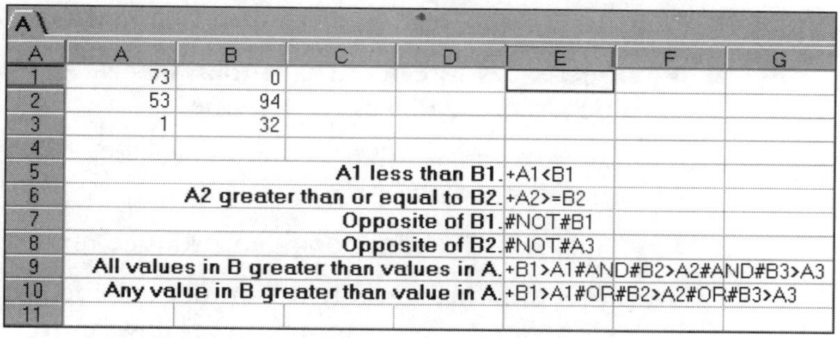

Writing Formulas

	A	B	C	D	E
1	73	0			
2	53	94			
3	1	32			
4					
5				A1 less than B1.	+A1<B1
6			A2 greater than or equal to B2.		+A2>=B2
7				Opposite of B1.	#NOT#B1
8				Opposite of B2.	#NOT#A3
9			All values in B greater than values in A.		+B1>A1#AND#B2>A2#AND#B3>A3
10			Any value in B greater than value in A.		+B1>A1#OR#B2>A2#OR#B3>A3
11					

Figure 7.3: **Experimenting with logical formulas**

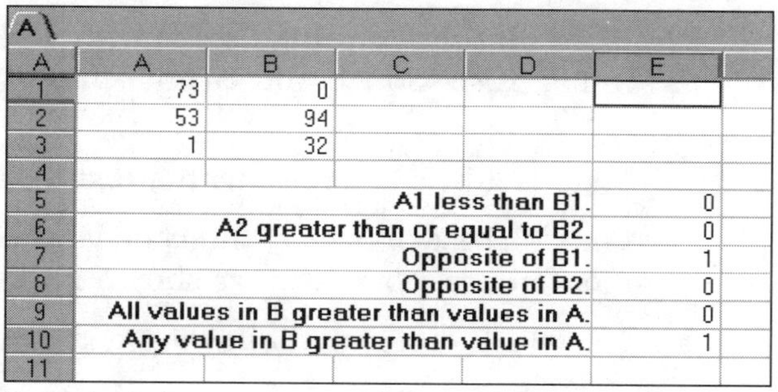

	A	B	C	D	E
1	73	0			
2	53	94			
3	1	32			
4					
5				A1 less than B1.	0
6				A2 greater than or equal to B2.	0
7				Opposite of B1.	1
8				Opposite of B2.	0
9			All values in B greater than values in A.		0
10			Any value in B greater than value in A.		1
11					

Figure 7.4: **The results of logical formulas**

> **NOTE** As illustrated in Figure 7.3, you can display formulas on a sheet by selecting a range, clicking the Format button on the status bar, and choosing the Formula option. You might want to display formulas temporarily in order to investigate the structure of calculations on a sheet.

In the next section, you'll see that 1-2-3 also recognizes formulas that produce labels, or text values.

Text Formulas

A text formula combines two or more labels to produce a new text value. Lotus 1-2-3 has one text operation, represented by the ampersand (&) character. The & operator joins two text values. The 1-2-3 documentation refers to & as the text operator, but in other software environments you may know this operation as concatenation.

The items joined in a text formula may include any of the following:

- References to cells that contain labels. As always, a cell reference can appear as an address or a name.

- Literal strings—that is, sequences of characters enclosed in double quotation marks ("").

- Built-in 1-2-3 functions that produce text values.

Each data item in a text formula is joined to the previous item by the & operator. For example, the following formula joins labels stored in cells A1 and A2 with a literal string value:

```
+A1&" and "&A2
```

Note that the formula begins with a plus sign, just like a numeric formula. Also notice the blank spaces enclosed within the quotation marks.

Here is a brief exercise with a text formula:

1. On a blank worksheet, enter the labels from the first several lines of the Conference worksheet, as shown in rows 1 through 5 of Figure 7.5.

2. In cell A7, enter the following text formula:

```
+B1&", invites you to attend '"&B4&"' in "&B5&"."
```

As usual, you can use the pointing technique to enter the cell references into the formula. Figure 7.5 shows the result of this formula—a sentence displayed across row 7.

	A	B	C	D	E	F	G	H
1		Computing Conferences, Inc.						
2		Profit Projection for a One-Day Seminar						
3								
4	Conference	Computing for Video Stores						
5	Place:	St. Louis						
6								
7	Computing Conferences, Inc., invites you to attend 'Computing for Video Stores' in St. Louis.							
8								
9								
10								
11								

Figure 7.5: **Experimenting with concatenation**

3. Change the label in cell B4 to **Computing for Lawyers**. Then change the label in cell B5 to **New York**. After each of these changes, 1-2-3

recalculates the value of the text formula in cell A7. The result is shown in Figure 7.6.

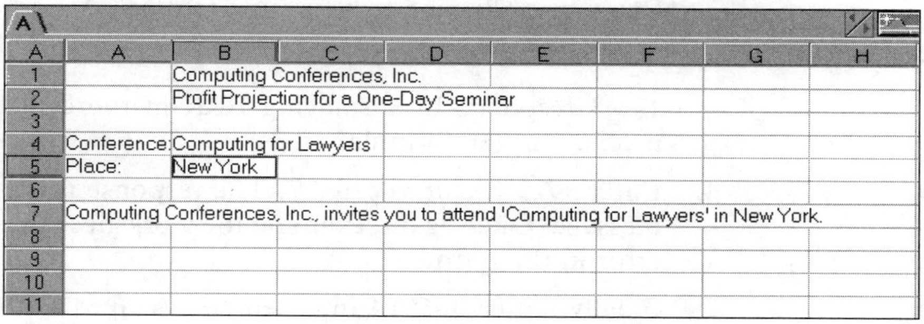

	A	B	C	D	E	F	G	H
1		Computing Conferences, Inc.						
2		Profit Projection for a One-Day Seminar						
3								
4	Conference	Computing for Lawyers						
5	Place:	New York						
6								
7	Computing Conferences, Inc., invites you to attend 'Computing for Lawyers' in New York.							
8								
9								
10								
11								

Figure 7.6: **Changing the result of the text formula**

You'll learn much more about text formulas when you examine 1-2-3's built-in text functions in Chapter 8.

Finding Errors in Formulas

Occasionally 1-2-3 responds to a new formula entry by displaying ERR in the formula's cell. As you can guess, the ERR message means that there is an error in your formula. Because of the error, 1-2-3 can't calculate the formula's result. Sometimes the error is in the formula itself, and sometimes the problem is in the data that the formula reads from other cells. Either way, the appearance of the ERR value in a cell means that you need to go back and investigate the formula and perhaps other entries on your sheet.

A number of problems can cause the ERR result. Here are three common ones:

▶ A reference to an undefined range name

▶ An inappropriate mix of data types in a formula

▶ An attempt to divide by zero in a numeric formula

In the following exercise, you'll simulate these three error conditions by entering formulas that are devised to produce intentional ERR values. Then you'll go through the steps to correct the errors by changing values on the sheet:

1. On a blank sheet, enter the label **Lotus 1-2-3 for** in A1, and **Windows** in A2. Then enter the value **95** in A3 and **0** in A4.

2. Select cell A1, choose Range ➤ Name, and enter **TITLE1** as the name for this cell. Click OK or press ↵ to confirm.

3. Enter the following text formula into cell A6:

    +TITLE1&" "&TITLE2

    1-2-3 responds by displaying ERR in the cell. Can you identify the problem in the formula?

4. Enter **+A2&A3** into cell A7. The response is the same—another ERR message. Once again, examine the worksheet's data and try to find the error in the formula.

5. Finally, enter **365/A4** into cell A8. A third ERR message appears in column A:

	A	B
1	Lotus 1-2-3 for	
2	Windows	
3	95	
4	0	
5		
6	ERR	
7	ERR	
8	ERR	
9		
10		

Here is what the worksheet's three formulas look like displayed in the Formula format:

	A	B
1	Lotus 1-2-3 for	
2	Windows	
3	95	
4	0	
5		
6	+TITLE1&" "&TITLE2	
7	+A2&A3	
8	365/A4	
9		
10		

6. Now begin correcting the conditions that produce the three ERR values. First, select cell A2 and choose Range ➤ Name. Enter **TITLE2** as the range name for the cell.

As soon as you complete this step, 1-2-3 recalculates the formula in cell A6, which previously contained a reference to an undefined range name. Now the formula's result appears as a text value.

7. Select cell A3 and enter 95 as a label rather than a value: Begin the entry by pressing the spacebar; 1-2-3 switches into the Label mode. Next type **95** and press ↵. Now 1-2-3 recalculates the text formula in cell A7, which previously contained an unusable reference to a numeric value.

8. Finally, select cell A4 and enter a value of 5.

    In response, 1-2-3 recalculates the numeric formula in cell A8. Because the denominator is no longer zero, 1-2-3 successfully calculates the numeric result of the formula. Here are the results of all three formulas after you complete these corrections:

	A	B
1	Lotus 1-2-3 for	
2	Windows	
3	95	
4		5
5		
6	Lotus 1-2-3 for Windows	
7	Windows 95	
8		73
9		
10		

As you know from your experience with the Conference worksheet, formulas are often interconnected in a complex system of calculations. If 1-2-3 detects an error in one formula, all dependent formulas are also evaluated as ERR. As a result, a single error condition can produce ERR messages all over your worksheet. Conversely, a single correction can take away all of the ERR messages.

Using Functions

A useful function library is one of the most important features of any spreadsheet program. The functions in 1-2-3 include groups of special-purpose tools designed for particular fields, such as accounting, engineering, and statistics. Other functions are designed for much more general use. Functions are among the tools you'll use most frequently in the 1-2-3 spreadsheet.

A library of almost three hundred functions seems dauntingly hard to master. But as you work with 1-2-3 you'll gradually identify the dozen or two functions that are most useful to you in your own sheets; these are the ones you'll become most adept at using. You can learn about other functions when occasions arise that call for their use.

Entering a Function into a Cell

1-2-3 offers detailed and substantial help when you need to learn how to use a new function. Help comes in a variety of forms:

▶ **Function selector.** You can click the Function selector button on the edit line to see a list of commonly used functions. When you select a function name from the list, 1-2-3 enters the function into the current cell along with convenient placeholders for the arguments you need to supply. If the function you want to use is not in the list, choose the List All option to view the @Function List dialog box, which contains a complete list of all the 1-2-3 functions:

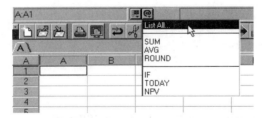

▶ **The @Function List dialog box.** Alternatively, you can type the @ character into a cell as the start of a function entry, and then press the F3 function key to view the @Function List dialog box. When you select a name from the list, 1-2-3 copies the function to the edit line and supplies placeholders for arguments:

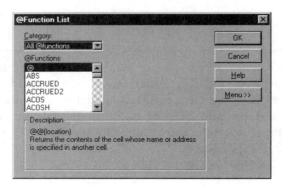

▶ **The Help Key.** Once a function name is displayed in a cell, you can place the flashing insertion point next to the name and press the F1 function key to go directly to the help topic for the function.

For example, imagine that you're building a sheet like the one in Figure 7.7 to calculate the monthly payment on a bank loan. You're ready to enter the formula for calculating the payment in cell B4. You know that 1-2-3 has a function that will do the job, but you can't recall the name of the function or how it's used. Here are the steps you take to get help:

1. With B4 selected as the current cell, type the @ character to begin a function entry.

2. Press the F3 function key. In response, 1-2-3 displays the @Function List dialog box. Press P to scroll quickly down the alphabetically ordered list of function names. Press the down-arrow key several times until the PMT function is highlighted in the list, as shown in Figure 7.7.

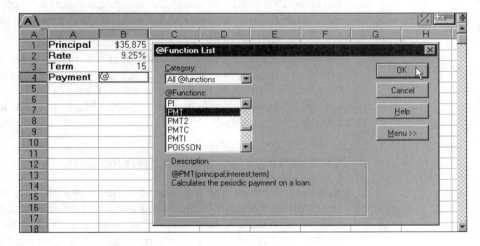

Figure 7.7: **Using the @Function List dialog box**

3. Press ↵ to select this function. In response, 1-2-3 enters the function's name into the current cell. Now use your mouse to move the flashing insertion point to a position just after the function name, and press the F1 function key to view the help topic for this function. The Help window appears on the screen, as shown in Figure 7.8. This Help topic describes @PMT and some related functions in detail, giving you all the information you need to use these functions successfully.

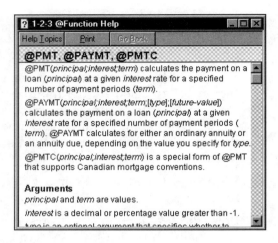

Figure 7.8: **Getting help with @ functions**

4. After you've read the information, press Escape to close the Help window and return to your work in 1-2-3. Then continue entering the function into the cell.

Of course, if you already know exactly how a function works, you can enter the function's name and arguments directly from the keyboard without using either of these help features. But even experienced spreadsheet users rely on the 1-2-3 Help system for reviewing the details of functions.

Customizing the Function Selector List

Because the function selector list initially contains only a half-dozen function names, you'll probably want to add the functions that you use most frequently. Using the @Function List dialog box, you can easily expand or modify the Function selector list. For example, suppose you want to add the @PMT function to the list. Here are the steps:

1. Click the Function selector button on the edit line, and choose List All. The @Function List dialog box appears, as shown back in Figure 7.7.
2. Press P and then ↓ several times until the PMT function is highlighted in the @Functions box.

3. Click the Menu button. The dialog box displays the Current menu box, with a list of all the functions that are currently included in the Function selector list.

4. Scroll down to the end of the Current menu box, and highlight the last entry in the list.

5. Click the >> button, located just to the right of the @Functions box. In response, 1-2-3 adds the PMT function to the bottom of the Current menu list, as shown in Figure 7.9.

6. Click OK to close the dialog box.

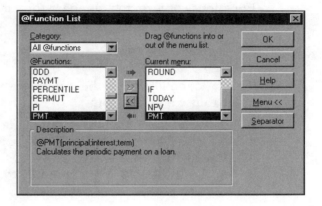

Figure 7.9: Customizing the @Function selector list

Now you can click the Function selector button to see the new entry in the list. Whenever you want to use the PMT function in a worksheet, you can select it instantly from this list:

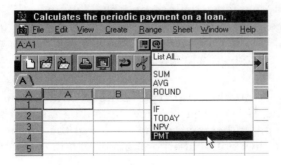

> **TIP** Notice two additional buttons on the @Function List dialog box in Figure 7.9. The << button deletes a function from the Current menu list. The Separator button adds a separator line so you can easily create groups of functions in your customized list. Before clicking either of these buttons, highlight the position in the Current menu list where you want the change to take place.

The Elements of a Function

Functions conform to a standard format, with only a few variations. To examine the elements of this format, take another look at the PMT function:

`@PMT(PRINCIPAL,RATE/12,TERM*12)`

This function illustrates the general features you need to understand in order to use any function:

- A function name consists of the @ character, followed by the predefined name for the function itself. If you misspell a function name, 1-2-3 won't recognize your entry. To avoid this problem, use the Function selector or press the F3 function key to view the @Function List dialog box.

- Immediately following the function name, an open parenthesis character marks the beginning of the argument list. A close parenthesis character goes at the end of the list.

- Between the parentheses you enter the function's arguments. Each argument is separated from the next with a comma, a semicolon, or the separator character defined in the Windows 95 Regional Settings Properties. A given argument can be expressed in any form that produces the required type of data. For example, an argument can appear as a cell reference, a range name, an expression, or even as another function name.

- The correct number and type of arguments is defined for each function in the 1-2-3 library. A few functions take no argument. Do not enter the parentheses after the names of these functions. A few other functions have optional arguments or varying lists of arguments.

You'll see many examples of this function format and its variations in Chapter 8.

Summary

Formulas and functions are the tools you use to develop the computational basis of a worksheet. Formulas may contain combinations of literal values, operators, references to cells or ranges, and functions. 1-2-3's built-in function library is a vast collection of tools, some for general use, others for special purposes.

Each category of formulas has its own set of operators in 1-2-3:

- Numeric formulas use the familiar operators *, /, +, and –, along with the ^ operator for exponentiation.

- Logical formulas produce values of true or false, represented numerically by 1 and 0. There are two groups of logical operators: Relational operators determine equality or inequality; they are =, <>, <, >, <=, and >=. The three logical operators modify or combine logical expressions; they are #NOT#, #AND#, and #OR#.

- Finally, 1-2-3 has one text operator, &, which joins two labels or strings.

As you experiment with formulas and functions, you can often use 1-2-3's drag-and-fill operation as a technique to generate sample data. In the "fill by example" procedure, you begin by entering values or labels that represent the beginning of a series of data; then you use drag-and-fill to extend the series over a larger range. 1-2-3's built-in SmartFill lists represent commonly used labels such as the days of the week and the months of the year. Using the SmartFill Setup dialog box, you can easily develop custom SmartFill lists of your own.

In Chapter 8 you'll continue exploring the 1-2-3 function library.

CHAPTER 8

Categories of Functions

Fast Track

To multiply pairs of numbers and then find the sum of all the products, 245
organize the values in adjacent rows or columns and use the @SUMPRODUCT function to perform the calculations.

To calculate accelerated depreciation amounts for a series of years, 248
use one of the available depreciation functions: @SLN, @SYD, @DDB, @DB, or @VDB.

To switch 1-2-3 into the manual recalculation mode, 262
choose File ➤ User Setup ➤ 1-2-3 Preferences, click the Recalculation tab, and select the Manual option.

To convert a formula to its current value before completing the formula entry, 263
press the F9 function key before you press ↵.

To convert a range of existing formulas into their current value, 264
select the range and press Ctrl+C to copy the information to the Clipboard. Then choose Edit ➤ Paste Special and click the Formulas as values option. Click OK to complete the conversion.

To rearrange a group of records in random order,	**264**
use the @RAND function to create a column of random numbers next to the records. Then choose Range ➤ Sort and specify the column of random numbers as the key to the sort.	
To display the current date and/or time on a sheet,	**269**
enter the @TODAY or @NOW function in a cell on the sheet, and format the resulting value to display the date and/or time.	
To find specific chronological information about a date,	**270**
enter the target value in a format that 1-2-3 recognizes as a date, and then use the @DATEINFO function to compute one of 13 items of information about the date.	
To evaluate an entry on a sheet and return one of two values depending on the result,	**277**
use the @IF function. The first argument of this function is a logical expression that produces a value of true or false. The second and third arguments are values that can be returned as the result of the function. If the expression is true, @IF returns the second argument; if false, the third.	
To convert the alphabetic case of a string,	**282**
use the @PROPER, @UPPER, and @LOWER functions.	
To convert a number to a string,	**284**
use the @STRING function.	
To convert a string of digits to a number,	**284**
use the @VALUE function.	
To find a value in a look-up table on your worksheet,	**285**
use the @HLOOKUP and @VLOOKUP functions.	

1-2-3's function library is divided into categories—statistical, financial, mathematical, engineering, calendar, logical, text, database, lookup, and information. To see these categories, click the function selector on the edit line and choose List all. In the @Function List dialog box, click the small down-arrow button at the right side of the Category list:

There is nothing absolute about these categories. You are likely to find useful tools in unexpected places among them. You may also find yourself mixing functions from different categories to solve individual problems on a worksheet.

This chapter presents a selective survey of some of the most useful functions. You'll study additional functions in other chapters. In addition, Appendixes A through H at the end of this book provide a reference guide to the entire function library.

Statistical Functions

The statistical functions are tools for investigating groups of numbers. For example, you can use these functions to count the number of entries in a list; to find the sum, the average, the largest value, and the smallest value of a list; and to calculate the statistical values known as variance and standard deviation. In addition, there are many other statistical functions designed for specialized uses. Here are brief descriptions of ten commonly used functions in this category:

Function	Description
@COUNT	Counts the number of cells that contain entries in a range.
@SUM	Finds the total of a list of numbers.

Statistical Functions

@AVG — Calculates the average value of a list of numbers.

@MIN *and* @MAX — Find the smallest and largest numeric values in a list.

@VAR *and* @VARS — Represent two different ways of calculating the *variance*, a measure of how the numbers in a list diverge from the average. A large variance means great divergence, and a small variance means little divergence. The @VAR function performs the calculation known as the *population* variance, whereas the @VARS function performs the *sample* variance.

@STD *and* @STDS — Calculate the standard deviation, the square root of the variance. @STD supplies the standard deviation for a population—that is, the square root of @VAR. @STDS produces the result for a sample, the square root of @VARS.

@SUMPRODUCT — As its name indicates, performs two operations in one efficient step. First, the function multiplies corresponding values in a range, and then it finds the sum of all the multiplication products.

These functions accept lists of numeric arguments that can include ranges, individual cell references, literal numeric values, calculated values, and range names. The exception is @SUMPRODUCT, which accepts only ranges as arguments. Statistical functions can also operate on three-dimensional ranges—that is, ranges across multiple sheets in a workbook.

NOTE For a detailed look at statistical functions, see Appendix G.

The sheet in Figure 8.1 illustrates the statistical functions. The managers at Computing Conferences, Inc., have compiled a list of conferences conducted in 1996, along with the number of people who attended each conference. As you can see, column A on the sheet displays the city in which each conference was held, column B gives the date, and column C the number of participants. Columns D and E supply a variety of statistics about the conferences and the attendance records—including the number of conferences, the total attendance for all conferences, the average attendance, and the largest and smallest attendance records. In addition, the worksheet shows the variance and the standard deviation calculations, produced with both methods. In Figure 8.2 you can see the functions that produce all these statistics. Notice that the column of attendance records, C6..C19, has the range name ATTENDANCE.

	A	B	C	D	E
1			Computing Conferences, Inc.		
2			Attendance at Conferences Conducted in 1996		
3			Computing for Video Stores		
4					
5	Place	Date	Attendance	Statistics	
6	Chicago	08-Jan-96	154		
7	St. Louis	20-Jan-96	119	Number of conferences:	14
8	Indianapolis	14-Feb-96	174	Total attendance:	1994
9	New York	06-Mar-96	201	Average attendance:	142
10	Boston	24-Mar-96	136	Largest attendance:	235
11	Washington, D.C.	02-Apr-96	172	Smallest attendance:	86
12	Atlanta	10-May-96	112		
13	Miami	27-May-96	97	Variance(n):	1632.53
14	Dallas	02-Jun-96	86	Standard deviation (n):	40.40
15	Albuquerque	28-Jun-96	104	Variance (n-1):	1758.11
16	Las Vegas	04-Sep-96	235	Standard deviation (n-1):	41.93
17	Los Angeles	10-Oct-96	119		
18	San Francisco	28-Oct-96	137		
19	Seattle	04-Nov-96	148		

Figure 8.1: Using 1-2-3's statistical functions

Finally, Figure 8.3 provides an example of the @SUMPRODUCT function. Column D in this sheet shows the individual attendance prices for each of the conferences held in 1996. The following @SUMPRODUCT function appears in cell F11:

    @SUMPRODUCT(C6..C19, D6..D19)

The first range argument in this function represents the attendance records, and the second argument contains the prices. The function multiplies each attendance record by the corresponding price, and finds the sum of all the products. The result is displayed as $434,920.

Statistical Functions

	A	B	C	D	E
1		Computing Conferences, Inc.			
2		Attendance at Conferences Conducted in 1996			
3		Computing for Video Stores			
4					
5	Place	Date	Attendance	Statistics	
6	Chicago	08-Jan-96	154		
7	St. Louis	20-Jan-96	119	Number of conferences:	@COUNT(ATTENDANC
8	Indianapolis	14-Feb-96	174	Total attendance:	@SUM(ATTENDANCE)
9	New York	06-Mar-96	201	Average attendance:	@AVG(ATTENDANCE)
10	Boston	24-Mar-96	136	Largest attendance	@MAX(ATTENDANCE)
11	Washington, D.C.	02-Apr-96	172	Smallest attendance:	@MIN(ATTENDANCE)
12	Atlanta	10-May-96	112		
13	Miami	27-May-96	97	Variance(n):	@VAR(ATTENDANCE)
14	Dallas	02-Jun-96	86	Standard deviation (n):	@STD(ATTENDANCE)
15	Albuquerque	28-Jun-96	104	Variance (n-1):	@VARS(ATTENDANCE
16	Las Vegas	04-Sep-96	235	Standard deviation (n-1):	@STDS(ATTENDANCE
17	Los Angeles	10-Oct-96	119		
18	San Francisco	28-Oct-96	137		
19	Seattle	04-Nov-96	148		

Figure 8.2: A formula view of the statistical functions used in Figure 8.1

	A	B	C	D	E	F
1		Computing Conferences, Inc.				
2		Attendance at Conferences Conducted in 1996				
3		Computing for Video Stores				
4						
5	Place	Date	Attendance	Price		
6	Chicago	08-Jan-96	154	$195		
7	St. Louis	20-Jan-96	119	$195		
8	Indianapolis	14-Feb-96	174	$195		Total Attendance
9	New York	06-Mar-96	201	$225		Revenues:
10	Boston	24-Mar-96	136	$225		
11	Washington, D.C.	02-Apr-96	172	$225		$434,920
12	Atlanta	10-May-96	112	$225		
13	Miami	27-May-96	97	$225		
14	Dallas	02-Jun-96	86	$195		
15	Albuquerque	28-Jun-96	104	$195		
16	Las Vegas	04-Sep-96	235	$245		
17	Los Angeles	10-Oct-96	119	$245		
18	San Francisco	28-Oct-96	137	$245		
19	Seattle	04-Nov-96	148	$195		

Figure 8.3: Using the @SUMPRODUCT function to calculate total attendance revenues

Financial Functions

The financial functions represent the formulas for calculations such as depreciation, loan payments, present value and future value, and investment analyses.

> **NOTE** Appendix E presents a detailed look at the financial functions.

Depreciation Functions

Depreciation refers to any one of several standard methods for allocating the expense of a large purchase over the useful life of the asset. Because depreciation has an impact on taxes, businesses are always concerned with finding the most advantageous way to calculate this expense among the permitted methods.

Five depreciation methods are available as functions in 1-2-3. The straight-line method, represented by the function named @SLN, is the simplest. It assigns equal portions of the asset's cost to each year of useful life. Four other methods represent various approaches to accelerated depreciation—the process of assigning greater portions of the expense to the earlier years of useful life, and lesser portions to later years. These methods are:

▶ The sum-of-the-years'-digits method, calculated by the @SYD function

▶ The double-declining-balance method, calculated by the @DDB function

▶ The fixed-declining-balance method, calculated by the @DB function

▶ The variable-rate declining balance method, calculated by the @VDB function

Arguments of the depreciation functions

These functions have common arguments, which can be represented as cost, salvage, life, and period:

▶ *Cost* is the original purchase price of the asset.

- *Life* is the defined useful life of the asset, in years.
- *Salvage* is the remaining value of the asset at the end of the useful life.
- *Period* is the target year for which you want to calculate the depreciation.

The @SLN function takes only the first three arguments, because the result of straight-line depreciation is the same for each year of useful life:

    @SLN(*cost,salvage,life*)

The @SYD, @DDB, and @DB functions calculate distinct amounts for each year of useful life. The target year, *period*, therefore appears as the fourth argument:

    @SYD(*cost,salvage,life,period*)

    @DDB(*cost,salvage,life,period*)

    @DB(*cost,salvage,life,period*)

The @VDB function is the most complex of all. It takes two period arguments, representing the start and the end of the target period; this allows you to calculate the depreciation expense for a portion of a year. In addition, @VDB takes two optional arguments, factor and switch:

    @VDB(*cost,salvage,life,period1,period2,factor,switch*)

The *factor* argument is the percentage by which the remaining value of the asset is multiplied to calculate the accelerated depreciation for a given period. For example, you might enter a value of 150% or 175% for this argument. If you omit *factor*, the default is 200%; in this case, @VDB produces the same result as @DDB. In the *switch* argument you specify whether you want @VDB to switch to straight-line depreciation at the point when it is advantageous to do so. Supplying a switch value of 0 (or omitting the argument altogether) instructs 1-2-3 to make the switch; a value of 1 prevents the switch.

Figure 8.4 shows examples of all five depreciation methods, calculated for an asset with a four-year useful life. Here are the steps for producing this sample worksheet on your own computer:

1. Enter the labels, data, and column headings as they appear in rows 1 through 6 of Figure 8.4.

2. Enter the integers 1 through 4 to represent the year numbers in cells A7 to A10.

3. Arrange and format all these entries as you see them in Figure 8.4. Then select the range B7..F10, click the Format button in the status bar, and choose the US Dollar format.

	A	B	C	D	E	F
1	Asset	Computer System				
2	Cost	$9,600.00				Depreciation
3	Life	4 years				factor
4	Salvage	$1,600.00				175%
5						
6	Year	SLN	SYD	DDB	DB	VDB
7	1	$2,000.00	$3,200.00	$4,800.00	$3,466.15	$4,200.00
8	2	$2,000.00	$2,400.00	$2,400.00	$2,214.67	$2,362.50
9	3	$2,000.00	$1,600.00	$800.00	$1,415.05	$1,328.91
10	4	$2,000.00	$800.00	$0.00	$904.14	$108.59
11						

Figure 8.4: *1-2-3's five depreciation methods*

4. Select the range A2..A4 and choose the Range ➤ Name command. Keep the default To the right option in the For cells box, and click the Use Labels button. Then click Done. This action assigns the range names COST, LIFE, and SALVAGE to the appropriate cells in column B.

5. Select cell F3 and choose Range ➤ Name again. This time choose the Below option in the For cells box, click the Use Labels button, and click Done to confirm. This action assigns the name FACTOR to cell F4.

6. In cell B7, enter the formula for the straight-line depreciation method:

    @SLN($COST,$SALVAGE,$LIFE)

    Notice the absolute references to range names. This format is necessary for the upcoming copy operation.

7. In cell C7, enter the formula for the sum-of-the-years'-digits method:

    @SYD($COST,$SALVAGE,$LIFE,A7)

8. In cell D7, enter the formula for the double-declining-balance method:

    @DDB($COST,$SALVAGE,$LIFE,A7)

9. In cell E7, enter the formula for the fixed-declining-balance method:

    @DB($COST,$SALVAGE,$LIFE,A7)

10. In cell F7, enter the formula for the variable-rate declining balance method:

    @VDB($COST,$SALVAGE,$LIFE,A7-1,A7,$FACTOR)

11. Use the Copy Down command to copy the five depreciation formulas down their respective columns: Select the range B7..F10, and click the selection with the right mouse button. Then choose Copy Down from the resulting shortcut menu.

Try making changes in the basic data—the cost, the salvage value, and the depreciation factor—and watch as 1-2-3 recalculates the depreciation schedules. If you increase the useful life value, you also have to add a new row to the depreciation table for each year's increase.

Other Financial Functions

Here is a selection of other financial functions available in 1-2-3:

@PV	The present value function
@NPV	The net present value function
@FV	The future value function
@PMT	The payment function
@CTERM *and* @TERM	The investment term functions
@RATE	The interest rate function
@IRR	The internal rate of return function

Most of these functions take an interest rate as one of several arguments. You can supply this argument as a decimal value such as .085 or as a percentage such as 8.5%. Of course, you can also provide the rate argument as a reference to a cell that contains the interest rate.

WARNING If a financial function gives a value that you know is incorrect, you should double-check the interest rate argument. Make sure you have not inadvertently supplied a rate argument that is off by a factor of 100—such as 8.5 instead of .085 or 8.5%.

The @PV and @NPV functions

The @PV function finds the present value of a series of future periodic income amounts, where each amount is the same. The present value calculation takes into account the time value of money at a given interest rate. @PV takes three arguments:

    @PV(*payment,rate,term*)

The *payment* argument is the income amount that will be received at the end of each period in the term. The *rate* argument is the periodic rate of return. The periods of the *rate* and the *term* must be the same.

The @NPV function finds the net present value of a series of future periodic cash flow amounts, positive or negative. @NPV takes two arguments, a rate and a range of cash flow amounts:

```
@NPV(rate,cashflows)
```

The sheet in Figure 8.5 uses the @PV and @NPV functions to compare the following two five-year investments: Investment #1 provides five annual income amounts of $10,000 at the end of each year. Investment #2 provides an initial amount of $5,000 at the end of the first year, and then a final amount of $50,000 at the end of the fifth year. Using a rate of 8.5% for the comparison, which is the better investment?

	A	B	C	D	E
1	Comparing Investments				
2					
3	Investment #1			Investment #2	
4					
5	Payment	$10,000		Year	
6	Years	5		1	$5,000
7	Rate	8.5%		2	$0
8	Present Value	$39,406.42		3	$0
9				4	$0
10				5	$50,000
11					
12				Net Present	
13				Value	$37,860.57
14					

Figure 8.5: Using @PV and @NPV to compare investments

The @PV function in cell B8 gives the present value of the first investment:

```
@PV(B5,B7,B6)
```

The @NPV function in cell E13 gives the present value of the second investment:

```
@NPV(B5,E6..E10)
```

As you can see, the first investment has a greater present value, even though the net income of the second investment is $5,000 more than the first.

The @FV function

The @FV function finds the future value of a series of equal periodic payments at a fixed periodic interest rate. @FV takes three arguments:

```
@FV(payment,rate,term)
```

The future value is equal to the amount of the periodic payments, plus the accumulated interest over the specified term.

Here's an illustration of the @FV function: The parents of a new baby girl have decided to deposit $1,500 in an account at the end of each year until their child is ready to go to college. How much will the account be worth at the end of 18 years, if the interest rate is 6%, compounded annually?

The @FV function in cell B7 is as follows:

```
@FV(PAYMENT,RATE,TERM)
```

(The labels in column A have been assigned as the names of the corresponding cells in column B.) There will be $46,358.48 in the account at the end of the 18-year term:

A	B	C
College Education Fund		
Payment	$1,500	per year
Rate	6%	annually
Term	18	years
Future Value	$46,358.48	

The @PMT function

The @PMT function finds the fixed periodic payment amount required to pay back a loan. @PMT takes three arguments:

```
@PMT(principal,rate,term)
```

When you use @PMT to find the monthly payment for a bank loan, you must supply the monthly interest rate, and the term in months.

In the following example, the principal of the loan is $135,950. The rate is 7.75% and the term is 30 years. The formula in cell B6 is:

```
@PMT(PRINCIPAL,RATE/12,TERM*12).
```

Notice that the annual rate is divided by 12 to produce the monthly rate, and the term in years is multiplied by 12 to find the term in months. The monthly payment is $973.96:

	A	B	C
1	Monthly Payment		
2			
3	Principal	$135,950	
4	Rate	7.75%	
5	Term	30	years
6	Payment	$973.96	

The @CTERM and @TERM functions

The @CTERM function finds the number of compounding periods required to reach a specified future value from a one-time investment amount, given a fixed interest rate. This function takes three arguments:

@CTERM(*rate,futurevalue,presentvalue*)

The @TERM function finds the number of equal payments required to reach a specified future value, given a fixed interest rate. @TERM also takes three arguments:

@TERM(*payment,rate,futurevalue*)

The following worksheet compares these two functions, analyzing two different scenarios for attaining a future value of $25,000. Under the first scenario, a one-time amount of $15,000 is deposited in an account at the beginning of the period. Under the second scenario, $1,000 is deposited in an account at the end of each year. In both cases, the accounts yield 6% interest annually. How long will it take each investment to reach the goal of $25,000?

	A	B	C	D	E	F
1	Time Needed to Save $25,000					
2						
3	Single Deposit			Annual Deposits		
4						
5	Deposit	$15,000		Payment	$1,000	annually
6	Rate	6%		Rate	6%	
7	Goal	$25,000		Goal	$25,000	
8	Term		9 years	Term	16	years
9						

The following @CTERM function is stored in cell B8:

@CTERM(B6,B7,B5)

In this case, the required term is approximately 9 years. (The value in B8 has been rounded by formatting.) The following @TERM function is stored in cell E8:

@TERM(E5,E6,E7)

Given annual deposits of $1,000, the account balance would reach $25,000 in approximately 16 years.

The @RATE function

The @RATE function calculates the interest rate corresponding to a fixed future return from a current investment amount. The function takes three arguments:

@RATE(*futurevalue, presentvalue, term*)

Here is an illustration of the @RATE function: A friend asks to borrow $15,000 from you now, and promises to pay you $25,000 at the end of four years. What will be the annual interest rate that you will earn from the loan?

	A	B
1	Calculating the Interest Rate	
2		
3	Present Value	$15,000
4	Future Value	$25,000
5	Term	4
6	Rate	13.62%

The function @RATE(B4,B3,B5) is entered into cell B6. The resulting annual interest rate is 13.62%.

The @IRR function

The @IRR function gives the internal rate of return from a series of positive and negative cash flow amounts. The internal rate of return is defined as the interest rate that gives a net present value of zero. @IRR takes two arguments, a rate and a range of cash flow amounts:

@IRR(*guess, cashflows*)

In the first argument you supply a reasonable guess for the internal rate of return. 1-2-3 uses this guess as a starting point for the iterative process that calculates the IRR. The second argument is a worksheet range that contains the positive and negative cash flow amounts.

The following example uses @IRR to find the internal rate of return for a six-year investment project. In the first year, an output of $80,000 is required to start the investment. The five subsequent years produce various income amounts: $15,000 at the end of the second year, $20,000 at the end of the third and fourth years, and $25,000 at the end of the fifth and sixth years. What is the calculated IRR for this sequence of cash flow amounts?

	A	B	C	D
1	Internal Rate of Return			
2				
3	Year	Cash Flow		
4	1	($80,000)		
5	2	$15,000		
6	3	$20,000	IRR	NPV
7	4	$20,000	9.00%	0.00%
8	5	$25,000		
9	6	$25,000		
10				

The following entry is stored in cell C7.

@IRR(0.1,B4..B9)

The guess supplied as the first argument is 10%. The range of cash flow amounts is B4..B9. @IRR calculates the internal rate of return as 9%. To confirm that this figure matches the IRR definition, the following formula appears in cell D7.

@NPV(C7,B4..B9)

Given the calculated internal rate of return, the @NPV function gives an approximate result of zero.

Mathematical Functions

Lotus 1-2-3 has a standard set of mathematical functions, including the trigonometric, logarithmic, and exponential functions. In addition, several of the mathematical functions have important roles in everyday business worksheets. For example, the @RAND function produces random numbers, which you can use to supply random data for testing formulas or to rearrange data in a random order; and the @INT and @ROUND functions are useful for converting real numbers to integers or for rounding numbers to a specified decimal place. In the sections ahead you'll see examples of these functions.

> TIP 1-2-3 also has a set of specialized engineering functions, including Bessel, Beta, Gamma, and error functions. Read about these in Appendix D of this book, or choose Help ➤ Help Topics, click the Index tab, and enter **engineering @functions** as the search key.

Trigonometric Functions

1-2-3 has a full set of trigonometric and inverse trigonometric functions. The trigonometric functions take arguments expressed in radians. The inverse functions produce radian values. A *radian* is a multiple of π, where the range 0 to $2*\pi$ is equivalent to 0 to 360 degrees. For example, $\pi/4$ is equal to 45 degrees, and $\pi/2$ is equal to 90 degrees. To simplify the task of supplying arguments in radians, 1-2-3 has a built-in @PI function; this function gives the value of π as:

    3.14159265358979

In addition, 1-2-3 supplies two relevant conversion functions. @DEGTORAD computes the radian equivalent of a degree measurement, and @RADTODEG gives the degree equivalent of a radian measurement.

Figure 8.6 shows @SIN, @COS, and @TAN values for a range of radian arguments from $-\pi/2$ to $+\pi/2$. The sine and cosine values move through their familiar wave patterns in this range: sine goes from -1 to 0 to 1, and cosine goes from 0 to 1 to 0. The result of the tangent function approaches infinity for arguments approaching $+\pi/2$, and negative infinity for arguments approaching $-\pi/2$.

	A	B	C	D	E	F	G	H
1				Trigonometric Functions				
2								
3		Radians	Sine	Cosine			Radians	Tangent
4	-0.5000	-1.5708	-1.0000	0.0000			Radians	Tangent
5	-0.4375	-1.3744	-0.9808	0.1951		-0.4375	-1.3744	-5.0273
6	-0.3750	-1.1781	-0.9239	0.3827		-0.3750	-1.1781	-2.4142
7	-0.3125	-0.9817	-0.8315	0.5556		-0.3125	-0.9817	-1.4966
8	-0.2500	-0.7854	-0.7071	0.7071		-0.2500	-0.7854	-1.0000
9	-0.1875	-0.5890	-0.5556	0.8315		-0.1875	-0.5890	-0.6682
10	-0.1250	-0.3927	-0.3827	0.9239		-0.1250	-0.3927	-0.4142
11	-0.0625	-0.1963	-0.1951	0.9808		-0.0625	-0.1963	-0.1989
12	0.0000	0.0000	0.0000	1.0000		0.0000	0.0000	0.0000
13	0.0625	0.1963	0.1951	0.9808		0.0625	0.1963	0.1989
14	0.1250	0.3927	0.3827	0.9239		0.1250	0.3927	0.4142
15	0.1875	0.5890	0.5556	0.8315		0.1875	0.5890	0.6682
16	0.2500	0.7854	0.7071	0.7071		0.2500	0.7854	1.0000
17	0.3125	0.9817	0.8315	0.5556		0.3125	0.9817	1.4966
18	0.3750	1.1781	0.9239	0.3827		0.3750	1.1781	2.4142
19	0.4375	1.3744	0.9808	0.1951		0.4375	1.3744	5.0273
20	0.5000	1.5708	1.0000	0.0000				

Figure 8.6:   **Examples of the trigonometric functions**

Inverse trigonometric functions

The inverse trigonometric functions take single numeric arguments and return angles in radians. For example, Figure 8.7 shows the arcsine and arccosine values for a range of decimal arguments between –1 to 1. The arcsine value goes from –p/2 to p/2 for this range of arguments, and the arccosine value goes from p down to zero. Here are the functions entered into cells B4 and C4:

@ASIN(A4)

@ACOS(A4)

To produce the table, these functions were copied down columns B and C.

Figure 8.7 also shows examples of arctangent functions. As you can see, the arctangent approaches $-\pi/2$ for large negative arguments, and $+\pi/2$ for large positive arguments. Here is the formula stored in cell F4:

@ATAN(E4)

Mathematical Functions

	A	B	C	D	E	F	G	H	I	J	K
1			Inverse Trigonometric Functions								
2											
3	Argument	ASIN	ACOS		Argument	ATAN		x	y	ATAN2	
4	-1.0000	-1.5708	3.1416		-100000	-1.5708		-0.5	-1.0	-2.0344	
5	-0.8750	-1.0654	2.6362		-10000	-1.5707		-1.0	-1.0	-2.3562	
6	-0.7500	-0.8481	2.4189		-1000	-1.5698		-1.0	-0.5	-2.6779	
7	-0.6250	-0.6751	2.2459		-100	-1.5608		-1.0	0.0	3.1416	
8	-0.5000	-0.5236	2.0944		-10	-1.4711		-1.0	0.5	2.6779	
9	-0.3750	-0.3844	1.9552		-1	-0.7854		-1.0	1.0	2.3562	
10	-0.2500	-0.2527	1.8235		-0.1	-0.0997		-0.5	1.0	2.0344	
11	-0.1250	-0.1253	1.6961		0	0.0000		0.0	1.0	1.5708	
12	0.0000	0.0000	1.5708		0.1	0.0997		0.5	1.0	1.1071	
13	0.1250	0.1253	1.4455		1	0.7854		1.0	1.0	0.7854	
14	0.2500	0.2527	1.3181		10	1.4711		1.0	0.5	0.4636	
15	0.3750	0.3844	1.1864		100	1.5608		1.0	0.0	0.0000	
16	0.5000	0.5236	1.0472		1000	1.5698		1.0	-0.5	0.4636	
17	0.6250	0.6751	0.8957		10000	1.5707		1.0	-1.0	-0.7854	
18	0.7500	0.8481	0.7227		100000	1.5708		0.5	-1.0	-1.1071	
19	0.8750	1.0654	0.5054					0.0	-1.0	-1.5708	
20	1.0000	1.5708	0.0000								

Figure 8.7: **Examples of inverse trigonometric functions**

The @ATAN2 function supplies radian angles in a four-quadrant x-y coordinate system. This function takes two numeric arguments, forming a coordinate pair:

    @ATAN2(x, y)

The result of @ATAN2 is the angle formed by two lines in the coordinate system: the x axis extending horizontally to the right from the origin, and the line from (0,0) to (x,y). Figure 8.7 shows a range of examples. The formula in cell J4 is as follows:

    @ATAN2(H4,I4)

> **TIP** In addition to the examples you've seen here, 1-2-3 also supplies secant, cosecant, and cotangent functions, along with the equivalent inverse trigonometric functions.

Exponential and Logarithmic Functions

The exponential and logarithmic functions are @EXP and @LN, both based on the natural constant e; and @LOG, based on 10. The @EXP function calculates exponents of e, where the value of e is represented as:

    2.71828182845905

@EXP takes one numeric argument, *x*, and supplies the value of e to the *x* power. The @LN function finds the natural logarithm of its argument. @LN takes one argument, *x*, and supplies the power of e that produces *x*. The @LOG function gives the base-10 logarithm. @LOG takes one numeric argument, *x*, and returns the power of 10 that gives *x*. Figure 8.8 shows a range of examples for all three of these functions.

A	B	C	D	E	F	G	H	I
1			The Exponential, Logarithmic, and Square Root Functions					
2								
3	x	EXP(x)		x	LN(x)	LOG(x)	x	SQRT(x)
4	-1.00	0.3679		0.50	-0.6931	-0.3010	0.25	0.5000
5	-0.75	0.4724		1.00	0.0000	0.0000	0.50	0.7071
6	-0.50	0.6065		1.50	0.4055	0.1761	0.75	0.8660
7	-0.25	0.7788		2.00	0.6931	0.3010	1.00	1.0000
8	0.00	1.0000		2.50	0.9163	0.3979	1.25	1.1180
9	0.25	1.2840		3.00	1.0986	0.4771	1.50	1.2247
10	0.50	1.6487		3.50	1.2528	0.5441	1.75	1.3229
11	0.75	2.1170		4.00	1.3863	0.6021	2.00	1.4142
12	1.00	2.7183		4.50	1.5041	0.6532	2.25	1.5000
13	1.25	3.4903		5.00	1.6094	0.6990	2.50	1.5811
14								

Figure 8.8: Examples of @EXP, @LN, @LOG, and @SQRT

The @SQRT function gives the square root of its numeric argument. The argument must be greater than zero. The last column in Figure 8.8 shows examples of @SQRT.

The @RAND Function

The @RAND function produces random numbers. The function takes no argument, and supplies a random decimal value between 0 and 1. If you want to generate random numbers in another range, you can multiply @RAND by the maximum value in the range. For example, the following formula produces random numbers between 0 and 100:

    @RAND*100

To produce random integers, you can use 1-2-3's built-in @INT function with @RAND. @INT eliminates the decimal portion of a real number and supplies the integer portion. For instance, the following formula gives random integers between 0 and 100:

    @INT(@RAND*100)

This is an example of a formula in which one function appears as the argument of another function. You'll see other examples as you continue in this chapter.

Figure 8.9 shows four columns of random numbers, generated using the @RAND and @INT functions. Column A contains random decimal values between 0 and 1; column B, random numbers between 0 and 100; column C, random integers between 0 and 10; and column D, random integers between 0 and 1000. To produce these numbers, the four formulas shown in row 3 were copied down their respective columns.

	A	B	C	D
1		The @RAND Function		
2				
3	@RAND	@RAND*100	@INT(@RAND*10)	@INT(@RAND*1000)
4	0.93893081086638	44.9915794399528	2	837
5	0.610138231241209	73.4756472862678	1	315
6	0.593252470993089	5.20394030269419	8	679
7	0.794279980843086	62.6246673812273	2	514
8	0.463638029742817	32.7846762876886	6	240
9	0.364365887532181	12.0543671828016	5	525
10	0.897471753366977	97.7492413473079	1	835
11	0.807758838780112	71.499324204167	9	973
12	0.00280337734278449	89.1418994353814	8	349
13	0.116363000178879	7.90381045448771	3	197
14	0.712944006413661	39.3423085749812	2	314
15				

Figure 8.9: Examples of the @RAND function

@RAND and automatic recalculation

The @RAND function is commonly used for producing random test data and for arranging records in random order. But before you use @RAND for these applications, you should consider the implications of 1-2-3's automatic recalculation mode. 1-2-3 recalculates the formulas on a sheet whenever a change occurs in the data that the formulas depend on. The @RAND function takes no argument, and is therefore independent of any particular data value on the worksheet. However, whenever 1-2-3 recalculates any formula on the worksheet, it also recalculates all cells that contain @RAND entries. For this reason, the random values on the worksheet appear to be unstable: They change whenever the worksheet is recalculated. This can be a problem if you are trying to perform a test with a fixed set of random numbers.

There are two different ways of solving this problem. One way is to switch 1-2-3 out of its automatic recalculation mode while you use the @RAND function, and the other way is to convert @RAND function entries into simple numeric values. You can switch out of automatic recalculation mode by choosing File ➤ User Setup ➤ 1-2-3 Preferences, clicking the Recalculation tab, and then selecting the Manual option:

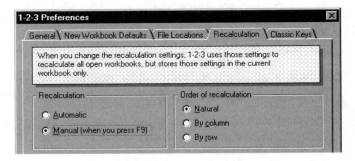

In the manual recalculation mode, 1-2-3 recalculates formulas on the worksheet only when you instruct it to do so. You force a recalculation by pressing the F9 function key. When formulas need to be recalculated—normally after a change in the worksheet's data—1-2-3 displays the word "Calc" on the status bar, just to the left of the mode indicator. Ignore the Calc message if you are working with a particular set of random numbers that you want to keep. Press F9 only when you want to change the set of random numbers on your worksheet.

Try this exercise with the @RAND function, starting in the default Automatic recalculation mode:

1. On a blank worksheet, enter **@RAND** into cell A1. A random number between 0 and 1 appears in the cell.

2. Now enter a value of **1** in cell A2. Even though this new entry has no relationship to the formula in cell A1—or to any other formula, since none other currently appears in the worksheet—1-2-3 recalculates the @RAND function anyway. A new random number appears in cell A1. This change could be disconcerting if you were using random numbers as test data on your worksheet. You'd prefer to have the opportunity to examine the results of one random scenario before suddenly jumping to a new one.

3. Now choose File ➤ User Setup ➤ 1-2-3 Preferences and click the Recalculation tab. Click the Manual option to switch into the manual recalculation mode. Click OK to confirm the change.

4. Now enter a value of **2** into cell A2. In the manual mode, 1-2-3 does not automatically recalculate any formula on the worksheet. The random number displayed in cell A1 does not change. Notice the word "Calc" at the right side of the status bar. This tells you that 1-2-3 has not recalculated the worksheet, because of the manual recalculation mode.

5. Press the F9 function key to force a recalculation. A new random number appears in cell A1, and the word "Calc" disappears from the status line.

6. Continue experimenting with this worksheet in the manual mode, if you wish. When you are finished, choose File ➤ User Setup ➤ 1-2-3 Preferences again, click the Recalculation tab, and switch 1-2-3 back into the Automatic mode. Then close this workbook without saving it.

By the way, the Recalculation settings apply to all worksheets that are open at the time you select a setting. The setting is actually saved for the current workbook.

The second way to prevent 1-2-3 from recalculating random numbers is to convert a @RAND function entry into a simple numeric value entry. As a result of this conversion, a worksheet cell will contain a random number that was generated by @RAND, but the @RAND function itself will not be present in the cell. You can accomplish this conversion either before or after you complete the @RAND entry. To convert a function or formula to a value during the entry process, you simply press the F9 function key before pressing ↵. After a function or formula is already entered into a cell, you can make the same conversion by using the Edit ➤ Paste Special command.

You'll experiment with both of these techniques in the following exercise:

1. Select cell A1 on a blank worksheet, and type **@RAND** as a formula entry. Do not press ↵.

2. Press the F9 function key. In response, 1-2-3 converts the @RAND function into a random numeric value entry.

3. Now press ↵. The random number in A1 is static, because the entry is a value rather than a formula.

4. In cell A2 type the **@RAND** function. Press ↵ to complete the entry. (Do not press F9 this time.)

5. Select A2..A10 and click the selection with the right mouse button. In the resulting shortcut menu, choose Copy Down. When you complete the copy operation, a different random number appears in each of the cells in the range.

6. With the range A2..A10 still selected, press Ctrl+C to copy the selection to the Clipboard. Then choose Edit ➤ Paste Special. In the resulting dialog box, select the option labeled "Formulas as values":

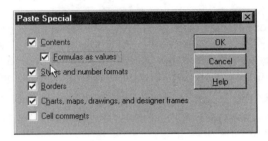

7. Click OK or press ↵ to confirm this option.

Back on your worksheet, the entries in the selected range are now numeric value entries, not functions. You can confirm this by selecting any cell in the range and examining the contents box. You'll see a long decimal number in the box, not a @RAND entry.

Using random numbers

Now consider a situation in which you might use the @RAND function on a sheet. Imagine that you have a group of employees whom you evaluate formally once a year. You hold individual evaluation meetings in September. To avoid conducting these meetings in the same alphabetical order each year, you want a way to rearrange the list of employees in random order.

The list of employee names appears in columns B and C in the worksheet shown in Figure 8.10. The list is currently in alphabetical order. Here are the steps you take to rearrange the list randomly:

1. Enter the formula @INT(@RAND*50) in cell A1. Select the range A1..A15, and click the selection with the right mouse button. Choose Copy Down from the resulting shortcut menu. A random integer between 0 and 50 appears in each cell, as in Figure 8.10. (The random numbers on your worksheet will be different from the ones in this figure.)

Mathematical Functions 265

	A	B	C
1	17	Alcott	M.
2	48	Burton	C.
3	0	Calloway	D.
4	30	Dalton	R.
5	3	Everett	V.
6	29	Fine	M.
7	41	Graves	A.
8	18	Hines	D.
9	31	Jackson	N.
10	14	Kelley	N.
11	41	Larson	W.
12	23	Madison	I.
13	37	Nelson	P.
14	9	Oliver	A.
15	34	Parker	H.

Figure 8.10: Using random numbers to rearrange a list of names

2. Select the range A1..A15 and press Ctrl+C. Choose the Edit ➤ Paste Special command, select Formulas as values, and click OK. Back on the worksheet, the random numbers in column A are now simple value entries rather than function entries.

3. Select the range A1..C15. Choose Range ➤ Sort. The Sort dialog box appears on the screen. Click the >> button and then click OK to sort the data by the random numbers in column A:

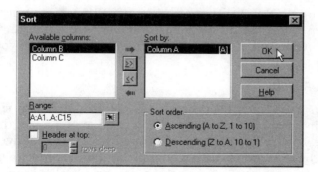

Back on the worksheet, the list of employee names is now rearranged randomly according to the random numbers you entered into column A, as shown in Figure 8.11. Once you've completed your employee evaluation, you can use the Range ➤ Sort command to realphabetize the list of employees.

	A	B	C
1	0	Calloway	D.
2	3	Everett	V.
3	9	Oliver	A.
4	14	Kelley	N.
5	17	Alcott	M.
6	18	Hines	D.
7	23	Madison	I.
8	29	Fine	M.
9	30	Dalton	R.
10	31	Jackson	N.
11	34	Parker	H.
12	37	Nelson	P.
13	41	Graves	A.
14	41	Larson	W.
15	48	Burton	C.
16			
17			

Figure 8.11: The randomly arranged employee list

More Mathematical Functions

Among the remaining tools in this category are three miscellaneous but important functions named @ROUND, @MOD, and @ABS.

The @ROUND function

The @ROUND function takes two numeric arguments. The first argument, x, is the number that you want to round, and the second, n, is an integer representing the decimal place at which you want the rounding to occur:

@ROUND(x, n)

If n is positive, rounding takes place at the right side of the decimal point. For example, if you enter a value of 2 for n, the function rounds the value x to the nearest hundredth. If n is negative, rounding occurs at the left side of the decimal point. For example, if you enter −1 for n, the function rounds x to the nearest multiple of ten. Finally, a value of zero for n results in rounding to the nearest whole integer.

The worksheet in Figure 8.12 shows examples of the @ROUND function. Column A in this worksheet contains a series of random numbers between 0 and 100. In columns B through E, these numbers are rounded to the nearest thousandth, the nearest hundredth, the nearest tenth, the nearest integer, and the nearest multiple of ten, respectively. Here are the formulas in cells A4, B4, C4, D4, and E4:

@RAND*100

@ROUND(A4,3)

@ROUND(A4,2)

@ROUND(A4,1)

@ROUND(A4,0)

@ROUND(A4,-1)

These formulas are copied down the worksheet, to the range A5..E13.

	A	B	C	D	E	F
1		The @ROUND Function				
2						
3	RAND * 100	n = 3	n = 2	n = 1	n = 0	n = -1
4	60.51822	60.518	60.52	60.5	61	60
5	29.67818	29.678	29.68	29.7	30	30
6	1.20317	1.203	1.2	1.2	1	0
7	21.68289	21.683	21.68	21.7	22	20
8	24.31975	24.32	24.32	24.3	24	20
9	42.02632	42.026	42.03	42	42	40
10	36.38729	36.387	36.39	36.4	36	40
11	61.20233	61.202	61.2	61.2	61	60
12	27.60388	27.604	27.6	27.6	28	30
13	38.36190	38.362	38.36	38.4	38	40

Figure 8.12: Experimenting with the @ROUND function

NOTE 1-2-3 has several other functions related to rounding, including @ROUNDDOWN, @ROUNDUP, @ROUNDM, @EVEN, @ODD, @INT, and @TRUNC. You can read about all of these tools in Appendix G.

The @MOD function

The @MOD function performs division between two integers, but unlike the division operator, @MOD supplies the remainder from the division, not the quotient. @MOD is known as the modulus function. It takes two arguments, the numerator and the denominator of the division operation:

@MOD(x, y)

If *y* divides evenly into *x* with no remainder, @MOD supplies a value of zero. Otherwise, @MOD returns the remainder from the division. For example, try entering @MOD(25,9) into a cell. The result is 7. The division of 9 into 25 gives a value of 2 with a remainder of 7.

@MOD is useful in a variety of applications. For example, suppose you have an alphabetized list of one hundred employees, with employee numbers that range from 1 to 100. For evaluation purposes, you want to divide this list randomly into five groups of 20 employees each. If the employee numbers are displayed in column A (from A1 to A100), you can copy the following formula down column B to assign each employee a group number from 1 to 5:

@MOD(A1,5)+1

NOTE Two other functions that produce results from division operations are @MODULO and @QUOTIENT. Read about these in Appendix G.

The @ABS function

The @ABS function gives the absolute value of a number. @ABS takes one numeric argument, x:

@ABS(*x*)

Whether *x* is positive or negative, @ABS returns the unsigned (positive) equivalent of the argument.

Use this function when the sign of a numeric value is not relevant to your worksheet. When you subtract one number from another, the result may be positive or negative, depending upon which number is larger; applying @ABS to the subtraction guarantees a positive result. For example, the following worksheet displays the difference in days between two dates:

	A	B
1	28-Nov-97	
2	08-Jun-97	
3	Difference in days:	
4		173
5		

Cell B4 contains a formula for finding the number of days between the two dates:

@ABS(A2–A1)

This formula gives a positive number of days, regardless of which day is later in time.

Date and Time Functions

1-2-3 has a useful set of chronological functions for working with date and time values. You can use functions in this category to:

- Read the current date and time from the system calendar and clock
- Get information about existing date and time values
- Convert other types of data into date and time values
- Perform date arithmetic

Two functions supply values representing the current date and time:

Function	Results
@TODAY	Returns a date number representing the current date. For example, a return value of 35273 represents the date 27-Jul-96. @TODAY takes no argument.
@NOW	Returns a combined date-and-time number representing both the current date and the current time. For example, a return value of 34493.25 represents the date 27-Jul-96 at 6:00 AM. @NOW takes no argument.

Several functions supply information about a date value or a time value. Among these are the following:

Function	Arguments and Results
@DAY	Takes a date number as its argument and returns an integer from 1 to 31 representing the day of the month.
@WEEKDAY	Takes a date number argument and returns an integer from 0 to 6, representing a day from Monday to Sunday.

Function	Description
@MONTH	Takes a date number argument and returns an integer from 1 to 12 representing the month.
@YEAR	Takes a date number argument and returns a two-digit integer representing the year.
@DATEINFO	Takes two arguments, a date and an attribute number from 1 to 13. As shown in Figure 8.13, this function returns a specific item of information about the date, depending upon the attribute number you supply.
@HOUR	Takes a decimal time number as its argument and returns an integer from 0 to 23 representing the hour.
@MINUTE	Takes a time number argument and returns an integer from 0 to 59 representing the minutes.
@SECOND	Takes a time number argument and returns an integer from 0 to 59 representing the seconds.

	A	B	C	D	E	F	G	H	I	J
1				The @DATEINFO Function						
2										
3	Information for this date:									
4	27-Jul-96									
5										
6		Attribute		Result		Explanation				
7		1		Sat		Abbreviated day of the week.				
8		2		Saturday		Day of the week.				
9		3		5		Integer representing the day of the week.				
10		4		30		Week of the year.				
11		5		Jul		Abbreviated month.				
12		6		July		Month.				
13		7		31		Number of days in this month.				
14		8		4		Number of days remaining in this month.				
15		9		35277		Date number for the last day of this month.				
16		10		3		The current quarter.				
17		11		1		Leap year indicator. (0 = no; 1 = yes)				
18		12		209		Day of the year.				
19		13		157		Number of days remaining in this year.				

Figure 8.13: *The information available from the @DATEINFO function*

These functions also accept combined date-and-time arguments, in the form supplied by the @NOW function.

The following functions convert numeric values or strings into dates or strings:

Function	Arguments and Results
@DATE	Takes three integer arguments representing the year, the month, and the day, and returns the corresponding date number. For example, @DATE(96,7,27) gives the date number 35273.
@DATEVALUE	Takes a string argument in a format that 1-2-3 can recognize as a date, and returns the corresponding date number. For example, @DATEVALUE("27-Jul-96") supplies the number 35273.
@DATESTRING	Converts a date value into a text date. For example, @DATESTRING(35273) returns 07/27/96 as a label.
@TIME	Takes three numeric arguments representing the hour, the minutes, and the seconds, and returns the corresponding decimal time number. For example, @TIME(4,30,0) gives the value 0.1875.
@TIMEVALUE	Takes a string argument in a format that 1-2-3 can recognize as a time, and returns the corresponding time number. For example, @TIMEVALUE("4:30 AM") gives the value 0.1875.

Finally, several functions perform special date arithmetic operations. Among them are these three:

Function	Use
@DATEDIF	Takes two dates and a format specifier as its arguments, and returns the difference between the two dates in days, months, or years, depending on the *format* argument. The first two arguments are date numbers, and the third is a string. Figure 8.14 provides a more thorough explanation of this function.
@DAYS360	Takes two date numbers as arguments, and returns the number of days between the two dates, using a standard algorithm based on a 360-day year.

@D360   Also takes two date numbers as arguments, and calculates the number of days between the two dates, based on a year of twelve months with 30 days each.

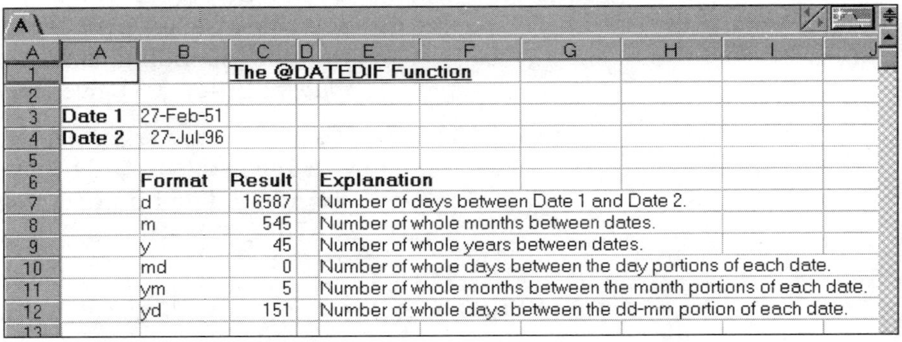

	Format	Result	Explanation
			The @DATEDIF Function
Date 1	27-Feb-51		
Date 2	27-Jul-96		
	d	16587	Number of days between Date 1 and Date 2.
	m	545	Number of whole months between dates.
	y	45	Number of whole years between dates.
	md	0	Number of whole days between the day portions of each date.
	ym	5	Number of whole months between the month portions of each date.
	yd	151	Number of whole days between the dd-mm portion of each date.

Figure 8.14:   *Using the @DATEDIF function*

TIP Several other date functions perform calculations for specialized business uses: @DAYS uses one of five algorithms to find the number of days between two dates. @NETWORKDAYS finds the number of workdays (not counting weekends and holidays) between two dates. @WORKDAY finds a workday that is a specified number of days from a given date. @NEXTMONTH finds the date that is a specified number of months from a given date. See Appendix B for information about all these functions.

Working with Date and Time Functions

In the upcoming exercises you'll see worksheet examples of date and time functions. To start, here's a simple experiment with the @NOW function and the six functions that supply information about date and time values—@DAY, @MONTH, @YEAR, @HOUR, @MINUTE, and @SECOND:

1. On a new blank worksheet, type the @NOW function into cell B1. (Recall that the function takes no argument.) To convert the function to a value, press the F9 key before you press ↵. A number representing the current date and time appears in B1. Using the Range ➤ Name command, assign the name DATETIME to this cell.

2. In cells B2 through B7, enter the following six functions:

   @DAY(DATETIME)

   @MONTH(DATETIME)

   @YEAR(DATETIME)

   @HOUR(DATETIME)

   @MINUTE(DATETIME)

   @SECOND(DATETIME)

These six functions give the components of the date and time value displayed in cell B1.

Here is an example of this experiment:

	A	B
1	Now	35273.348
2	Day	27
3	Month	7
4	Year	96
5	Hour	8
6	Minute	21
7	Second	3
8		

Of course, the date-and-time values shown here will be different from the ones on your own worksheet.

In Figure 8.15 you see a practical use of the @MONTH and @DAY functions, along with an example of the @TODAY function in a formula. The worksheet shows a list of employees; their names are displayed in column A and their birth dates in column B. Column C contains a formula that calculates each employee's age. The formula (@TODAY–B4)/365 is entered in cell C4—for the first employee—and then copied down the column. (The Fixed format with no decimal places has been applied to the column of data.) Examine this formula carefully. The expression in parentheses finds an employee's age in days by subtracting the employee's birth date from today's date:

   @TODAY–B4

Dividing this number of days by 365 gives the employee's age in years.

NOTE The @DATEDIF function is another way to carry out this calculation. Decide for yourself whether you prefer to use @DATEDIF or your own formulas for finding the difference between two dates.

	A	B	C	D	E
1		Employees' Birthdays			
2					
3	Name	Date of Birth	Age	Mo	Day
4	Graves, A.	23-Jun-35	61	6	23
5	Alcott, M.	05-Aug-39	57	8	5
6	Parker, H.	08-May-45	51	5	8
7	Dalton, R.	06-Jul-47	49	7	6
8	Hines, D.	27-Oct-51	45	10	27
9	Oliver, A.	03-Sep-54	42	9	3
10	Jackson, N.	19-Jun-59	37	6	19
11	Everett, V.	02-Dec-59	37	12	2
12	Larson, W.	07-Aug-65	31	8	7
13	Nelson, P.	02-Jan-67	30	1	2
14	Madison, I.	07-Apr-68	28	4	7
15	Burton, C.	05-Aug-69	27	8	5
16	Fine, M.	01-Feb-70	27	2	1
17	Kelley, N.	08-Nov-71	25	11	8
18	Calloway, D.	03-Mar-72	24	3	3

Figure 8.15: Using the @TODAY function to calculate employees' ages

Notice that this list is arranged by the employees' ages, in descending order—that is, from the oldest employee to the youngest, or from the earliest birth date to the most recent. Imagine the following situation: The company where these employees work has a policy of giving each employee an extra vacation day per year on the employee's birthday. To monitor these vacation days, the employees' manager would like to rearrange the employee list in order of calendar birthdays, from the first birthday in January to the last birthday in December. Accomplishing this calls for the use of the @MONTH and @DAY functions:

1. Enter the function **@MONTH(B4)** in cell D4, and the function **@DAY(B4)** in cell E4. Copy these two formulas down their respective columns, to the range D5..E18. Together, these two functions give the month and day of each employee's birthday, as shown in Figure 8.15.

2. Select the range A4..E18 and choose Range ➤ Sort. Select Column D in the Available columns list, and click the >> button twice. Columns D and E move to the Sort by list. (Make sure that the Header at top option is not checked.) Click OK or press ↵ to complete the operation.

As a result, 1-2-3 sorts the list by employees' birthdays, from January to December. As you can see in Figure 8.16, columns D and E show the month and the day of each birthday through the course of the calendar year. The manager can now use this worksheet to anticipate each employee's extra vacation day.

	A	B	C	D	E
1		Employees' Birthdays			
2					
3	Name	Date of Birth	Age	Mo	Day
4	Nelson, P.	02-Jan-67	30	1	2
5	Fine, M.	01-Feb-70	27	2	1
6	Calloway, D.	03-Mar-72	24	3	3
7	Madison, I.	07-Apr-68	28	4	7
8	Parker, H.	08-May-45	51	5	8
9	Jackson, N.	19-Jun-59	37	6	19
10	Graves, A.	23-Jun-35	61	6	23
11	Dalton, R.	06-Jul-47	49	7	6
12	Alcott, M.	05-Aug-39	57	8	5
13	Burton, C.	05-Aug-69	27	8	5
14	Larson, W.	07-Aug-65	31	8	7
15	Oliver, A.	03-Sep-54	42	9	3
16	Hines, D.	27-Oct-51	45	10	27
17	Kelley, N.	08-Nov-71	25	11	8
18	Everett, V.	02-Dec-59	37	12	2

Figure 8.16: *Using @MONTH and @DAY to sort the employee list by birthdays*

In some worksheet applications you might prefer to enter the day, month, and year components of dates in three separate columns, as shown in columns A, B, and C of the following sheet:

	A	B	C	D
1	Day	Month	Year	Date
2	31	1	63	31-Jan-63
3	28	2	61	28-Feb-61
4	21	3	93	21-Mar-93
5	5	4	71	05-Apr-71
6	9	5	88	09-May-88
7	30	6	55	30-Jun-55
8	24	7	88	24-Jul-88
9	17	8	76	17-Aug-76
10				

This arrangement may sometimes be more efficient for input purposes, especially when dates have to be read from hand-written forms and entered manually into a worksheet. Given a list of dates in this three-column format, you can use 1-2-3's @DATE function to convert the date components into date numbers—so that you can ultimately perform date arithmetic operations on the worksheet. For example, the formula entered into cell D2 is:

```
@DATE(C2,B2,A2)
```

After copying this formula down column D, you can select an appropriate date display format.

You may need to perform another kind of conversion on a sheet that contains dates or times entered as labels. In particular, this may happen if you load data into a 1-2-3 worksheet from a different software environment. The following sheet shows the date and time label formats that 1-2-3 can successfully convert into date and time numbers:

	A	B	C	D	E
1	Date String	Date Number		Time String	Time Number
2	1-Dec-96	35400		4:30:00 PM	0.6875
3	1-Dec	35400		4:30 PM	0.6875
4	Dec-96	35400		16:30:00	0.6875
5	12/1/96	35400		16:30	0.6875
6	12/1	35400			
7					

Column A of this worksheet contains examples of five date formats 1-2-3 recognizes. The @DATEVALUE function converts these labels into date numbers. The formula @DATEVALUE(A2) has been entered into cell B2 and copied down column B. Column D of the same worksheet shows examples of four time formats that 1-2-3 recognizes. In this case, the @TIMEVALUE function converts these labels into decimal time numbers. The formula @TIMEVALUE(D2) in cell E2 has been copied down column E.

The @DAYS360 and @D360 functions are available for special financial contexts in which date arithmetic is based on a 360-day year. The worksheet in Figure 8.17 shows examples of these tools. Columns A and B in this worksheet show two lists of dates. Columns C, D, and E display the results of the three techniques for finding the difference in days between pairs of dates. Here are the three formulas in cells C4, D4, and E4:

```
+B4-A4

@DAYS360(A4,B4)

@D360(A4,B4)
```

Of course, only the first of these formulas finds the exact number of days between two dates. The @DAYS360 and @D360 find approximations of the difference, for the convenience of particular financial applications. As you can see, the three formulas produce different results.

	A	B	C	D	E
1			Difference Between Two Dates		
2					
3	Date 1	Date 2	Subraction	DAYS360	D360
4	15-Jan-85	22-May-86	492	487	487
5	04-Sep-86	31-Aug-83	-1100	-1083	-1084
6	31-Oct-92	28-Feb-94	485	478	478
7	07-Jul-91	02-Nov-86	-1708	-1685	-1685
8	31-Oct-93	30-Oct-93	-1	0	0
9	11-Dec-85	27-Feb-82	-1383	-1364	-1364
10	18-Feb-89	06-Mar-87	-715	-702	-702
11	18-Feb-86	31-Aug-95	3481	3433	3432
12	30-Apr-95	30-Jun-93	-669	-660	-660
13	21-Jan-86	05-Jan-94	2906	2864	2864
14					
15					

Figure 8.17: **Comparing date arithmetic tools**

Logical Functions

1-2-3 has an interesting assortment of logical functions that supply information about a worksheet. Like logical formulas, these functions give values of 1 or 0, representing true or false. For example, the @ISNUMBER function takes a cell address as its argument, and returns a value of 1 (true) if the cell contains a value or is blank. If the cell contains a label, @ISNUMBER returns a value of 0 (false).

The @IF function

Perhaps the most important tool in the logical function category is the @IF function. This function evaluates a logical expression and chooses between one of two values, depending on whether the expression is true or false. The @IF function takes three arguments:

@IF(*expression*,*value1*,*value2*)

The first argument is the logical expression that @IF evaluates. You can use operators that you studied in Chapter 7 to build a logical expression for the @IF function—the relational operators =, <>, <, >, <=, and >=; and the logical operators #NOT#, #AND#, and #OR#.

The second and third arguments of the @IF function are the data items that the function chooses between. If the logical expression in the first argument is evaluated as true, @IF returns *value1*. If the logical expression is false, @IF gives *value2*. In other words, when you enter the @IF function into a worksheet cell, you can expect the function to display either *value1* or *value2* in the cell.

Try the following simple example:

1. Enter a value of **0** in cell A1 of a blank worksheet.
2. Enter the following formula in cell A2:

    ```
    @IF(A1=0,"zero","not zero")
    ```

    The word "zero" appears in cell A2.

3. Now select cell A1 again and enter a value of **10**. The display in cell A2 changes to "not zero."

The @IF function evaluates the expression A1=0 to decide which label to display in cell A2.

The *value1* and *value2* arguments in the @IF function can be strings enclosed in quotes, as in the previous example, or they can appear as values or calculations. For a more interesting example of the @IF function, consider the following sheet:

	A	B	C
1	Billing Date	Date + 30	Due Date
2	17-Jan-97	Sunday	Monday, February 17, 1997
3	28-Jan-97	Thursday	Thursday, February 27, 1997
4	07-Feb-97	Sunday	Monday, March 10, 1997
5	20-Feb-97	Saturday	Saturday, March 22, 1997
6	14-Mar-97	Sunday	Monday, April 14, 1997
7	25-Mar-97	Thursday	Thursday, April 24, 1997
8			

Imagine that the calculations on this worksheet are part of a billing application. Column A contains a list of dates on which a company has sent bills to its customers. Normally each invoice is payable in 30 days. However, if a 30-day due date falls on a Sunday, the formula in column C adds an additional day to produce a Monday due date. Here is the @IF function that performs this calculation in cell C2:

```
@IF(@WEEKDAY(A2+30)=6,A2+31,A2+30)
```

Logical Functions

This formula is copied down column C, to the range C3..C7. The first argument in the @IF function is an expression that determines whether the 30-day due date falls on a Sunday:

```
@WEEKDAY(A2+30)=6
```

The argument of the @WEEKDAY function adds 30 to the date in column A. If this calculated date falls on a Sunday (with a @WEEKDAY result of 6) the @IF function chooses the *value1* argument, a 31-day due date:

```
A2+31
```

But if the @WEEKDAY function shows that the 30-day due date is not a Sunday, the *value2* argument is chosen:

```
A2+30
```

For comparison, column B shows the day of the week on which the due date would fall if the formula simply added 30 days to the billing date. As you can see, the @IF function has added 31 days whenever column B shows an entry of Sunday.

Note that column C of this sheet illustrates an interesting format that is available for displaying dates. In the InfoBox for range properties, the formula is represented as "Tuesday, December 31, 1996":

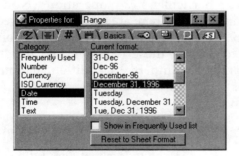

The use of the @IF function can become even more complex than this example. In some applications, you might write additional "nested" @IF functions in the positions of the *value1* and *value2* arguments of an initial @IF function. This can result in multifaceted decision-making processes for a worksheet.

Text Functions

A large library of text functions gives you the power to manipulate the contents of labels and strings in your worksheets. Text-related tasks require careful attention to detail. But some of the text functions prove to be useful worksheet tools, as you'll see in upcoming exercises.

Categories of text functions include:

- Substring functions, which find or extract sequences of characters from within existing labels
- Alphabetic case functions, which change letters to uppercase or lowercase
- Conversion functions, which produce text from numeric values, or numbers from text entries
- A miscellaneous variety of other text functions

NOTE See Appendix H for a complete explanation of text functions.

Examples of some of these functions appear in Figure 8.18. This worksheet is organized as follows: Cell A1 contains the label "Lotus 1-2-3 for windows 95." Each function example in the worksheet uses this label to illustrate a particular string operation. (Notice two odd details about the string in cell A1: There are two spaces between *for* and *windows*, and the word *windows* is not capitalized. Some functions in the worksheet illustrate ways to correct these details.) The results of the function examples appear in Column B. In addition, Column C shows complete text copies of the functions.

Substring functions

The first five examples in the worksheet show the substring functions:

Function	Arguments and Results
@LEFT	Supplies a copy of a substring from the beginning of a string. @LEFT takes two arguments, a string and an integer: @LEFT(*string*, *n*). The function supplies the first *n* characters of a string. For example, @LEFT(A1,5) displays the string "Lotus" in Figure 8.18.

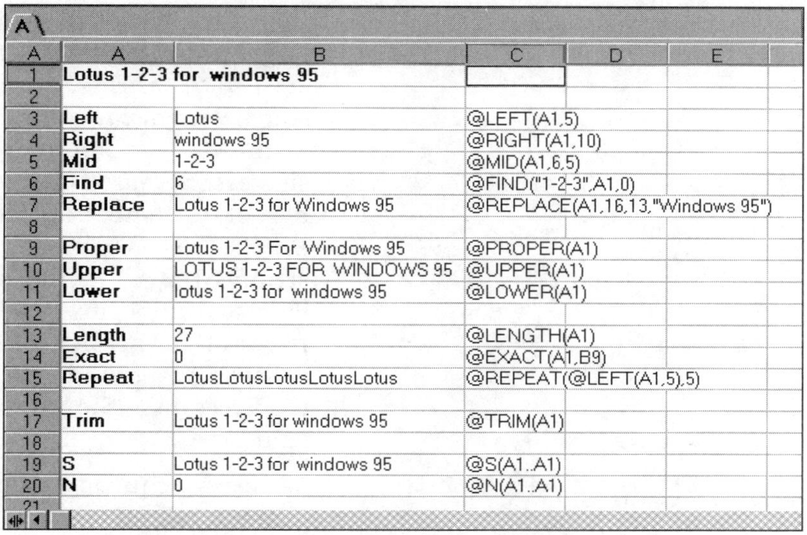

Text Functions

	A	B	C	D	E
1	Lotus 1-2-3 for windows 95				
2					
3	Left	Lotus	@LEFT(A1,5)		
4	Right	windows 95	@RIGHT(A1,10)		
5	Mid	1-2-3	@MID(A1,6,5)		
6	Find	6	@FIND("1-2-3",A1,0)		
7	Replace	Lotus 1-2-3 for Windows 95	@REPLACE(A1,16,13,"Windows 95")		
8					
9	Proper	Lotus 1-2-3 For Windows 95	@PROPER(A1)		
10	Upper	LOTUS 1-2-3 FOR WINDOWS 95	@UPPER(A1)		
11	Lower	lotus 1-2-3 for windows 95	@LOWER(A1)		
12					
13	Length	27	@LENGTH(A1)		
14	Exact	0	@EXACT(A1,B9)		
15	Repeat	LotusLotusLotusLotusLotus	@REPEAT(@LEFT(A1,5),5)		
16					
17	Trim	Lotus 1-2-3 for windows 95	@TRIM(A1)		
18					
19	S	Lotus 1-2-3 for windows 95	@S(A1..A1)		
20	N	0	@N(A1..A1)		
21					

Figure 8.18: **Experiments with text functions**

@RIGHT — Supplies a copy of a substring from the end of a string. @RIGHT also takes two arguments: @RIGHT(*string*, *n*). The function supplies the last *n* characters of *string*. For example, @RIGHT(A1,10) displays the string "windows 95" in Figure 8.18.

@MID — Supplies a copy of a substring from a position inside a string. @MID takes three arguments, a string and two integers: @MID(*string*, *pos*, *n*). The function copies *n* characters from string, starting from the position identified as *pos*. For example, @MID(A1,6,5) displays the string "1-2-3" in cell B5 of Figure 8.18. Note that the first character in a string has a *pos* value of 0; this value is sometimes called the *offset number*. The offset number for a character in a string is one less than the character's actual position in the string. For example, the seventh character in a string has a *pos* value of 6.

@FIND Identifies the position of a substring inside a larger string. @FIND takes three arguments: @FIND(*substring*, *string*, *pos*). The function searches for *substring* inside *string*, starting the search at the *pos* character in *string*. If the search is successful, @FIND returns the offset number of the substring. For example, @FIND ("1-2-3",A1, 0) in cell B7 searches for the string "1-2-3" in the label stored in cell A1. The search begins at the beginning of the label. It results in a value of 6, the offset where the substring is found. (If the @FIND search is unsuccessful, the function returns an ERR value.)

@REPLACE Writes a sequence of characters over existing characters in a string. @REPLACE takes four arguments: @REPLACE(*string*, *pos*, *n*, *substring*). The function replaces *n* characters of *string*, starting from *pos*. The substring argument supplies the replacement characters. For example, @REPLACE(A1,16,13,"Windows 95") replaces the final characters of the string.

Alphabetic case functions

The next three examples in Figure 8.18 show the alphabetic case functions @PROPER, @UPPER, and @LOWER. Each of these three functions takes a single string argument, and returns a copy of the same string with specified changes in the alphabetic case:

Function	Result
@PROPER	Capitalizes the first letter in each word of its string argument
@UPPER	Capitalizes all the letters in the string
@LOWER	Changes all the letters in the string to lowercase

Miscellaneous functions

The remaining six functions illustrated in Figure 8.18 perform a variety of string operations:

Function	Arguments and Results
@LENGTH	Supplies the length, in characters, of a string. @LENGTH takes one string argument. For example, @LENGTH(A1) displays 27 as the length of the string in cell B13 of Figure 8.18.
@EXACT	Compares two strings and determines whether or not they are the same. @EXACT returns a value of 1 (true) if its two string arguments are identical, or a value of 0 (false) if they are not. For example, @EXACT(A1,B9) returns a value of 0.
@REPEAT	Generates a new string consisting of multiple copies of a string argument. The function takes two arguments: @REPEAT(*string*, *n*). The first argument is the string to be repeated, and the second argument is an integer that specifies the number of repetitions. For example, @REPEAT(@LEFT(A1,5),5) produces five copies of the label "Lotus."
@TRIM	Removes extraneous spaces from a string—that is, spaces at the beginning and the end of the string, and multiple consecutive spaces inside the string. For example, @TRIM(A1) removes the extra space between "for" and "windows."
@S	Returns the label located in the first corner of a range. If this cell does not contain a label, @S returns an empty string. For example, the function @S(A1..A1) in B19 copies the label from cell A1.
@N	Returns the numeric value located in the first corner of a range. If this cell does not contain a value, @N returns a value of zero. For example, the function @N(A1..A1) in B20 returns a value of zero.

Among the remaining text functions, four perform conversions from one data type to another and give you access to the character code used in Lotus 1-2-3 for Windows:

Function	Arguments and Results
@CHAR	Takes an integer as its argument and supplies the corresponding character from the Lotus *Multibyte Character Set*. This character code, known by its abbreviation LMBCS, represents all the characters that can be produced and displayed in 1-2-3. Figure 8.19 shows an excerpt from the LMBCS code.
@CODE	Supplies the LMBCS code number of a given character. @CODE takes one string argument, and gives the code number of the first character in the string.
@STRING	Produces a string from a numeric value. @STRING takes two arguments: @STRING(*value*, *n*). The *value* argument is the number to be converted to a string, and the *n* argument specifies the number of decimal places that will be displayed in the result. For example, @STRING(123.456,1) produces the string "123.5" as its result.
@VALUE	Performs the opposite conversion, producing a number from a string of digits. The single argument of @VALUE must be a string that 1-2-3 can read as a number. For example, @VALUE ("9876") produces the number 9876.

The worksheet in Figure 8.20 shows two short experiments with the @STRING and @VALUE functions. The @STRING function is important in situations where you need to incorporate a numeric value into a string. The & operation will not join a string and a number. Before you can perform the concatenation, you must use @STRING to convert the number into a string. For example, cell A1 in the figure contains the calculated number of days between today's date and December 25; the following string formula combines this number with two strings to form the sentence displayed in cell A2:

```
+"There are "&@STRING(A1,0)&" shopping days 'til Christmas."
```

	A	B	C	D	E	F	G	H	I	J
1	33	!	52	4	71	G	90	Z	109	m
2	34	"	53	5	72	H	91	[	110	n
3	35	#	54	6	73	I	92	\	111	o
4	36	$	55	7	74	J	93	]	112	p
5	37	%	56	8	75	K	94	^	113	q
6	38	&	57	9	76	L	95	_	114	r
7	39	'	58	:	77	M	96	`	115	s
8	40	(	59	;	78	N	97	a	116	t
9	41	)	60	<	79	O	98	b	117	u
10	42	*	61	=	80	P	99	c	118	v
11	43	+	62	>	81	Q	100	d	119	w
12	44	,	63	?	82	R	101	e	120	x
13	45	-	64	@	83	S	102	f	121	y
14	46	.	65	A	84	T	103	g	122	z
15	47	/	66	B	85	U	104	h	123	{
16	48	0	67	C	86	V	105	i	124	|
17	49	1	68	D	87	W	106	j	125	}
18	50	2	69	E	88	X	107	k	126	~
19	51	3	70	F	89	Y	108	l	127	▮

Figure 8.19: An excerpt from the LMBCS code

	A	B	C	D
1	150			
2	There are 150 shopping days 'til Christmas.			
3				
4	We received 107 units @ $1.25 per unit.			
5				
6	107	units		
7	$1.25	per unit		
8	$133.75	total cost		
9				

Figure 8.20: Experimenting with @STRING and @VALUE

Conversely, you may sometimes need to convert a string of digits into a number so you can perform arithmetic operations on the value. The @VALUE function does this. For example, consider the sentence displayed in cell A4 of Figure 8.20: "We received 107 units @ $1.25 per unit." In order to perform arithmetic operations on the two numbers in this string, you have to extract the strings of digits and convert them into numeric values. The formulas in cells A6 and A7 illustrate the technique:

```
@VALUE(@MID(A4,12,3))

@VALUE(@MID(A4,25,4))
```

The argument in each of these @VALUE functions is a @MID function that extracts a string of digits from the sentence in cell A4. @VALUE then makes the conversion from string to number. After this conversion, the numbers can be formatted and used in numeric formulas; for example, cell A8 contains the formula +A6*A7.

Lookup Functions

The lookup functions make up an important category that includes tools such as @CHOOSE, @INDEX, @HLOOKUP, and @VLOOKUP. These functions allow you to select a data item from a table that you enter into a range of your worksheet—or, in the case of @CHOOSE, from a list that is contained within the arguments of the function itself. Using these functions requires some careful planning, because you have to begin by developing the list or table of data. But once you have organized your worksheet appropriately, these functions prove to be very powerful tools, as you'll see in this chapter's final exercises.

The @CHOOSE function

@CHOOSE is the easiest function to use in this category. It takes one numeric argument, n, followed by a list of data values or references to cells:

```
@CHOOSE(n, datalist)
```

The purpose of *n* is to select one of the values in *datalist*. The value of *n* must be within the range from 0 up to the number of entries in the list, minus 1. Using *n* as an offset number, @CHOOSE returns the *n*th value in the list.

For example, suppose you're using a worksheet to plan the visual elements of a graphic design. Each row of the worksheet describes the characteristics of one part of your design—position, shape, color, and so on. You've used numeric codes from 0 to 4 for five colors you're planning to use in the design—blue, green, red, yellow, and purple—and you've entered one of these codes into column B for each element of your design. Now you want to translate these codes into the names of colors. To do so, you'll enter and copy this formula into C2 and copy the formula down column C:

```
@CHOOSE(B2,"blue","green","red","yellow","purple")
```

The @INDEX function

By contrast, the @INDEX function selects a label or value from a table on your worksheet. @INDEX takes three required arguments and one optional argument. Here is its format with three arguments:

    @INDEX(range, column, row)

The *range* argument is the location of the table where @INDEX reads a data item. The *column* and *row* arguments identify a column and a row as offsets within a range. The *column* argument ranges from 0 up to the number of columns in the table, minus 1. Likewise, the *row* argument ranges from 0 up to the number of rows in the table, minus 1. The fourth optional argument is an integer representing the sheet that contains the lookup table:

    @INDEX(range, column, row, sheet)

This argument allows you to build the lookup table in a different sheet location than the function itself.

For example, suppose you've entered the names of five colors (blue, green, red, yellow, and purple) into a column range named COLORS on your graphic design worksheet. The following @INDEX function is an alternative approach for translating the color codes in column B into color names:

    @INDEX($COLORS,0,B1)

This function uses each code number in column B as an index into the color table stored in the $COLORS range.

The @HLOOKUP and @VLOOKUP functions

Finally, the @HLOOKUP and @VLOOKUP functions read values from specially organized lookup tables. The first row or column of a lookup table contains a range of reference values that are central to the process of searching for a target data item in the table.

For example, consider the Conference Room Price Table, shown in the lower part of the worksheet in Figure 8.21. The conference planners at Computing Conferences, Inc., use this table to determine the price of a downtown conference room for a one-day event. As you can see, the price of a conference room varies by the number of people attending and by the date of the event. To find the correct price for an expected attendance size, *n*, you begin by looking across the first row of the table, which contains a range of attendance figures from 1 to 300. Find the largest value in this row that is less than or equal to *n*. This value heads the column in which you will find the price for the conference room. Next, look down the column to the row containing the year of the conference. The correct price is found in the cell at the intersection of the attendance column and date row.

	A	B	C	D	E	F	G	H
1		Computing Conferences, Inc.						
2		Conference Room Expense						
3								
4	Conference:	Computing for Video Stores						
5	Place:	St. Louis						
6	Date:	15-Oct-97			Expected Attendance			
7					Min	Max		
8	Price:	$195			80	150		
9								
10		Conference room cost:			$1,750.00	$2,300.00		
11								
12								
13								
14		Conference Room Price Table						
15		Attendance -->	1	35	75	100	150	200	300
16		1996 Price	$400	$600	$1,500	$1,750	$2,000	$3,000	$3,500
17		1997 Price	$450	$700	$1,750	$1,899	$2,300	$3,400	$3,700
18		1998 Price	$500	$750	$1,900	$2,000	$2,500	$3,500	$3,850

Figure 8.21: **Using the @HLOOKUP function**

The @HLOOKUP function automates this search. The function takes three arguments—a look-up value, a table range, and a row offset:

@HLOOKUP(*n*, *table*, *row*)

The first argument, *n*, is the value that the function looks for in the first row of the lookup table. The second argument, *table*, is the range of the lookup table itself, and the third argument, *row*, is the target row offset in the table.

In Figure 8.21, the @HLOOKUP function is used in cells E10 and F10 to find the conference room costs corresponding to the minimum and maximum attendance estimates. The table in the range B15..H18 is assigned the name ROOM. The two attendance estimates are in E8 and F8. Here is the function in cell E10:

@HLOOKUP(E8,$ROOM,2)

In this example, E8 is the attendance estimate that the function looks for in the first row of the ROOM range. A row offset of 2 gives the correct row for a 1997 conference date. In short, the @HLOOKUP function finds the conference room price corresponding to an estimated attendance of 80 people. In the first row of the look-up table, the largest value that is less than or equal to 80 is the attendance figure of 75 in cell D15. Searching down column D to the 1997 row, the function finds the correct price for the conference room, $1,750 in cell D17.

The @VLOOKUP function performs an equivalent data search, but in a vertically organized look-up table:

@VLOOKUP(*n*, *table*, *column*)

This function searches for *n* in the first column of table. The third argument, *column*, gives the column offset in the look-up table.

You can also enter labels rather than numbers in the first row or column of a look-up table. In this case, the first argument in the @HLOOKUP and @VLOOKUP functions is a string:

@HLOOKUP(*string*, *table*, *row*)

@VLOOKUP(*string*, *table*, *column*)

The @HLOOKUP function looks for a label that exactly matches *string* in the first row of the look-up table. Likewise, the @VLOOKUP function looks for a match for *string* in the first column of the table.

The @HLOOKUP and @VLOOKUP functions are versatile and powerful, especially in applications that require very large look-up tables. Of course, the classic example is an income tax table, in which the first column contains a range of income levels, and the first row contains taxpayer categories. The @VLOOKUP function is ideally suited to read tax amounts from such a table.

Summary

The 1-2-3 function library includes almost three hundred tools that can be entered into cells by themselves or used in formulas. Here is a brief summary of the function categories presented in this chapter:

▶ The statistical functions include tools designed to calculate totals, averages, counts, and maximum and minimum values, along with the more advanced statistical calculations known as variance and standard deviation.

- The financial functions include calculations for depreciation methods; present value and future value; payment, term, and rate values; and the internal rate of return.

- Mathematical functions include built-in formulas for trigonometric, logarithmic, and exponential values, plus an assortment of other important tools: a random number generator, integer and rounding functions, and the absolute value and modulus operations.

- The date and time functions include tools that supply the current date and time, functions that give information about date and time values, conversion functions, and date arithmetic functions.

- An important logical function for spreadsheet use is @IF, which evaluates a logical expression and returns one of two values as its result.

- The text functions include tools that work with substrings, alphabetic case functions, and functions that convert between numeric and string values.

- The lookup functions include important tools that read values from tables and lists on the worksheet.

CHAPTER 9

Introduction to Charts

Fast Track

To create a chart from a table of worksheet data,   296
select an appropriate range of worksheet data, choose Create ➤ Chart, and drag the mouse pointer over the area where you want to display the chart.

To create more room for displaying a chart,   301
pull down the View menu and choose a Hide command, temporarily removing the SmartIcons, the status bar, or the edit line from the Desktop.

To display titles and labels in a chart,   301
select a sheet range that includes descriptive labels along with the numeric data. 1-2-3 automatically determines how to use sheet labels for the elements of the chart.

To resize a chart,   302
select the chart and use the mouse to drag any one of the selection handles displayed around the perimeter of the chart.

To move a chart to a new position on a sheet,   302
select the chart and use the mouse to drag the chart's border to a new position.

To open the InfoBox for chart properties,   304

select a chart by clicking along its border, then choose Chart ➤ Chart Properties.

To change the properties of a particular chart element,   304

pull down the Properties for list on the title bar of the chart InfoBox, and choose the chart element that you want to change. Alternatively, click any chart element with the right mouse button and choose the Properties command from the resulting shortcut menu.

To change the format of numbers displayed along a bar chart's y-axis,   305

click the axis with the right mouse button and choose the Y-Axis Properties command from the resulting shortcut menu. Click the Number Format tab in the resulting InfoBox, and choose a format.

To switch to a different chart type,   308

select the chart you want to change and choose Chart ➤ Chart Type. In the InfoBox, select a chart type and click a chart style button.

To redefine data series by rows or by columns,   308

select the chart that you want to redefine, and choose Chart ➤ Ranges. In the Ranges tab of the resulting InfoBox, click the Options button. In the Range Options dialog box, select an option from the Assign Ranges list, and click OK.

To redraw a chart for new data in the underlying worksheet table,   310

simply enter the new data. 1-2-3 automatically redraws the chart to match the changes in the data.

To add a drawn object to a chart or a worksheet,   311

choose the appropriate command from the Create menu—for example, Create ➤ Text or Create ➤ Drawing ➤ Arrow. Drag the mouse pointer through the area where you want to display the object.

IN business, technology, and everyday life, charts have a universal appeal. People often prefer to look at pictorial representations of numbers rather than the numbers themselves. Grasping the sense of a table of numbers requires time, effort, and concentration—but a chart has an instant impact. When you look at a chart, you can answer many questions about the data, almost before you can even ask the questions: Which data item is the smallest and which is the largest? Is there a downward or upward trend over time? Are there any atypical values that don't conform to the trends of the other data? How significant is a given value in relation to the total? The answers to these and many other questions are visibly clear in a chart of numeric data.

Producing a chart in 1-2-3 is simple, yet you can create an extraordinary variety of visual effects. There are several major chart types to choose from. The most familiar are bar charts, line charts, area charts, and pie charts; these are available in both two-dimensional and three-dimensional versions. In addition, you can create XY charts, mixed charts, high-low-close-open charts, doughnut charts, and radar charts for special kinds of data.

A chart resides on a sheet in 1-2-3—on the same sheet that displays the chart's underlying data, or on another sheet that you select. A chart is an object that can be moved and resized within the sheet that contains it.

When you select a chart, 1-2-3 replaces the Range menu with the Chart menu, which contains a variety of commands for refining and modifying the appearance of a chart:

In addition, distinct sets of chart-related status bar buttons and SmartIcons appear on the Desktop, as shown in Figure 9.1. Of particular interest is the Chart Properties SmartIcon; clicking this tool opens the InfoBox for chart properties:

Like other InfoBoxes you've seen, this box provides access to many properties and settings in a single convenient location. It gives you efficient and powerful ways to change the appearance of a chart.

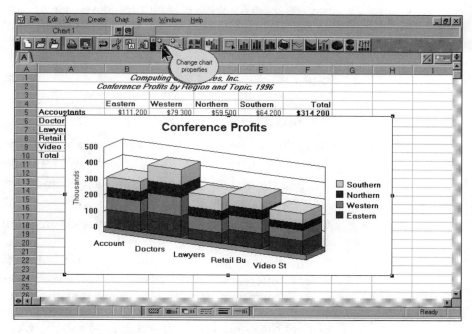

Figure 9.1: When you select a chart, 1-2-3 displays a distinct set of status bar buttons and SmartIcons.

You can also use a variety of simple mouse and keyboard actions to refine and clarify the visual impact of a chart. For example, you can:

- Click any chart element with the right mouse button to view a shortcut menu of commands that apply to the selected object
- Drag individual elements of a chart to new positions
- Add drawn objects to a chart—special graphic objects such as arrows and text boxes, designed to highlight or emphasize specific elements of the chart

In this chapter you'll learn to create effective graphic representations of data, using charts and drawn objects.

Developing a Chart

A chart is linked to data on a sheet and is saved as part of a workbook file. A sheet can have multiple charts, each identified by a unique name. To create a chart, you begin by developing the table of data that the chart will ultimately represent. Once the sheet is ready, you follow a pattern of simple steps to develop your chart:

1. Select the range of data.
2. Choose Create ➤ Chart, or click the Chart SmartIcon on the Range SmartIcon bar.
3. Drag the mouse over the worksheet area where you want to display the chart. When you release the mouse button, the chart appears.
4. Change the chart's type, style, and appearance in any way that meets your requirements.
5. Optionally, print the chart—either by itself or with its underlying worksheet data.

In an initial series of exercises presented in this chapter, you'll create several different charts from one fairly simple worksheet example. The sheet, shown in Figure 9.2, is a one-year profit summary from Computing Conferences, Inc. The sheet's columns show the profits from each of the company's four regions—Eastern, Western, Northern, and

Southern. The rows represent the conference topics—that is, the various types of computer-training conferences that the company conducts in each region—for accountants, doctors, lawyers, retail businesses, and video stores.

	A	B	C	D	E	F
1		Computing Conferences, Inc.				
2		Conference Profits by Region and Topic, 1996				
3						
4		Eastern	Western	Northern	Southern	Total
5	Accountants	$111,200	$79,300	$59,500	$64,200	**$314,200**
6	Doctors	$131,900	$116,900	$77,500	$96,700	**$423,000**
7	Lawyers	$63,500	$81,500	$54,000	$88,400	**$287,400**
8	Retail Business	$92,800	$88,600	$57,900	$78,400	**$317,700**
9	Video Stores	$88,300	$63,200	$41,900	$61,900	**$255,300**
10	Total	**$487,700**	**$429,500**	**$290,800**	**$389,600**	**$1,597,600**
11						

Figure 9.2: **The Conference Profits worksheet**

To prepare for the exercises ahead, your first job is to create a copy of this data table for yourself. On a blank sheet, enter the titles in cells A1 and A2, and center these labels over the range A1..F2. Enter the region headings in row 4, and the conference topic categories in column A. Then enter the profit amounts in the range B5..E9. To calculate the row and column of totals, simply enter the label **Total** in cells A10 and F5. 1-2-3 enters the appropriate @SUM formulas in row 10 and column F. Format the table as you see it in Figure 9.2.

The numbers from which you'll create your first chart are located in the range B5..E9. The labels for this data are in column A and row 4. Before you create a chart from this worksheet, consider the two different ways in which 1-2-3 might translate this data into a chart.

Understanding Data Series

Suppose you're planning to create a vertical bar chart from the Profits worksheet. The height of each bar in the chart will represent the profit level from one conference topic in a particular region. Because the worksheet contains four columns by five rows of numbers, there will be twenty bars in a chart to represent all the data.

Within this context, there are two ways to organize the chart—by conference topic or by region. Grouping together all the bars for a given conference topic, 1-2-3 produces a chart that looks like this:

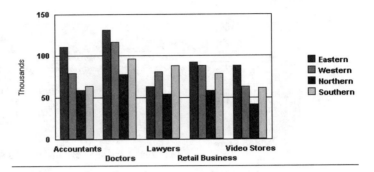

In this chart, each group of bars represents the four regional profit figures for one conference topic. The values displayed along the y-axis (the chart's vertical axis) show the profit levels. The labels along the x-axis (the horizontal axis) identify the conference topics, and the legend at the right side of the chart shows the color codes used to represent each region. This chart makes it easy to see which region has the highest profit for a particular type of conference. The regions make up the four distinctly colored data series in this chart.

By contrast, the following chart organizes the bars by region:

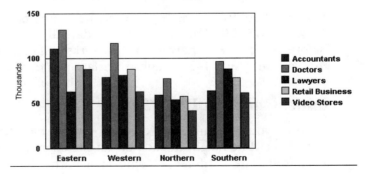

In this chart, each group of bars represents the five conference topics for a given region. The labels along the x-axis identify the regions, and the legend shows the color code for each conference topic. This chart shows the most profitable and the least profitable conference topic in each region. The conference topics make up the five data series in this chart.

TIP As you can see already, charts come with their own special vocabulary. Here's a quick review of the terms you've encountered so far: The x-axis is the horizontal axis along the bottom of a chart. The y-axis is the vertical axis at the left side of a chart. A data series is a distinct visual way of representing one range of data that the chart is based on. The legend is a box that identifies the colors, shades, or shapes that represent data series in the chart.

In short, 1-2-3 can create the data series for a chart from the rows or the columns of a worksheet table. Which of these two charts will 1-2-3 create initially? The answer depends on the number of rows and columns of numeric data in the table itself:

▶ If the number of rows is greater than the number of columns, the data series in the chart are based on columns of numeric data. This is the default in the Profits worksheet: There are five rows of conference topics and four columns of regional data. The initial chart is therefore based on regions.

▶ If the number of columns is greater than or equal to the number of rows, the data series are based on rows of data.

Look back at the Profits worksheet (see Figure 9.2) and the two column charts you can create from it; you'll quickly see the distinction between these two schemes. With this much background information, you're ready to create your first chart.

TIP Whether 1-2-3 initially creates a chart by rows or by columns, you can easily switch between the two ways of organizing charts using the InfoBox for chart properties, as you'll learn later in this chapter.

Creating the Profits Chart

By carefully selecting all the relevant information on the underlying sheet, you can instantly create a chart that contains all the elements you want. Try it now:

1. Select the range A1..E9 on the Profits worksheet. This range includes the title, subtitle, row and column headings, and the actual numeric data. (It doesn't include the row and the column of totals, which will not be part of this chart.)

2. Choose Create ➤ Chart or click the Chart SmartIcon. Then move the mouse pointer back into the worksheet area, to cell A11. Notice that the pointer takes the shape of a small chart icon with a cross marker.

3. Hold down the left mouse button and drag the pointer from cell A11 down to cell H23. A dotted boundary marks the large rectangle where your chart will appear.

4. Release the mouse button. 1-2-3 immediately draws a chart based on the data in the Profits worksheet, as you can see in Figure 9.3.

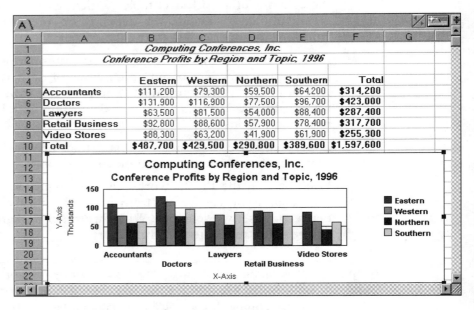

Figure 9.3: *The first chart from the Profits worksheet*

NOTE After you choose Create ➤ Chart, you can define the size and shape of your chart by dragging the mouse over an area on your sheet, as in the previous exercise. But if you're willing to accept a default size for the chart, you can simply click the mouse at a position on the sheet. The spot where you click becomes the upper-left corner of the chart frame.

> **TIP** If you don't select a chartable range of data before choosing Create ➤ Chart, 1-2-3 displays the Chart Assistant dialog box. This dialog box prompts you to select an appropriate range of data as the basis for a chart. Then you click OK to create the chart.

Take a careful look at the chart you've created. 1-2-3 has made appropriate use of all the information you've selected on the Profits worksheet:

▶ The labels stored in cells A1 and A2 of the sheet have become the chart's title and subtitle.

▶ The column headings in row 4 are displayed in the chart's legend, which identifies the colors that represent the four regions of data.

▶ The conference topics in column A appear along the x-axis to identify the five groups of bars in the chart.

All these elements have been included in your chart automatically, as a result of the worksheet range you selected before clicking the Chart SmartIcon. In a few seconds you've created a chart that is nearly ready to be used as a tool for presenting your data.

> **TIP** To give yourself more room to view both a chart and the data it's based on, you may want to hide, temporarily, the edit line, the SmartIcons, and the status bar. Choose View ➤ Hide SmartIcons, View ➤ Hide Edit Line, and View ➤ Hide Status Bar to do so. You can always bring these elements back onto the Desktop by choosing the appropriate View ➤ Show commands. In the meantime, you'll use menu commands—rather than SmartIcons or status bar buttons—to perform operations on your chart.

Moving and Resizing a Chart

1-2-3 gives you many interesting ways to refine and enhance charts. Notice the selection handles, the small black squares displayed around the perimeter of the chart object. These indicate that the chart is selected and ready to be modified in any number of ways. For example, you can change the size and dimensions of the chart, and you can move it to a new location. In the following steps, you'll increase the height of the chart and then you'll move it further down the worksheet so that you can view the chart and data at the same time:

1. Position the mouse pointer over the selection handle located just above the chart title. When you do so, the pointer takes the shape of a cross with four arrowheads, pointing up, down, left, and right. This icon indicates that you can resize the chart:

   ```
   500 | $290,800
        ⤯
   Conferences,
   ```

2. Hold down the left mouse button and drag the chart's border up to the bottom of row 7 in the worksheet.

3. Release the mouse button. When you do so, 1-2-3 immediately redraws the chart within the new dimensions of the resized chart box.

4. Position the mouse pointer at any blank spot inside the chart box. Hold down the left mouse button and begin dragging the pointer down. The pointer takes the shape of a closed fist holding onto a rectangle.

5. Drag the chart border down to the bottom of row 10, and release the mouse button. The chart is now displayed just beneath the worksheet data.

6. Position the mouse pointer over the down-arrow button at the bottom of the vertical scroll bar, and click the left mouse button three times. This action scrolls the worksheet so that you can see the data and the chart, as in Figure 9.4.

The larger chart results in a clearer presentation, yet still gives you room to view the data along with the chart. Now you'll try changing the appearance and format of specific elements within the chart.

TIP To deselect a chart, click any cell in the sheet that contains the chart. To select the chart again, click along the chart's border or at an empty area within the chart box.

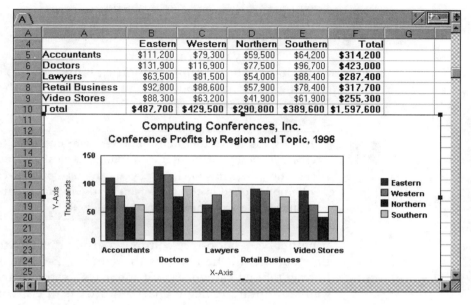

Figure 9.4: Moving and resizing the chart area

Changing the Elements of the Chart

Looking closely at the chart, you may find several items that you'd like to change. For example, 1-2-3 has supplied generic titles for the chart axes—currently these titles are displayed as Y-Axis and X-Axis. You may want to change these to titles that have meaning for your particular graph; alternatively, you have the option of deleting one or both of the titles to make more room for the data series themselves. In addition, it would be nice to apply a currency format to the numbers that appear along the vertical axis. And you may want to experiment with a new position for the legend.

To change the format or appearance of an item in a chart, you can pull down the Chart menu and choose the appropriate command. For example:

▶ The Chart ➤ Title command allows you to change the content and position of the chart's title and subtitle.

▶ Chart ➤ Legend is for changing the appearance and position of the legend.

▶ Chart ➤ Axes and Grids commands control the format of the two axes, and the labels and titles displayed along the axes.

Alternatively, you can use shortcut menus to make changes in chart items. To do so, position the mouse pointer over an object in the chart, click the right mouse button, and select from the shortcut menu of relevant commands.

> **TIP** As you move the mouse pointer from one item to another inside the chart, you'll see the pointer icon change to a variety of different shapes, representing the kinds of changes you can make on a given item. For example, when positioned over a text element, the mouse pointer takes the shape of a small white arrowhead with an *A* below it.

Whether you choose a command from the Chart menu or from a shortcut menu, the result is the same: 1-2-3 opens an InfoBox containing tabbed categories of properties for the chart element that you want to modify. Once a chart InfoBox is open, you can switch from one set of properties to another by pulling down the Properties for list in the title bar:

As you can see, this list contains the names of the various chart elements that can be modified. Choose the name of an item, and the InfoBox displays the relevant property settings.

You'll use the chart InfoBox in the following exercise, as you go about changing the appearance of your chart:

1. Position the mouse pointer over the X-Axis title and click the right mouse button. In the resulting shortcut menu, choose the X-Axis Properties command. 1-2-3 displays the chart InfoBox, with X-axis selected in the Properties for list.

2. Click the Titles tab. In the Show title box, type the new title as **Conference Topics**:

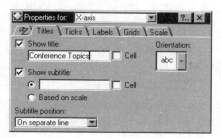

3. Press ↵. The new title appears beneath the x-axis.

4. Click the Font tab (the first tab in the InfoBox). In the Style list, click the Bold option:

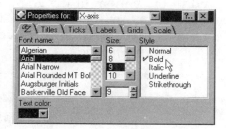

You can select a font, a point size, a set of style attributes, and a color for any text that appears in the chart.

5. Pull down the Properties for list in the title bar of the InfoBox and choose the Y-Axis item. Click the Titles tab and then click the Show title option to remove the check from the corresponding box. This action deletes the y-axis title from the chart area.

6. Click the Number Format tab (the second tab in the InfoBox). In the Format type list choose Currency; then choose US Dollar in the Current format list. Change the Decimal places setting to **0**:

7. Finally, pull down the Properties for list in the title bar of the InfoBox, and choose Legend. Click the Options tab if necessary. In the Position group, click the option button that represents the lower-center position for the legend:

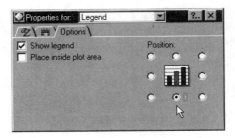

Now you can close the InfoBox. As a result of your last step, 1-2-3 has moved the legend to the bottom of the graph area, as shown in Figure 9.5. Suppose you're not satisfied with this final change. Click the Undo SmartIcon now (or choose Edit ➤ Undo Chart Edit); the legend moves back to its original position.

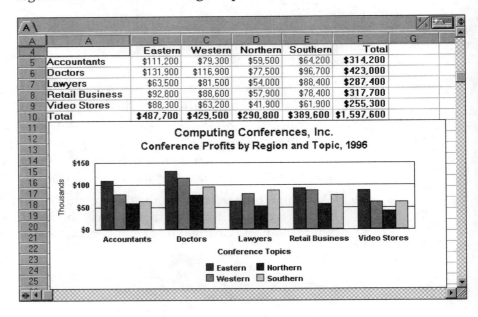

Figure 9.5:   *Moving the legend below the chart*

Figure 9.6 shows the chart at this point in your work. In a very short time, you've made some small but important changes in several elements of the chart, including axis titles, axis labels, and the legend. You've seen that charting is a direct, efficient process in 1-2-3. Now you'll experiment with different ways of organizing and presenting your chart.

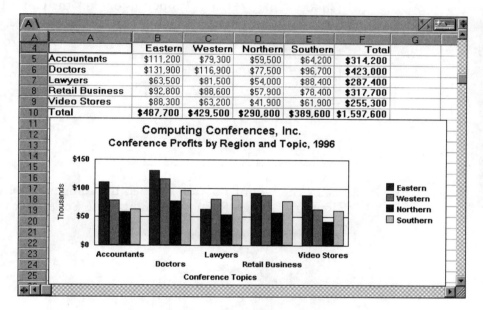

Figure 9.6: Making changes in the elements of a chart

Changing the Data Series and the Chart Type

In the next exercise you'll transform this chart into a stacked bar chart, where the height of one bar represents the total profit for a given region, and the stacked components in a bar represent the profits from individual conference topics within a region. This change involves two main steps. First you'll switch from column-oriented to row-oriented data series. Then you'll change to a stacked bar chart. Along the way, you'll also experiment with the option of a three-dimensional chart. Although these steps will produce very dramatic revisions in the chart's appearance, you'll see that they are just as simple to carry out as the changes you've already made.

Once again you can choose settings for these operations from the chart InfoBox:

1. If the chart is not currently selected, click the mouse pointer along the border or at any empty position inside the chart box. 1-2-3 once again displays selection handles around the border of the chart.

2. Choose Chart ➤ Chart Properties or click the Chart Properties Smart-Icon. Click the Ranges tab in the resulting InfoBox:

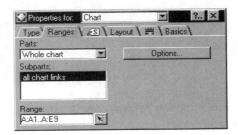

3. Click the Options button to open the Range Options dialog box. Pull down the Assign Ranges list and choose Series by row; then click OK:

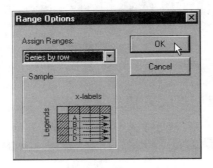

1-2-3 rearranges the chart into four groups of bars, where each group represents regional profits. Because the four region names are now displayed along the x-axis, you can see that the axis title "Conference Topics" is no longer appropriate.

4. Pull down the Properties for list in the title bar of the chart InfoBox and choose X-axis. Click the Titles tab and then click the Show title option to remove the check from the corresponding check box. The x-axis title disappears from the chart.

5. Pull down the Properties for list again and choose Chart. If necessary, click the Type tab. In the Chart type list, click the Stacked Bar option. Then click the button representing a three-dimensional stacked bar, just to the right of the Chart type list:

Close the InfoBox. Figure 9.7 shows the result of your work in this exercise. You've achieved the effect that you wanted: Each stacked bar represents one of the four regions, and each portion of a given bar represents one of the conference topics. This presentation makes it easy to compare the profits of the four regions and the profits from specific conference topics within a region.

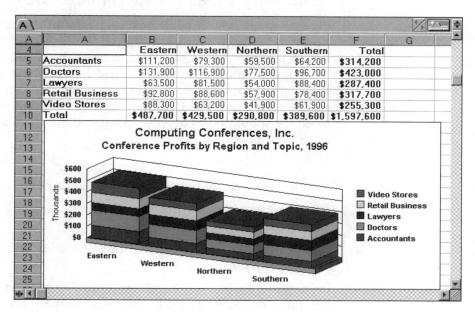

Figure 9.7: **Creating a stacked bar chart**

TIP Interestingly, the chart InfoBox gives you a simple way to view a data table inside the chart frame. With the chart selected, choose Chart ➤ Table, and then check the Show data table option in the resulting InfoBox. Close the InfoBox. Beneath the chart, 1-2-3 displays the data values that the chart represents. You can choose Edit ➤ Undo Chart Edit to restore the chart to its previous appearance.

 TIP The Type tab in the InfoBox for chart properties gives you options for changing a vertical bar chart to a horizontal chart. Click the chart with the right mouse button, and choose Chart Properties from the shortcut menu. Click the Type tab. At the right side of the InfoBox, click one of the horizontal bar chart options. Then close the InfoBox. In the resulting chart, the bars extend from the left side of the chart to the right instead of from bottom to top. Choose Edit ➤ Undo Chart Edit to switch back to a vertical chart. The Horizontal option is available for other chart types as well.

Performing What-If Experiments with a Chart

What happens now if you make a change in the original data on the sheet to which the charts are linked? For example, imagine this situation: After creating these charts, one of the managers at Computing Conferences, Inc., discovers a clerical error. The profit amount for video store training conferences in the Southern region has been underreported by $100,000. Instead of the current $61,900, the figure in cell E9 should be $161,900. What will the chart look like when this figure is corrected?

To find out, follow these steps:

1. Double-click cell E9 to switch into the Edit mode.

2. Press the Home key to move the flashing insertion point to the beginning of the entry in the cell.

3. Type **1** from the keyboard, and press ↵ to enter the corrected profit value, $161,900.

   As shown in Figure 9.8, 1-2-3 has redrawn the chart in response to the correction on the worksheet. Now the Southern region has the highest profits of the four regions.

Developing a Chart   311

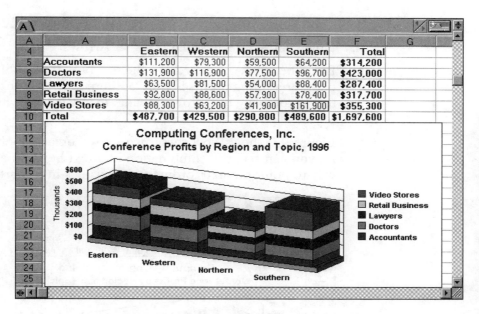

Figure 9.8:   *The stacked bar chart, redrawn in response to new data*

To focus attention on a particular value in the chart, you can add a block of text and an arrow that points from the text to the appropriate item in the chart. These are examples of drawn objects, which you can place anywhere on a chart or sheet. In the next section you'll try your hand at adding such objects to the stacked bar chart.

Adding Drawn Objects to a Chart

Drawn objects can be displayed in any size and at any position in a chart. You may need to experiment for a while before you're satisfied with the results of your work in the upcoming exercise. You'll begin by adding a block of text to the chart, and then you'll draw an arrow from the text to the chart. The purpose of these additions is to highlight the unusually high profits for the Video conferences in the Southern region:

1. Choose Create ➤ Text.
2. Drag the mouse pointer to form a rectangle in the blank space at the upper-right corner of the chart area. Release the mouse button.

3. Type **Congratulations** and press ↵. Then type **Video Group!**.
4. Now choose Create ➤ Drawing ➤ Arrow.
5. Drag the mouse pointer from the text box down to the top stack of the bar representing profits in the Southern region. Release the mouse button to complete the arrow drawing, then click elsewhere to deselect the object.

Figure 9.9 shows how these two drawn objects look inside the chart. As you can see, the combination of a text box and an arrow is a good way to point out extraordinary data values in a chart or a worksheet.

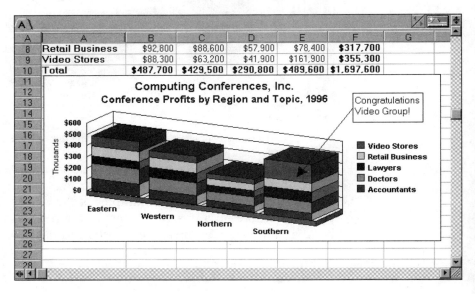

Figure 9.9: **Adding a text block and an arrow to the chart**

This is the end of your work with the Profits sheet and chart. Choose File ➤ Save to save the worksheet file to disk. If you like, you can try printing the worksheet with its chart. Choose File and click Print in the resulting dialog box.

Summary

A chart resides on a worksheet in 1-2-3 and is saved as part of the worksheet file. You can produce a chart from a range that includes labels, numeric values, and titles. After selecting an appropriate range, you choose Create ➤ Chart or click the Chart SmartIcon and then drag the mouse through the sheet area where you want to display the chart. 1-2-3 determines how to use the data in the sheet for the elements of the chart, including titles, axis labels, data series, and a legend.

When a chart object is selected, 1-2-3 replaces the Range menu with the Chart menu and also displays distinct SmartIcons and status bar buttons for modifying, refining, and enhancing the elements of a chart. In particular, the Chart ➤ Chart Properties command opens the Info-Box for chart properties. The Type tab provides a variety of chart types, including bar, line, area, and pie charts.

1-2-3 defines the data series for a chart depending on the row-and-column arrangement of the underlying data table. But once a chart is created, you can redefine the data series for the chart by row or by column. The choice between row and column data series often determines the focus and emphasis of the chart itself.

Drawn objects such as text blocks and arrows can be useful additions to a chart. A block of text with an arrow is a way of focusing attention on a particular element of the chart itself. To add one of these objects to a chart or a sheet, simply choose the appropriate command from the Create menu and then drag the mouse pointer over the area where you want to display the object.

CHAPTER 10

Chart Types and Maps

Fast Track

To switch between stacked and unstacked layouts in a line chart,   319

select the chart, and choose Chart ➤ Plot. Click the Layout tab. Then pull down the Lines list and choose either the Stacked or Not Stacked option.

To assign a new name to a chart,   321

select the chart and choose Chart ➤ Chart Properties. Click the Basics tab. In the Chart name text box, enter a new name for the chart and press ↵.

To use the Go To dialog box to select a chart,   321

press F5 or Ctrl+G to open the dialog box. Pull down the Type of object list and choose Chart. Then select the target chart in the Names list.

To create a pie chart,   322

select a row or column of labels and a corresponding row or column of numeric data. (The two ranges need not be contiguous. To select noncontiguous ranges, hold down the Ctrl key while you drag the mouse over the second range.) Choose Create ➤ Chart and drag the mouse pointer to create the chart. Then choose Chart ➤ Chart Type and choose the Pie option in the Chart type list.

To explode a pie chart wedge, 327

use your mouse to drag the wedge away from the circumference of the other wedges.

To set the default chart type, 329

select a chart and then choose Chart ➤ Chart Style ➤ Set Default Chart. In the Set Default Chart dialog box, choose a basic chart type and style and click OK.

To switch to a mixed chart format, 332

select the chart you want to modify, and choose Chart ➤ Chart Type. Select the Mixed option in the Chart type list. Then choose Chart ➤ Series. In the Options tab, select the data series for which you want to change the chart type. Check the Plot against 2nd Y-axis option. Pull down the Mixed type list, and choose the type for the target series.

To create a map, 339

enter a list of state or country names (or map code abbreviations) into a range, along with a corresponding range of numeric data. Select the entire range of names and values, and choose Create ➤ Map. Move the mouse pointer to the worksheet position where you want to display the map and click the left mouse button.

To zoom in on a portion of a map, 339

hold down the Ctrl-key and the left mouse button, and drag the mouse pointer around the map area that you want to zoom. Then release the mouse button.

To complete your introduction to charting, this chapter surveys the chart types available in 1-2-3. As you'll learn by studying a variety of examples, some charts are of general use for depicting almost any two-dimensional table of numeric data; others are best suited to very specific categories and arrangements of information.

You'll also explore 1-2-3's mapping feature, a dramatic tool for presenting geographically-oriented data. In a map, 1-2-3 sets up a color code to represent ranges of numeric data and assigns these colors appropriately to individual locations in the map. Maps are easy to create, and provide a very impressive medium for national or global information.

This chapter guides you through a series of exercises with charts and maps.

Working with Other Chart Types

Throughout Chapter 9 you worked with one of the simplest but most commonly used of chart types, the bar chart. Now you'll review the other types available in 1-2-3, including line charts, area charts, pie and doughnut charts, XY charts, mixed charts, HLCO charts, and radar charts.

Creating Line Charts and Area Charts

Line and area charts are useful for illustrating the upward or downward trends in data over time. Both types are available in two-dimensional and three-dimensional formats, and can be produced in unstacked and stacked versions. In an unstacked chart, each point on a line represents an actual value from the corresponding data range. In a stacked chart, the values of each data range are added to the accumulated values of previous data ranges, so that the top line of the chart represents the totals of all the data ranges.

For example, the worksheet at the top of Figure 10.1 shows a table of yearly regional profit figures over a five-year period. Below the data table you see a line chart created from this profit table. Each line in the chart represents regional profit variations. Notice that some of the lines cross each other one or more times; this is typical of an unstacked line chart. By contrast, Figure 10.2 shows the stacked version of the same chart, and Figure 10.3 shows a stacked area chart. In both of these stacked charts, the upward trend of the top line shows the combined profits for the four regions over the five-year period.

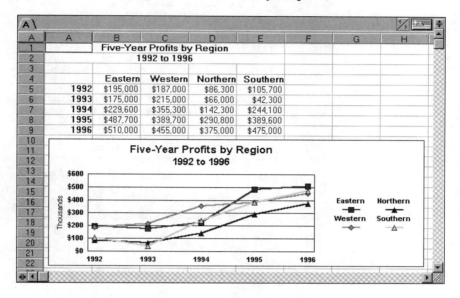

Figure 10.1: *An unstacked line chart of regional profits over a five-year period*

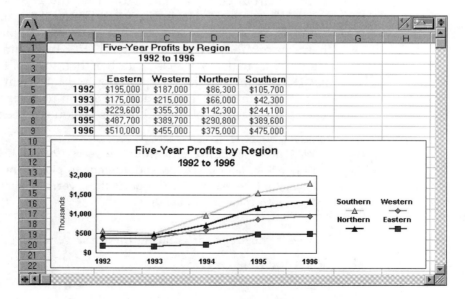

Figure 10.2: *A stacked line chart, showing combined profit growth over the period*

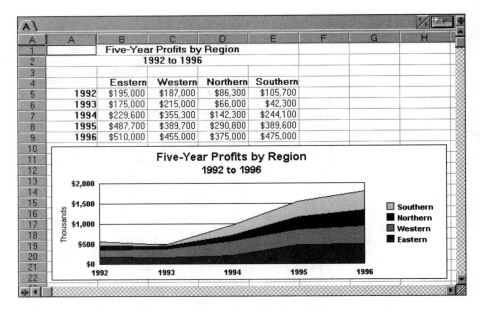

Figure 10.3: A stacked area chart of the same regional profit data

You'll create these three charts in the upcoming exercise. Start your work by producing the data table that the charts will be based on. Enter the numeric data table from Figure 10.1 onto a blank worksheet. Enter the title and subtitle into cells A1 and A2, and center them horizontally over the range A1..E2. In column A, enter the five years (1992 to 1996) as labels rather than values. (Type the first year as **"1992**, using the double quotation mark to right-justify the label in its cell, and then use a drag-and-fill action to enter the remaining four dates.) Format the labels and values as you see them in Figure 10.1.

 WARNING If you were to enter the years 1992 to 1996 as numeric values rather than labels, 1-2-3 would attempt to plot them as data series in the chart itself. To make 1-2-3 recognize these years as labels for the x-axis, enter them into column A as labels.

Here are the steps for creating the three versions of the line chart:

1. Select the range A1..E9.

2. Choose Create ➤ Chart, or click the Chart SmartIcon.

3. Drag the mouse pointer to form a rectangular frame in the area beneath the data table. 1-2-3 creates the default bar chart from the data.

4. Click the Y-Axis title to select it, and then press the Delete key to remove it from the chart. Then select the X-Axis title and delete it as well.

5. Choose Chart ➤ Chart Type. Choose the Line option in the Chart type list in the Type tab:

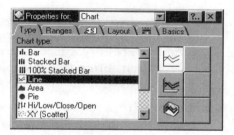

The chart now looks like the one in Figure 10.1. (If the InfoBox obstructs your view of the chart, you can drag the box to a different position on the Desktop. Alternatively, double-click the InfoBox title bar to collapse the box. Double-click the title bar again to reopen the InfoBox when you're ready to use it again.)

6. Pull down the Properties for list in the title bar of the chart InfoBox, and choose Plot:

7. In the InfoBox for plot properties, click the Layout tab if necessary. (Plot refers to the area of the chart that contains the actual graph. The Layout tab allows you to switch between an unstacked and stacked line

chart.) To view the line chart as it is shown in Figure 10.2, pull down the Lines list and choose the Stacked option:

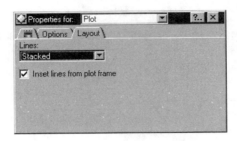

8. Pull down the Properties for list in the InfoBox again, and choose Chart. Click the Type tab if necessary. Select the Area option in the Chart type list. This action transforms the example into the stacked area chart you see in Figure 10.3.

A stacked area chart is similar to a stacked line chart, except that the areas beneath the lines are filled in with shades or colors. In this area chart (see Figure 10.3), the area between the x-axis and the top line of the chart represents the total profit for all four regions in a given year.

TIP The SmartIcon bar for charts contains a variety of one-click tools that you can use to switch from one chart type to another. For example, you'll find SmartIcons representing the bar, line, area, and pie chart types. You'll also see SmartIcons representing several three-dimensional charting options. These SmartIcons are useful for quick changes in the basic format of a chart. But there are a couple of reasons why you might favor using the InfoBox for chart properties—rather than SmartIcons—for refining the appearance of a chart. First, the InfoBox contains many detailed options and settings that are not available as SmartIcons. And second, you may sometimes want to hide the SmartIcons altogether (by choosing View ➤ Hide SmartIcons) as a way to maximize the amount of Desktop space for creating and viewing charts. To see the SmartIcons again, choose View ➤ Show SmartIcons.

Assigning a Name to a Chart

Next you'll add a second graph to this same worksheet. But before you do, there are a few additional tasks to take care of. 1-2-3 assigns a default name—in the form of Chart 1, Chart 2, and so on—to each new chart you create on a sheet. You can use the InfoBox for chart properties to assign a more descriptive name to a chart. In the steps ahead, you'll change the name of the current chart and you'll move it to a new location on the worksheet; you'll also save your work to disk:

1. If the chart InfoBox is not already open, select the chart you've created and choose Chart ➤ Chart Properties.

2. Click the Basics tab. As you can see, the default name for this chart is Chart 1:

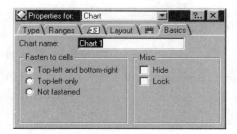

3. Enter **FiveYears** into the Chart name text box, and press ↵. Close the InfoBox. On the Edit line you can now see FiveYears as the name in the selection indicator. (If the Edit line is hidden from view, choose View ➤ Show Edit Line to see it.):

4. Now use the mouse to drag the chart down the worksheet to a location just below row 26. Then press the Home key to return the cell pointer to A1.

5. Choose File ➤ Save As and enter **Profits5** into the File name text box.

6. Click Save or press ↵. 1-2-3 saves your worksheet as Profits5.123.

    The Go To dialog box presents a list of all the current charts by name, and gives you a way to select any chart in the list. There are three ways to open this dialog box: Choose Edit ➤ Go To, press F5, or press Ctrl+G. To see the current list of chart names, pull down the Type of object list and choose Chart. Highlight the name of a chart in the Names list and click OK:

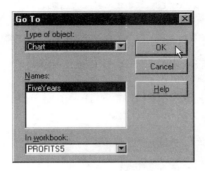

Back on the sheet, 1-2-3 selects and scrolls to the chart you've chosen.

Now you're ready to add another chart to the Profits5 worksheet. In upcoming exercises you'll learn how to create pie charts and doughnut charts.

Creating Pie Charts

A pie chart depicts one range of numeric data. The wedges (or "slices") of the pie show how each individual data value relates to the total and how each value compares in importance with all the other values. Pie charts are available in two-dimensional and three-dimensional formats.

In its simplest format, a pie chart uses only two columns of data—a row or column of labels for the legend, and another row or column containing the numeric data to be depicted in the chart. For example, Figure 10.4 shows a pie chart created from the total annual profits in the four regions of the Profit5 worksheet. Each wedge of the chart represents one of the four regions, as identified in the legend. The labels displayed alongside each wedge show the dollar profit represented by the wedge, and the percentage of the total; for example:

$1,602,000

30%

Working with Other Chart Types

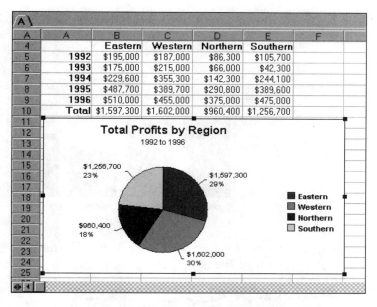

Figure 10.4: A pie chart representing total regional profits over a five-year period

Here are the steps for creating a chart like this one on your own Profits5 worksheet:

1. Press Home to select cell A1. Then scroll the sheet vertically so that row 4 is at the top of the worksheet window. Enter the word **Total** in cell A10. In response, 1-2-3 enters the total regional profit figures at the bottom of the table. Format these values as you see them in Figure 10.4.

2. Select B4..E4. Then hold down the Ctrl key and select B10..E10. The selection consists of two noncontiguous rows containing the data for a pie chart—a row of labels and a row of numeric data:

	A	B	C	D	E
4		Eastern	Western	Northern	Southern
5	1992	$195,000	$187,000	$86,300	$105,700
6	1993	$175,000	$215,000	$66,000	$42,300
7	1994	$229,600	$355,300	$142,300	$244,100
8	1995	$487,700	$389,700	$290,800	$389,600
9	1996	$510,000	$455,000	$375,000	$475,000
10	Total	$1,597,300	$1,602,000	$960,400	$1,256,700
11					

3. Choose Create ➤ Chart or click the Chart SmartIcon, and then drag the mouse to form a rectangular frame beneath the data table. When you release the mouse button, 1-2-3 initially creates a bar chart:

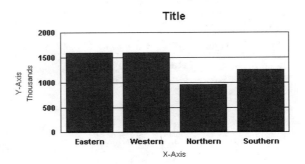

4. Choose Chart ➤ Chart Type. In the Type tab of the chart InfoBox, choose Pie as the chart type:

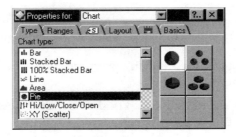

In response, 1-2-3 creates a pie chart in its initial format:

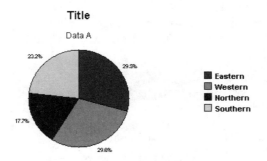

Now you need to supply a title for the chart and revise the labels that appear next to each wedge.

5. On the title bar of the chart InfoBox, pull down the Properties for list and choose Title. You'll see text boxes for three title lines:

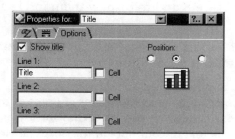

6. In the Line 1 box, enter **Total Profits by Region** and press ↵.

7. Click the Cell option next to the Line 2 box, placing a check in the corresponding check box. This option tells 1-2-3 that you want to take the chart's subtitle from a label stored in a cell on the worksheet. Enter **A2** as the cell reference in the Line 2 box and press ↵. In response, 1-2-3 copies the contents of cell A2—the label "1992 to 1996"—to the second title line of the chart.

8. Click this second title line on the chart itself. Selection handles appear around the title. Back in the InfoBox, click the Fonts tab and choose 9 as the point size and Normal as the style for the second title line:

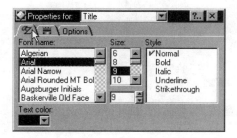

9. A third title line, "Data A" appears just above the pie chart itself. Click this title to select it and press the Delete key to remove it.

10. Pull down the Properties for list on the InfoBox title bar, and choose Pie Labels. 1-2-3 displays selection handles around the four percentage figures displayed next to each wedge. Click the Font tab and choose 8 as the point size for these labels. Click the Number Format tab and enter **0** in the Decimal places box.

11. Click the Options tab and select the Show value labels option. A check appears in the corresponding check box. On the chart, the actual values

represented by each wedge appear above the percentages. Use the Font and Number Format tabs in the InfoBox to change the point size of these labels to 8 and to display them in US Dollar format with no decimals.

Your chart and worksheet now look about the same as Figure 10.4. Click the Save button to save your work to disk.

> **TIP** You can place as many as three lines of notes at the bottom of a chart. To do so, choose Note from the Properties for list on the title bar of the InfoBox. Enter the text of your note in the boxes labeled Line 1, Line 2, and Line 3. By default, notes are displayed at the lower-right corner of the chart area, but you can move them by clicking one of the three option buttons labeled Position.

Three-Dimensional Pie Charts and Doughnut Charts

For a variation on the pie chart format, try creating a three-dimensional chart. Choose Chart ➤ Chart Type. In the InfoBox, click the button representing the 3-D pie chart:

Here's the resulting chart:

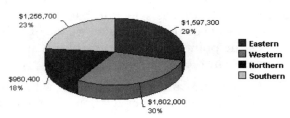

Yet another option is the doughnut chart type. A doughnut chart is shaped like a pie with a hole in the middle. To see an example, choose Doughnut in the Chart type list:

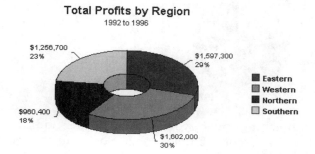

After examining this new chart, select the Pie option again and click the button representing the two-dimensional chart.

Exploding a Wedge on a Pie Chart

Sometimes you may want to place special emphasis on a particular wedge of a pie chart—the largest or smallest wedge, or the wedge that is the most important to a particular audience. One way to do this is to explode the wedge, separating it from the circumference of the rest of the pie.

You can use your mouse to drag a wedge slightly away from its original position in the chart. For example, suppose you want to explode the wedge representing the Northern region in the Profits pie chart. Here are the steps:

1. Position the mouse pointer over the wedge.

2. Hold down the left mouse button and drag the wedge slightly away from the center of the pie chart. A dotted border represents the new position of the wedge:

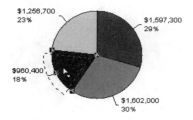

3. Release the mouse button. 1-2-3 redraws the pie chart with the exploded wedge in its new position:

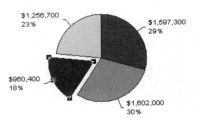

As a finishing touch, you might consider adding some drawn objects to the chart—for example, a text block and an arrow to further identify the exploded wedge.

> **TIP** You can explode all the wedges of a pie chart by the same amount. In the Properties for list on the InfoBox title bar, choose Plot. Click the Layout tab. In the text box labeled "Explode slices %," enter the percentage by which you want to explode the wedges. Try out different percentages until you find the visual effect you're looking for.

Multiple Pie Charts

1-2-3 also gives you the option of creating multiple pies within a single chart frame, to represent several rows or columns of data at once. For example, Figure 10.5 shows how this option might be used to represent the figures from all four regions of the profit table. To create this chart, select the entire table in the range A1..E9. Choose Create ➤ Chart and click at a position on the sheet. Then choose Chart ➤ Chart Type, select the Pie option, and click the button representing multiple pie charts:

Notice that you can choose between two-dimensional and three-dimensional charts in this format.

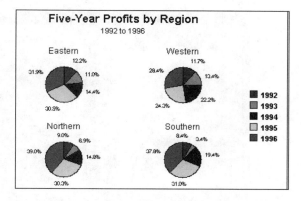

Figure 10.5: **Creating multiple pie charts from a range of data**

Setting the Default Chart Type

You've now seen examples of the most commonly used chart types, including bar, line, area, pie, and doughnut charts. As you know, 1-2-3 initially uses the bar chart as the selected type for all new charts you create. In other words, the bar chart is the default type when you first start creating charts in 1-2-3. Given a chart in the default type, you can switch to a new type by choosing the Chart ➤ Type command or clicking an appropriate SmartIcon.

NOTE In previous versions of 1-2-3, the default chart type was known as the *preferred* chart type.

What if you want to create several charts in a type that's not the default setting? For example, suppose you're planning a series of pie charts to represent various data ranges in a profit worksheet. You face the inconvenience of starting each new chart as a bar chart and then switching to the pie chart type.

For situations like this, 1-2-3 gives you the option of changing the default chart type setting to one of the basic types and styles. To do so, use the Set Default Chart dialog box:

1. Select a chart on the current sheet. As a result, the Chart menu appears on the menu bar.

2. Choose Chart ➤ Chart Style ➤ Set Default Chart. The Set Default Chart dialog box appears on the Desktop:

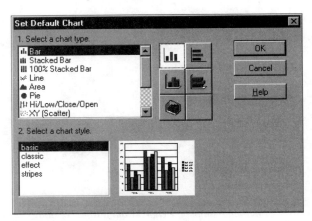

3. Choose a chart type and click a style button. (Keep the "basic" selection in the list labeled "Select a chart style.") Then click OK.

The default chart type you've selected is applied to any new charts you subsequently create. This setting remains in effect until you change it again.

> **TIP** You can create custom chart style definitions, based on charts you've already created and formatted; and you can designate a custom style as the default type. Select the chart that will serve as the pattern for a style you want to create, and choose Chart ➤ Chart Style ➤ Create. Optionally, click the check box labeled "Make this your Default Chart" on the Create Chart Style dialog box. When you click OK, the Save As dialog box appears. Enter a name for the new chart style, and click Save.

> **TIP** To apply a custom style to an existing chart, click the Style tab on the chart InfoBox, choose the style, and click Apply.

Next you'll take a look at several of the more complex chart types available in 1-2-3, including XY, mixed, and radar charts.

Creating XY Charts

An XY chart—also known as a scatter chart—plots one range of values as a function of another, and portrays the mathematical relationship between the two sets of numbers. The first data range supplies the x-coordinate of each plotted point in the chart and a second data range supplies the corresponding y-coordinate.

For example, Computing Conferences, Inc., has developed the sheet in Figure 10.6 to explore the correlation between conference attendance and advertising. Column C shows the amounts spent on advertising for a series of conferences, and column D shows the attendance levels for the same conferences. An XY chart created from this information appears in Figure 10.7. Each point on the chart represents an advertising amount and the attendance level as an x, y ordered pair of values in the coordinate system. The chart seems to suggest a positive correlation—attendance goes up as more money is spent on advertising.

	A	B	C	D
1	Computing Conferences, Inc.			
2	Attendance and Advertising			
3	Computing for Video Stores			
4				
5	Place	Date	Advertising	Attendance
6	Chicago	09-Jan-96	$5,000	154
7	St. Louis	21-Jan-96	$3,500	119
8	Indianapolis	15-Feb-96	$6,000	174
9	New York	07-Mar-96	$6,000	201
10	Boston	25-Mar-96	$3,500	136
11	Washington, D.C.	03-Apr-96	$5,000	172
12	Atlanta	11-May-96	$3,500	112
13	Miami	18-May-96	$1,000	97
14	Dallas	03-Jun-96	$1,000	86
15	Albuquerque	29-Jun-96	$1,000	104
16	Las Vegas	05-Sep-96	$7,500	235
17	Los Angeles	11-Oct-96	$1,500	119
18	San Francisco	29-Oct-96	$2,500	137
19	Seattle	05-Nov-96	$3,500	148
20				

Figure 10.6: A worksheet containing attendance and advertising data

If you want to try developing this chart on your own computer, begin by creating the worksheet in Figure 10.6. Here are the beginning steps for creating the chart:

1. Select the range C5..D19, which contains the two columns of numeric data—the advertising expenditures and the corresponding attendance levels.

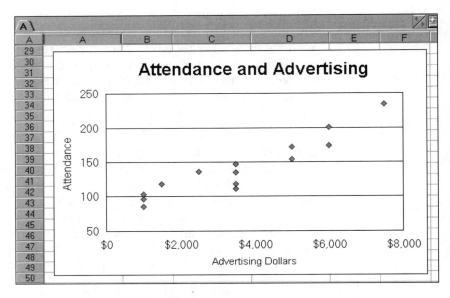

Figure 10.7: An XY chart correlating conference attendance with advertising dollars

2. Choose Create ➤ Chart or click the Chart SmartIcon. Drag the mouse to form an appropriate frame in the area beneath the data table. When you release the mouse button, 1-2-3 creates a chart in the default format.

3. Choose Chart ➤ Type, and select the XY (Scatter) option in the Chart type list:

Creating Mixed Charts

A mixed chart superimposes a line chart over a bar chart. The two chart types represent different sets of data and can be scaled independently.

For example, Figure 10.8 shows a mixed chart created from the attendance-and-advertising worksheet shown in Figure 10.6.

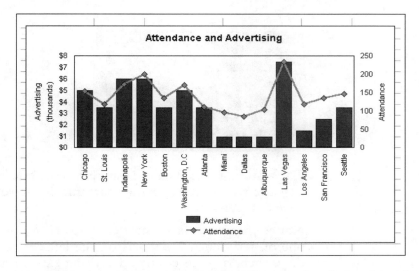

Figure 10.8: A mixed chart showing advertising expenditures as a bar chart, and attendance as a line chart

To prepare the data table for this chart, select the range A1..D19 from the sheet shown in Figure 10.6. Press Ctrl+C to copy this range to the Clipboard. Create a blank sheet; with the cell pointer at A1, press Ctrl+V to paste a copy of the data to the sheet. Select column B (containing the conference dates) and choose Range ➤ Delete Columns to remove this column from the data table. Then proceed as follows to get started on the chart:

1. Select the range A5..C19 in the sheet.
2. Choose Create ➤ Chart, or click the Chart SmartIcon. Drag the mouse pointer to define a rectangular area for the new chart. 1-2-3 initially creates a chart in the default format.
3. Choose Chart ➤ Chart Type. In the Chart type list, choose Mixed.
4. Pull down the Properties for list in the InfoBox title bar, and choose Series. Click the Options tab if necessary.
5. Pull down the list at the top of the Options tab and choose the second entry, Attendance.

6. Click the Plot against 2nd Y-axis option, placing a check in the corresponding check box, and choose the Line option from the Mixed type list:

The resulting mixed chart is similar to the one in Figure 10.8. You can now use other settings in the chart InfoBox to refine the chart's appearance and content.

Notice that the mixed chart contains two y-axes, one on the left and one on the right. The y-axis on the left contains a scale of values for the bar chart representing advertising expenditures. The y-axis on the right is the scale for the line chart, which represents attendance.

Creating HLCO Charts

A high-low-close-open chart is also known as a "stock market chart." This chart type displays vertical lines representing pairs of high and low values. In addition, special markings along each vertical line represent opening and closing values. The HLCO chart is a special form of the mixed chart type; it uses ranges that supply several kinds of data:

▶ A range of labels that will appear along the x-axis.

▶ Two numeric ranges representing high and low values.

▶ Two numeric ranges representing closing and opening values.

▶ An additional numeric range that becomes a bar chart, located beneath the high-low lines.

▶ A numeric range that supplies average readings. This data series becomes a line chart that runs through the high-low lines.

All of these ranges have typical uses for reporting stock market data: The high-low lines represent stock prices, as do the opening and closing values; the bar chart beneath the lines represents trading volume; and the horizontal line chart represents stock averages.

But you may find other uses for the HLCO chart. For example, consider the weather worksheet shown in Figure 10.9. This worksheet contains data ranges displaying daily high and low temperatures, morning and evening readings, daily rainfall, and average temperatures. Using these six columns as the data ranges, 1-2-3 creates the HLCO chart shown in Figure 10.10.

	A	B	C	D	E	F	G
1			One Week of February Weather				
2			San Francisco				
3							
4		High	Low	6:00 AM	6:00 PM	Rainfall (in.)	Avg. Temp.
5	Mon	53	32	43	50	0.75	41
6	Tue	76	35	51	62	1.25	49
7	Wed	71	38	59	67	1.25	54
8	Thu	55	30	39	50	2.00	40
9	Fri	50	28	39	50	1.25	38
10	Sat	59	29	43	55	2.25	43
11	Sun	68	37	49	60	2.00	49

Figure 10.9:   Weather data

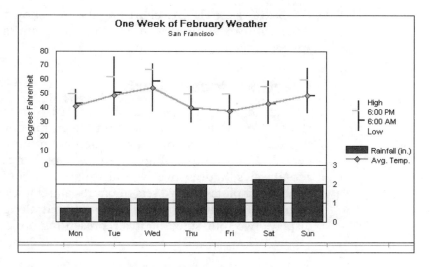

Figure 10.10:   An HLCO chart from the weather data in Figure 10.9

If you want to try creating this HLCO chart, open a new worksheet and enter the table of weather data into a range at the top of the sheet, as shown in Figure 10.9. Then follow these steps:

1. Select the range A4..G11.

2. Choose Create ➤ Chart or click the Chart SmartIcon. Drag the mouse pointer to define a rectangular frame beneath the data table. When you release the mouse button, 1-2-3 draws a chart in the current default format.

3. Choose Chart ➤ Chart Type, and click the High/Low/Close/Open option in the Chart type list. The chart InfoBox offers two styles of HLCO charts; keep the first of the two types as the selection:

1-2-3 draws an HLCO chart like the one shown in Figure 10.10. Use other InfoBox settings to modify the titles and axis labels of the chart appropriately.

Creating Radar Charts

Yet another chart type available in 1-2-3 is the radar chart. Radar charts plot numeric data around a central point and are useful for showing data projections against actual amounts for a particular time period. For example, Figure 10.11 shows a table of projected and actual sales figures over a four-quarter period. The accompanying radar chart plots the two sets of figures along lines that represent the four quarters. By connecting the points plotted along these lines, the chart displays two four-sided figures representing projected and actual sales.

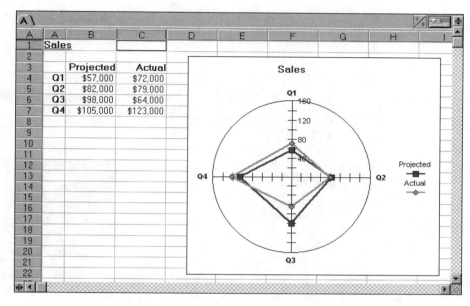

Figure 10.11: *A radar chart comparing sales projections with actual sales data*

Maps

In addition to the standard chart types, 1-2-3 provides a dramatic way to illustrate geographic data. Using 1-2-3's mapping feature, you can portray geographic information related to business, industry, natural resources, economics, politics, populations and cultures, languages, history, health statistics, religions, or any other relevant topic. For example, you might use a map to depict business activity in any region of the globe—from states across the United States to countries around the world. Like the other chart types you've examined in this chapter, maps are easy to create from any appropriate range of worksheet data.

Figure 10.12 shows a map of business activity by Computing Conferences, Inc., in eleven Western states. Specifically, it shows the number of conferences that the company conducted in each state during 1996. As you can see in the map's legend, 1-2-3 organizes the numeric data into six bins (0 to 12, 13 to 24, 25 to 36, and so on) and assigns a unique color code to each bin. Thanks to this coding, you can instantly assess the level of business activity in any state pictured in the map.

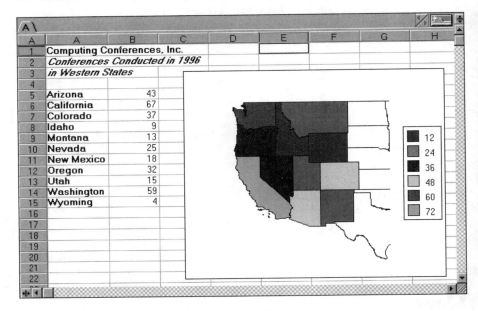

Figure 10.12: A map showing business activity in Western states

Mapping is nearly automatic in 1-2-3. When you select a range of data for a map, 1-2-3 examines the names of states or countries that you supply, and determines which map to add to your worksheet.

TIP If you prefer, you can use abbreviated map codes instead of the full names of states or countries in the worksheet for a map. For example, use AZ, CA, and CO for Arizona, California, and Colorado.

NOTE If the data range for a map contains a geographic name that 1-2-3 doesn't recognize, The Region Check dialog box appears on the Desktop, giving you the chance to verify the accuracy of the name in question. This often occurs as the result of a simple misspelling. To fix the problem, select the correct name from the Known map region list, and click OK.

Creating a Map

In the following exercise you'll see how easy it is to create a map, as you go through the steps to duplicate the one shown in Figure 10.12. Begin your work by opening a new sheet and creating the data table in the range A1..Bl5. Then proceed as follows:

1. Select the range A5..B15.
2. Choose Create ➤ Map or click the Create Map SmartIcon.
3. Drag the mouse to form a rectangular frame for the new map. Release the mouse button, and 1-2-3 draws the initial version of the map:

4. Click the map's title ("USA by State") with the right mouse button, and choose the Clear command from the resulting shortcut menu. This action deletes the title from the map.

5. Position the mouse pointer above and to the left of the map area (just off the northwest corner of Washington state) and hold down the Ctrl key. Then hold down the left mouse button, and drag the mouse down and to the right until you see a dotted border around the eleven western states that are the subject of this map:

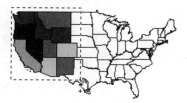

6. Release the mouse button, and 1-2-3 performs a zoom operation, increasing the size of the map area that you've marked off.

Using the zoom operation, you can create maps of any selected geographical region in the world. Figure 10.13 shows another example, a population map of West Africa. Given the list of countries and population figures in the range A3..B17, 1-2-3 initially creates a map of the world:

Using the zoom operation you can increase the size of the focus area in West Africa, producing the map in Figure 10.13. You may have to complete more than one zoom action to produce exactly the geographic focus that you are searching for.

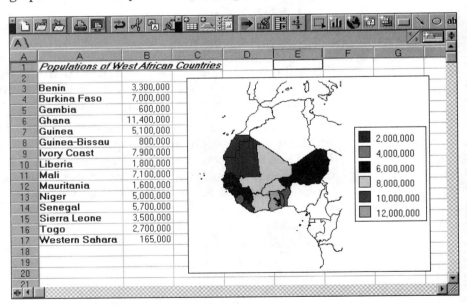

Figure 10.13: *A population map of West Africa*

Summary

Each of the chart types available in 1-2-3 is suited to a particular arrangement of data. For example, line and area charts typically depict data values that change over time. Pie charts and doughnut charts show the importance of individual data items in relation to the total of all the data. In an XY chart, sets of paired data values are plotted as points against an x-y coordinate system. A mixed chart shows a combination of bar and line charts. The HLCO chart displays high and low values as vertical lines, with closing and opening points marked along the length of each line. Finally, a radar chart plots points around a center point and can prove useful for comparing projected and actual data sets.

Maps are a dramatic form of charting available in 1-2-3. In a map, you can depict geographic data related to business, economics, politics, populations, or any other topic. 1-2-3 creates maps automatically from a range of worksheet data that includes recognizable geographic names.

CHAPTER 11
Database Tables

Fast Track

To create a database table,   344
enter a row of field names at the top of the table range, and then enter the records in consecutive rows immediately after the field names.

To create a complete database,   348
consider the option of organizing the information into two or more related database tables. You can enter each table on a different sheet of a workbook. Two related tables typically have at least one field in common.

To create a calculated field,   349
enter the formula as the field entry in the first record, then copy the formula down the field column to all the records of the database.

To identify the distinct tables of a database,   352
assign a range name to each table, using the Range ➤ Name command. Include the row of field names and all records in the target range. If each table is stored on its own sheet, it is also helpful to assign an appropriate name to each tab in the workbook.

To sort a database table, 353

choose Range ➤ Sort and specify the table range. In the Sort by box, develop a list of one or more sort keys. Choose Ascending or Descending for each key. If the specified database range includes field names, click the Header at top option. Click OK to carry out the sort.

To modify the characteristics of 1-2-3's default sort order, 361

choose File ➤ User Setup ➤ 1-2-3 Preferences, and change the settings in the Sorting group. In particular, you can switch the numbers before words and blank cells to the top options off or on. (Both options are checked by default.) You can also choose a sort order that is appropriate for a language other than English.

A database is a collection of information, systematically organized to provide convenient access to individual records. Business databases are created for a variety of subjects, including inventory, product lines, sales transactions, business assets, employee directories, client lists, regional offices, sales people, and so on.

The Lotus database software is ideal for managing such information. The commands on 1-2-3's Create ➤ Database menu (Figure 11.1) use Lotus Approach, a separate SmartSuite application, to perform important database tasks. Each of the commands in the Create ➤ Database menu ultimately inserts an Approach object in the current 1-2-3 workbook. For example, the Create ➤ Database ➤ Query Table command develops a query for an existing database table stored on a sheet. A query is a selection of data copied from the original database.

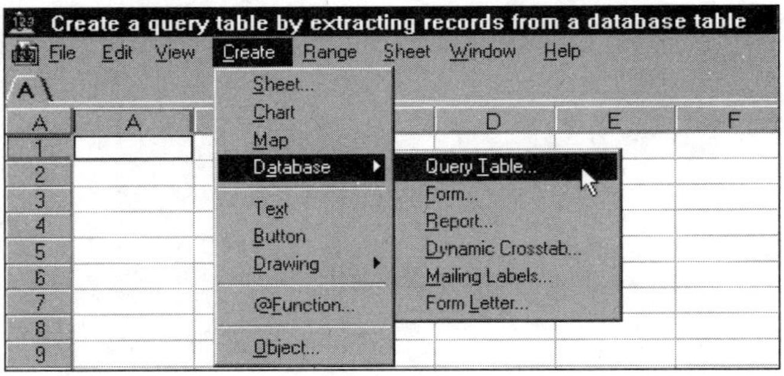

Figure 11.1: The Create ➤ Database commands

In this chapter and the next you'll learn how to organize a 1-2-3 database and you'll explore some of the basic operations available for database tables and query tables.

Creating a Database Table

A database table is an arrangement of records and fields stored in the rows and columns of a sheet. A record contains all the information describing a single item in the database—for example, a product, a transaction, an event, a property, an employee, a client, a regional office, or a sales person. Records are stored in consecutive rows of the worksheet. All the information for a given record is displayed in one row.

A field is one category of information for each record in the database—for example, the product name, the transaction date, the event location, the property value, the employee's salary, the client's business address, the office manager, or the sales region. Fields appear side by side in adjacent columns of the worksheet. Each entry in a given column belongs to the same field and the same data type. At the top of each field column, just above the first record in the database, is a field name, a label that identifies the field.

In short, a database table is a collection of records organized into distinct fields of information and stored in a worksheet. Every database table begins with a row of field names. For successful database operations, a consistent data type within each field is an essential part of database design.

The best way to clarify these terms and concepts is to consider an example. In the exercises of this chapter you'll once again look into the business files of Computing Conferences, Inc., this time to examine the company's database of conference instructors. This database contains information about computer specialists and educators around the country whom the company engages to present specific topics at training conferences.

Figure 11.2 shows the beginning of the database, displayed at the top of a sheet. Each record in the database is stored in a row of the sheet and contains all the information about one instructor. The first record is in row 4. There are eleven fields, displayed across the worksheet in columns A through K. The field names are in row 3. As you can see, a complete record consists of one entry for each of the eleven fields.

The first five fields supply an instructor's number, name, and location. The **ID** field is an identification number, **Last** is the instructor's last name, and **First** is the initial of the first name. **City** is the instructor's home location, and **Region** is a single letter—N, S, E, or W—designating one of the company's four regions.

The next four fields describe an instructor's work and experience. **Specialty** is the instructor's primary area of expertise—Spreadsheet, Database, WP (for word processing), Accounting, Networks, or Programming; **Rate** is the instructor's current hourly rate for conference presentations, an amount that varies from one instructor to the next; the **Hrs** field gives the total number of conference hours the instructor has worked; and **Contract** is the date of the instructor's first work contract with the company.

The last two fields are columns of data calculated from other fields. **Yrs** is the number of years since the instructor's first conference job; and **OK** is a rating of A, B, or C, indicating the instructor's level of experience. If the instructor has worked for Computing Conferences, Inc. for less than a year, the entry in this field is New.

	A	B	C	D	E	F	G	H	I	J	K
1				Instructor Database							
2											
3	ID	Last	First	City	Region	Specialty	Rate	Hrs	Contract	Yrs	OK
4	D-140	Abrams	P.	Atlanta	S	Database	$125	29	20-Oct-95	1.3	B
5	W-154	Alexander	E.	Los Angeles	W	WP	$150	10	14-Jun-96	0.6	New
6	S-125	Ashford	W.	Washington, D.C.	E	Spreadsheet	$150	145	10-May-92	4.7	A
7	S-126	Ballinger	I.	Boston	E	Spreadsheet	$150	40	12-Feb-92	5.0	C
8	W-145	Banks	S.	St. Louis	S	WP	$150	55	10-Jun-95	1.6	A
9	W-130	Burke	C.	Miami	S	WP	$100	41	22-May-93	3.7	B
10	D-141	Cheung	F.	Las Vegas	W	Database	$125	61	15-May-95	1.7	A
11	D-143	Cody	L.	Los Angeles	W	Database	$75	43	20-Jun-95	1.6	B
12	A-146	Daniels	A.	Atlanta	S	Accounting	$125	24	09-May-96	0.7	New
13	W-119	Davis	G.	San Francisco	W	WP	$150	149	09-Jul-92	4.6	A
14	N-115	Dixon	G.	Las Vegas	W	Networks	$150	59	09-May-91	5.7	B
15	S-120	Edmonds	R.	Indianapolis	N	Spreadsheet	$75	35	27-Sep-92	4.3	C
16	T-128	Eng	R.	Albuquerque	S	Programming	$75	75	11-Oct-92	4.3	B
17	D-105	Fitzpatrick	P.	New York	E	Database	$125	164	07-Nov-91	5.2	A
18	S-131	Garcia	A.	Seattle	N	Spreadsheet	$100	17	02-Jul-93	3.6	C
19	W-114	Garrison	V.	Boston	E	WP	$125	207	06-May-91	5.7	A
20	S-127	Gill	P.	Los Angeles	W	Spreadsheet	$100	35	22-Jun-92	4.6	C
21	S-156	Hale	S.	San Francisco	W	Spreadsheet	$75	28	09-Jun-96	0.6	New
22	S-149	Harris	P.	Dallas	S	Spreadsheet	$150	17	12-Feb-96	1.0	New

Figure 11.2: **The beginning of the instructor database**

As you'll see in this chapter, field names play an important role in database operations. Each field has a unique name. For convenience, you should try to write field names that are clear, concise, and easy to remember.

> **TIP** Field names need not be restricted to a single word. For example, you could write Last Name, First Name, Home Region, Hourly Rate, and Years of Work as field names in the Instructor database. But it's often more convenient to write short, one-word field names, because in the long run they're easier for you to use in database operations.

Figure 11.3 shows the remainder of the database table, describing the instructors who work for Computing Conferences, Inc., in the four regions. There are over fifty records in the table. In this particular listing, the records are arranged in alphabetical order by the instructors' names. Notice that the entries in a given field column all belong to the same data type and are formatted consistently. The first six fields are labels. The next four are numeric fields—the hourly rate, formatted as a dollar amount; the hours, an integer; the first contract date, a date number formatted in a date display format; and the years, formatted as a numeric value with one decimal place. The last field, OK, is a label.

	A	B	C	D	E	F	G	H	I	J	K
23	D-109	Hayes	S.	San Francisco	W	Database	$75	95	07-Feb-91	6.0	B
24	T-136	Hermann	J.	Los Angeles	W	Programming	$125	74	24-May-94	2.7	B
25	S-132	Jones	L.	Atlanta	S	Spreadsheet	$125	5	10-Feb-93	4.0	C
26	W-116	Jordan	E.	Dallas	S	WP	$100	17	06-Oct-91	5.3	C
27	W-115	Kim	E.	Washington, D.C.	E	WP	$100	137	11-Oct-91	5.3	B
28	N-144	King	T.	New York	E	Networks	$75	13	06-Jan-95	2.1	C
29	D-136	Koenig	O.	Albuquerque	S	Database	$125	20	02-May-94	2.8	C
30	S-111	Kwat	O.	New York	E	Spreadsheet	$100	71	21-Jun-91	5.6	B
31	D-123	Lambert	S.	Dallas	S	Database	$150	145	26-Jun-92	4.6	A
32	D-134	Lee	H.	Seattle	N	Database	$150	21	17-Dec-93	3.1	C
33	W-150	Leung	M.	Chicago	N	WP	$100	17	26-Mar-96	0.9	New
34	W-112	Manning	P.	Atlanta	S	WP	$75	71	09-Nov-91	5.2	B
35	W-107	Martinez	G.	Las Vegas	W	WP	$150	178	15-Mar-91	5.9	A
36	N-129	McKay	J.	Washington, D.C.	E	Networks	$150	35	09-May-92	4.7	C
37	W-124	Meyer	J.	New York	E	WP	$150	85	05-May-92	4.7	B
38	A-135	Meyer	L.	New York	E	Accounting	$100	57	17-Aug-93	3.5	B
39	P-148	Miranda	O.	Las Vegas	W	Programming	$75	9	04-Jan-96	1.1	C
40	S-153	Michols	B.	Albuquerque	S	Spreadsheet	$150	19	28-Feb-96	0.9	New
41	N-118	O'Neil	P.	Atlanta	S	Networks	$75	5	01-May-92	4.8	C
42	A-103	Perez	D.	Las Vegas	W	Accounting	$100	5	11-Jul-91	5.6	C
43	W-113	Porter	D.	Seattle	N	WP	$125	59	02-Aug-91	5.5	B
44	D-139	Porter	M.	Washington, D.C.	E	Database	$150	26	28-Mar-94	2.8	B

	A	B	C	D	E	F	G	H	I	J	K
45	T-133	Ramirez	F.	Boston	E	Programming	$150	73	08-Feb-93	4.0	B
46	S-155	Roberts	P.	Chicago	N	Spreadsheet	$100	10	21-Aug-96	0.4	New
47	D-137	Sanchez	W.	Indianapolis	N	Database	$100	47	16-Apr-94	2.8	B
48	N-101	Schwartz	B.	Boston	E	Networks	$150	178	02-Mar-91	5.9	A
49	W-151	Schwartz	P.	Indianapolis	N	WP	$150	23	10-May-96	0.7	New
50	D-104	Taylor	F.	Boston	E	Database	$100	17	24-Oct-91	5.3	C
51	D-142	Thomas	t.	St. Louis	S	Database	$150	35	23-Dec-95	1.1	A
52	S-108	Tong	C.	St. Louis	S	Spreadsheet	$150	35	12-Nov-91	5.2	C
53	N-152	Tong	P.	San Francisco	W	Networks	$150	23	13-May-96	0.7	New
54	N-110	tong	W.	Los Angeles	W	Networks	$100	83	09-May-91	5.7	B
55	S-122	Vasquez	T.	Las Vegas	W	Spreadsheet	$75	5	27-Apr-92	4.8	C
56	T-102	Vaughn	A.	Washington, D.C.	E	Programming	$75	53	11-Sep-91	5.4	B
57	T-147	Webb	F.	New York	E	Programming	$125	32	27-Jan-96	1.0	A
58	D-106	Weinberg	P.	Miami	S	Database	$75	59	18-Jan-91	6.0	B
59	D-121	Williams	C.	Chicago	N	Database	$150	30	02-Oct-92	4.3	C
60											

Figure 11.3: *The remainder of the instructor database table*

Creating a Database

For the exercises of this chapter, you'll need a copy of the Instructor database table on a sheet of your own; but to avoid spending too much time creating this example, you can enter a shortened form of the database. The short version, shown in Figure 11.4, contains a selection of 17 record entries in rows 4 through 20.

	A	B	C	D	E	F	G	H	I	J	K
1				Instructor Database							
2											
3	ID	Last	First	City	Region	Specialty	Rate	Hrs	Contract	Yrs	OK
4	S-149	Harris	P.	Dallas	S	Spreadsheet	$150	17	12-Feb-96		
5	A-146	Daniels	A.	Atlanta	S	Accounting	$125	24	09-May-96		
6	A-103	Perez	D.	Las Vegas	W	Accounting	$100	5	11-Jul-91		
7	W-113	Porter	D.	Seattle	N	WP	$125	59	02-Aug-91		
8	N-101	Schwartz	B.	Boston	E	Networks	$150	178	02-Mar-91		
9	S-155	Roberts	P.	Chicago	N	Spreadsheet	$100	10	21-Aug-96		
10	S-125	Ashford	W.	Washington, D.C.	E	Spreadsheet	$150	145	10-May-92		
11	D-106	Weinberg	P.	Miami	S	Database	$75	59	18-Jan-91		
12	W-119	Davis	G.	San Francisco	W	WP	$150	149	09-Jul-92		
13	W-124	Meyer	J.	New York	E	WP	$150	85	05-May-92		
14	W-145	Banks	S.	St. Louis	S	WP	$150	55	10-Jun-95		
15	D-137	Sanchez	W.	Indianapolis	N	Database	$100	47	16-Apr-94		
16	D-139	Porter	M.	Washington, D.C.	E	Database	$150	26	28-Mar-94		
17	T-133	Ramirez	F.	Boston	E	Programming	$150	73	08-Feb-93		
18	D-143	Cody	L.	Los Angeles	W	Database	$75	43	20-Jun-95		
19	S-127	Gill	P.	Los Angeles	W	Spreadsheet	$100	35	22-Jun-92		
20	T-128	Eng	R.	Albuquerque	S	Programming	$75	75	11-Oct-92		

Figure 11.4: **The short version of the instructor database table**

To create the shortened database, start with a new blank workbook and click the New Sheet button to insert sheet B. You'll enter the instructor database into worksheet B, saving worksheet A for a later exercise. Enter the title **Instructor Database** into cell B:A1, and center it horizontally across columns A through K. Enter the field names into row 3, cells A3 through K3. Then enter the first nine fields of information into columns A through F. Copy each record exactly as you see it in Figure 11.4, applying appropriate formats as you go. Finally, choose the File ➤ Save As command, and save this file as INSTRUCT.123.

The Yrs and OK fields, in columns J and K, are calculated fields in the instructor database table. They are blank in Figure 11.4; you'll fill them in next.

Creating Calculated Fields

You can write a formula to calculate the data for any field in a database table. To create a calculated field, you enter the formula as the field entry for the first record in the database, then you copy the formula down the field column—just as you would do in an ordinary worksheet application. Formulas for calculated fields often contain references to values in other fields of the database table. As you would expect, 1-2-3 recalculates a field formula whenever you make a change in the data that the formula uses.

The Yrs field in the Instructor database table shows the number of years an instructor has worked with Computing Conferences, Inc. The number would normally be calculated as the difference between today's date and the date in the Contract field, as in the following formula:

    (@TODAY-I4)/365

This formula finds the difference, in days, between today's date (@TODAY) and the first contract date (I4); then the result is divided by 365 to calculate the difference in years. The advantage of this formula in a database is that 1-2-3 can recalculate the Yrs field each time the value of @TODAY changes—that is, every day. This means that the values in the Yrs field are always up to date.

But for the exercises in this chapter, you'll replace this formula with one that supplies a fixed date instead of @TODAY:

    (@DATE(97,1,31)-I4)/365

By making this small adjustment, you'll be able to duplicate each database example exactly as it appears in this chapter.

> **TIP** The @DATEDIF function is an alternate tool for finding the difference in years between two dates.

The value in the OK field for a given instructor is based on the instructor's experience level—specifically, the average number of conference hours the instructor has worked per year since the initial contract:

▶ An instructor who has worked an average of 30 hours or more per year receives an OK rating of A.

▶ An instructor who has worked fewer than 30 hours but at least 9 hours per year receives a rating of B.

- An instructor who has worked fewer than 9 hours per year receives a rating of C.
- An instructor who has worked for less than a year receives a "New" entry in this field instead of an A, B, or C rating.

Here are the steps for entering these two formulas into the first record of the database table and copying them down their respective field columns:

1. Enter the following formula into cell J4 to calculate the number of years since the initial contract:

    (@DATE(97,1,31)-I4)/365

2. Enter this formula carefully into cell K4:

    @IF(J4<1,"New",@IF(H4/J4>=30,"A",@IF(H4/J4<9,"C","B")))

    This formula uses a sequence of nested @IF functions to select a label of New, A, B, or C for the OK field. The outermost @IF function enters a label of New if the value of the Yrs field is less than 1. Otherwise, the middle @IF function enters A if the average yearly work hour amount (H4/J4) is greater than or equal to 30. Finally, if neither of these first two conditions is true, the innermost @IF function chooses between labels C and B, depending upon whether the average work hour figure is less than or greater than 9.

3. To copy these two formulas down columns J and K, respectively, select the range J4..K20, click the selection with the right mouse button, and choose the Copy Down command from the resulting quick menu.

4. Use the appropriate panels of the Status bar (or the InfoBox for range properties) to assign an appropriate format to the values in column J—fixed, with one digit after the decimal point. When you complete this step, the two calculated fields, Yrs and OK, appear as shown in Figure 11.5.

5. Choose File ➤ Save to update the file on disk.

Creating Multiple Tables in a Database

In 1-2-3 a database may consist of a single table or a collection of two or more tables. Given a database containing multiple tables, you can use a *join* operation to match records from related tables and build new combinations of data.

Creating a Database Table

	A	B	C	D	E	F	G	H	I	J	K
1					Instructor Database						
2											
3	ID	Last	First	City	Region	Specialty	Rate	Hrs	Contract	Yrs	OK
4	S-149	Harris	P.	Dallas	S	Spreadsheet	$150	17	12-Feb-96	1.0	New
5	A-146	Daniels	A.	Atlanta	S	Accounting	$125	24	09-May-96	0.7	New
6	A-103	Perez	D.	Las Vegas	W	Accounting	$100	5	11-Jul-91	5.6	C
7	W-113	Porter	D.	Seattle	N	WP	$125	59	02-Aug-91	5.5	B
8	N-101	Schwartz	B.	Boston	E	Networks	$150	178	02-Mar-91	5.9	A
9	S-155	Roberts	P.	Chicago	N	Spreadsheet	$100	10	21-Aug-96	0.4	New
10	S-125	Ashford	W.	Washington, D.C.	E	Spreadsheet	$150	145	10-May-92	4.7	A
11	D-106	Weinberg	P.	Miami	S	Database	$75	59	18-Jan-91	6.0	B
12	W-119	Davis	G.	San Francisco	W	WP	$150	149	09-Jul-92	4.6	A
13	W-124	Meyer	J.	New York	E	WP	$150	85	05-May-92	4.7	B
14	W-145	Banks	S.	St. Louis	S	WP	$150	55	10-Jun-95	1.6	A
15	D-137	Sanchez	W.	Indianapolis	N	Database	$100	47	16-Apr-94	2.8	B
16	D-139	Porter	M.	Washington, D.C.	E	Database	$150	26	28-Mar-94	2.8	B
17	T-133	Ramirez	F.	Boston	E	Programming	$150	73	08-Feb-93	4.0	B
18	D-143	Cody	L.	Los Angeles	W	Database	$75	43	20-Jun-95	1.6	B
19	S-127	Gill	P.	Los Angeles	W	Spreadsheet	$100	35	22-Jun-92	4.6	C
20	T-128	Eng	R.	Albuquerque	S	Programming	$75	75	11-Oct-92	4.3	B

Figure 11.5: Entering the calculated fields into the database table. The data values in the Yrs and OK fields are supplied by formulas.

Anticipating this option, you'll now enter a second database table in worksheet A, which you've left empty up to now. This new table, shown in Figure 11.6, contains information about the regional offices of Computing Conferences, Inc. The Office database table has only four records, one for each of the four regional offices. There are seven fields in the database: **Region**, an entry of N, S, E, or W; **Address**, **City**, **State**, and **Zip**, which together provide the complete address for a regional office; **Phone**, the voice phone number; and **Manager**, the name of the person in charge of operations at the particular office.

	A	B	C	D	E	F	G
1	Regional Offices						
2							
3	Region	Address	City	State	Zip	Phone	Manager
4	E	222 Allen Street	New York	NY	10103	(212) 555-4678	Campbell, R.
5	N	Mills Tower, Suite 992	Chicago	IL	60605	(312) 555-8803	Logan, C.
6	S	11 Maple Street	Dallas	TX	75210	(214) 555-6754	Harvey, J.
7	W	432 Market Avenue	Los Angeles	CA	90028	(213) 555-9974	Garcia, M.

Figure 11.6: The Office database table

Notice that this new table and the Instructor table have one field in common, Region. This field allows you to correlate records in the two tables. For example, imagine the steps you might take to find the name of the regional manager who supervises a particular instructor. You would begin by searching for the instructor's name in the instructor table. After locating the correct record, you would make note of the instructor's region. Then you would switch over to the office database, look up the office record corresponding to the same region, and find the manager's name in the Manager field.

In Chapter 12 you'll learn how to accomplish this sequence of steps in a query operation that joins data from multiple database tables. For now, create the Office database table in sheet A. Enter the title, **Regional Offices**, into cell A1; seven field names into row 3; and the four records in rows 4 through 7. Enter the zip codes and phone numbers as labels rather than values. Format the information as it is shown in Figure 11.6, and then choose File ➤ Save to update the workbook on disk.

Defining Range Names for Database Tables

Now this file consists of two database tables—the Office table in sheet A, and the Instructor table in sheet B. Creating range names will simplify your work in upcoming exercises with these two tables. In the following steps, you'll assign a range name to each table; in addition, you'll assign meaningful names to the two sheet tabs.

1. On sheet A, select the range A3..G7, which contains the entire Office table, including the field names. Choose Range ➤ Name and assign the name OFFICEDB (for "Office database") to this range:

2. Double-click the A tab on the tab line just above the worksheet area. Type **Offices** as the new name for this sheet, and press ↵.

3. Click the B tab to activate the second sheet. Select the range B:A3..B:K20. This range contains the entire Instructor database table, including the field names. Choose Range ➤ Name and assign the name INSTRUCTDB ("Instructors database") to this range.

4. Double-click the B tab and type **Instructors** as the new name for this sheet. Press ↵ to confirm the name change.

5. Choose File ➤ Save to update the workbook file to disk.

To confirm that you've defined these range names correctly, click the Navigator button on the edit line, or press F5 to open the Go To dialog box. In either list you'll see the names you've defined:

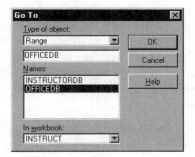

Notice that both names are available regardless of which sheet is currently active in the workbook. As always, the Navigator and the Go To command are convenient tools for jumping from one named range to another in a workbook. You'll use the OFFICEDB and INSTRUCTDB range names in sorting and query operations that require references to the database tables.

Sorting a Database

Once you create a database, you may want to sort the records, rearranging them in a new order. You accomplish this operation by choosing the Range ➤ Sort command.

You can probably imagine several useful new arrangements for the records in the Instructor database. For example, you might decide to sort the database in alphabetical order by instructors' ID numbers; in numerical order by their hourly rates; or in chronological order by their first contract dates. In each of these examples, the specified field—ID, Rate, or Contract—is the key to the sort.

> TIP Range ➤ Sort is not exclusively for use in databases. You can use this command to sort the data in any range of rows, whether or not they form a database.

Given a sorting key and a database range to be sorted, the Data Sort command can arrange the records in ascending or descending order. The difference depends on the type of data stored in the key field and on the standard sort order that is currently in effect. Here is how 1-2-3 sorts data by default:

▶ **Labels.** If the key field contains labels, an ascending sort arranges the records in alphabetical order, from A to Z. If two labels are identical except for alphabetic case, lowercase letters are placed before uppercase letters. Labels that begin with digits are placed before labels that begin with letters. A descending sort produces the reverse order, from Z to A, followed by labels that begin with digits.

▶ **Numeric values.** If the key field contains numeric values, an ascending sort arranges the records from the smallest value to the largest; and a descending sort arranges the records from the largest to the smallest.

▶ **Date numbers.** If the key contains dates that have been entered as 1-2-3 date numbers, an ascending sort arranges the database from the earliest to the latest date; and a descending sort arranges the records from the latest to the earliest date.

> NOTE By default, blank cells are arranged first in an ascending sort, and last in a descending sort. But this sort order can be changed, using the File ➤ User Setup ➤ 1-2-3 Preferences command, as you'll learn at the end of this chapter.

Using the Sort Command

When you choose Range ➤ Sort, the Sort dialog box appears:

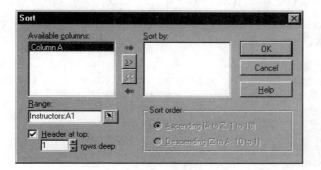

For a database sort, you need to supply several items of information:

▶ In the Range box, specify the range of records that you want to sort.

▶ In the Available columns list, select the column or columns that will serve as the keys to the sort. By clicking the >> button, you can move the selected columns over to the Sort by list. (Conversely, click the << button to move columns out of the Sort by list; you may need to take this step to empty the list after a previous sort.)

▶ For each key, make a choice between the Ascending and Descending options in the Sort order group.

▶ If the database range you have specified includes a row of field names, check the Header at top option.

 WARNING In the process of sorting a database, you must take care not to move the row of field names away from its correct position at the top of the table. By checking the Header at top option in the Sort dialog box, you identify the top row as the location of the field names and you avoid sorting this row in with the records. If you inadvertently move the field names in a sort, click the Undo SmartIcon (or choose Edit ➤ Undo Range Sort) immediately after the sort operation.

In the following exercise you'll sort the Instructor database in ascending chronological order by contract dates:

1. Click the Instructors tab if necessary, and choose Range ➤ Sort.
2. Activate the Range box by pressing Alt+R or by clicking inside the text box.
3. Press the F3 function key. In response, 1-2-3 displays the Range Names dialog box on the screen, with a list of the range names you've defined in your database workbook:

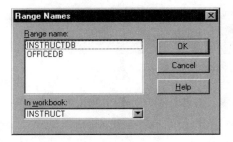

Click the name INSTRUCTDB, representing the table of instructors. Click OK. The Range Names box disappears and 1-2-3 enters the name into the Range box.

4. The Available columns list shows the columns included in the database table. Scroll down the list and select Column I, which is the location of the Contract field. Click the >> button to move this column into the Sort by list. The default ascending order is indicated by the notation [A].

5. If the Header at top option is not checked, click it once. A check appears in the corresponding check box. At this point in your work, the Sort dialog box appears as follows:

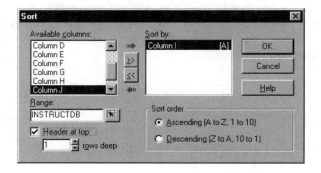

6. Click OK to complete the sort operation.

The sorted database appears in Figure 11.7. As you can see in column I, 1-2-3 has rearranged the instructor records in order of contract dates, from the earliest to the most recent.

ID	Last	First	City	Region	Specialty	Rate	Hrs	Contract	Yrs	OK
D-106	Weinberg	P.	Miami	S	Database	$75	59	18-Jan-91	6.0	B
N-101	Schwartz	B.	Boston	E	Networks	$150	178	02-Mar-91	5.9	A
A-103	Perez	D.	Las Vegas	W	Accounting	$100	5	11-Jul-91	5.6	C
W-113	Porter	D.	Seattle	N	WP	$125	59	02-Aug-91	5.5	B
W-124	Meyer	J.	New York	E	WP	$150	85	05-May-92	4.7	B
S-125	Ashford	W.	Washington, D.C.	E	Spreadsheet	$150	145	10-May-92	4.7	A
S-127	Gill	P.	Los Angeles	W	Spreadsheet	$100	35	22-Jun-92	4.6	C
W-119	Davis	G.	San Francisco	W	WP	$150	149	09-Jul-92	4.6	A
T-128	Eng	R.	Albuquerque	S	Programming	$75	75	11-Oct-92	4.3	B
T-133	Ramirez	F.	Boston	E	Programming	$150	73	08-Feb-93	4.0	B
D-139	Porter	M.	Washington, D.C.	E	Database	$150	26	28-Mar-94	2.8	B
D-137	Sanchez	W.	Indianapolis	N	Database	$100	47	16-Apr-94	2.8	B
W-145	Banks	S.	St. Louis	S	WP	$150	55	10-Jun-95	1.6	A
D-143	Cody	L.	Los Angeles	W	Database	$75	43	20-Jun-95	1.6	B
S-149	Harris	P.	Dallas	S	Spreadsheet	$150	17	12-Feb-96	1.0	New
A-146	Daniels	A.	Atlanta	S	Accounting	$125	24	09-May-96	0.7	New
S-155	Roberts	P.	Chicago	N	Spreadsheet	$100	10	21-Aug-96	0.4	New

Figure 11.7: The Instructor database sorted chronologically by contract date

Sorting by More Than One Key Field

Sometimes a single key is not enough to produce a complete or useful sort. When two or more records have the same entry in the primary key field, you need to choose a secondary key to decide the order of these matching records. One simple example of this occurs in the Instructor database: There are two instructors with the last name of Porter. When you sort the records alphabetically by instructors' names, you need to select the Last field as the first, or primary, key, and the First field as the second key, to make sure that these two names appear in the correct order. Try this second sorting exercise now:

1. Choose Range ➤ Sort. The sort range and Sort by column from the previous sort are still shown in the dialog box. Select Column H in the Available columns list and click the << button once to move

Column I out of the Sort by list. The Header at top option should still be checked.

2. In the Available columns list select Column B and then click the >> button twice. The Sort dialog box appears as follows:

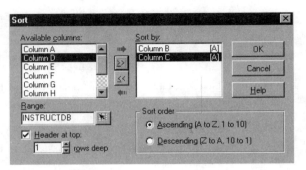

3. Click OK to complete the sort.

The resulting sort is shown in Figure 11.8. The records are now arranged by the Last and First fields. In particular, notice in rows 14 and 15 that the two Porters are in the correct order—first D. Porter of Seattle, then M. Porter of Washington, D.C.

	A	B	C	D	E	F	G	H	I	J	K
1					Instructor Database						
2											
3	ID	Last	First	City	Region	Specialty	Rate	Hrs	Contract	Yrs	OK
4	S-125	Ashford	W.	Washington, D.C.	E	Spreadsheet	$150	145	10-May-92	4.7	A
5	W-145	Banks	S.	St. Louis	S	WP	$150	55	10-Jun-95	1.6	A
6	D-143	Cody	L.	Los Angeles	W	Database	$75	43	20-Jun-95	1.6	B
7	A-146	Daniels	A.	Atlanta	S	Accounting	$125	24	09-May-96	0.7	New
8	W-119	Davis	G.	San Francisco	W	WP	$150	149	09-Jul-92	4.6	A
9	T-128	Eng	R.	Albuquerque	S	Programming	$75	75	11-Oct-92	4.3	B
10	S-127	Gill	P.	Los Angeles	W	Spreadsheet	$100	35	22-Jun-92	4.6	C
11	S-149	Harris	P.	Dallas	S	Spreadsheet	$150	17	12-Feb-96	1.0	New
12	W-124	Meyer	J.	New York	E	WP	$150	85	05-May-92	4.7	B
13	A-103	Perez	D.	Las Vegas	W	Accounting	$100	5	11-Jul-91	5.6	C
14	W-113	Porter	D.	Seattle	N	WP	$125	59	02-Aug-91	5.5	B
15	D-139	Porter	M.	Washington, D.C.	E	Database	$150	26	28-Mar-94	2.8	B
16	T-133	Ramirez	F.	Boston	E	Programming	$150	73	08-Feb-93	4.0	B
17	S-155	Roberts	P.	Chicago	N	Spreadsheet	$100	10	21-Aug-96	0.4	New
18	D-137	Sanchez	W.	Indianapolis	N	Database	$100	47	16-Apr-94	2.8	B
19	N-101	Schwartz	B.	Boston	E	Networks	$150	178	02-Mar-91	5.9	A
20	D-106	Weinberg	P.	Miami	S	Database	$75	59	18-Jan-91	6.0	B
21											

Figure 11.8: *Sorting the database by two keys. Notice that the two instructors named Porter are sorted in the correct order.*

Multiple Sort Keys

The Data Sort command allows you to select more than just two key fields. For example, imagine that you have sorted the database by the Region field as the primary key and the City field as the secondary key, as shown in Figure 11.9. Examining the result of this sort, you realize that you would like to be able to sort the records within each city in alphabetical order by the Specialty field. In other words, your goal is three sorting keys: First the Region field, then the City field, and finally the Specialty field.

To sort by more than two keys, you simply continue developing a list of keys in the Sort by box. For example, to carry out the three-key sort by the Region, City, and Specialty fields, choose Range ➤ Sort, and move Columns E, D, and F into the Sort by box:

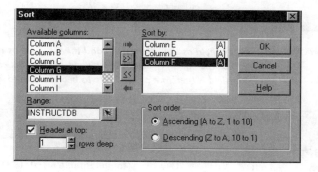

Click OK to complete the sort operation. The sorted database appears in Figure 11.10. You can see that the database has indeed been sorted by three keys: First the records are arranged by region. Then, within each region, they are arranged by city. And where there are duplicate city entries, the records are always arranged by the instructors' specialties.

As you've seen, 1-2-3 retains your previous sorting instructions each time you choose Data ➤ Sort. If you want to start over again with a new set of sort keys, you click the << button to move previous keys out of the Sort by box. Take a minute now to sort the database once again by instructors' names. Choose Range ➤ Sort and click << three times. Then move Column B and Column C into the Sort by box and click OK. Choose File ➤ Save to save this version of the workbook to disk.

Chapter 11 Database Tables

B	A	B	C	D	E	F	G	H	I	J	K
1					Instructor Database						
2											
3	ID	Last	First	City	Region	Specialty	Rate	Hrs	Contract	Yrs	OK
4	N-101	Schwartz	B.	Boston	E	Networks	$150	178	02-Mar-91	5.9	A
5	T-133	Ramirez	F.	Boston	E	Programming	$150	73	08-Feb-93	4.0	B
6	W-124	Meyer	J.	New York	E	WP	$150	85	05-May-92	4.7	B
7	D-139	Porter	M.	Washington, D.C.	E	Database	$150	26	28-Mar-94	2.8	B
8	S-125	Ashford	W.	Washington, D.C.	E	Spreadsheet	$150	145	10-May-92	4.7	A
9	S-155	Roberts	P.	Chicago	N	Spreadsheet	$100	10	21-Aug-96	0.4	New
10	D-137	Sanchez	W.	Indianapolis	N	Database	$100	47	16-Apr-94	2.8	B
11	W-113	Porter	D.	Seattle	N	WP	$125	59	02-Aug-91	5.5	B
12	T-128	Eng	R.	Albuquerque	S	Programming	$75	75	11-Oct-92	4.3	B
13	A-146	Daniels	A.	Atlanta	S	Accounting	$125	24	09-May-96	0.7	New
14	S-149	Harris	P.	Dallas	S	Spreadsheet	$150	17	12-Feb-96	1.0	New
15	D-106	Weinberg	P.	Miami	S	Database	$75	59	18-Jan-91	6.0	B
16	W-145	Banks	S.	St. Louis	S	WP	$150	55	10-Jun-95	1.6	A
17	A-103	Perez	D.	Las Vegas	W	Accounting	$100	5	11-Jul-91	5.6	C
18	S-127	Gill	P.	Los Angeles	W	Spreadsheet	$100	35	22-Jun-92	4.6	C
19	D-143	Cody	L.	Los Angeles	W	Database	$75	43	20-Jun-95	1.6	B
20	W-119	Davis	G.	San Francisco	W	WP	$150	149	09-Jul-92	4.6	A

Figure 11.9: **The Region field as the primary key and the City field as the secondary key. Notice that the Specialty field is not always in alphabetical order within a given city; this field is therefore a candidate to become a third key to the sort.**

B	A	B	C	D	E	F	G	H	I	J	K
1					Instructor Database						
2											
3	ID	Last	First	City	Region	Specialty	Rate	Hrs	Contract	Yrs	OK
4	N-101	Schwartz	B.	Boston	E	Networks	$150	178	02-Mar-91	5.9	A
5	T-133	Ramirez	F.	Boston	E	Programming	$150	73	08-Feb-93	4.0	B
6	W-124	Meyer	J.	New York	E	WP	$150	85	05-May-92	4.7	B
7	D-139	Porter	M.	Washington, D.C.	E	Database	$150	26	28-Mar-94	2.8	B
8	S-125	Ashford	W.	Washington, D.C.	E	Spreadsheet	$150	145	10-May-92	4.7	A
9	S-155	Roberts	P.	Chicago	N	Spreadsheet	$100	10	21-Aug-96	0.4	New
10	D-137	Sanchez	W.	Indianapolis	N	Database	$100	47	16-Apr-94	2.8	B
11	W-113	Porter	D.	Seattle	N	WP	$125	59	02-Aug-91	5.5	B
12	T-128	Eng	R.	Albuquerque	S	Programming	$75	75	11-Oct-92	4.3	B
13	A-146	Daniels	A.	Atlanta	S	Accounting	$125	24	09-May-96	0.7	New
14	S-149	Harris	P.	Dallas	S	Spreadsheet	$150	17	12-Feb-96	1.0	New
15	D-106	Weinberg	P.	Miami	S	Database	$75	59	18-Jan-91	6.0	B
16	W-145	Banks	S.	St. Louis	S	WP	$150	55	10-Jun-95	1.6	A
17	A-103	Perez	D.	Las Vegas	W	Accounting	$100	5	11-Jul-91	5.6	C
18	D-143	Cody	L.	Los Angeles	W	Database	$75	43	20-Jun-95	1.6	B
19	S-127	Gill	P.	Los Angeles	W	Spreadsheet	$100	35	22-Jun-92	4.6	C
20	W-119	Davis	G.	San Francisco	W	WP	$150	149	09-Jul-92	4.6	A

Figure 11.10: **Sorting the database by three key fields—Region, City, and Specialty**

Changing 1-2-3's Default Sort Order

The sort order refers to 1-2-3's default techniques for sorting a database. This order may include a variety of special characteristics. For example, when a key field contains some label entries that begin with digits and others that begin with letters of the alphabet, the digits are sorted to the top of the list in an ascending sort.

You can see an example of this situation by looking back at the Office database table in Figure 11.6. The Address field contains three labels that begin with digits, and one that begins with a letter. If you sort this table by the Address field, the resulting order conforms to the "numbers before words" default. To demonstrate that this is so, try the following brief exercise:

1. Choose Range ➤ Sort.
2. Select the Range box, press F3, and double-click the OFFICEDB entry in the Range Names dialog box. 1-2-3 copies this name into the Range text box.
3. Select Column B in the Available columns list and click the >> key once. The Sort dialog box now looks like this:

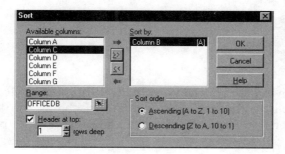

4. Click OK to complete the sort.

    Figure 11.11 shows the Office database, sorted by the Address field. You can see the result of 1-2-3's default sort order: The addresses that begin with digits come first, followed by the address that begins with a letter.

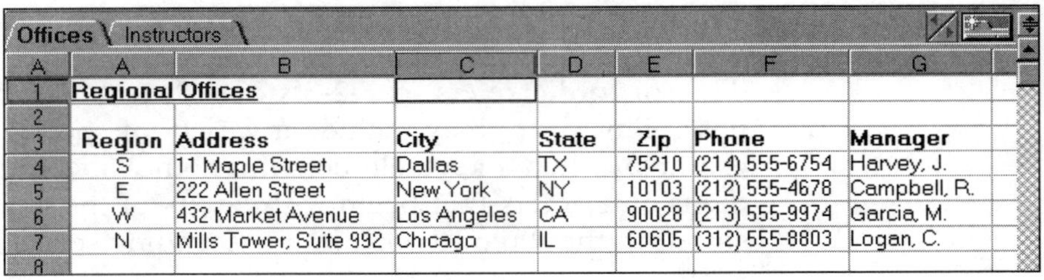

	A	B	C	D	E	F	G
1	Regional Offices						
2							
3	Region	Address	City	State	Zip	Phone	Manager
4	S	11 Maple Street	Dallas	TX	75210	(214) 555-6754	Harvey, J.
5	E	222 Allen Street	New York	NY	10103	(212) 555-4678	Campbell, R.
6	W	432 Market Avenue	Los Angeles	CA	90028	(213) 555-9974	Garcia, M.
7	N	Mills Tower, Suite 992	Chicago	IL	60605	(312) 555-8803	Logan, C.

Figure 11.11: *A demonstration of the "numbers before words" sort order*

Except for the purposes of this experimental exercise, it is perhaps unlikely that you would actually want to sort the office database by the Address field, because the four addresses in the table are all in different cities. But a sort by addresses may be realistic in a database containing many addresses in the same city.

In some specific cases you may want to change 1-2-3's default sort order. To do so, choose File ➤ User Setup ➤ 1-2-3 Preferences and click the General tab if necessary. At the lower-left corner of the dialog box, you'll see the options available for modifying sort operations:

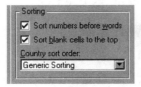

By removing the checks from the Sort numbers before words and Sort blank cells to the top options, you can change two of 1-2-3's default sort order characteristics. In the Country sort order list you can choose options that conform to sorting standards for languages other than English.

Summary

A 1-2-3 database table is a collection of records that you enter into consecutive rows of a worksheet. Each table begins with a row of field names. The entries within a field all belong to the same data type. A database may consist of one or more such tables.

You use the Range ➤ Sort command to rearrange the records of a database table in alphabetical, numeric, or chronological order. The Sort dialog box allows you to define multiple sorting keys, with options for ascending or descending sorts. By checking the Header at top option, you avoid sorting the row of field names into the body of the database table.

The Create ➤ Database menu (shown back in Figure 11.1) contains commands representing a variety of important database operations. As you'll learn in Chapter 12, 1-2-3 calls on the resources of the Lotus Approach application to perform all of these operations.

CHAPTER 12
Database Queries

FAST TRACK

To create a query table, 367

choose Create ➤ Database ➤ Query Table and specify a database range. Click OK and then click the mouse on the sheet location where you want to display the query table. In the Worksheet Assistant dialog box, develop a list of fields for the query table, and click Done. The query object appears on your worksheet, and is linked to the original database table.

To display records that match one simple criterion, 369

select an existing query and choose Query Table ➤ Edit. Then choose Browse ➤ Find ➤ Find Using Worksheet. In the blank cells displayed in query table, enter the value you want to search for beneath the appropriate field name, and press ↵. The matching records appear in the query table.

To find records that match a complex combination of criteria, 370

select the target query, choose Query Table ➤ Edit, and choose Browse ➤ Find ➤ Find Assistant. In the Find Assistant dialog box, choose Basic Find and click Next. In the Condition 1 tab, choose a field name and an operator, and then enter a search value for selecting records. To add another criterion to the expression, click the button labeled "Find on Another Field." In the next Condition panel, choose an AND or an OR connector, and then specify another field, operator, and matching value. Continue this process until you've entered all the necessary criteria. Then click Done. The records that match your criteria will appear in the query table.

To delete records that match the stated criteria,   **374**

select an existing query and choose Query ➤ Edit. Then choose Browse ➤ Delete Found Set. On the resulting dialog box, click Yes if you're sure you want to carry out the deletion. There is no Undo command for this operation.

To use the Query by Box feature for expressing criteria,   **375**

select a query table, choose Query Table ➤ Edit, and then choose Browse ➤ Find ➤ Find Assistant. In the Find/Sort Assistant dialog box, choose the Find using Query by Box option and click Next. In the Query by Box tab, choose a field and an operator and enter a matching value for each separate criterion. Then click And or Or to connect with the next criterion. The Description box displays a graphic representation of the criteria you're building.

To revise the criteria displayed graphically in the Query by Box feature,   **377**

use your mouse to drag any criterion to a new position in the Description box, thus creating a new relationship between the criteria.

To revise database records that match the stated criteria,   **377**

simply edit the data that appears in the query table. The changes are copied to the linked database table.

To combine information from multiple databases,   **378**

select an existing query and choose Query Table ➤ Edit. Then choose Edit ➤ Open Into Full Window to view the query in the Lotus Approach application window. In Approach, choose Create ➤ Join. On the Join dialog box, click Open, and open the database table that you want to connect with the existing table. Back in the Join dialog box, drag the related field from one field list to another, creating a line that represents the relationship between the two tables. Click OK. Then choose Worksheet ➤ Add Field and drag any target field names from the Add Field box to the query table. Choose File ➤ Exit and Return to Lotus 1-2-3 when you've completed the join. Choose Query Table ➤ Refresh to update the query in 1-2-3.

A query is an important feature for working with the databases you develop in 1-2-3. In a query table you view a copy of database records, selected by conditions you express. The table can be used for finding, deleting, copying, and revising records. To create a query—and to perform the operations you request—1-2-3 employs the resources of Lotus Approach, the database management program included in SmartSuite 97.

The criteria for selecting records in a query can be simple or complex. For example, in the instructor database that you developed in Chapter 11, you might write criteria to look for any of the following combinations of records:

▶ Instructors in the Southern region

▶ Instructors in the Southern region who specialize in spreadsheets or databases

▶ A Los Angeles instructor who specializes in spreadsheets

▶ Cities where programming or networking experts are available

▶ Western region instructors whose hourly rate is less than or equal to $100 per hour

▶ Spreadsheet experts who have an A rating in the OK field

▶ Southern or Eastern database experts who have an A or B rating and work for less than $100 per hour

▶ Eastern region instructors who have worked at least four years for Computing Conferences, Inc., and have an A or B rating

To simplify the process of developing queries like these, Lotus provides a variety of tools for expressing criteria—in words and in graphics. Using these tools, you can quickly build efficient and reliable queries.

In short, a query table is an Approach object that resides on a 1-2-3 sheet and is linked to the source database. The object itself can be moved, copied, reformatted, resized, or deleted as a unit. It displays a copy of a database, or a copy of selected fields and records from a database. In this chapter you'll explore the general characteristics of query tables. Along the way you'll see examples of several important query operations:

▶ Locating records that match the criteria you express

▶ Copying records from a query to a new sheet location

▶ Deleting database records that match specific criteria

- Updating the contents of a database by revising the records in a query table
- Joining the information from two or more related database tables

> **NOTE** Chapter 13 covers additional query operations, including the use of a query table to work with data from an external database.

Creating and Using a Query

As your first experiment with a query table, suppose you want to list the names and specialties of the instructors in the Southern region. In other words, you want to examine records that contain an entry of "S" in the Region field. Any record in which this condition is true will be selected for your query; other records will remain unselected.

Reopen the INSTRUCT.123 file, and begin this exercise by placing two new sheets in the workbook. Click the Instructors tab and then click the New Sheet button twice, adding sheets C and D. These sheets will give you a place to experiment with queries. You'll display a query table on sheet C and later you'll try copying data from the query to sheet D.

Here's how to create the initial query table:

1. Click the tab for sheet C, and then choose Create ➤ Database ➤ Query Table (or click the Create Query SmartIcon on the Range SmartIcon bar). A dialog box named Query Table Assistant appears on the Desktop.

2. Select the range box (labeled "A 1-2-3 range") and press F3 to open the Range Names dialog box. Highlight INSTRUCTDB in the Range name list and click OK. This range name is copied to the Query dialog box. You're now ready to create a query based on the Instructors table:

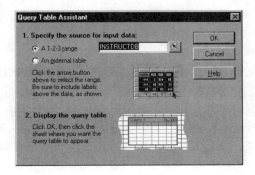

3. Click OK on the Query Table Assistant dialog box. A message box instructs you to click on the sheet location where you want to place the query table:

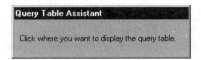

4. Click the mouse near the upper-left corner of sheet C. The next dialog box to appear is called the Worksheet Assistant. It contains a list of all the fields in the Instructor table, and an Add button for selecting the fields that you want to display in your query.

5. Select Last in the Fields list and click the Add button. The field name appears in the box labeled "Fields to place on view." Repeat this action to add First, Region, and Specialty to the list:

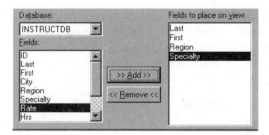

6. Click the Done button. An object named Query Table 1 appears on sheet C, and a variety of menus and buttons from Lotus Approach appear at the top of the Desktop.

7. Double-click the title bar of the query object. The InfoBox for query properties appears on the Desktop. Click the Basics tab if necessary. In the text box labeled "Query table name" enter the word **Instructors**. Then close the InfoBox. The new name appears on the title bar of the query object. Use your mouse to resize the query object, as shown in Figure 12.1.

Copying Selected Data to an Output Range

Keep in mind that this query table is an Approach object, linked to the database table that resides on the Instructors sheet. For the moment, the query shows the selected field entries for all the records in the table.

Figure 12.1: A query object created from the Instructors database table

Your next tasks are to issue the instructions for selecting the records from the Southern region, and then to copy the records to sheet D. To accomplish this, follow these steps:

1. Choose Browse ➤ Find ➤ Find Using Worksheet. The query table now shows only a blank row of cells beneath the field names; this format is designed to accept specifications for the data you want to find:

2. Select the cell beneath the Region field name, and type the uppercase letter **S**. Then press ↵. In response, the query table displays the names and specialties of the five instructors from the Southern region:

   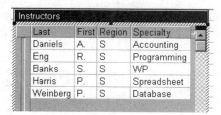

3. Now double-click the title bar of the query table. In the query InfoBox click the Output range tab.

4. In the range box labeled "Copy query table results to range (optional)" type the reference D:A1. Select the option button labeled "Variable—Changes to show all results":

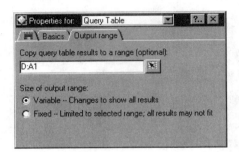

5. Close the InfoBox and click the tab for sheet D. As you can see, the data selection has been copied to the sheet:

TIP The query is linked to the original database table and to the output range on sheet D. If you edit the data in the query table, your changes are copied to both the database and the output range.

Finding Records That Match Multiple Criteria

In the previous exercise, you used the query table itself to specify a simple selection criterion. For developing more complex criteria, 1-2-3 and Approach provide a more elaborate tool called the Find/Sort Assistant. You'll explore this tool next.

Suppose you want to find a subset of the previous selection—specifically, all the Southern instructors who have OK ratings of A or B. You might express this criterion as:

Region = S and (OK = A or OK = B)

In other words, a record must have a value of S in the Region field and a value of either A or B in the OK field. Using the Find/Sort Assistant to build criteria, you'll find a variety of simple techniques to establish And and Or conditions.

To carry out this exercise, you'll use the query table that you've already created on sheet C:

1. Click the tab for sheet C. Select the query object by clicking its title bar. Then reactivate the query by choosing Query Table ➤ Edit. The Browse menu appears on the menu bar, and a selection of query-related buttons appear above the workbook tabs.

2. Choose Browse ➤ Find ➤ Find Assistant or click the Find Assistant button. As shown in Figure 12.2, the Find/Sort Assistant dialog box contains tabs representing the steps for performing a record search in your query table. The first tab, Find Type, contains a list of the various procedures you can use. The list is labeled "Type of find," and is located at the right side of the dialog box. For this exercise, keep the default selection, Basic Find.

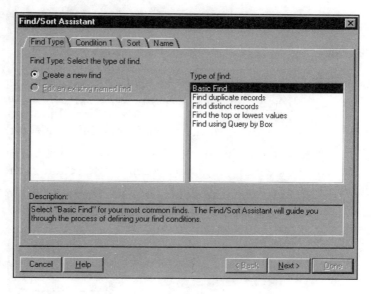

Figure 12.2: **The first step in the Find/Sort Assistant**

3. Click the Next button, located at the lower-right corner of the dialog box. The Condition 1 tab is designed for you to develop a first selection criterion. Select Region in the Fields list. In the Operator list, keep the first selection, "is exactly equal to." In the first cell of the Values

list, enter **S**. When you complete this condition, read the text provided in the Description box (Figure 12.3) to confirm that you've created the criterion you want.

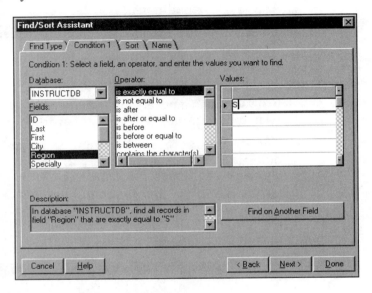

Figure 12.3: **Developing a first selection criterion**

4. Click the button labeled "Find on Another Field." A new tab named Condition 2 is created. At the top of the panel you can choose between "Find fewer records (AND)" or "Find more records (OR)" as a connector with the previous condition. Keep the default AND selection.

5. Scroll down the Fields list and choose the OK field. Again keep the default "is exactly equal to" selection in the Operator list.

6. Activate the Values list, and enter **A** in the first cell and **B** in the second cell. As you can see in the Description box, this creates an *or* condition ("equal to A or B"):

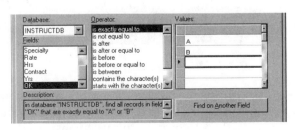

7. Click the Done button.

The query table now shows the three records that match the criteria. All three records are in the Southern region:

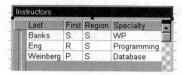

But the table does not yet show the OK field, so you can't confirm that your second search criterion has worked properly. You can solve this problem by adding a field to the query table:

1. Widen the query table by positioning the mouse pointer over the selection handle on the right border; when the pointer changes to a two-headed arrow, hold down the left mouse button and drag the handle to the right.

2. Inside the query table, click the Specialty field name with the right mouse button, and choose Add Field from the resulting shortcut menu:

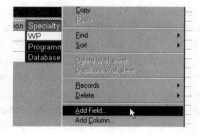

3. In the Add Field dialog box, select the OK field. Then hold down the left mouse button and drag this field name into the query table, to a position just to the right of the Specialty field:

4. Release the mouse button to complete the drag operation. Close the Add Field dialog box by clicking the X at the right side of the title bar.

The OK field now appears as part of the query table. You can see that the selection is correct. The table contains the three Southern-region instructors who have OK ratings of A or B:

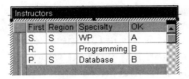

TIP You can remove a field from a query table simply by dragging the field name to a position outside the query box.

Using a Query to Delete Records

The Browse ➤ Delete Found Set command removes a selection of records from the linked database table. Like delete operations in any software environment, this command requires some care. Accidental or incorrect use of the command can result in large losses of data. For this reason, you should save your database just before you use the Delete command. If Delete produces unexpected results—or if you change your mind about the deletion—you can close the current worksheet window without saving it, and then reopen the original version from disk.

As an experiment with the Delete command, imagine that you've decided to drop instructors who have OK ratings of C. In the following steps you'll proceed just to the point of deletion, and then you'll back out of the operation to avoid any actual changes in your database table:

1. Choose the Browse ➤ Find ➤ Find using Worksheet command.
2. In the query table, enter **C** in the cell located beneath the OK field name, and press ↵. The query table shows the two instructors who have OK ratings of C:

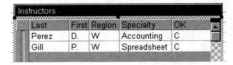

3. Choose Browse ➤ Delete Found Set. The following warning box appears on the Desktop:

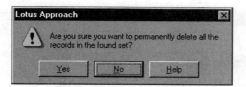

If you were to click the Yes button at this point, the query would delete the two selected records from the linked database table that resides on sheet B. The deletion would be permanent; no Undo command is available for this operation. To complete this exercise, click the No button to cancel the deletion.

Because a query table is linked to the original database table, you can use the query to make other kinds of changes in the information stored in a database. For example, you can select records that you wish to revise, and make the necessary data changes directly in the query table. The revisions are automatically carried forward to the source database table and to any output table you've created from the query. You'll experiment with this operation in the next section. You'll also explore the Query by Box feature, another tool for building search criteria.

Updating the Linked Database Table

Here are the general steps for revising a database from a query:

1. Create a query table that contains the records you want to modify.
2. Make any changes you want in the content of these selected records.
3. Check the original database table to confirm that you've made the intended revisions.

Consider the following situation for testing this procedure. The Western region has just completed a series of training conferences focusing on spreadsheets and word processing. The regional instructors specializing in these fields each worked for ten hours at the conferences. Your job is to locate the records for these instructors and increase the entries in their Hrs fields. Proceed as follows:

1. Select the query table on sheet C and choose Browse ➤ Find ➤ Find Assistant, or click the Find Assistant button.

2. In the first tab of the Find/Sort Assistant dialog box, choose Find using Query by Box in the Type of find list:

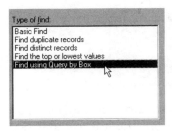

3. Click the Next button. The Query by Box tab provides a graphical technique for building complex criteria. For each criterion expression, you specify a field, an operator, and a value; multiple criteria can be connected as And or Or conditions.

4. For your first criterion, pull down the Field list and choose Region. Keep the default operator, the = sign. In the Value box enter **W** for the Western region. In the description box, you can see how your criterion is expressed:

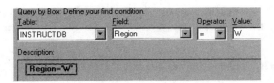

5. Click the And button to prepare for the next criterion.

6. Pull down the Field list and choose Specialty. Keep = as the operator, and type **Spreadsheet** in the Value box.

7. Click the Or button. Select the contents of the Value box, and replace its contents with the new entry **WP**. Here is how these conditions are expressed in the Description box:

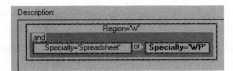

In short, this query will search for instructors in the Western region who specialize in either spreadsheets or word processing.

8. Click the Done button.

Creating and Using a Query

 TIP As you build complex expressions in the Query by Box tool, you may sometimes want to change the relationships between criteria. To do so, you can use your mouse to drag an expression to a new location. For example, in the exercise above, you could drag the expression Specialty = 'WP' to a position outside of the group of criteria in which it's located. Doing so results in a new *or* relationship and an entirely new meaning for the query. A good way to learn how to revise criteria is to experiment with mouse actions inside the Query by Box tool and then study the resulting queries.

Back in the query table, you can see the two records that match the criteria you've expressed:

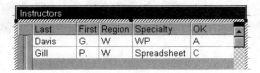

These are indeed the records you want to revise, but the target field—**Hrs**—isn't displayed in the query. In the next steps, you'll remove the OK field, add the Hrs field, and make the data revisions:

1. Click the OK field name, and drag the name to a position outside of the query table. Release the mouse pointer, and the OK field is removed from the table.

2. Click the Specialty field name with the right mouse button, and choose Add Field from the resulting shortcut menu.

3. From the Add Field dialog box, drag the Hrs field into the query table. Then close the Add Field box. The query now displays the information you want to revise:

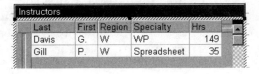

4. Inside the query table itself, select the Hrs entry for the instructor named Davis, and enter a new value of **159**. Likewise, select the Hrs entry for Gill and enter a new value of **45**. In both cases, these values are ten hours greater than the previous entries.

In response, 1-2-3 copies the revised records to the database table. Now click the Instructors tab to see what's happened to the original database table. The records for Davis and Gill have been updated from the changes you made in the query table, as shown in Figure 12.4. (The two records have been highlighted in this figure for clarity.)

	A	B	C	D	E	F	G	H	I	J	K
1				Instructor Database							
2											
3	ID	Last	First	City	Region	Specialty	Rate	Hrs	Contract	Yrs	OK
4	S-125	Ashford	W.	Washington, D.C.	E	Spreadsheet	$150	145	10-May-92	4.7	A
5	W-145	Banks	S.	St. Louis	S	WP	$150	55	10-Jun-95	1.6	A
6	D-143	Cody	L.	Los Angeles	W	Database	$75	43	20-Jun-95	1.6	B
7	A-146	Daniels	A.	Atlanta	S	Accounting	$125	24	09-May-96	0.7	New
8	W-119	Davis	G.	San Francisco	W	WP	$150	159	09-Jul-92	4.6	A
9	T-128	Eng	R.	Albuquerque	S	Programming	$75	75	11-Oct-92	4.3	B
10	S-127	Gill	P.	Los Angeles	W	Spreadsheet	$100	45	22-Jun-92	4.6	C
11	S-149	Harris	P.	Dallas	S	Spreadsheet	$150	17	12-Feb-96	1.0	New
12	W-124	Meyer	J.	New York	E	WP	$150	85	05-May-92	4.7	B
13	A-103	Perez	D.	Las Vegas	W	Accounting	$100	5	11-Jul-91	5.6	C
14	W-113	Porter	D.	Seattle	N	WP	$125	59	02-Aug-91	5.5	B
15	D-139	Porter	M.	Washington, D.C.	E	Database	$150	26	28-Mar-94	2.8	B
16	T-133	Ramirez	F.	Boston	E	Programming	$150	73	08-Feb-93	4.0	B
17	S-155	Roberts	P.	Chicago	N	Spreadsheet	$100	10	21-Aug-96	0.4	New
18	D-137	Sanchez	W.	Indianapolis	N	Database	$100	47	16-Apr-94	2.8	B
19	N-101	Schwartz	B.	Boston	E	Networks	$150	178	02-Mar-91	5.9	A
20	D-106	Weinberg	P.	Miami	S	Database	$75	59	18-Jan-91	6.0	B

Figure 12.4: Updating a database from changes in a query table

Joining Two Database Tables

Using a join operation, you can combine information from related database tables. For example, the INSTRUCT.123 workbook contains two tables—the Offices table on the first sheet and the Instructors table on the second sheet. These two tables are related by their Region fields. To locate the regional office for a given instructor, you could manually search through the two tables for the information you need. But the join operation simplifies and automates this process by creating a table that combines the information from the two tables.

In a join query for this database, 1-2-3 uses the common field to correlate information from the two tables. To see exactly how this works, suppose you want to create a table that includes instructor names along with the names of the corresponding regional managers and the phone numbers of regional offices. In the upcoming exercise, you'll revise the query table so that it shows fields from all the records in the Instructors database table, and you'll use a join operation to add information from the Offices database table:

1. Click the tab for sheet C and select the query table by clicking its title bar. Then choose Query Table ➤ Edit.

2. Select the Specialty field and drag it out of the query table. Release the mouse button to remove the field. Repeat this action to remove the Hrs field from the query. Now only three fields remain, Last, First, and Region.

3. Choose Edit ➤ Open Into Full Window. This command displays the query object inside the Lotus Approach application window. Maximize the window, as shown in Figure 12.5.

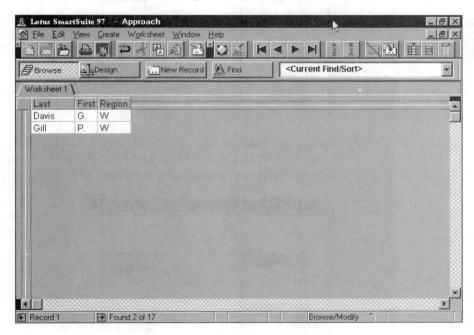

Figure 12.5: **Working with the query table inside Lotus Approach**

4. Choose Worksheet ➤ Find ➤ Find All. As a result, the query shows the First, Last, and Region fields for all the records of the Instructors table.

5. Choose Create ➤ Join. In the Join dialog box, click the Open button. The Open dialog box appears on the Desktop.
6. Pull down the Files of type list and choose 1-2-3 Ranges (*).
7. If necessary, choose Instruct.123 from the Look In box. In response, the Open dialog box displays the named ranges in the INSTRUCT.123 file.
8. Select the range name OfficeDB, and click Open. Back in the Join dialog box, you can now see field lists representing both the Instructors and the Offices database tables:

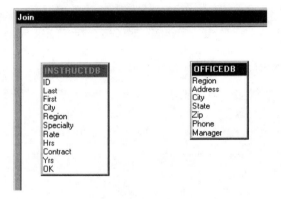

9. Select the Region field in the INSTRUCTDB box, and drag it to the Region field in the OFFICEDB box. Release the mouse button, and a line is drawn to connect the two related fields:

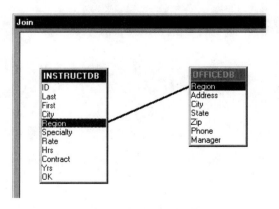

10. Click OK on the Join dialog box. Your query is now linked to both the Instructors and Offices database tables.

11. The Add Field box is automatically opened. Pull down the table list and choose OFFICEDB. The Field list displays the field names of the Offices table:

12. Use your mouse to drag the Phone field name from the Add Field box to the position just to the right of the Region field. Then drag the Manager field from the Add Field box to the position next to the Phone field. Close the Add Field box.

    The result of your work appears in Figure 12.6. The joined query now shows the office phone number and the manager's name for each of the instructors in the database.

    Now choose File ➤ Exit and Return to 1-2-3 to switch back to the 1-2-3 application. The query on sheet C contains the same information as shown back in Figure 12.6. You can now use the query InfoBox to make a copy of the joined query on sheet D:

1. Choose Query Table ➤ Query Table Properties, and click the Output range tab on the resulting InfoBox.

2. Enter D:A5 in the range box. Then close the InfoBox.

3. Click tab D. The joined database table appears as shown in Figure 12.7.

    If you wish, continue experimenting with join operations, using the query displayed on sheet C. (Later in this chapter, you'll see the result of another join procedure, producing an address table for the instructor database.) When you're finished, close the INSTRUCT.123 workbook without saving the work you've done in this chapter. You'll need the Offices and Instructors database tables intact and unchanged for exercises in Chapter 13.

Worksheet 1

Last	First	Region	Phone	Manager
Ashford	W.	E	(212) 555-4678	Campbell, R.
Banks	S.	S	(214) 555-6754	Harvey, J.
Cody	L.	W	(213) 555-9974	Garcia, M.
Daniels	A.	S	(214) 555-6754	Harvey, J.
Davis	G.	W	(213) 555-9974	Garcia, M.
Eng	R.	S	(214) 555-6754	Harvey, J.
Gill	P.	W	(213) 555-9974	Garcia, M.
Harris	P.	S	(214) 555-6754	Harvey, J.
Meyer	J.	E	(212) 555-4678	Campbell, R.
Perez	D.	W	(213) 555-9974	Garcia, M.
Porter	D.	N	(312) 555-8803	Logan, C.
Porter	M.	E	(212) 555-4678	Campbell, R.
Ramirez	F.	E	(212) 555-4678	Campbell, R.
Roberts	P.	N	(312) 555-8803	Logan, C.
Sanchez	W.	N	(312) 555-8803	Logan, C.
Schwartz	B.	E	(212) 555-4678	Campbell, R.
Weinberg	P.	S	(214) 555-6754	Harvey, J.

Figure 12.6: ***The result of the join operation. Each record now contains information from both the Instructors database table and the Offices database table.***

Offices \ Instructors \ C \ D \

D	A	B	C	D	E
4					
5	Last	First	Region	Phone	Manager
6	Ashford	W.	E	(212) 555-4678	Campbell, R.
7	Banks	S.	S	(214) 555-6754	Harvey, J.
8	Cody	L.	W	(213) 555-9974	Garcia, M.
9	Daniels	A.	S	(214) 555-6754	Harvey, J.
10	Davis	G.	W	(213) 555-9974	Garcia, M.
11	Eng	R.	S	(214) 555-6754	Harvey, J.
12	Gill	P.	W	(213) 555-9974	Garcia, M.
13	Harris	P.	S	(214) 555-6754	Harvey, J.
14	Meyer	J.	E	(212) 555-4678	Campbell, R.
15	Perez	D.	W	(213) 555-9974	Garcia, M.
16	Porter	D.	N	(312) 555-8803	Logan, C.
17	Porter	M.	E	(212) 555-4678	Campbell, R.
18	Ramirez	F.	E	(212) 555-4678	Campbell, R.
19	Roberts	P.	N	(312) 555-8803	Logan, C.
20	Sanchez	W.	N	(312) 555-8803	Logan, C.
21	Schwartz	B.	E	(212) 555-4678	Campbell, R.
22	Weinberg	P.	S	(214) 555-6754	Harvey, J.
23					
24					

Figure 12.7: ***Copying a joined query table to a sheet***

Other Database Objects

In addition to query tables, the Create ➤ Database menu gives you access to five other objects that can be linked to a 1-2-3 database and displayed on a sheet:

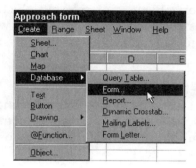

These are all Approach objects—that is, objects that 1-2-3 creates and manages through the resources of the Lotus Approach database management program. Here are brief descriptions of each type of object:

▶ A form is a tool for viewing and editing individual records, one at a time. Some or all of the fields of a database table are arranged inside the form. You can use the form to scroll from one record to the next, to revise individual data items in a particular record, and to append new records to the database table.

▶ A report is typically a column-oriented list of all or some of the records from a database table. The records in a report can be grouped by categories—for example, by regions or by specialties. Within categories, a report can display totals or other calculated values—for example, the total hours of instruction completed by all the instructors in a region, or the average hourly rate for instructors within a specialty area.

▶ A dynamic crosstab is a two-dimensional table of database calculations, where two text fields provide the row and column categories, and a numeric field is the object of the calculations in the body of the table. For example, in Chapter 13 you'll see a dynamic crosstab table that shows the average hourly instruction rate by region (in columns) and by specialty (in rows).

▶ Mailing labels are typically names and addresses from a database table, formatted for convenient printing onto gummed labels. You'll see an example later in this chapter.

▶ A form letter is a text document in which fields of information can be inserted from the records of a database table. Typically one copy of the document is produced for each record. Because each copy contains specific information from one record, the document gives the impression of having been individually produced.

You'll work with report objects and crosstab objects in Chapter 13. The following sections provide short examples of two other Approach objects, forms and mailing labels.

Using a Form

If you're developing a large database, you may find the row-column orientation of a 1-2-3 worksheet to be inconvenient for data entry. A form provides a useful alternative. To create a form for an existing table, follow these general steps:

1. Select the database table (including field names), and choose Create ➤ Database ➤ Form.

2. The Create Form dialog box appears. Confirm that the database range is correct, and click OK:

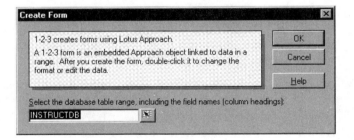

3. Click the mouse at the sheet location where you want to display the form. The Form Assistant dialog box appears, with two tabs representing the two steps for defining a form.

4. In the Step 1: Layout tab, select among the available layout options for a form. Also, enter a title for your form in the text box labeled "View name & title." Then click Next.

5. In the Step 2: Fields tab, select a field from the Fields list, and click Add; then repeat this action for each field you want to include in the form. Click Done when you've added all the fields you want, as shown in Figure 12.8.

Other Database Objects 385

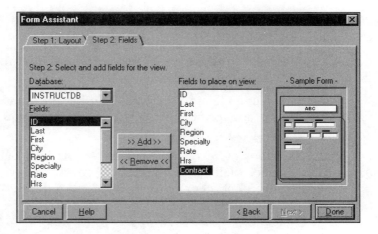

Figure 12.8:   Selecting the fields for a form

For example, Figure 12.9 shows a form for the fields of the Instructors database table. While the form is active, you can click the Previous Record or Next Record button (or press PgUp or PgDn on the keyboard) to scroll from one record to another in the database. You can also select individual field entries in a form and revise them; your changes are copied to the original database table. Finally, you can choose Browse ➤ New Record (or click the New Record button) to insert a blank record at the current position in the database table. Then you can complete the new record by entering data for each displayed field in the form.

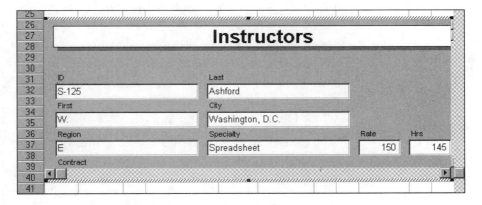

Figure 12.9:   A form for the Instructors database table

Creating Mailing Labels

The steps for creating other objects in the Create ➤ Database are very similar to those you've just seen for the form object. For example, here is how you create mailing labels:

1. Select a table of addresses or other information that you want to organize and print onto labels. Make sure you include the row of field names in the selection.

2. Choose Create ➤ Database ➤ Mailing Labels. The Create Mailing Label dialog box appears; confirm that you've selected the correct range, and click OK:

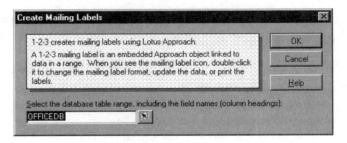

3. Click the mouse at the worksheet location where you want to display the mailing label object.

4. When the Mailing Label Assistant appears on the screen (Figure 12.10), select an address layout.

5. For each position in the Field placement template, select a field name and click the Add button to copy the name to its correct place.

6. For further control over the format of your labels, click the Options tab and change the settings and measurements as appropriate. In particular, you can enter values for the number of labels across and down on a printed page of labels.

7. Click Done to create the labels.

For example, suppose you've used a join operation to create the table of instructor names and regional addresses shown in Figure 12.11. You can follow the steps outlined above to create a set of mailing labels for all the instructors in the database; when you're done, the labels appear in the Lotus Approach window as shown in Figure 12.12. Click the

Other Database Objects

Print Preview SmartIcon to see how they will look when printed on paper (Figure 12.13).

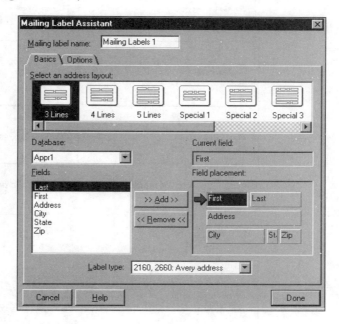

Figure 12.10: The Mailing Label Assistant dialog box

	A	B	C	D	E	F
1	Last	First	Address	City	State	Zip
2	Ashford	W.	222 Allen Street	New York	NY	10103
3	Banks	S.	11 Maple Street	Dallas	TX	75210
4	Cody	L.	432 Market Avenue	Los Angeles	CA	90028
5	Daniels	A.	11 Maple Street	Dallas	TX	75210
6	Davis	G.	432 Market Avenue	Los Angeles	CA	90028
7	Eng	R.	11 Maple Street	Dallas	TX	75210
8	Gill	P.	432 Market Avenue	Los Angeles	CA	90028
9	Harris	P.	11 Maple Street	Dallas	TX	75210
10	Meyer	J.	222 Allen Street	New York	NY	10103
11	Perez	D.	432 Market Avenue	Los Angeles	CA	90028
12	Porter	D.	Mills Tower, Suite 992	Chicago	IL	60605
13	Porter	M.	222 Allen Street	New York	NY	10103
14	Ramirez	F.	222 Allen Street	New York	NY	10103
15	Roberts	P.	Mills Tower, Suite 992	Chicago	IL	60605
16	Sanchez	W.	Mills Tower, Suite 992	Chicago	IL	60605
17	Schwartz	B.	222 Allen Street	New York	NY	10103
18	Weinberg	P.	11 Maple Street	Dallas	TX	75210

Figure 12.11: An address table for the Instructor database, created by a join operation

Figure 12.12: A set of mailing labels created from the address table

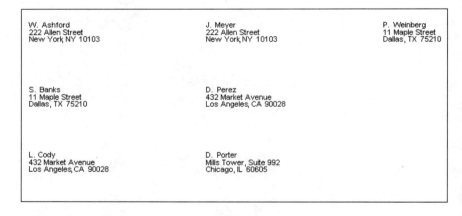

Figure 12.13: A preview of the printed mailing labels

Summary

The Create ➤ Database ➤ Query Table command creates an Approach object known as a query table. You can use a query to perform a number of important operations on a 1-2-3 database table. For example, you can express criteria for selecting records and copy the selection to a new worksheet location; delete records from the original database table; edit records and automatically pass the changes onto the linked table; and perform a join operation to combine information from two or more database tables.

Other objects provided in the Create ➤ Database menu include forms, reports, dynamic crosstabs, mailing labels, and form letters. All of these are Approach objects, which are displayed on a form in 1-2-3, and are linked to a 1-2-3 database table. Using a variety of easy-to-follow Assistant dialog boxes, you can create these objects quickly and efficiently.

CHAPTER 13

Database Calculations

FAST TRACK

To use statistical database functions such as @DSUM or @DAVG,   393

supply three arguments: the database range, the target field name enclosed in quotes, and an expression that supplies a criterion or multiple criteria for selecting records from the range. 1-2-3 applies the function to the records that meet the criteria.

To read field entries from an individual record,   397

use the @DGET function with a criterion that uniquely identifies the target record.

To perform a join operation with the @DGET function,   397

list two or more table references as the initial arguments of the function, and write a criterion expression that joins the tables by a common field. An additional criterion must uniquely identify a target record.

To create a report with groups and totals   399

choose Create ➤ Database ➤ Report and specify the range of the source database table. Click OK and then click the mouse pointer at the sheet location where you want to display the report. In the steps of the Report Assistant, enter a title for your report and choose Columnar with groups & totals as the layout option. Then select the fields that will appear in the report, the field by which the report will be grouped, and the summary field that will become the object of calculations in the report. Also choose the calculation option. Then click Done. The report is displayed at the sheet location you've specified.

To create a summary report containing calculations but no record details, 403

select Summary Only as the layout option in Step 1 of the Report Assistant. Then choose a field for grouping the report, a summary field for calculations, and a calculation option. Click Done to produce the report.

To revise the format or content of an existing report object, 403

double-click the report object to switch to Lotus Approach. Use the Design features in Approach to make changes in the report.

To create a crosstab object from a database table, 403

choose Create ➤ Database ➤ Dynamic Crosstab. In the Dynamic Crosstab dialog box, enter the range name of the database table from which you want to create the crosstab, and click OK. Then click on the sheet location where you want to display the crosstab object. In the steps of the Crosstab Assistant, select a field for the table's row headings, a field for the column headings, a field that will be the subject of the crosstab table, and the calculation option (Sum, Average, Count, and so on). Click Done to complete the process. 1-2-3 creates a crosstab object at the sheet location you've specified.

To create a query for an external database, 406

choose Create ➤ Database ➤ Query Table and click the option labeled "An external table." Click the sheet location where you want to display the query object. Then, in the Open dialog box, choose the database type and select the file that you want to open. In the next dialog box, select the fields that you want to include in the query table and click Done. The query table appears at the sheet location you've specified.

IN addition to the query operations you've already explored, 1-2-3 has several other important features designed to help you work with the information in a database. Using a variety of built-in functions and menu commands, you can:

- Calculate statistical values and other numeric data from selected groups of records
- Create reports from a database table, grouping information by category and summarizing the numeric fields in each group
- Create crosstab tables to display totals, averages, or other values in a two-dimensional table format
- Perform queries on an *external* database, a file developed in a database management environment other than 1-2-3

To explore these procedures, you'll continue working with the Instructor database for Computing Conferences, Inc. Open the INSTRUCT.123 file now. The instructor database table is on sheet B, and is identified by the range name INTRUCTDB. You'll use this table again in exercises presented throughout this chapter.

Calculations on Numeric Fields

Given a database table containing one or more numeric fields, you can perform a variety of statistical calculations on selected records. For example, suppose you're focusing on one of the four regions in the Instructor database and you want to find answers to questions like these:

- What's the average number of hours an instructor has worked in this region? What are the lowest and highest number of hours for a given instructor, and the total hours for a region?
- What is the average hourly rate for instructors in the region?
- What is the average rate for each specialty area, such as databases, spreadsheets, word processing, and so on?

There are several general approaches to answering questions like these. First, 1-2-3 has a useful group of statistical functions that operate on database records. You use these tools to perform statistical calculations selectively on records that meet specific criteria. In addition, you can use the Create ➤ Database ➤ Report and Create ➤ Database ➤ Dynamic Crosstab commands to create tables of statistics from your database.

NOTE See Appendix C for a complete reference guide to the database functions.

Understanding the Database Functions

1-2-3 supplies a group of functions for calculating statistical values on records in a database. Given a selection of records that you specify by criteria, here is what these functions do:

Function	Use
@DSUM	Finds the total of the numeric entries in a field.
@DCOUNT	Counts nonblank entries in a field.
@DPURECOUNT	Finds the number of numeric values in a field.
@DAVG	Computes the average of the values in a field.
@DMAX	Finds the largest value in a field.
@DMIN	Finds the smallest value in a field.
@DVAR and @DVARS	Compute the variance, using the population or sample method.
@DSTD and @DSTDS	Compute the standard deviation using the population or sample method.

These database functions represent the same statistical formulas as the equivalent worksheet functions, @SUM, @COUNT, @AVG, and so on. The difference is that the database functions perform their calculations on a selection of records in a database table. You define this selection by writing criteria designed to select the records you want to work with.

Using the Database Functions

In general, the statistical database functions take three arguments:

- **Database.** The first argument is the input range—that is, the range or name of the database table itself.
- **Field.** The second argument identifies the field on which the calculation will be performed. This argument typically appears as a field name in quotes, but you can also supply this value as an offset number from 0 to *n*-1, where *n* is the number of fields in the database.
- **Criteria.** The third argument expresses the criterion or criteria for selecting records from the database.

For example, consider the following @DSUM function:

```
@DSUM(INSTRUCTDB,"Hrs",REGION="S")
```

This function selects all the records in the Instructor database that match the criterion REGION="S"—that is, all the instructors in the southern region. Then, within this selection of records, the function finds the sum of all the entries in the Hrs field.

> **TIP** Actually, the initial argument of the database functions can include references to multiple tables (separated by commas, semicolons, or the defined argument separator for your system). The use of multiple tables is an opportunity to perform special *join* operations using the database functions. You'll see an example shortly.

The following worksheet shows the result of the @DSUM function, along with five other database functions—@DCOUNT, @DAVG, @DMIN, @DMAX, and @DSTD:

	A	B	C	D	E	F	G
1	Conference Hours in Region:			S			
2							
3	Number of instructors		5		Lowest instructor hours		17
4	Average instructor hours		46.00		Highest instructor hours		75
5	Total instructor hours		230		Standard deviation		21.98

The calculations focus on the work hours recorded for the instructors in the Southern region. As you can see, this worksheet shows the number of instructors in the region (5), the average number of conference hours worked by these instructors (46), the total hours they've worked (230), the smallest number of hours worked by an individual instructor (17), the largest number of hours worked (75), and the standard deviation calculated for this set of data (displayed as 21.98). The six database functions that produce these calculations all use the value in cell D1 to select records. Notice that this cell currently contains the label S; the cell's range name is REG.

To create this example for yourself, begin by adding a third sheet to the INSTRUCT.123 file. Click the New Sheet button once. Double-click the C tab and enter **Hours** as the new sheet's title. Enter all the labels shown in columns A and E. Use Range ➤ Name to assign a name of **Reg** to cell D1. Then enter these database formulas into cells C3, C4, and C5, respectively:

```
@DCOUNT(INSTRUCTDB,"Hrs",REGION=REG)
@DAVG(INSTRUCTDB,"Hrs", REGION=REG)
@DSUM(INSTRUCTDB,"Hrs", REGION=REG)
```

And enter these formulas into cells G3, G4, and G5:

```
@DMIN(INSTRUCTDB,"Hrs", REGION=REG)
@DMAX(INSTRUCTDB,"Hrs", REGION=REG)
@DSTD(INSTRUCTDB,"Hrs", REGION=REG)
```

Notice the criterion in each of the six database functions:

```
REGION=REG
```

Because cell D1 is named REG and contains the label S, this expression is equivalent to:

```
REGION="S"
```

In other words, this criterion selects all the database records in the Southern region.

In a sense, the database functions perform individual queries. They use a criterion to select records from the database, and they read data from a specific field. Because the criterion in this particular example depends on the value stored in the cell named REG, 1-2-3 automatically recalculates the six functions if you change the value in the cell. To see how this recalculation works, select cell D1 and enter the new label E. Then examine the result. The Hours worksheet now contains statistical data about the instructors in the Eastern region:

Offices	Instructors	Hours				
C	A	B	C	D	E	F	G
1	Conference Hours in Region:			E		
2						
3	Number of instructors		5		Lowest instructor hours	26
4	Average instructor hours		101.40		Highest instructor hours	178
5	Total instructor hours		507		Standard deviation	53.91
6						

Now try entering labels representing the remaining two regions, N and W, into cell D1. With each change, 1-2-3 recalculates all six formulas on the sheet.

NOTE In the earliest versions of 1-2-3 (before Release 4.0), you could not use an expression like Region="S" as the criterion in the final argument of the database functions. Instead, you had to create a separate *criteria range* on a worksheet in order to use these functions. A criteria range consists of a row of field names followed by one or more rows of entries that 1-2-3 can read as criteria for selecting records from the target database. In older versions of 1-2-3, the final argument of a database function was always a reference to a criteria range. Lotus 1-2-3 97 still *allows* this usage; if you use old worksheets that are organized in this way, the database functions will still work. But you'll generally find that the use of criteria expressions is much more convenient in the database functions. Oddly enough, the @DPURECOUNT function is a holdout—it still requires a criteria range, not a criteria expression, as its final argument.

TIP In functions like @DCOUNT, @DAVG, @DSUM, @DMIN, @DMAX, and @DSTD, you can omit the third argument altogether. If you do so, the functions perform their statistical calculations on all the records of the target database. (The @DPURECOUNT function is an exception; it always requires a criteria range as its third argument.)

An additional tool available in 1-2-3's collection of database functions is @DGET. This function reads and returns individual field entries from a database. It is useful when you need to build a worksheet that lists values from a single record.

The @DGET Function

The @DGET function takes the same three arguments as other database functions you've examined—a database range, a field name, and a criteria expression. For a successful use of the @DGET function, however, the expressions in the criteria range must select a single record from the database. @DGET returns a label or a value from a specified field in this selected record. If two or more records match the criteria, @DGET returns an ERR value.

The following simple worksheet shows some examples of the @DGET function:

	B	C	D
6			
7		Name:	Cody
8		City:	Los Angeles
9		Specialty:	Database
10		Rate:	$75
11		Manager:	Garcia, M.
12			

Cell D7 is named INSTNAME, and contains the name of one of the instructors in the database. The cells D8, D9, and D10 contain @DGET functions that use this cell in criteria expressions to select a single record from the database:

```
@DGET(INSTRUCTDB,"City",LAST=INSTNAME)
@DGET(INSTRUCTDB,"Specialty",LAST=INSTNAME)
@DGET(INSTRUCTDB,"Rate",LAST=INSTNAME)
```

In each case, the function's first argument is a reference to the database table itself, and the second argument identifies a field as the target for the data query—City, Specialty, or Rate. The third argument is the criterion LAST=INSTNAME. In other words, each function finds a particular data entry from the record in which the Last field matches the value in the cell named INSTNAME. As you can see, the results of the functions are Los Angeles from the City field, Database from the Specialty field, and $75 from the Rate field—all from the record for the instructor named Cody.

The @DGET formula in cell D11 illustrates the use of multiple table references in a database function. In this case, the function performs a kind of join operation to find the name of the instructor's regional manager, from the Manager field in the Offices table. Here is the formula entry:

```
@DGET(INSTRUCTDB,OFFICEDB,"Manager",
LAST=INSTNAME#AND#INSTRUCTDB.REGION=OFFICEDB.REGION)
```

The two database tables are identified by their defined names, INSTRUCTDB and OFFICEDB. The target field—from which a data value will be retrieved—is the Manager field in the Offices table. The criteria argument contains two separate expressions, connected by the #AND# operator. The first expression identifies the instructor name:

```
LAST=INSTNAME
```

And the second expression matches the Region field in the Instructors table with the Region field in the Offices table:

```
INSTRUCTDB.REGION=OFFICEDB.REGION
```

This final criterion provides the definition for joining the two tables. Because each table has a Region field, the TABLE.FIELD notation is used to identify the field in a given table.

Try entering these four @DGET formulas into your own copy of the Hours sheet (sheet C). Don't forget to assign the name INSTNAME to cell D7. Then experiment with the @DGET function by entering a new name into cell D7. For example, if you enter the name **Daniels**, 1-2-3 immediately recalculates the @DGET functions to display entries from the record for the instructor named Daniels:

Offices \ Instructors \ **Hours** \			
C	B	C	D
6			
7		**Name:**	Daniels
8		**City:**	Atlanta
9		**Specialty:**	Accounting
10		**Rate:**	$125
11		**Manager:**	Harvey, J.
12			

Finally, try one more experiment with this worksheet. Enter the name **Porter** in cell D7. As you may recall, the database contains two instructors named Porter. Because the criterion now selects more than one record, the four @DGET functions all return values of ERR:

	B	C	D
6			
7		Name:	Porter
8		City:	ERR
9		Specialty:	ERR
10		Rate:	ERR
11		Manager:	ERR
12			

Whenever you use the @DGET function you have to keep in mind this unique characteristic: The function operates successfully only on a single selected record.

The database functions are not the only tools available for producing calculations from a database table. For some applications you may prefer using special objects offered in the Create ➤ Database menu to produce tables of calculations. In the upcoming sections you'll learn to work with computed values in a database report, and you'll find out how to create a crosstab table.

Creating a Report with Groups and Totals

A report is an Approach object that's linked to a 1-2-3 database table. You can design a report to organize information in groups of records and to display statistical values that summarize numeric fields in each group. To create a report, choose the Create ➤ Database ➤ Report command and then work through the steps of the Report Assistant.

For example, suppose you need a document showing the hourly rates charged by regional instructors, along with the average rate for each region. An easy way to produce this output is to create a grouped report. You'll experiment with reports in the following exercise:

1. Click the New Sheet button to create sheet D in your database workbook. Double-click the new sheet's tab and enter **Reports** as the sheet's name.

2. Choose Create ➤ Database ➤ Report. In the Create Report dialog box, enter **INSTRUCTDB** in the range box. Then click OK:

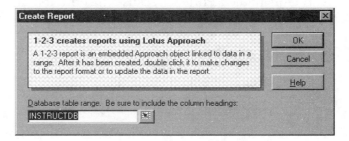

3. Click the mouse pointer in cell A1 of the Reports sheet. The first step of the Report Assistant dialog box appears on the Desktop.

4. In the text box labeled "View name & title" enter **Average Hourly Rates by Region** as the report's title. In the Layout list, choose "Columnar with groups & totals" (Figure 13.1). Then click Next.

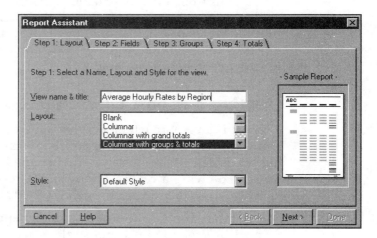

Figure 13.1: **Step 1 of the Report Assistant. Enter a name for your report and choose a layout.**

5. In the Step 2 panel, select Last in the Fields list, and click the Add button to copy the field name to the box labeled "Fields to place on view." Repeat this action for the First, City, and Rate fields, as shown in Figure 13.2. Then click Next.

6. In the Step 3 panel, select Region in the Fields list, and click the Add button to copy the name to the Group fields list (Figure 13.3). As a

result, the records in your report will be grouped by region. Click the Next button.

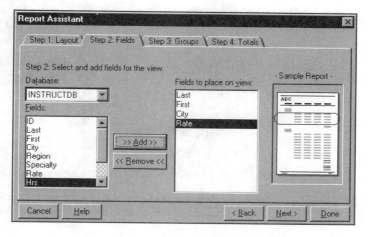

Figure 13.2: **Step 2 of the Report Assistant.** *Select the fields that will be included in the report.*

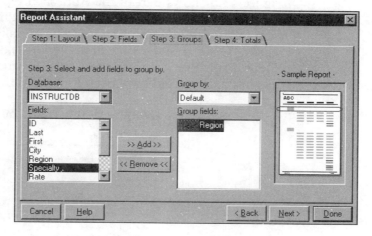

Figure 13.3: **Step 3 of the Report Assistant.** *Select the field by which the records will be grouped.*

7. In the Step 4 panel, pull down the list labeled "Calculate the" and choose Average. Then choose Rate in the Fields list and click the Add button to copy the name to the Summary fields list (Figure 13.4). As a result, your report will show the average hourly rate for each region.

Chapter 13 Database Calculations

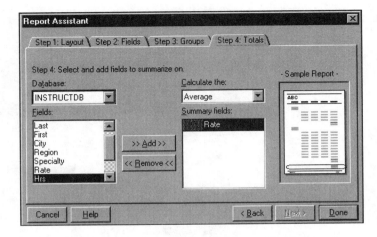

Figure 13.4: *Step 4 of the Report Assistant. Select the numeric field that will become the object of calculations in the report, and choose the type of calculation.*

8. Click the Done button.

   Figure 13.5 shows part of the Approach report that results from these steps. As you can see, the report lists the name, city, and hourly rate of each instructor in a given region, and supplies the average rate for the region. This particular view of the report is displayed when you choose File ➤ Print Preview from the Lotus Approach menu bar. (The numbers in the Rate field have been formatted to display dollars and cents.)

Average Hourly Rates by Region

Last	First	City	Rate
E			
Ashford	W.	Washington, D.C.	$150
Porter	M.	Washington, D.C.	$150
Schwartz	B.	Boston	$150
Ramirez	F.	Boston	$150
Meyer	J.	New York	$150
			$150.00
N			
Porter	D.	Seattle	$125
Sanchez	W.	Indianapolis	$100
Roberts	P.	Chicago	$100
			$108.33
S			
Daniels	A.	Atlanta	$125
Eng	R.	Albuquerque	$75.
Banks	S.	St. Louis	$150
Harris	P.	Dallas	$150
Weinberg	P.	Miami	$75.
			$115.00

Figure 13.5: *A report that groups instructors by region and shows the average hourly instruction rate in each region*

You can use the options of the Report Assistant to produce other kinds of reports. For example, suppose you want a list of average rate calculations for each specialty area, without any other record details. To produce such a report you could choose the Summary Only option in Step 1 of the Report Assistant:

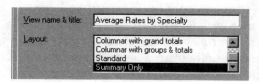

In subsequent steps, choose Specialty as the field for grouping the report, Rate as the summary field, and Average as the calculation. The resulting report might look something like this:

Average Rates by Specialty

	Rate
Accounting	$112.50
Database	$100.00
Networks	$150.00
Programming	$112.50
Spreadsheet	$125.00
WP	$143.75
	$122.06

This report shows the average rate in each specialty area. As you can see, a summary report is an efficient way to generate statistical information about specific groups of records in a database.

 TIP To view or revise the content or format of a report, double-click the report object in 1-2-3. This action switches you to Lotus Approach, where you can choose commands to fine-tune the appearance of your report. For example, you might want to change the format of numeric values that appear in the report, enter a new title, or adjust the positions of certain elements in the report.

Using the Crosstab Command

The Create ➤ Database ➤ Dynamic Crosstab command is another important feature for calculating statistics from a database. Using this command, you can create a two-dimensional table of database calculations (for example, sum, average, count, maximum, and minimum), where the row and column headings are entries from two fields and the numeric entries in the body of the table are calculated from a third field.

For example, suppose you want to build a table that shows the average hourly rate for instructors by specialty and region. The specialty areas will appear as row headings in the first column of the table, and the regions will appear as column headings in the first row. To create this kind of table manually from a large database table could require a considerable amount of time and effort; but using the Crosstab command, you can complete the task in minutes. Here are the steps:

1. Create another new sheet in your database workbook, and name it Crosstab.

2. Choose Create ➤ Database ➤ Dynamic Crosstab. In the Dynamic Crosstab dialog box, enter **INSTRUCTDB** as the database range. Then click OK:

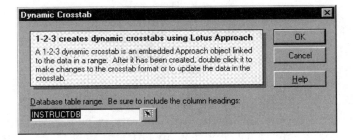

3. Click the mouse pointer in cell A1 of the new sheet you've created for the crosstab object.

4. The Crosstab Assistant dialog box appears on the Desktop. In the Step 1 panel, choose Specialty as the field for the rows of the crosstab. Then click Next.

5. In the Step 2 panel, choose Region as the field for the columns of the crosstab. Then click Next.

6. In the Step 3 panel, choose Rate as the numeric field for the crosstab, and choose Average as the calculation to be applied to the field. Then click Done.

At this point the crosstab object appears on your sheet. Again, you can revise the format of this object by switching to the Approach application. Here is what the crosstab looks like after the numbers have been formatted to appear as currencies:

	E Rate	N Rate	S Rate	W Rate	Total Rate
Accounting			$125.00	$100.00	$112.50
Database	$150.00	$100.00	$75.00	$75.00	$100.00
Networks	$150.00				$150.00
Programming	$150.00		$75.00		$112.50
Spreadsheet	$150.00	$100.00	$150.00	$100.00	$125.00
WP	$150.00	$125.00	$150.00	$150.00	$143.75
Total	$150.00	$108.33	$115.00	$106.25	$122.06

As you can see, the crosstab shows the average hourly rate for each specialty in each region. Blank cells indicate that a particular specialty area is not available in a given region. In addition, there is a row of values (labeled "Total") showing the average rate for each region, and a column showing the average rate for each specialty.

In this exercise you've created a crosstab from a very small number of records. But the crosstab operation takes place just as efficiently on a large database. For example, here is the same crosstab table, created for the complete version of the Instructor database shown back in Chapter 11:

	E Rate	N Rate	S Rate	W Rate	Total Rate
Accounting	$100		$125	$100	$108
Database	$125	$133	$125	$92	$120
Networks	$125		$75	$150	$129
Programming	$117		$75	$100	$104
Spreadsheet	$133	$92	$144	$83	$115
WP	$125	$125	$106	$150	$125
Total	$123	$117	$119	$115	$119

In the complete database, regions may have multiple instructors for a given specialty; accumulating the data is therefore a larger task. But the crosstab table is still developed quickly and efficiently.

Finally, you can use 1-2-3 to gain access to databases created in other database management applications. In the final section of this chapter you'll look at an example of external database query.

Querying an External Database

To work with data from an external database, use the Create ➤ Database ➤ Query Table command. In the Query Table Assistant dialog box, you specify an external table as the source for the query, rather than a 1-2-3 range. Then, in an Open dialog box, you choose the type of database file you want to open, and you find and select the file name itself. Otherwise, the general steps for working with external queries are the same as for a database table on a 1-2-3 sheet. Furthermore, you can perform the same operations, such as editing data, deleting records, and finding records that match specific criteria.

The following exercise shows you how to create a query table from an external database. As you read through these steps, imagine that the original instructor database from Computing Conferences, Inc., is a dBASE IV database file stored on disk as INSTRUCT.DBF. With such a file stored on your own system, you would proceed as follows to create a linked query object:

1. Choose Create ➤ Database ➤ Query Table. The Query Table Assistant appears.

2. Select the option button labeled "An external table" and then click OK:

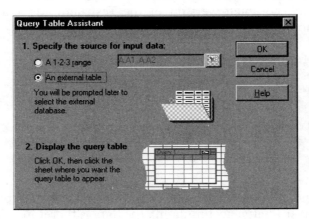

3. A small message box prompts you to "Click where you want to display the query table." Follow this instruction by positioning the mouse pointer over the sheet location where you want the query object to appear, and clicking the left mouse button once.

4. The Open dialog box appears on the Desktop. The default external file type is dBase IV (*.DBF). If you want to open a file of a different type, pull down the Files of type list and make a selection:

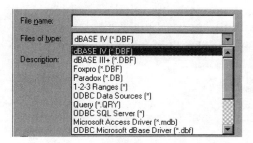

5. Use the file and folder list in the top half of the Open dialog box to find the location of the source database file, and select the file that you want to open:

6. Click the Open button.

7. The Worksheet Assistant dialog box appears next on the Desktop, with a list of all the field names in the external database you've chosen. Make selections from this list, and click the Add button for each field that you want to include in your query table:

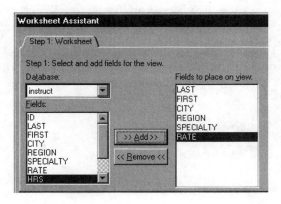

Chapter 13   *Database Calculations*

8. Click the Done button. The query table is displayed and activated at the sheet location you've specified. Selection handles appear around the perimeter of the query, and the Browse menu appears on the menu bar.

9. To change the query's name, click the object's title bar with the right mouse button and choose Query Table Properties from the resulting shortcut menu. Enter a new name in the Query table name text box:

The new name appears in the title bar for the query table:

Now suppose you want to find a specific selection of records from the external INSTRUCT.DBF database. To do so, you use either of the Browse ➤ Find commands, just as you learned to do with a 1-2-3 database table. For example, here's how you can find the spreadsheet specialists from the Southern and Western regions:

1. Choose Browse ➤ Find ➤ Find Assistant. When the Find/Sort Assistant dialog box appears, choose the Find using Query by Box option, and click Next.

2. Use the tools of the Query by Box panel to create the following query:

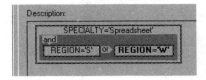

3. Click Done. To deactivate the query object, click its title bar with the right mouse button and choose Bring to Front. The object shows the resulting data selection:

InstDBF				
LAST	FIRST	CITY	REGION	SPECIALTY
Harris	P.	Dallas	S	Spreadsheet
Gill	P.	Los Angeles	W	Spreadsheet

In addition to the Find operations, you can use familiar menu commands to accomplish other tasks with an external query:

▶ Copy the current query table to a range on a 1-2-3 sheet. (Choose Query Table ➤ Query Properties and click the Output range tab on the query InfoBox. Enter a reference to the range where you want to copy the data.) Once you've completed this step, you can use the resulting data range to perform the other database operations provided in the Create ➤ Database menu; for example, you can create reports and crosstab tables using the data you've copied from the external database.

▶ Make changes in the data, and pass those changes on to the external database. (Choose Query Table ➤ Edit and modify the data directly in the query table. The external database is automatically updated.)

▶ Delete records from the external database. (Choose Browse ➤ Delete Record or Browse ➤ Delete Found Set.) Keep in mind that you cannot undo this operation.

▶ Redisplay the entire record set after a Find operation has selected records that match specific criteria. (Choose Browse ➤ Find ➤ Find All.)

Summary

To calculate statistics from a database, you use database functions such as @DSUM, @DAVG, @DCOUNT, @DMIN, and @DMAX. These functions calculate totals, averages, or other statistical values from numeric field entries in selected database records. Each of the statistical database functions takes three arguments: a database range or name, a field name or offset number, and an expression that provides the criterion or criteria for selecting records. To perform a join operation, you can list multiple tables as the initial arguments of the database functions.

There are several other good ways to perform calculations from the information stored in a database. You can use the Create ➤ Database ➤ Report command to generate a report object using the resources of Lotus Approach. In a report, you can organize records in groups or categories and display calculated values (totals, averages, etc.) for numeric fields in each group. Alternatively, a summary report shows only the overall calculations, without any detailed information from the records themselves. Finally, the Create ➤ Database ➤ Dynamic Crosstab command creates a two-dimensional table of statistics based on numeric entries in two fields.

An external database is a file that originates from a database management application other than 1-2-3. Use the Create ➤ Database ➤ Query Table command to create query tables for an external database.

CHAPTER 14

Scripts

Fast Track

To record a script, 415

choose Edit ➤ Scripts & Macros ➤ Record Script to turn the recorder on. Enter a name for your script and choose a workbook location. Then click Record to start recording. Perform the worksheet actions that you want to record. Then choose Edit ➤ Scripts & Macros ➤ Stop Recording to complete the process and to view the recording in the script editor.

To revise a script that you've just recorded, 417

make changes in the lines of script that appear in the script editor window, the upper panel of the LotusScript IDE.

To delete a script from the script library, 418

activate the workbook that contains the script. Then choose Edit ➤ Scripts & Macros ➤ Show Script Library Editor to open the IDE. From the Script list, choose the name of the script you want to delete. In the script editor, select the entire text of the script, then press Delete on the keyboard.

To run a script, 419

open or activate the workbook that contains the script. Then choose Edit ➤ Scripts & Macros ➤ Run. In the resulting dialog box, select the name of the script you want to run, and click the Run button.

To create an Action menu with a list of global script commands, **421**

choose Edit ➤ Scripts & Macros ➤ Global Script Options. In the resulting dialog box, select the workbook that contains the target scripts. Then select the name of the script that you want to add to the Action menu, and click the Edit Options button. In the Edit Script Options dialog box, check the Menu commands on Actions menu box. Enter a name for the command that will represent the current script, and a short line of help text to explain the use of the command. Then click OK on the Edit Script Options dialog box. Repeat these steps for any other scripts that you want to add to the Action menu. Then click Done on the Global Script Options dialog box.

To create a Ctrl+key shortcut for running a global script, **422**

open or activate the workbook that contains the script. Then choose Edit ➤ Scripts & Macros ➤ Global Script Options. In the resulting dialog box, select the name of the script for which you want to create a shortcut key, and click the Edit Options button. In the Edit Script Options dialog box, check the Quick key box and enter a shortcut letter in the Ctrl+ box. Then click OK on the Edit Script Options dialog box and click Done on the Global Script Options dialog box.

To call a script as a procedure from another script, **423**

in a procedure you're developing in the script editor, write a line consisting of the name of the script you want to call.

To create a SmartIcon to represent a script, **425**

choose File ➤ User Setup ➤ SmartIcons Setup. Click the Edit Icon button, and choose an existing icon to use as a pattern for your new icon. Click OK, and you'll see an enlargement of the icon you've chosen. Edit this image in any way you wish to create an appropriate image for your new SmartIcon. Click the Save As button, and create a file name for the new icon. Then click the Attach Script button and choose an existing script to associate with the new icon. Enter a bubble-help message for the SmartIcon, and click Save. Then click Done. Back in the SmartIcons Setup dialog box, drag a copy of the new SmartIcon to any bar of your choice. Click OK to complete the procedure.

SCRIPTS are custom-made tools designed to automate your activities in 1-2-3. You can create your own scripts to carry out any variety of everyday tasks—entering data and formulas onto a sheet, performing sequences of menu commands, applying combinations of formats to a range, copying formulas across a range, creating objects such as charts and maps, and accomplishing almost any other common sequence of steps in a 1-2-3 workbook. When you run a script, the designated actions are carried out, typically on the current sheet. The end result is the same as it would be if you performed the identical tasks manually, using the keyboard and the mouse.

At another level of complexity, scripts can evolve into elaborate programs for controlling the 1-2-3 environment. The processes defined in such programs can include repetition, decisions, input and output, and detailed management of objects. Scripts are written in a sophisticated programming language called LotusScript. For producing and testing LotusScript programs, 1-2-3 provides a complete integrated development environment, known simply as the IDE. This environment includes a script editor for writing, viewing, and revising the LotusScript statements that make up a program.

But even without programming, you can use LotusScript to develop important tools for your work in 1-2-3. A feature called the script recorder—available from the Edit ➤ Scripts & Macros ➤ Record Script command—automatically creates scripts for you, reproducing the steps you perform to complete a particular task. The recorder translates each step into the appropriate LotusScript statements.

Using the recorder is simple. After choosing the Record Script command, you supply a name and a location for the script you want to create. Then you start the recording, and you proceed through the actions that you want to translate into the lines of a script. When you finally stop the recording, the editor displays a new script representing your actions. You can devise a variety of convenient ways to run a script you've recorded—including a keyboard shortcut (Ctrl+key), a menu command, and even a custom SmartIcon.

Every script is stored as part of a workbook and is available for use whenever the workbook is open. One workbook can store multiple scripts. In some cases you might create scripts to work specifically with the data or objects contained in a particular workbook. But more often you're likely to develop general-purpose scripts for use at any time during your work in 1-2-3.

One convenient way to organize these tools is to create a single workbook for storing your own personal library of general-purpose scripts. The entire library is then available for use when you open the workbook that contains them. This is the approach you'll take in this chapter's exercises, as you learn how to record and use scripts.

> **NOTE** Lotus 1-2-3 97 Edition is the first release to include LotusScript. Previous versions provided a more elementary set of programming tools, called the macro language. If you have a library of favorite macros, you can still use them in this version of 1-2-3. But for developing new programs, you'll find LotusScript, the script recorder, and the IDE to be easier, more powerful, and more versatile.

Recording Scripts

Begin your work by creating and saving a workbook for storing the scripts you'll develop in this chapter. Call the workbook MyScripts. You'll also create a second workbook, Untitled, for temporary use in the upcoming exercise:

1. Choose File ➤ New Workbook, and click the Create a Blank Workbook button on the New Workbook dialog box. The new workbook appears on the Desktop.

2. Choose File ➤ Save As and enter **MyScripts** as the file name for the new workbook.

3. Click the Save button. The file is saved as MyScripts.123. You'll use this workbook only for storing scripts, not for data. But you'll need a second workbook for use during the script-recording process. (Pull down the Window menu to find out if another workbook is currently open. If an Untitled workbook is already available, you can skip the next step.)

4. Choose File ➤ New Workbook again, and open another blank workbook. You'll use this Untitled workbook to perform actions while you record your first script. Later you'll close this workbook without saving it.

If SmartIcons are not currently displayed on your Desktop, choose View ➤ Show SmartIcons to display them.

Now you can use the recorder to create scripts and store them in the MyScripts workbook. In the first exercise you'll create and test a simple script designed to enter a company's name into a selected cell on a worksheet and to apply specific style attributes to the text. In the following steps, the name Computing Conferences, Inc. is used as the company, but you can substitute the name of your own company if you wish:

1. Select any cell on sheet A of the Untitled workbook.

2. Choose Edit ➤ Scripts & Macros ➤ Record Script. The Record Script dialog box appears on the Desktop:

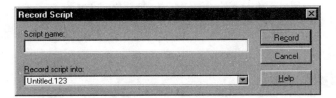

3. Pull down the list labeled "Record script into" and choose MyScripts as the workbook for storing the script:

4. Select the Script name text box and enter **CompanyName** as the name of the script you're about to create.

5. Click the Record button. A floating SmartIcon bar appears on the Desktop, with two buttons—the Stop Recording SmartIcon and the Pause/Restart Recording SmartIcon:

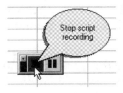

6. Now begin the actions that you want to record. Press Ctrl+B to apply the boldface style to the current cell. Then press Ctrl+I for italics and Ctrl+U for underlining.

7. Type **Computing Conferences, Inc.** (or the name of your own company) and then press ↓.

8. Click the Stop Recording SmartIcon, or choose Edit ➤ Scripts & Macros ➤ Stop Recording.

   When you stop the recorder, 1-2-3 automatically switches you into the LotusScript integrated development environment. The IDE is divided into two panels. The upper panel is the script library editor, which displays the script you've just created:

   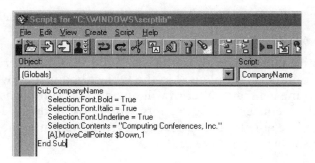

   The lower panel is called the browser; it contains a collection of tools designed to help you build and test a new script.

Examining the Lines of a Recorded Script

Take a moment to examine the script that the recorder has generated. It is a standalone procedure, organized as a *sub*. In a long programming project, you can use subs to divide your work into small and manageable parts. But in this example the sub stands by itself as a complete script, ready to perform a specific task on a worksheet.

Inside the script editor, the first line indicates that the name of the sub is CompanyName:

    Sub CompanyName

The final line marks the end of the sub:

    End Sub

The lines between Sub and End Sub represent specific worksheet actions. Without dwelling much on details of the LotusScript programming language, you can easily guess the action that each line represents. The first three change property settings of the current selection on a sheet, applying the bold, italic, and underlining styles:

```
Selection.Font.Bold = True

Selection.Font.Italic = True

Selection.Font.Underline = True
```

The next line assigns a label to the current cell:

```
Selection.Contents = "Computing Conferences, Inc."
```

And the last line moves the pointer down by one cell:

```
[A].MoveCellPointer $Down,1
```

Notice that CompanyName is defined as a *global* script, as indicated by the notation "(Globals)" in the Object box just above the script editor. This means that the script will operate successfully as a general-purpose tool whenever the MyScripts workbook is open. It also means that you'll be able to define special keyboard and menu options for running the script, as you'll learn later.

In this first exercise you've recorded a simple script that enters a formatted label into a cell on a sheet. Now you're ready to test the script you've created. Choose File ➤ Close Script Editor to exit the IDE and return to your worksheet. 1-2-3 has stored your script as part of the MyScripts workbook.

TIP To re-examine a script, activate the workbook that contains it, and choose Edit ➤ Scripts & Macros ➤ Show Script Editor to reopen the IDE. From the Script list at the top of the editor, choose the name of the script that you want to see. To delete a script, select the entire text of the script in the editor window, and press Delete on the keyboard.

When you save the MyScripts workbook, the script will be saved with it:

1. Choose Window ➤ MyScripts to activate the workbook containing your script.
2. Choose File ➤ Save, or click the Save SmartIcon.
3. Choose Window ➤ Untitled to activate the other open workbook. Although this is the workbook you used while you were recording, the script itself is not attached to this workbook in any way. To demonstrate that this is the case, you'll now close the Untitled workbook without saving it.

4. Choose File ➤ Close. On the resulting dialog box, click the No button to confirm that you want to discard the Untitled workbook.

5. Choose File ➤ New Workbook and create a new Untitled workbook for the next exercise.

Running a Script

There are several ways to run a script, depending on features that you'll learn to develop in this chapter. But the tool that is always available for running scripts—without any further preparation—is the Edit ➤ Scripts & Macros ➤ Run command.

In the upcoming exercise you'll try running the CompanyName script. Keep in mind that this script is available for use as long as the MyScripts workbook is open.

1. Select cell A1 on sheet A of the Untitled workbook.

2. Choose Edit ➤ Scripts & Macros ➤ Run. The Run Scripts & Macros dialog box appears on the Desktop. Pull down the From list, and choose the MyScripts.123 file. The list box shows the name of the script currently stored in the workbook:

3. Because CompanyName is the only script in the list at the moment, simply click the Run button to run it.

The script results in the actions you've planned. The current cell in the active sheet is formatted (bold, italics, underlining), and the company name is entered into the cell:

Before you explore the other techniques for running scripts, take a moment now to record a second script, this one designed to enter the company address into a range of cells:

1. Select cell A:A2 on the Untitled sheet.

2. Choose Edit ➤ Scripts & Macros ➤ Record Script.

3. In the Record Script dialog box, enter **CompanyAddress** as the name of the script you're about to create. In the Record scripts into list, choose MyScripts. Then click the Record button.

4. Back on the Untitled sheet, type the first line of the company address as **432 Market Avenue** (or type the first line of your own business address). Then press ↵.

5. In cell A3 type the second line of the address, **Los Angeles, CA 90028** (or complete your own address). Press ↵.

6. Click the Stop Recording button, or choose Edit ➤ Scripts & Macros ➤ Stop Recording. The LotusScript IDE reopens onto the Desktop, and displays the script you've just created:

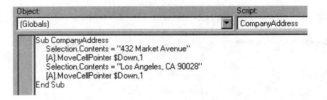

7. To confirm that two scripts are now stored in the MyScripts workbook, pull down the Scripts list. You'll see the names of the two programs you've recorded, CompanyAddress and CompanyName:

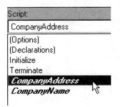

8. Choose File ➤ Close Script Editor to exit from the IDE and return to your worksheet.

Next you'll next try your hand at defining menu commands and keyboard shortcuts for running the scripts.

Creating an Action Menu and Shortcuts

You can easily add an Action menu to the 1-2-3 menu bar and fill it with commands representing your most commonly used global scripts. Optionally, you can also create Ctrl+key shortcuts for global scripts. The Global Script Options dialog box is the tool for defining these features.

In the next exercise you'll create Action menu commands and keyboard shortcuts to represent both the CompanyName and CompanyAddress scripts:

1. Choose Edit ➤ Scripts & Macros ➤ Global Script Options. The Global Script Options dialog box appears on the screen. Pull down the list labeled "Edit options for script from" and choose MyScripts. The Scripts list shows the names of the two programs you've stored in the workbook:

2. Select CompanyName in the Scripts box, and click the Edit Options button. The Edit Script Options dialog box appears, with several options for the CompanyName script:

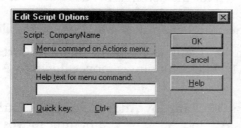

3. Click the check box labeled "Menu command on Actions menu." In the text box just below, enter **Company Name** as the menu command. Then, in the text box labeled "Help text for menu command," enter this sentence as the Help text: **Enter the company name into the current cell**.

4. Click the check box labeled "Quick key" and enter the letter **N** in the Ctrl+ text box.

5. Click OK. The Global Script Options dialog box regains control, and the options you've entered for the CompanyName script are displayed in the lower part of the dialog box.

6. In the Scripts list, select CompanyAddress and click the Edit Options button.

7. Click the Menu command on Actions menu check box, and enter **Company Address** as the menu command. Then enter **Enter the company address, starting from the current cell** as the help text.

8. Click the Quick key check box, and enter the letter **A** in the Ctrl+ text box.

9. Click OK on the Edit Script Options dialog box and click Done on the Global Script Options dialog box.

Now you run these two scripts using the convenient features you've just developed. Notice that a new menu named Actions now appears on the menu bar. Pull down the menu (by clicking it or by pressing Alt+A) and you see the following list of commands:

When you select one of the commands, the title bar displays the help text that you've written for the command. Also note that the menu list shows the two shortcut keys, Ctrl+N and Ctrl+A. To try out these features, create a new sheet in the Untitled workbook and follow these steps:

1. Choose Actions ➤ Company Name, or press Ctrl+N, to display the name in cell A1. The cell pointer moves down to A2 after the entry is completed.

2. Choose Actions ➤ Company Address, or press Ctrl+A, to display the address in cells A2 and A3. The cell pointer moves down to cell A4.

In effect, you've incorporated your own custom-made scripts into the 1-2-3 menu system. This results in a spreadsheet that is more clearly responsive to your own requirements.

> **NOTE** The Ctrl+key shortcuts you define for scripts take precedence over 1-2-3's built-in keyboard shortcuts. For example, Ctrl+B is normally the shortcut for applying the bold style to a cell or range. But if you assign this same shortcut to a script, Ctrl+B instead runs the script; the Bold shortcut is therefore unavailable. Avoid using Ctrl+key shortcuts for scripts that will override your favorite built-in shortcuts.

You can also run one script from within another. In programming terms, this is known as a *procedure call*. In the next section you'll create a short script from scratch, without the use of the recorder, and you'll see the significance of procedure calls.

Using Scripts as Procedures

When one script calls another, LotusScript performs all the instructions of the called script and then returns control to the caller. A call instruction is simply a line that refers to the target script by name. Organizing a detailed script into small procedures is an effective way to avoid writing duplicate instructions for the same task.

In the next exercise you'll develop a new script named CompanyHeading, which enters the company name, the region name, and the company address onto a sheet, starting from the current cell. To produce the name and the address, you'll write calls to the CompanyName and CompanyAddress scripts:

1. Choose Window ➤ MyScripts to activate the MyScripts.123 workbook. Then choose Edit ➤ Scripts & Macros ➤ Show Script Editor to open the LotusScript IDE.

2. From the script editor's menu bar, choose Create ➤ Sub. The Create Sub dialog box appears:

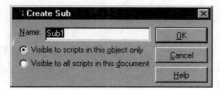

3. In the Name box, enter **CompanyHeading** as the name of the script you're about to create. Then click the option labeled "Visible to all scripts in this document." Click the OK button. In response, the editor creates the first and last lines of a new global sub for you and places the flashing cursor on the blank line between them:

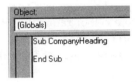

4. Enter four new lines into the script, as shown here:

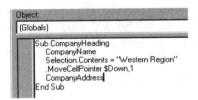

The first and last of these new lines are calls to the scripts that you've already created. The two lines in between are designed to include the region name in the heading that will be the output of this script. (Don't omit the initial period at the beginning of the MoveCellPointer line.) Note that you can enter a different text item between quotes on the Selection.Contents line, to create a heading for your own company.

5. Choose File ➤ Close Script Editor to return to the current sheet.

Create a new sheet in the Untitled workbook and try running the CompanyHeading script. Choose Edit ➤ Scripts & Macros ➤ Run, select the MyScripts.123 workbook in the From list, and select CompanyHeading from the list of script names. Then click Run. Here is the result:

From its output, you can see that the CompanyHeading script combines the actions of your two other scripts, CompanyName and CompanyAddress.

TIP When you write a script from scratch instead of recording it, consider including comments inside the script. A comment is a line of explanatory text that LotusScript ignores at the time the script is run. To designate a comment, begin the line with a single-quote character ('). Then write any information that you think might be useful to you at some future time when you decide to review or modify the script itself. Experienced programmers recognize the importance of fluent and extensive commenting inside the text of a program.

Creating a SmartIcon for a Script

Another significant step you can take in customizing 1-2-3 is to create a SmartIcon to represent a script you've written. Any script that you use frequently is a good candidate for a SmartIcon. For example, in the upcoming exercise you'll create a new SmartIcon to represent the CompanyHeading script you just developed.

Developing an icon for a script is a detailed process, but it is not very difficult. The File ➤ User Setup ➤ SmartIcons Setup command provides all the resources you need to complete the task. Using this command, you can:

▶ Design a graphic to be displayed on the face of the new SmartIcon. (You can create your own graphic design from scratch or you can start with an existing graphic and revise it for your own use.)

▶ Attach a script to the SmartIcon.

▶ Write a brief description that will appear in a help bubble when the SmartIcon is selected.

The following steps suggest one way to create an appropriate Company Heading SmartIcon as a new tool in the bar of Range SmartIcons. The icon developed in this exercise is a picture of a computer screen displaying the letters CC (for "Computer Conferences"). If you prefer, try your hand at designing an icon that serves as a logo for your own company:

1. Choose Window ➤ MyScripts to activate the MyScripts.123 workbook. Then choose File ➤ User Setup ➤ SmartIcons Setup.

2. In the SmartIcons Setup dialog box, choose Range in the Bar name list. Then click the Edit Icon button.

3. Scroll down the list of available icons, and select the Print Preview SmartIcon. The following message box appears:

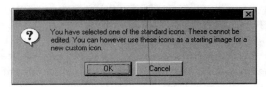

4. Click OK to confirm that you want to create a new icon, starting from the selected image. When you do so, the Picture editor box displays an enlarged image of the Print Preview SmartIcon:

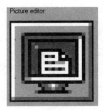

5. To prepare for editing the image, select two colors in the box labeled "Mouse button colors." Click the down-arrow button next to the Left color selection, and choose powder blue from the resulting color palette. Then click the down-arrow button next to the Right color selection, and choose red from the color palette. When you complete these steps, the Mouse button colors box shows your current color selections:

6. Inside the Picture editor box, use the left mouse button, click by click, to fill the background of the computer with the powder blue color selection. Then use the right mouse button to draw two red C's over the blue background:

7. Click the Save As button at the bottom of the Edit SmartIcons dialog box. In the File name text box, enter CC as the name for this bitmap file; then click Save. Your new SmartIcon graphic is saved as CC.BMP.

8. Now click the Attach Script button, at the lower-left corner of the Edit SmartIcons dialog box. In the resulting Attach Script dialog box, click the Script option if necessary. The MyScripts.123 workbook should already be referenced in the From text box. Select CompanyHeading in the Script name list. Then click Attach:

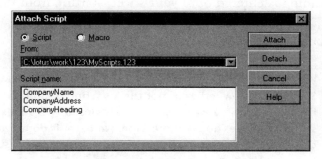

9. Back in the Edit SmartIcons dialog box, locate the Description box, just beneath the Picture editor. Enter the following text as the bubble-help message: **Enter the Company Heading**.

10. Click Save and then click Done. The SmartIcons Setup dialog box regains control.

11. Then scroll to the bottom of the Available icons list. Drag a copy of the new Company Heading SmartIcon to the beginning of the Range preview bar:

12. Click OK to confirm your new SmartIcon.

Back on the Desktop, activate the Untitled workbook and select a cell location where you'd like to enter the company heading. Then position the mouse pointer over the Company Heading SmartIcon. The bubble help shows the brief description you wrote for the new SmartIcon:

Click the icon to run the CompanyHeading script. The complete heading is entered onto your sheet, starting from the current cell.

Now activate the MyScripts.123 workbook and choose File ➤ Save to update the file on disk.

> **WARNING** The new SmartIcon you've created remains part of the Range SmartIcon bar whether or not the MyScripts.123 file is open. But if you click the icon at a time when MyScripts is closed, 1-2-3 fails to find the relevant script and issues an error message. No harm is done; you simply click OK to close the error message box. But you cannot successfully run the CompanyHeading script until you open the MyScripts workbook.

Designing Scripts for Other Actions

The scripts you've created up to this point have performed a limited variety of simple actions: entering labels into cells, applying formats to cells, and controlling the movement of the cell pointer. These few actions scarcely begin to illustrate the capacity of the LotusScript language. Scripts can perform virtually any operation that you normally accomplish manually with the mouse and the keyboard. For example, in this chapter's final exercise you'll create a new script that enters a formula into a cell, copies the formula to a range, and carries out a combination of menu commands to make important changes in the resulting entries.

You'll also experiment with yet another way to run a script. So far you've devised several tools for running the scripts you've created, including Action menu commands, keyboard shortcuts, and a custom-made SmartIcon. Now you'll see that a script can be attached to a specific object on a sheet. The attached script will be performed whenever a designated event occurs on the target object. Specifically, in the upcoming exercise you'll create a command button on a sheet, and attach a script to the button. To run the script, you simply click the button.

Creating a Random-Number Script

Suppose you're developing some sheets on which you regularly need to generate ranges of random integers in order to test certain formulas and commands. Your work would go much faster if you could develop a one-step tool to carry out the following actions:

1. Enter @RAND formulas into a selected range of cells.

2. Convert the formulas to values so that they won't be recalculated each time a change occurs on the sheet.

   Clearly this is a good job for a script. Given a selection of cells, the script should begin by entering a formula and then copying the formula across and down the range. Then the script should carry out a Paste Special command to convert the copied formulas to values.

   To create this script you'll begin by recording a sequence of actions that you perform yourself. Then you'll revise the resulting script as necessary. Here are the steps:

1. Create a new sheet in the Untitled workbook. Select any two-dimensional range of cells. The active cell is at the upper-left corner of the selected range.

2. Choose Edit ➤ Scripts & Macros ➤ Record Script. In the Record Script dialog box, enter **RandRange** as the name of your script. Choose MyScripts in the Record script into list. Click the Record button to begin recording your script.

3. Type the formula **@INT(@RAND*100)+1** into the active cell. (This formula generates random integers from 1 to 100.) Then press Ctrl+↵ to enter the formula without moving the cell pointer or changing the range selection.

4. Choose Edit ➤ Copy Down and then Edit ➤ Copy Right. These two commands fill the selected range with copies of the random-integer formula.

5. Choose Edit ➤ Copy and then Edit ➤ Paste Special. In the Paste Special dialog box, check the Contents option and the Formulas as values option, and uncheck all other options. Then click OK:

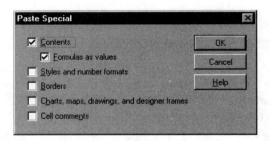

6. Click the Stop Recording SmartIcon. The LotusScript IDE appears on the Desktop, and the editor displays the script you've just recorded.
7. The first line of the macro contains a reference to a specific cell, enclosed in square brackets. Delete the reference and change it to the keyword **Selection**. After this small revision, the script appears as follows:

```
Sub RandRange
    Selection.Contents = "@int(@rand*100)+1"
    Selection.CopyFill $Down
    Selection.CopyFill $Right
    Selection.CopyToClipboard
    Selection.Paste ,False,PasteData + PasteFormulas,,,,
End Sub
```

8. Select the five lines located between Sub and End Sub, and press Ctrl+C to copy these lines to the Windows Clipboard. Then choose File ➤ Close Script Editor to exit from the IDE and return to your worksheet.

Now you can delete the range of random numbers you generated in the Untitled workbook while you were recording the script, and press the Home key to move the cell pointer to A1 of the current sheet. You're ready to create a button on the sheet to represent the RandRange script.

Creating a Button for a Script

Like a command button on a dialog box, a button on a sheet is designed to be clicked in order to carry out a particular action. You create a button on a sheet either by choosing the Create ➤ Button

Designing Scripts for Other Actions

command or by clicking the Create Button SmartIcon on the Range SmartIcon Bar. Then you use the mouse to specify the size and position of the button. In subsequent steps, you attach a script to the button—to define the action that the button will carry out; and you change the caption displayed on the face of the button.

Here are the steps for creating a Random Range button on the current sheet:

1. Choose Create ➤ Button. Then position the mouse pointer near the lower-right corner of the sheet window, hold down the left mouse button, and drag the mouse to form a small rectangular shape. When you release the mouse button, a button object named Button 1 appears on your sheet:

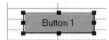

2. You get only a fleeting glimpse of this new button, because 1-2-3 immediately opens the LotusScript IDE window for the Untitled workbook. Just above the script editor, the Object list shows Button 1 as the current selection and the Script box displays the word Click. The script editor displays the Sub and End Sub lines for a Button 1 script named Click. By creating this script, you define the action that will result from a click on the button:

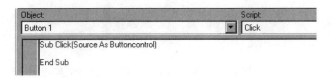

3. Press Ctrl+V (or choose Edit ➤ Paste) to paste a copy of the lines you selected in the RandRange script. Here's the resulting script:

```
Sub Click(Source As Buttoncontrol)
    Selection.Contents = "@int(@rand*100)+1"
    Selection.CopyFill $Down
    Selection.CopyFill $Right
    Selection.CopyToClipboard
    Selection.Paste ,False,PasteData + PasteFormulas,,,,
End Sub
```

4. Now choose File ➤ Close Script Editor to return to your sheet. Button 1 should still be surrounded by selection handles.

5. Choose Drawing ➤ Drawing Properties to open the InfoBox for the object. In the Text box enter the words **Random Fill** as the new caption to be displayed on the surface of the button:

6. Close the InfoBox and click any cell on the sheet to deselect the new button.

You can now test the Random Fill button by selecting a range on the sheet and then clicking the button once with the mouse. Here's the result:

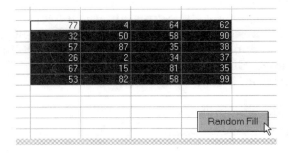

As you can see, the Random Fill button has performed its attached script, filling the selected range with random integers.

> **TIP** A button is a good tool to represent any script you develop for use only on a specific sheet. For instance, suppose you've created some scripts that perform operations on a database table. You might add one or more buttons to the sheet that contains the table, to give the user an easy way to run your scripts.

You can now save the Untitled workbook to disk if you wish, or you can close it without saving. Either way, the RandRange macro is still available in the MyScripts workbook. Take this opportunity to update the latest version of MyScripts to disk. Along with the other scripts you've developed, RandRange is available for use whenever you open MyScripts.

Summary

A script is a program that performs a particular action in the 1-2-3 environment. Scripts can carry out data entry tasks, specific menu commands, mouse and keyboard operations, or detailed sequences of programmed activities. LotusScript is the built-in programming language in which scripts are written. The integrated development environment (the IDE) provides all the features necessary for developing scripts.

Every script is saved as part of a workbook. For storing the general-purpose scripts that you develop, you should consider creating your own script library workbook. All of your scripts are available for use whenever the workbook file is open. Each workbook has its own IDE window for viewing and writing scripts.

Using the script recorder, you can create scripts quickly and easily. Simply turn the recorder on (Edit ➤ Scripts & Macros ➤ Record Script), supply a name and a storage location for your script, and then perform the worksheet steps that you want to record in your script. The recorder translates your actions into lines of script. When you're finished, stop the recorder (Edit ➤ Scripts & Macros ➤ Stop Recording). The IDE window opens automatically, giving you the opportunity to review the recorded script and revise it if necessary.

Once you've created a global script, you can devise a variety of convenient ways to run it. For example, in the Global Script Options dialog box you define menu commands and keyboard shortcuts for running scripts. Or you can use the various tools of the SmartIcons Setup dialog box to create a new SmartIcon to represent a script. Alternatively, you might consider creating a button for running a script that is designed to perform tasks on a particular sheet.

PART 3

More 1-2-3 Features

CHAPTER 15

Versions and Team Computing

Fast Track

To create versions on a worksheet containing a combination of data and formulas, 444
select the data range for which you want to define different versions, and choose Range ➤ Version ➤ New Version. In step 1 of the New Version dialog box, enter a range name and a version name. In step 2, enter a comment to describe the version, and click Done. Back on the sheet, enter a value inside the version frame.

To choose a version directly from the worksheet, 447
click the button at the upper-right corner of the version frame, and choose the version you want to switch to.

To hide a version frame without deleting the versions themselves, 447
click the version frame with the right mouse button, and choose Hide Version Name & Border from the resulting shortcut menu.

To display a version frame on the worksheet if the frame is hidden, 448
select the cell or range that contains versions, and choose Range ➤ Version ➤ Version Properties. In the resulting InfoBox, check the option labeled "Show name and borders."

To switch to a combination of versions, 449

choose Range ➤ Version ➤ Display Version. Choose the range containing a version you want to display. Then choose the version name, and click Display. Repeat this process for any combination of versions you want to choose.

To organize several versions in a group, 451

choose Range ➤ Version ➤ Version Groups. In the resulting dialog box, click the New Group button. Enter a name for the new group. Then drag a combination of versions from the Available versions box to the Versions in group box. Enter a brief comment to describe the purpose of the group, and click OK. Back in the Version Groups dialog box, click New Group again and repeat the process if you want to create additional groups. Then click Done.

To switch to the data represented by a version group, 452

choose Range ➤ Version ➤ Version Groups. Select the name of the group you want to switch to, and click the Display Group button.

To create a summary report, giving the results from a selection of versions, 454

choose Range ➤ Version ➤ Report. Begin by selecting the range and versions from which you want to generate the report. Then enter the range of one or more dependent formulas whose results you want to include in the report. Click OK, and 1-2-3 creates a new workbook in which to generate the report.

To send copies of a workbook document via e-mail to people at different sites, 456

open the target worksheet, and select the range of information that you want to send. Then choose File ➤ TeamReview. Choose either the Formulas and values or the Values only option and click OK. 1-2-3 generates a temporary workbook to serve as the transfer document; make any changes in the workbook as necessary. Then click Send. In the TeamMail dialog box, develop a list of recipients, and choose between sequential routing or direct mail to each recipient. Then click Send.

1-2-3's Range ➤ Version commands gives you convenient ways to store and compare different versions of data in a single worksheet. Versions are designed for sheets that contain both data and formulas. When you switch from one version of the data to another, 1-2-3 automatically recalculates all formulas that are dependent on the revised data. Versions are therefore an ideal way to explore projections or "scenarios," given the input of diverse data sets.

Using the commands of the Range ➤ Version menu, you can:

▶ Create different versions of key data on a sheet

▶ Switch quickly from one version to another

▶ Delete a version that becomes irrelevant to your work

▶ Organize several interrelated versions as a group, and switch easily from one group to another

▶ Create summary reports comparing the results of different versions

If you are working with other people to develop a worksheet, versions of data may come from a variety of sources. In this case, 1-2-3 has several important features that can help you manage the logistics of team computing. For Lotus Notes users, the File ➤ TeamConsolidate commands are designed for worksheet collaboration over a network. Alternatively, the File ➤ TeamReview command allows you to distribute a worksheet by e-mail over the Internet. Recipients supply their own data and return it to you. You can then store each person's changes as a version on your worksheet.

In this chapter you'll examine the 1-2-3 commands for creating and managing versions. The chapter ends with an overview of team computing.

Preparing a Sample Worksheet

In this chapter's exercises you'll work with an abbreviated form of the Conference worksheet that you first developed in Chapters 3 through 6. Figure 15.1 shows this new version of the worksheet. You can create it by reentering all the data and formulas into a new worksheet. If you choose this approach, Figure 15.2 shows the formulas you should enter into column H. Save this new file as CONF2.123.

Preparing a Sample Worksheet

	A	B	C	D	E	F	G	H
1	Computing for Video Stores			Projected Revenues				
2	Place	St. Louis			Attendance			$12,675.00
3	Date	15-Oct-97			Video Sales		$35.00	$1,137.50
4	Attendance	65			Total Revenues			$13,812.50
5	Price	$195.00						
6					Projected Expenses — Fixed			
7					Conference Room			$1,500.00
8					Video Production			$1,000.00
9					Promotion			$3,500.00
10					Travel			$800.00
11					Total Fixed Expenses			$6,800.00
12								
13					Projected Expenses — Variable by Attendance			
14					Conference Materials		$8.25	$536.25
15					Coffee and Pastries		$3.25	$211.25
16					Box Lunch		$4.75	$308.75
17					Total Variable Expenses			$1,056.25
18								
19					Projected Profit			$5,956.25

Figure 15.1: **The shortened version of the Conference worksheet**

	B	C	D	E	F	G	H	I
1	r Video Stores		Projected Revenues					
2	St. Louis			Attendance			+$B$5*B4	
3	15-Oct-97			Video Sales		$35.00	+G3*B4/2	
4	65			Total Revenues			@SUM(H2..H3)	
5	$195.00							
6				Projected Expenses — Fixed				
7				Conference Room			1500	
8				Video Production			1000	
9				Promotion			3500	
10				Travel			800	
11				Total Fixed Expenses			@SUM(H7..H10)	
12								
13				Projected Expenses — Variable by Attendance				
14				Conference Materials		$8.25	+B$4*$A:$G14	
15				Coffee and Pastries		$3.25	+B$4*$A:$G15	
16				Box Lunch		$4.75	+B$4*$A:$G16	
17				Total Variable Expenses			@SUM(H14..H16)	
18								
19				Projected Profit			+H4-(H11+H17)	

Figure 15.2: **The formulas in column H of the CONF2.123 file**

Alternatively, you can copy a range of data from the original CONF.123 file and then reformat and reorganize the worksheet to match Figure 15.1. The File ➤ Open command contains a Combine option that simplifies this task. This operation copies data to the current worksheet from a file stored on disk. Here's an outline of this approach:

1. If necessary, choose File ➤ New Workbook to open a new blank workbook. Click the Create a Blank Workbook button on the New Workbook dialog box.

2. Choose File ➤ Open. Find the directory location of the original CONF.123 file, and select the file in the File name box. Then check the option labeled "Combine with current workbook" at the lower-left corner of the Open dialog box, and click the Combine button:

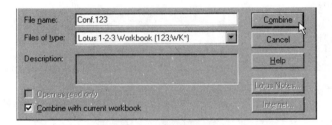

3. The Combine 1-2-3 File dialog box appears. Click the Range option and enter **A5..F34** as the range from which to copy data:

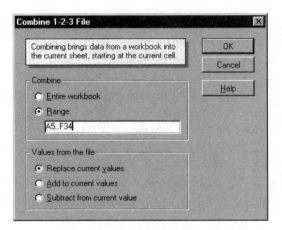

4. Click OK to complete the operation. In response, 1-2-3 copies the data from CONF.123 to your current worksheet.

5. Delete the final column of data and the extra blank rows from the worksheet. Enter the label **Attendance** in cell A4. Then move ranges of data to their new positions on the worksheet, as shown in Figure 15.1.

As you do so, 1-2-3 automatically makes the appropriate adjustments in the worksheet's formulas. (In the end, the formulas in column H should be the same as shown in Figure 15.2.)

6. Confirm that these adjustments have been made correctly by entering a new attendance projection of **65** in cell B4; in response, 1-2-3 recalculates the worksheet formulas that depend on this value, including the bottom-line profit.

7. To complete your work, apply the appropriate formats and styles to the sheet. Then choose the File ➤ Save As command and save the workbook as CONF2.123.

You'll use this sheet for exercises throughout this chapter and the next.

Understanding Versions

By creating versions, you can save many different variations and combinations of data within a single workbook. Versions prove most effective on a sheet that contains a combination of data and formulas. With defined versions, you quickly switch to a different data set—or to a combination of several data sets—and view the new calculations that result on your worksheet. Whenever you find yourself changing the data on a worksheet frequently over time—and wishing you could keep records of previous data sets—the Version commands provide the tools you need.

The Range ➤ Version Commands

The commands of the Range ➤ Version menu are designed to help you create, view, and organize versions:

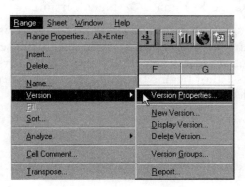

Here is a preview of the commands you'll be working with in this chapter:

▶ The Version Properties command opens the InfoBox for range properties and displays the Versions tab. Given a defined version in the current range, the InfoBox shows the version name, the name and address of its range, and any attached comment:

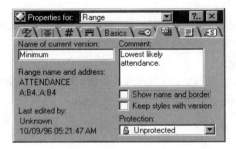

If there is no defined version for the current range, the InfoBox tells you so, and gives you the opportunity to create a new version:

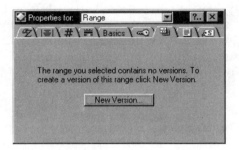

Clicking the New Version button results in the same set of dialog boxes as choosing Range ➤ Version ➤ New Version.

▶ The New Version command starts the Version Assistant, which guides you through the steps of defining a version. If the selection on the current sheet consists of a single cell for which no version is yet defined, the Version Assistant begins by asking you to confirm a single-cell version, or to select a larger range for the version:

Understanding Versions

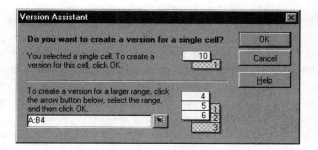

Either way, the New Version dialog box appears next, with two tabbed steps for eliciting the version name, the attached comments, and a variety of other information needed for the version definition. You'll learn more about this process in an upcoming exercise.

▶ The Display Version command gives you the opportunity to explore all the versions defined in the current workbook. In the Display Version dialog box you select the range that you want to examine, and then you select one of the versions defined for that range. When you click the Display button, the sheet in the background shows the selected version, along with any recalculations that result from the version change.

▶ The Delete Version command allows you to remove version definitions from the current workbook. To do so, you select a range and a version, and click the Delete button. While the Delete Version dialog box remains open, you can continue deleting any combination of versions.

▶ The Version Groups command is a means of placing several versions together in a group. Given a group definition, you can switch to all these versions in one step by selecting the group and clicking the Display Group button. (In previous versions of 1-2-3, version groups were known as "scenarios.")

▶ The Report command creates a summary of several selected versions. You choose the range for which you want to create the report, and you select the versions that you want to include. You also specify a particular formula whose results you want to explore in the report. The Report command creates a new workbook to display the summary. For each version you've selected, the report displays the current data in the version, and the result of the target formula under this version.

TIP By defining a set of versions for a contiguous range of cells, you can quickly change the values of all the cells at once when you switch to a new version. An alternative approach is to define distinct versions for each individual cell in a range, and then to use the Version Groups command to create associations between different versions. While the latter approach requires additional steps, it is also more versatile, because you can create groups from any combination of versions. Keep these two approaches in mind as you learn more about versions in upcoming exercises.

Defining Versions

The best way to learn to create and use versions is to begin experimenting on a worksheet you've already developed. The shortened Conference worksheet, CONF2.123, is an ideal example. Suppose that the managers at Computing Conference, Inc., are experimenting with various pricing levels and attendance estimates in an attempt to predict the profitability of a given conference. Specifically, they want to study the result of varying three values on the CONF2 worksheet: the per-person price for attending the conference, the attendance estimate, and the unit price of the conference video. The managers want to try several different versions of the data, as illustrated in the following table:

	Minimum	Medium	Maximum
Attendance	65	95	135
Price	$195	$225	$245
Video	$35	$40	$50

Although this table contains only nine data values, the numbers can be combined in many different ways on the Conference worksheet. For example, you might want to examine the result of combining all the minimum or all the maximum values, or you might want to see what happens to the profit when you combine the minimum price with the maximum attendance. The Version commands put all these possibilities at your fingertips.

In the following exercise, you'll set up these versions on the Conference worksheet and you'll learn how to use the Version commands to experiment with the results:

1. Select cell B4, the location of the attendance estimate. The value stored in this cell is currently 65, and the cell is unnamed at the moment.

When you define a version for a range, you also create a range name if one does not already exist.

2. Choose Range ➤ Version ➤ New Version. The Version Assistant window appears on the screen, asking you if you want to create a version for a single cell. Click OK to confirm, and the New Version dialog box appears:

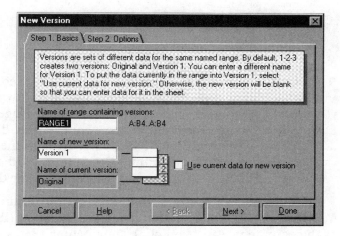

3. In the text box labeled "Name of range containing versions" enter **Attendance**. As a result, 1-2-3 assigns this range name to cell B4.

4. Select the Name of new version box and enter **Minimum** as the version name. Notice that the check box labeled "Use current data for new version" is unchecked by default. Keep it this way. You'll enter the data value for this version later, on the sheet itself.

5. Click Next to go to the next step of the New Version dialog box. In the Comment box, enter **Lowest likely attendance.** as a brief explanation for this version. The check box labeled "Show name and borders around version" is checked by default; leave it checked for the moment:

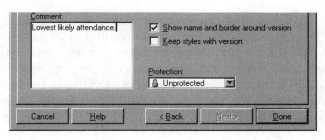

6. Click Done to complete the definition of this first version. Back on the sheet, a frame appears around cell B4, indicating the existence of versions. Double-click inside the cell that this frame contains, and type **65** as the data value for the Minimum version. Press ↵ to confirm:

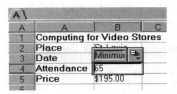

7. Repeat steps 1 through 6, above, to create a second version. (The Version Assistant dialog box, described in Step 2, does not appear as you create this second version. In addition, the range name, ATTENDANCE, is already recorded in the New Version dialog box, so you don't have to enter it in Step 3.) Enter **Medium** as the name for the new version, and **Medium attendance estimate.** as the comment. After you click the Done button, enter **95** as the value for this new version.

8. Again following Steps 1 through 6, create a third version. Enter **Maximum** as the new version name and **Highest likely attendance.** as the comment. After you click Done, enter **135** as the data value for the third version.

You've now created three versions for the Attendance cell. Back on the sheet, click the button at the upper-right corner of the version frame, and 1-2-3 shows you a list of the names you've defined:

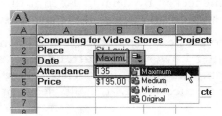

Notice that there are actually four versions in this list. 1-2-3 automatically creates a version named Original to represent the data value that was originally stored in the cell or range before you defined the first version. In this particular example, Original turns out to be a redundancy, because it has the same data value as the version you've named Minimum. But on some sheets, you might find it useful to retain this extra version for an initial data value.

Choosing a Version

To switch data on the worksheet—that is, to view the effect of any version on the bottom-line profit—you simply select one of the names in the version list. For example, try pulling down the versions list and choosing the Medium version. When you do so, 1-2-3 enters the medium attendance estimate into cell B4 and instantly recalculates all the formulas that depend on that value. As you can see in Figure 15.3, the entire worksheet shows the result of the change.

Figure 15.3: **Viewing the result of a selected version. When you select a name in the version list, the sheet instantly shows you the result of the change in data.**

Before you start creating versions for the price entry in cell B5, you should hide the frame for the attendance versions. To do so, click the frame with the right mouse button, and choose Hide Version Name & Border from the resulting shortcut menu:

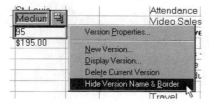

Hiding the frame does not affect the version definitions themselves; it simply returns your sheet back to its usual appearance. Given a range that contains version definitions, you can restore the version frame at any time by clicking the range with the right mouse button and choosing Show Version Name & Border from the shortcut menu.

TIP Notice the other commands available on the shortcut menu for a version: The Version Properties command opens the range InfoBox and displays the Versions tab. The New Version command starts the steps for creating a new version. Display Version shows a list of the versions defined in the workbook, and gives you the opportunity to choose one. The Delete Current Version command removes the definition for the version that's currently displayed in the target cell. And, as you've seen, the Hide Version Name & Border command removes the frame around the current version.

TIP Another way to show or hide the version frame is to select the target cell or range and choose Range ➤ Version ➤ Version Properties. In the Versions tab of the resulting InfoBox, click the check box labeled "Show name and borders." When the option is checked, the frame appears; when it is not checked, the target range returns to its usual appearance.

Defining Additional Versions

Next you'll define versions for the conference price in cell B5 and the video price in cell G3. In each case, you'll follow the same steps you used to create three versions of the attendance estimate. When you create the first version for the conference price in cell B5, enter **Price** as the range name for the cell. Here are the values, version names, and comments to enter for this cell:

Value	Version Name	Comment
$195	Minimum	1995 pricing
$225	Medium	1996 pricing
$245	Maximum	1997 pricing

For the first version for the per-unit video price in cell G3, enter **Video** as the range name. Then enter the following values, version names, and comments for the cell:

Value	Version Name	Comment
$35	Minimum	1995 pricing
$40	Medium	1996 pricing
$50	Maximum	1997 pricing

Now hide all the version frames, so that the sheet has the same general appearance that it had before you started creating versions. You've defined nine different versions of the data on the Conference sheet. To view any one of these versions, you can restore the appropriate version frame and select a name:

1. Click the target cell with the right mouse button and choose Show Version Name & Border.
2. Click the button at the upper-right corner of the version frame and select a version name from the resulting list.

Spend some time now experimenting with this process. Each time you choose a new version, 1-2-3 recalculates all the formulas that depend on the new data value, and displays the new results.

If you want to look at several versions in succession, the Display Version command provides an easier approach.

Displaying Versions

Choose the Range ➤ Version ➤ Display Version command to open the Display Version dialog box. As you can see in Figure 15.4, this window gives you quick access to all the versions you've created. To view the calculated results from a combination of versions, follow the steps inside the dialog box:

1. Pull down the list labeled "Display a version for range" and choose the name of the cell or range for which you want to view a version. In response, the Version list shows information about all the versions defined for the selected range.
2. Select the name of the version that you want to switch to.

3. Click the Display button.
4. Repeat steps 1 through 3 to select a version for any combination of ranges in the Display versions for range list.
5. Click the Done button to close the Display Version dialog box.

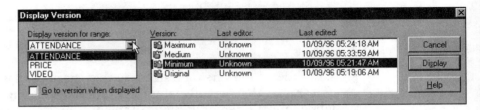

Figure 15.4: The Display Version dialog box, with lists of all the versions you've created in the Conference worksheet

For example, suppose you want to see the bottom-line calculation—that is, the projected profit, in cell H19—under the Medium versions for the attendance, price, and video entries. To switch to this value quickly, follow these steps:

1. Choose Range ➤ Version ➤ Display Version.
2. Select ATTENDANCE in the Display version for range list and click Medium in the Version list. Then click Display.
3. Select PRICE in the Display version for range list and click Medium in the Version list. Click Display.
4. Select VIDEO in the Display version for range list and click Medium in the Version list. Click Display.
5. Click the Done button.

Here is the result, displayed in a window that's been split horizontally:

A	B	C	D	E	F	G	H
Computing for Video Stores			Projected Revenues				
Place	St. Louis			Attendance			$21,375.00
Date	15-Oct-97			Video Sales		$40.00	$1,900.00
Attendance	95			Total Revenues			$23,275.00
Price	$225.00						

A	B	C	D	E	F	G	H
			Projected Profit				$14,931.25

As you can see, the three Medium versions—figures of 95 for attendance, $225 for the price, and $40 for the video—result in a projected profit of $14,931.25. Before you read on, you might want to try some additional experiments with the Display Version dialog box, switching to other combinations of data in the Conference sheet.

Creating Groups of Versions

A group gives you a quick way to switch to several different versions in one step. In a group you combine two or more versions to produce a particular result on your worksheet. When you choose the group, all the versions are selected at once.

Suppose the managers at Computing Conferences, Inc., would like to compare two combinations of data, which they refer to as the Highest Price and Medium Price groups:

▶ In the Highest Price group, they'll apply the maximum conference price per person; as a result of the high price, they anticipate only medium attendance at the event.

▶ In the Medium Price group, they'll use the middle conference price; as a result, they expect the maximum attendance.

They'll select the medium video price for both of these groups. Their question is obvious: Which of these strategies results in the highest profit?

Use the Range ➤ Version ➤ Version Groups command to define groups and to select a group for display. Here are the steps for defining the Highest Price and Medium Price groups:

1. Choose Range ➤ Version ➤ Version Groups. The Version Groups dialog box appears on the Desktop.

2. Click the New Group button, at the right side of the dialog box. The New Version Group dialog box appears.

3. In the text box labeled "Name of version group," enter **Highest Price** as the name of the group you're about to create.

4. In the Available versions box, select the Medium version under the ATTENDANCE heading, and drag it to the Versions in group box. (Alternatively, select the version and click the >> button to move it into the box to the right.)

5. Scroll down the Available versions list, and select the Maximum PRICE version; then drag this version to the Versions in group list. Perform the same action on the Medium VIDEO version. When you're finished, the Versions in group list appears as follows:

6. In the Comments box, enter **Expect only medium attendance.**

7. Click OK to complete the group definition. Back in the Version Groups dialog box, the newly defined group is displayed as follows:

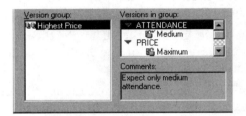

8. Click the New Group button to open the New Version Group dialog box again. Enter **Medium Price** as the name of the second group.

9. Move the Maximum ATTENDANCE, Medium PRICE, and Medium VIDEO versions into the Versions in group box from the Available versions box:

10. Enter **Expect maximum attendance.** into the Comments box, and click OK to return to the Version Groups dialog box.

Now that you've defined the two target groups, you can use the Version Groups dialog box to switch from one group to another, and you can view the results on the sheet in the background. Move the dialog box toward the lower-left corner of the Desktop so that you can see most of the information on the sheet. You can now switch quickly between these two groups by following two simple steps:

1. Select the name of a group in the Version group list.
2. Click the Display Group button, near the upper-right corner of the Version Groups dialog box.

For example, Figure 15.5 shows the result of the Highest Price group, and Figure 15.6 shows the result of the Medium Price group. Examining the Projected Profit value at the lower-right corner of the sheet in both figures, you can see that the Medium Price group results in a much higher profit calculation than the Highest Price group.

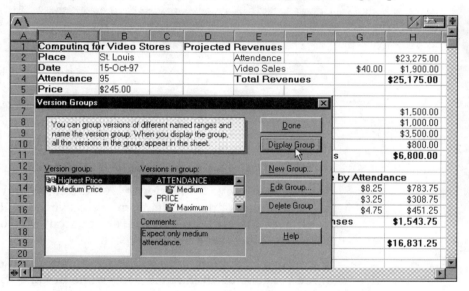

Figure 15.5: **The Highest Price group results in a calculated profit of $16,831.25.**

If the projections represented by these two version groups are valid, the managers at Computing Conferences, Inc., might conclude that the better strategy is to hold the attendance price at a medium level in an effort to attract a larger audience.

After examining the results of the two version groups, click the Done button to close the Version Groups dialog box.

Chapter 15   *Versions and Team Computing*

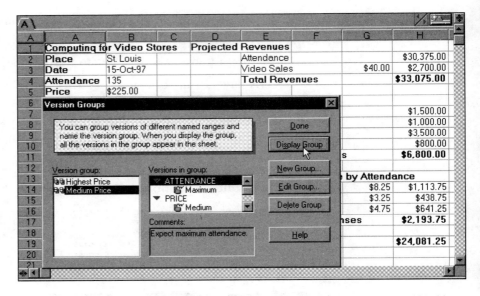

Figure 15.6: The Medium Price group gives a calculated profit of $24,081.25, considerably higher than the other group.

Creating a Report from Versions

Finally, the Range ➤ Version ➤ Report command allows you to create a summary of the results from several versions. 1-2-3 creates a new worksheet for each report you create from versions. You can then reformat, save, and print the report.

For example, suppose you want to compare profit calculations for the three versions of attendance data, while holding the conference price and the video price constant at their medium levels. Here are the steps for producing a report for this comparison:

1. Using the Range ➤ Version ➤ Display Version command, switch to the Medium versions for both Price and Video. Then close the Display Version dialog box.

2. Choose Range ➤ Version ➤ Report. The Version Report dialog box appears.

3. Pull down the Report on this range list and choose ATTENDANCE. Under this range name, click the Maximum, Medium, and Minimum versions in the Include these versions box. When you do so, a check mark appears to the left of each selected version:

4. In the Show in report group, keep the Version data option checked; this ensures that you will see the Attendance data as part of the report. Uncheck the option labeled "Creator, editors, and dates."

5. Click inside the range box labeled "Results of dependent formulas in this range." Then move the mouse pointer to cell H19, and click the cell once. A reference to H19 appears in the range box:

6. Keeping the default By columns selection in the Arrange report group, click OK to complete this process.

1-2-3 opens a new workbook and creates the report on sheet A. You can reformat this sheet in any way you like to produce a readable report, as shown here:

	A	B	C	D
1	File	C:\LOTUS\WORK\123\CONF2.123		
2	Named range	ATTENDANCE (A:B4)		
3				
4	Version name	Medium	Maximum	Minimum
5	Version cells			
6				
7	A:B4	95	135	65
8				
9	Formula results			
10				
11	A:H19	$14,931.25	$24,081.25	$8,068.75

This report compares the profit calculations resulting from each of the three attendance versions. When you've finished looking at it, you can save it to disk or close it without saving. Then activate the CONF2.123 file, choose File ➤ Save As, and save your work as VERSIONS.123. (This step leaves the original CONF2.123 file intact and unrevised for upcoming exercises.)

Developing Versions by Team

As you develop a complex sheet in 1-2-3, you may find yourself consulting many different people to acquire the data you need for your work. Information may originate from the person who works in the office next to yours, from colleagues across town, or from regional offices around the world. Given these various sources, your job is to compile the data into a single worksheet, perhaps defining versions to represent different points of view.

Through a variety of *team computing* features, 1-2-3 provides strategies for coordinating data exchange between people at different locations. You can use these strategies to gather relevant information for a particular worksheet project. In team computing, versions can prove to be an essential tool for organizing the input you receive.

One of 1-2-3's distribution techniques for team computing is represented by the File ➤ TeamReview command. Using this command, you can send and receive workbooks via your Internet e-mail system. If you are the originator of a workbook, you develop a list of recipients.

You also decide whether the workbook will be routed in sequence from one person to the next, or go to every recipient at the same time. After supplying their own input, the people on your list may also use e-mail to send the workbook on to other recipients or back to you.

For example, to initiate a TeamReview operation, you begin with the following steps:

1. Open the target workbook, and select the range of data that you want to send to members of your team.

2. Choose File ➤ TeamReview. The TeamReview dialog box gives you the choice between sending formulas along with data values, or values alone. Choose between these options, and click OK:

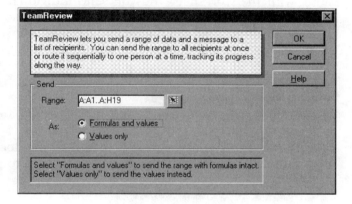

3. 1-2-3 creates a new workbook file to serve as the distribution document; the target range is copied to the file. You can make changes in the data as necessary, and then click the Send button:

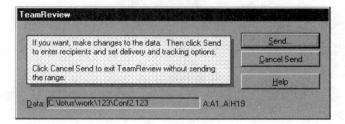

4. In the TeamMail dialog box you develop a list of recipients for the workbook. By clicking the mail button just to the right of a Recipient

cell, you can choose a name and address from your personal address book or from a network address book:

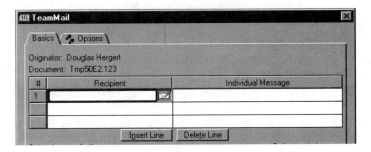

5. Along with the worksheet you can send individual messages to each recipient and a group message to everyone. You also choose the distribution mode—routing the document sequentially from one person to the next, or sending it to everyone at once:

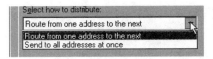

6. The Options tab gives you control over how the document's progress can be tracked and routed as it goes from person to person:

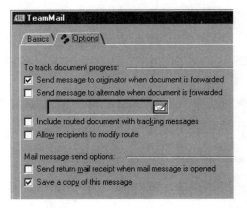

7. When you've completed your list of recipients and chosen the appropriate options, click the Send button to begin the TeamReview process.

As data comes back to you from the members of the team, you can merge their input into a central workbook, creating a different version to represent each person's data.

> **TIP** If you are on a network that uses Lotus Notes software, choose the File ➤ TeamConsolidate ➤ Share Sheets using Lotus Notes command to manage the distribution of a 1-2-3 document.

Summary

The Range ➤ Version commands allow you to save multiple versions of data for a worksheet and to organize your versions into groups. Once you've created versions on a sheet, you can switch easily from one version to another and view the results calculated from dependent formulas. You can also organize a set of versions as a group. By selecting a new group, you change the data of all the included versions at once. A version report summarizes the results of selected versions.

These are excellent tools to use whenever you need to save and investigate different sets of data in a single sheet. If the version data comes from people at different sites, you can use 1-2-3's team computing commands to manage the distribution of documents and data from one person to another. For example, the TeamReview command employs Internet e-mail to distribute a worksheet among the members of a team.

CHAPTER 16
Worksheet Tools

Fast Track

To build a workbook based on a SmartMaster,   463
choose File ➤ New Workbook and select a SmartMaster from the New Workbook dialog box.

To create a one-variable what-if table,   467
enter a column of input values at the left side of the table range, and enter one or more formulas at the top of each column in the table range. Decide on an input cell where 1-2-3 will substitute the input values one at a time to develop the what-if table. Select the table range, and choose Range ➤ Analyze ➤ What-If Table. Select 1 as the number of input cells and enter a reference to the input cell in the Input cell 1 box.

To create a two-variable what-if table,   470
enter a column of values at the left side of the table range for a first input cell, and a row of values at the top of the table range for a second input cell. Enter the target formula into the upper-left corner of the table range. Select the table range, and choose Range ➤ Analyze ➤ What-If Table. Select 2 as the number of input cells, and enter references into the Input cell 1 and Input cell 2 boxes.

To find the input value that yields a target result from a worksheet formula, 474

choose the Range ➤ Analyze ➤ Backsolver command. Specify the formula location, the target result, and the adjustable cell, and click OK.

To count the number of values that belong to specified numeric categories, 476

create a bin range that defines the categories. Then select the values range, and choose Range ➤ Analyze ➤ Distribution. Enter a reference to the bin range and click OK.

To analyze the mathematical correlation between two or more ranges of values, 479

choose Range ➤ Analyze ➤ Regression. Enter the X-range, Y-range, and output range, and click OK.

To solve simultaneous equations on a worksheet, 485

enter the coefficients of the variables as a square matrix on the worksheet. Then enter the constant values from the right side of each equation as a one-column matrix. Use the Range ➤ Analyze ➤ Invert Matrix command to create the inverse of the coefficient matrix. Then use the Range ➤ Analyze ➤ Multiply Matrix command to perform matrix multiplication between the inverse matrix and the constant matrix. The result of the multiplication is the solution matrix.

To copy columns of data to a range of rows, or to copy rows to a range of columns, 487

select the source range and choose the Range ➤ Transpose command. Enter a reference to the upper-left corner of the destination range into the To text box, and click OK.

To designate the levels of an outline, 492

select a range of rows and choose Sheet ➤ Outline ➤ Demote rows, or select a range of columns and choose Sheet ➤ Outline ➤ Demote Columns.

1-2-3 furnishes several powerful tools designed to help you create, analyze, and organize worksheets:

▶ SmartMasters are professional-quality templates you can use as the basis for creating a variety of practical business worksheets.

▶ The commands of the Range ➤ Analyze menu perform advanced analytical calculations on numeric information in a sheet. Among these you'll find the versatile What-If Table command, the Backsolver, and the matrix arithmetic calculators.

▶ Outlining is a way to focus on the information that's most important to you on a sheet, while temporarily hiding intermediate details. The outlining commands are located in the Sheet ➤ Outline menu.

This chapter presents these important features as independent topics that you can read in any order you wish.

Using SmartMasters

Much of the work that people do in spreadsheets falls into certain generic categories. Budgets, expense reports, invoices, purchase orders, time sheets, financial statements, loan amortizations, sales records—these worksheets are reinvented time and time again by business people everywhere.

1-2-3 supplies standard forms of these worksheets in a library of templates known as SmartMasters. Each SmartMaster creates a professionally-designed worksheet, complete with formulas, instructions, sample data, scripts, and one-click techniques for accomplishing major tasks.

When you open a new workbook based on a SmartMaster, 1-2-3 copies all the information from the SmartMaster to your new file. You can then begin entering data and completing operations on the worksheet. When you're done, you save the worksheet under a file name of your choice. The original SmartMaster template is left intact for future reuse.

Creating a Worksheet from a SmartMaster

Choose the File ➤ New Workbook command (or click the New Workbook SmartIcon) to display the New Workbook dialog box with its list of SmartMasters. You can browse through the list for a preview of what each of these tools does. When you highlight a name in the list, the Description box provides some brief notes about the SmartMaster you've selected.

> **NOTE** If no dialog box appears when you choose File ➤ New Workbook, you need to reset an option in the 1-2-3 Preferences dialog box in order to see the list of SmartMasters. Choose File ➤ User Setup ➤ 1-2-3 Preferences. In the General tab of the resulting dialog box, place a check in the option labeled "Show New Workbook dialog," and then click OK. Next time you choose File ➤ New Workbook (or click the New Workbook SmartIcon), you'll see the dialog box and the list of SmartMasters.

For example, here is the description of a SmartMaster designed for loan amortizations:

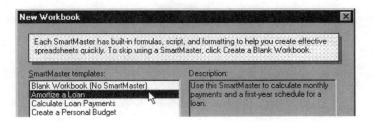

These are the general steps for creating a new worksheet based on a SmartMaster:

1. Choose File ➤ New Workbook.

2. In the New Workbook dialog box, scroll down the list of SmartMasters until you see the one you want. Click its name to select it.

3. Click OK. 1-2-3 opens a new workbook and copies data, formats, formulas, and script programs from the template to the worksheet.

4. Begin entering your own data into the sheet that the SmartMaster provides.

For example, Figure 16.1 shows a workbook based on the Loan Amortization SmartMaster. The input area—where you enter the information about a particular loan or mortgage—is displayed in a version frame, just above the New Loan button. To calculate data for a particular loan, click New Loan and begin entering the loan parameters into the box—the principal, the interest rate, the term, and so on. As you do so, the SmartMaster recalculates the range of values labeled Key Figures and builds the Payments table shown in the lower part of the sheet. When you've completed the worksheet, you can choose File ➤ Save As and enter a new name for your file.

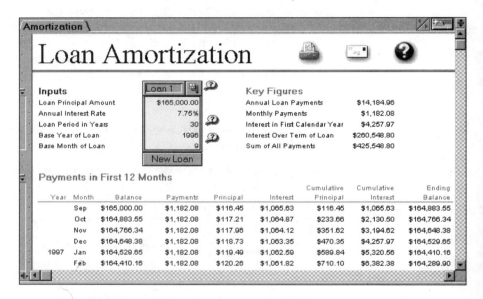

Figure 16.1: *A sheet produced by the Mortgage Amortization SmartMaster. To create a payment table for a particular mortgage, you simply begin entering data in the Inputs box.*

Although each SmartMaster has its own organization and purpose, the worksheet files produced by SmartMasters have similar features. For example, SmartMasters typically come with information about usage and input requirements.

The Range ➤ Analyze Menu

The six commands in the Range ➤ Analyze menu provide a variety of mathematical techniques for analyzing data in a worksheet:

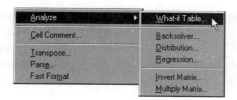

Here are brief summaries of these commands:

Command	Description
What-If Table	Recalculates worksheet formulas while varying the data in one, two, or three input cells; generates a table from the results.
Backsolver	Finds the numeric input value that produces a desired result in a selected worksheet formula.
Distribution	Counts the number of entries that belong to specified numeric categories.
Regression	Examines the correlation between sets of numeric data, in a series of calculations known as regression analysis.
Invert Matrix	Produces the inverse of a square matrix.
Multiply Matrix	Performs matrix multiplication between two matrices. You can use the two matrix operations together to find solutions for simultaneous equations.

In the upcoming sections you'll see examples of each of these commands. To prepare for the exercises ahead, open CONF2.123, which contains the shortened Conference sheet that you developed in Chapter 15.

Using the What-If Table Command

The What-If Table command is a tool for exploring multiple what-if scenarios on a worksheet. It is particularly useful with formulas that are dependent on specific input values.

For example, most of the formulas on the shortened Conference sheet—including the bottom-line profit calculation—depend directly or indirectly on the attendance level and the per-person attendance price. These two input values appear in cells B4 and B5, respectively; and the profit is in cell H19:

	A	B	C	D	E	F	G	H
1	Computing for Video Stores			Projected Revenues				
2	Place	St. Louis			Attendance			$12,675.00
3	Date	15-Oct-97			Video Sales		$35.00	$1,137.50
4	Attendance	65			Total Revenues			$13,812.50
5	Price	$195.00						
18								
19				Projected Profit				$5,956.25
20								

(Rows 6 through 17 have been temporarily hidden in this view of the sheet.) By entering new numeric values in B4 and B5, you can explore individual changes in the profit under different projections for attendance and price. But in some applications you may want to build an entire table of what-if projections. For example, here is a table of profit calculations, given a range of attendance and price levels for a particular conference:

	A	B	C	D	E
1	Profits				
2			Price		
3			$145	$170	$195
4	Attendance	65	$2,706.25	$4,331.25	$5,956.25
5		75	$4,168.75	$6,043.75	$7,918.75
6		85	$5,631.25	$7,756.25	$9,881.25
7		95	$7,093.75	$9,468.75	$11,843.75
8		105	$8,556.25	$11,181.25	$13,806.25
9		115	$10,018.75	$12,893.75	$15,768.75
10		125	$11,481.25	$14,606.25	$17,731.25

This is a two-variable table. Each profit calculation is the result of a change in both the attendance projection and the price. To create this table manually you would have to enter many different values into cells B4 and B5, and then copy each of the resulting profit calculations to your table from cell H19. Fortunately, this is exactly the kind of task that the What-If Table command is designed to automate.

Choose the Range ➤ Analyze ➤ What-If Table command now to take a first look at the dialog box for this feature. Notice the three option buttons located just beneath the explanation box. These allow you to build tables with one, two, or three variables:

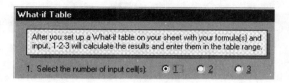

In upcoming sections you'll learn to create all three types of what-if tables. For now, click Cancel to close the dialog box.

Creating a One-Variable What-If Table

To create a one-variable what-if table you begin by identifying three ranges of information:

▶ A column of input values that 1-2-3 can insert one at a time into the worksheet calculations

▶ The input location where these values will be substituted

▶ The formula that 1-2-3 will recalculate for each new input entry

For example, Figure 16.2 shows a range of attendance projections in A10..A18 of the Conference sheet. The goal of the upcoming operation is to calculate the profit corresponding to each of these attendance values. To produce this information, 1-2-3 needs to insert each of the attendance figures into the input cell, B4, and then recalculate the formula that gives the profit. Accordingly, the formula in B9 is a reference to the cell that contains profit formula: +H19.

You'll begin the following exercise by entering the range of attendance estimates on your own copy of the Conference sheet. Then you'll use the Range ➤ Analyze ➤ What-If Table command to compute the profit figures:

1. Enter **45** into cell B10 and **55** in cell B11. Then select B10..B11 and use the drag-and-fill mouse technique to extend this series of values down to cell A18, as shown in Figure 16.2.

2. Select cell B9. Click the Format panel on the status bar and choose the Formula format so you'll be able to see the formula itself. Then enter **+H19** into B9.

Chapter 16   Worksheet Tools

Figure 16.2:   Preparing for a one-variable what-if table. The formula format has been applied to cell B9 so you can see exactly how the table is created.

3. Enter the labels **Attendance** and **Profit** into cells A8 and B8, respectively, and format them as shown in Figure 16.2. Apply the US Dollar style to the range B10..B18.

4. Select the range A9..B18.

5. Choose Range ➤ Analyze ➤ What-If Table. The What-If Table dialog box appears. Keep the 1 option as the selection for the number of input cells.

6. Enter a reference to cell **A:B4** in the Input cell 1 box. The dialog box now appears as follows:

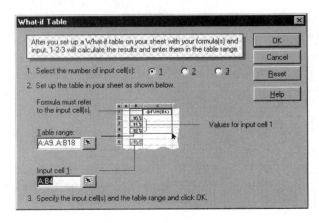

7. Click OK to confirm. Back on the sheet, move the cell pointer to A7, out of the way of the what-if table.

8. Choose the File ➤ Save As command and save this worksheet as WHATIF.123. (The original file, CONF2.123, remains unchanged on disk for upcoming exercises.)

As a result of these steps, 1-2-3 fills in the what-if table with a range of profit calculations in B10..B18:

	A	B	C
1	Computing for Video Stores		
2	Place	St. Louis	
3	Date	15-Oct-97	
4	Attendance	65	
5	Price	$195.00	
6			
7			
8	Attendance	Profit	
9		+H19	
10	45	$2,031.25	
11	55	$3,993.75	
12	65	$5,956.25	
13	75	$7,918.75	
14	85	$9,881.25	
15	95	$11,843.75	
16	105	$13,806.25	
17	115	$15,768.75	
18	125	$17,731.25	
19			

Each of these figures represents the value that would appear in cell H19 if you were to enter the corresponding attendance value into cell B4. The What-If Table command has generated the entire column of figures in a single operation.

This command also allows you to create one-variable what-if tables for more than one formula at a time. For example, suppose you want to add a column to display the variable expenses corresponding to each of the projected attendance levels:

1. Enter the formula **+H17** into cell C9.

2. Select the range A9..C18, and choose Range ➤ Analyze ➤ What-If Table again. Specify **A:B4** as the input cell, and click OK. The results of this second formula appear in the range C10..C18:

			Variable
7			
8	Attendance	Profit	Expenses
9		+H19	+H17
10	45	$2,031.25	$731.25
11	55	$3,993.75	$893.75
12	65	$5,956.25	$1,056.25
13	75	$7,918.75	$1,218.75
14	85	$9,881.25	$1,381.25
15	95	$11,843.75	$1,543.75
16	105	$13,806.25	$1,706.25
17	115	$15,768.75	$1,868.75
18	125	$17,731.25	$2,031.25
19			

Using the F8 Function Key to Recalculate a What-If Table

The entries that 1-2-3 places in the what-if table are values, not formulas; they are therefore not subject to automatic recalculation when you make changes on the worksheet. However, 1-2-3 gives you a convenient way to repeat the last What-If Table operation: Simply press the F8 function key. For example, suppose you make some changes in the column of input values in A10..A18. After you revise the entries in this range, pressing F8 produces a new version of the what-if table.

Try this exercise:

1. Use the drag-and-fill operation to enter a new range of attendance projections into A10..A18—values from **60** to **220** in step increments of **20**.

2. Press the F8 function key.

   The new what-if table appears as follows:

	Attendance	Profit	Variable Expenses
9		+H19	+H17
10	60	$4,975.00	$975.00
11	80	$8,900.00	$1,300.00
12	100	$12,825.00	$1,625.00
13	120	$16,750.00	$1,950.00
14	140	$20,675.00	$2,275.00
15	160	$24,600.00	$2,600.00
16	180	$28,525.00	$2,925.00
17	200	$32,450.00	$3,250.00
18	220	$36,375.00	$3,575.00

Creating a Two-Variable Table

To prepare a two-variable table, you begin by entering a column of values for the first input cell and a row of values for the second input cell. For example, suppose you want to generate a profit table for a range of attendance projections and a range of prices. To do so, you enter the attendance values down a column, just as you did for the one-variable table. Then you enter the range of prices across a row at the top of the table range. In the upper-left corner cell of the table range you enter the formula that 1-2-3 will use for calculating the what-if table.

In the following exercise, you'll generate a two-variable what-if table on sheet B of the WHATIF.123 workbook:

1. Click the New Sheet button to add sheet B to the file.

2. In cell B:A2, enter the formula **+A:H19**. Apply the Formula format and the bold style to this cell.

3. Enter the **Prices** as a right-aligned label in B:B1. Then enter **Attendance** into cell B:A1. Apply the bold style to both labels.

4. Use the drag-and-fill operation to enter a column of attendance projections into the range B:A3..B:A12—values from **45** to **135** in increment steps of **10**.

5. Use drag-and-fill again to enter a row of prices in the range B:B2..B:F2—values from **145** to **245** in increments of **25**.

6. Select the range B:B2..B:F12 and apply the US Dollar format.

7. Select the range B:A2..B:F12, and choose Range ➤ Analyze ➤ What-If Table. Notice that the range you've selected appears in the Table range box.

8. Click 2 as the number of input cells.

9. Enter **A:B4** as the reference for Input cell 1, and **A:B5** as the reference for Input cell 2, as shown here:

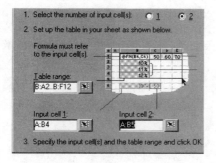

10. Click OK to confirm.

    Here is the resulting what-if table:

B	A	B	C	D	E	F
1	Attendance	Prices				
2	+A:H19	$145.00	$170.00	$195.00	$220.00	$245.00
3	45	($218.75)	$906.25	$2,031.25	$3,156.25	$4,281.25
4	55	$1,243.75	$2,618.75	$3,993.75	$5,368.75	$6,743.75
5	65	$2,706.25	$4,331.25	$5,956.25	$7,581.25	$9,206.25
6	75	$4,168.75	$6,043.75	$7,918.75	$9,793.75	$11,668.75
7	85	$5,631.25	$7,756.25	$9,881.25	$12,006.25	$14,131.25
8	95	$7,093.75	$9,468.75	$11,843.75	$14,218.75	$16,593.75
9	105	$8,556.25	$11,181.25	$13,806.25	$16,431.25	$19,056.25
10	115	$10,018.75	$12,893.75	$15,768.75	$18,643.75	$21,518.75
11	125	$11,481.25	$14,606.25	$17,731.25	$20,856.25	$23,981.25
12	135	$12,943.75	$16,318.75	$19,693.75	$23,068.75	$26,443.75

As you can see, 1-2-3 has calculated fifty different what-if scenarios in the conference worksheet. The profit figures resulting from these scenarios are displayed in the range B:B3..B:F12.

Creating a Three-Variable Table

A three-variable what-if table is organized over a three-dimensional sheet range. Each sheet in the range contains a column of entries for the first input cell and a row of entries for the second input cell, just as in a two-variable table. But instead of entering a formula in the upper-left corner of the table, you enter a value for the third input cell. Each sheet in the three-dimensional range displays a different value in this cell. You then specify the formula for the what-if table in the What-If Table dialog box rather than in the table range itself.

For example, sheets C, D, and E in Figure 16.3 have been designed as the basis for a three-variable what-if table. The purpose of this example is to generate profit scenarios by varying the values in three input cells: the attendance estimate (A:B4), the per-person admission price (A:B5), and the cost of renting a conference room (A:H7). The range B3..B6 on each of the three sheets displays a column of attendance projections, and the range C2..G2 displays a row of conference prices. In cell B2, each sheet contains a different dollar amount for the conference room rental.

Conf2: Window 3 (Sheet E)

	A	B	C	D	E	F	G	H
1		Room	Price					
2	Attendance	$2,500	$145	$170	$195	$220	$245	
3		65						
4		85						
5		105						
6		125						

Conf2: Window 2 (Sheet D)

	A	B	C	D	E	F	G	H
1		Room	Price					
2	Attendance	$2,000	$145	$170	$195	$220	$245	
3		65						
4		85						
5		105						
6		125						

Conf2: Window 1 (Sheet C)

	A	B	C	D	E	F	G	H
1		Room	Price					
2	Attendance	$1,500	$145	$170	$195	$220	$245	
3		65						
4		85						
5		105						
6		125						

Figure 16.3: **Preparing for a three-variable what-if table. Cell B2 represents the third variable in each sheet.**

Here are the steps for creating this three-variable what-if table in your own copy of the WHATIF.WK4 worksheet:

1. With the cell pointer located in sheet B, click the New Sheet button three times to add sheets C, D, and E to the file.

2. Enter the labels and values into sheet C, and format them as they appear in Figure 16.3. Then use copy-and-paste operations to copy the contents of sheet C to sheets D and E. Enter a new value of **$2,000.00** into cell D:B2 and a new value of **$2,500.00** into cell E:B2.

3. Select the three-dimensional range C:B2..E:G6. To do so, begin by selecting the two-dimensional range C:B2..C:G6 on sheet C; then hold down the Shift and Ctrl keys while you press the PgUp key twice. When you release all the keys, the three-dimensional range is selected.

4. Choose Range ➤ Analyze ➤ What-If Table. Notice that a reference to the three-dimensional range appears in the Table range box.

5. Choose the 3 option for the number of input cells.

6. Enter **A:H19** into the Formula cell text box; this is a reference to the profit formula in worksheet A.

7. Enter **A:B4** in the Input cell 1 box, **A:B5** in the Input cell 2 box, and **A:H7** in the Input cell 3 box. These are references to the attendance projection, the per-person admission price, and conference room cost, respectively. When you finish all these entries, the What-If Table dialog box appears as follows:

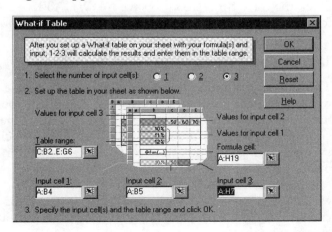

8. Click OK to confirm the entries in the dialog box.

Figure 16.4 shows the what-if table that 1-2-3 creates in response to these steps. In this example, 1-2-3 has calculated 60 different scenarios of the conference worksheet and has copied the profit figure from each scenario to the what-if table.

Conf2: Window 3

	A	B	C	D	E	F	G	H
1		Room	Price					
2	Attendance	$2,500	$145	$170	$195	$220	$245	
3		65	$1,706.25	$3,331.25	$4,956.25	$6,581.25	$8,206.25	
4		85	$4,631.25	$6,756.25	$8,881.25	$11,006.25	$13,131.25	
5		105	$7,556.25	$10,181.25	$12,806.25	$15,431.25	$18,056.25	
6		125	$10,481.25	$13,606.25	$16,731.25	$19,856.25	$22,981.25	

Conf2: Window 2

	A	B	C	D	E	F	G	H
1		Room	Price					
2	Attendance	$2,000	$145	$170	$195	$220	$245	
3		65	$2,206.25	$3,831.25	$5,456.25	$7,081.25	$8,706.25	
4		85	$5,131.25	$7,256.25	$9,381.25	$11,506.25	$13,631.25	
5		105	$8,056.25	$10,681.25	$13,306.25	$15,931.25	$18,556.25	
6		125	$10,981.25	$14,106.25	$17,231.25	$20,356.25	$23,481.25	

Conf2: Window 1

	A	B	C	D	E	F	G	H
1		Room	Price					
2	Attendance	$1,500	$145	$170	$195	$220	$245	
3		65	$2,706.25	$4,331.25	$5,956.25	$7,581.25	$9,206.25	
4		85	$5,631.25	$7,756.25	$9,881.25	$12,006.25	$14,131.25	
5		105	$8,556.25	$11,181.25	$13,806.25	$16,431.25	$19,056.25	
6		125	$11,481.25	$14,606.25	$17,731.25	$20,856.25	$23,981.25	

Figure 16.4: **A three-variable what-if table**

Click the Save SmartIcon to save the WHATIF.123 workbook to disk for future reference. You can then close the workbook.

Using the Backsolver Command

The Backsolver is a simple but valuable tool to use when you want to work backward through a worksheet scenario—specifically when you have determined a bottom-line figure as your projection or goal, and you want to discover the input value necessary to achieve this goal. For example, suppose you want to find the admission price required to produce a total profit of $10,000 on the Conference sheet, at the current attendance estimate of 65. One way to find the correct price would be to experiment with new entries in cell B5 until you find the value that gives a profit of $10,000. But this trial-and-error approach would take time.

The 1-2-3 Backsolver performs this task for you more efficiently. To use this command successfully, you supply three items of information:

▶ A worksheet cell that contains the target formula for the Backsolver operation

▶ The projected value that you want this formula to yield

▶ The cell (or cells) containing the input that 1-2-3 will adjust in order to achieve the specified result from the target formula

In the following exercise you'll experiment with the Backsolver on the Conference sheet:

1. Reopen the CONF2.123 workbook from disk.
2. Choose Range ➤ Analyze ➤ Backsolver.
3. In the text box labeled "Make the formula in this cell," enter a reference to **H19**, the cell that contains the profit formula.
4. Enter **10000** in the text box labeled "Equal to this value." This is the value that you want the profit formula to yield.
5. In the By changing cell(s) text box, enter a reference to cell **B5**, which contains the current admission price; this is the cell that you want 1-2-3 to adjust in order to achieve the desired profit projection. The Backsolver dialog box now appears as follows:

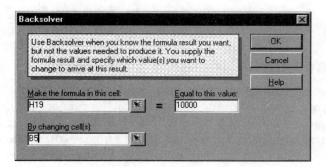

6. Click OK to perform the Backsolver operation.

When you complete this operation, the worksheet looks like Figure 16.5. As you can see, an admission price of $257.21 is necessary to achieve a profit of $10,000. To avoid changing the original CONF2.123 file, save this version of the worksheet under a new name, or close it without saving.

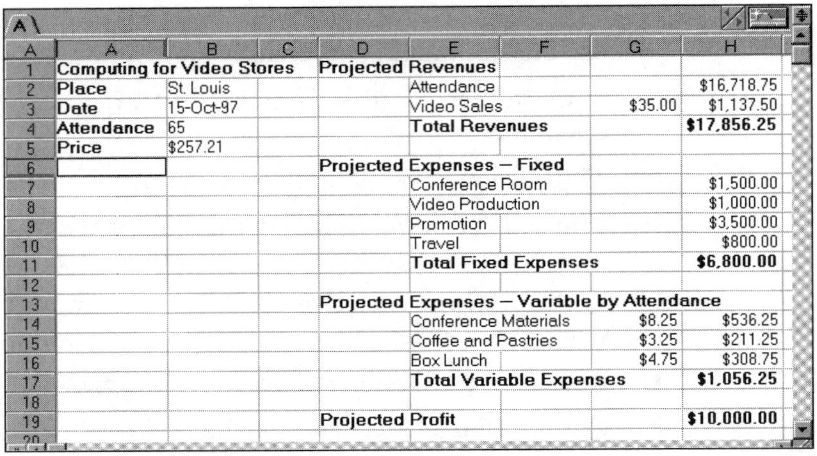

	A	B	C	D	E	F	G	H
1	**Computing for Video Stores**			**Projected Revenues**				
2	**Place**	St. Louis			Attendance			$16,718.75
3	**Date**	15-Oct-97			Video Sales		$35.00	$1,137.50
4	**Attendance**	65			**Total Revenues**			**$17,856.25**
5	**Price**	$257.21						
6				**Projected Expenses – Fixed**				
7					Conference Room			$1,500.00
8					Video Production			$1,000.00
9					Promotion			$3,500.00
10					Travel			$800.00
11					**Total Fixed Expenses**			**$6,800.00**
12								
13				**Projected Expenses – Variable by Attendance**				
14					Conference Materials		$8.25	$536.25
15					Coffee and Pastries		$3.25	$211.25
16					Box Lunch		$4.75	$308.75
17					**Total Variable Expenses**			**$1,056.25**
18								
19				**Projected Profit**				**$10,000.00**

Figure 16.5: ***Using the Backsolver. 1-2-3 has found the admission price necessary to reach a profit of $10,000.***

TIP The Backsolver allows you to enter a range of cells in the By changing cell(s) text box. If you do so, 1-2-3 adjusts all the values in the range proportionally to achieve the result you want. For example, using the Conference sheet, you could try entering a range of B4..B5 in the By changing cell(s) text box. In response, the Backsolver would adjust both the attendance level and the admission price to achieve a bottom line profit of $10,000.

Using the Distribution Command

The Distribution command counts the number of entries that fall within specified numeric categories. To prepare for this command, you begin by entering a series of numbers into a column of the worksheet. These numbers, known as the bin range, express the numeric intervals into which you want to distribute a range of values. Then you select the values range—that is, the worksheet range that is the subject of the frequency distribution. Given these two ranges, the Data Distribution command creates a new column of numbers representing the frequency count.

For example, Figure 16.6 shows a use of this command on the Yrs field in the Instructor database, which you developed in Chapter 11. Four fields have been copied to this sheet from the database. As you'll recall, Yrs represents the number of years each instructor has worked for

Computing Conferences, Inc. The purpose of this particular worksheet is to count the number of instructors whose length of employment falls within each of several categories: one year or less, one to two years, two to three years, and so on. The bin range representing these categories appears in F7..F12.

A	B	C	D	E	F	G
1	Instructor Database					
2						
3	ID	Last	First	Yrs	Frequency Distribution	
4	S-125	Ashford	W.	4.7		
5	W-145	Banks	S.	1.6	Years as	Number of
6	D-143	Cody	L.	1.6	Instructor	Instructors
7	A-146	Daniels	A.	0.7	1	3
8	W-119	Davis	G.	4.6	2	2
9	T-128	Eng	R.	4.3	3	2
10	S-127	Gill	P.	4.6	4	1
11	S-149	Harris	P.	1.0	5	5
12	W-124	Meyer	J.	4.7	6	3
13	A-103	Perez	D.	5.6		1
14	W-113	Porter	D.	5.5		
15	D-139	Porter	M.	2.8		
16	T-133	Ramirez	F.	4.0		
17	S-155	Roberts	P.	0.4		
18	D-137	Sanchez	W.	2.8		
19	N-101	Schwartz	B.	5.9		
20	D-106	Weinberg	P.	6.0		

Figure 16.6: **Using the Data Distribution command. The bin range is F7..F12. The values range is D4..D20.**

Once you have established the bin range, using the Data Distribution command is simple. Here are the steps to produce the frequency distribution shown in G7..G13:

1. Select the values range, in this case the data in the Yrs field, D4..D20.

2. Choose Range ➤ Analyze ➤ Distribution. The range you've selected appears in the text box labeled "Range of values to count."

3. Enter **A:F7..A:F12** in the Bin range text box, as shown here:

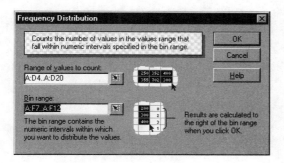

4. Click OK to complete the operation.

The command enters the frequency distribution into the column located immediately to the right of the bin range. In Figure 16.6, you can see that there are three instructors who have worked for one year or less, two who have worked between one and two years, and so on. In addition, you'll notice that the frequency distribution range contains one more entry than the bin range. The final entry shows the number value-range entries found to be greater than the last entry in the bin range. In this example, there is one instructor who has worked for more than six years.

Using the Regression Command

Regression analysis is an attempt to discover the strength of the mathematical correlation between two or more sets of data. For example, column B of the following worksheet shows the amount that Computing Conferences, Inc. has spent on advertising for several recent computer-training conferences, and column C shows the attendance at those same conferences:

	A	B	C
1	Computing Conferences, Inc.		
2	Attendance and Advertising		
3	*Computing for Video Stores*		
4			
5	Date	Advertising	Attendance
6	09-Jan-96	$5,000	154
7	21-Jan-96	$3,500	119
8	15-Feb-96	$6,000	174
9	07-Mar-96	$6,000	201
10	25-Mar-96	$3,500	136
11	03-Apr-96	$5,000	172
12	11-May-96	$3,500	112
13	18-May-96	$1,000	97
14	03-Jun-96	$1,000	86
15	29-Jun-96	$1,000	104
16	05-Sep-96	$7,500	235
17	11-Oct-96	$1,500	119
18	29-Oct-96	$2,500	137
19	05-Nov-96	$3,500	148
20			

The general question posed by this worksheet is clear: Does attendance go up when the company spends more money on advertising? In other words, is there a correlation between advertising and attendance? In an analysis of this particular example, attendance is referred to as the dependent variable, because the goal of the analysis will be to discover the extent to which advertising affects attendance. Accordingly, advertising is called the independent variable.

You might recall working with this same data in Chapter 10 while you were studying the variety of 1-2-3 chart types. Specifically, Figure 10.7 displays an XY chart in which advertising dollars are plotted against attendance in an x-y coordinate system. This graph seems to show a relationship between the two data sets. In effect, an XY chart is a pictorial form of regression analysis. Suppose you were to draw a straight diagonal line somewhere through the middle of the plotted points in Figure 10.7; you might then formulate an approximate equation describing the relationship between advertising and attendance.

The general equation for a straight line is:

$$y = mx + b$$

where

▶ y is the dependent variable,

▶ x is the independent variable,

▶ m is the slope of the straight line that represents the relationship, and

▶ b is the y-intercept, or the value of y when x is zero.

To the extent that the equation you develop is a reliable description of the relationship between the two variables, you can use this equation to make predictions about the dependent variable.

The Range ➤ Analyze ➤ Regression command performs this same kind of analysis, but produces specific mathematical results rather than graphic approximations. Regression allows you to select a range containing one or more independent variables (known as the X-range) and one dependent variable (known as the Y-range). In addition, you specify an output range where the command can display the results of its analysis.

Here is the Regression dialog box, filled in with appropriate ranges for an analysis of the advertising and attendance worksheet:

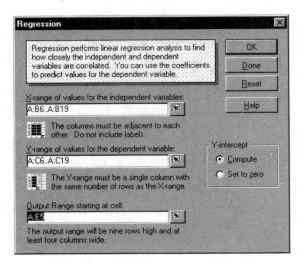

The X-range text box contains a reference to the range of advertising data in column B, and the Y-range text box contains a reference to the range of attendance data in column C. Cell E5 is specified as the upper-left corner of the output range. In addition, the Y-intercept box presents two option buttons, giving you a choice between calculating the actual y-intercept (the Compute option) or hypothesizing a value of zero for the y-intercept (the Set to zero option). For the advertising and attendance data, you want 1-2-3 to calculate the actual y-intercept; in theory, this value represents the expected attendance level when no money is spent on advertising.

Here are the results of the regression analysis:

	Regression Output:
Constant	74.84
Std Err of Y Est	15.78
R Squared	0.869
No. of Observations	14
Degrees of Freedom	12
X Coefficient(s)	0.019
Std Err of Coef.	0.002

At the top of the output table, the Constant value (displayed as 74.84) is the y-intercept. Near the bottom of the table, the X Coefficient(s) value (displayed as 0.019) is the slope of the line that theoretically describes the relationship between the two variables. Rounding the constant, you can formulate the following equation for the line:

```
y = 0.019x + 75
```

or

```
attendance = 0.019*advertising + 75
```

You can substitute actual advertising amounts into this equation to calculate the corresponding attendance projection. For example, according to this equation, attendance should be at a level of 75 people when no money is spent on advertising, and approximately 150 people when $4,000 is spent.

Other Values in the Regression Output

The Regression command also displays output values that tell you the extent to which you can rely on this particular regression analysis as a tool for predicting the behavior of the dependent variable:

▶ **R Squared.** The R Squared value is a general measurement of the reliability of the analysis. For a strong correlation between the dependent and independent variables, the R Squared value is close to 1; for a weak correlation, the value is close to zero.

▶ **Std Err of Y Est.** The value labeled Std Err of Y Est (standard error of the y estimate) indicates the range of accuracy for calculated values of y. In the advertising example, the Std Err of Y Est value is approximately 16. This implies that any attendance value you calculate from the equation is accurate within a range of plus-or-minus 16.

▶ **Std Err of Coef.** The value labeled Std Err of Coef. (standard error of the x coefficient) indicates the reliability of the slope calculation. The smaller this value is in relation to the X Coefficient(s), the better the reliability.

Using the Matrix Commands

A group of numbers arranged in rows and columns is called a matrix. In mathematics, a matrix is represented as a rectangular array of numbers enclosed in parentheses. In a worksheet, a matrix is an ordinary table of numbers in a range where you can appropriately use 1-2-3's matrix commands.

The Range ➤ Analyze menu contains two matrix commands, named Invert Matrix and Multiply Matrix. You can use these commands to solve simultaneous equations in business, financial, or technical applications. A set of simultaneous equations has a common group of unknown values, known as variables. In typical examples, each equation has the same number of variables, and the number of equations is equal to the number of unknowns. For instance, in a set of four simultaneous equations, each equation has the same four variables. To solve these equations, you must find a set of four numeric values that satisfy all four equations.

Consider the example shown in Figure 16.7. The central office of Computing Conferences, Inc., has incurred expenses in four categories of curriculum development, designing courses for accountants, doctors, lawyers, and video store owners. These expenses will be shared among the company's four regions in relation to each region's profits. The table of numbers in the range B5..E8 represents the profits earned from regional conferences in the four topic areas. Column F shows the expenses for curriculum development. The problem of this worksheet is to find the fixed percentage of each region's profits to charge for curriculum costs.

	A	B	C	D	E	F
1	Distributing the Cost of Curriculum Development					
2						Cost of
3		Profits by Region				Curriculum
4	Topic	Eastern	Western	Northern	Southern	Development
5	Accountants	$111,200	$79,300	$59,500	$64,200	$8,058.76
6	Doctors	$131,900	$116,900	$77,500	$96,700	$10,852.33
7	Lawyers	$63,500	$81,500	$54,000	$88,400	$7,376.34
8	Video Stores	$88,300	$63,200	$41,900	$161,900	$9,619.99
9						
10						
11						
12						
13						
14						
15						
16	Region	% of Profit				
17	Eastern					
18	Western					
19	Northern					
20	Southern					
21						

Figure 16.7: Setting up the curriculum expense worksheet. The goal is to find the percentage of each region's profits to charge for curriculum development.

This problem can be expressed as a group of four simultaneous equations with four unknowns. In this case, the unknowns are the percentages to charge the four regions—that is, the fixed amount by which each region's profit figures should be multiplied to find the correct share of the curriculum expense. In the following equations, these unknowns are represented as E, W, N, and S:

```
111200*E +  79300*W + 59500*N +  64200*S =  8058.76
131900*E + 116900*W + 77500*N +  96700*S = 10852.33
 63500*E +  81500*W + 54000*N +  88400*S =  7376.34
 88300*E +  63200*W + 41900*N + 161900*S =  9619.99
```

Accordingly, the goal of the worksheet in Figure 16.7 is to find values for E, W, N, and S that satisfy all four equations.

To prepare for the upcoming exercise, enter the values and labels of the curriculum expense worksheet onto a new blank worksheet of your own, and format the data as shown in Figure 16.7. Save the workbook as CURREXP.123.

Understanding Matrix Arithmetic

Before using the Matrix commands, you may find it helpful to review briefly the mathematical background of matrices. The worksheet in Figure 16.8 displays a group of matrices generated from the curriculum expense problem:

▶ **Coefficient matrix.** In the range A2..D5, the coefficient matrix is the table of regional profits, the numbers by which the four variables are multiplied in the simultaneous equations.

▶ **Constant matrix.** The constant matrix, shown in the range F2..F5, is the column of values from the right side of each equation, the expense amounts for curriculum development.

Here is a summary of the two operations you can perform on matrices using the Matrix commands:

▶ The Range ➤ Analyze ➤ Invert Matrix command can be performed on a square matrix—that is, any matrix that contains an equal number of rows and columns. The result of this operation is a second matrix that has the same dimensions as the first. For example, the inverse of the coefficient matrix appears in the range A8..D11 in Figure 16.8.

Chapter 16   Worksheet Tools

	A	B	C	D	E	F	G
1	Coefficient Matrix					Constant Matrix	
2	111200	79300	59500	64200		8058.76	
3	131900	116900	77500	96700		10852.33	
4	63500	81500	54000	88400		7376.34	
5	88300	63200	41900	161900		9619.99	
6							
7	Inverse Matrix						
8	-0.0000001	0.00001888	-0.0000316	0.00000605			
9	-0.0000959	0.00009898	-0.0000348	-0.0000021			
10	0.00014481	-0.0001587	0.0001002	-0.0000173			
11	0.00000002	-0.0000079	0.0000049	0.00000818			
12							
13	Identity Matrix					Solution Matrix	
14	1	0	0	0		0.02861811	
15	0	1	0	0		0.02470488	
16	0	0	1	0		0.01687767	
17	0	0	0	1		0.02979918	
18							

Figure 16.8:   **Matrices and matrix arithmetic**

▶   The Range ➤ Analyze ➤ Matrix Multiply operation is performed between two matrices and results in a third matrix. The number of columns in the first matrix must be the same as the number of rows in the second matrix. In this operation, 1-2-3 multiplies values in each row of the first matrix by the corresponding values in each column of the second matrix; the sums of these products become the elements of the third matrix. If the first matrix in the operation has r1 rows and c1 columns, and the second matrix has r2 rows and c2 columns, the resulting matrix will have r1 rows and c2 columns.

By definition, the result of multiplying a matrix by its own inverse matrix is the identity matrix. As you can see in the range A14..D17 of Figure 16.8, an identity matrix consists of values of 0 and 1, where the values of 1 are arranged in a diagonal from the upper-left to the lower-right corners of the matrix.

The identity matrix suggests an approach to solving the simultaneous equations. If the four equations can be rearranged so that one variable in each equation has a coefficient of 1 and the remaining variables have coefficients of 0, the resulting constants on the right sides of the equations are the solutions to the problem. Keep in mind that the identity matrix is the result of multiplying the coefficient matrix by its own inverse. This implies the basic rule that you use to solve simultaneous equations: The one-column solution matrix is found by multiplying the inverse of the coefficient matrix by the constant matrix, the column of values from the right sides of the original equations.

For example, consider the solution matrix displayed in the range F14..F17 in Figure 16.8. This column of values is the result of using the Multiply Matrix command to multiply the inverse matrix in the range A8..D11 by the constant matrix in F2..F5. Each element in the solution matrix is the value for one of the four variables, E, W, N, or S.

Solving the Simultaneous Equations

Returning now to the original curriculum expense worksheet, CUREXP .123 (see Figure 16.7), here are the steps for finding the correct percentage for each region:

1. Select the range of profit figures, in B5..E8.
2. Choose Range ➤ Analyze ➤ Invert Matrix. In the resulting dialog box, the selected range is displayed in the From text box.
3. In the To box, enter a reference to cell B11, as shown here:

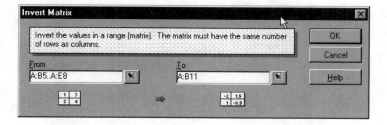

This is the upper-left corner of the range where 1-2-3 will generate the inverse matrix.

4. Click OK, and the inverse matrix appears on the worksheet, as shown in Figure 16.9.
5. Now select the inverse matrix, in the range B11..E14.
6. Choose Range ➤ Analyze ➤ Multiply Matrix. In the resulting dialog box, the selected range (of the inverse matrix) appears in the First Matrix text box.

7. Enter the range of the constant matrix, F5..F8, in the Second Matrix text box. Then enter B17 in the Resulting Matrix text box:

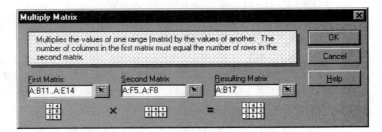

Click OK to complete the operation.

8. Select the range of the solution matrix, B17..B20. Click the Format button on the status bar, and select the Percent format. Your sheet now appears as shown in Figure 16.10.

9. Click the Save SmartIcon to save your work to disk.

	A	B	C	D	E	F
1	Distributing the Cost of Curriculum Development					
2						Cost of
3		Profits by Region				Curriculum
4	Topic	Eastern	Western	Northern	Southern	Development
5	Accountants	$111,200	$79,300	$59,500	$64,200	$8,058.76
6	Doctors	$131,900	$116,900	$77,500	$96,700	$10,852.33
7	Lawyers	$63,500	$81,500	$54,000	$88,400	$7,376.34
8	Video Stores	$88,300	$63,200	$41,900	$161,900	$9,619.99
9						
10						
11		-0.0000001	0.00001888	-0.0000316	0.00000605	
12		-0.0000959	0.00009898	-0.0000348	-0.0000021	
13		0.00014481	-0.0001587	0.0001002	-0.0000173	
14		0.00000002	-0.0000079	0.0000049	0.00000818	
15						
16	Region	% of Profit				
17	Eastern					
18	Western					
19	Northern					
20	Southern					
21						

Figure 16.9: *Generating the inverse matrix*

In effect, you have now solved the four simultaneous equations. The values in the range B17..B20 show the percentage to take from each region's profits to cover the shared expense of curriculum development.

Now suppose you want to produce a table that shows the actual curriculum expense amount to be charged against the earnings for each conference topic in each region. For this table, you need to display the four percentages across a row, rather than down a column as they currently appear. The Range ➤ Transpose command is a convenient tool for accomplishing this task.

	A	B	C	D	E	F
1	Distributing the Cost of Curriculum Development					
2						
3		Profits by Region				Cost of Curriculum
4	Topic	Eastern	Western	Northern	Southern	Development
5	Accountants	$111,200	$79,300	$59,500	$64,200	$8,058.76
6	Doctors	$131,900	$116,900	$77,500	$96,700	$10,852.33
7	Lawyers	$63,500	$81,500	$54,000	$88,400	$7,376.34
8	Video Stores	$88,300	$63,200	$41,900	$161,900	$9,619.99
9						
10						
11		-0.0000001	0.00001888	-0.0000316	0.00000605	
12		-0.0000959	0.00009898	-0.0000348	-0.0000021	
13		0.00014481	-0.0001587	0.0001002	-0.0000173	
14		0.00000002	-0.0000079	0.0000049	0.00000818	
15						
16	Region	% of Profit				
17	Eastern	2.86%				
18	Western	2.47%				
19	Northern	1.69%				
20	Southern	2.98%				
21						

Figure 16.10: *Producing the solution matrix. The values in the range B17..B20 represent the percentages of profit to charge for curriculum development.*

Using the Transpose Command

The Range ➤ Transpose command copies the row entries of a source range to the columns of a destination range, or, conversely, the column entries of a source to the rows of a destination. If the source range contains formulas, the Transpose command replaces those formulas with their current values in the destination range. (The original formulas in the source range are not affected.) This command also copies formats and display styles from the source to the destination range.

To produce the detailed table of curriculum expenses, you want to copy the percentages currently displayed in the column range

B17..B20 to the row range B10..E10. (Note that these entries are simple values, not formulas.) Because you have no further use for the inverse matrix in the curriculum expense worksheet, you'll begin this next exercise by deleting the matrix:

1. Select the range B11..E14. Press the Delete key on your keyboard to erase the entries in this entire range.

2. Select the range of labels in A5..A8 and press Ctrl+C. Then select cell A11 and press Ctrl+V to copy these labels to the range A11..A14.

3. Select the range of percentages in B17..B20 and choose Range ➤ Transpose. The selected range appears in the text box labeled "Transpose the range." Enter B10 into the text box labeled "Put the results in," as shown here:

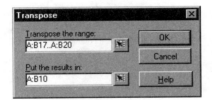

Click OK to complete the operation. The column of percentages has now been transposed to a row.

4. Enter the formula **+B5*B$10** into cell B11.

5. Select the range B11..B14. Click the range with the right mouse button and choose Copy Down from the resulting shortcut menu.

6. Select the range B11..E14. Click the range with the right mouse button and choose Copy Right from the shortcut menu.

7. Enter the word **Total** into cell F10. In response, 1-2-3 generates a column of totals in F11..F14.

8. Apply the US Dollar format to the values in B11..F14. Then move the cell pointer to F1, out of the way of any data. Your worksheet now appears as shown in Figure 16.11.

9. Click the Save SmartIcon to save your work to disk.

Notice that the expense totals you've produced in the range F11..F14 are the same as the original curriculum costs that you entered into F5..F8. These matching values confirm your solution for the simultaneous equations.

Outlining

	A	B	C	D	E	F
1	Distributing the Cost of Curriculum Development					
2						
3		Profits by Region				Cost of Curriculum
4	Topic	Eastern	Western	Northern	Southern	Development
5	Accountants	$111,200	$79,300	$59,500	$64,200	$8,058.76
6	Doctors	$131,900	$116,900	$77,500	$96,700	$10,852.33
7	Lawyers	$63,500	$81,500	$54,000	$88,400	$7,376.34
8	Video Stores	$88,300	$63,200	$41,900	$161,900	$9,619.99
9						
10		2.86%	2.47%	1.69%	2.98%	Total
11	Accountants	$3,182.33	$1,959.10	$1,004.22	$1,913.11	$8,058.76
12	Doctors	$3,774.73	$2,888.00	$1,308.02	$2,881.58	$10,852.33
13	Lawyers	$1,817.25	$2,013.45	$911.39	$2,634.25	$7,376.34
14	Video Stores	$2,526.98	$1,561.35	$707.17	$4,824.49	$9,619.99
15						
16	Region	% of Profit				
17	Eastern	2.86%				
18	Western	2.47%				
19	Northern	1.69%				
20	Southern	2.98%				
21						

Figure 16.11: Producing the curriculum expense table. The column of percentages has been transposed into a row in B10..E10.

Outlining

Finally, outlining is yet another feature you can use to organize and clarify the information on a sheet. The Sheet ➤ Outline menu provides the commands for planning an outline:

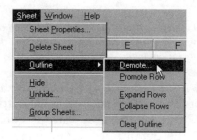

On a sheet that has many rows and columns of "detail" data, along with rows and columns that serve to summarize the data, outlining gives you a convenient way to hide the details so you can focus on the summary.

For example, consider the profits sheet for Computer Conferences, Inc., shown in Figure 16.12. For each of the four regions, the sheet shows profit figures organized by conference topics (in rows) and by the four quarters of the year (in columns). Given all this detail, you may have trouble focusing on exactly the information that you need—say, the total quarterly profits for each region, or the total profits by conference topics. Outlining gives you a way to solve this problem by temporarily hiding the details that you don't need to see.

	A	B	C	D	E	F	G
1	PROFITS		Quarter 1	Quarter 2	Quarter 3	Quarter 4	TOTAL
2	Eastern						
3		Accountants	$23,562	$19,871	$32,871	$34,896	$111,200
4		Doctors	$37,131	$29,355	$41,231	$24,183	$131,900
5		Lawyers	$12,339	$22,122	$8,712	$20,327	$63,500
6		Video Stores	$21,991	$19,831	$16,889	$29,589	$88,300
7		TOTAL	$95,023	$91,179	$99,703	$108,995	$394,900
8	Western						
9		Accountants	$18,933	$16,551	$21,852	$21,964	$79,300
10		Doctors	$28,751	$31,831	$27,669	$28,649	$116,900
11		Lawyers	$18,779	$23,669	$16,839	$22,213	$81,500
12		Video Stores	$15,896	$17,532	$13,554	$16,218	$63,200
13		TOTAL	$82,359	$89,583	$79,914	$89,044	$340,900
14	Northern						
15		Accountants	$14,773	$12,779	$16,733	$15,215	$59,500
16		Doctors	$18,740	$16,834	$19,833	$22,093	$77,500
17		Lawyers	$13,221	$14,833	$11,337	$14,609	$54,000
18		Video Stores	$9,821	$8,678	$11,669	$11,732	$41,900
19		TOTAL	$56,555	$53,124	$59,572	$63,649	$232,900
20	Southern						
21		Accountants	$16,844	$12,664	$16,833	$17,859	$64,200
22		Doctors	$24,558	$21,833	$24,838	$25,471	$96,700

Figure 16.12: A Profits sheet with many rows and columns of detail data, along with a few rows and columns of summary data. This sheet is a good candidate for outlining.

Once you've planned an outline on the profit sheet, you can collapse the sheet to hide details or you can expand it to redisplay details. Figures 16.13, 16.14, and 16.15 show various collapsed views of the data. In Figure 16.13 the detail lines for individual conference topics have been collapsed. In Figure 16.14 the quarterly profit columns are hidden from view. And in Figure 16.15 both row and column details are collapsed, leaving only the regional totals.

Outlining takes only a few short steps in 1-2-3. The first step is simply to examine your sheet and determine the best ways to organize the outline. How many levels of outlining are appropriate for your sheet? Which rows and columns might you want to hide from view temporarily? Where are the summary rows and columns in relation to the detail data? These are the questions you'll answer for yourself at the outset.

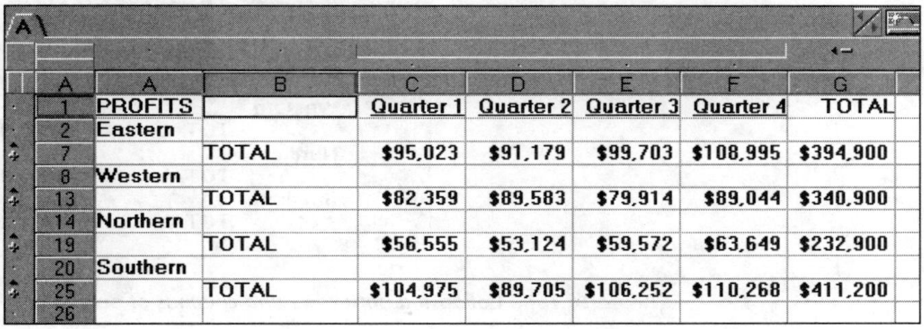

	A	B	C	D	E	F	G
1	PROFITS		Quarter 1	Quarter 2	Quarter 3	Quarter 4	TOTAL
2	Eastern						
7		TOTAL	$95,023	$91,179	$99,703	$108,995	$394,900
8	Western						
13		TOTAL	$82,359	$89,583	$79,914	$89,044	$340,900
14	Northern						
19		TOTAL	$56,555	$53,124	$59,572	$63,649	$232,900
20	Southern						
25		TOTAL	$104,975	$89,705	$106,252	$110,268	$411,200
26							

Figure 16.13: **Collapsing rows of detail data**

	A	B	G
1	PROFITS		TOTAL
2	Eastern		
3		Accountants	$111,200
4		Doctors	$131,900
5		Lawyers	$63,500
6		Video Stores	$88,300
7		TOTAL	$394,900
8	Western		
9		Accountants	$79,300
10		Doctors	$116,900
11		Lawyers	$81,500
12		Video Stores	$63,200
13		TOTAL	$340,900
14	Northern		
15		Accountants	$59,500
16		Doctors	$77,500
17		Lawyers	$54,000
18		Video Stores	$41,900
19		TOTAL	$232,900
20	Southern		
21		Accountants	$64,200

Figure 16.14: **Collapsing columns of detail data**

Once you've decided how the outline should work, you can use the Info-Box for sheet properties to display an outline frame around the perimeter of your sheet; as you'll see shortly, this frame contains the tools you use to control the status of the outline. The InfoBox also gives you the opportunity to establish the orientation between detail and summary data.

	A	B	G
1	PROFITS		TOTAL
2	Eastern		
7		TOTAL	$394,900
8	Western		
13		TOTAL	$340,900
14	Northern		
19		TOTAL	$232,900
20	Southern		
25		TOTAL	$411,200
26			

Figure 16.15: **Collapsing both rows and columns of detail data**

Choose Sheet ➤ Sheet Properties to display the InfoBox, and click the Outline tab. You'll see two check boxes for displaying the outline frame—one for rows and one for columns:

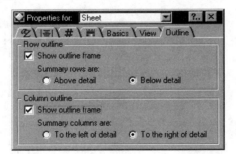

After placing checks in the outline frame boxes, you need to make sure that the summary/detail orientation option is correct. For example, on the profit sheet, the summary totals for each region are located below the topic detail rows; and the summary column is to the right of the quarterly detail columns. Accordingly, you choose the Below detail option for the row outline, and the option labeled "To the right of detail" for the column outline.

The next step is to identify the rows and columns that can be collapsed:

▶ Select a range of rows and choose Sheet ➤ Outline ➤ Demote Rows.

▶ Select a range of columns and choose Sheet ➤ Outline ➤ Demote Columns.

When you complete these actions, the outline frame shows exactly which rows and columns have been assigned to a particular outline level. For example, here is how demoted rows are represented on the frame:

In the profits sheet, all the rows containing conference topic details can be demoted to the same outline level—that is, rows 3 to 6 in the Eastern region, 9 to 12 in the Western region, 15 to 18 in the Northern region, and 21 to 24 in the Southern region. Likewise, the columns containing quarterly details—columns C, D, E, and F—should be demoted to their own outline level.

Finally, you can collapse and expand data simply by clicking the buttons that represent the levels of your outline. For rows, these buttons are located at the top of the vertical outline frame; for columns, they appear at the left side of the horizontal outline frame:

To collapse all the rows of topic detail, as shown back in Figure 16.13, you simply click the first button in the row outline frame. To collapse all the columns of quarterly detail, as shown in Figure 16.14, you click the upper button in the column outline frame. To collapse rows and columns, as in Figure 16.15, click both buttons.

Conversely, you can expand the outline—redisplaying the detail rows and columns—by clicking the second button on the row outline frame and the lower button on the column outline frame.

TIP You can collapse an individual range of rows or columns by clicking the corresponding arrowhead along the outline frame.

TIP To return your sheet to its original unoutlined state, choose Sheet ➤ Outline ➤ Clear Outline. To hide the outline frame without clearing the outline definition itself, open the InfoBox for sheet properties and remove the checks from the outline frame options.

Summary

Beyond basic spreadsheet operations, 1-2-3 provides a selection of tools that help you develop, analyze, and organize information on a sheet. For example, SmartMasters are templates you can use to create professionally designed workbooks for specific business purposes.

The Range ➤ Analyze menu contains a variety of commands that perform advanced mathematical calculations in appropriately organized sheets. The What-If Table command produces one-, two-, and three-variable what-if tables representing multiple worksheet scenarios. The Backsolver command finds the input value that produces a specified bottom-line result from a formula on your sheet. The Distribution command counts the entries that fit into numerical categories in a bin range. The Regression command analyzes the correlation between a dependent variable and one or more independent variables. The Invert Matrix and Multiply Matrix commands are tools to use for solving simultaneous equations, represented as matrix tables in a worksheet.

Outlining is a method of organizing tabular information into levels of detail and summary. Using the Sheet ➤ Outline commands, you can temporarily hide rows or columns of detail information and focus on the more important summary data.

CHAPTER 17

Links between Files

FAST TRACK

To create a link between the current workbook and a second workbook,   *499*

enter a formula that includes a file reference to the second workbook. The complete notation for a file reference contains the drive name, directory path, file name, and extension of the second workbook, all enclosed in pairs of angle brackets, (<<>>). The file reference is followed by an ordinary range reference, in the form <<file>>range. The purpose of the link is to copy data from the source workbook to the current destination workbook, and to update the destination whenever the data changes on the source.

To use the Range Names list box to create a reference to an open file,   *500*

begin the formula entry with an appropriate operator, then press the F3 function key to view the Range Names dialog box. Select the name of a file from the In workbook list to view the range names defined in the file. Select the name that you want to include in the reference. In response, 1-2-3 enters a complete file reference and range name into the formula.

To create a link to a disk file that is not currently open,   *501*

type the complete file reference and range reference directly from the keyboard.

To update a destination file if the linked source file is not currently open, *506*

open the destination file from disk. Under manual updating, choose Edit ➤ Manage Links to update the newly opened file.

To create a workbook that displays the sum of data contained in other workbooks, *510*

choose the File ➤ Open command, select the name of a source file, check the Combine with current workbook option, and click the Combine button. In the Combine 1-2-3 File dialog box, choose the Add to current values option, and click OK. Repeat these steps for each file that you want to add to the current workbook. This command does not establish links.

To create an OLE link in which a 1-2-3 workbook is the server, *511*

Select a range of data in the workbook and press Ctrl+C. Then move to the second application and select the location where you want to transfer the data. In the second application, choose the Paste Link option. (For example, in WordPad, choose Edit ➤ Paste Special, and then click the Paste Link option button.)

COMPLEX record-keeping tasks sometimes require input from various locations and from different events during the business year. As a result, the information related to a particular topic may appear in multiple workbook files. For example, sales data may be stored in several regional files; accounting figures in twelve monthly workbooks; and financial records in file categories such as revenues, expenses, deprecations, and deductions.

To coordinate and summarize information like this, you need ways to consolidate data from separate files. Accordingly, 1-2-3 allows you to establish links between workbooks. Workbook links are expressed as special formulas that include file references along with range references. In response to such a formula, 1-2-3 copies data from the file named in the reference. The workbook that contains a link formula is the destination, and the workbook named in the reference is the source file.

You can use links to create a master workbook file that combines information from several other files. For example, the following workbooks are designed to incorporate the data stored in groups of files:

- A national sales file brings together data from regional offices.
- A year-end file displays totals from twelve monthly accounting files.
- A profit workbook calculates the bottom line from data stored in various financial files.

To develop these workbooks, you write formulas to link the individual source files to the master workbook. If you later make changes in the data stored in one of the source files, 1-2-3 can update the destination file by transferring the new data to the cell that contains the link formula. In this chapter you'll learn to write formulas to integrate data from multiple workbooks.

An analogous feature in the Windows 95 environment is known as Object Linking and Embedding (OLE). With programs that support OLE, you can establish links between documents created in different Windows applications. A 1-2-3 workbook can be the server (the application that supplies data) or the client (the application that requests data). OLE is the final topic of this chapter.

Creating Links between Workbooks

In this chapter's exercises, you'll be working with a group of files from the four regions of Computing Conferences, Inc. Suppose that the company's central office has asked each of the regional managers to prepare a monthly business summary workbook. As you can see in Figure 17.1, each of these sample workbooks contains five items of information about a given region's business activities for the month of February 1997:

▶ The number of computer-training conferences conducted in the region

▶ The total number of people who attended these conferences

▶ The dollar revenues from the conferences

▶ The total expenses associated with conducting the conferences

▶ The total profit for the month

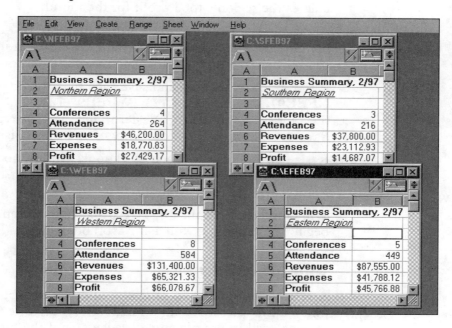

Figure 17.1: **Monthly business summaries from the four regions**

The sample files in Figure 17.1 have been sized and positioned so that the contents of all four files can be seen at once. To prepare for your work in this chapter, begin by creating copies of these four files on your own computer. Here is an outline of the steps for creating each file; you'll perform these steps four times to develop the set of four files:

1. If necessary, use the File ➤ New command to open a new workbook.

2. Enter the appropriate labels into column A of the new workbook, and apply the boldface, italic, and underlining styles shown in Figure 17.1.

3. Select the range A4..A8 and choose the Range ➤ Name command. Make sure that the For cells box displays the To the right option, and click the Use Labels button. Then click OK.

4. Enter the first four numeric data items into column B: the number of conferences, the attendance, the revenue amount, and the expenses.

5. Enter the formula **+REVENUES−EXPENSES** into cell B8. This calculates the region's total profit for the month.

6. Apply the US Dollar format to the range B6..B8. Increase the widths of columns A and B so that the labels and values in the range A4..B8 can be viewed within their respective cells.

7. Choose File ➤ Save As and save each file under its appropriate name: **NFEB97.123**, **SFEB97.123**, **WFEB97.123**, and **EFEB97.123**, for the Northern, Southern, Western, and Eastern regions, respectively. Save the files in the root directory of your hard disk.

8. Resize and reposition each workbook window so that you can view all four files at once, in an arrangement similar to what you see in Figure 17.1.

With these sample files displayed on your screen, you are ready to begin experimenting with 1-2-3 workbook links.

Using File References

A reference to a cell or range on another workbook consists of two parts: a file reference and a range reference. The file name and path are enclosed in double angle brackets, and the range appears immediately after:

```
<<file>>range
```

For example, the following formula copies the entry from cell A:A1 in a file named SUMMARY:

```
+<<C:\SUMMARY.123>>A:A1
```

When you enter this formula into a cell in the current workbook, the contents of cell A1 in the SUMMARY workbook appear in the destination cell. Note that the file reference must include a complete path name and file name, including the extension.

To enter a reference to a file that is not open, you type the complete reference directly from the keyboard. But if the source file is open, you can use pointing techniques to create the reference. If you've arranged your workbooks so that the source and destination files are both in view, you can easily use your mouse to create the reference: Begin your formula with an operator (+, for example) and then click the mouse at the target location of the source workbook. In response, 1-2-3 enters a complete file reference and range reference into the current cell in the destination workbook.

If the target cell has a range name in the source file, you can use the F3 function key to select a range name while you're building a formula. This is probably the clearest and simplest way to establish a link between two open files. Because you've taken the trouble to define range names in the regional business summary files currently displayed on your screen, you can use this technique in the upcoming exercise.

Building a "Totals" Workbook

Your goal in this exercise is to create a new workbook file that displays the total of the numeric figures in these four regional files. Here are the steps:

1. Select the range A1..A8 in any one of the four files, and then press Ctrl+C.

2. Click the minimize icon button on each of the four workbooks in turn to reduce the files to title bars at the bottom of the 1-2-3 window.

3. Choose the File ➤ New Workbook command and click Create a Blank Workbook. With the cell pointer at A:A1 of the new workbook, press Ctrl+V to paste the labels into column A of the new workbook. Enter the new label **Totals for Four Regions** in cell A2.

4. Resize the new workbook to approximately the same dimensions as the other four workbooks, and move the workbook to a position near the center of the screen. Increase the widths of columns A and B to 12.

5. Choose File Save As, and save the file to the root directory of your hard disk as TOTFEB97.123. Then select cell B4.

6. Type the + key and press the F3 function key to view the Range Names list. Click the down-arrow button at the right side of the In workbook box. The resulting drop-down list contains the names of the five open workbook files:

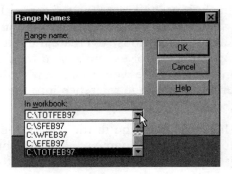

(Although only four of the names are in view at once, the list is scrollable. Use the list's vertical scroll bar to view the fifth file name.)

7. Select C:\EFEB97 from the list. When you do so, the Range name list box displays a list of the names defined in this file:

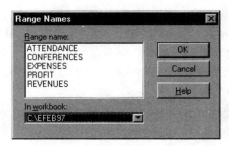

8. Select the range name CONFERENCES and click OK. A complete reference to the cell appears as follows in the contents box on the edit line:

```
+<<C:\EFEB97.123>>CONFERENCES
```

Creating Links between Workbooks

9. Now repeat steps 6, 7, and 8 three times, each time selecting a different file reference from the Range Names list box: first C:\NFEB97, then C:\SFEB97, and finally C:\WFEB97. (Don't forget to type + between each reference.) As you complete these steps, 1-2-3 builds the following formula:

   +<<C:\EFEB97.123>>CONFERENCES+

   <<C:\NFEB97.123>>CONFERENCES+

   <<C:\SFEB97.123>>CONFERENCES+

   <<C:\WFEB97.123>>CONFERENCES

   This formula finds the sum of the values stored in the cells named CONFERENCES in the four source workbooks.

10. Press ↵ to complete the formula entry. When you do so, the TOTFEB97.123 workbook appears as shown in Figure 17.2. As you can see, a total of 20 conferences were conducted in the four regions during the month of February 1997.

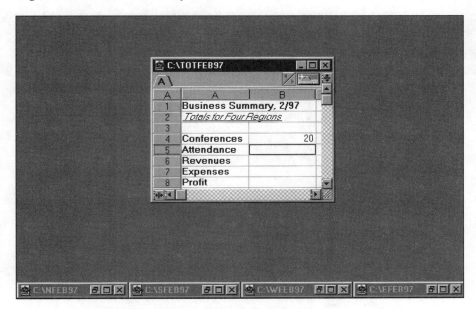

Figure 17.2: Entering a formula that finds the sum of the Conferences entries in the four regional workbooks

11. Select the range B4..B8 on the TOTFEB97 workbook. Click the selection with the right mouse button, and choose Copy Down from the

resulting quick menu. In response, 1-2-3 copies the formula from cell B4 down to the cells in the range B5..B8. Because the original formula contains relative references to cells in the source workbooks, the references in the new copied formulas are automatically adjusted according to their positions in the column. For example, here is the formula that 1-2-3 copies into cell B8 to calculate the total profit from the four regional files:

```
+<<C:\EFEB97.123>>PROFIT+
<<C:\NFEB97.123>>PROFIT+
<<C:\SFEB97.123>>PROFIT+
<<C:\WFEB97.123>>PROFIT
```

12. Apply the Comma format (with no decimal places) to cell B5 and the US Dollar format to the range B6..B8.

13. Choose File ➤ Save or click the Save SmartIcon to save your work to disk.

When you complete these steps, the TOTFEB97.123 workbook appears as follows:

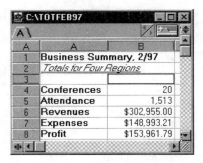

A quick look back at the workbooks in Figure 17.1 confirms that 1-2-3 has successfully computed the totals of the data in the four source workbooks: the total number of conferences in the four regions, the total attendance, the total revenues, expenses, and profit.

Revising a Source Workbook

Now if you revise the data in any one of the source workbooks, 1-2-3 automatically updates the corresponding formulas in TOTFEB97.123. For example, suppose you reach this point in your work only to discover that one of the conferences conducted in the Southern region was inadvertently omitted from SFEB97.123. Here is the corrected workbook:

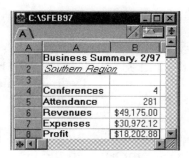

As you can see, the entries in cells B4, B5, B6, and B7 have been changed, and 1-2-3 has recalculated the formula in cell B8. Make these changes now in your own copy of SFEB97.123:

1. Double-click the bar representing SFEB97.123 to view the open file once again on the screen.

2. Make the four new entries in the range B4..B7. Notice that the value in B8 is automatically recalculated.

3. Choose File ➤ Save to save the new version of the file to disk. Then click the Minimize button on the SFEB97.123 window to reduce the file once again to a bar on the Desktop.

Now look at what has happened to TOTFEB97.123:

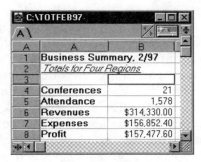

All the values in the range B4..B8 have been revised to reflect the changes in the source file. This demonstrates the advantage of linked workbooks: The destination file is updated when you revise the data in one or more source files.

To prepare for the next exercise, save the current version of TOT-FEB97.123 and then close the file. Also close all the source files except the workbook for the Northern region, NFEB97.123.

Updating Files

Sometimes you might find yourself making revisions on a source workbook at a time when the linked destination workbook is not open. Conversely, you might later open the destination file when the source files are not open. The destination file can still be updated to reflect new data in the source.

The sequence of updating is controlled by an option in the File ➤ User Setup ➤ 1-2-3 Preferences command. In the General tab, the option labeled "Update links when opening workbooks" can be checked or unchecked:

When the option is unchecked, updating is manual; you have explicit control over the timing of updates. This can be an advantage in some cases. For example, when you first open a destination workbook, you may want an opportunity to see what the former data looked like before you change to the latest data. But you can check the Update links option to switch to automatic updating. If you do so, 1-2-3 updates all the links from the source files as soon as you open the destination file. The data in the newly opened workbook is revised accordingly.

To prepare for the upcoming exercise, make sure 1-2-3 is set for manual updating. Choose File ➤ User Setup ➤ 1-2-3 Preferences. In the General tab, find the check box labeled "Update links when opening workbooks." If it is checked, click it once to remove the check. Then click OK.

Under manual updating, you use the Edit ➤ Manage Links to ensure that the destination file accurately reflects the data in the source files. For example, in the following steps you'll make a single revision in the data contained in NFEB97.123, and then you'll close the file; when you reopen the TOTFEB97.123 file, you'll have the opportunity to experiment with the Edit ➤ Manage Links command:

1. Double-click the bar representing NFEB97.123 to view the open workbook file.

2. Enter the new value **56200** in cell B6. The entry is displayed in the currency format, as $56,200.00. In addition, 1-2-3 recalculates the formula in cell B8, increasing the profit for the Northern region by $10,000:

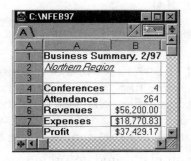

3. Choose File ➤ Save to update this file to disk, then close the file.

4. Open TOTFEB97.123 from disk. The file's contents are still the same as before. The workbook has not yet been updated to reflect the latest changes you made in NFEB97.123.

5. Choose Edit ➤ Manage Links. The Manage Links dialog box appears.

6. Pull down the Link type list and choose the 1-2-3 file Links option. When you do so, the dialog box displays a list of all the source files that are linked to TOTFEB97.123:

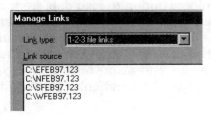

7. Click the Update All Now button, and then click Done to close the Links dialog box. When you look again at the TOTFEB97 workbook, you'll see that 1-2-3 has successfully updated the data from workbook files on disk:

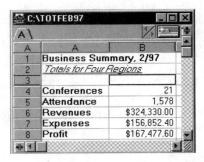

8. Choose File ➤ Save to store the new version of this file to disk. Then close the file.

In summary, the TOTFEB97.123 workbook consolidates the data from the four regional source files, and can be updated whenever the data in one of these source files changes. Workbook links can be updated automatically or manually, depending on the setting of the Update links option in the 1-2-3 Preferences dialog box.

You should turn the automatic update option on now before you continue with your work in this chapter. Choose File ➤ User Setup ➤ 1-2-3 Preferences, and check the option labeled "Update links when opening workbooks." Then click OK.

Another way to create a "totals" workbook that is similar in appearance to the TOTFEB97.123 file—but rather different in operation—is with the Combine option on the File ➤ Open dialog box.

Combining Files

You can use the Combine option to read data from a workbook file on disk and incorporate the data into the current workbook. This operation does not create a link between the current file and the file on disk; it merely transfers data statically and enters the data onto the current workbook. You used this command once in Chapter 15, when you copied part of the CONF.123 workbook to a new file.

Creating Links between Workbooks

The Combine operation can also add data to values contained in specified cells of the current workbook. This process requires some careful planning to make sure the data values from disk are added to the correct locations on the current workbook. But the Add option is useful when you want to create a "totals" workbook without establishing links between source and destination workbooks.

Here is a brief exercise with this feature:

1. With the cell pointer located at A1 on a new Untitled workbook, choose File ➤ Open. In the Open File dialog box, select the root directory of your hard disk so you can see a list of the files you've been working with in this chapter:

2. Select EFEB97.123 in the list, and then check the option labeled "Combine with current workbook" at the lower-left corner of the Open dialog box. Click the Combine button. The Combine 1-2-3 File dialog box appears.

3. For this first operation, keep the default Replace current values option, and click the OK button. 1-2-3 copies the contents of the EFEB94 file to the Untitled workbook.

4. Repeat steps 1 through 3 for the remaining three source files, NFEB97.123, SFEB97.123, and WFEB97.123, but each time choose the Add to current values option on the Combine 1-2-3 File dialog box:

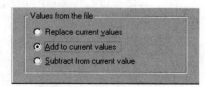

Each operation adds the data from one of these files to the current workbook.

When you complete these steps, the data displayed in the workbook is the same as in the TOTFEB97 file. But notice the important difference: The TOTFEB97 workbook contains formulas that link it to the source workbooks; but this new Untitled workbook contains only data, with no links. (You can now close this experimental workbook without saving it.)

Creating Links between Documents

In the Windows environment you can easily copy data values from 1-2-3 workbooks to documents you create in other applications. The Clipboard is the key to this procedure:

1. Select a range of data in a 1-2-3 workbook.
2. Choose the Edit ➤ Copy command or press Ctrl+C. This copies the data to the Clipboard.
3. Activate the other Windows application, and move to the location where you want to copy the data.
4. Choose the Edit ➤ Paste command or press Ctrl+V. This command pastes the data from the Clipboard to the selected location in the second application.

The Edit ➤ Paste command simply makes a copy of the data itself in the new location.

A more powerful option, available in 1-2-3 and in many other Windows applications, is Paste Link. This feature uses Object Linking and Embedding (OLE) to establish a link between documents created in two different applications. In an OLE link, the source document is known as the server, and the destination document is known as the client. While a link is active, data changes that take place in the server can automatically be sent to the client.

Transferring Data from a Workbook

For example, Figure 17.3 shows the 1-2-3 application window alongside Microsoft WordPad, a simple word-processing program that comes with Windows 95. The two application windows have been resized so that each takes up about half the screen. In the 1-2-3 window you can see the TOTFEB97.123 workbook. In the WordPad document window you see the beginning of a memo directed to the regional managers of Computing Conferences, Inc.

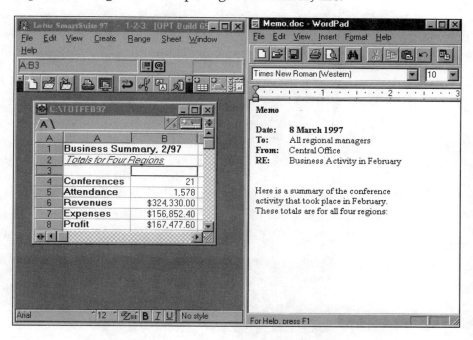

Figure 17.3: *Preparing to create a link between documents in two applications*

Imagine that you are writing this memo, and you have reached the point where you want to insert the data from the TOTFEB97.123 workbook into the word-processed document. Because you are anticipating possible changes in the workbook data, you want to establish a link between the workbook and the document. Here are the steps you take:

1. Activate the workbook window, and select the range A4..B8.

2. Pull down the Edit menu in 1-2-3 and choose the Copy command, or simply press Ctrl+C.

3. Activate the WordPad window and move the cursor to the end of the memo text.

4. Pull down the Edit menu in WordPad and choose the Paste Special command.

5. In the Paste Special dialog box, select the Paste Link option:

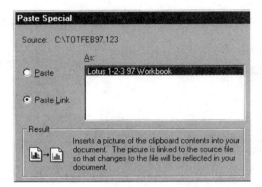

As you can see, the As box identifies the type of document you are linking to your WordPad file; in addition, the Result box gives a clear explanation of the type of link you are creating.

6. Click OK. The data from the 1-2-3 workbook appears as a table at the bottom of the WordPad document, as shown in Figure 17.4.

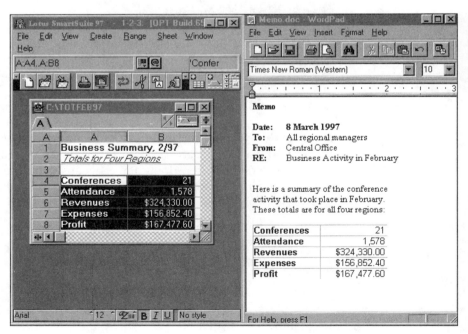

Figure 17.4: **The result of the link**

Now imagine that your phone rings just as you are completing your work on the memo. It is Mary Garcia, the manager of the Western region. She's calling to let you know that she inadvertently omitted a $7,000 expense item for advertising in her February workbook. No problem, you tell her; you can fix the error right away. You continue your work as follows:

7. Activate the 1-2-3 window and open the WFEB97.123 workbook. Select cell B7. As you can see in Figure 17.5, the current expense amount displayed in the cell is $65,321.33.

8. Enter the revised figure into the cell, $72,321.33. Choose File ➤ Save to save the WFEB97.123 workbook to disk; then close the file. Notice that the TOTFEB97.123 workbook is updated automatically; its data now reflects the increased expense figure from the Western region, and the resulting decrease in total profit:

	A	B
1	Business Summary, 2/97	
2	Totals for Four Regions	
3		
4	Conferences	21
5	Attendance	1,578
6	Revenues	$324,330.00
7	Expenses	$163,852.40
8	Profit	$160,477.60

9. Choose File ➤ Save to save TOTFEB97.123 to disk, and then close the file. Choose File ➤ Exit 1-2-3 to end this session with 1-2-3.

10. The WordPad window remains on the Desktop. From the WordPad menu, choose Edit ➤ Links. As shown in Figure 17.6, the Links dialog box identifies the link to the 1-2-3 workbook. Select this link description by clicking it once. Notice that you can choose between the Automatic or Manual options for updating the link. If Automatic is the current selection, the WordPad window should already show the latest version of the data. Otherwise, if the selection is Manual, continue to the next step.

11. Click the Update Now button, and then click Close. As shown in Figure 17.7, the latest version of the data appears in the WordPad document, thanks to the link between the document and the TOTFEB97.123 workbook.

514 **Chapter 17** **Links between Files**

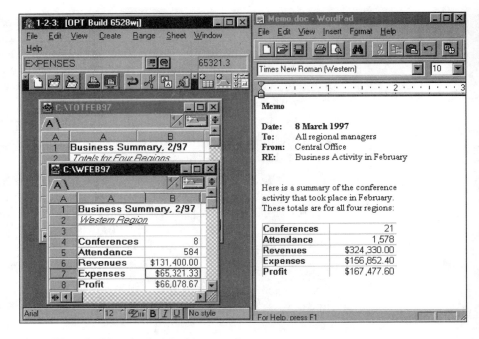

Figure 17.5: **Revising the data in the source document**

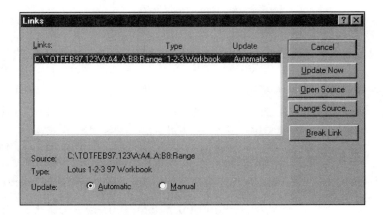

Figure 17.6: **WordPad's Links dialog box**

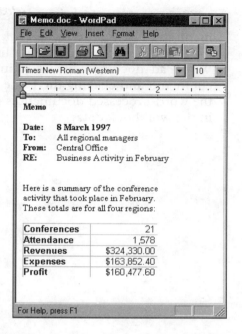

Figure 17.7: **The WordPad document is updated with the latest information from the linked 1-2-3 workbook.**

Summary

The purpose of establishing a link between two files is to exchange data between the files and to ensure that the destination file will be updated when there is a change in the source file.

A link between two workbooks is expressed as a formula that includes both a file reference and a range reference. The workbook containing the formula is the destination file, and the workbook named in the file reference is the source file. Updates can be manual or automatic in 1-2-3, depending on the setting of the Update links option in the 1-2-3 Preferences dialog box. Under manual updating, you choose the Edit ➤ Manage Links command to update a newly opened destination file.

Thanks to the Windows protocols known as Object Linking and Embedding, you can also establish links between documents that are created in different Windows applications. To create such a link, you choose the Edit ➤ Copy command to copy data from the source document to the Clipboard. Then you move to the destination document and choose the Paste Link option from the second application. For example, you can create a link between a 1-2-3 workbook and a WordPad document by choosing WordPad's Edit ➤ Paste Special command and clicking the Paste Link option. While the link is active, the word-processed document is updated whenever you make changes in the workbook data.

PART 4

Appendixes

APPENDIX A:
An Overview of 1-2-3's Functions

As discussed in Chapters 7 and 8, 1-2-3 97 Edition comes with a function library that contains well over 200 functions. This library includes groups of special-purpose functions designed for particular fields of work, such as accounting, engineering, and statistics, while other functions are designed for much more general use and can be valuable to almost any user of 1-2-3.

Few users could hope to swiftly master such a cornucopia of functions—but fortunately, very few users need to do so. Most users quickly identify the fistful of functions most useful to them or to their businesses and become adept in using them. 1-2-3 provides a number of tools to help you enter and use functions.

The appendixes of this book are set up to help you find out immediately about the functions you need and how to use them. This section looks in detail at each of 1-2-3's functions, discussing their syntax and purpose and illustrating their use. For convenience, the functions are divided by group into individual appendixes, as shown in the following list:

Function Category	Appendix
Calendar functions	B
Database functions	C
Engineering functions	D
Financial functions	E
Information functions	F
Logical functions	F

Function Category	Appendix
Lookup functions	F
Mathematical functions	G
Statistical functions	G
Text functions	H

The next section of this appendix, "Using Functions," provides a quick recapitulation of how to enter and use functions. For a more detailed discussion of this topic, see Chapter 7.

The final section of this appendix, "1-2-3 Functions Quick Reference," provides an alphabetical list of 1-2-3's functions, together with a brief description of what each does and the page on which you can find a more detailed discussion of each.

Using Functions

This section of the appendix provides a quick summary of how to enter functions into cells and how to use functions.

Entering Functions into Cells

As discussed in Chapter 7, 1-2-3 offers several ways of entering a function into a cell:

▶ Type in the function and its arguments. This is the swiftest and easiest way of entering functions into worksheets and is best suited for those functions with fewer arguments. For example, if your worksheet contains a range named SQUIRRELS, you can find out the average of the values in the range (excluding any labels) by entering the following function statement into a cell:

   @PUREAVG(SQUIRRELS)

▶ Click the Function selector button on the edit line to see a list of commonly used functions. When you select a function name from the list, 1-2-3 enters the function into the current cell along with convenient placeholders for the arguments you need to supply. If the function you want to use is not in the list, choose the List All option to display the @Function List dialog box with the complete list of all the 1-2-3 functions.

> **TIP** As discussed in Chapter 7, you can customize the list of functions in the Function selector by choosing the List All option from the Function selector drop-down list and choosing the Menu>> button in the @Function List dialog box, then using the Add and Remove buttons in the expanded @Function List dialog box.

▶ Display the @Function List dialog box by typing @ into a cell and pressing the F3 function key, then choose a function from the @Function List dialog box. 1-2-3 copies the function to the edit line and supplies placeholders for arguments.

Getting Help with Functions

The easiest way to get help with functions is to enter the function into a cell using any of the methods described in the previous section, then press the F1 function key. 1-2-3 will take you directly to the help topic for that function.

When you've finished with the help topic, press Escape or double-click the control-menu box in the Help window to close Help and return to your worksheet.

Alternatively, you can search for and select information about the desired @function directly from the 1-2-3 Help system.

The Elements of a Function

1-2-3's functions conform to a standard format, as you can see by looking at the following example:

@DATEDIF(*start-date*,*end-date*,*format*)

▶ A function name consists of the @ character, followed by the predefined name for the function itself—in this case, **DATEDIF**.

▶ Immediately following the function name, an open parenthesis character marks the beginning of the argument list. A close parenthesis character goes at the end of the list.

▶ Between the parentheses you enter the function's arguments. Each argument is separated from the next with an argument separator (such as a comma or a semicolon), but no spaces. Each argument can be expressed in any form that produces the required type of data. For example, an argument can appear as a cell reference, a range name, an expression, or even as another function name; the *start-date* argument for the @DATEDIF function could be a cell reference such as **A1**, an expression that produced a date number, or another date function.

▶ The correct number and type of argument is defined for each function in the 1-2-3 library. For example, the @DATEDIF function shown here requires three arguments—*start-date*, *end-date*, and *format*—and will not run without them. A few functions (for example, @ERR and @NA) take no argument and therefore need no parentheses. Many other functions have optional arguments in addition to their required arguments. While you need not include any of the optional arguments when you enter such a function, if you do use any of the optional arguments, you must use all the optional arguments that precede it so that 1-2-3 can correctly identify all the arguments you enter.

1-2-3 Functions Quick Reference

Table A.1 provides an alphabetical list of 1-2-3's functions, together with a brief description of what each does.

Table A.1:   1-2-3 Functions Quick Reference

Function	Returns
@@	The contents of the cell specified by means of a reference through the contents of another cell
@ACCRUED	The accrued interest for a security of a given value
@ACCRUED2	The accrued interest for a security of a given value, using Japanese conventions
@ACOSH	The arc hyperbolic cosine of the given angle
@ACOT	The arc cotangent of the given angle
@ACOTH	The arc hyperbolic cotangent of the given angle
@ACSC	The arc cosecant of the given angle

Table A.1: 1-2-3 Functions Quick Reference (continued)

Function	Returns
@ACSCH	The arc hyperbolic cosecant of the given angle
@ASEC	The arc secant of the given angle
@ASECH	The arc hyperbolic secant of the given angle
@ASIN	The arc sine of the given angle
@ASINH	The arc hyperbolic sine of the given angle
@ATAN	The arc tangent of the given angle
@ATAN2	The arc tangent of the given angle determined by the x and y coordinates using the tangent y/x ($n1/n$)
@ATANH	The arc hyperbolic tangent of the given angle
@AVEDEV	The average of the absolute deviations of the values in the given list
@AVG	The average of the values contained in the given list
@BESSELI	The modified Bessel integer function $In(x)$
@BESSELJ	The Bessel integer function $Jn(x)$
@BESSELK	The modified Bessel integer function $Kn(x)$
@BESSELY	The Bessel integer function $Yn(x)$
@BETA	The Beta integer function
@BETAI	The incomplete Beta integer function
@BINOMIAL	The binomial probability mass function or the cumulative binomial distribution
@CELL	Information about the upper-left cell in a reference; for example, the cell's contents, color, or file name
@CELLPOINTER	Information about the current cell's formatting, location, or contents

Table A.1:   1-2-3 Functions Quick Reference (continued)

Function	Returns
@CHAR	The character of the Lotus Multibyte Character Set (LMBCS) that corresponds to the number code specified
@CHIDIST	The one-tailed probability of the chi-square distribution
@CHITEST	The independence of the data in a given range or the goodness of fit for the data in two given ranges
@CHOOSE	A value or label from a list or range of values
@CLEAN	The specified text string with all nonprinting characters removed from it
@CODE	The code for the Lotus Multibyte Character Set (LMBCS) code that corresponds to the first character in a text string
@COLS	The number of columns in a range
@COMBIN	The binomial coefficient for two specified values
@COORD	A cell reference from given values for *worksheet*, *column*, and *row*
@CORREL	The correlation coefficient of the values for two given ranges
@COS	The cosine of the given angle
@COSH	The hyperbolic cosine of the given angle
@COT	The cotangent of the given angle
@COTH	The hyperbolic cotangent of the given angle
@COUNT	The number of nonblank cells in the given list
@COV	Either the population or the sample covariance of the values in two given ranges

Table A.1: 1-2-3 Functions Quick Reference (continued)

Function	Returns
@CRITBINOMIAL	The largest integer for which the cumulative binomial distribution is less than or equal to alpha
@CSC	The cosecant (the reciprocal of the sine) of the given angle
@CSCH	The hyperbolic cosecant (the reciprocal of the hyperbolic sine) of the given angle
@CTERM	The number of compounding periods required for a one-time investment earning a fixed periodic interest rate to reach a specified future value
@D360	The number of days between two date numbers
@DATALINK	The data specified as a result of creating an OLE2 relationship
@DATE	A date number from three integer arguments representing the year, the month, and the day
@DATECONVERT	The Hijri (Arabic), Farsi (Iranian), or Hebrew (Israeli) to and from Gregorian date conversions
@DATEDIF	The number of days, months, or years between two date numbers
@DATEINFO	Various kinds of information about a date number
@DATESTRING	Text that resembles its equivalent date
@DATEVALUE	A date number from a text string
@DAVG	The average of selected values in a database range
@DAY	An integer from 1 to 31, representing the day of the month

Table A.1: 1-2-3 Functions Quick Reference (continued)

Function	Returns
@DAYS	The number of days between two date numbers using a user-specified *basis* for day-count
@DAYS360	The number of days between two dates based on a 360-day year (12 months of 30 days each)
@DB	The depreciation value of an asset, calculated using the declining-balance method
@DCOUNT	The number of selected values in a database range
@DDB	The depreciation value of an asset, calculated using the double-declining-balance method
@DECILE	A given decile
@DECIMAL	A signed decimal value from a hexadecimal string
@DEGTORAD	The value in radians of the angle given in degrees
@DEVSQ	The sum of squared deviations of the values in the given list from their mean (average)
@DGET	The field item from a single database record selected by the expressions in the criteria range
@DMAX	The largest value among selected entries in a database range
@DMIN	The smallest value among selected entries in a database range
@DPURECOUNT	The number of cells in a database that contain a value in the specified field that match specified criteria
@DSTD	The population standard deviation of selected values in a database range

Table A.1: 1-2-3 Functions Quick Reference (continued)

Function	Returns
@DSTDS	The sample standard deviation of selected values in a database range
@DSUM	The sum of selected values in a database range
@DURATION	The annual duration for a security that pays periodic interest
@DVAR	The population variance of selected values in a database range
@DVARS	The sample variance of selected values in a database range
@EDIGIT	Converts an Arabic number to a Thai number
@ERF	The error function
@ERFC	The complementary error function
@ERFD	The derivative of the error function
@ERR	The value ERR (for forcing an error condition in formulas when a certain result would be undesirable)
@EVEN	The nearest even integer to the number; positive values are rounded up and negative values are rounded down
@EXACT	1 (TRUE) if the two specified sets of characters match exactly; 0 (FALSE) if the two sets do not match exactly
@EXP	The value of the constant e (approximately 2.718282, the base of the natural logarithm) raised to the specified power

Table A.1: 1-2-3 Functions Quick Reference (continued)

Function	Returns
@EXP2	The value of the constant *e* (approximately 2.718282, the base of the natural logarithm) raised to the power (*numeric-value*^2)
@FACT	The factorial of the given number (the product of all positive integers from 1 to the number)
@FACTLN	The natural logarithm of the factorial of a number
@FALSE	The logical value 0 (FALSE), the opposite of the logical value 1 (TRUE)
@FDIST	The F-distribution of probability for the two given ranges (for determining the degree to which two samples vary)
@FIND	The character position in a given text string at which 1-2-3 finds the first occurrence of the specified search text, the search beginning at the given position
@FINDB	The byte position in a given text string at which 1-2-3 finds the first occurrence of the specified search text, the search beginning at the given position
@FORCAST	A forecast estimate based on trends between values in two equally sized groups of cells
@FTEST	The associated probability of an F probability test for the two given ranges (to test if two samples have different variances)
@FULLP	Converts single-byte characters to Kanji double-byte characters

Table A.1: 1-2-3 Functions Quick Reference (continued)

Function	Returns
@FV	The future value of a series of equal periodic payment amounts over term periods at a fixed periodic interest rate
@FV2	The future value of a series of equal periodic payment amounts over term periods at a fixed periodic interest rate, using Japanese conventions
@FVAL	The future value of an item based on the present value
@FVAMOUNT	The future value of a sum at a rate for a number of periods
@GAMMA	The Gamma function
@GAMMAI	The incomplete Gamma function
@GAMMALN	The natural logarithm of the Gamma function
@GEOMEAN	The geometric mean of the values in the given list
@GRANDTOTAL	The sum of all the cells in the given list that contain the function @SUBTOTAL
@HALFP	Converts Kanji double-byte characters to single-byte characters
@HARMEAN	The harmonic mean of the values in the given list
@HEX	A hexadecimal string from a signed decimal value
@HLOOKUP	The contents of the cell indicated by a specified key in a specified row of a horizontal lookup table
@HOUR	An integer from 0 to 23, representing the hour

Table A.1:   1-2-3 Functions Quick Reference (continued)

Function	Returns
@IF	The result given for *true* if the given condition evaluates as TRUE (not equaling zero) or the result given for *false* if condition evaluates as FALSE (equaling zero)
@INDEX	The contents of the cell located at the intersection of a specified column, row, and worksheet of a range
@INFO	System information for the current 1-2-3 session, such as the current directory path or the current operating system
@INT	The integer value of the given number, disregarding any fractional portion
@IPAYMT	The cumulative interest on a loan
@IRATE	A value equivalent to the periodic interest rate of an investment
@IRR	The internal rate of return from a series of positive and negative cash-flow amounts
@ISAAF	1 (TRUE) if the given name is that of a defined add-in function for 1-2-3; 0 (FALSE) if it is not
@ISAPP	1 (TRUE) if the given name is that of a defined add-in application for 1-2-3; 0 (FALSE) if it is not
@ISBETWEEN	1 (TRUE) if the given value is between two boundaries; 0 (FALSE) if it is not
@ISEMPTY	1 (TRUE) if the specified location is a blank cell; 0 (FALSE) if it is not blank
@ISERR	1 (TRUE) if the given value is the value ERR and 0 (FALSE) if *value* is not the value ERR

Table A.1: 1-2-3 Functions Quick Reference (continued)

Function	Returns
@ISFILE	1 (TRUE) if the specified file name exists and 0 (FALSE) if it does not exist
@ISMACRO	1 (TRUE) if the specified name is a defined add-in macro command and 0 (FALSE) if it is not
@ISNA	1 (TRUE) if the specified value is the value NA and 0 (FALSE) if value is not the value NA
@ISNUMBER	1 (TRUE) if the specified value contains a value, NA, ERR, or a blank cell; 0 (FALSE) if the specified value is text or a cell containing a label or a formula that results in a label
@ISRANGE	1 (TRUE) if the specified range is a defined range name or valid range address; 0 (FALSE) if it is not
@ISSTRING	1 (TRUE) if the specified value is text or a cell that contains a label or a formula that results in a label; 0 (FALSE) if the specified value is a value, ERR, NA, or a blank cell
@KURTOSIS	The kurtosis of the values in the given range—the concentration of a distribution around the mean of a range of values
@LARGE	The nth largest value in the given range
@LEFT	The specified number of the first (leftmost) characters in a given text string
@LEFTB	The specified number of the first (leftmost) bytes in a given text string
@LENGTH	The number of characters in a string
@LENGTHB	The number of bytes in a string
@LN	The natural logarithm of the given value

Table A.1:   1-2-3 Functions Quick Reference (continued)

Function	Returns
@LOG	The common or base-10 logarithm (base 10) of the given value
@LOWER	The given string with all letters converted to lowercase
@MATCH	The offset position in a range of the cell containing specified contents
@MAX	The largest value in the given list
@MAXLOOKUP	An absolute reference to the cell containing the largest value in a list of ranges
@MDURATION	The modified annual duration for a security that pays periodic interest
@MEDIAN	The median value in the given list
@MID	The specified number of characters from a text string, beginning with the character at the offset specified
@MIDB	The specified number of bytes from a text string, beginning with the byte at the offset specified
@MIN	The smallest value in the given list
@MINLOOKUP	An absolute reference to the cell containing the smallest value in a list of ranges
@MINUTE	An integer from 0 to 59, representing the minutes
@MIRR	The modified internal rate of return for a series of positive and negative cash-flow amounts
@MOD	The *modulus* (remainder) after the given number is divided by the given divisor, using the sign of the given number

Table A.1: **1-2-3 Functions Quick Reference (continued)**

Function	Returns
@MODULO	The *modulus* (remainder) after the given number is divided by the given divisor, using the sign of the given divisor
@MONTH	An integer from 1 to 12, representing the month
@N	The entry in the first cell of a specified range as a value
@NA	The value NA ("not available") indicating that no value is available; for use as a placeholder for key cells that need to be filled for a formula to be valid
@NETWORKDAYS	The number of working days (days excluding weekends and holidays) between two date numbers
@NEXTMONTH	The date number for the date that falls a specified number of months before or after a given date
@NORMAL	The normal distribution function for the specific mean (average) and standard deviation
@NOW	A date number and time number representing the current date and the current time
@NPER	The number of periods required to reach a specified future value at a given interest rate
@NPV	The net present value of a series of positive or negative future periodic cash-flow amounts
@NSUM	The sum of the values in a list, starting at a given offset, located at a given interval
@NUMBERSTRING	The Kanji spelled-out text for a given number

Table A.1: 1-2-3 Functions Quick Reference (continued)

Function	Returns
@ODD	The given value rounded away from 0 to the nearest odd integer; positive values are rounded up and negative values are rounded down
@PAYMT	The payments necessary to reach a specified principal over a given term at a fixed interest rate
@PERCENTILE	The xth sample percentile among the values in the given range
@PERMUT	The number of permutations (ordered sequences) of objects that can be selected from a given number of objects
@PMT	The periodic payment required to pay back a loan over a given term at a fixed interest rate
@PMT2	The periodic payment required to pay back a loan over a given term at a fixed interest rate, using Japanese conventions
@PMTC	The periodic payment required to pay back a loan over a given term at a fixed interest rate (@PMTC is a version of @PMT adjusted for Canadian mortgage conventions)
@PMTI	The interest amount of a loan over a given term at a fixed interest rate and with identical payments
@POISSON	The Poisson distribution (for predicting the number of events that will occur over a specific period of time)
@PPAYMT	The principal value of payments made on a loan
@PRANK	The percentile of the given value among the values in the given range

Appendix A   An Overview of 1-2-3's Functions

Table A.1:   1-2-3 Functions Quick Reference (continued)

Function	Returns
@PRICE	The price per $100 of value for investments that pay a periodic interest
@PRICE2	The price per $100 of value for investments that pay a periodic interest, using Japanese conventions
@PRODUCT	The product of the values in the given list
@PROPER	The given string with all the letters converted to initial capital style (i.e., the first letter of each word in uppercase and the remaining letters all lowercase)
@PUREAVG	The average of the values contained in the given list, ignoring cells in the range that contain labels
@PURECOUNT	The number of nonblank cells in the given list, ignoring cells in the range that contain labels
@PUREMAX	The largest value
@PUREMEDIAN	The median value
@PUREMIN	The smallest value in the given list, ignoring cells that contain labels
@PURESTD	The population standard deviation of the values in the given list, ignoring cells that contain labels
@PURESTDS	The sample standard deviation of the values in the given list, ignoring cells that contain labels
@PUREVAR	The population variance in the given list, ignoring cells that contain labels
@PUREVARS	The sample population variance in the given list, ignoring cells that contain labels

Table A.1:   1-2-3 Functions Quick Reference (continued)

Function	Returns
@PV	The present value of a series of equal future cash-flow amounts
@PV2	The present value of a series of equal future cash-flow amounts, using Japanese conventions
@PVAL	The present value of an investment
@PVAMOUNT	The present value of a sum over a given number of future periods discounted at a given interest rate
@QUARTILE	A given quartile
@QUOTIENT	The integer result of the given number divided by the given divisor
@RADTODEG	The value in degrees of a value given in radians
@RANGENAME	The name of the range in which a given cell is located
@RANK	The rank of the given value relative to other values in the range
@RATE	The interest rate that will produce a fixed future return from an initial investment over a specified term
@REFCONVERT	The corresponding numbers (1–256) for the 1-2-3 column or worksheet letters (A–IV) to numbers from 1 through 256, and the corresponding column or worksheet letters for the numbers 1–256
@REGRESSION	The statistic specified from a multiple linear regression
@REPEAT	The specified string repeated the specified number of times

Table A.1:   1-2-3 Functions Quick Reference (continued)

Function	Returns
@REPLACE	The specified text string with the given replacement characters added or appended
@REPLACEB	The specified text string with the given replacement bytes added or appended
@RIGHT	The specified number of characters last (rightmost) in a text string
@RIGHTB	The specified number of bytes last (rightmost) in a text string
@ROUND	The given number rounded to the nearest specified multiple of the power of 10
@ROUNDDOWN	The given value rounded down to the nearest multiple of the specified power
@ROUNDM	The given value rounded to the nearest specified multiple
@ROUNDUP	The given value rounded up to the nearest multiple of the specified power
@ROWS	The number of rows in a given range
@S	The entry in the first cell of a given range as a label. If the entry is a value, @S returns a blank cell
@SCENARIOINFO	Information about a scenario—for example, the user who last modified a scenario or the latest comment attached to a scenario
@SCENARIOLAST	The name of the scenario that was last displayed in a file during the current 1-2-3 session
@SEC	The secant (the reciprocal of the cosine) of the given angle
@SECH	The hyperbolic secant (the reciprocal of the hyperbolic cosine) of the given angle

Table A.1: 1-2-3 Functions Quick Reference (continued)

Function	Returns
@SECOND	An integer from 0 to 59, representing the seconds
@SEMEAN	The standard error of the sample mean (or average) for the values in the given range
@SERIESSUM	The sum of a power series
@SETSTRING	A label the specified number of characters long consisting of the specified text string and enough blank spaces to align the text string with the chosen alignment
@SHEETS	The number of worksheets in a given range
@SIGN	The sign of the given number
@SIN	The sine of the given angle
@SINH	The hyperbolic sine of the given angle
@SKEWNESS	The skewness of the values in the given range—the symmetry of a distribution around its mean (average)
@SLN	The depreciation of an asset, using the straight-line method
@SMALL	The *n*th smallest value in the given range
@SPI	The interest portion of a payment where principal is always the same
@SQRT	The positive square root of the given value
@SQRTPI	The square root of the given value multiplied by p
@STD	The population standard deviation of the values in the given list
@STDS	The sample standard deviation of the values in the given list

Table A.1: 1-2-3 Functions Quick Reference (continued)

Function	Returns
@STRING	The specified value converted to a label using the format specified
@SUBTOTAL	The total of the values in a list. @SUBTOTAL also indicates to @GRANDTOTAL which subtotals to include in the grand total
@SUM	The sum of the values in the given list
@SUMNEGATIVE	The sum of the negative values in the given list
@SUMPOSITIVE	The sum of the positive values in the given list
@SUMPRODUCT	The sum of the products of values in corresponding cells in multiple ranges
@SUMSQ	The sum of the squares of the values in the given list
@SUMXMY2	The sum of the squared differences after the values in one range have been subtracted from the corresponding cells in another range
@SYD	The depreciation of an asset, using the sum-of-the-years'-digits method
@TAN	The tangent of the given angle
@TANH	The hyperbolic tangent of the given angle
@TDATESTRING	The short format Thai date string that represents a given value
@TDIGIT	A Thai number converted to an Arabic number
@TDIST	The Student's *t*-distribution (the distribution of the ratio of a standardized normal distribution to the square root of the quotient of a chi-square distribution by the number of its degrees of freedom)
@TDOW	An internal date converted to a Thai date name

Table A.1:   1-2-3 Functions Quick Reference (continued)

Function	Returns
@TERM	The number of equal payment amounts required to reach a specified future value at a fixed interest rate
@TERM2	The number of equal payment amounts required to reach a specified future value at a fixed interest rate, using Japanese conventions
@TFIND	The Thai character position in a given text string at which 1-2-3 finds the first occurrence of the specified search text, the search beginning at the given position
@TIME	A decimal time number from three numeric arguments representing the hour, the minutes, and the seconds
@TIMEVALUE	A decimal time number from a string argument entered in one of four forms that 1-2-3 recognizes
@TLDATESTRING	The long format Thai date which represents a given internal date
@TLEFT	The specified number of the first (leftmost) characters in a given Thai text string
@TLENGTH	The number of characters in a Thai string
@TMID	The specified number of characters from a Thai text string, beginning with the character at the offset specified
@TNUMBERSTRING	The spelled-out text for a given Thai number
@TODAY	A date number representing the current date
@TREPLACE	The specified Thai text string with the given replacement characters added or appended

Table A.1: 1-2-3 Functions Quick Reference (continued)

Function	Returns
@TRIGHT	The specified number of characters last (rightmost) in a Thai text string
@TRIM	The specified text string with all leading, trailing, and consecutive space characters stripped from it
@TRUE	The logical value 1 (TRUE)
@TRUNC	The given value truncated to the number of decimal places specified
@TTEST	The associated probability of a Student's t-test on the data in two given ranges (to establish whether two samples are likely to have come from the same two underlying populations)
@UPPER	The specified string with all its letters converted to uppercase
@VALUE	The value corresponding to a number entered as a text string in one of the four formats 1-2-3 recognizes
@VAR	The population variance in the given list of values
@VARS	The sample population variance in the given list of values
@VDB	The depreciation of an asset, using the variable-declining-balance method
@VERSIONCURRENT	The name of the current version in a range
@VERSIONDATA	The contents of a specified cell in a version
@VERSIONINFO	Information about a version—for example, the name of the user who created it or who last modified it

Table A.1: 1-2-3 Functions Quick Reference (continued)

Function	Returns
@VLOOKUP	The contents of the cell indicated by a given key in a specified column of a vertical lookup table
@WEEKDAY	An integer from 0 through 6, representing the day of the week (0 = Monday, 6 = Sunday)
@WEIGHTAVG	The weighted average of values in a data range
@WORKDAY	The date number for the date that falls a specified number of working days before or after a given date
@XINDEX	The contents of the cell located at the intersection of a specified column_heading, row_heading, and worksheet_heading of a range
@XIRR	The internal rate of return from a series of inflows and outflows
@XNPV	The net present value of a series of inflows and outflows
@YEAR	An integer representing the year
@YIELD	The yield on an interest-bearing security
@YIELD2	The yield on an interest-bearing security, using Japanese conventions
@ZTEST	The associated probability of a z-test on one or two populations (for judging the likelihood that a particular observation is drawn from a particular population)

APPENDIX B
Calendar Functions Reference

1-2-3 for Windows offers a full set of 26 calendar functions for working with date and time values. These functions convert dates and times to serial numbers with which you can perform date and time arithmetic. As discussed in Chapter 8, the calendar functions fall into the following categories:

▶ Functions that supply the current date and time

▶ Functions that give information about existing time and date values

▶ Functions that convert other types of data into date and time values

▶ Functions that perform date arithmetic

The next section gives a quick overview of the calendar functions. In the section after that, you will find detailed descriptions of the calendar functions.

 NOTE See "Date and Time Functions" in Chapter 8 for a general explanation of how to use calendar functions.

Overview of the Calendar Functions

For quick reference, Table B.1 lists the 26 calendar functions in their five categories, with page numbers indicating their detailed discussions in the next section of this appendix, "Descriptions of the Calendar Functions."

Table B.1:   Calendar Functions Quick Reference

Function	Returns
Current Date and Time Calculations	
@NOW	A date number and time number representing the current date and the current time
@TODAY	A date number representing the current date
Information about Date and Time Values	
@DATEINFO	Various kinds of information about a date number
@DAY	An integer from 1 to 31, representing the day of the month
@HOUR	An integer from 0 to 23, representing the hour
@MINUTE	An integer from 0 to 59, representing the minute
@MONTH	An integer from 1 to 12, representing the month
@SECOND	An integer from 0 to 59, representing the second
@WEEKDAY	An integer from 0 through 6, representing the day of the week (0 = Monday, 6 = Sunday)
@YEAR	An integer representing the year
Conversion of Data into Date and Time Values	
@DATE	A date number from three integer arguments representing the year, the month, and the day
@DATESTRING	Text that resembles its equivalent date
@DATEVALUE	A date number from a text string
@TIME	A decimal time number from three numeric arguments representing the hour, the minute, and the second

Table B.1: **Calendar Functions Quick Reference (continued)**

Function	Returns
Conversion of Data into Date and Time Values	
@TIMEVALUE	A decimal time number from a string argument entered in one of four forms that 1-2-3 recognizes
Date Arithmetic	
@D360	The number of days between two date numbers
@DATEDIF	The number of days, months, or years between two date numbers
@DAYS	The number of days between two date numbers using a user-specified *basis* for day-count
@DAYS360	The number of days between two dates based on a 360-day year (12 months of 30 days each)
@NETWORKDAYS	The number of working days (days excluding weekends and holidays) between two date numbers
@NEXTMONTH	The date number for the date that falls a specified number of months before or after a given date
@WORKDAY	The date number for the date that falls a specified number of working days before or after a given date
International Date Conversions	
@DATECONVERT	The Hijri (Arabic), Farsi (Iranian), or Hebrew (Israeli) to and from Gregorian date conversions
@TDATESTRING	The short format Thai date string that represents the given internal date value

Table B.1: Calendar Functions Quick Reference (continued)

Function	Returns
International Date Conversions	
@TDOW	The Thai date name for an internal date
@TLDATESTRING	The long format Thai date string that represents the given internal date value

NOTE The @DATECONVERT, @TDATESTRING, @TDOW, and @TLDATESTRING functions are new in 1-2-3 97 Edition. As it works out, all four of these new functions have been provided in 1-2-3 to allow international conversions of dates. @DATECONVERT converts Hijri, Farsi, and Hebrew numeric text to and from Gregorian date formats. The @TDATESTRING, @TDOW, and @TLDATESTRING functions all provide conversions to and from the different Thai numeric formats.

Descriptions of the Calendar Functions

This section contains a detailed description of each calendar @ function.

@D360(start-date,end-date)

The @D360 function returns the number of days between two dates, *start-date* and *end-date*, which are both date numbers based on a 360-day year (12 months of 30 days apiece, as per the 1990 modifications to the Securities Industry Association's 1986 edition of Standard Security Calculation Methods).

For example, to calculate the number of days between January 1, 1997 (date number 35431) and May 27, 1997 (date number 35577) you could use:

```
@D360(35431,35577)
```

The answer returned is 146 days. Note that this total includes the start date and the end date.

Appendix B   **Calendar Functions Reference**

 WARNING @D360 and @DAYS360 may return different answers for the same data when either *start-date* or *end-date* is the last day of the month.

Figure B.1 illustrates the different values produced by @D360, @DAYS360, and @DAYS. The cells contain the following function statements:

Cell	Statement
C6	@D360(A6,B6)
D6	@DAYS360(A6,B6)
E6	@DAYS(A6,B6)
F6	@DAYS(A6,B6,1)
G6	@DAYS(A6,B6,2)
H6	@DAYS(A6,B6,3)

Note the different values produced by the four permutations of @DAYS.

See Also   @DATE, @DATEDIF, @DAYS

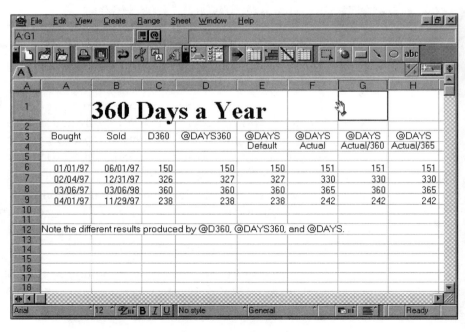

Figure B.1:   *@D360, @DAYS360, and @DAYS produce different results.*

@DATE(year,month,day)

The @DATE function returns the date number for the *year*, *month*, and *day* entered. Turning a date into a date number that 1-2-3 can use is usually the first step in using dates in arithmetic operations, and you'll probably find yourself using the @DATE function frequently.

The arguments for @DATE are as follows:

Argument	Description
year	An integer from 0 through 199. Zero represents 1900, 199 represents 2099, 97 represents 1997, and so on.
month	An integer from 1 through 12. One represents January, 12 represents December.
day	An integer from 1 through 31 (or 28, 29, or 30, depending on the number of days in the month). If you try to enter a date that doesn't exist—for example, February 30—1-2-3 will return an error.

Consider the following example of the @DATE function:

```
@DATE(97,6,3)
```

This returns 35584, the date number for June 3, 1997. To make the results of @DATE appear in a date format (such as 03-Jun-97), format the cell by using the Format selector in the status bar or the Number Format dialog box.

You can use @DATE with algebraic symbols for calculations. For example, to find the date five days before May 9, 1987, you could use

```
@DATE(87,5,9)-5
```

which returns 31901, the date number for May 4, 1987. You might be tempted to use @DATE to calculate the date a bill is due or overdue, but you'd do better to use the @WORKDAY function instead, which you can set up to exclude weekends and holidays from the calculation.

See Also   @DATEVALUE, @NOW, @TIME

WARNING How well does 1-2-3 handle February 29 on leap years? Perfectly, apart from February 29, 1900, a day that 1-2-3 assigns but which did not take place, as 1900 was not a leap year. So if you're using dates between January 1, 1900 and March 1, 1900, you'll need to subtract 1 from any results to get the correct date. Otherwise, don't worry.

@DATEDIF(start-date,end-date,format)

The @DATEDIF function returns the number of years, months, or days between two date numbers, where *start-date* and *end-date* are date numbers and *format* is a text code that specifies the format in which to calculate and return the result. Following are the *format* text codes:

Format	Returns the Number of
y	Years
m	Months
d	Days
md	Days, ignoring months and years
ym	Months, ignoring years
yd	Days, ignoring years

TIP Use the @DATE function together with @DATEDIF to keep your worksheets neat: Use @DATEDIF(@DATE(64,11,28),@DATE(100,1,1),"y") rather than @DATEDIF(23709,36526).

For example, you could use @DATEDIF to calculate the length of time between November 28, 1964 and January 1, 2000 in several different ways. This returns 35, the number of years between November 28, 1964 and January 1, 2000:

    @DATEDIF(@DATE(64,11,28),@DATE(100,1,1),"y")

This returns 421, the number of months between November 28, 1964 and January 1, 2000:

    @DATEDIF(@DATE(64,11,28),@DATE(100,1,1),"m")

This returns 12817, the number of days between November 28, 1964 and January 1, 2000:

Descriptions of the Calendar Functions

    @DATEDIF(@DATE(64,11,28),@DATE(100,1,1),"d")

This returns 4, the number of days (ignoring months and years) between November 28, 1964 and January 1, 2000:

    @DATEDIF(@DATE(64,11,28),@DATE(100,1,1),"md")

This returns 1, the number of months (ignoring years) between November 28, 1964 and January 1, 2000:

    @DATEDIF(@DATE(64,11,28),@DATE(100,1,1),"ym")

This returns 34, the number of days (ignoring years) between November 28, 1964 and January 1, 2000:

    @DATEDIF(@DATE(64,11,28),@DATE(100,1,1),"yd")

Figure B.2 illustrates the use of @DATEDIF in a human-resources worksheet. Cell F5 contains the function statement

    @DATEDIF(D5,@TODAY,"y")

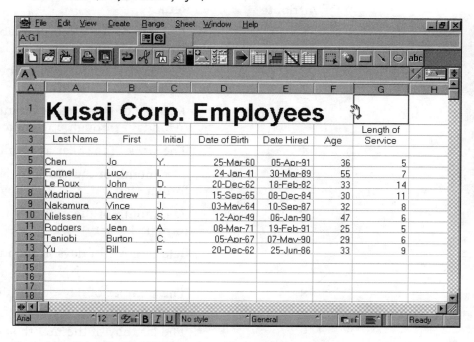

Figure B.2:   Using the @DATEDIF function with the @TODAY function to calculate the number of years between two dates

to calculate the difference between the employee's date of birth and the present date and return the result—the employee's age—in years; this formula is copied down the column to produce the ages of the other employees. Similarly, cell G5 calculates the employee's length of service in years by using

    @DATEDIF(E5,@TODAY,"y")

to calculate the difference in years between the employee's date of hire and the present date.

See Also   @D360, @DAYS, @DAYS360

@DATEINFO(date,attribute)

The @DATEINFO function returns information about *date*, where *date* is a date number and *attribute* is one of the following:

Attribute	Returns
1	The day of the week as a label in short format (Mon)
2	The day of the week as a label in long format (Monday)
3	The day of the week as an integer from 0 (Monday) through 6 (Sunday)
4	The week of the year as an integer from 1 to 53
5	The month of the year as a label in short format (Jan)
6	The month of the year as a label in long format (January)
7	The number of days in the month specified by *date*
8	The number of days left in the month specified by *date*
9	The last day of the month specified by *date*
10	The Quarter *date* is in, as an integer from 1 (Q1) through 4 (Q4)
11	One if the year specified by *date* is a leap year; 0 if the year is not a leap year

Descriptions of the Calendar Functions

Attribute	Returns
12	The day of the year specified by *date*, as a number from 1 to 366
13	The number of days left in the year specified by *date*, as a number

For example, to find the date of the last day of the month in which date number 23699 fell, you could use

    @DAY(@DATEINFO(23699,9))

and get the result 30, the date of the last day of November 1964.

@DATESTRING(date-number)

The @DATESTRING function returns from *date-number* a label that resembles its equivalent date (using the default International Date format), where *date-number* is a date number. For example,

    @DATESTRING(34819)

returns 04/30/95 if the default International Date format is *mm/dd/ty*.

See Also   @DATE, @DATEVALUE

> **TIP** To change the default International Date format, choose Tools ➤ User Setup ➤ International and choose a format from the Format drop-down list in the International dialog box.

@DATEVALUE(text)

The @DATEVALUE function returns the date number for the date specified in *text*, where *text* is a date expressed as text within double quotation marks (""), a formula that results in text, the address or name of a cell that contains a label, or a formula that results in a label.

If you use text, it must be in one of the five 1-2-3 date formats:

Date Format	Example
Day-Month-Year	27-May-63
Day-Month	27-May
Month-Year	May-63

Date Format	Example
Long International Date	5/27/63
Short International Date	5/27

Note that in the Day-Month and Short International Date formats, the year is not specified.

For example, the following statement returns **23158**:

   @DATEVALUE("5/27/63")

(Note that the double quotation marks ("") are necessary to stop 1-2-3 from dividing the values 5, 27, and 63.) To return an actual date from an @DATEVALUE calculation (rather than returning a date number), format the appropriate cell with one of the date formats by using the Format selector in the status bar.

Why use @DATEVALUE rather than @DATE? You may find @DATEVALUE especially valuable with data imported from another application that uses a format unsuitable for @DATE. For example, a word-processing application might not support the date format 95,3,15 that @DATE needs. Figure B.3 shows the use of @DATEVALUE to convert date strings to date serial numbers. Cell A5 contains the function statement

   @DATEVALUE(B5)

to return the date number for the text string in cell B5.

See Also   @DATE

@DAY(date-number)

The @DAY function returns the day of the month represented by *date-number*, a value from 1 (January 1, 1900) through 73050 (December 31, 2099). @DAY returns a value from 1 through 31 representing the day of the month. For example, date number 34666 is November 28, 1994, so

   @DAY(34666)

returns 28. Alternatively, you can combine @DAY with other date functions:

   @DAY(@DATE(94,11,28))

Descriptions of the Calendar Functions

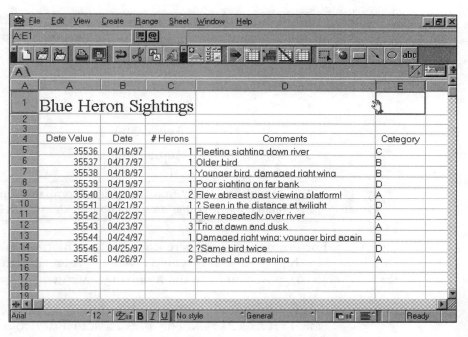

Figure B.3: Using @DATEVALUE to convert date strings to date serial numbers

This statement also returns 28. You can use @DAY with cell addresses. You can also use @DAY(@NOW) to return the current day of the month. For example, if run on December 31, 1994,

    @DAY(@NOW)

would return 31.

> **NOTE** You may find @DAY most useful for supplying the day argument for use with other 1-2-3 date @functions.

See Also   @MONTH, @WEEKDAY, @YEAR

@DAYS(start-date,end-date,[basis])

The @DAYS function returns the number of days between two dates using a user-specified *basis* for day-count. *start-date* and *end-date* are both date numbers; @DAYS will return a positive result if *start-date* is before *end-date*, a negative result if *start-date* is after *end-date*, or 0 if *start-date* and *end-date* are the same. *basis* is the type of day-count basis:

Basis	Meaning
0	30/360
1	Actual/actual
2	Actual/360
3	Actual/365

TIP As with the @DAY function, you will probably find @DAYS most useful in conjunction with other date functions, such as @DATE, as illustrated below.

For example, if you were born on June 3, 1936 and wanted to calculate how many days you'd lived by your sixtieth birthday (June 3, 1996), you could use the following statement:

    @DAYS(@DATE(36,6,3),@DATE(96,6,3),1)

which returns 21549. This uses an actual day count, denoted by *basis* being 1.

If you wanted to calculate the number of days between two dates based on a 360-day year consisting of twelve months of thirty days each, you could use

    @DAYS(@DATE(94,11,28),@DATE(95,5,27))

See Figure B.1 for an illustration of the @DAYS function.

See Also   @D360, @DATEDIF, @DAYS360

@DAYS360(start-date,end-date)

The @DAYS360 function returns the number of days between two dates, *start-date* and *end-date*, based on a 360-day year (12 months of 30 days each). *start-date* and *end-date* are date numbers. @DAYS360 calculates a result according to the standards of the U.S. securities industry, conforming to the 1990 modifications of the Securities Industry Association's 1986 edition of Standard Security Calculation Methods.

WARNING Because of their different calculation methods, @AND360 and @DAYS360 will typically return different results when either *start-date* or *end-date* is the last day of a month.

For example, the following statement calculates the number of days between the Fourth of July 1994 and Christmas Day 1994 (the result is 171 days):

    @DAYS360(34519,34693)

Usually, you will find it more convenient to combine @DAYS360 with other date @functions:

    @DAYS(@DATE(94,7,4), @DATE(94,12,25))

which of course gives the same result. See Figure B.1 for an illustration of the @DAYS function.

See Also   @DATEDIF, @DAYS

@HOUR(time-number)

The @HOUR function returns an integer value from 0 (midnight) through 23 (11 P.M.), the hour corresponding to *time-number*. *time-number* is a value between 0.0000000 (which represents midnight) and 0.999994 (which represents 11:59:59 P.M.; 0.999995 and above return 0, midnight, again).

For example, this statement returns 12 (noon):

    @HOUR(0.5)

Consider using @HOUR with other time @functions that supply a time number. For example, this function statement returns 17, the seventeenth hour of the day:

    @HOUR(@TIMEVALUE("5:15pm"))

See Also   @MINUTE, @SECOND

TIP Since @HOUR returns only an hour value, it is most useful for projects that require times calculated in hours without minutes. For example, a law firm might use @HOUR to calculate billable hours to clients (and it might be tempted to use it in conjunction with @ROUNDUP rather than @ROUNDDOWN). Other uses include calculating hourly wages and the like.

@MINUTE(time-number)

The @MINUTE function returns an integer between 0 and 50 for the minute corresponding to *time-number*. *time-number* is a value between 0.0000000 (which represents midnight) and 0.999994 (which represents 11:59:59 P.M.; 0.999995 and above return 0, midnight, again).

For example, this statement returns 55, the fifty-fifth minute of the hour:

    @MINUTE(0.58)

Consider using @MINUTE with other time @functions that supply a time number. For example, this function statement returns 15, the fifteenth minute of the hour:

    @MINUTE(@TIMEVALUE("5:15pm"))

See Also   @HOUR, @SECOND

@MONTH(date-number)

@MONTH returns the month of the year from *date-number* as a value from 1 (January) through 12 (December). *date-number* is a value from 1 (January 1, 1900) through 73050 (December 31, 2099).

For example, as 34700 is the date number for January 1, 1995, the following statement returns 1, representing January, the first month of the year:

    @MONTH(34700)

> **TIP** You'll usually find it easier to use another date function to provide *date-number* than entering *date-number* directly. For example, use @MONTH in combination with @DATE or another date function—@MONTH(@DATE (95,1,1)) or the like.

To return the current month, use @MONTH in combination with @NOW:

    @MONTH(@NOW)

This statement would return 7 if the current month were July.

See Also   @DAY, @YEAR

@NETWORKDAYS(start-date,end-date, [holidays-range],[weekends])

The @NETWORKDAYS function returns the number of working days between *start-date* and *end-date*. The number of working days is considered to be the number of days excluding weekends and holidays.

The arguments for @NETWORKDAYS are as follows:

Argument	Description
start-date	A date entered as a date number (e.g., 34666 for November 28, 1994). *start-date* counts as a day in the @NETWORKDAYS calculation.
end-date	A date entered as a date number (e.g., 35031 for November 28, 1995). *end-date* counts as a day in the @NETWORKDAYS calculation.
holidays-range	The name or address of a range containing date numbers that specify holidays to exclude from the calculation of working days. *holidays-range* is an optional argument and can contain date numbers, formulas that produce date numbers, and range addresses or range names containing date numbers.
weekends	An optional argument to specify which days of the week are considered weekend days, entered as text, where the days are represented as listed below. The default setting is "56" to indicate that Saturday and Sunday are considered weekend days.

0 = Monday

1 = Tuesday

2 = Wednesday

3 = Thursday

4 = Friday

5 = Saturday

6 = Sunday

7 = no holidays |

WARNING Note that you cannot use an optional argument unless you use those that precede it. For example, you cannot use *weekends* in @NETWORK-DAYS if you do not specify *holidays-range*. To include weekends in the calculation without using holidays, you can specify a blank cell for the *holidays-range* value.

For example, suppose you need to calculate the number of working days in December 1997. Your company generously gives December 24, 25, 26, and 31 as holidays, so you enter these in a range that you call HOLIDAYS (well, why not?). Everyone in the company works a five-day week, with Friday and Saturday off, which gives "45" as the *weekends* argument. So the calculation looks like this:

```
@NETWORKDAYS(@DATE(97,12,1),@DATE(97,12,31),HOLIDAYS,"45")
```

which gives 21, the number of working days excluding holidays and the specified weekend days.

See Also   @D360, @DAYS, @DAYS360, @NEXTMONTH

@NEXTMONTH(start-date,months, [day-of-month],[basis])

The @NEXTMONTH function returns the date number for the date that falls a specified number of months before or after *start-date*.

The arguments for the @NEXTMONTH function are as follows:

Argument	Description
start-date	A date entered as a date number.
months	An integer indicating the number of months before or after *start-date* that you want to calculate. A positive integer indicates months after *start-date*; a negative integer indicates months before *start-date*.
day-of-month	A value (0, 1, or 2) specifying the day of the month you want the result of @NEXTMONTH to fall on, as follows: 0 returns the date that falls on the same day of the month as *start-date* (the default setting if

Descriptions of the Calendar Functions

you omit the *day-of-month* argument). For example, if *start-date* represents February 15 and *months* is 1, @NEXTMONTH will return the date number for March 15. If the new month does not have the relevant day of the month (for example, if *start-date* is 31 and the new month is February, April, June, September, or November, none of which has a thirty-first day), @NEXTMONTH will return the date for the last day of the month (i.e., February 28 or 29, April 30, and so on). 1 returns the date that is the first day of the month. 2 returns the date that is the last day of the month.

basis A value (0, 1, 2, or 3) to specify the day-count basis to use for the calculation. *basis* is an optional argument and the values are as follows: 0 specifies a 30/360 day count. 1 specifies an actual/actual day count. This is the default if you omit the *basis* argument. 2 specifies an actual/360 day count. 3 specifies an actual/365 day count.

WARNING Note that you cannot use an optional argument unless you use those that precede it. For example, you cannot use the optional argument *basis* in @NEXTMONTH if you do not specify *day-of-month*.

For example, to work out the date of the last day of the month that's six months after July 4, 1997, you would use this statement:

```
@NEXTMONTH(@DATE(97,7,4),6)
```

This returns 35799, the date number for...wait, for what? It would be clearer to combine @NEXTMONTH with the @DATESTRING function:

```
@DATESTRING(@NEXTMONTH(@DATE(97,7,4),6))
```

This returns 01/04/98, which is indeed the date value 35799.

See Also @D360, @DAYS360, @NETWORKDAYS, @WORKDAY

@NOW

The @NOW function returns the date number as determined by your computer's built-in clock. The date number includes a time number. The date number is the integer portion and the time number is the decimal portion. For example, if today's date is November 11, 1994 and the time is 11:00 A.M., then the @NOW function returns 34649.4583, of which 34649 represents November 11, 1994, and .4583 represents 11:00 A.M. For a more user-friendly display, choose a date or time format in the Format Number dialog box (Style ➤ Format Number). In a date-formatted cell, @NOW will display only the date; in a time-formatted cell, @NOW will display only the time.

TIP If you find yourself getting improbable values from function statements using @NOW, check your recalculation settings in the Recalculation dialog box and check your computer's clock setting.

Note that @NOW function statements will be recalculated every time you recalculate your worksheet, either automatically (if you choose Automatic in the Recalculation dialog box that you reach via Tools ➤ User Setup ➤ Recalculation ➤ Automatic) or manually (by pressing F9 or by clicking the Recalculate SmartIcon).

Two frequent uses of @NOW are to time-stamp worksheets or to calculate elapsed time.

See Also   @TODAY

@SECOND(time-number)

The @SECOND function returns an integer between 0 and 59 for the seconds corresponding to *time-number*. *time-number* is a value between 0.0000000 (which represents midnight) and 0.999994 (which represents 11:59:59 P.M.; 0.999995 and above return 0, midnight, again).

For example, this statement returns 17, the seventeenth second of the minute:

    @SECOND(@TIMEVALUE("10:15:17PM"))

See Also   @HOUR, @MINUTE

@TIME(hour,minutes,seconds)

The @TIME function returns the time number for the specified hour, minutes, and seconds.

The arguments for the @TIME function are as follows:

Argument	Description
hour	An integer from 0 (midnight) through 23 (11:00 P.M.)
minutes	An integer from 0 through 59
seconds	An integer from 0 through 59

For example, this statement returns 0.55, the time for 13:12:00:

    @TIME(13,12,00)

Format the relevant cell to display a time number by using the Format selector in the status bar or by choosing Style ➤ Number Format and choosing a format from the Number Format dialog box.

Perhaps more useful than a single time on its own is the use of @TIME to calculate the amount of time elapsed. For example, if a temporary worker in your office worked from 7:45 A.M. to 1:15 P.M., you could calculate his or her pay (at a meager $13.40 per hour, including an exorbitant agency fee) by subtracting the start time from the end time and multiplying the result by the hourly pay rate, as follows:

    @TIME(13,15,0)-@TIME(7,45,0)*13.4*24

This produces $73.70.

See Also @TIMEVALUE

@TIMEVALUE(text)

The @TIMEVALUE function returns the time number for *text*. *text* can be a time entered as text within double quotation marks (""), a formula resulting in text, or the address of a cell containing a label or a formula resulting in a label. Text for *text* must conform to one of 1-2-3's four time formats:

22:15:17 P.M.
22:15 P.M.
22:15:17
22:15

For example, this statement returns 0.604167, the time value for 2:30 P.M.:

    @TIMEVALUE("14:30")

Similarly, if the cell named APPOINTMENT contains the label 15:45, this statement returns 0.65625, the time value for 3:45 P.M.:

    @TIMEVALUE(APPOINTMENT)

To make the time value appear in a time format, choose a suitable format by using the Format selector in the status bar.

> **TIP** @TIMEVALUE may appear to have little advantage over @TIME—or indeed may appear completely pointless—until you find yourself stuck with times entered as labels in a worksheet or imported in label format from another program, such as a word-processing application or presentation. For most conventional purposes, you'll probably find it easiest to enter times in the 22,15,17 format that @TIME uses.

See Also   @TIME

@TODAY

The @TODAY function calculates the date number as determined by your computer's built-in clock, without a time value. It is equivalent to @INT(@NOW). Not surprisingly, @TODAY has no arguments.

> **TIP** If you find yourself getting improbable values from @TODAY function statements, check to see if someone's been messing with the clock on your computer.

Note that @TODAY function statements will be recalculated every time you recalculate your worksheet, either automatically (choose Automatic in the Recalculation dialog box that you reach via Tools ➤ User Setup ➤ Recalculation ➤ Automatic) or manually (by pressing F9 or by clicking the Recalculate SmartIcon).

For example, on New Year's Day, 1996, this statement will return 35065:

    @TODAY

To display the date in a user-friendly format, format the cell for Date by using the Format selector in the status bar, or use the @DATE STRING function in combination with @TODAY:

    @DATESTRING(@TODAY)

See Also   @NOW, @TIME

@WEEKDAY(date-number)

The @WEEKDAY function returns the day of the week from *date-number* as an integer from 0 (Monday) through 6 (Sunday). *date-number* is a value from 1 (January 1, 1900) through 73050 (December 31, 2099).

For example, this statement returns 3, indicating that April 19, 2001, is a Thursday:

    @WEEKDAY(37000)

TIP Usually you'll find the @WEEKDAY function more useful in combination with other date functions that supply a date number. For example, if you are planning the mother of all parties and want to know what day of the week December 31, 1999, will fall on, use @WEEKDAY(@DATE(99,12,31)) to find the answer—Friday (how appropriate!).

See Also   @MONTH, @YEAR

@WORKDAY(start-date,days,[holidays-range], [weekends])

The @WORKDAY function returns the date number for the date that falls a specified number of working days before or after *start-date*. You can instruct @WORKDAY to ignore weekends and various holidays.

The arguments for @WORKDAY are as follows:

Argument	Description
start-date	A date entered as a date number (e.g., 34666 for November 28, 1994). *start-date* counts as a day in the @WORKDAYS calculation.

end-date	A date entered as a date number (e.g., 35031 for November 28, 1995). *end-date* counts as a day in the @WORKDAYS calculation.
holidays-range	The name or address of a range containing date numbers that specify holidays to exclude from the calculation of working days. *holidays-range* is an optional argument and can contain date numbers, formulas that produce date numbers, and range addresses or range names containing date numbers.
weekends	An optional argument to specify which days of the week are considered weekend days, entered as text, where the days are represented as listed below. The default setting is "56" to indicate that Saturday and Sunday are considered weekend days. 0 = Monday 1 = Tuesday 2 = Wednesday 3 = Thursday 4 = Friday 5 = Saturday 6 = Sunday 7 = no holidays

WARNING Note that you cannot use an optional argument unless you use those that precede it. For example, you cannot use *weekends* in @WORKDAY if you do not specify *holidays-range*. To include weekends in the calculation without using holidays, you can specify a blank cell for the *holidays-range* value.

For example, say you want to calculate ten working days as a payment period for the invoices you are sending out on February 28, 1997. You have a company holiday (Founder's Day) on March 3, which you enter in a range named HOLIDAYS; and the problem is further complicated by the company's working Tuesday to Friday, with Sunday and Monday off, which gives you a *weekends* value of "06". Use this function statement:

    @WORKDAY(@DATE(97,2,28),10,HOLIDAYS,"06")

It returns 35501, the date number for March 14, 1997. To better see the due date for the invoices, weave the @DATESTRING function into the statement:

    @DATESTRING(@WORKDAY(@DATE(97,2,28),10,HOLIDAYS,"06"))

This statement returns 03/14/97.

See Also   @D360, @DAYS360

@YEAR(date-number)

The @YEAR function returns the year from *date-number* as an integer from 0 (representing 1900) to 199 (representing 2099). *date-number* is an integer, or the address or name of a cell that contains an integer, from 1 (January 1, 1900) through 73050 (December 31, 2099).

For example, if you knew the date number for November 28, 1994 was 34666, you could use

    @YEAR(34666)

to return the year for that date, 94. Usually, though, it would be more useful to use @YEAR in combination with @DATE to produce the date number and then extract the year from it:

    @YEAR(@DATE(94,11,28))

> **TIP** To return the year as a conventional and user-friendly four-digit number rather than as a two-digit number, simply add 1900 to the result of @YEAR. For example, use @YEAR(@DATE(94,11,28))+1900 to return 1994 rather than 94. To return the present year, use @YEAR with @NOW—@YEAR(@NOW) or @YEAR(@NOW)+1900.

See Also   @DAY, @MONTH

APPENDIX C

Database Functions Reference

1-2-3's eleven database functions perform statistical calculations and queries on database tables, scanning the specified database tables and selecting the records that match the specified criteria before performing the calculations on them.

Most of the database functions are database variations of other 1-2-3 functions. The main difference between similarly named database functions (such as @DAVG and @DMIN) and statistical functions (such as @AVG and @MIN) is that the database functions operate on selected field entries in a database table rather than simply operating on lists.

TIP Note that functions that refer to external database tables are recalculated each time any value in the worksheet changes—unlike functions that refer to database tables in a single worksheet file, which are recalculated only when a value changes on which the function depends.

This appendix is divided into three sections. The first section, "Overview of the Database Functions," provides a reference table of the database functions. The second section, "Arguments for the Database Functions," lists the arguments for the database functions, since nearly all of them take exactly the same arguments. The third section, "Descriptions of the Database Functions," discusses each database function in detail and gives examples.

NOTE Chapters 11, 12 and 13 explain how to work with databases in 1-2-3.

This appendix uses a sample file of Frequently Accessed Newsgroups on the Internet to illustrate the various database functions. The worksheet includes:

- The location of each newsgroup in the Location column
- The name of the newsgroup in the Newsgroup column
- The date of the first access to the newsgroup in the First Access column
- The date of the last (i.e., the latest) access to the newsgroup in the Last Access column
- The total number of times the newsgroup has been accessed in the Total column
- Other information as necessary to illustrate the database functions

Overview of the Database Functions

For quick reference, Table C.1 lists the database functions.

Table C.1: Database Functions Quick Reference

Function	Returns
@DAVG	The average of selected values in a database range
@DCOUNT	The number of selected values in a database range
@DGET	The field item from a single database record selected by the expressions in the criteria range
@DMAX	The largest value among selected entries in a database range
@DMIN	The smallest value among selected entries in a database range
@DPURECOUNT	The number of a cells in a database that contain a value in the specified field that match specified criteria

Table C.1: **Database Functions Quick Reference (continued)**

Function	Returns
@DSTD	The population standard deviation of selected values in a database range
@DSTDS	The sample standard deviation of selected values in a database range
@DSUM	The sum of selected values in a database range
@DVAR	The population variance of selected values in a database range
@DVARS	The sample variance of selected values in a database range

Arguments for the Database Functions

All the 1-2-3 database functions take the same arguments. Table C.2 summarizes those arguments to avoid numbing repetition through the rest of this appendix.

Table C.2: **Arguments for the Database Functions**

Argument	Description
input	The name or address of a range containing a database table, the name of an external table, or the name of a query table enclosed in double quotation marks ("").
field	The name of the field, enclosed in double quotation marks (""), on which you want the function to operate. Note that if *input* is from an external table, *field* must be from that table too. If you are using more than one *input* argument and *field* appears in more than one input table (in other words, it is not unique), you need to specify *field* as the name of the table, followed by a period and the field name. For example, if the tables

Table C.2: Arguments for the Database Functions (continued)

Argument	Description
	DESKTOPS and LAPTOPS both contained a PROCESSOR field, you would specify "LAPTOPS.PROCESSOR" to indicate the PROCESSOR field in the LAPTOPS table.
criteria	A criteria formula or the name or address of a range that contains a criteria formula. If you use only one table for input, you can omit criteria.

Descriptions of the Database Functions

This section contains detailed descriptions of each database @function. For details of the arguments for the database @functions, see Table C.2 in the previous section.

@DAVG(input,field,[criteria])

The @DAVG function calculates the average of the values in a field of a database table that meet specified *criteria*. The arguments for the @DAVG function are discussed in Table C.2 in the previous section.

For example, column G in Figure C.1 shows the use of @DAVG to produce averages from a database table. Cell G6 contains the function statement

```
@DAVG(A3..E18,"total",LOCATION="alt")
```

to find the average number of times the newsgroups in the Location "Alt": 27 have been accessed. Similarly, cells G8, G10, and G12 contain the following function statements, respectively:

```
@DAVG(A3..E18,"total",LOCATION="biz")
@DAVG(A3..E18,"total",LOCATION="misc")
@DAVG(A3..E18,"total",LOCATION="rec")
```

These statements find the average number of accesses to the newsgroups in the Locations "Biz," "Misc," and "Rec," respectively. Cell

G14 contains a function statement to produce the average number of accesses for all newsgroups:

```
@DAVG(A3..E18,"total")
```

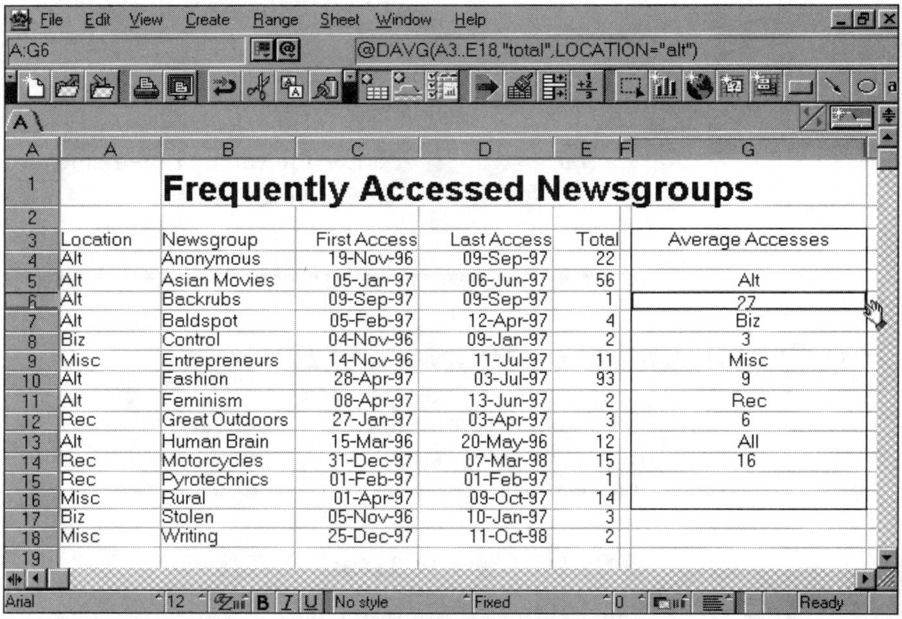

A	A	B	C	D	E	F	G
1		Frequently Accessed Newsgroups					
2							
3	Location	Newsgroup	First Access	Last Access	Total		Average Accesses
4	Alt	Anonymous	19-Nov-96	09-Sep-97	22		
5	Alt	Asian Movies	05-Jan-97	06-Jun-97	56		Alt
6	Alt	Backrubs	09-Sep-97	09-Sep-97	1		27
7	Alt	Baldspot	05-Feb-97	12-Apr-97	4		Biz
8	Biz	Control	04-Nov-96	09-Jan-97	2		3
9	Misc	Entrepreneurs	14-Nov-96	11-Jul-97	11		Misc
10	Alt	Fashion	28-Apr-97	03-Jul-97	93		9
11	Alt	Feminism	08-Apr-97	13-Jun-97	2		Rec
12	Rec	Great Outdoors	27-Jan-97	03-Apr-97	3		6
13	Alt	Human Brain	15-Mar-96	20-May-96	12		All
14	Rec	Motorcycles	31-Dec-97	07-Mar-98	15		16
15	Rec	Pyrotechnics	01-Feb-97	01-Feb-97	1		
16	Misc	Rural	01-Apr-97	09-Oct-97	14		
17	Biz	Stolen	05-Nov-96	10-Jan-97	3		
18	Misc	Writing	25-Dec-97	11-Oct-98	2		
19							

Figure C.1: ***Using the @DAVG function to produce averages for a database table***

See Also @AVG, @PUREAVG

@DCOUNT(input,field,[criteria])

The @DCOUNT function returns the number of nonblank cells in a *field* of a database *input* table that meet specified *criteria*. The arguments for the @DCOUNT function are discussed in Table C.2.

For example, Figure C.2 shows a database of Frequently Accessed Newsgroups. Cell G5 contains a statement that returns 15, the count of newsgroups accessed:

```
@DCOUNT(A2..E17,"Newsgroup")
```

Cell G7 contains a statement that returns 7, the count of Alt newsgroups within the Location list:

```
@DCOUNT(A2..E17,"Location",LOCATION="Alt")
```

Cell G9 contains a statement that returns 3, the count of Misc newsgroups within the Location list:

```
@DCOUNT(A2..E17,"Location",LOCATION="Misc")
```

Cell G11 contains a statement that returns 3, the count of Rec newsgroups within the Location list:

```
@DCOUNT(A2..E17,"Location",LOCATION="Rec")
```

And cell G13 contains a statement that returns 2, the count of Biz newsgroups within the Location list:

```
@DCOUNT(A2..E17,"Location",LOCATION="Biz")
```

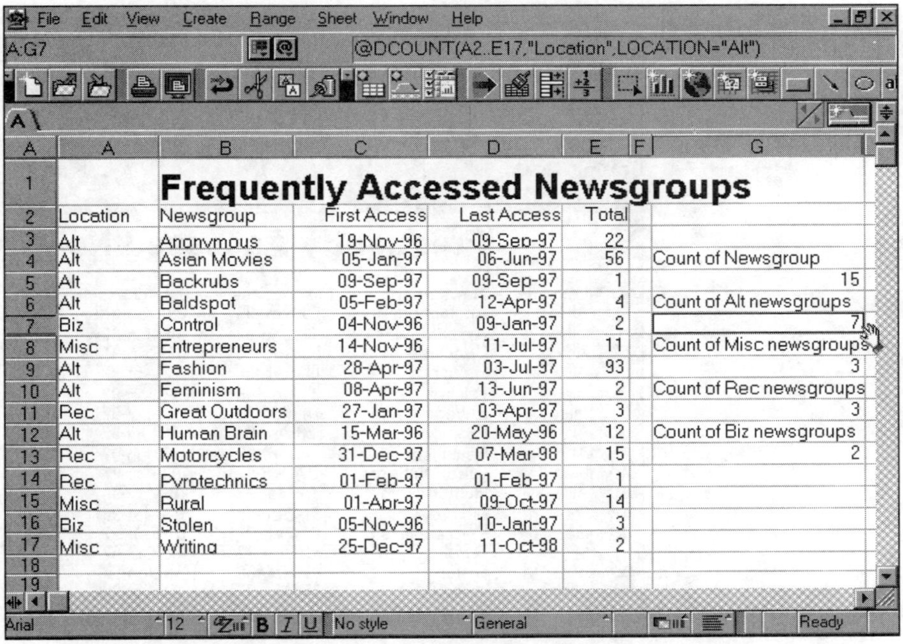

	A	B	C	D	E	F	G
1		Frequently Accessed Newsgroups					
2	Location	Newsgroup	First Access	Last Access	Total		
3	Alt	Anonymous	19-Nov-96	09-Sep-97	22		
4	Alt	Asian Movies	05-Jan-97	06-Jun-97	56		Count of Newsgroup
5	Alt	Backrubs	09-Sep-97	09-Sep-97	1		15
6	Alt	Baldspot	05-Feb-97	12-Apr-97	4		Count of Alt newsgroups
7	Biz	Control	04-Nov-96	09-Jan-97	2		7
8	Misc	Entrepreneurs	14-Nov-96	11-Jul-97	11		Count of Misc newsgroups
9	Alt	Fashion	28-Apr-97	03-Jul-97	93		3
10	Alt	Feminism	08-Apr-97	13-Jun-97	2		Count of Rec newsgroups
11	Rec	Great Outdoors	27-Jan-97	03-Apr-97	3		3
12	Alt	Human Brain	15-Mar-96	20-May-96	12		Count of Biz newsgroups
13	Rec	Motorcycles	31-Dec-97	07-Mar-98	15		2
14	Rec	Pyrotechnics	01-Feb-97	01-Feb-97	1		
15	Misc	Rural	01-Apr-97	09-Oct-97	14		
16	Biz	Stolen	05-Nov-96	10-Jan-97	3		
17	Misc	Writing	25-Dec-97	11-Oct-98	2		
18							
19							

Figure C.2: ***Using the @DCOUNT function to return the number of nonblank fields that meet specific criteria***

See Also @COUNT, @DPURECOUNT, @PURECOUNT

@DGET(input,field,[criteria])

The @DGET function retrieves a value or label from a *field* of a database table that meets specified *criteria*. Use @DGET to retrieve a single value that meets particular *criteria*. You can use the result of @DGET in a macro or in a function. The arguments for @DGET are discussed in Table C.2.

> **WARNING** Be careful when specifying criteria for @DGET, because @DGET will return ERR if more than one entry meets the given criteria.

For example, Figure C.3 uses @DGET as follows to retrieve information about the Baldspot newsgroup in the Frequently Accessed Newsgroups database. The function statement in cell G6 returns Alt, the Location of the Baldspot newsgroup:

```
@DGET(A3..E18,"Location",NEWSGROUP="Baldspot")
```

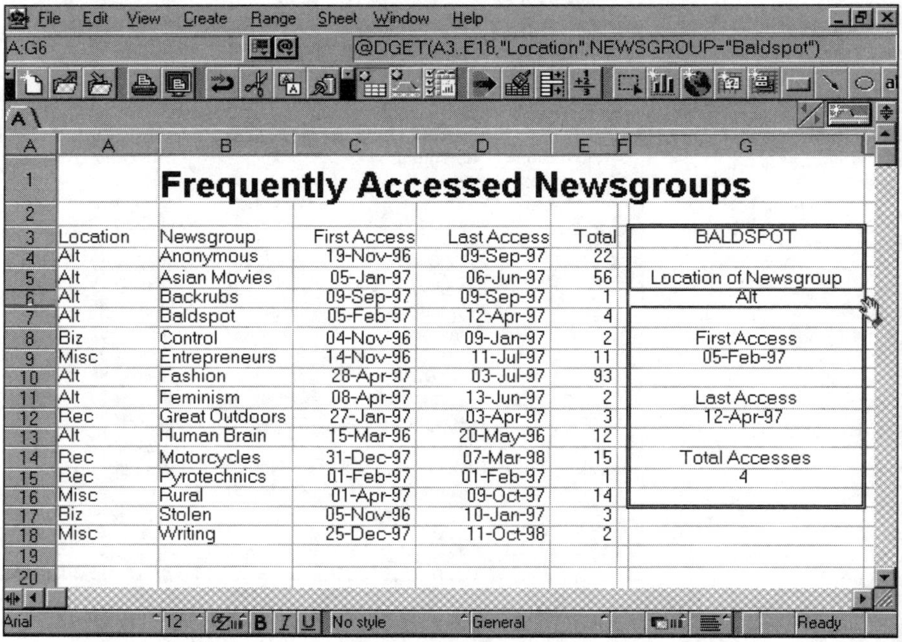

Figure C.3: Using the @DGET function to retrieve single values from a database

The function statement in cell G9 returns 05-Feb-94, the First Access date for Baldspot (the cell is formatted to present a date format rather than a date number):

    @DGET(A3..E18,"First Access",NEWSGROUP="Baldspot")

Cell G12 contains this function statement:

    @DGET(A3..E18,"Last Access",NEWSGROUP="Baldspot")

It returns 12-Apr-94, the Last Access date for the newsgroup. Finally, cell G15 contains a statement that returns 4, the Total number of accesses for the newsgroup:

    @DGET(A3..E18,"Total",NEWSGROUP="Baldspot")

See Also   @CHOOSE, @HLOOKUP, @INDEX, @VLOOKUP, @XINDEX

@DMAX(input,field,[criteria])

The @DMAX function retrieves the largest value in a *field* of a database table that meets the specified *criteria*. The arguments for the @DMAX function are discussed in Table C.2.

While an obvious use for @DMAX would be to retrieve the highest sales figure from a range, you can also use @DMAX to retrieve the most recent date or time from a list of dates or times.

For example, in Figure C.4, cell G6 contains a function statement that retrieves the latest Last Access date for the database:

    @DMAX(A3..E18,"Last Access")

Cell G8 retrieves the latest Last Access date to an Alt newsgroup in the database:

    @DMAX(A3..E18,"Last Access",LOCATION="ALT")

And cell G10 retrieves the most accessed Rec newsgroup in the database:

    @DMAX(A3..E18,"Total",LOCATION="REC")

See Also   @MAX, @PUREMAX

Appendix C   Database Functions Reference

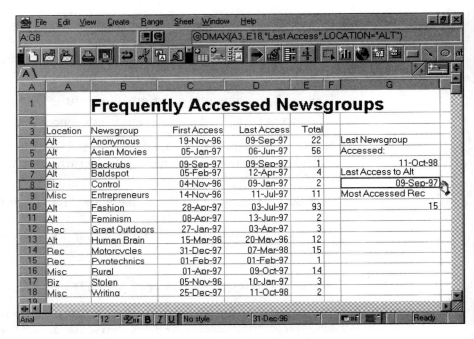

Figure C.4:   *Using the @DMAX function to retrieve values from a database*

@DMIN(input,field,[criteria])

The @DMIN function retrieves the smallest value in a *field* of a database table that meets specified *criteria*. The arguments for the @DMIN function are discussed in Table C.2.

You can use @DMIN not only to retrieve, say, the lowest sales figure from a range, but also to retrieve the earliest date or time from a list of dates or times.

For example, in Figure C.5, cell G6 contains a function statement that retrieves the earliest First Access date for the database:

```
@DMIN(A3..E18,"First Access")
```

Cell G8 retrieves the latest First Access date to a Rec newsgroup in the database:

```
@DMIN(A3..E18,"First Access",LOCATION="Rec")
```

And cell G10 retrieves the number of accesses to the least accessed Biz newsgroup in the database:

```
@DMIN(A3..E18,"Total",LOCATION="Biz")
```

See Also   @MIN, @PUREMIN

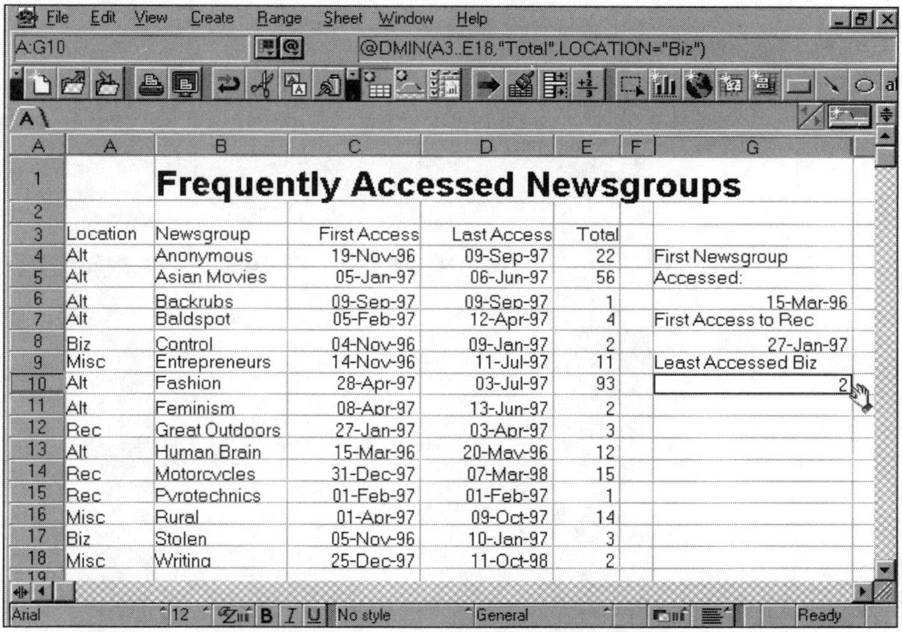

Figure C.5:   *Using the @DMIN function to retrieve values from a database*

@DPURECOUNT (input,field,[criteria])

The @DPURECOUNT function returns the number of cells that contain values in a *field* of a database table that meet specified *criteria*. The arguments for @DPURECOUNT are discussed in Table C.2. Note, however, that unlike the other database functions, @DPURECOUNT requires *criteria* every time. @DPURECOUNT's *criteria* must satisfy the following rules:

▶ *criteria* must be the name or address of a range containing two or more rows. This range *must not* be a 3-D range.

▶ *criteria*'s first row must list some or all of the field names from a database table.

- *criteria*'s second (and subsequent) rows must contain the criteria: values, labels, formulas, functions, or logical expressions.

For example, Figure C.6 shows a query table with *criteria* set as follows:

- *Field* was set to Location.
- *Operator* was set to =.
- *Value* was set to Biz.

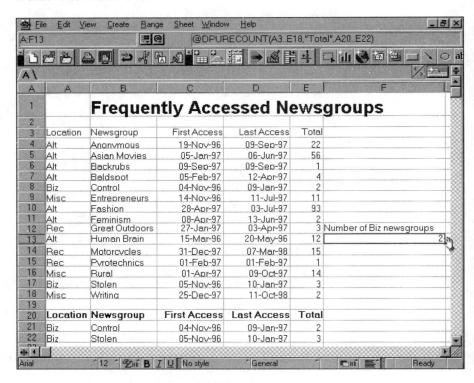

Figure C.6: *Using the @DPURECOUNT function to return the number of nonblank cells that meet specific criteria*

Cell F13 contains this function statement to return the number of Biz newsgroups included in the database:

```
@DPURECOUNT(A3..E18,"Total",A20..E22)
```

The result is 2.

See Also @COUNT, @DCOUNT, @PURECOUNT

@DSTD(input,field,[criteria])

The @DSTD function returns the population standard deviation of the values in a *field* of a database *input* table that meet specified *criteria*. The population standard deviation assumes that the values selected represent the entire population; if the values do not represent the whole population, the standard deviation will return a biased result. (For sample standard deviation, use @DSTDS rather than @DSTD.) The arguments for @DSTD are discussed in Table C.2.

NOTE Standard deviation is the square root of the variance of all individual values from the mean.

For example, Figure C.7 shows a Frequently Accessed Newsgroups database with costs included. In cell D19, this function statement returns the standard deviation of the Cost field:

```
@DSTD(A3..F18,"Cost")
```

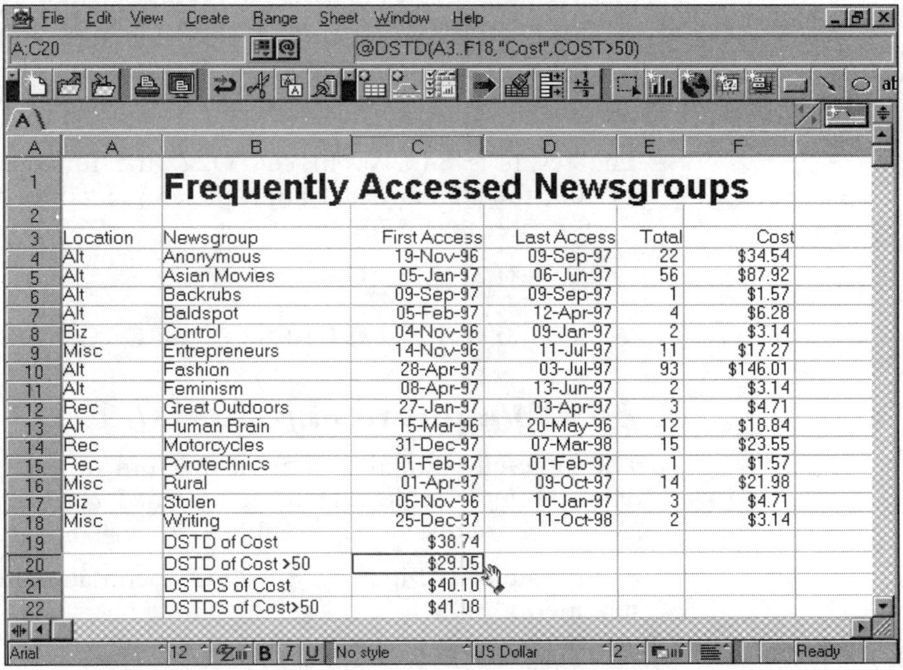

	A	B	C	D	E	F
1		Frequently Accessed Newsgroups				
2						
3	Location	Newsgroup	First Access	Last Access	Total	Cost
4	Alt	Anonymous	19-Nov-96	09-Sep-97	22	$34.54
5	Alt	Asian Movies	05-Jan-97	06-Jun-97	56	$87.92
6	Alt	Backrubs	09-Sep-97	09-Sep-97	1	$1.57
7	Alt	Baldspot	05-Feb-97	12-Apr-97	4	$6.28
8	Biz	Control	04-Nov-96	09-Jan-97	2	$3.14
9	Misc	Entrepreneurs	14-Nov-96	11-Jul-97	11	$17.27
10	Alt	Fashion	28-Apr-97	03-Jul-97	93	$146.01
11	Alt	Feminism	08-Apr-97	13-Jun-97	2	$3.14
12	Rec	Great Outdoors	27-Jan-97	03-Apr-97	3	$4.71
13	Alt	Human Brain	15-Mar-96	20-May-96	12	$18.84
14	Rec	Motorcycles	31-Dec-97	07-Mar-98	15	$23.55
15	Rec	Pyrotechnics	01-Feb-97	01-Feb-97	1	$1.57
16	Misc	Rural	01-Apr-97	09-Oct-97	14	$21.98
17	Biz	Stolen	05-Nov-96	10-Jan-97	3	$4.71
18	Misc	Writing	25-Dec-97	11-Oct-98	2	$3.14
19		DSTD of Cost	$38.74			
20		DSTD of Cost >50	$29.05			
21		DSTDS of Cost	$40.10			
22		DSTDS of Cost>50	$41.08			

Figure C.7: ***Using the @DSTD function to return the population standard deviation***

The result is $38.74. The function statement in cell D20 returns $29.05, the standard deviation of the Cost field for Cost greater than $50:

    @DSTD(A3..F18,"Cost",Cost>50)

See Also   @DSTDS, @PURESTD, @PURESTDS, @STD, @STDS, @DVAR

@DSTDS(input,field,[criteria])

The @DSTDS function calculates the sample standard deviation of sample values in a field of a database table that meet specified criteria. The arguments for @DSTDS are discussed in Table C.2.

> **TIP** Use @DSTDS to return an unbiased standard deviance for sample values that do not represent the whole population. If your values represent the whole population, use @DSTD instead of @DSTDS.

For example, Figure C.7 shows the Frequently Accessed Newsgroups database with costs included. The function statement in cell D21 returns the standard deviation of sample values for the Cost field:

    @DSTDS(A3..F18,"Cost")

The result is $40.10. In cell D22, the function statement returns $41.08, the standard deviation of sample values of the Cost field for Cost greater than $50:

    @DSTDS(A3..F18,"Cost",Cost>50)

See Also   @DVAR, @PURESTD, @PURESTDS, @STD, @STDS

@DSUM(input,field,[criteria])

The @DSUM function returns the sum of the values in a *field* of a database *input* table that meet specified *criteria*. The arguments for @DSUM are discussed in Table C.2.

For example, in Figure C.8, cell C19 contains the following function statement:

    @DSUM(A3..F18,"Cost")

Descriptions of the Database Functions

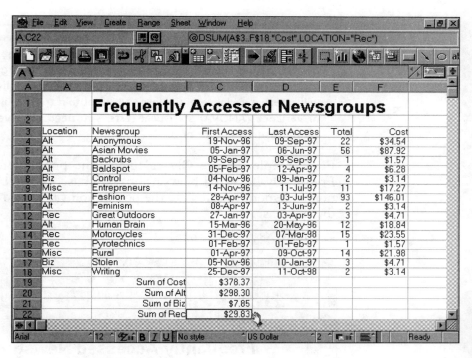

Figure C.8: Using the @DSUM function

It returns the sum of the values in the Cost field of the Frequently Accessed Newsgroups database: $378.37. The function statement in cell C20 returns $298.30, the sum of the values in the Cost field for Alt newsgroups:

```
@DSUM(A3..F18,"Cost",Location="Alt")
```

See Also @SUM

@DVAR(input,field,[criteria])

The @DVAR function returns the population variance of the values in a *field* of a database *input* table that meet specified *criteria*. The arguments for @DVARS are discussed in Table C.2.

The population variance assumes that the values selected represent the entire population; if the values do not represent the whole population, the population variance will return a biased result, and you should use the sample variance instead (the @DVARS function).

NOTE **Variance—the square of standard deviation—measures the degree to which individual values in a list vary from the average of all the values in the list. A lower variance indicates a more reliable average or mean, since the individual values vary from it less. If all the values in a list are equal, @DVAR will return a variance of 0. Note that to obtain true results in several analysis of variance (ANOVA) statistical tests, you need to have variance—i.e., you cannot use a variance of 0.**

For example, Figure C.9 calculates the population variance for the Frequently Accessed Newsgroups database. Cell C19 contains a function statement to calculate the population variance of the Total field of the database:

```
@DVAR(A3..F18,"Total")
```

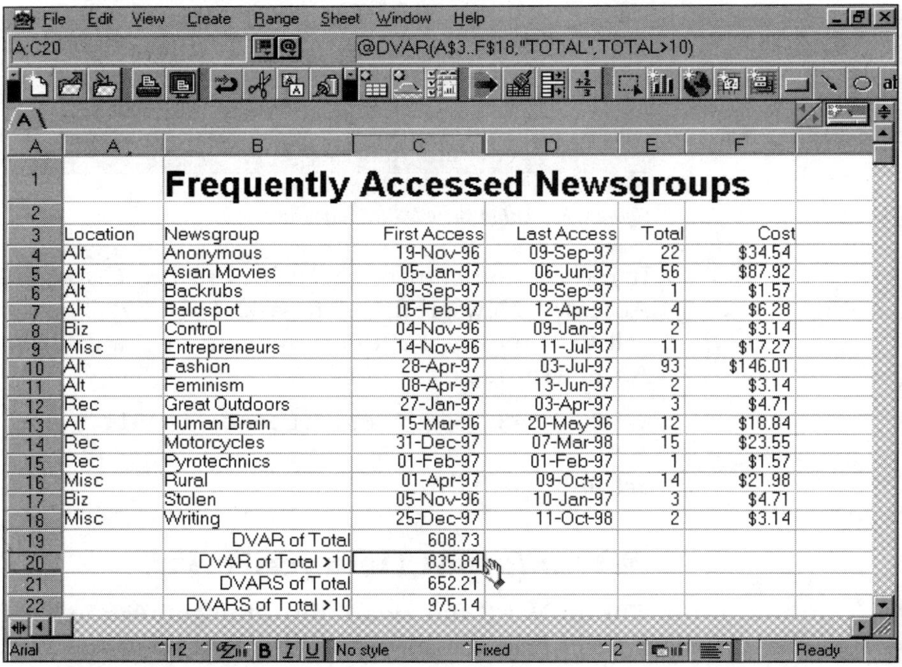

	A	B	C	D	E	F
1		Frequently Accessed Newsgroups				
2						
3	Location	Newsgroup	First Access	Last Access	Total	Cost
4	Alt	Anonymous	19-Nov-96	09-Sep-97	22	$34.54
5	Alt	Asian Movies	05-Jan-97	06-Jun-97	56	$87.92
6	Alt	Backrubs	09-Sep-97	09-Sep-97	1	$1.57
7	Alt	Baldspot	05-Feb-97	12-Apr-97	4	$6.28
8	Biz	Control	04-Nov-96	09-Jan-97	2	$3.14
9	Misc	Entrepreneurs	14-Nov-96	11-Jul-97	11	$17.27
10	Alt	Fashion	28-Apr-97	03-Jul-97	93	$146.01
11	Alt	Feminism	08-Apr-97	13-Jun-97	2	$3.14
12	Rec	Great Outdoors	27-Jan-97	03-Apr-97	3	$4.71
13	Alt	Human Brain	15-Mar-96	20-May-96	12	$18.84
14	Rec	Motorcycles	31-Dec-97	07-Mar-98	15	$23.55
15	Rec	Pyrotechnics	01-Feb-97	01-Feb-97	1	$1.57
16	Misc	Rural	01-Apr-97	09-Oct-97	14	$21.98
17	Biz	Stolen	05-Nov-96	10-Jan-97	3	$4.71
18	Misc	Writing	25-Dec-97	11-Oct-98	2	$3.14
19		DVAR of Total	608.73			
20		DVAR of Total >10	835.84			
21		DVARS of Total	652.21			
22		DVARS of Total >10	975.14			

Figure C.9: ***Calculating population variance and sample variance with the @DVAR and @DVARS functions***

The result is 608.73. Cell C20 calculates the population variance of the Total field over 10:

```
@DVAR(A3..F18,"Total",Total>10)
```

The result is 835.84.

See Also   @DSTD, @DSTDS, @DVARS, @PUREVAR, @VAR

@DVARS(input,field,[criteria])

The @DVARS function returns the sample variance of the values in a *field* of a database *input* table that meet specified *criteria*. The arguments for @DVARS are discussed in Table C.2.

The sample variance assumes that the values selected represent only a sample of the entire population; if the values represent the whole population, you should use the population variance instead (the @DVAR function).

For example, Figure C.9 calculates the sample variance for the Frequently Accessed Newsgroups database. Cell C21 contains a statement to calculate the sample variance of the Total field of the database:

```
@DVARS(A3..F18,"Total")
```

The result is 652.21. Cell C22 calculates the sample variance of the Total field over 10:

```
@DVARS(A3..F18,"Total",Total>10)
```

The result is 975.14.

See Also   @DSTD, @DVAR, @PUREVAR, @VAR

APPENDIX D
Engineering Functions Reference

1-2-3's fifteen engineering functions perform engineering calculations, such as calculating Bessel functions; numeric-type conversions, such as converting hexadecimal numbers to decimal numbers (and vice versa); and advanced mathematical operations, such as calculating power series.

Overview of the Engineering Functions

For quick reference, the fifteen engineering functions are listed in Table D.1. Each of them is discussed in detail in the next section, "Descriptions of the Engineering Functions."

Table D.1: Engineering Functions Quick Reference

Function	Returns
@BESSELI	The modified Bessel integer function $I_n(x)$
@BESSELJ	The Bessel integer function $J_n(x)$
@BESSELK	The modified Bessel integer function $K_n(x)$
@BESSELY	The Bessel integer function $Y_n(x)$
@BETA	The Beta integer function
@BETAI	The incomplete Beta integer function
@DECIMAL	A signed decimal value from a hexadecimal string
@ERF	The error function

Table D.1: Engineering Functions Quick Reference (continued)

Function	Returns
@ERFC	The complementary error function
@ERFD	The derivative of the error function
@GAMMA	The Gamma function
@GAMMAI	The incomplete Gamma function
@GAMMALN	The natural logarithm of the Gamma function
@HEX	A hexadecimal string from a signed decimal value
@SERIESSUM	The sum of a power series

A quick look at their names and definitions reveals that the engineering functions are specialized beyond the needs of the average user, but they can prove invaluable to engineers. Before you skip this section completely, though, note that the engineering functions include @HEX and @DECIMAL, functions which may prove of use to the non-engineer. These two functions allow you to convert hexadecimal numbers (which are used by computer programmers *inter alia*) to decimal numbers and vice versa. If you need to tinker with memory addresses in your PC, @HEX and @DECIMAL can come in handy.

The @HEX function converts normal decimal numbers (in base 10) to hexadecimal numbers. For example, to discover the hexadecimal equivalent of 180, you could use

```
@HEX(180)
```

which returns B4. The @DECIMAL function converts hexadecimal numbers into normal decimal numbers (in base 10) and is essentially the opposite of the @HEX function. For example, to find the decimal equivalent of the hexadecimal number FFFF0000, you could use

```
@DECIMAL("FFFF0000")
```

which returns –65,536.

Descriptions of the Engineering Functions

This section contains detailed descriptions of each engineering function.

@BESSELI(numeric_value,order)

The @BESSELI function calculates the modified Bessel function of integer order I*order*(*numeric_value*), in which *numeric_value* is the value at which to evaluate the function and is any value, and *order* is the order of the function and can be any positive integer including 0. For example, this function statement returns 0.504724:

    @BESSELI(4,5)

See Figure D.1 for an illustration of the Bessel functions; note the very different results produced from the same *order* and *numeric_value*.

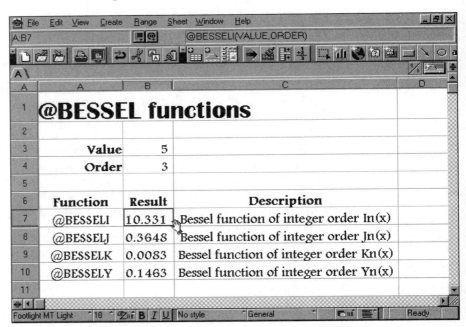

Figure D.1: *Using the @BESSEL functions*

NOTE Bessel functions are primarily used for problems involving cylindrical symmetry, in connection with wave propagation, fluid motion, elasticity, and diffusion. 1-2-3's Bessel functions approximate their functions to within $\pm 5 \times 10^{-8}$.

See Also   @BESSELJ, @BESSELK, @BESSELY

@BESSELJ(numeric_value,order)

The @BESSELJ function calculates the Bessel function of integer order J$order$(*numeric_value*), in which *numeric_value* is the value at which to evaluate the function and is any value, and *order* is the order of the function and can be any positive integer. For example, this function statement returns –0.06604:

    @BESSELJ(4,1)

The @BESSELJ function approximates to within $\pm 5*10^{-8}$. See Figure D.1 for an illustration of the Bessel functions; note the very different results produced from the same *order* and *numeric_value*.

See Also @BESSELI, @BESSELK, @BESSELY

@BESSELK(numeric_value,order)

The @BESSELK function calculates the modified Bessel function of integer order K$order$(*numeric_value*), in which *numeric_value* is the value at which to evaluate the function and is any value, and *order* is the order of the function and can be any positive integer including 0. For example, this function statement returns 0.25376:

    @BESSELK(2;2)

The @BESSELK function approximates to within $\pm 5*10^{-8}$. See Figure D.1 for an illustration of the Bessel functions; note the very different results produced from the same *order* and *numeric_value*.

See Also @BESSELI, @BESSELJ, @BESSELY

@BESSELY(numeric_value,order)

The @BESSELY function calculates the Bessel function of integer order Y$order$(*numeric_value*), in which *numeric_value* is the value at which to evaluate the function and is any value, and *order* is the order of the function and can be any positive integer. For example, this function statement returns –46.914:

    @BESSELY(2,6)

See Also @BESSELI, @BESSELJ, @BESSELK

NOTE The Bessel function of integer order Y$n(x)$ is also called the *Neumann function*. It approximates to within $\pm 5*10^{-8}$. See Figure D.1 for an illustration of the Bessel functions; note the very different results produced from the same *order* and *numeric_value*.

@BETA(numeric_value1,numeric_value2)

The @BETA function calculates the Beta function, where *numeric_value1* and *numeric_value2* are any values. For example, this function statement produces a result of 2.846527:

    @BETA(1.5,0.3)

NOTE @BETA produces a result accurate to within at least six significant digits.

See Also   @BETAI, @GAMMA

@BETAI(numeric_value1,numeric_value2, numeric_value3)

The @BETAI function calculates the incomplete Beta function, where *numeric_value1* and *numeric_value2* are any values, and *numeric_value3* is any value from 0 to 1. For example, this function statement produces a result of 0.984375:

    @BETAI(2,4,0.75)

NOTE Like @BETA, @BETAI produces a result accurate to within at least six significant digits.

See Also   @BETA, @GAMMA

@DECIMAL(hexadecimal)

The @DECIMAL function converts a hexadecimal value to its signed decimal equivalent, where *hexadecimal* is a value from 00000000 through FFFFFFFF.

hexadecimal should be entered as text, within double quotation marks (""); can be up to eight characters long; and can contain only numbers from 0 through 9 and letters from A through F (entered as uppercase or lowercase—@DECIMAL is not case-sensitive, so ffff0000 is the same value as FFFF0000).

For example, this function statement returns 123:

    @DECIMAL("7B")

But this one returns ERR because it lacks the double quotation marks (""):

    @DECIMAL(7B)

Be careful to include the double quotation marks when using the @DECIMAL function—it's very easy to forget them, particularly as @HEX, the sister function of @DECIMAL, does not need them. Figure D.2 shows a worksheet with a chart that uses the @DECIMAL function to convert hexadecimal values to decimal values.

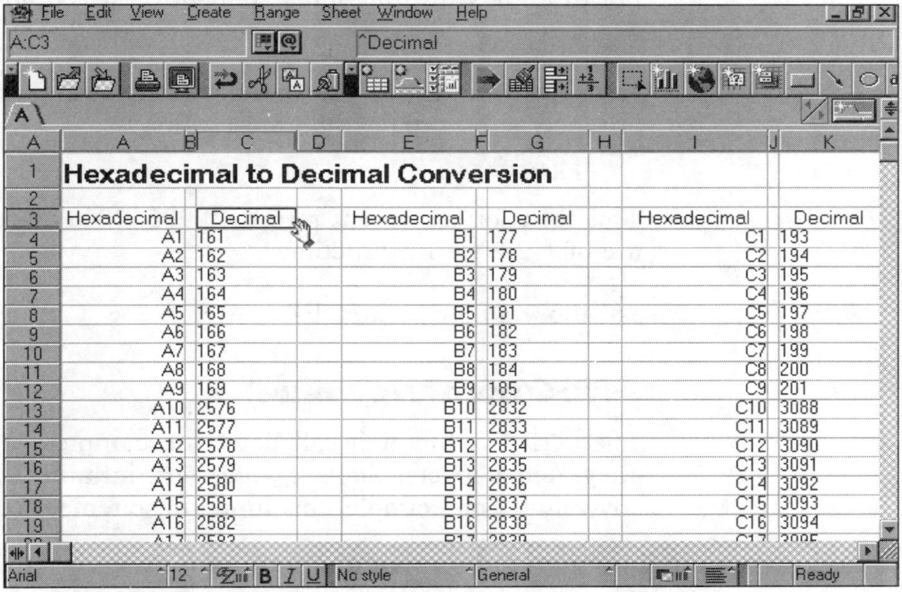

Figure D.2: Using the @DECIMAL function to create a chart showing the decimal equivalents of hexadecimal values. Note that @DECIMAL needs the hexadecimal argument to be entered in double quotation marks (" ").

See Also   @HEX

NOTE Hexadecimal values 00000000–7FFFFFFF represent 0 and all positive decimal values; hexadecimal values 80000000–FFFFFFFF represent negative decimal values.

@ERF(lower-limit,[upper-limit])

The @ERF function is an approximation function that returns the error function integrated between *lower-limit* and *upper-limit*:

▶ *Lower-limit* is any value representing the lower boundary for integrating @ERF.

▶ *Upper-limit* is any value specifying the upper boundary for integrating @ERF.

You can omit *upper-limit*, in which case @ERF integrates between 0 and *lower-limit*.

For example, this function statement returns 0.00466:

    @ERF(2,3)

Note that omitting the second argument—the *upper-limit* argument—produces substantially different results:

    @ERF(2)

This function statement returns 0.995322. Figure D.3 illustrates the use of 1-2-3's error functions.

See Also   @ERFC, @ERFD

@ERFC(numeric_value)

The @ERFC function calculates the complementary error function, integrated between *numeric_value* and infinity. *numeric_value* can be any value. For example, this function statement returns 0.05624:

    @ERFC(1.35)

To return the error function of the absolute value of a cell, use @ERFC in combination with @ABS:

    @ERFC(@ABS(Z255))

Figure D.3 illustrates the use of 1-2-3's error functions.

See Also @ERF, @ERFD

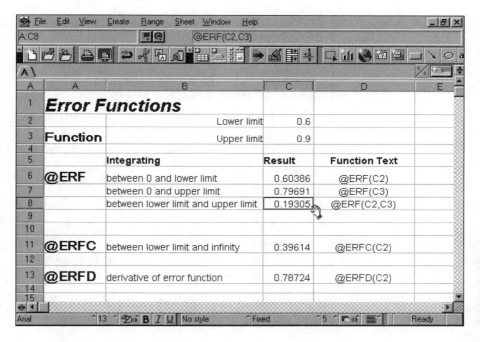

Figure D.3: Using 1-2-3's error functions

@ERFD(numeric_value)

The @ERFD function calculates the derivative of the error function using the formula $(2/@SQRT(@PI))*@EXP(-x^2)$. *numeric_value* can be a value from approximately –106.560 to approximately 106.560; if *numeric_value* is smaller than –106.560 or larger than 106.560, the @ERFD calculation is too large for 1-2-3 to store, and you'll see ERR.

> **WARNING** If *numeric_value* is outside the range –15.102 to 15.102 (i.e., between –106.560 and –15.102 or between 15.102 and 106.560), 1-2-3 will be able to calculate the result of @ERFD but it will not be able to display it. You'll see a series of asterisks in the cell instead.

For example, this function statement returns 0.000139, the derivative of the error function of 3:

    @ERFD(3)

Figure D.3 illustrates the use of 1-2-3's error functions.

See Also   @ERF

@GAMMA(numeric_value)

The @GAMMA function calculates the Gamma distribution function to within six significant figures, where *numeric_value* is any value except 0 and negative integers. For example, this function statement returns 6:

    @GAMMA(4)

See Also   @BETA, @BETAI, @GAMMAI, @GAMMALN

@GAMMAI (numeric_value1,numeric_value2, [complement])

The @GAMMAI function returns the incomplete gamma function to within six significant figures. The arguments for @GAMMAI are as follows:

Argument	Description
numeric_value1	A positive value
numeric_value2	A positive value or 0
complement	(optional) 0 or 1 to specify how 1-2-3 calculates the @GAMMAI function: 0 = P(*numeric_value1,numeric_value*). This is the default if you omit the complement argument. 1 = Q(*numeric_value1, numeric_value*). This equals 1–P(*numeric_value1,numeric_value*).

For example, this function statement returns 0.714943:

    @GAMMA(5,6)

This one returns 0.285057:

    @GAMMAI(5,6,1)

See Also   @GAMMA, @GAMMALN

@GAMMALN(numeric_value)

The @GAMMALN function calculates the natural logarithm of the gamma function, where *numeric_value* is a value greater than 0. For example, this function statement returns 39.33988:

    @GAMMALN(20)

See Also   @GAMMA, @GAMMAI

@HEX(number)

The @HEX function converts a decimal number to its hexadecimal equivalent. *number* can be any value between –2,147,483,648 and 2,147,483,647. If *number* is not an integer, 1-2-3 will truncate it to an integer. For example, this function statement returns E4, the hexadecimal equivalent of 228:

    @HEX(228)

This one returns FFFFFFFC, the hexadecimal equivalent of –4:

    @HEX(-4)

Figure D.4 shows a worksheet with a chart that uses the @HEX function to convert decimal values to hexadecimal values.

> **NOTE** Hexadecimal values 00000000–7FFFFFFF represent 0 and all positive decimal values; hexadecimal values 80000000–FFFFFFFF represent negative decimal values.

See Also   @DECIMAL

Appendix D   Engineering Functions Reference

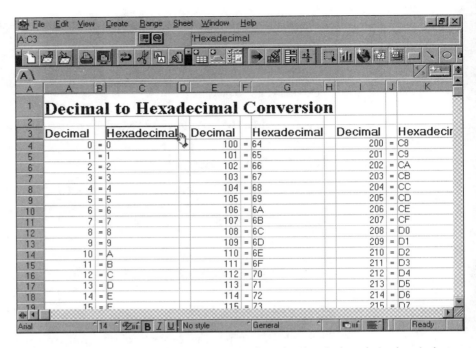

Figure D.4: Using the @HEX function to create a chart showing the hexadecimal equivalents of decimal values

@SERIESSUM(value,power,increment,coefficients)

The @SERIESSUM function calculates the sum of a power series. The arguments for the @SERIESSUM function are as follows:

Argument	Description
value	A value indicating the input value for the power series.
power	A value indicating the initial power to which to raise value.
increment	A value indicating the increment by which to increase value for each term in the series.

coefficients The address or name of a range containing the coefficients by which @SERIESSUM multiplies each successive power of value. The number of cells that coefficients contains determines the number of terms in the series. If coefficients is a range consisting of six cells, there will be six terms in the power series.

For example, say you have a range named POWER that consists of five cells, which contain the values 1, 2, 3, 4, and 5. With an input *value* of 3, a *power* of 4, and an increment of 2, this function statement returns 2914623:

```
@SERIESSUM(3,4,2,POWER)
```

Figure D.5 illustrates this function statement.

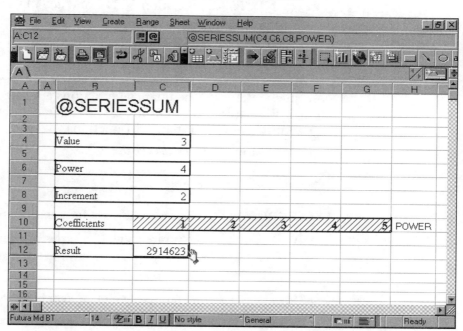

Figure D.5: *Using the @SERIESSUM function to return the sum of a power series*

APPENDIX E

Financial Functions Reference

1-2-3's financial functions include functions to calculate discounted cash flow (for example, @IRR and @NPV), loan amortization (@NPER), depreciation (@DB and @SYD), investment analysis (@RATE), and annuities (@FV).

Overview of the Financial Functions

For quick reference, the financial functions are listed here in Table E.1 in their five categories. They are discussed in detail in the next section, "Descriptions of the Financial Functions."

Table E.1: **Financial Functions Quick Reference**

Function	Returns
@ACCRUED	The accrued interest for a security of a given value
@FV	The future value of a series of equal periodic payment amounts over term periods at a fixed periodic interest rate
@FVAL	The future value of an item based on the present value
@FVAMOUNT	The future value of a sum to be received for a specified number of periods in the future and discounted at a specified interest rate
@IPAYMT	The cumulative interest on a loan

Table E.1: **Financial Functions Quick Reference (continued)**

Function	Returns
@IRATE	A value equivalent to the periodic interest rate of an investment
@NPER	The number of periods required to reach a specified future value at a given interest rate
@PAYMT	The payments necessary to reach a specified principal over a given term at a fixed interest rate
@PMT	The periodic payment required to pay back a loan over a given term at a fixed interest rate
@PMTC	The periodic payment required to pay back a loan over a given term at a fixed interest rate (@PMTC is a version of @PMT adjusted for Canadian mortgage conventions)
@PMTI	The interest paid with each fixed periodic payment on a loan at a specified interest rate
@PPAYMT	The principal value of payments made on a loan
@PRICE	The price per $100 of value for investments that pay a periodic interest
@PV	The present value of a series of equal future cash-flow amounts
@PVAL	The present value of an investment
@PVAMOUNT	The present value of a sum to be received for a specified number of periods in the future and discounted at a specified interest rate
@SPI	The interest paid with each fixed principal payment on a loan at a specified interest rate
@TERM	The number of equal payment amounts required to reach a specified future value at a fixed interest rate

Appendix E Financial Functions Reference

Table E.1: Financial Functions Quick Reference (continued)

Function	Returns
Bonds	
@ACCRUED	The accrued interest for a security of a given value
@DURATION	The annual duration for a security that pays periodic interest
@MDURATION	The modified annual duration for a security that pays periodic interest
@PRICE	The price per $100 of value for investments that pay a periodic interest
@YIELD	The yield on an interest-bearing security
Capital-Budgeting Tools	
@IRR	The internal rate of return from a series of positive and negative cash-flow amounts
@MIRR	The modified internal rate of return for a series of positive and negative cash-flow amounts
@NPV	The net present value of a series of positive or negative future periodic cash-flow amounts
@XIRR	The internal rate of return from a series of inflows and outflows
@XNPV	The net present value of a series of inflows and outflows
Depreciation	
@DB	The depreciation value of an asset, calculated using the declining-balance method
@DDB	The depreciation value of an asset, calculated using the double-declining–balance method
@SLN	The depreciation of an asset, using the straight-line method

Table E.1:   *Financial Functions Quick Reference (continued)*

Function	Returns
Depreciation	
@SYD	The depreciation of an asset, using the sum-of-the-years'-digits method
@VDB	The depreciation of an asset, using the variable-declining-balance method
Annuities	
@CTERM	The number of compounding periods required for a one-time investment earning a fixed periodic interest rate to reach a specified future value
@RATE	The interest rate that will produce a fixed future return from an initial investment over a specified term
International Financial Functions	
@ACCRUED2	The accrued interest for a security of a given value, using Japanese conventions
@FV2	The future value of a series of equal periodic payment amounts over term periods at a fixed periodic interest rate, using Japanese conventions
@PMT2	The periodic payment required to pay back a loan over a given term at a fixed interest rate, using Japanese conventions
@PRICE2	The price per $100 of value for investments that pay a periodic interest, using Japanese conventions
@PV2	The present value of a series of equal future cash-flow amounts, using Japanese conventions
@TERM2	The number of equal payment amounts required to reach a specified future value at a fixed interest rate, using Japanese conventions
@YIELD2	The yield on an interest-bearing security, using Japanese conventions

Descriptions of the Financial Functions

This section contains detailed descriptions of 1-2-3's financial functions.

 NOTE Chapter 8 explains the financial functions as well.

@ACCRUED(settlement,issue,first-interest, coupon,[par],[frequency],[basis])

The @ACCRUED function returns the accrued interest for securities with periodic interest payments. @ACCRUED works for short, standard, and long coupon periods.

The arguments for the @ACCRUED function are as follows:

Argument	Description
settlement	A date number indicating the security's settlement date. Note that *settlement* must be greater than *issue* for 1-2-3 to produce a valid result; if it is less, @ACCRUED will return ERR.
issue	A date number indicating the security's issue date or dated date.
first-interest	A date number indicating the security's first interest date. Note that *first-interest* must be greater than *issue* for 1-2-3 to produce a valid result; if it is less, @ACCRUED will return ERR.
coupon	Zero or a positive value, indicating the security's annual coupon rate.
par	A value indicating the security's par value. The par value is the amount of principal paid at maturity; the default setting if you omit the *par* argument is 100.
frequency	1, 2, 4, or 12, specifying the number of coupon payments per year as follows: 1 Annual

2 Semiannual (this is the default if *frequency* is omitted)
4 Quarterly
12 Monthly

basis   An optional value specifying the type of day-count to use, as follows:
0 30/360 (this is the default if you omit *basis*)
1 Actual/actual
2 Actual/360
3 Actual/365

WARNING Note that you cannot use an optional argument unless you use those that precede it. For example, you cannot use *basis* in @ACCRUED if you do not specify *frequency*, and you cannot use *frequency* if you do not specify *par*.

For example, Figure E.1 illustrates a bond with a settlement date of November 28, 1996; an issue date of April 1, 1995; a first-interest date of June 1, 1995; a coupon rate of 8.125 percent; a par of 100; a quarterly frequency; and a 30/360 day-count basis. To work out the result, you could enter this formula:

```
@ACCRUED(@DATE(98,11,28),@DATE(97,4,1),@DATE(97,6,1),
0.08125,100,4,0)
```

It results in 1.96354. But you would probably find it much easier to enter the values into a range of cells (here these values are entered into cells B3..B9) and set up a function statement to provide a result for whatever values you enter in those cells. In Figure E.1, cell B11 contains the function statement

```
@ACCRUED(B3,B4,B5,B6,B7,B8,B9)
```

It produces the same result, 1.96354, but is much easier to work with and more flexible. Creating this type of spreadsheet can help you greatly with projects requiring swift what-if analyses.

See Also   @ACCRUED2, @PRICE, @YIELD, @YIELD2

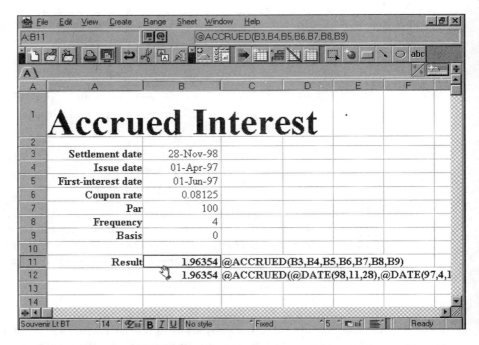

Figure E.1: *Using the @ACCRUED function to return the accrued interest for securities with periodic interest payments*

@CTERM(interest,future-value,present-value)

The @CTERM function returns the number of compounding periods required for an investment of the amount *present-value* to grow to the amount *future-value* while earning a fixed rate of *interest* per compounding period.

present-value and *future-value* are any values. Both must be either positive or negative. *interest* can be any value greater than −1 except 0.

For example, suppose the high-risk bonds in which you just invested a $25,000 windfall have hit a good streak, returning 22 percent annually (a rate of 0.22). If this rate holds (fat chance), how long will it take you to double your windfall? You could use this function statement to find out:

```
@CTERM(.22,50000,25000)
```

The answer is 3.49 years. Not bad at all.

Descriptions of the Financial Functions

To run @CTERM calculations using interest compounded monthly or daily instead of yearly, divide both the interest rate and the result by 12 or 360, respectively, as in these examples:

@CTERM(.22/12,50000,25000)/12

@CTERM(.22/360,50000,25000)/12

See Also   @NPER, @TERM

@DB(cost,salvage,life,period)

The @DB function returns the depreciation allowance of an asset using the fixed-declining balance method. This method slows the rate of depreciation in comparison to the double-declining balance method, so more depreciation expense occurs (and can be written off) in later periods. Depreciation stops when the asset's book value (its total cost minus its total depreciation) reaches the salvage value.

The arguments for the @DB function are as follows:

Argument	Description
cost	The amount originally paid for the asset, entered as any positive value or 0. (Note that if cost is given as 0, @DB will give a result of 0.)
salvage	The estimated value of the asset at the end of its useful life, entered as any positive value or 0. @DB will return a negative value if *salvage* is greater than *cost*.
life	The number of periods the asset takes to depreciate from its *cost* value to its *salvage* value. *life* is any value greater than or equal to 1 and less than or equal to *period*.
period	The time for which you want to find the depreciation allowance, entered as a value greater than or equal to 1.

NOTE The *life* and *period* arguments must be expressed in the same units (usually years) for the @DB function to produce a usable result.

For example, the 100-MHz Pentium on which you're running 1-2-3 cost you $3,000 a few days ago. Its useful life is five years, after which it will have a salvage value of $600. To calculate the depreciation expense for the third year, you could use this function statement:

```
@DB(3000,600,5,3)
```

The expense would be $433.72. Figure E.2 illustrates the depreciation on the Pentium computer for its five-year life span.

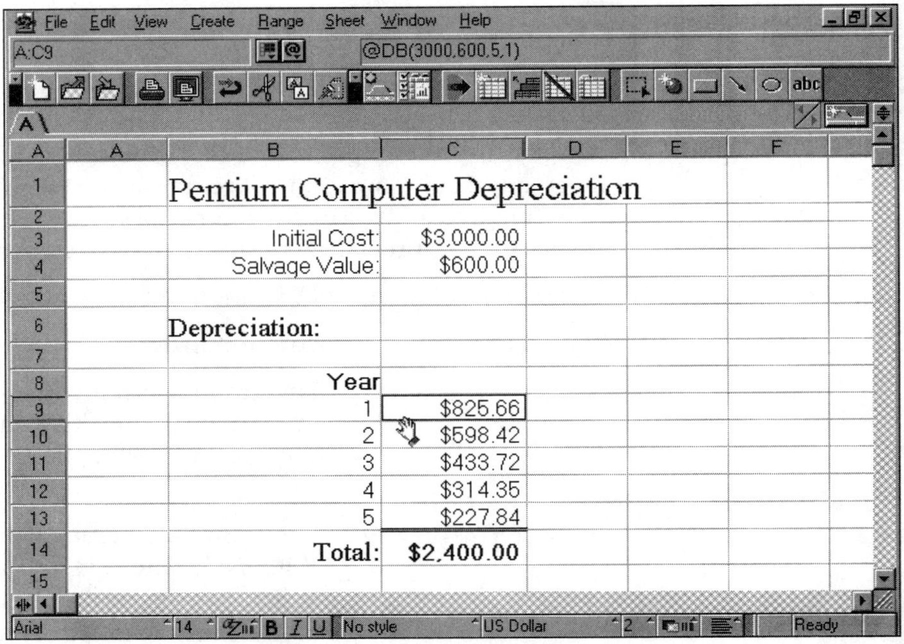

Figure E.2: Using the @DB function to calculate depreciation on a computer system

See Also   @DDB, @SLN, @SYD, @VDB

@DDB(cost,salvage,life,period)

The @DDB function returns the depreciation allowance of an asset using the double-declining balance method. (Chapter 8 offers worksheet examples using the depreciation functions.)

Descriptions of the Financial Functions

TIP The difference between the fixed-declining balance method (calculated by the function @DB) is that the double-declining balance method accelerates the rate of depreciation so that more depreciation expense occurs (and can be written off) in earlier periods than in later ones. As with the fixed-declining balance method, in the double-declining balance method, depreciation stops when the book value of the asset (the asset's total cost minus its total depreciation over all prior periods) reaches the salvage value.

The arguments for the @DDB function are as follows:

Argument	Description
cost	The amount originally paid for the asset, entered as any positive value or 0. (Note that if cost is given as 0, @DB will give a result of 0.)
salvage	The estimated value of the asset at the end of its useful life, entered as any positive value or 0. @DB will return a negative value if *salvage* is greater than *cost*. (Note that *salvage* can be the same as *cost*, though not greater.)
life	The number of periods the asset takes to depreciate from its *cost* value to its *salvage* value. *life* is any value greater than or equal to 2 and less than or equal to *period*.
period	The time for which you want to find the depreciation allowance, entered as a value greater than or equal to 1.

NOTE The *life* and *period* arguments must be expressed in the same units (usually years) for the @DB function to produce a usable result. Note also that you may want to use @VDB rather than @DDB to accurately depreciate an asset that has a relatively low salvage value.

For example, that $3,000, 100-MHz Pentium you just depreciated in the @DB section produces very different figures when depreciated with the double-declining balance method. Using the format

@DDB(3000,600,5,4)

you would establish the third-year depreciation for the Pentium to be $432.00, as shown in Figure E.3.

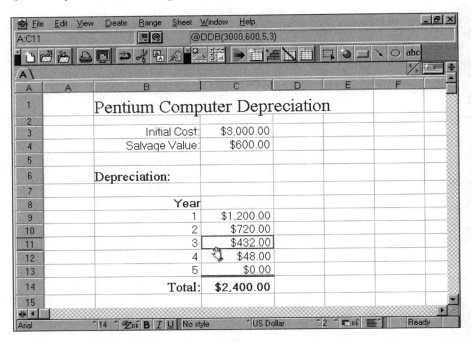

Figure E.3: Depreciation using the @DDB function produces very different results from depreciation using the @DB function.

See Also   @DB, @SLN, @SYD, @VDB

@DURATION(settlement,maturity,coupon,yield, [frequency],[basis])

The @DURATION function returns the annual duration for a security that pays periodic interest. (*Duration* is the weighted average term to maturity of the cash flows of a security.)

The arguments for @DURATION are as follows:

Argument	Description
settlement	A date number representing the security's settlement date.

maturity	A date number representing the security's maturity date. *maturity* must be greater than settlement; otherwise @DURATION will return ERR.
coupon	Any positive value (or 0) representing the security's annual coupon rate.
yield	Any positive value (or 0) representing the annual yield.
frequency	An optional value specifying the number of coupon payments per year, as follows: 1 Annual 2 Semiannual (this is the default if *frequency* is omitted) 4 Quarterly 12 Monthly
basis	An optional value specifying the type of day-count to use, as follows: 0 30/360 (this is the default if you omit *basis*) 1 Actual/actual 2 Actual/360 3 Actual/365

WARNING You cannot use an optional argument unless you use those that precede it. For example, you cannot use *basis* in @DURATION if you do not specify *frequency*.

For example, say you have a security with a February 1, 1995 settlement date and a July 1, 1999 maturity date. The quarterly coupon rate is 2.85 percent, and the annual yield is 6.5 percent. The bond uses an actual/365 day-count basis. You could determine the security's annual duration by using this function statement:

    @DURATION(@DATE(95,2,1),@DATE(99,7,1),0.0285,0.065,4,3)

It returns 4.127.

See Also @ACCRUED, @MDURATION, @PRICE, @YIELD

TIP To work out the modified annual duration for a security, use @MDURATION instead of @DURATION.

@FV(payments,interest,term)

The @FV function returns the future value of an investment, based on a series of equal payments, earning a constant rate of *interest*, over the number of *payment* periods in *term*. *payments* and *term* can be any values; *interest* is a value greater than –1. (See Chapter 8 for more examples of using the @FV function.)

TIP The @FV function is included in this release of 1-2-3 for backward compatibility with previous releases. This release also contains @FVAL, a significantly improved version of @FV that adds an optional *type* argument to specify whether the investment is an ordinary annuity or an annuity due. See the next section, "@FVAL," for details. If you don't need the extra options that @FVAL includes, however, @FV still works perfectly well and is easier to type—so there's really no reason to stop using it.

For example, you reckon to add $5,000 to your 401K plan, where it should earn 13 percent interest every year for the next ten years. To calculate how much it will be worth at the end of that time, you could use this function statement:

    @FV(5000,0.13,10)

It returns a paltry $92,098.75. Twenty years—@FV(5000,0.13,20)—produces a much more promising $404,734.14. Ah well, investing always was a long-term game....

See Also @FV2, @FVAL, @FVAMOUNT, @NPV, @PV, @PVAL, @PVAMOUNT

@FVAL(payments,interest,term,[type], [present-value])

@FVAL is an improved version of the @FV function and calculates the future value of an investment with a specified present-value over a specified term, based on periodic, constant payments and earning a periodic interest rate. By specifying a value for *type*, you can have @FVAL calculate for either an ordinary annuity or an annuity due.

The arguments for @FVAL are similar to those for @FV:

Argument	Description
payments	A value indicating the fixed, periodic payment. Note that *payments* cannot change during the life of the annuity.
interest	A value greater than −1 indicating the constant interest rate per period.
term	A positive value indicating the total number of period payments. Note that *term* cannot be negative.
type	Zero or 1. *type* is an optional argument used to specify whether 1-2-3 calculates for an ordinary annuity or for an annuity due: 0 Indicates an ordinary annuity, in which the payments are due at the end of a period. This is the default if you omit the argument *type*. 1 Indicates an annuity due, in which the payments are due at the beginning of a period.
present-value	Any value representing the present value of the series of future payments. If you omit *present-value*, 1-2-3 uses the default value of 0. Note that, since *present-value* and *type* are both optional arguments, to use *present-value* you need to specify *type*.

WARNING Be careful when using @FVAL to use the same period for calculating *interest* as you used for *term*. When calculating a monthly payment, for instance, you will need to enter *interest* and *term* in monthly units—perhaps by multiplying the number of years in term by 12 and dividing the interest rate by 12.

To illustrate the difference between @FVAL and @FV, let's take the example used for @FV again: You plan to deposit $5,000 a year for the next ten years into your 401K plan, where it should earn 13 percent interest. To calculate how much it will be worth at the end of that time, based on payments made at the end of each year, you could use this function:

    @FVAL(5000,0.13,10)

It returns $92,098.75, the same as for @FV(5000,0.13,10). But if you make the payments at the beginning of each year, it returns $104,071.58:

    @FVAL(5000,0.13,10,1)

See Also   @FV, @NPV, @PV, @PVAL

@IPAYMT(principal,interest,term,start-period, [end-period],[type],[future-value])

The @IPAYMT function returns the cumulative interest payment of the periodic payment on a loan (*principal*), based on periodic, constant payments at a given interest rate over *term*. By contrast, the @PPAYMT function returns the principal payment on a loan (*principal*), based on periodic, constant payments at a given interest rate over *term*.

The arguments for @IPAYMT are as follows:

Argument	Description
principal	A value representing the amount borrowed.
term	Any value except zero, indicating the number of periods in the loan. Be sure to use the same units for *term* as you use for *interest*.
interest	A decimal or percentage value greater than −1, representing the fixed periodic interest rate for the loan. Use the same units for *interest* as you use for *term*.
start-period	A value greater than or equal to 1 (but not greater than *term*) representing the point in *term* at which the calculation of interest is to start.
end-period	A value greater than or equal to 1 (but not greater than *term*) representing the point in

	term at which the calculation of interest is to stop. The default setting for *end-period* (if you omit the argument) is the same as *start-period*.
type	Zero or 1. *type* is an optional argument used to specify whether 1-2-3 calculates for an ordinary annuity or for an annuity due: 0 Indicates an ordinary annuity, in which the payments are due at the end of a period. This is the default if you omit the argument *type*. 1 Indicates an annuity due, in which the payments are due at the beginning of a period.
future-value	Any value representing the future value of the series of payments. Note that this is an optional argument; if you do not specify *future-value*, 1-2-3 will use the default value of 0.

WARNING You cannot use an optional argument unless you use those that precede it. For example, you cannot use *type* in @IPAYMT if you do not specify *end-period*.

For example, suppose you were thinking of borrowing $25,000 for two years to buy a shiny new sport-utility vehicle with big tires. The best rate of interest you can get is 7.2 percent; how much money will you pay in interest in the first year? You would use this function statement to find out:

    @IPAYMT(25000,0.072,3,1)

The answer is $1,800.

See Also   @PMT, @PPAYMT

TIP To calculate the principal payment on a loan (rather than the interest payment), use the @PPAYMT function instead of the @IPAYMT function.

Appendix E Financial Functions Reference

@IRATE(term,payment,present-value,[type], [future-value],[guess])

The @IRATE function returns the necessary periodic interest rate to produce *future-value* from an annuity of *present-value* over the number of compounding periods in *term*.

The arguments for the @IRATE function are as follows:

Argument	Description
term	Any positive integer representing the number of periodic payments.
payment	A value expressing the amount of the periodic payments.
present-value	A value representing the current value of the investment.
type	Zero or 1. *type* is an optional argument used to specify whether 1-2-3 calculates for an ordinary annuity or for an annuity due:
	0 Indicates an ordinary annuity, in which the payments are due at the end of a period. This is the default if you omit the argument *type*.
	1 Indicates an annuity due, in which the payments are due at the beginning of a period.
future-value	Any value representing the future value of the series of payments. Note that this is an optional argument; if you do not specify *future-value*, 1-2-3 will use the default value of 0.
guess	A value from 0 through 1 representing your estimate of the interest rate. This is an optional argument; 1-2-3 uses the default setting of 0.1 (10 percent) if you omit the *guess* argument.

WARNING You cannot use an optional argument unless you use those that precede it. For example, you cannot use *guess* in @IRATE if you do not specify *future-value*.

For example, if you want to buy a new house for $200,000 and can afford payments of $1,500 for twenty years, you can figure out the interest rate needed by using this function statement:

    @IRATE(20*12,1500,200000,0,0)

It produces 0.005479—an interest rate of 0.05479 percent compounded monthly.

You can also use @IRATE with the *guess* argument, by starting with a *guess* value that seems reasonable. Note that there may be more than one possible solution, so keep trying values for *guess* if you get results less than 0 or greater than 1.

TIP @IRATE will return ERR if it cannot approximate the result to within 0.0000001 after thirty calculation iterations. If you find this happening with a number of your entries for *guess*, try using the @NPV function to establish a better value for *guess*. If you find @NPV returns a positive value, adjust your value for *guess* upwards; if @NPV returns a negative value, adjust your value for *guess* downwards. (When your *guess* is accurate, @NPV will return 0.)

See Also   @FV, @FVAL, @NPV, @PV, @PVAL, @RATE

@IRR(guess,range)

The @IRR function calculates the internal rate of return on an investment—the interest rate received for an investment consisting of payments (negative value) that occur at regular periods. You can use @IRR to calculate the profitability of an investment by discounting the investment's cash benefits over time to zero, including the initial cash cost of the investment.

TIP Typical uses for the internal rate of return are to rank different projects—for example, real-estate investments or joint ventures—by profitability and to make capital-asset budget decisions.

The internal rate of return tries to produce a single number summarizing the merits of a project, a single number not dependent on the interest rate (hence the appellation *internal*—the number depends solely on the cash flows of the project). The general rule of investment is to accept a project whose internal rate of return is greater than the discount rate, and to reject a project whose internal rate of return is less than the discount rate.

The arguments for the @IRR function are as follows:

Argument	Description
guess	A decimal or percentage value between 0 and 1 (e.g., 0.15 for 15 percent) representing your estimate of the internal rate of return.
range	The address or name of a range that contains the cash flows. Negative numbers represent cash outflows and positive numbers represent cash inflows. The first cash-flow amount in the range is usually a negative number (i.e., a cash outflow) representing the investment.

TIP For many calculations, you can leave *guess* at 0 (the default setting), but *guess* is more important when working with very large cash flows.

WARNING When using the @IRR function, beware that 1-2-3 includes any blank cells or labels contained in *range* in the calculation. It assigns the value 0 to blank cells and labels.

To assess an investment, you can combine @IRR with other financial functions (such as @NPV).

TIP @IRR will return ERR if it cannot approximate the result to within 0.0000001 after thirty calculation iterations. If you find this happening with a number of your entries for *guess,* try using the @NPV function to establish a better value for *guess*. If you find @NPV returns a positive value, adjust your value for *guess* upwards; if @NPV returns a negative value, adjust your value for *guess* downwards. (When your *guess* is accurate, @NPV will return 0.)

For example, Figure E.4 illustrates a project that involves an initial outlay of $100,000 and promises to bring in cash flows as shown in cells D5..D14. You could calculate the internal rate of return with the function statement that appears in cell C16:

```
@IRR(0,C4..C14)
```

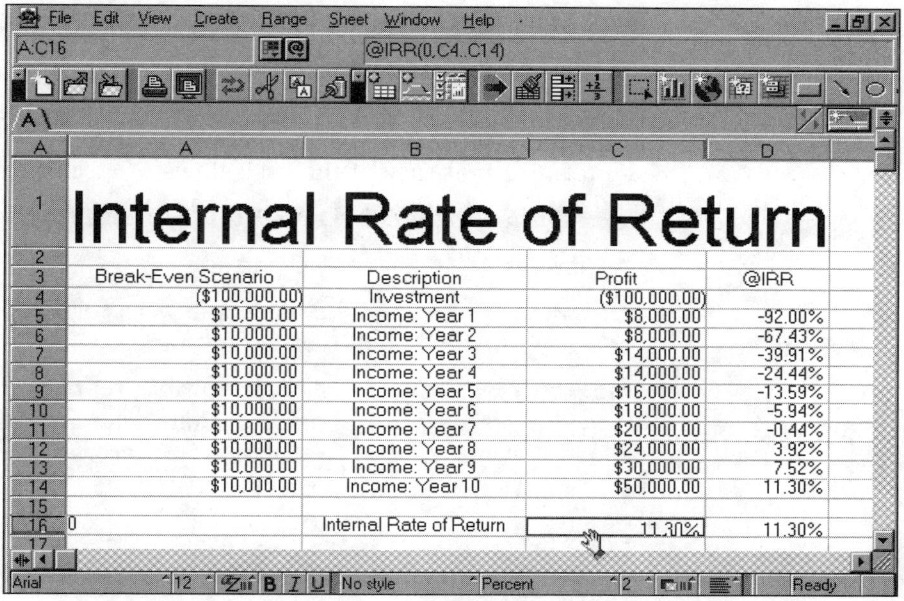

Figure E.4: *Using @IRR to assess the profitability of an investment*

This produces 11.30%. For comparison, cell A16 contains the function statement to calculate the internal rate of return for the break-even scenario:

```
@IRR(A4..A14)
```

It of course returns 0. (Cells D5 through D14 contain @IRR function statements to illustrate how the rate changes.)

Alternatively, you could enter the cash-flow values in a range called CASHFLOW and the *guess* value in a cell named GUESS, and use a function statement such as

```
@IRR(GUESS,CASHFLOW)
```

See Also   @FV, @FVAL, @MIRR, @NPV, @PV, @PVAL, @RATE @XIRR, @XNPV

NOTE For more examples of using this function, see Chapter 8.

@MDURATION(settlement,maturity,coupon,yield, [frequency],[basis])

The @MDURATION function returns the modified annual duration for a security that pays periodic interest. (*Duration* is the weighted average term to maturity of the cash flows of a security.)

The arguments for @MDURATION are as follows:

Argument	Description
settlement	A date number representing the security's settlement date.
maturity	A date number representing the security's maturity date. *maturity* must be greater than settlement; otherwise @MDURATION will return ERR.
coupon	Any positive value (or 0) representing the security's annual coupon rate.
yield	Any positive value (or 0) representing the annual yield.
frequency	1, 2, 4, or 12: an optional value specifying the number of coupon payments per year as follows: 1 Annual 2 Semiannual (this is the default if *frequency* is omitted) 4 Quarterly 12 Monthly
basis	An optional value specifying the type of day-count to use, as follows: 0 30/360 (this is the default if *basis* is omitted) 1 Actual/actual 2 Actual/360 3 Actual/365

WARNING You cannot use an optional argument unless you use those that precede it. For example, you cannot use *basis* in @MDURATION if you do not specify *frequency*.

For example, say you have a security with a February 1, 1995 settlement date and a July 1, 1999 maturity date. The quarterly coupon rate is 2.85 percent, and the annual yield is 6.5 percent. The bond uses an actual/365 day-count basis. You could determine the security's modified annual duration by using this function statement:

    @MDURATION(@DATE(95,2,1),@DATE(99,7,1),0.0285,0.065,4,3)

It returns 4.06066—substantially different from the 4.126652 that the @DURATION function produces for the same data.

TIP To work out the (unmodified) annual duration for a security, use @DURATION instead of @MDURATION.

See Also   @ACCRUED, @DURATION, @PRICE, @YIELD

@MIRR(range,finance-rate,reinvest-rate)

The @MIRR function calculates the modified internal rate of return on an investment—the interest rate received for an investment consisting of payments (negative value) that occur at regular periods.

The arguments for @MIRR are as follows:

Argument	Description
range	The address or name of a range that contains the cash flows. Negative numbers represent cash outflows and positive numbers represent cash inflows. The first cash-flow amount in the range is usually a negative number (i.e., a cash outflow) representing the investment.
finance-rate	A value indicating the interest rate paid on the money used in cash flows.

reinvest-rate	A value indicating the interest rate you receive on cash flows that you reinvest.
type	An optional argument specifying when the cash flow occurs, as follows: 0 Indicates a cash flow at the beginning of the period. This is the default if you omit the *type* argument. 1 Indicates a cash flow at the end of the period.

WARNING Note that any blank cells or labels within the *range* argument are included in the @MIRR calculation. They receive a value of 0.

You can combine the @MIRR function with other financial functions (for example, @NPV) to assess the profitability of an investment.

As an illustration of using the @MIRR function, assume you own a record store, Protozoa Records, that you purchased at the end of 1989 for $250,000. As shown in Figure E.5, you've made a steady profit, though your expenses have been growing steadily too. Your profit or loss is stored in the range PROFIT OR LOSS in the worksheet, currently cells D4..D12. Your finance rate is stored in the range named FINANCE RATE, and your reinvestment rate in the range named REINVESTMENT.

Cell D14 contains the function statement to work out the modified internal rate of return on your investment in Protozoa Records:

    @MIRR(PROFIT OR LOSS,FINANCE RATE,REINVESTMENT)

It returns 0.16136106, or 16.14 percent. Were you able to reinvest your profits at the end of the year rather than at the beginning, you could make rather more money:

    @MIRR(PROFIT OR LOSS,FINANCE RATE,REINVESTMENT,1)

This function statement returns 0.170603609, or 17.06 percent.

See Also   @IRR

Descriptions of the Financial Functions

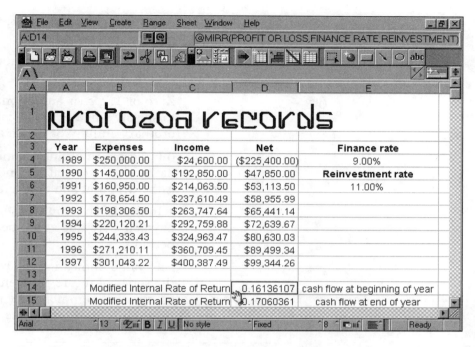

Figure E.5: *Using the @MIRR function to calculate the modified internal rate of return on an investment*

@NPER(payments,interest,future-value,[type], [present-value])

The @NPER function returns the number of periods required for a series of equal payments with a specified *present-value* to accumulate a *future-value* at a periodic rate of *interest*.

> **NOTE** The @NPER function is an enhanced version of the @TERM function. Unlike @TERM, you can specify a present value, and you can also specify a value for the *type* argument to make @NPER calculate for either an ordinary annuity or an annuity due.

The arguments for the @NPER function are as follows:

Argument	Description
payments	Any value except 0, indicating the value of the equal investments.

interest	Any value greater than −1, indicating the periodic interest rate.
future-value	A value indicating the amount you want to accumulate.
type	Zero or 1. *type* is an optional argument used to specify whether 1-2-3 calculates for an ordinary annuity or for an annuity due:
	0 Indicates an ordinary annuity, in which the payments are due at the end of a period. This is the default if you omit the argument *type*.
	1 Indicates an annuity due, in which the payments are due at the beginning of a period.
present-value	Any value, indicating the present value of the series of future payments. *present-value* is an optional argument; if you omit *present-value*, 1-2-3 uses the value of 0.

WARNING Note that you cannot use an optional argument unless you use those that precede it. For example, you cannot use *present-value* in @NPER if you do not specify *type*.

As an example of @NPER, assume that you have the princely sum of $1,776 in your savings account, where it earns a steady 8.25 percent interest. Being patriotic, you plan to deposit the same amount into the account at the end of each year. How long will it take you to reach your target of $17,760 for your sabbatical walk from Alaska to Tierra del Fuego? To find out, you use this function statement:

@NPER(1776,0.0825,17760,0,1776)

It returns 6.56 years. Bear in mind that the fractional part of the result means that you'll get the sabbatical funds only at the end of the sixth year.

You can use @NPER just as you would use @TERM—for example, to calculate the number of periods necessary to pay back a loan. For the loan of $25,000 you foolishly took out from a Vegas shark at a happy 25 percent interest, you might use the following function statement to find out how long it will take you to regain your feet if you can pay off $7,500 a year:

    @NPER(7500,0.25,-25000)

The answer is 8.03 years. Note that this function statement returns a negative value because the loan amount is entered as a negative value, −25000. Either ignore the negative—the number of years for the repayment is unfortunately always going to be positive—or add the @ABS function to the function statement to return a positive result:

    @ABS(@NPER(7500,0.25,-25000))

See Also   @CTERM, @TERM

@NPV(interest,range,[type])

The @NPV function calculates the net present value of a series of future estimated cash-flow values indicated by *range* discounted at a fixed periodic rate of *interest*.

> **TIP** The net present value of an investment is today's value of a series of future payments (negative cash flows) and income (positive cash flows). You can use @NPV either to evaluate an investment or to compare one investment with others by calculating the initial investment necessary to achieve a certain cash outflow at a certain rate.

The arguments for the @NPV function are as follows:

Argument	Description
interest	A value greater than −1 indicating the constant interest rate per period.
range	The range containing the cash flows, entered either as a range name or a range address. Note that *range* cannot be more than a single row or a single column—if it is, @NPV will return ERR.

type	Zero or 1. *type* is an optional argument used to specify whether 1-2-3 calculates for an ordinary annuity or for an annuity due:
	0 Indicates an ordinary annuity, in which the payments are due at the end of a period. This is the default if you omit the argument *type*.
	1 Indicates an annuity due, in which the payments are due at the beginning of a period.

Figure E.6 illustrates the use of @NPV to estimate the value of an investment discounted to today's dollars. The range named CASH (cells C3..C11) contains an initial investment of $66,000 and cash returns for the years 1995–2000 of $2,800.00, $5,320.00, $10,108.00, $19,205.20, $36,489.88, and $69,330.77, respectively. Cell C13 contains the function statement

@NPV(0.1,CASH)

It calculates the net present value of the investments at a 10 percent discount rate; the result is $7,202.56. If payments are made at the beginning of each period rather than at the end, the result is different:

@NPV(0.1,CASH,1)

This statement produces $7,922.82.

NOTE For more about @NPV, see Chapter 8.

See Also   @FV, @PV @XNPV

@PAYMT(principal,interest,term,[type], [future-value])

The @PAYMT function calculates the payment on a loan (principal) at a given rate of *interest* for a specified number of payment periods indicated by *term*.

NOTE The @PAYMT function is similar to the @PMT function but can calculate for either an ordinary annuity or an annuity due, depending on the *type* specified.

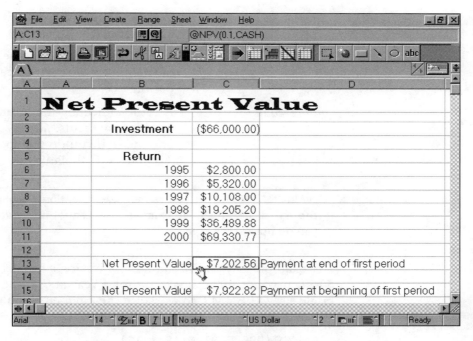

Figure E.6: *Using the @NPV function to calculate the net present value of an asset*

The arguments for the @PAYMT function are as follows:

Argument	Description
principal	A value indicating the amount borrowed.
interest	A decimal or percentage value greater than −1, indicating the interest rate of the loan. Note that the period used to calculate *interest* must be the same as the period used for *term*. If necessary, divide the annual interest rate by 12 to get the monthly interest and multiply the term by 12.
term	A value indicating the number of periods of the loan.
type	Zero or 1. *type* is an optional argument used to specify whether 1-2-3 calculates for an ordinary annuity or for an annuity due:
	0 Indicates an ordinary annuity, in which the payments are due at the end of a

	period. This is the default if you omit the argument *type*.
	1 Indicates an annuity due, in which the payments are due at the beginning of a period.
future-value	A value indicating the future value of the series of payments. *future-value* is an optional argument; if you do not specify *future-value*, 1-2-3 uses the default value of 0.

WARNING Note that you cannot use an optional argument unless you use those that precede it. For example, you cannot use *future-value* in @PAYMT if you do not specify *type*.

For example, say you're thinking of buying a hundred-CD changer for $799. If you want to finance it for a year at 7.75 percent interest, you could use @PAYMT to work out the payments you'd need to make on the first day of each month to pay it off:

@PAYMT(799,0.0775/12,1*12)

This returns a monthly payment of $69.41.

See Also   @IPAYMT, @PMT, @PMTC, @PPAYMT, @TERM

@PMT(principal,interest,term)

The @PMT function calculates the payment on a loan (*principal*) at a given rate of *interest* for a specified number of payment periods indicated by *term*.

TIP The @PMT function is included in 1-2-3 97 Edition for backward compatibility with older versions of 1-2-3. @PMT assumes that the investment being calculated is an ordinary annuity. Generally speaking, @PMT has been largely superseded by the @PAYMT function (discussed earlier in this appendix), which allows you to calculate for either an ordinary annuity or an annuity due. However, if you don't need the extra amenities that @PAYMT offers, @PMT remains a valid and viable function—and in fact is rather easier to use than @PAYMT, if only because it is shorter to type.

Descriptions of the Financial Functions

The arguments for the @PMT function are as follows:

Argument	Description
principal	A value indicating the amount borrowed.
interest	A decimal or percentage value greater than −1, indicating the interest rate of the loan. Note that the period used to calculate *interest* must be the same as the period used for *term*. If necessary, divide the annual interest rate by 12 to get the monthly interest and multiply the term by 12.
term	A value indicating the number of periods of the loan.

For example, suppose you're considering taking out a loan of $100,000 to expand your business of teaching sign language to primates. You'll be able to finance the loan for six years at 3.85 percent interest, and you'll be making payments on the last day of each month. To work out how much those payments will be, use this function statement:

    @PMT(100000,0.0385/12,6*12)

It returns $1557.69. Note that to calculate for payments at the beginning of each month rather than at the end of each month, you'd need to use the @PAYMT function rather than the @PMT function.

NOTE Chapter 8 also discusses the @PMT function.

See Also   @IPAYMT, @PAYMT, @PMTC, @PMTI, @PMT2, @PPAYMT, @SPI, @TERM

@PMTC(principal,interest,term)

The @PMTC function calculates the payment on a loan (*principal*) at a given rate of *interest* for a specified number of payment periods indicated by *term*. @PMTC is a variant of @PMT adapted to support Canadian mortgage conventions.

The arguments for the @PMTC function are as follows:

Argument	Description
principal	A value indicating the amount borrowed.
interest	A decimal or percentage value greater than −1, indicating the interest rate of the loan. Note that the period used to calculate *interest* must be the same as the period used for *term*. If necessary, divide the annual interest rate by 12 to get the monthly interest and multiply the term by 12.
term	A value indicating the number of periods of the loan.

As an illustration of @PMTC, consider the following example. You're considering taking out a mortgage of $200,000 to buy a house in either the U.S. or Canada. Either way, you'll be using U.S. dollars and suffering 9 percent interest for ten years. To find out how much you'd be paying on the loan each year in Canada, you could use the following function statement:

    @PMTC(200000,0.09,10)

This returns $20,818.86, a fairly painful blow to the third button of the financial waistcoat—but not nearly as bad as you'd be paying in the U.S.:

    @PMT(200000,0.09,10)

This returns $31,164.02. Time to emigrate and telecommute.

See Also   @IPAYMT, @PAYMT, @PMT, @PPAYMT, @TERM

@PPAYMT(principal,interest,term,start-period, [end-period],[type],[future-value])

The @PPAYMT function returns the principal payment on a loan (*principal*), based on periodic, constant payments at a given interest rate over *term*. The arguments for @PPAYMT are as follows:

Argument	Description
principal	A value representing the amount borrowed.

term	Any value except 0, indicating the number of periods in the loan. Be sure to use the same units for *term* as you use for *interest*.
interest	A decimal or percentage value greater than −1, representing the fixed periodic interest rate for the loan. Use the same units for *interest* as you use for *term*.
start-period	A value greater than or equal to 1 (but not greater than *term*) representing the point in *term* at which the calculation of interest is to start.
end-period	A value greater than or equal to 1 (but not greater than *term*) representing the point in *term* at which the calculation of interest is to stop. The default setting for *end-period* (if you omit the argument) is the same as *start-period*.
type	Zero or 1. *type* is an optional argument used to specify whether 1-2-3 calculates for an ordinary annuity or for an annuity due: 0 Indicates an ordinary annuity, in which the payments are due at the end of a period. This is the default if you omit the argument *type*. 1 Indicates an annuity due, in which the payments are due at the beginning of a period.
future-value	Any value representing the future value of the series of payments. Note that this is an optional argument; if you do not specify *future-value*, 1-2-3 will use the default value of 0.

WARNING Note that you cannot use an optional argument unless you use those that precede it. For example, you cannot use *type* in @PPAYMT if you do not specify *end-period*.

For example, suppose you were thinking of borrowing $25,000 for two years at 7.2 percent interest to buy a shiny new Monster Truck with jacked-up suspension and gigantic tires. How much money would you pay against the principal of the loan in the first year? To find out, you could use this function statement:

@PPAYMT(25000,0.072,3,1)

The answer is $7,761.

 TIP To calculate the interest payment on a loan (rather than the principal payment), use the @IPAYMT function instead of the @PPAYMT function.

See Also @IPAYMT, @PMT

@PRICE (settlement,maturity,coupon,yield, [redemption],[frequency],[basis])

The @PRICE function returns the price per $100 face value for securities that pay periodic interest. The arguments for the @PRICE function are as follows:

Argument	Description
settlement	A date number representing the security's settlement date.
maturity	A date number representing the security's maturity date. *maturity* must be greater than settlement; otherwise @PRICE will return ERR.
coupon	Any positive value (or 0) representing the security's annual coupon rate.
yield	Any positive value (or 0) representing the annual yield.
redemption	Any positive value (or 0) representing the security's redemption value per $100 face value. The default value for *redemption* is 100.
frequency	1, 2, 4, or 12: an optional value specifying the number of coupon payments per year as follows: 1 Annual

Descriptions of the Financial Functions

                                          2 Semiannual (this is the default if *frequency* is omitted)
                                          4 Quarterly
                                          12 Monthly

basis   An optional value specifying the type of day-count to use, as follows:
                                          0 30/360 (this is the default if you omit *basis*)
                                            1 Actual/actual
                                            2 Actual/360
                                            3 Actual/365

WARNING You cannot use an optional argument unless you use those that precede it. For example, you cannot use *basis* in @PRICE if you do not specify *frequency*, and you cannot use *frequency* if you do not specify *redemption*.

For example, say you needed to establish the price of a bond that has the following terms:

▶ A settlement date of April 1, 1994

▶ A maturity date of January 1, 2001

▶ A quarterly coupon rate of 4.5 percent

▶ An annual yield of 5.7 percent

▶ A redemption value of $120

▶ A quarterly frequency

▶ A 30/360 day-count basis

To establish the price of the bond, you could use this function statement:

    @PRICE(@DATE(94,4,1),@DATE(101,1,1),0.045,0.057,120,4,0)

It returns $106.96.

See Also   @ACCRUED, @DURATION, @MDURATION, @PRICE2, @YIELD

@PV(payments,interest,term)

The @PV function calculates the present value of an investment with a specified *future-value*, based on a series of equal cash flows, discounted at a periodic interest rate over the number of periods in *term*.

> **TIP** The @PV function is included in 1-2-3 97 Edition for compatibility with earlier versions of 1-2-3. It has been largely superseded by the @PVAL function, which allows you to specify a future value for the investment and to calculate either an ordinary annuity or an annuity due, depending on the value you specify for *type*. However, if you don't need the future value and annuity options that @PVAL offers, @PV remains a valid and viable function—there's no reason to stop using it if it fulfills your needs.

The arguments for the @PV function are as follows:

Argument	Description
payments	A value indicating the amount borrowed.
interest	A value greater than –1 indicating the constant interest rate per period. Note that the period used to calculate *interest* must be the same as the period used for *term*. If necessary, divide the annual interest rate by 12 to get the monthly interest and multiply the term by 12.
term	A positive value indicating the total number of period payments. Note that *term* cannot be negative.

The main use of the @PV function is to compare one investment with another. For example, say your spouse's devoted filling in of the ceaseless mailings from Publishers Clearing House has finally paid off, and you've hit a jackpot worth either $666,000 in one lump sum or $30,000 a year for the next twenty-five years of your natural term. To find out which is the better deal, check your interest rate (7 percent annually in this example), and then use this function statement:

```
@PV(30000,0.07,25)
```

It tells you that the twenty-five payments of $30,000 are worth only $349,706.50 in today's dollars.

Rather more practically, you could use @PV in conjunction with @PMT to work out how large a loan you can afford from the size of the monthly payment you can scrape together. And vice versa, of course—you could use @PMT to find out how painful your monthly payment will be for a loan of a given size.

NOTE See Chapter 8 for further practical examples of using @PV.

See Also   @FV @FVAL, @NPV, @PAYMT, @PMT, @PMTC, @PV2

@PVAL(payments,interest,term,[type], [future-value])

The @PVAL function calculates the present value of an investment with a specified *future-value*, based on a series of equal cash flows, discounted at a periodic interest rate over the number of periods in *term*.

TIP The @PVAL function is an enhanced version of the @PV function. @PVAL allows you to specify a future value for the investment; it is also able to calculate either an ordinary annuity or an annuity due, depending on the value you specify for *type*.

The arguments for the @PVAL function are as follows:

Argument	Description
payments	A value indicating the amount borrowed.
interest	A value greater than –1 indicating the constant interest rate per period. Note that the period used to calculate *interest* must be the same as the period used for *term*. If necessary, divide the annual interest rate by 12 to get the monthly interest and multiply the term by 12.
term	A positive value indicating the total number of period payments. Note that *term* cannot be negative.

type	Zero or 1. *type* is an optional argument used to specify whether 1-2-3 calculates for an ordinary annuity or for an annuity due: 0 Indicates an ordinary annuity, in which the payments are due at the end of a period. This is the default if you omit the argument *type*. 1 Indicates an annuity due, in which the payments are due at the beginning of a period.
future-value	Any value representing the present value of the series of future payments. If you omit *future-value*, 1-2-3 uses the default value of 0.

WARNING You cannot use an optional argument unless you use those that precede it. For example, you cannot use *future-value* in @PVAL if you do not specify *type*.

For example, the new workstation you're considering buying for running your company's Internet node costs $28,000 on the hoof, but you have the option of paying $1,400 a month at the beginning of each month for two years at 8 percent interest. Would the never-never be a better option for you? To calculate the total cost, use this function statement:

    @PVAL(1400,0.08/12,2*12,1)

It returns $31,161.13—not the greatest of deals for you. Paying at the end of each month would serve you a little better:

    @PVAL(1400,0.08/12,2*12,0)

This function statement returns $30,954.76.

See Also   @FV, @FVAL, @NPV, @PAYMT @PMT, @PMTC

@RATE(future-value,present-value,term)

The @RATE function calculates the periodic interest rate necessary for an investment of value *present-value* (present-value) to increase to a future value of *future-value* over the number of compounding periods in *term*. The arguments for the @RATE function are all values.

The @RATE function is a valuable instrument for examining investment opportunities. You could use it for anything from analyzing stocks professionally to choosing a better savings account.

For example, if you have $33,000 to invest and want to have $50,000 in three years. You could use the @RATE function as follows to find out what interest rate you need:

    @RATE(50000,33000,3)

This returns 0.148556—a rate of nearly 15 percent. This is going to be a high-risk investment. To discover the monthly interest rate, you could use

    @RATE(50000,33000,3*12)

which returns 0.011609, or 1.2 percent.

NOTE For another example of how the @RATE function works, see Chapter 8.

See Also   @IRATE

@SLN(cost,salvage,life)

The @SLN function calculates the straight-line depreciation allowance of an asset for one period. The asset has an initial value of *cost*, an expected useful *life* (the number of years over which the asset is to be depreciated), and a final value of *salvage*.

TIP Straight-line depreciation divides the depreciable cost equally into each period of the useful life of the asset. The depreciable cost is the actual cost of the item minus the salvage value of the item. Compare @SLN to 1-2-3's other depreciation functions: @DB, which uses the declining balance method; @DDB, which uses the double-declining balance method; and @SYD, which uses the sum-of-the-years'-digits method.

The arguments for the @SLN function are as follows:

Argument	Description
cost	Any value indicating the amount paid for the asset
salvage	Any value indicating the value of the asset at the end of its expected useful life

life	Any value greater than or equal to 1 indicating the number of periods the asset takes to depreciate to its salvage value
period	Any value greater than or equal to 1 indicating the time for which you want to find the depreciation allowance

For example, to calculate straight-line yearly depreciation on a color laser printer that cost $6,000, will have a useful life of seven years, and will be worth all of $500 after that, you could use this function statement:

    @SLN(6000,500,7)

It returns $785.71, the yearly depreciation on the printer.

NOTE See Chapter 8 for more examples of using @SLN.

See Also   @DB, @DDB, @SYD @VDB

@SYD(cost,salvage,life,period)

The @SYD function calculates the sum-of-the-years'-digits depreciation allowance of an asset that has an initial value of *cost*, an expected useful *life*, and a final value of *salvage*, over a specified *period*.

The arguments for the @SYD function are as follows:

Argument	Description
cost	Any value indicating the amount paid for the asset
salvage	Any value indicating the value of the asset at the end of its expected useful life
life	Any value greater than or equal to 1 indicating the number of periods the asset takes to depreciate to its salvage value
period	Any value greater than or equal to 1 indicating the time for which you want to find the depreciation allowance

TIP What's the difference between the @DB, @SYD, and @DDB functions? Compared to @DB, which calculates the fixed-declining balance method to calculate depreciation, @SYD (which uses the sum-of-the-years'-digits method to calculate depreciation) speeds the rate of depreciation so that more depreciation expense occurs in earlier periods than in later ones. @DDB, which uses the double-declining balance method to calculate depreciation, causes even more depreciation expense to occur in earlier periods than does @SYD. @SYD calculates the depreciable cost as the actual cost minus the salvage value. @SYD is particularly useful for occasions requiring a higher depreciation expense early in the life of an asset, such as in preparing tax returns.

For example, you could calculate the sum-of-the-years'-digits depreciation on your new Pentium computer system as illustrated in Figure E.7.

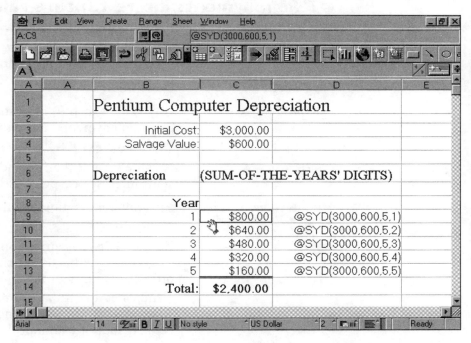

Figure E.7: Using the @SYD function to calculate the sum-of-the-years'-digits depreciation

You reckon the computer will have a useful life of five years; you paid $3,000 for it just a few days ago; and the salvage value is unlikely to be more than $600. To calculate the sum-of-the-years'-digits depreciation for the first year, use this function statement:

@SYD(3000,600,5,1)

It returns $800.00. (Cells C10, C11, C12, and C13 contain the same function statement except for the *period* argument, which is changed to 2, 3, 4, and 5, respectively.)

See Also   @DB, @DDB, @SLN, @VDB

NOTE For more about the @SYD function, see Chapter 8.

@TERM(payments,interest,future-value)

The @TERM function returns the number of periods required for a series of equal *payments* to increase to a *future-value* at a periodic rate of *interest*. The arguments for the @TERM function are as follows:

Argument	Description
payments	Any value except 0 indicating the fixed, periodic payments. Note that *payments* cannot change during the life of the annuity.
interest	A value greater than −1 indicating the constant interest rate per period.
future-value	Any value indicating the amount you want to accumulate.
type	Zero or 1. *type* is an optional argument used to specify whether 1-2-3 calculates for an ordinary annuity or for an annuity due: 0 Indicates an ordinary annuity, in which the payments are due at the end of a period. This is the default if you omit the argument *type*. 1 Indicates an annuity due, in which the payments are due at the beginning of a period.
present-value	Any value indicating the present value of the series of future payments. *present-value* is an optional argument; if you omit it, 1-2-3 uses the default value of 0.

WARNING You cannot use an optional argument unless you use those that precede it. For example, you cannot use *present-value* in @TERM if you do not specify *type*.

As an example of @TERM, assume that you're just firing up a 401K account and will be able to put $2,400 into it each year, where it will earn a steady 10.5 percent interest. Once your 401K reaches $250,000, you swear to yourself, you'll throw your job in and buy a salmon farm in Alaska. To calculate how far away your earthly paradise is, use this function statement:

```
@TERM(2400,0.105,250000)
```

It returns 24.84 years—rather a long way in the future. Suppose you reduce your target to $200,000:

```
@TERM(2400,0.105,200000)
```

Now the time is reduced only as far as 22.81 years. (This is a nice illustration of the benefits of starting your 401K plan as early as possible: With the same saving schedule, it will take you 20 years to reach $250,000, 31 years to reach $500,000, and only 38 years to reach $1 million.)

You can use @TERM to calculate the number of periods necessary to pay back a loan. As a domestic example, you could work out how long it would take your son to repay the $2,000 damage he did to your Porsche with the $240 a month he makes from his McJob, at the generous 3.5 percent interest rate you and he negotiated:

```
@TERM(240,0.035/12,2000)
```

This returns –8.25 months. Note that this function statement returns a negative value because the loan amount is entered as a negative value, –2000. Either ignore the negative—you know that the number of months for the repayment is going to be positive—or add the @ABS function to the function statement to return a positive result:

```
@ABS(@TERM(240,0.035/12,2000))
```

 NOTE Chapter 8 also discusses the @TERM function.

See Also   @CTERM, @TERM2

@VDB(cost,salvage,life,start-period,end-period, [depreciation-factor],[switch])

The @VDB function calculates the depreciation allowance of an asset for a period you specify with *start-period* and *end-period*, using the variable-rate declining balance method. The asset has an initial value of *cost*, an expected useful *life*, and a final *salvage* value.

The arguments for the @VDB function are as follows:

Argument	Description
cost	Any value indicating the amount paid for the asset. *cost* must be greater than *salvage*.
salvage	Any value indicating the value of the asset at the end of its expected useful life.
life	Any value greater than 0 indicating the number of periods the asset takes to depreciate to its salvage value.
start-period	Any value greater than or equal to 0 but less than or equal to *life*, indicating the point in the asset's life at which to begin calculating depreciation. *start-period* corresponds to the asset's life, relative to the fiscal period. Note that if both *start-period* and *end-period* have fractional parts, 1-2-3 uses the fractional part of *start-period*.
end-period	Any value greater than *start-period* indicating the point in the asset's life at which to stop calculating depreciation. *end-period* corresponds to the asset's life, relative to the fiscal period. Note that if both *start-period* and *end-period* have fractional parts, 1-2-3 uses the fractional part of *start-period*.
depreciation-factor	A value greater than or equal to 0 indicating the percentage of straight-line depreciation you want to use as the depreciation rate. *depreciation-factor* is an optional argument; if you omit it, @VDB will use the default value of 200 percent, the double-declining balance

Descriptions of the Financial Functions

	rate. Common rates for *depreciation-factor* are 1.25, 1.50, 1.75, and 2.
switch	Zero or 1, an optional argument used to prevent @VDB from switching to straight-line depreciation for the remaining useful life of the asset. Under normal circumstances in this type of calculation, declining-balance switches to straight-line depreciation when it is greater than declining-balance. 0 If switch = 0, @VDB automatically switches to straight-line depreciation when straight-line is greater than declining-balance. This is the default setting if you omit the *switch* argument. 1 If switch = 1, @VDB does not switch to straight-line depreciation, no matter what the relative values of straight-line depreciation and declining-balance depreciation.

WARNING You cannot use an optional argument unless you use those that precede it. For example, you cannot use *switch* in @VDB if you do not specify *depreciation-factor*.

For example, let's consider the Pentium computer system we looked at earlier in this appendix—a machine with an initial cost of $3,000, a salvage value of $600, and a life of six years. Figure E.8 shows a worksheet that calculates depreciation for the first month, the first year, the second year, and the second year with a depreciation factor of 1.75.

Cell B8 contains this function statement to calculate the depreciation for the first month:

    @VDB(3000,600,6*12,0,1)

Note the use of 6*12 in this cell for *life* to provide the number of months, which means that the 0 for *start-period* and the 1 for *end-period* also refer to months.

By contrast, cell B9 contains this function statement to calculate the depreciation for the first year:

    @VDB(3000,600,6,0,1)

Appendix E   Financial Functions Reference

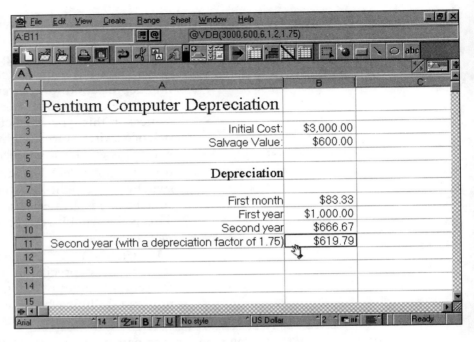

Figure E.8:   Using the @VDB function

Since *life* is the number of years, the 0 for *start-period* and the 1 for *end-period* also refer to years.

Similarly, cell B10 contains this function statement to calculate the depreciation for the second year:

    @VDB(3000,600,6,1,2)

By contrast, cell B11 calculates the depreciation for the second year with a depreciation fact of 1.75:

    @VDB(3000,600,6,1,2,1.75)

This produces a substantially different result—$619.79 rather than $666.67.

NOTE See Chapter 8 for more about the @VDB function.

See Also   @DDB, @SLN, @SYD

@YIELD(settlement,maturity,coupon,price, [redemption],[frequency],[basis])

The @YIELD function calculates the yield for securities that pay periodic interest. The arguments for the @YIELD function are as follows:

Argument	Description
settlement	A date number representing the security's settlement date.
maturity	A date number representing the security's maturity date. 1-2-3 will produce ERR for @YIELD if maturity is less than or equal to settlement.
coupon	Any positive value (or 0) representing the security's annual coupon rate.
price	Any positive value representing the security's price per $100 face value.
redemption	Any positive value (or 0) representing an optional argument that specifies the security's redemption value per $100 face value. This is an optional argument with a default of 100 if omitted.
frequency	1, 2, 4, or 12, to specify the number of coupon payments per year. This is an optional argument; the values have the following meanings: 1 Annual 2 Semiannual (this is the default value if you omit the *frequency* argument) 4 Quarterly 12 Monthly
basis	0, 1, 2, or 3, to specify the type of day-count basis to use. This is an optional argument; the values have the following meanings: 0 30/360 (this is the default value if you omit the *basis* argument) 1 Actual/actual 2 Actual/360 3 Actual/365

WARNING You cannot use an optional argument unless you use those that precede it. For example, you cannot use *basis* in @YIELD if you do not specify *frequency* and *redemption*.

For example, suppose you had a bond with the following details: a settlement date of January 1, 1990; a maturity date of January 1, 2000; a coupon rate of 6 percent; a price of $93.00; a redemption value of $100; a semiannual frequency; and an actual/actual day-count basis. You could calculate its yield with this function statement:

    @YIELD(@DATE(90,1,1),@DATE(100,1,1),0.06,93,100,2,1)

It returns 0.069844.

See Also @ACCRUED, @DURATION, @MDURATION, @PRICE

APPENDIX F

Information, Logical, and Lookup Functions Reference

This appendix examines three groups of 1-2-3's functions: the information functions, the logical functions, and the lookup functions.

The information functions fall into two general categories:

▶ Functions returning information about cells or ranges, the PC's operating system, or 1-2-3's tools

▶ Functions marking where information is missing from the worksheet or is incorrect

The logical functions calculate the results of logical formulas. Examples of the logical functions include @TRUE and @FALSE, which check to see whether a condition is true or false, respectively; @ISNUMBER, which checks to see if the contents of a cell (or a part of the contents) are a number; and @ISSTRING, which checks to see if the contents of a cell (or a part of the contents) is a string; and @ISEMPTY, which checks to see if a cell is empty.

The lookup functions find the contents of a cell. Examples of the lookup functions include @HLOOKUP and @VLOOKUP, which look up specified entries in a horizontal lookup table and a vertical lookup table, respectively; @MAXLOOKUP and @MINLOOKUP, which return an absolute reference (including the file name) to the cell that contains the largest value in a list of ranges and the smallest value in a list of ranges, respectively; and @MATCH, which returns the location of a cell whose contents match those specified.

Overview of the Information Functions

For quick reference, the information functions are listed here in Table F.1 and are discussed in detail in the next section of this appendix, "Descriptions of the Information Functions."

Table F.1:   *Information Functions Quick Reference*

Function	Returns
@CELL	Information about the upper-left cell in a reference; for example, the cell's contents, color, or file name
@CELLPOINTER	Information about the current cell's formatting, location, or contents
@COLS	The number of columns in a range
@COORD	A cell reference from given values for *worksheet*, *column*, and *row*
@DATALINK	Provides a mechanism for creating an OLE2 data advise relationship
@ERR	The value ERR (for forcing an error condition in formulas when a certain result would be undesirable)
@INFO	System information for the current 1-2-3 session, such as the current directory path or the current operating system
@NA	The value NA ("not available") indicating that no value is available; for use as a placeholder for key cells that need to be filled for a formula to be valid
@RANGENAME	The name of the range in which a given cell is located

Table F.1: Information Functions Quick Reference (continued)

Function	Returns
@REFCONVERT	The corresponding numbers (1–256) for the 1-2-3 column or worksheet letters (A–IV) to numbers from 1 through 256, and the corresponding column or worksheet letters for the numbers 1–256
@ROWS	The number of rows in a given range
@SCENARIOINFO	Information about a scenario—for example, the user who last modified a scenario or the latest comment attached to a scenario
@SCENARIOLAST	The name of the scenario that was last displayed in a file during the current 1-2-3 session
@SHEETS	The number of worksheets in a given range
@SOLVER	A value that gives information about the status of Solver
@VERSIONCURRENT	The name of the current version in a range
@VERSIONDATA	The contents of a specified cell in a version
@VERSIONINFO	Information about a version—for example, the name of the user who created it or who last modified it

Descriptions of the Information Functions

This section contains detailed descriptions of the information functions.

@CELL(attribute,location)

The @CELL function returns information about the upper-left cell in a reference, where *location* is the address or name of a range and *attribute* is one of the items shown in the list below.

Descriptions of the Information Functions

 NOTE For information about the current cell, use @CELLPOINTER instead of @CELL.

 NOTE *attribute* must be enclosed in double quotation marks ("") and can also be the address or name of a cell containing one of the items listed below.

Attribute	Returns This Information
address	The abbreviated absolute address—column letter and row number.
col	The column letter in the reference, expressed as a value from 1 through 256. Column A returns 1, column Z returns 26, column AA returns 27, etc.
color	1 if the cell is formatted in color for negative numbers, 0 if the cell is not.
contents	The contents of the cell (the upper-left cell in the reference).
coord	The full form of the absolute cell address—worksheet letter, column letter, and row number. Unlike "col", "coord" returns letters as letters rather than as numeric equivalents.
filename	The file name (including the full path) of the file that contains the cell referred to.
format	The cell format as follows:
	Currency returns C0 to C15 for 0 to 15 decimal places.
	Fixed returns F0 to F15 for 0 to 15 decimal places.
	General, a label, or a blank cell returns G.
	Percent returns P0 to P15 for 0 to 15 decimal places.
	Scientific returns S0 to S15 for 0 to 15 decimal places.
	Comma returns ,0 to ,15 for 0 to 15 decimal places.

± returns +.
Date format 11-Nov-97 returns D1.
Date format 11-Nov returns D2.
Date format Nov-97 returns D3.
Date format 12/11/97 returns D4.
Date format 12/11 returns D5.
Time format 10:15:00 AM returns D6.
Time format 10:15 AM returns D7.
Time format 22:15:00 returns D8.
Time format 15:30 returns D9.
Text returns T.
Hidden returns H.
Label returns L.
Automatic returns A.
Color for negative numbers returns—(two hyphens).
Parentheses returns 1 if the cell has parentheses and 0 if it does not.

prefix The label prefix character, as follows:
A left-aligned label returns '.
A right-aligned label returns ".
A centered label returns ^.
A repeating label returns \.
A nonprinting label returns |.
A blank cell or a cell containing a value returns a blank (an empty cell).

protect 1 if the cell is protected and 0 if it is not protected.

row The row number of the cell referred to, returned as a value from 1 through 8192.

sheet The letter of the worksheet containing the cell referred to, returned as a value from 1 through 256—1 for worksheet A, 27 for worksheet AA, and so on.

sheetname The name of the worksheet containing the cell referred to. If the worksheet is not named, the worksheet letter is returned instead.

type	The type of data the cell contains, as follows: A blank cell returns b. A cell containing a numeric value, a numeric formula, or a text formula returns v. A cell containing a label returns 1.
width	The column width as a number of characters (e.g., 25).

WARNING To make sure your results are up to date, always recalculate your work before using @CELL—this function does not automatically recalculate for you.

One use of @CELL well worth knowing is how to use it in conjunction with @IF and @ERR to ensure that you get the correct type of user input in a particular cell. For example, say you have a campaign spreadsheet with a cell called CONTRIBUTION. You could check that the user enters a value in CONTRIBUTION (and return that value) by using the following function statement:

    @IF(@CELL("type",CONTRIBUTION)="v",CONTRIBUTION,@ERR)

If the user does anything in CONTRIBUTION that would throw the spreadsheet a curveball, such as entering text or meanly leaving the cell blank, the cell will display ERR.

You can also use @CELL to direct the execution of macros by assigning different subroutines based on what the user enters in a cell. If you build an automated application, you can use @CELL to change cell attributes, again based on what the user enters into cells.

See Also @CELLPOINTER

@CELLPOINTER(attribute)

The @CELLPOINTER function returns information about the current cell's formatting, location, or contents. See the list in the entry for @CELL for the list of attributes for @CELLPOINTER.

WARNING To make sure your results are up to date, always recalculate your work before using @CELLPOINTER—this function does not automatically recalculate for you.

You can use @CELLPOINTER to determine which cell the cell pointer is currently in or to evaluate a formula based on the contents of the current cell. Once you have established what's in the cell, you can direct the macro accordingly.

For example, you could use the following function statement to test for a blank cell in a list of items and stop the macro if it encounters one:

    {IF @CELLPOINTER("type")="b"}{QUIT}

See Also   @@, @CELL

@COLS(range)

The @COLS function returns the number of columns in *range*, where *range* is the address or name of a range. For example, if you had a range named PENGUINS SEEN to which you added a new column each day with total numbers of penguins sighted that day, you could use @COLS to find out the number of columns in PENGUINS SEEN in order to print the appropriate range. You would use the following function statement:

    @COLS(PENGUINS SEEN)

> **TIP** Consider using @COLS when using a {FOR} statement in a macro to determine on how many columns the macro should repeat the series of actions.

See Also   @REFCONVERT, @ROWS, @SHEETS

@COORD(worksheet,column,row,absolute)

The @COORD function returns a cell reference from the values for *worksheet*, *column*, and *row*. The arguments for the @COORD function are as follows:

Argument	Description
worksheet	Any integer from 1 to 256, corresponding to the worksheet letter: 1 represents worksheet A, 2 represents worksheet B, and so on.
column	Any integer from 1 to 256, corresponding to the column letter: 1 represents column A, 2 represents column B, and so on.

Descriptions of the Information Functions

row	Any integer from 1 to 8192, corresponding to the row number.
absolute	Any integer from 1 to 8, specifying whether the cell reference is absolute, relative, or mixed, as follows: @COORD(2,2,2,1) returns $B:$B$2. @COORD(2,2,2,2) returns $B:B$2. @COORD(2,2,2,3) returns $B:$B2. @COORD(2,2,2,4) returns $B:B2. @COORD(2,2,2,5) returns B:$B$2. @COORD(2,2,2,6) returns B:B$2. @COORD(2,2,2,7) returns B:$B2. @COORD(2,2,2,8) returns B:B2.

NOTE If the values entered for *worksheet*, *column*, *row*, and *absolute* are not integers, 1-2-3 will truncate them to integers.

For example, to return the relative address of cell AA11 in worksheet W, you could use the following function statement:

```
@COORD(23,27,11,8)
```

You can use @COORD with @INDEX, @VLOOKUP, or @HLOOKUP to put together cell addresses from tables of values contained in the current file.

See Also @REFCONVERT

@DATALINK(app-name,topic-name,item-name, [format],[max-rows],[max-cols],[max-sheets])

The @DATALINK function establishes an OLE link in the current cell. You can then adjust the link by altering the arguments for @DATALINK. The arguments for @DATALINK are as follows:

Argument	Description
app-name	The text name of a Windows application that can act as a OLE server: for example, "CorelDRAW" or "Winword" (including

	the "", double quotation marks). This argument is provided for compatibility with earlier versions of 1-2-3.
topic-name	The name of the application file including its path (for example, "D:\SHARING\FUNNY-PIC .CDR" or "C:\WORD_DOX\HOT-LINKS.DOC"—again, including the double quotation marks) to which the OLE link is to be made. You can use "system" to link to the system topic.
item-name	The name of the item to which you want to link in the server application. This is the item in the server application file from which you want to transfer data through the link.
format	Text, WK1, or WK3, representing the Clipboard formats that can be used for the link. The *format* argument is optional; if you omit it, 1-2-3 will use the Text Clipboard format.
max-rows	The maximum number of rows for the destination range to occupy. If you omit the *max-rows* argument, 1-2-3 will use as many rows as the destination range takes up.
max-cols	The maximum number of columns for the destination range to occupy. If you omit the *max-cols* argument, 1-2-3 will use as many columns as the destination range takes up.
max-sheets	The maximum number of worksheets for the destination range to occupy. If you omit the *max-sheets* argument, 1-2-3 will use as many worksheets as the destination range takes up.

WARNING When using multiple links, make sure you never create a *circular link*—a link in which information is constantly updating itself. This sounds like a no-brainer, but given the complexity of workbooks that 1-2-3 lets you create, it can be surprisingly easy to do. If this does happen, 1-2-3 will grind for a while and then produce an error message.

@ERR

The @ERR function returns the value ERR. Use @ERR to force an error condition in formulas when a certain result would be undesirable. For example, if you were calculating the profit margin on a product, you might use @ERR as an argument with @IF to return an error if the values you entered resulted in a negative profit margin (assuming you wanted to make money, of course). For example, the following function statement returns ERR if the value in cell C9 is less than 0:

    @IF(C9<0;@ERR;C9)

Another use of @ERR is to check whether a formula refers to a particular cell indirectly. For example, if you suspect that a value in cell B11 is throwing a wrench into your calculations, but you're not sure that the formula refers to cell B11, you could enter @ERR in cell B11, recalculate, and check to see whether the formula displayed ERR.

See Also   @ISERR, @NA

@INFO(attribute)

The @INFO function returns system information for the current 1-2-3 session, such as the current directory path or the current operating system. *attribute* is a text string entered between double quotation marks ("") and is one of the following:

Attribute	Description
dbreturncode	Returns the most recent error code returned by the external DataLens *driver*. For example, 0.
dbdrivermessage	Returns the most recent DataLens message from an external database driver. This will be blank if there has been no message.
dbrecordcount	Returns the number of records extracted, modified, or inserted from the last query (either in the worksheet or in an external database). For example, 5.
directory	Returns the current path, including the drive letter. For example, C:\123R4W\WORK\.

macro-step	Returns Yes if Step mode is on; returns No if Step mode is off.
macro-trace	Returns Yes if the Macro Trace window is open; returns No if it is not open.
memavail	Returns the amount of available memory (RAM and virtual memory) in bytes. For example, 12439040.
mode	1-2-3's current mode, indicated as one of the following numeric codes: 0 Wait 1 Ready 2 Label 3 Menu 4 Value 5 Point 6 Edit 7 Error 8 Find 9 Files 10 Help 11 Stat 13 Names 99 All other modes (for example, modes defined by the user with {INDICATE})
origin	Returns the absolute address of the top-left cell in the current worksheet. For example, $ZA:$A$1. This can be very useful for checking which worksheet a macro is operating on before anything disastrous happens.
recalc	Returns the current recalculation mode for the worksheet as the label Automatic or the label Manual.
release	Returns the release number for the version of 1-2-3 for Windows you are using, in the following format: major release number, upgrade level, and version number. For example, 97.00.005.00.00.

Descriptions of the Information Functions

setup-user-name	Returns your e-mail or network user name. If 1-2-3 cannot find an e-mail or network user name, it will return the registered user name.
screen-height	Returns the height of the screen as a value in pixels. For example, 480 if you're using 640 × 480 resolution.
screen-width	Returns the width of the screen as a value in pixels. For example, 640 if you're using 640 × 480 resolution.
selection	Returns the address of the currently selected range, or the name of the currently selected chart, drawn object, or query table. For example, CHART 1.
selection-part	Returns the name of the selected part of a range or object. For example, 1-2-3 will display Legend labels if you have the legend labels of a chart selected.
selection-type	Returns the current selection type: Range, Draw, Query, or Chart.
system	Returns the name of the operating system. For example, MS Windows 4.0 build 67999999pcdos.
totmem	Returns the total memory available, in bytes. This includes both memory currently available (which you can establish using the *memavail* argument, described above) and memory being used. For example, 12420704.

TIP Be sure to recalculate your worksheets before using @INFO to make sure you get the correct results.

The @INFO function can be crucial to writing successful macros. For example, you could use @INFO("directory") with @IF to change the directory if the user had selected the wrong directory. Alternatively, you might use @INFO("numfile") with @IF to see how many files were open and close extraneous files to conserve memory for the task at hand.

Figure F.1 illustrates the most useful attributes for @INFO.

See Also   @CELL, @CELLPOINTER

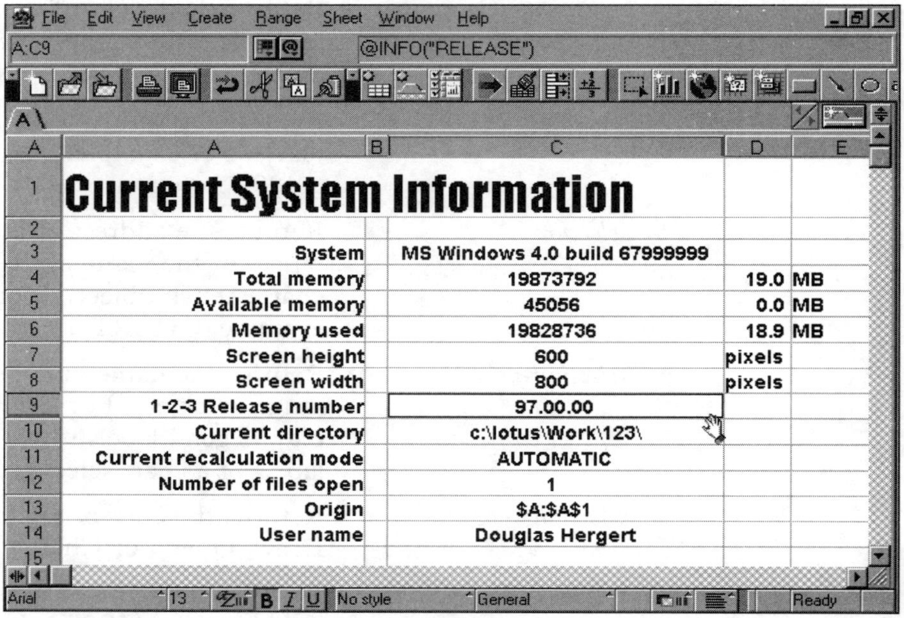

Figure F.1:   *Using the @INFO function to return information about your computer system and your work environment*

@NA

The @NA function returns the value NA ("not available") indicating that no value is available. The function has no arguments.

Use the @NA function when you're setting up a worksheet as a placeholder for key cells for which you do not yet have a valid entry. Any formulas that refer to the @NA in those cells will return NA, reminding you that the spreadsheet is not yet complete.

Figure F.2 illustrates this use of the @NA function. In the figure, a record store uses 1-2-3 to track its inventory and keep quarterly totals to see which artists to stock and which to drop. To make sure that the results in column E, the Q1 column, are accurate, @NA is entered in each of the cells that will contain the monthly sales figures. The @SUM function is entered in column E to keep the quarterly totals. If any of the cells needed for that total contains NA, the @SUM cell also shows NA to indicate that the figure is not available.

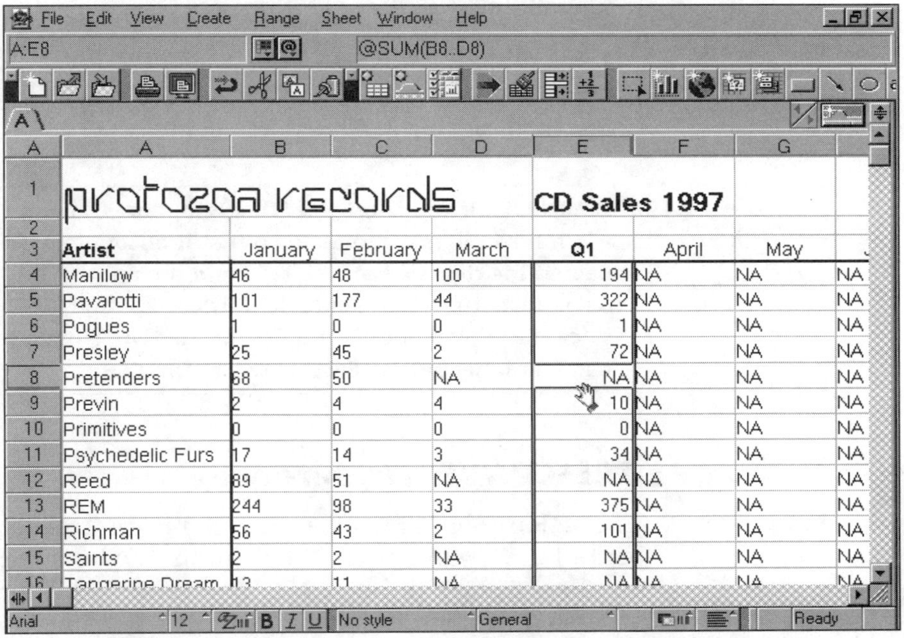

Figure F.2: Using the @NA function as a placeholder to remind you that key information is missing from a spreadsheet

You can also use the @NA function to make sure that a cell contains the type of information you want. For example, to make sure that you did not have a label in cell A1, you could use the following function statement:

    @IF(@CELL("type";A1)="l",@NA,A1)

This would return NA if cell A1 contained a label. Another use for @NA is to check which formulas depend on a particular cell.

See Also   @ERR, @ISNA

@RANGENAME(cell)

The @RANGENAME function returns the name of the range in which *cell* is located, where *cell* is a cell address or the name of a single-cell range. The file containing *cell* must be loaded in memory when you use @RANGENAME.

For example, if cell Z280 is in the range NISSAN, the following function statement will return NISSAN:

    @RANGENAME(Z280)

To find out the name of the range containing the current cell, you could use @CELLPOINTER in conjunction with @RANGENAME:

    @RANGENAME(@CELLPOINTER("address"))

WARNING If you enter a *cell* that is in more than one range, @RANGENAME will return the first range name that it encounters. For example, if you have named the range A1..A10 TITLES and the range A1..F1 MONTHS, so that cell A1 is in both TITLES and MONTHS, @RANGENAME will return MONTHS, since it is alphabetically the first of the two. Note also that if *cell* is not in a named range, @RANGENAME will return ERR.

@REFCONVERT(reference)

The @REFCONVERT function returns the corresponding numbers (1–256) for the 1-2-3 column or worksheet letters (A–IV) to numbers from 1 through 256, and returns the corresponding column or worksheet letters for the numbers 1–256.

reference specifies a 1-2-3 column or worksheet and can be:

▶ a letter from A through IV entered as text in double quotation marks ("")

▶ an integer from 1 through 256

@REFCONVERT is not case-sensitive, so that both the following function statements return 11:

    @REFCONVERT("k")

    @REFCONVERT("K")

See Also   @COLS, @COORD, @SHEETS

@ROWS(range)

The @ROWS function returns the number of rows in *range*, where *range* is a range address or a range name. For example, suppose you had a worksheet for keeping track of your prowess at baseball. If you had a

Descriptions of the Information Functions

range named RBI to which you added a new row after each baseball game with your number of runs batted in that day, you could use @ROWS to find out the number of rows in RBI in order to print the appropriate range by using the following function statement:

@ROWS(RBI)

> **TIP** Consider using @ROWS when using a {FOR} statement in a macro to determine on how many rows the macro should repeat the series of actions.

See Also   @COLS, @SHEETS

@SCENARIOINFO(option,name,[creator])

The @SCENARIOINFO function returns information about a scenario. The arguments for the @SCENARIOINFO function are as follows:

Argument	Description
option	Any of the following text arguments inside double quotation marks ("") to specify the information 1-2-3 is to return:
	"creator" returns the name of the person who created the scenario.
	"modifier" returns the name of the person who last modified the scenario.
	"created" returns the date and time the scenario was created, as a date and time number.
	"modified" returns a date and time number indicating the date and time the scenario was last modified.
	"comment" returns the comment for the scenario, up to a maximum of 512 characters; longer comments are truncated to 512 characters.
	"hidden" returns 0 (FALSE) if the scenario is not hidden or 1 (TRUE) if it is hidden.
	"protected" returns 0 (FALSE) if the scenario is not protected or 1 (True) if it is protected.

name	The name of the scenario, entered as text enclosed within double quotation marks (""). 1-2-3 will use the most recently created scenario if there are more than one with the same name.
creator	The name of the user who created the scenario, entered as text enclosed within double quotation marks (""). *creator* is an optional argument that you can enter to help 1-2-3 determine which scenario to use.

For example, if you had scenarios named Best Case Harvest (for your Lotus-Drinkers vineyard), you could retrieve the name of the user who created the latest Best Case Harvest scenario by using the following function statement:

    @SCENARIOINFO("Creator","Best Case Harvest")

Likewise, if your name were Hans Schleifenbaum, you could retrieve your latest comment on the Best Case Harvest scenario by using the following function statement:

    @SCENARIOINFO("comment","Best Case Harvest",
    "Hans Schleifenbaum")

See Also @VERSIONINFO

@SCENARIOLAST(file-name)

The @SCENARIOLAST function returns the name of the scenario that was last displayed in a file during the current 1-2-3 session. For *file-name*, enter the full name and extension of the file to test for within double quotation marks (""); if the file is not (or will not be) in the current directory, include the path name as well in *file-name*.

For example, if the last-displayed scenario in your file named HARVEST in the directory Z:\APPS\123R5W\WORK\WINERY\ was Gewuerztraminer, entering the following function statement would return Gewuerztraminer:

    @SCENARIOLAST("Z:\APPS\123R5W\WORK\WINERY\HARVEST.WK5")

WARNING @SCENARIOLAST will return ERR if no scenarios have been displayed in file name during the current 1-2-3 session.

See Also @SCENARIOINFO

@SHEETS(range)

The @SHEETS function returns the number of worksheets in *range*, where *range* is a range address or a range name.

For example, if your company kept its forecast in a file called FORE-CAST.WK5 that contained a growing number of worksheets featuring (among other ranges) a range named PERSONNEL, you could find out the number of worksheets that PERSONNEL spanned by using the following function statement:

    @SHEETS(PERSONNEL)

TIP The @SHEETS function also comes in useful with a {FOR} statement in a macro to determine on how many sheets the macro should repeat the series of actions.

See Also @COLS, @REFCONVERT, @ROWS

@VERSIONCURRENT(range)

The @VERSIONCURRENT function returns the name of the current version in *range*, where *range* is the name or address of a range for which you need to find the version name.

For example, if you have a worksheet with a range named CD OUTPUT, the following function statement would return the name of the current version in the CD OUTPUT range:

    @VERSIONCURRENT(CD OUTPUT)

If there were no current version, @VERSIONCURRENT would return ERR.

@VERSIONDATA(option,cell,version-range, name,[creator])

The @VERSIONDATA function returns the contents of a specified cell in a version. The arguments for the @VERSIONDATA function are as follows:

Argument	Description
option	"formula" or "value", text entered in double quotation marks ("") indicating the information for @VERSIONDATA to return from the cell, as follows:
	"formula" returns as a label the formula contained in the cell. If no formula is in the cell, @VERSIONDATA returns ERR.
	"value" returns the result of a formula contained in the cell, or the value or label contained in the cell. If the cell is blank, @VERSIONDATA returns an empty string.
cell	The name or address of the cell whose contents 1-2-3 returns. For @VERSIONDATA to work, *cell* must be located within *version-range*.
version-range	The name of the existing named range containing the version.
name	Text entered in double quotation marks ("") indicating the name of the version. @VERSIONDATA will return the most recently created version if more than one version has the same name.
creator	Text entered in double quotation marks ("") indicating the name of the user who created the version. *creator* is an optional argument that you can use to help @VERSIONDATA establish which version to use or delete. As with *name*, @VERSIONDATA will return the most recently created version if the same creator created more than one version with the same name.

For example, if users in your company, Mile-High Balloon Club, had versions named Stormy, you could retrieve the formula in cell B:C14 of the most recently created Stormy version in the range PROFIT by using

    @VERSIONDATA("formula",B:C14,PROFIT,"Stormy")

Likewise, if your name were Chief Goldblum, you could retrieve the value or label in cell A:A1 of the version named Stormy most recently created by Chief Goldblum in the range PROFIT by using the following function statement:

    @VERSIONDATA("value",A:A1,PROFIT,"Stormy","Chief Goldblum")

See Also   @VERSIONINFO

@VERSIONINFO(option,name,[creator])

The @VERSIONINFO function returns information about a version. The arguments for the @VERSIONINFO function are as follows:

Argument	Description
option	Any of the following text arguments inside double quotation marks ("") to specify the information 1-2-3 is to return:
	"creator" returns the name of the person who created the version.
	"modifier" returns the name of the person who last modified the version.
	"created" returns the date and time the version was created, as a date and time number.
	"modified" returns a date and time number indicating the date and time the version was last modified.
	"comment" returns the comment for the version, up to a maximum of 512 characters; longer comments are truncated to 512 characters.
	"hidden" returns 0 (FALSE) if the version is not hidden or 1 (TRUE) if it is hidden.
	"protected" returns 0 (FALSE) if the version is not protected or 1 (True) if it is protected.

name	The name of the version, entered as text enclosed within double quotation marks (""). 1-2-3 will use the most recently created version if there are more than one with the same name.
creator	The name of the user who created the version, entered as text enclosed within double quotation marks (""). *creator* is an optional argument that you can enter to help 1-2-3 determine which version to use.
version-range	The name of the existing named range that contains the version.

For example, if you had versions named Strong Dollar (for Neuschwanstein Tours Inc.), you could retrieve the name of the user who created the latest Strong Dollar version by using the following function statement:

```
@VERSIONINFO("Creator","Strong Dollar")
```

Likewise, if your name were Ludwig the Mad of Bavaria, you could retrieve your latest comment on the Strong Dollar version by using the following function statement:

```
@VERSIONINFO("comment","Strong Dollar","Ludwig the Mad of Bavaria")
```

See Also @SCENARIOINFO

Overview of the Logical Functions

For quick reference, the logical functions are listed here in Table F.2. They are discussed in detail in the next section of this appendix, "Descriptions of the Logical Functions."

Table F.2: **Logical Functions Quick Reference**

Function	Returns
@FALSE	The logical value 0 (FALSE), the opposite of the logical value 1 (TRUE)
@IF	The result given for true if the given condition evaluates as TRUE (not equaling zero) or the result given for false if condition evaluates as FALSE (equaling zero)

Table F.2: **Logical Functions Quick Reference (continued)**

Function	Returns
@ISAAF	1 (TRUE) if the given name is that of a defined add-in function for 1-2-3; 0 (FALSE) if it is not
@ISAPP	1 (TRUE) if the given name is that of a defined add-in application for 1-2-3; 0 (FALSE) if it is not
@ISBETWEEN	1 (TRUE) if the given value is between two boundaries; 0 (FALSE) if it is not
@ISEMPTY	1 (TRUE) if the specified location is a blank cell; 0 (FALSE) if it is not blank
@ISERR	1 (TRUE) if the given value is the value ERR and 0 (FALSE) if value is not the value ERR
@ISFILE	1 (TRUE) if the specified file name exists and 0 (FALSE) if it does not exist
@ISMACRO	1 (TRUE) if the specified name is a defined add-in macro command and 0 (FALSE) if it is not
@ISNA	1 (TRUE) if the specified value is the value NA and 0 (FALSE) if value is not the value NA
@ISNUMBER	1 (TRUE) if the specified value contains a value, NA, ERR, or a blank cell; 0 (FALSE) if the specified value is text or a cell containing a label or a formula that results in a label
@ISRANGE	1 (TRUE) if the specified range is a defined range name or valid range address; 0 (FALSE) if it is not
@ISSTRING	1 (TRUE) if the specified value is text or a cell that contains a label or a formula that results in a label; 0 (FALSE) if the specified value is a value, ERR, NA, or a blank cell
@TRUE	The logical value 1 (TRUE)

Descriptions of the Logical Functions

This section contains detailed descriptions of the logical functions that 1-2-3 offers.

> **NOTE** See "Logical Functions" in Chapter 8 for a general-purpose discussion of these functions.

@FALSE

The @FALSE function returns the logical value 0 (FALSE), the opposite of the logical value 1 (TRUE). @FALSE has no arguments.

For example, the following function statement returns TRUE if the value in cell C11 is greater than that in cell D11 and FALSE if it is not:

    @IF(C11>D11,@TRUE,@FALSE)

> **TIP** While it might be easier to enter 0 than enter @FALSE when writing formulas for evaluating logical conditions, you'll probably find that having @FALSE in the formulas makes them easier to read later.

See Also   @TRUE

@IF(condition,true,false)

The @IF function evaluates the specified *condition* and returns the result given for *true* if *condition* evaluates as TRUE (not equaling zero) or the result given for *false* if *condition* evaluates as FALSE (equaling zero). *condition* is typically a logical formula, but it can also be any formula, number, text within double quotation marks (""), or the name or address of a cell.

> **TIP** Note that blank cells, text, ERR, and NA all equal zero when used as a condition and thus equal FALSE.

true and *false* can be values, text within double quotation marks (""), or the addresses or names of cells containing values or labels.

Descriptions of the Logical Functions

To prevent division by zero and the ERR values that result, you can use @IF with other functions, such as @SUM. For example, if you need to use @SUM in a spreadsheet that may not at any given point have values entered in all the cells you want to sum, you can use a function statement like the following:

    @IF(@SUM(Z20..Z28),@SUM(Z20..Z28)," ")

rather than a function statement like this:

    @SUM(Z20..Z28)

The first of these two function statements has the advantage that if there are no values in cells Z20..Z28, @IF will return a blank cell rather than 0. This is particularly useful if you need to perform a further operation (such as division) with the result of the @SUM calculation.

Figure F.3 shows the @IF function used for a basic small-business budget spreadsheet. Cell D5 contains a function statement to display *On Target* if the Actual expense in cell C5 is the same as or less than the Plan expense in cell B5 and *Overrun* if Actual is greater than Plan:

    @IF(B5>C5,"On Target","Overrun")

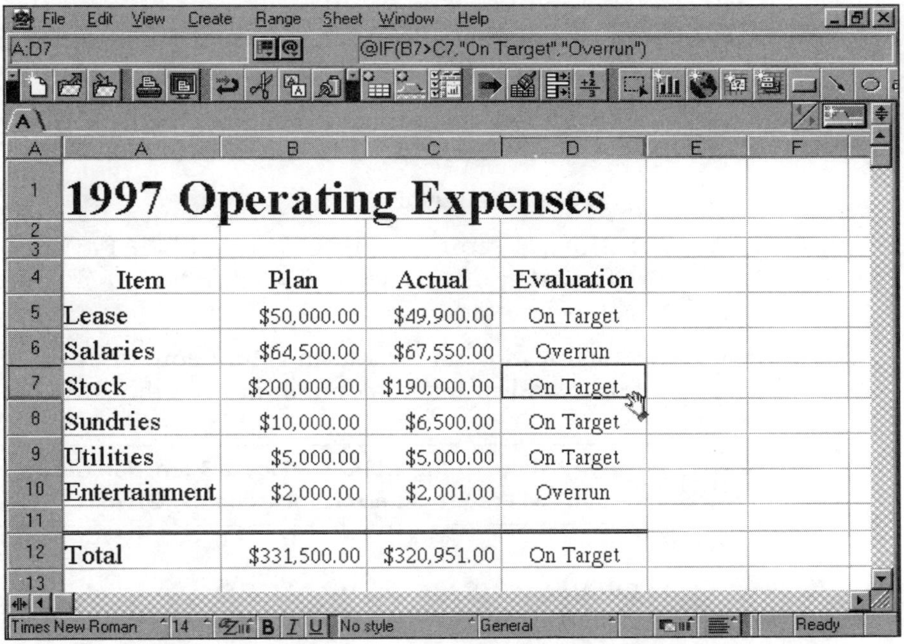

Item	Plan	Actual	Evaluation
Lease	$50,000.00	$49,900.00	On Target
Salaries	$64,500.00	$67,550.00	Overrun
Stock	$200,000.00	$190,000.00	On Target
Sundries	$10,000.00	$6,500.00	On Target
Utilities	$5,000.00	$5,000.00	On Target
Entertainment	$2,000.00	$2,001.00	Overrun
Total	$331,500.00	$320,951.00	On Target

1997 Operating Expenses

Figure F.3: Using the @IF function to display different labels for a budget spreadsheet

Cell D11, which appears blank in the spreadsheet, shows the use of nested @IF functions. It contains the following function statement:

```
@IF(@IF(B11>C11,"On Target","Overrun"),@IF(B11>C11,"On Target","Overrun"),"")
```

This displays a blank cell if there are no entries in cells B11 and C11, or, if there are entries, it displays *On Target* or *Overrun* depending on whether the Actual expense is less than or equal to, or greater than, the Plan expense.

You can also use the @IF function in combination with the @ERR function to check for missing data or for errors. For example, in a payments spreadsheet, you might want 1-2-3 to reject entries with negative or zero values. A simple function statement would do the trick:

```
@IF(A1<=0,@ERR,A1)
```

If the amount entered in cell A1 is less than or equal to zero, the cell will display ERR; otherwise, it will display the amount entered in cell A1.

@ISAAF(name)

The @ISAAF function tests to see if *name* is a defined add-in function for 1-2-3. *name* is the name of the add-in function and should be entered as text within double quotation marks ("").

For example, if you have defined @BREAKEVEN as an add-in function, you can test for it by entering the following function statement:

```
@ISAAF("BREAKEVEN")
```

1-2-3 will return 1 (TRUE) if @BREAKEVEN is a defined add-in @function; otherwise, 1-2-3 will return 0 (FALSE). Note that the @ sign is omitted.

When testing for an add-in @function, omit the @ sign. When testing for an add-in macro command, omit the curly braces ({}).

WARNING Using @ISAAF on a 1-2-3 function (as opposed to an add-in function) will return an error. For example, @ISAFF("ISAFF") returns ERR.

See Also @ISAPP, @ISMACRO

@ISAPP(name)

The @ISAPP function tests to see if *name* is a defined add-in application for 1-2-3 currently loaded in memory. *name* is the name of the add-in application and should be entered as text within double quotation marks ("").

For example, if you have defined @BUDGET as an add-in application and loaded it using Tools ➤ Add-in ➤ Load, you can test for it by entering the following function statement:

    @ISAPP("BUDGET")

1-2-3 will return 1 (TRUE) if BUDGET is a defined add-in application and is loaded into memory; otherwise, 1-2-3 will return 0 (FALSE).

WARNING @ISAPP will return 0 (FALSE) for add-in applications not loaded using Tools ➤ Add-in ➤ Load.

@ISBETWEEN(value;bound1;bound2;[inclusion])

The @ISBETWEEN function checks to see if a value is between *bound1* and *bound2*. It returns a 1 if the condition is true and a 0 if it is not.

WARNING @ISBETWEEN will return ERR if the data types of *bound1* and *bound2* are not the same.

For example, if cell A1 contains 123, A2 contains 100, and A3 contains 150 the following function statement will return 1 (TRUE):

    @ISBETWEEN(A1;A2;A3)

@ISEMPTY(location)

The @ISEMPTY function checks to see if *location* is a blank cell, where *location* is the name or address of one cell. If *location* is blank, @ISEMPTY returns 1 (TRUE); if *location* is not a blank, @ISEMPTY returns 0 (FALSE).

WARNING @ISEMPTY will return 0 (FALSE) if you specify a range for *location*, even if all the cells in *location* are blank.

For example, if cell A1 contains the label Porcupines, cell B1 is blank, and cell C1 contains the value 3023, the following function statement will return 0 (FALSE):

    @ISEMPTY(A1)

@ISEMPTY(C1) will also return 0 (FALSE), but @ISEMPTY(B1) will return 1 (TRUE).

@ISERR(value)

The @ISERR function tests *value* for the value ERR. *value* can be any value, location, text, or condition. @ISERR returns 1 (TRUE) if *value* is the value ERR and returns 0 (FALSE) if *value* is not the value ERR.

One popular and practical use of @ISERR is to avoid division-by-zero errors, as shown in Figure F.4. Column G of the First Grade Test Results worksheet contains a function statement to divide the sum of the results from the four tests (in columns B, C, D, and E) by the number of students in the class (in column F). The function statement is arranged to display "Missing Information" if the relevant cell in column F is empty, to provide a divide-by-zero error:

    @IF(@ISERR(@SUM(B7..E7)/F7),"Missing
    Information",@SUM(B7..E7)/F7)

If a value does appear in cell F7, 1-2-3 will carry out the calculation, as it has for the other classes in the column.

See Also @ISNA

@ISFILE(file-name,[type])

The @ISFILE checks to see if the file named *file-name* exists in memory or on disk, where *file-name* is the full name (including extension and including path if the file is not in the current directory) of the file enclosed in double quotation marks (""). *type* specifies whether 1-2-3 searches for *file-name* in memory or on disk:

▶ If *type* = 0, 1-2-3 searches in memory.
▶ If *type* = 1, 1-2-3 searches on disk.

0 is the default if you omit the *type* argument.

@ISFILE returns 1 (TRUE) if *file-name* exists and 0 (FALSE) if *file-name* does not exist.

Descriptions of the Logical Functions

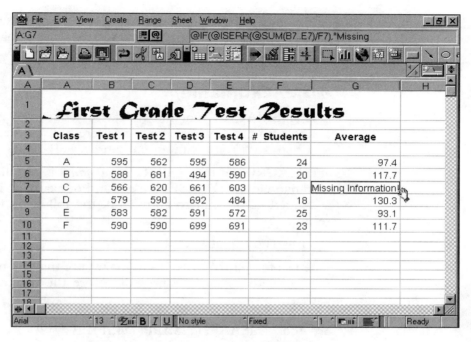

Figure F.4: Using the @ISERR function to avoid a divide-by-zero error

For example, if the file OVERRUNS.WK5 is stored in the F:\FINANCE\123R5W\DATA directory, you could check for it by entering the following function statement:

```
@ISFILE("F:\FINANCE\123R5W\DATA\OVERRUNS.WK5",1)
```

This would return 1 (TRUE). To check to see if OVERRUNS.WK5 were in memory, you could use instead this function statement:

```
@ISFILE("F:\FINANCE\123R5W\DATA\OVERRUNS.WK5")
```

You could use @ISFILE in combination with @IF if you needed to make sure that, say, certain network files were available to one of your colleagues. Using a number of function statements such as the following to return Available for files that were available and Not Available for files that were not would be much quicker than checking manually for the files:

```
@IF(@ISFILE("Z:\PLANNING\BUDGET\1997_Q1.WK5",1),"Availab
le","Not Available")
```

Alternatively, you might want to check to make sure particular files from which you needed to extract data were loaded into memory before running a particular macro.

@ISMACRO(name)

The @ISMACRO function checks to see if *name* is a defined add-in macro command, where *name* is entered as text within double quotation marks ("") but without curly braces ({}).

@ISMACRO returns 1 (TRUE) if *name* is a defined add-in macro command and 0 (FALSE) if it is not. For example, if {REDEFINE} is a defined add-in macro command, the following function statement returns 1:

   @ISMACRO("REDEFINE")

One use for @ISMACRO is to make sure that the other macros that a macro needs to call are present before the macro starts running in earnest.

See Also   @ISAAF, @ISAPP, @ISFILE

@ISNA(value)

The @ISNA function tests *value* for the value NA, where *value* is any value, location, text, or condition. @ISNA returns 1 (TRUE) if *value* is the value NA and 0 (FALSE) if *value* is not the value NA.

For example, if cell Z15 contains the value NA (produced by the @NA function), the following function statement returns 1 (TRUE):

   @ISNA(Z15)

You can use @ISNA in a way similar to how the @ISERR function is used.

See Also   @ISERR

@ISNUMBER(value)

The @ISNUMBER function checks to see if *value* contains a value, where *value* is any value, location, text, or condition. @ISNUMBER returns 1 (TRUE) if *value* contains a value, NA, ERR, or a blank cell;

@ISNUMBER returns 0 (FALSE) if *value* is text or a cell containing a label or a formula that results in a label.

> **WARNING** Be aware that NA and ERR are actually numeric values in 1-2-3—that is why they return 1 (TRUE) for @ISNUMBER. If your calculations will be thrown off by having NA or ERR instead of a value, consider using @ISNA and @ISERR to check for their presence. If a blank cell will upset matters, use @ISEMPTY to check for that too.

You can perform some calculations more reliably if you first check to see that a cell contains a number. Alternatively, you could stop a calculation or a macro and display an error message if a crucial cell is missing a value or contains a label instead.

> **WARNING** Note that *value* must be a single cell. If *value* is a range consisting of more than one cell, @ISNUMBER will return 0 (FALSE) no matter what the first cell in the range (or, indeed, any of the cells in the range) contains.

For example, if cell H78 contains the value 999666, the following function statement returns 1 (TRUE):

    @ISNUMBER(H78)

See Also   @CELL, @CELLPOINTER, @ISEMPTY, @ISSTRING

@ISRANGE(range)

The @ISRANGE function checks to see if *range* exists as a defined range name or valid range address, where *range* can be any text or range address.

> **TIP** A valid range address is one with worksheet and column letters from A through IV and row numbers from 1 through 8192. For example, A:AB8190..AC8200 is not a valid range address. On the other hand, Z:A1 *is* a valid range address, even though it is a single cell.

@ISRANGE returns 1 (TRUE) if *range* is a defined range name or valid range address and 0 (FALSE) if it is not. For example, if the worksheet contains a range called EXECUTION, the following function statement returns 1 (TRUE):

    @ISRANGE(EXECUTION)

By using @ISRANGE in combination with @IF, you can direct macros after checking whether an entry is a valid range name or not.

> **TIP** @ISRANGE works only with files in memory. Consider using @ISFILE to make sure that the relevant file is in memory before using @ISRANGE.

See Also   @ISSTRING

@ISSTRING(value)

The @ISSTRING function checks to see if *value* contains text or a label, where *value* is any value, location, text, or condition. @ISSTRING returns 1 (TRUE) if *value* is text or a cell that contains a label or a formula that results in a label and 0 (FALSE) if *value* is a value, ERR, NA, or a blank cell.

When using @ISSTRING to check for a literal string, enclose *value* in double quotation marks (""); when using @ISSTRING to check for a range name, there is no need for quotation marks. For example, you could run the following function statement for a worksheet that contains a range named NEW ORDER:

    @ISSTRING("New Order")

This would return 1 (TRUE), as would the following function statement:

    @ISSTRING(NEW ORDER)

See Also   @CELL, @CELLPOINTER, @ISNUMBER

@TRUE

The @TRUE function returns the logical value 1 (TRUE). The function has no arguments.

The 1 that @TRUE returns is a valid 1 that you can use in calculations, as illustrated in the foolish personal finance worksheet in Figure F.5.

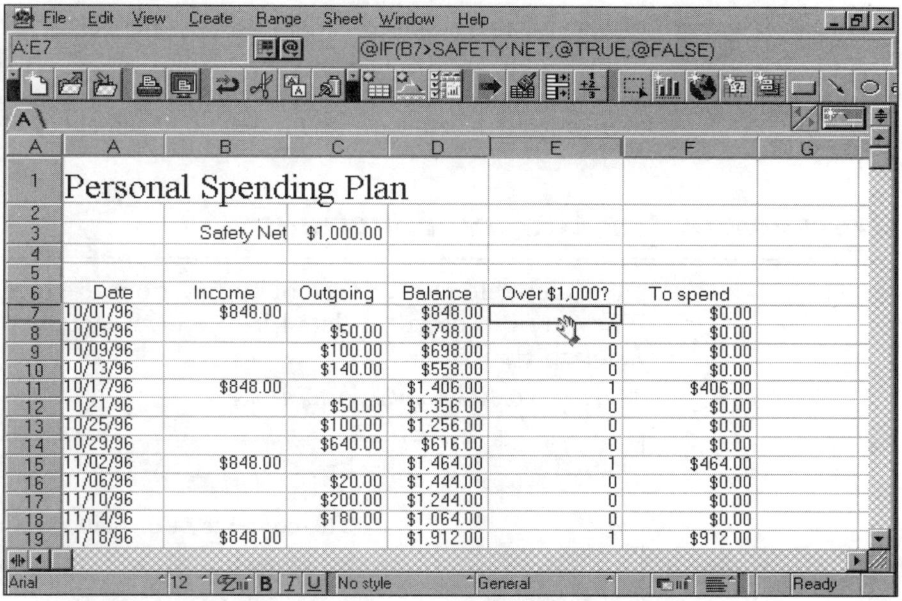

Descriptions of the Logical Functions

Figure F.5: Using the @TRUE function

In this worksheet, you have set up a simple budgeting spreadsheet to track income and expenses and keep a running total of what's left in your bank account. To give yourself an incentive, you've set up a mechanism to allow you to splurge on frivolities when the balance rises above your designated safety net of $1,000. Column E contains the following function statement in cell E7:

    @IF(B7>SAFETY NET,@TRUE,@FALSE)

This will return 1 (TRUE) if your balance is above the safety net and 0 if it is not; this function statement is copied down the column. Column F contains the following function statement in cell F7:

    (+D7--$SAFETY NET)*E7

This will calculate the amount of money you have to squander—the value of 1 (TRUE) or 0 (FALSE) multiplied by the amount over $1,000 in the account.

See Also   @FALSE

TIP While it might be easier to enter 1 than enter @TRUE when writing formulas for evaluating logical conditions, you'll probably find that having @TRUE in the formulas makes them easier to read later. This applies in spades when you're working with formulas that somebody else wrote.

Overview of the Lookup Functions

For quick reference, the Lookup functions are listed here in Table F.3. They are discussed in detail in the next section, "Descriptions of the Lookup Functions."

Table F.3:   Lookup Functions Quick Reference

Function	Returns
@@	The contents of the cell specified by means of a reference through the contents of another cell
@CHOOSE	A value or label from a list or range of values
@HLOOKUP	The contents of the cell indicated by a specified key in a specified row of a horizontal lookup table
@INDEX	The contents of the cell located at the intersection of a specified column, row, and worksheet of a range
@MATCH	The offset position in a range of the cell containing specified contents
@MAXLOOKUP	An absolute reference to the cell containing the largest value in a list of ranges
@MINLOOKUP	An absolute reference to the cell containing the smallest value in a list of ranges
@N	The entry in the first cell of a specified range as a value
@VLOOKUP	The contents of the cell indicated by a given key in a specified column of a vertical lookup table
@XINDEX	The contents of the cell located at the intersection of a specified column_heading, row_heading, and worksheet_heading of a range

Descriptions of the Lookup Functions

This section of the appendix contains detailed descriptions of the lookup functions that 1-2-3 offers.

> **NOTE** See "Lookup Functions" in Chapter 8 for a general-purpose discussion of these functions.

@@(location)

The @@ function retrieves the contents of the cell specified in *location* by means of a reference through the contents of another cell. *location* can be the address or name of a cell containing a cell address or name, or a formula returning the address or name of a cell.

@@ is mysterious at first sight, but straightforward with an example. If cell D1 contains the value 44, and cell B1 contains the label 'D1 (note the apostrophe), you could enter the following function statement in cell A1:

    @@(B1)

This would return the contents of cell D1: 44. Note that *location* must be a valid cell address or range name for a single-cell range; otherwise, @@ will return ERR.

The @@ function is most useful for worksheets that contain several formulas that use the same argument—an argument that you need to change now and then. For example, in Figure F.6, cell F5 contains the following function statement:

    +E5*@@(D$15)

This pulls the reference-cell information from cell D15 to calculate the commission for the salespeople. Since cell D15 contains 'G11, the value in cell G11—13.00%—is used in the calculation. You can easily change all the formulas in the Commission column at once by changing the label in cell D15.

> **TIP** Note that you will need to press F9 to recalculate an @@ formula if the *location* argument refers to a cell containing a formula; otherwise the @@ formula will return 0.

See Also @CHOOSE, @HLOOKUP, @INDEX, @VLOOKUP

Appendix F Information, Logical, and Lookup Functions Reference

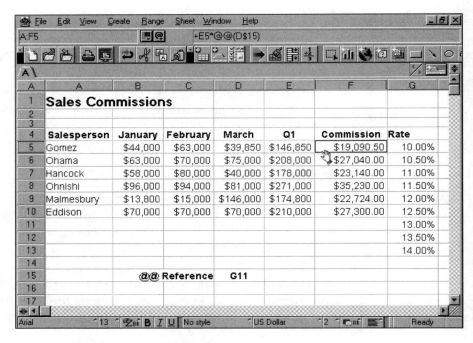

Figure F.6: Using the @@ function to change several formulas at once

@CHOOSE(value, list)

The @CHOOSE function returns a value or label from a *list*, which is a group of values or the addresses or names of cells that contain values or labels. *value* indicates the offset number of the item's position in *list*.

For example, the worksheet shown in Figure F.7 contains a list of labels in the range B1..E1 and a list of their offset numbers (0, 1, 2, 3) in the range B2..E2. To pull the label from D1, one could use the following function statement, since D2 contains 2, which is the offset number for D1 in *list*:

    @CHOOSE(D2,B1,C1,D1,E1)

See Also   @HLOOKUP, @INDEX, @MATCH, @VLOOKUP, @XINDEX

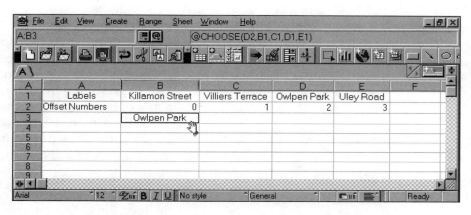

Figure F.7:   Using the @CHOOSE function to pull a label from a specified cell

@HLOOKUP(key,range,row-offset)

The @HLOOKUP function returns the contents of the cell indicated by *key* in a specified row of a horizontal lookup table, *range*. The horizontal lookup table is a range with either value information in ascending order or labels in the first row.

@HLOOKUP works by comparing *key* to the index values in each cell in the first row of the horizontal lookup table. When 1-2-3 finds the cell containing *key* (or, for a value entered for *key*, the value closest to but not larger than *key*), it moves down that column to the cell indicated by *row-offset* and returns the contents of that cell.

The arguments for the @HLOOKUP function are as follows:

Argument	Description
key	A value or text, depending on what the first row of the horizontal lookup table contains, as follows:
	Values. If the first row of the horizontal lookup table contains values, *key* can be any value greater than or equal to the first value in range. If *key* is smaller than the first value in range, @HLOOKUP returns ERR. If *key* is larger than the last value contained in the first row of *range*, @HLOOKUP will stop at the last cell in the row specified by row-offset and return the contents of that cell as the answer.

Argument	Description
	Labels. If the first row of the horizontal lookup table contains labels, *key* can be text enclosed in double quotation marks (""), a formula resulting in text, or the address or name of a cell that contains a label or a formula resulting in a label. @HLOOKUP will return ERR if *key* does not exactly match the contents of a cell in the first row of *range*.
range	A range address or range name indicating the location of the horizontal lookup table. Note that 1-2-3 will use only the first worksheet in a 3D range entered for range.
row-offset	A number indicating the offset position of the row in *range*.

For example, Figure F.8 shows a company's Length of Service spreadsheet for employees of different salary grades. You could use @HLOOKUP to track how many employees of a particular grade have been at the company for a particular length of time. For example, you could use the following statement to find out how many Grade 2 employees have been at the company for five years:

```
@HLOOKUP("Grade 2",A3..G17,5)
```

This function statement returns 20.

See Also   @CHOOSE, @INDEX, @MATCH, @MAXLOOKUP, @MINLOOKUP, @VLOOKUP, @XINDEX

@INDEX(range,column,row,[worksheet])

The @INDEX function returns the contents of the cell located at the intersection of a specified *column*, *row*, and *worksheet* of a *range*. (The *worksheet* argument is optional.)

The arguments for @INDEX are as follows:

Argument	Description
range	Any range address or range name.
column	The offset number of the column for @INDEX to use.

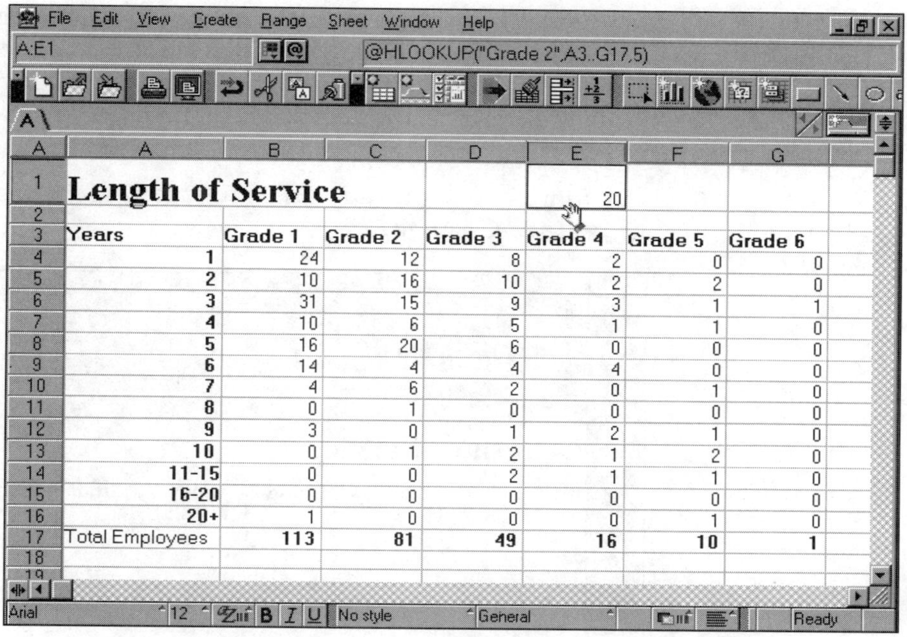

A	A	B	C	D	E	F	G
1	**Length of Service**				20		
2							
3	Years	Grade 1	Grade 2	Grade 3	Grade 4	Grade 5	Grade 6
4	1	24	12	8	2	0	0
5	2	10	16	10	2	2	0
6	3	31	15	9	3	1	1
7	4	10	6	5	1	1	0
8	5	16	20	6	0	0	0
9	6	14	4	4	4	0	0
10	7	4	6	2	0	1	0
11	8	0	1	0	0	0	0
12	9	3	0	1	2	1	0
13	10	0	1	2	1	2	0
14	11-15	0	0	2	1	1	0
15	16-20	0	0	0	0	0	0
16	20+	1	0	0	0	1	0
17	Total Employees	113	81	49	16	10	1
18							

Figure F.8: ***Using the @HLOOKUP function***

row Either the offset number of the row for @INDEX to use, or the address or name of a cell containing 0 or a positive integer.

worksheet The offset number of the worksheet for @INDEX to use. This is an optional argument; if you don't specify the worksheet, 1-2-3 will use the first worksheet in *range*.

For example, consider the Length of Service worksheet shown in Figure F.9. In this figure, cell B19 contains the following function statement:

```
@INDEX(A3..G17,D19,F19)
```

This defines the range on which @INDEX operates and uses the values stored in cell D19 (representing the Grade of the employees) and cell F19 (representing the length of service of the employees) to quickly return the relevant value from the worksheet: 4. In the figure, cell D19 contains 4, specifying the fourth column offset from the beginning of the range, and cell F19 contains 6, specifying the sixth row offset from the top of the range. By changing the values in cells D19 and F19, you can easily look up information in other cells. For example, to look up the number of Grade 5 employees with 20 or more years of service at the company, you could enter 5 in cell D19 and 13 in cell F19.

For more about the @INDEX function, including some examples of its use, see Chapter 8.

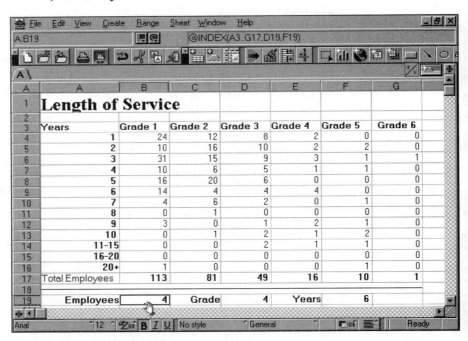

Figure F.9: Using the @INDEX function to return the contents of a cell by specifying the relative positions of the rows and columns

TIP @INDEX is similar in use to three other 1-2-3 @ functions: @XINDEX, @HLOOKUP, and @VLOOKUP. The differences between these four functions are as follows: @XINDEX is for locating a cell using text or values in *column_heading, row_heading,* and *worksheet_heading* rather than specifying offset numbers for *column, row,* or *worksheet.* @HLOOKUP and @VLOOKUP are for locating cells by identifying the column or row in which they are located, then specifying an offset number from the row heading or column heading. @INDEX is for locating a cell in a lookup table by specifying its exact location without reference to the row heading or column heading.

See Also @CHOOSE, @HLOOKUP, @MATCH, @MAXLOOKUP, @MINLOOKUP, @VLOOKUP, @XINDEX

@MATCH (cell-contents,range,[type])

The @MATCH function returns the offset position of the cell containing *cell-contents* in *range*. The arguments for the @MATCH function are as follows:

Argument	Description
cell-contents	The value or text to find. You can use wildcard characters if *cell-contents* is text.
range	Any range name or address.
type	0, 1, or 2 to specify how 1-2-3 compares *cell-contents* with the contents of the cells in *range*, as follows: 0 If *type* = 0, @MATCH returns the first cell whose contents match cell-contents. 1 If *type* = 1, @MATCH returns the cell that contains the largest value less than or equal to *cell-contents*. 1 is the default setting if you omit the *type* argument. When *type* = 1, 1-2-3 sorts *range* in ascending order. 2 If *type* = 2, @MATCH returns the cell that contains the smallest value greater than or equal to *cell-contents*. When *type* = 2, 1-2-3 sorts *range* in descending order.

TIP The major difference between @MATCH and functions such as @HLOOKUP and @VLOOKUP is that @MATCH returns the position of the match item found rather than the item itself. Thus you could use @MATCH to find, say, an instance of a particular value or text and report its position, but not to bring that value or text into another calculation or string.

Note that @MATCH searches *range* from top to bottom in a column and from left to right. If *range* is a multisheet range, @MATCH searches the first worksheet in the range as described in the previous sentence before going to the second worksheet, and so forth. @MATCH stops the search when it encounters a match or reaches the end of *range*.

> **WARNING** @MATCH will return ERR if *range* does not include a match for *cell-contents*. @MATCH will also return ERR if *type* = 1 and the first cell in *range* contains a value greater than *cell-contents*, or if *type* = 2 and the first cell in *range* contains a value less than *cell-contents*.

See Also @CHOOSE, @HLOOKUP, @INDEX, @MAXLOOKUP, @MINLOOKUP, @VLOOKUP

@MAXLOOKUP(range-list)

The @MAXLOOKUP function returns an absolute reference to the cell containing the largest value in a list of ranges, *range-list*, which can be any combination of range names or addresses separated by argument separators. The absolute reference includes the file name.

> **NOTE** @MAXLOOKUP ignores labels and blank cells in the *range-list* argument and will return NA if none of the cells in *range-list* contains values.

For example, suppose you teach five classes and keep the scores for the students in the files YEAR_1.WK5, YEAR2_WK5, YEAR_3.WK5, YEAR_4.WK5, and YEAR_5.WK5 in your 1-2-3 \WORK\ directory. You built the files from the same template, so they have the same layout; each has a range named AVERAGE SCORE that contains the average scores for the students over all the tests in the year. To find the highest score for a student in any of the years, you could use

```
@MAXLOOKUP(<<YEAR_1.WK5>>AVERAGE
SCORE,<<YEAR2_WK5>>AVERAGE SCORE,<<YEAR_3.WK5>>AVERAGE
SCORE,<<YEAR_4.WK5>>AVERAGE SCORE,<<YEAR_5.WK5>> AVERAGE
SCORE)
```

See Also @CHOOSE, @HLOOKUP, @INDEX, @MATCH, @VLOOKUP, @XINDEX

@MINLOOKUP(range-list)

The @MINLOOKUP function returns an absolute reference to the cell containing the smallest value in a list of ranges, *range-list*, which can be any combination of range names or addresses separated by argument separators. The absolute reference includes the file name.

Descriptions of the Lookup Functions

NOTE @MINLOOKUP ignores labels and blank cells in *range-list* and will return NA if none of the cells in *range-list* contain values.

For example, you keep the test scores for the students in the five classes you teach in the files YEAR_1.WK5, YEAR2_WK5, YEAR_3.WK5, YEAR_4.WK5, and YEAR_5.WK5 in your 1-2-3 \WORK\ directory. Since you built the files from the same template, they're laid out the same; each has a range named AVERAGE SCORE that contains the average scores for the students over all the tests in the year. To find the lowest score for a student in any of the years—perhaps for special tutoring—you could use this function statement:

```
@MINLOOKUP(<<YEAR_1.WK5>>AVERAGE
SCORE,<<YEAR2_WK5>>AVERAGE  SCORE,<<YEAR_3.WK5>>AVERAGE
SCORE,<<YEAR_4.WK5>>AVERAGE  SCORE,<<YEAR_5.WK5>> AVERAGE
SCORE)
```

See Also   @CHOOSE, @HLOOKUP, @INDEX, @MATCH, @VLOOKUP, @XINDEX

@N(range)

The @N function returns the entry in the first cell of *range* as a value. @N returns the value 0 if the entry in the first cell of *range* is a label. *range* can be a cell address, a range address, or a range name. For example, if cell B100 contains 98.4, this function statement returns 99.4:

```
@N(B100..B200)+1
```

Although at first sight the uses of @N may seem limited, the function has two common uses. First, you can use it to return a value from a cell containing a label, when returning a label would upset a calculation and return ERR. Second, you use @N in macros to check that a user enters a value where you need one. For example,

```
{IF @N(C1)=0}{BEEP}
```

would cause a macro to beep if a user entered a label in cell C1 (because @N returns 0 for a label).

See Also   @ISNUMBER, @ISSTRING, @S

@VLOOKUP(key,range,row-offset)

The @VLOOKUP function returns the contents of the cell indicated by *key* in a specified column of a vertical lookup table, *range*. The vertical lookup table is a range with either value information in ascending order or labels in the first column.

@VLOOKUP works by comparing *key* to the index values in each cell in the first column of the vertical lookup table. When 1-2-3 finds the cell containing *key* (or, for a value entered for *key*, the value closest to but not larger than *key*), it moves across that row to the cell indicated by *column-offset* and returns the contents of that cell.

The arguments for the @VLOOKUP function are as follows:

Argument	Description
key	A value or text, depending on what the first column of the vertical lookup table contains, as follows:
	Values. If the first column of the vertical lookup table contains values, *key* can be any value greater than or equal to the first value in *range*. If *key* is smaller than the first value in *range*, @VLOOKUP returns ERR. If *key* is larger than the last value contained in the first column of *range*, @VLOOKUP will stop at the last cell in the column specified by *column-offset* and return the contents of that cell as the answer.
	Labels. If the first column of the vertical lookup table contains labels, *key* can be text enclosed in double quotation marks (""), a formula resulting in text, or the address or name of a cell that contains a label or a formula resulting in a label. @VLOOKUP will return ERR if *key* does not exactly match the contents of a cell in the first column of *range*.
range	A range address or range name indicating the location of the vertical lookup table.

Descriptions of the Lookup Functions

	Note that 1-2-3 will use only the first worksheet in a 3D range entered for *range*.
column-offset	A number indicating the offset position of the column in *range*.

For example, Figure F.10 shows a company's Length of Service spreadsheet for employees of different salary grades. You could use @VLOOKUP to track how many employees with a particular length of service have attained a specified salary grade. For example, you could use this function statement to find out how many 11 to 15-year employees have reached salary grade 5:

```
@VLOOKUP("11-15",A3..G17,5)
```

The answer is 1.

See Also @CHOOSE, @HLOOKUP, @INDEX, @MATCH, @MAXLOOKUP, @MINLOOKUP, @XINDEX

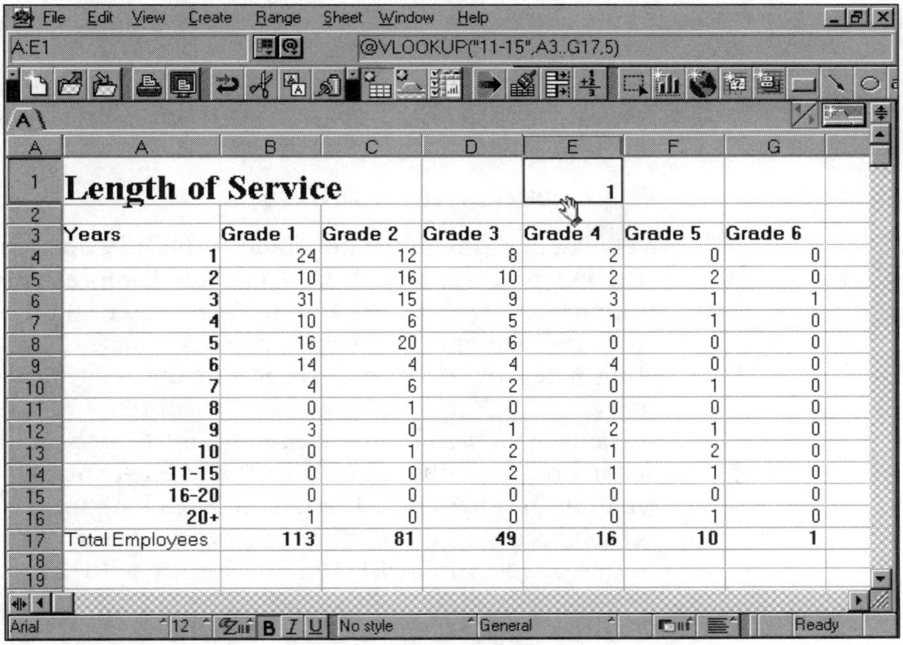

Years	Grade 1	Grade 2	Grade 3	Grade 4	Grade 5	Grade 6
1	24	12	8	2	0	0
2	10	16	10	2	2	0
3	31	15	9	3	1	1
4	10	6	5	1	1	0
5	16	20	6	0	0	0
6	14	4	4	4	0	0
7	4	6	2	0	1	0
8	0	1	0	0	0	0
9	3	0	1	2	1	0
10	0	1	2	1	2	0
11-15	0	0	2	1	1	0
16-20	0	0	0	0	0	0
20+	1	0	0	0	1	0
Total Employees	113	81	49	16	10	1

Figure F.10: Using the @VLOOKUP function

@XINDEX(range,column,row,[worksheet])

The @XINDEX function returns the contents of the cell located at the intersection of a specified *column_heading*, *row_heading*, and *worksheet_heading* of a *range*. (The *worksheet* argument is optional.)

The arguments for @XINDEX are as follows:

Argument	Description
range	Any range address or range name.
column_heading	A value or text representing the contents of a cell in the first row of *range*.
row_heading	A value or text representing the contents of a cell in the first column of *range*.
worksheet_heading	A value or text representing the contents of the first cell in *range*. This is an optional argument; if you don't specify the worksheet, 1-2-3 will use the first worksheet in *range*.

For example, consider the Length of Service worksheet shown in Figure F.11. In this figure, cell B19 contains the following function statement:

```
@XINDEX(A3..G17,D19,F19)
```

This defines the range on which @INDEX operates (A3..G17). It uses the labels stored in cell D19 (Grade 3, representing the Grade of the employees) and cell F19 ('11-15, representing the length of service of the employees; note the apostrophe to make this a label rather than letting it return −4) to quickly return the relevant value from the worksheet: 2. @XINDEX returns the contents of the cell referenced by Grade 3 in the column heading and '11-15 in the row heading. By changing the values in cells D19 and F19, you can easily look up information in other cells. For example, to look up the number of Grade 5 employees with 20 or more years of service at the company, you could enter Grade 5 in cell D19 and '20+ in cell F19.

See Also @CHOOSE, @HLOOKUP, @MATCH, @MAXLOOKUP, @MINLOOKUP, @VLOOKUP

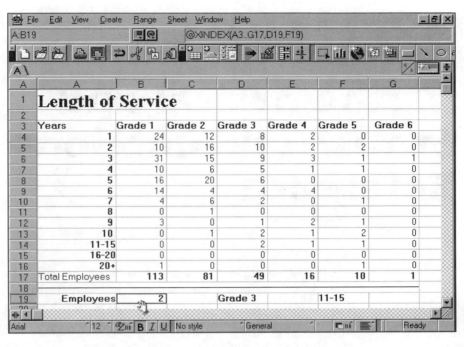

Figure F.11: **Using the @XINDEX function to return the contents of a cell by specifying the column heading and row heading**

 WARNING @XINDEX is similar in use to three other 1-2-3 @ functions: @INDEX, @HLOOKUP, and @VLOOKUP. The differences between these four functions are as follows: @INDEX is for locating a cell by specifying offset numbers for column and row rather than specifying text or values in a row-heading or column-heading cell. @HLOOKUP and @VLOOKUP are for locating cells by identifying the column or row in which they are located, then specifying an offset number from the row heading or column heading. @INDEX is for locating a cell in a lookup table by specifying its exact location without reference to the row heading or column heading.

APPENDIX G
Mathematical and Statistical Functions Reference

THIS appendix looks at two of the most important groups of 1-2-3's functions—the mathematical and statistical functions.

The mathematical functions, which include functions such as @COS (for calculating the cosine of an angle), @DEGTORAD (for converting degrees to radians), and @EVEN (for returning the next even number), simplify a number of mathematical operations.

The statistical functions, which include functions such as @CHIDIST (for calculating a chi-distribution) and @WEIGHTAVG (for calculating weighted averages), perform calculations on lists of values.

Overview of the Mathematical Functions

1-2-3 provides a comprehensive set of mathematical functions that will take care of almost any basic or specialized mathematical operations. The mathematical functions fall into five categories:

- **Conversion functions.** For example, @DEGTORAD, which converts degrees to radians.
- **General mathematical functions.** For example, @RAND, which generates a random number.
- **Hyperbolic functions.** For example, @TANH, which calculates the hyperbolic tangent of a given angle.

- **Rounding functions.** For example, @TRUNC, which truncates a value to the number of decimal places requested.
- **Trigonometric functions.** For example, @SIN, which calculates the sine of a given angle.

For quick reference, the mathematical functions are listed in Table G.1.

Table G.1: **Mathematical Functions Quick Reference**

Function	Returns
@ABS	The absolute value of the given number
@ACOS	The angle that is the arc cosine of the given number
@ACOSH	The arc hyperbolic cosine of the given angle
@ACOT	The arc cotangent of the given angle
@ACOTH	The arc hyperbolic cotangent of the given angle
@ACSC	The arc cosecant of the given angle
@ACSCH	The arc hyperbolic cosecant of the given angle
@ASEC	The arc secant of the given angle
@ASECH	The arc hyperbolic secant of the given angle
@ASIN	The arc sine of the given angle
@ASINH	The arc hyperbolic sine of the given angle
@ATAN	The arc tangent of the given angle
@ATAN2	The arc tangent of the given angle determined by the x and y coordinates using the tangent y/x ($n1/n$)
@ATANH	The arc hyperbolic tangent of the given angle
@COS	The cosine of the given angle
@COSH	The hyperbolic cosine of the given angle
@COT	The cotangent of the given angle
@COTH	The hyperbolic cotangent of the given angle

Table G.1: Mathematical Functions Quick Reference (continued)

Function	Returns
@CSC	The cosecant (the reciprocal of the sine) of the given angle
@CSCH	The hyperbolic cosecant (the reciprocal of the hyperbolic sine) of the given angle
@DECILE	A selected decile
@DEGTORAD	The value in radians of the angle given in degrees
@EVEN	The nearest even integer to the number; positive values are rounded up and negative values are rounded down
@EXP	The value of the constant *e* (approximately 2.718282, the base of the natural logarithm) raised to the specified power
@EXP2	The value of the constant *e* (approximately 2.718282, the base of the natural logarithm) raised to the power (*numeric-value^2*)
@FACT	The factorial of the given number (the product of all positive integers from 1 to the number)
@FACTLN	The natural logarithm of the factorial of a number
@INT	The given number as a whole number, disregarding any fractional portion
@LARGE	The *n*th largest value in the given range
@LN	The natural logarithm of the given value
@LOG	The common or base-10 logarithm (base 10) of the given value
@MOD, @MODULO	The *modulus* (remainder) after the given number is divided by the given divisor
@ODD	The given value rounded away from 0 to the nearest odd integer; positive values are rounded up and negative values are rounded down

Table G.1: **Mathematical Functions Quick Reference** (continued)

Function	Returns
@PI	The value of the mathematical constant
@QUARTILE	A selected quartile
@QUOTIENT	The integer result of the given number divided by the given divisor
@RADTODEG	The value in degrees of a value given in radians
@RAND	A random value between 0 and 1 calculated to seventeen decimal places
@ROUND	The given number rounded to the nearest specified multiple of the power of 10
@ROUNDDOWN	The given value rounded down to the nearest multiple of the specified power
@ROUNDM	The given value rounded to the nearest specified multiple
@ROUNDUP	The given value rounded up to the nearest multiple of the specified power
@SEC	The secant (the reciprocal of the cosine) of the given angle
@SECH	The hyperbolic secant (the reciprocal of the hyperbolic cosine) of the given angle
@SEMEAN	The standard error of the sample mean (or average) for the values in the given range
@SIGN	The sign of the given number
@SIN	The sine of the given angle
@SINH	The hyperbolic sine of the given angle
@SMALL	The nth smallest value in the given range
@SQRT	The positive square root of the given value
@SQRTPI	The square root of the given value multiplied by pi

Table G.1: Mathematical Functions Quick Reference

Function	Returns
@SUBTOTAL	The total of the values in a list. @SUBTOTAL also indicates to @GRANDTOTAL which subtotals to include in the grand total
@SUM	The sum of the values in the given list
@SUM-PRODUCT	The sum of the products of values in corresponding cells in multiple ranges
@SUMSQ	The sum of the squares of the values in the given list
@SUMXMY2	The sum of the squared differences after the values in one range have been subtracted from the corresponding cells in another range
@TAN	The tangent of the given angle
@TANH	The hyperbolic tangent of the given angle
@TRUNC	The given value truncated to the number of decimal places specified

Descriptions of the Mathematical Functions

This section contains detailed descriptions of the mathematical functions.

> **NOTE** See "Mathematical Functions" in Chapter 8 for a general-purpose description of these functions.

@ABS(number)

The @ABS function calculates the absolute value of *number*, where *number* is any number. Absolute values are always positive. For example, the following function statement returns 33 if cell C119 contains –33 or 33:

@ABS(C119)

To return a negative value, use –@ABS instead of @ABS. For example, the following function statement returns –33 if cell C119 contains –33 or 33:

    -@ABS(C119)

> **NOTE** See Chapter 8 for more information about this function.

@ACOS(number)

The @ACOS function calculates the angle that is the arc cosine of *number*, where *number* is a value between –1 and 1. An arc cosine is an inverse cosine that produces its result as an angle in radians, between 0 and π, representing an angle between 0 and 180 degrees. For example, the following function statement returns 0.85 (rounded to two decimal places), the cosine of which is 0.66:

    @ACOS(0.66)

See Chapter 8 for more information about this and other inverse trigonometric functions.

> **NOTE** You can convert the number in radians into an angle by using the @RADTODEG function.

See Also   @ACOSH, @COS, @RADTODEG

@ACOSH(number)

The @ACOSH function calculates the arc hyperbolic cosine using the hyperbolic cosine *number* of an angle, where *number* is a value of 1 or greater. An arc hyperbolic cosine is an inverse hyperbolic cosine; the result is in radians. For example, the following function statement returns 1.762747:

    @ACOSH(3)

You can use @RADTODEG to convert the result of @ACOSH from radians to degrees—in this case, 101 degrees.

See Also   @ACOS, @COS, @COSH, @RADTODEG

@ACOT(number)

The @ACOT function calculates the arc cotangent using the cotangent *number* of an angle, where *number* is the cotangent of an angle, a value between $-2*\pi$ and $2^{32}*\pi$. An arc cotangent is an inverse cotangent; the result is in radians from 0 to π, representing an angle between 0 and 180 degrees. For example, if the cotangent of angle *number* is 1.43, the following function statement returns 0.61:

    @ACOT(1.43)

You can use @RADTODEG to convert the result in radians to degrees—in this case, @RADTODEG (0.61) gives a result of 34.97 degrees.

See Also   @ACOTH, @COT

@ACOTH(number)

The @ACOTH function calculates the arc hyperbolic cotangent using the hyperbolic cotangent *number* of an angle, where *number* is a value less than –1 or greater than 1. An arc hyperbolic cotangent is an inverse hyperbolic cotangent; the result is in radians. For example, the following function statement produces –0.35:

    @ACOTH(-3)

You can use @RADTODEG to convert the result in radians to degrees—in this case, @RADTODEG (–0.35) gives a result of –20 degrees.

See Also   @ACOT, @COTH

@ACSC(number)

The @ACSC function calculates the arc cosecant using the cosecant *number* of an angle, where *number* is less than or equal to –1, or equal to or greater than 1. The result is an angle in radians from $-\pi/2$ through $\pi/2$, representing an angle between –90 and 90 degrees. For example, if the cosecant of angle *number* is 1.5, the following function statement returns 0.728 radians:

    @ACSC(1.5)

You can use @RADTODEG to convert the result in radians to degrees—in this case, @RADTODEG(0.729728) returns a result of 41.8 degrees.

See Also   @ACSCH, @CSC

@ACSCH(numeric-value)

The @ACSCH function calculates the arc hyperbolic cosecant using the hyperbolic cosecant *number* of an angle, where *number* is any value other than 0. An arc hyperbolic cosecant is an inverse hyperbolic cosecant; the result is in radians. For example, the following function statement produces 0.247:

    @ACSCH(4)

You can use @RADTODEG to convert the result in radians to degrees—in this case, @RADTODEG (0.247) gives a result of 14.2 degrees.

See Also   @ACSC, @CSCH

@ASEC(numeric-value)

The @ASEC function calculates the arc secant using the secant *number* of an angle, where *number* is less than or equal to –1 or equal to or greater than 1. (The arc secant is the inverse secant.) The result is an angle in radians from 0 to π, representing an angle between 0 and 180 degrees. For example, if the secant of angle *number* is 1, the following function statement returns 0 radians:

    @ASEC(1)

You can use @RADTODEG to convert the result in radians to degrees, though in this case you hardly need to—as you might guess, @RADTODEG(0) gives a result of 0 degrees.

See Also   @ASECH, @SEC

@ASECH(numeric-value)

The @ASECH function calculates the arc hyperbolic secant using the hyperbolic secant *number* of an angle, where *number* is a value greater than 0 and less than or equal to 1. An arc hyperbolic secant is an inverse hyperbolic secant; the result is in radians. For example, the following function statement returns 0.896:

    @ASECH(0.7)

You can use @RADTODEG to convert the result in radians to degrees—in this case, @RADTODEG (0.896) gives a result of 51.3 degrees.

See Also   @ASEC, @SECH

@ASIN(numeric-value)

The @ASIN function calculates the arc sine of *n*, where *number* is a value between –1 and 1. The arc sine is the inverse sine; the result is an angle in radians from $-\pi/2$ to $\pi/2$, representing an angle between –90 and 90 degrees. For example, to calculate the arc sine of 0.75, you could use the following function statement:

    @ASIN(0.75)

This returns 0.8481. You can use @RADTODEG to convert the result in radians to degrees—in this case, @RADTODEG(0.8481) returns 43 degrees.

NOTE See Chapter 8 for more information about this and other inverse trigonometric functions.

See Also   @ASINH, @SIN

@ASINH(numeric-value)

The @ASINH function calculates the arc hyperbolic sine using the hyperbolic sine *number* of an angle, where *number* is any value. An arc hyperbolic sine is an inverse hyperbolic sine; the result is in radians. For example, the following function statement produces 1.82:

    @ASINH(3)

You can use @RADTODEG to convert the result in radians to degrees—in this case, @RADTODEG (1.82) gives a result of 104.25 degrees.

See Also   @ASIN, @SINH

@ATAN(numeric-value)

The @ATAN function calculates the arc tangent of *n*, where *number* is the tangent of any angle and is any value. The arc tangent is the inverse

Descriptions of the Mathematical Functions

tangent; the result is an angle in radians from $-\pi/2$ to $\pi/2$, representing an angle between –90 and 90 degrees. For example, if you know the tangent of angle *number* is 3/1 (i.e., 3), you can calculate the arc tangent of 3 by using the following function statement:

    @ATAN(3)

This returns 1.249. You can then use @RADTODEG to convert the result in radians to degrees—in this case, @RADTODEG(1.249) returns 71.62 degrees.

See Also   @ATAN2, @ATANH, @TAN

@ATAN2(numeric-value1,numeric-value2)

The @ATAN2 function calculates the arc tangent of the angle determined by the x and y coordinates (*numeric-value1* and *numeric-value2*) using the tangent y/x (*n1/n*). @ATAN2 produces a result of an angle in radians between $-\pi$ and π, an angle between –180 and 180 degrees. For example, using coordinates with the same value, 50 degrees, the following function statement gives an angle of 45 degrees:

    @RADTODEG(@ATAN2(50,50))

See Chapter 8 for more information about this and other inverse trigonometric functions.

NOTE @ATAN 2 returns 0 if y = 0 and returns ERR if both x = 0 and y = 0.

Depending on whether the values of the x and y coordinates are positive or negative, @ATAN2 can result in values for all four quadrants:

x	y	Value Range	Quadrant
Positive	Positive	$0-\pi/2$	I
Negative	Positive	$\pi/2-\pi$	II
Negative	Negative	$-\pi--\pi/2$	III
Positive	Negative	$-\pi/2-0$	IV

NOTE In quadrants I and IV, @ATAN2 produces the same results as @ATAN. For example, when x is positive (e.g., 4) and y is positive (e.g., 5), both @ATAN2(4,5) and @ATAN(5/4) produce 0.8961, which produces (using @RADTODEG) an angle of 51.34 degrees.

See Also   @ATAN, @TAN

@ATANH(numeric-value)

The @ATANH function calculates the arc hyperbolic tangent using the hyperbolic tangent *number* of an angle, where *number* is a value between –1 and 1. An arc hyperbolic tangent is an inverse hyperbolic tangent; the result is in radians. For example, this function statement gives a result of –0.79281:

    @ATANH(-0.66)

You can use @RADTODEG to convert the result in radians to degrees—in this case, @RADTODEG (–0.79281) gives an angle of –45.42 degrees.

See Also   @ATAN, @ATAN2, @TANH

@COS(numeric-value)

The @COS function returns the cosine of *numeric-value*, which is an angle measured in radians and which is a value between $-2^{32}*\pi$ and $2^{32}*\pi$. @COS returns a value from –1 through 1.

NOTE The cosine is the ratio of the side adjacent an acute angle of a right triangle to the hypotenuse.

For example, to calculate the cosine of an angle of 6 radians, you would use the following function statement:

    @COS(6)

This produces a result of 0.96017. You could then use @RADTODEG to convert this result to degrees, as in the following function statement:

    @RADTODEG(0.96017)

This gives an angle of 55.014 degrees. Alternatively, you could combine @COS and @RADTODEG to produce this result more concisely:

    @RADTODEG(@COS(6))

You can use @DEGTORAD to convert degrees to radians. To produce the cosine of an angle—for example, a 50-degree angle—use @COS in combination with @DEGTORAD:

    @COS(@DEGTORAD(50))

> **NOTE** See Chapter 8 for more information about this and other trigonometric functions.

See Also   @ACOS, @COSH, @DEGTORAD

@COSH(numeric-value)

The @COSH function returns the hyperbolic cosine of *numeric-value*, which can be any value from approximately –11355.1371 through 11355.1371. @COSH produces as a result a value greater than or equal to 1. For example, the following function statement returns 29937.07:

    @COSH(11)

> **WARNING** Using @COSH with large numbers is liable to produce numbers too large for 1-2-3 to store or display. If this happens, try using @COSH in combination with other @functions, such as @DEGTORAD, to return a value you can display and use. For example, use @COSH(@DEGTORAD(11111)) rather than @COSH(11111) to produce a displayable result.

See Also   @ACOS, @COS

@COT(numeric-value)

The @COT function returns the cotangent of *numeric-value*, which is an angle measured in radians and which is a value between $-2^{32}*\pi$ and $2^{32}*\pi$.

For example, to calculate the cotangent of an angle of 4 radians, you would use the following function statement:

    @COT(4)

This produces a result of 0.8637. You could then use @RADTODEG to convert this result to degrees:

    @RADTODEG(0.8637)

This gives an angle of 49.49 degrees. Alternatively, you could combine @COT and @RADTODEG to produce this result rather more neatly:

    @RADTODEG(@COT(4))

You can use @DEGTORAD to convert degrees to radians. To produce the cotangent of an angle—for example, a 50-degree angle—use @COT in combination with @DEGTORAD:

    @COT(@DEGTORAD(50))

NOTE The cotangent is the ratio of the side adjacent an acute angle of a right triangle to the opposite side. The cotangent of an angle is the reciprocal of the tangent of the same angle.

See Also   @ACOT, @COTH, @TAN

@COTH(numeric-value)

The @COTH function returns the hyperbolic cotangent of *numeric-value*, which can be any value from approximately –11355.1371 through 11355.1371 except for 0. For example, the following function statement returns 1.00497:

    @COTH(3)

To calculate the hyperbolic cotangent of a 45-degree angle, use @COTH combined with @DEGTORAD:

    @COTH(@DEGTORAD(45))

This returns 1.525.

See Also   @ACOTH, @COT, @TANH

@CSC(numeric-value)

The @CSC function returns the cosecant (the reciprocal of the sine) of angle *numeric-value*, where *numeric-value* is an angle measured in radians and is any value from $-2^{32}*\pi$ through $2^{32}*\pi$ except 0 and multiples of π. @CSC results in either a value greater than or equal to 1, or a value less than or equal to -1.

For example, the following function statement returns 7.086.

    @CSC(3)

You can use @DEGTORAD with @CSC to determine the cosecant of an angle that you know in degrees:

    @CSC(@DEGTORAD(45))

This returns 1.414, the cosecant of a 45-degree angle.

See Also   @ACSC, @CSCH, @SIN

@CSCH(numeric-value)

The @CSCH function returns the hyperbolic cosecant (the reciprocal of the hyperbolic sine) of angle *numeric-value*, which is any value from approximately -11355.1371 through 11355.1371 with the exception of 0. For example, the following function statement returns 0.0366:

    @CSCH(4)

> **WARNING** Using @CSCH with large numbers is liable to produce numbers too large for 1-2-3 to store or display. If this happens, try using @CSCH in combination with other @functions, such as @DEGTORAD, to return a value you can display and use. For example, use @CSCH(@DEGTORAD(11111)) rather than @CSCH(11111) to produce a displayable result.

You can use @DEGTORAD with @CSCH to determine the hyperbolic cosecant of an angle that you know in degrees:

    @CSCH(@DEGTORAD(45)) = 1.825306

This returns 1.1512, the hyperbolic cosecant of a 45-degree angle.

See Also   @ACSCH, @CSC, @SINH

@DECILE(tile;range)

The @DECILE function returns a given decile, where *tile* is an integer from 0 through 10, as listed below, and *range* is the address or name of the range that contains the target values.

Tile	Returns	Same as...
0	minimum	@PERCENTILE(0.0,*range*) or @MIN(*range*)
1	decile one	@PERCENTILE(0.1,*range*)
2	decile two	@PERCENTILE(0.2,*range*)
3	decile three	@PERCENTILE(0.3,*range*)
4	decile four	@PERCENTILE(0.4,*range*)
5	median	@PERCENTILE(0.5,*range*) or @MEDIAN(*range*)
6	decile six	@PERCENTILE(0.6,*range*)
7	decile seven	@PERCENTILE(0.7,*range*)
8	decile eight	@PERCENTILE(0.8,*range*)
9	decile nine	@PERCENTILE(0.9,*range*)
10	maximum	@PERCENTILE(1.0,*range*) or @MAX(*range*)

For example, where the range "RANGE1" contains the following data:

34

12

60

128

67

350

206

@DECILE(0;RANGE1) returns 12.0.

@DECILE(1;RANGE1) returns 25.2.

@DECILE(2;RANGE1) returns 39.2.

> **TIP** Blank cells and labels are calculated by @DECILE as 0.

See Also @QUARTILE

@DEGTORAD(degrees)

The @DEGTORAD function converts the value *degrees* to radians. For example, the following function statement returns 1.5708:

    @DEGTORAD(90)

You can combine @DEGTORAD with other mathematical functions—for example, to calculate the sine of an angle:

    @SIN(@DEGTORAD(75))

This returns 0.966, the sine of a 75-degree angle.

See Also @RADTODEG

@EVEN(numeric-value)

The @EVEN function rounds the value *numeric-value* away from zero to the nearest even integer. Positive values are rounded up; negative values are rounded down. *numeric-value* can be any value. For example, the following function statement returns 2:

    @EVEN(1.0000001)

And the following function statement returns –6:

    @EVEN(-4.4)

> **NOTE** If *numeric-value* is an even integer, @EVEN(*numeric-value*) will return the same integer: @EVEN(2) will return 2, while @EVEN(2.000000001) will return 4. Consider using @ROUND, @ROUNDUP, or @ROUNDDOWN before using @EVEN.

See Also @INT, @ODD, @ROUND, @ROUNDDOWN, @ROUNDM, @ROUNDUP, @TRUNC

@EXP(numeric-value)

The @EXP function returns the value of the constant *e* (approximately 2.718282, the base of the natural logarithm) raised to the power *numeric-value*. *Numeric-value* can be any value between approximately –11355.1371 and approximately 11356.5234; if *numeric-value* is outside this range of values, @EXP will return ERR because the calculation will be too big for 1-2-3 to store. If *numeric-value* is smaller than approximately –227.956 or larger than approximately 230.259, 1-2-3 will be able to calculate the result but will not be able to display it; you'll see a series of asterisks in the cell instead.

For example, the following function statement returns 66.686:

    @EXP(4.2)

NOTE See Chapter 8 for more information about this function.

See Also @EX, @EXP2, @LN

@EXP2(numeric-value)

The @EXP2 function returns the value of the constant *e* (approximately 2.718282, the base of the natural logarithm) raised to the power (*numeric-value*^2).

numeric-value can be a value from approximately –106.570 to approximately 106.570; if *numeric-value* is smaller than –106.570 or larger than 106.570, the @EXP2 calculation is too large for 1-2-3 to store, and you'll see ERR.

WARNING If *numeric-value* is outside the range –15.098 to 15.098 (i.e., between –106.570 and –15.098 or between 15.098 and 106.570), 1-2-3 will be able to calculate the result of @EXP2 but it will not be able to display it. You'll see a series of asterisks in the cell instead.

For example, this function statement returns 0.99005:

    @EXP2(0.1)

See Also @EXP

@FACT(number)

The @FACT function calculates the factorial of *number*. The factorial is the product of all positive integers from 1 to *number*—the factorial of 2 is 2 (1*2), the factorial of 3 is 6 (1*2*3), and so on. *number* can be 0 or any positive integer; if you enter a number that is not an integer, 1-2-3 will truncate it to an integer.

> **WARNING** 1-2-3 cannot calculate or store the factorial for *number* greater than or equal to 1755, and will return ERR. 1-2-3 can calculate but not display the factorial for *number* greater than or equal to 70; you will see a series of asterisks in the cell to indicate that 1-2-3 cannot display the number.

For example, the following function statement returns 362880:

    @FACT(9)

See Also @FACTLN, @PRODUCT

@FACTLN(number)

The @FACTLN function returns the natural logarithm of the factorial of *number*. The factorial is the product of all positive integers from 1 to *number*—the factorial of 2 is 2 (1*2), the factorial of 3 is 6 (1*2*3), and so on. *number* can be 0 or any positive integer; if you enter a number that is not an integer, 1-2-3 will truncate it to an integer.

For example, the following function statement returns 42.33562, the natural logarithm of the factorial of 20—the same as @LN(@FACT(20):

    @FACTLN(20)

See Also @FACT, @LN

@INT(numeric-value)

The @INT function returns the integer value of *numeric-value*, disregarding any fractional portion, where *numeric-value* can be any value.

> **WARNING** Use @INT only when the fractional portion of a number is irrelevant to your purposes. *Do not* use @INT when you simply need to display only the integers from a calculation in a particular cell. Use Style ➤ Number Format instead, choose Fixed, and reduce the number of decimal places to zero.

For example, the boss gives you $75 to arrange a department party. If each gateau costs $6.63, how many can you get? (Let's ignore tax for the moment.) You could use the following function statement to produce the answer, which turns out to be 11:

    @INT(75/6.63)

(If you simply divided 75 by 6.63, you'd get 11.31222—a difficult number of gateaux to buy exactly.)

See Also   @EVEN, @ODD, @ROUND, @ROUNDDOWN, @ROUNDM, @ROUNDUP, @TRUNC

@LARGE(range,number)

The @LARGE function returns the *n*th largest value in *range*. *range* is the name or address of a range containing values. *number* is any positive integer but cannot be larger than the number of values in *range*, or @LARGE will return ERR.

For example, if you wanted to automatically track the largest deposits (or withdrawals) you made into (or from) your bank account, you could use the @LARGE function as illustrated in Figure G.1.

In the Bank Account worksheet, cell F1 contains the function statement:

    @LARGE(D4..D20,1)

This returns the first largest value from the range D4..D20. If the range D4..D20 were named EXPENDITURE, one could retrieve, say, the second largest value in the range by using the following function statement:

    @LARGE(EXPENDITURE,2)

See Also   @MAX, @MIN, @PUREMAX, @PUREMIN, @SMALL

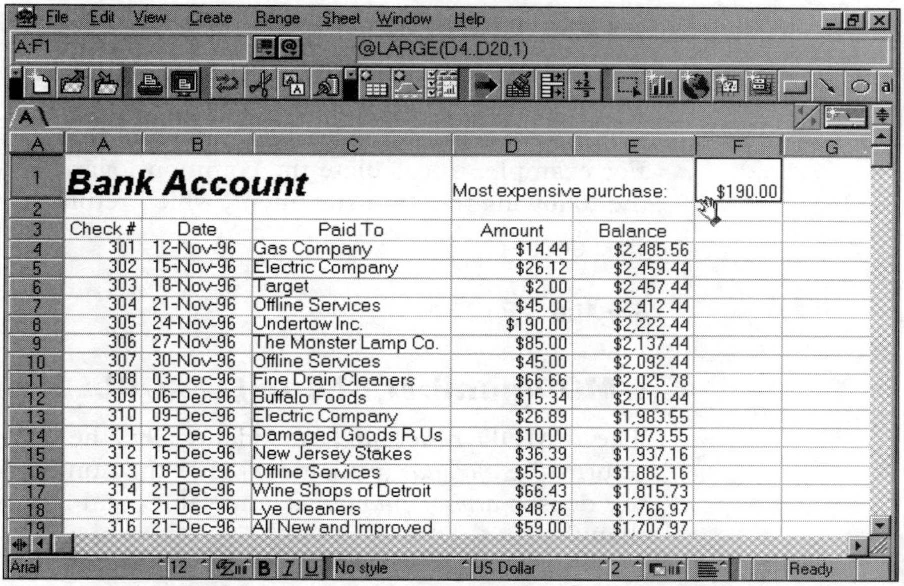

Descriptions of the Mathematical Functions

Figure G.1: Using the @LARGE function to return the nth largest values from a range

@LN(numeric-value)

The @LN function returns the natural logarithm of *numeric-value*. *numeric-value* must be a value greater than 0; if *numeric-value* is less than 0, @LN will return ERR.

TIP Natural logarithms are based on the constant *e*, which is approximately 2.718282. The @LN function is the inverse of the @EXP function.

For example, to calculate the natural logarithm of *e*, you could use the following function statement, which returns 1.098612:

    @LN(3)

See Chapter 8 for more information about this function.

See Also   @EXP, @L, @LOG

@LOG(numeric-value)

The @LOG function returns the common or base-10 logarithm (base 10) of *numeric-value*, where *numeric-value* is a value greater than 0. (If *numeric-value* is a value less than or equal to 0, @LOG returns ERR.) For example, to calculate the common logarithm of 3, you could use the following function statement, which returns 0.477121:

    @LOG(3)

See Also   @LN

@MOD(number,divisor), @MODULO(number,divisor)

The @MOD function (and, identically, the @MODULO function) returns the *modulus* (remainder) after the number *number* is divided by the divisor *divisor*. *number* is any value, and *divisor* is any value other than 0.

> **TIP**   @MOD always returns a result with the same sign (+ or –) as the sign of *number*. For example, if *number* is negative, the modulus will also be negative. If *number* is 0, @MOD returns 0.

For example, the following function statement returns 2, because 2 is the remainder when 11 is divided by 3:

    @MOD(11,3)

You can use the @MOD function to calculate the day of the week: Enter a date number as *number* in the @MOD function statement and 7 (days in the week) as the *divisor*. The remainder indicates the day of the week, from 0 (indicating Saturday) through 6 (indicating Friday). For example, to calculate the day of the week on which November 5, 1997, falls, you could use the following function statement:

    @MOD(@DATE(97,11,5),7)

This returns 1, indicating that November 5, 1997, will fall on a Sunday.

See Chapter 8 for more information about @MOD.

See Also   @QUOTIENT

@ODD(numeric-value)

The @ODD function returns the value *numeric-value* rounded away from 0 to the nearest odd integer—positive values are rounded up; negative values are rounded down. *numeric-value* can be any value; if *numeric-value* is an odd integer, @ODD(*numeric-value*) returns *numeric-value*.

For example, the following function statement returns 5:

    @ODD(3.03)

And this function statement returns –25:

    @ODD(-25)

See Also   @EVEN, @INT, @ROUND, @ROUNDDOWN, @ROUNDM, @ROUNDUP, @TRUNC

@PI

The @PI function returns the value of the mathematical constant π, the ratio of the circumference of a circle to its diameter. π is approximately 3.14159265358979324.

For example, to calculate the circumference of a circle that had a radius of 4, you could use the following function statement:

    @PI*4^2

This returns 50.26548, the area of the circle.

> **NOTE** See Chapter 8 for more information about this and other trigonometric functions.

@QUARTILE(tile;range)

The @QUARTILE function returns a given quartile, where:

tile is an integer from 0 to 4, as below, and *range* is the address or name of the range that contains the values.

Tile	Returns	Same as...
0	minimum	@PERCENTILE(0.0,*range*) or @MIN(*range*)

1	quartile one	@PERCENTILE(0.25,*range*)
2	median	@PERCENTILE(0.50,*range*)
3	quartile three	@PERCENTILE(0.75,*range*)
4	maximum	@PERCENTILE(1.00,*range*) or @MAX(*range*)

For example, where the range "RANGE1" contains the following data:

34

12

60

128

67

350

206

@QUARTILE(0;RANGE1) returns 12.

@QUARTILE(1;RANGE1) returns 47.

@QUARTILE(2;RANGE1) returns 67.

@QUARTILE(3;RANGE1) returns 167.

@QUARTILE(4;RANGE1) returns 350.

TIP Blank cells and labels are calculated by @QUARTILE as 0.

See Also @DECILE

@QUOTIENT(number,divisor)

The @QUOTIENT function returns the integer result of *number* divided by *divisor*, where *number* is a value and *divisor* is a value other than 0.

For example, to divide 113 by 5 and ignore the remainder of the division, you could use the following function statement, which returns 22 rather than 22.6:

```
@QUOTIENT(113,5)
```

See Also @MOD

Descriptions of the Mathematical Functions

TIP @QUOTIENT returns 0 if *number* is 0, and ERR if *divisor* is 0.

@RAND

The @RAND function generates and returns a random value between 0 and 1 calculated to seventeen decimal places. For example, entering a @RAND function statement in a cell might return numbers such as the following:

0.4055564102742618

0.0685917209221942914

0.932591693444453037

You can see from these examples that @RAND produces values with differing numbers of decimal places.

NOTE @RAND generates a new random value for each @RAND function statement each time 1-2-3 recalculates your work, whether the recalculation is automatic or manual. Each time you enter a new @RAND statement in a worksheet, all the other @RAND statements are recalculated.

To give yourself more flexibility when working with this @RAND function, you can use these three techniques:

▶ To return random values in different intervals, multiply @RAND by the size of the interval. For example, to produce numbers between 100 and 1,000, multiply @RAND by 99:

@RAND*99

▶ To prevent @RAND from updating a particular random value when the worksheet is recalculated, press F2 and then F9 with the relevant cell selected to fix the value.

▶ To generate random whole numbers, use the @INT function or the @ROUND function in conjunction with @RAND:

@ROUND(@RAND*9,1)

@INT(@RAND)

NOTE See Chapter 8 for further examples of using the @RAND function.

@RADTODEG(radians)

The @RADTODEG function converts radians to degrees, where *radians* is any value. For example, the following function statement returns 114.5916:

    @RADTODEG(2)

You can also use the @RADTODEG function together with other mathematical functions to return a value in degrees rather than in radians, which many of the mathematical functions return. The following list gives some examples of functions with which you can use @RADTODEG; look under the listing for each function for details of usage.

@RADTODEG(@ACOS(0.45))

@RADTODEG(@ACOT(3.1))

@RADTODEG(@ACSC(2.8))

@RADTODEG(@ASEC(2))

@RADTODEG(@ASIN(0.5))

@RADTODEG(@ATAN(4))

@RADTODEG(@ATAN2(5,5))

@RADTODEG(@COS(85))

See Also   @DEGTORAD

@REGRESSION(x-range,y-range, attribute,[compute])

The @REGRESSION function performs multiple linear regression and returns the statistic specified. The arguments for the @REGRESSION function are as follows:

Argument	Description
x-range	The name or address of a range containing the independent variables. *x-range* can contain up to 75 columns and 8,192 rows.
y-range	The name or address of a single-column range containing the set of values for the dependent variable. *y-range* must have the same number of rows as *x-range*.

attribute   1, 2, 3, 4, 5, 01–175, or 201–275, indicating which regression output value @REGRESSION is to calculate, as follows:

1 If *attribute* = 1, @REGRESSION calculates constant calculation.

2 If *attribute* = 2, @REGRESSION calculates the standard error of Y estimate constant calculation.

3 If *attribute* = 3, @REGRESSION calculates the R squared constant calculation.

4 If *attribute* = 4, @REGRESSION calculates the number of observations calculation.

5 If *attribute* = 5, @REGRESSION calculates the degrees of freedom calculation.

01–175 If *attribute* = 01 to 175, @REGRESSION calculates the x coefficient (slope) for the independent variable specified by *attribute*. @REGRESSION numbers the independent variables in *x-range*, starting with the number 1, from top to bottom in a column and from left to right. For example, to find the x coefficient for the independent variable in column A, use the attribute 100; to find the x coefficient for the independent variable in column F, use 105.

201–275 If *attribute* = 201 to 275, @REGRESSION calculates the standard error of coefficient for the independent variable specified by *attribute*. @REGRESSION numbers the independent variables in *x-range*, starting with the number 1, from top to bottom in a column and from left to right. For example, to find the standard error of coefficient for the independent variable in column A, use 201 as the *attribute*; to find the standard error of coefficient for the independent variable in column D, use 203 as the *attribute*.

compute	Zero or 1, indicating the Y intercept, as follows: 0 If *compute* = 0, @REGRESSION uses 0 as the Y intercept. 1 If *compute* = 1, @REGRESSION calculates the Y intercept; this is the default if you omit the optional *compute* argument.

@ROUND(numeric-value,number)

The @ROUND function rounds the value *numeric-value* to the nearest multiple of the power of 10 specified by *number*. The arguments for the @ROUND function are as follows:

Argument	Description
numeric-value	Any value indicating the number to be rounded.
number	A value from −100 through 100 that specifies how to round the number, as per the following list: **Positive.** If *number* is positive, @ROUND rounds the decimal portion of the number. If *number* is 1, @ROUND rounds *numeric-value* to the nearest tenth; if *number* is 2, @ROUND rounds *numeric-value* to the nearest hundredth; if *number* is 3, @ROUND rounds *numeric-value* to the nearest thousandth, etc. **Negative.** If *number* is negative, @ROUND rounds the integer portion of the number. If *number* is −1, @ROUND rounds *numeric-value* to the nearest ten; if *number* is −2, @ROUND rounds *numeric-value* to the nearest hundred; if *number* is −3, @ROUND rounds *numeric-value* to the nearest thousand, etc. **Zero.** If *number* is 0, @ROUND rounds *numeric-value* to the nearest integer.

Descriptions of the Mathematical Functions

WARNING Note that the @ROUND function actually changes the number, which in many cases is not desirable. If you simply want to change the display of a number to a given number of decimal places, change the number format of the cell rather than using @ROUND.

For example, if a function in cell A1 returned a decimal number that you needed to round to the nearest integer, you could use the following function statement:

    @ROUND(A1,0)

See Chapter 8 for a thorough discussion of @ROUND, including examples of its use.

See Also   @EVEN, @INT, @ODD, @ROUNDDOWN, @ROUNDM, @ROUNDUP, @TRUNC

@ROUNDDOWN(numeric-value,[number], [direction])

The @ROUNDDOWN function rounds the value *numeric-value* down to the nearest multiple of the power of 10 specified by *number*. The arguments for the @ROUNDDOWN function are as follows:

Argument	Description
numeric-value	Any value indicating the number to be rounded.
number	A value from −100 through 100 that specifies how to round the number, as per the following list. This is an optional argument; @ROUNDDOWN uses 0 if you omit it. **Positive.** If *number* is positive, @ROUNDDOWN rounds the decimal portion of the number. If *number* is 1, @ROUNDDOWN rounds *numeric-value* to the nearest tenth; if *number* is 2, @ROUNDDOWN rounds *numeric-value* to the nearest hundredth; if *number* is 3, @ROUNDDOWN rounds *numeric-value* to the nearest thousandth, etc.

| | **Negative.** If *number* is negative, @ROUNDDOWN rounds the integer portion of the number. If *number* is −1, @ROUNDDOWN rounds *numeric-value* to the nearest ten; if *number* is −2, @ROUNDDOWN rounds *numeric-value* to the nearest hundred; if *number* is −3, @ROUNDDOWN rounds *numeric-value* to the nearest thousand, etc.
Zero. If *number* is 0, @ROUNDDOWN rounds *numeric-value* to the nearest integer. |
|---|---|
| *direction* | Zero or 1, indicating how to round negative values. This is an optional argument; @ROUNDDOWN uses 0 if you omit it. Note that the *direction* argument has no effect on positive numbers.
0 If *direction* = 0, @ROUNDDOWN rounds negative values down.
1 If *direction* = 1, @ROUNDDOWN rounds negative values up. |

For example, if you had a formula in cell Z280 that calculated a price, you could use @ROUNDDOWN to round it down to the nearest cent with the following function statement:

```
@ROUNDDOWN(Z280,2)
```

WARNING Do not use the @ROUNDDOWN function if you simply want to change the display of a number—change the number format of the cell using the Format selector or Style ➤ Number Format. Use @ROUNDDOWN only when you want to round down the number itself.

See Also @EVEN, @INT, @ODD, @ROUND, @ROUNDM, @ROUNDUP, @TRUNC

@ROUNDM(numeric-value, multiple, [direction])

The @ROUNDM function rounds the value *numeric-value* to the nearest *multiple*. *numeric-value* and *multiple* are any values that have the

Descriptions of the Mathematical Functions

same sign; *direction* is an optional argument indicating whether to round *numeric-value* up or down as follows:

0 If *direction* = 0, @ROUNDM rounds *numeric-value* to the nearest multiple. This is the default setting if you omit the *direction* argument.

1 If *direction* = 1, @ROUNDM rounds *numeric-value* up.

–1 If *direction* = –1, @ROUNDM rounds *numeric-value* down.

Figure G.2 illustrates the use of @ROUNDM. For example, cell B5 contains the following function statement:

@ROUNDM(987.654,0.05,1)

This rounds the numeric value 987.654 up to the nearest 0.05.

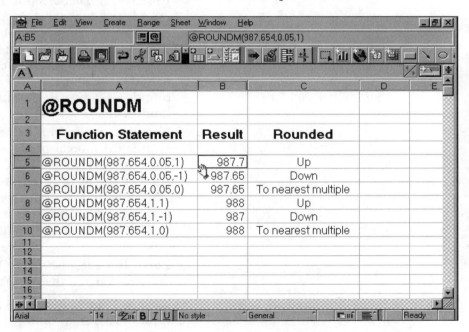

Figure G.2: Using the @ROUNDM function to round a numeric value to the nearest multiple

See Also   @EVEN, @INT, @ODD, @ROUND, @ROUNDDOWN, @ROUNDUP, @TRUNC

@ROUNDUP(numeric-value,[number],[direction])

The @ROUNDUP function rounds the value *numeric-value* up to the nearest multiple of the power of 10 specified by *number*. The arguments for the @ROUNDUP function are as follows:

Argument	Description
numeric-value	Any value indicating the number to be rounded.
number	A value from –100 through 100 that specifies how to round the number, as per the following list. This is an optional argument; @ROUNDUP uses 0 if you omit it. **Positive.** If *number* is positive, @ROUNDUP rounds the decimal portion of the number. If *number* is 1, @ROUNDUP rounds *numeric-value* to the nearest tenth; if *number* is 2, @ROUNDUP rounds *numeric-value* to the nearest hundredth; if *number* is 3, @ROUNDUP rounds *numeric-value* to the nearest thousandth, etc. **Negative.** If *number* is negative, @ROUNDUP rounds the integer portion of the number. If *number* is –1, @ROUNDUP rounds *numeric-value* to the nearest ten; if *number* is –2, @ROUNDUP rounds *numeric-value* to the nearest hundred; if *number* is –3, @ROUNDUP rounds *numeric-value* to the nearest thousand, etc. **Zero.** If *number* is 0, @ROUNDUP rounds *numeric-value* to the nearest integer.
direction	Zero or 1, indicating how to round negative values. This is an optional argument; @ROUNDUP uses 0 if you omit it. Note that the *direction* argument has no effect on positive numbers. 0 If *direction* = 0, @ROUNDUP rounds negative values up. 1 If *direction* = 1, @ROUNDUP rounds negative values down.

Descriptions of the Mathematical Functions

For example, if you had a formula in cell Z280 that calculated a price, you could use @ROUNDUP to round it up to the nearest ten cents with the following function statement:

@ROUNDUP(Z280,1,0)

> **WARNING** The @ROUNDUP function changes the number itself, not its display. Do not use @ROUNDUP if you simply want to change the way a number appears in a cell—change the number format of the cell using the Format selector or Style ➤ Number Format instead.

See Also   @EVEN, @INT, @ODD, @ROUND, @ROUNDDOWN, @ROUNDM, @TRUNC

@SEC(numeric-value)

The @SEC function returns the secant of the angle represented by *numeric-value*, where *numeric-value* is an angle measured in radians and is any value from $-2^{32}*\pi$ through $2^{32}*\pi$. The secant is the reciprocal of cosine and is the ratio of the hypotenuse to the side adjacent to an acute angle of a right triangle.

For example, to discover the secant of an angle of 24 radians, you could use the following function statement:

@SEC(24)

This returns 2.357495, the secant of an angle of 24 radians.

To find the secant of an angle measured in degrees, you can combine @SEC with @DEGTORAD, as in the following function statement, which finds the secant of a hundred-degree angle:

@SEC(@DEGTORAD(100))

See Also   @ASEC, @ASECH, @COS, @DEGTORAD, @SECH

@SECH(numeric-value)

The @SECH function returns the hyperbolic secant (the reciprocal of the hyperbolic cosine) of the angle represented by *numeric-value*, where *numeric-value* is a value between approximately –1135.571 and approximately 1135.571. @SECH results in a value greater than 0 or less than or equal to 1.

For example, to calculate the hyperbolic secant of an angle of 3, you could use the following function statement:

    @SECH(3)

This returns 0.09932792. To find the hyperbolic secant of an angle measured in degrees, you can combine @SECH with @DEGTORAD, as in the following function statement, which finds the hyperbolic secant of a 60-degree angle:

    @SECH(@DEGTORAD(60))

See Also   @ASECH, @DEGTORAD, @SEC

@SIGN(numeric-value)

The @SIGN function returns the sign of *numeric-value*, any number, as follows:

- @SIGN returns 1 if *numeric-value* is positive.
- @SIGN returns 0 if *numeric-value* is 0.
- @SIGN returns –1 if *numeric-value* is negative.

For example, the following function statement returns 1 when cell AK47 contains a positive value:

    @SIGN(AK47)

@SIN(numeric-value)

The @SIN function returns the sine of the angle represented by *numeric-value*, where *numeric-value* is an angle measured in radians and is any value from $-2^{32}\ast\pi$ through $2^{32}\ast\pi$. The sine is the ratio of the side opposite an acute angle of a right triangle to the hypotenuse.

For example, to calculate the sine of an angle of 2 radians, you could use the following function statement:

    @SIN(2)

This returns 0.909297. Alternatively, you can use @SIN to find out the sine of an angle in degrees. For example, to calculate the sine of a 45-degree angle, you could combine @SIN with @DEGTORAD and use the following function statement:

    @SIN(@DEGTORAD(45))

This returns 0.707107.

> **NOTE** See Chapter 8 for more information about this and other trigonometric functions.

See Also @ASIN, @DEGTORAD, @SINH

@SINH(numeric-value)

The @SINH function returns the hyperbolic sine of the angle represented by *numeric-value*, where *numeric-value* is a value between approximately –1135.571 and approximately 1135.571. For example, the following function statement returns 1.175201:

    @SINH(1)

To establish the hyperbolic sine of an angle measured in degrees, use @SINH together with @DEGTORAD, as in the following function statement, which returns the hyperbolic sine of a 50-degree angle:

    @SINH(@DEGTORAD(50))

See Also @ASINH, @DEGTORAD, @SIN

@SEMEAN(range)

The @SEMEAN function returns the standard error of the sample mean (or average) for the values in *range*, where *range* is a range name or address.

For example, if the range named DETROIT PARTS contains the values 10, 22, 6, 34, 17, and 44, you could use the following function statement to return the standard error of the sample mean:

    @SEMEAN(DETROIT PARTS)

This returns 5.924056.

See Also @GEOMEAN, @HARMEAN, @PURESTD, @STD

@SMALL(range,number)

The @SMALL function returns the *n*th smallest value in *range*. *range* is the name or address of a range containing values. *number* is any positive integer but cannot be smaller than the number of values in *range*, or @SMALL will return ERR.

For example, if you wanted to automatically track the smallest deposits (or withdrawals) you made into (or from) your bank account, you could use the @SMALL function as illustrated in Figure G.3.

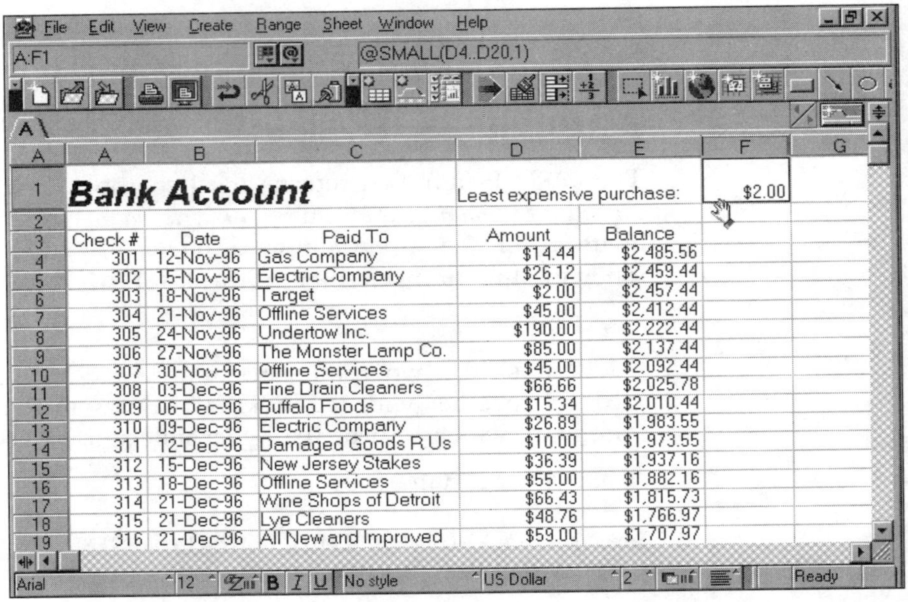

Check #	Date	Paid To	Amount	Balance
301	12-Nov-96	Gas Company	$14.44	$2,485.56
302	15-Nov-96	Electric Company	$26.12	$2,459.44
303	18-Nov-96	Target	$2.00	$2,457.44
304	21-Nov-96	Offline Services	$45.00	$2,412.44
305	24-Nov-96	Undertow Inc.	$190.00	$2,222.44
306	27-Nov-96	The Monster Lamp Co.	$85.00	$2,137.44
307	30-Nov-96	Offline Services	$45.00	$2,092.44
308	03-Dec-96	Fine Drain Cleaners	$66.66	$2,025.78
309	06-Dec-96	Buffalo Foods	$15.34	$2,010.44
310	09-Dec-96	Electric Company	$26.89	$1,983.55
311	12-Dec-96	Damaged Goods R Us	$10.00	$1,973.55
312	15-Dec-96	New Jersey Stakes	$36.39	$1,937.16
313	18-Dec-96	Offline Services	$55.00	$1,882.16
314	21-Dec-96	Wine Shops of Detroit	$66.43	$1,815.73
315	21-Dec-96	Lye Cleaners	$48.76	$1,766.97
316	21-Dec-96	All New and Improved	$59.00	$1,707.97

Figure G.3: ***Using the @SMALL function to return the nth smallest values from a range***

In the Bank Account worksheet, cell F1 contains the function statement

```
@SMALL(D4..D20,1)
```

to return the first smallest value from the range D4..D20. If the range D4..D20 were named EXPENDITURE, one could retrieve, say, the second smallest value in the range by using this function statement:

```
@SMALL(EXPENDITURE,2)
```

See Also @LARGE, @MAX, @MIN, @PUREMAX, @PUREMIN

@SQRT(numeric-value)

The @SQRT function returns the positive square root of *numeric-value*, where *numeric-value* is a positive value. (If *numeric-value* is a negative value, @SQRT returns ERR.)

For example, to calculate the square root of the value in cell M61, you could use the following function statement:

    @SQRT(M61)

If cell M61 contained the value 169, this function statement would return 13.

@SQRTPI(numeric-value)

The @SQRTPI function returns the square root of *numeric-value* multiplied by π, where *numeric-value* is any positive value or 0. (If *numeric-value* is a negative value, @SQRTPI returns ERR.)

For example, the following function statement calculates the square root of 20*π:

    @SQRTPI(20)

The result is 7.926655.

See Also   @PI, @SQRT

@SUBTOTAL(list)

The @SUBTOTAL function fulfills a double function: It adds together the values in a *list*, producing the total, and indicates to the @GRAND TOTAL function which cells @GRANDTOTAL should sum. For @SUBTOTAL, *list* can be the following in any combination, separated by separator characters:

- Numbers
- Numeric formulas
- Range addresses or range names containing numbers or numeric formulas

Figure G.4 illustrates the use of the @SUBTOTAL function in a spreadsheet containing an output report for carved bears for the years 1985–1997. As you can see in the figure, cell B8 contains the following function statement to create a subtotal from the cells B5..B7:

    @SUBTOTAL(B5..B7)

Cell A16 contains the following function statement to sum up all the subtotals into a grand total:

    @GRANDTOTAL(B8..L13)

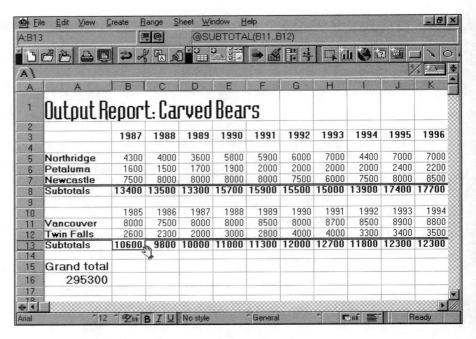

Figure G.4: Using the @SUBTOTAL function to produce subtotals, which are then added together into a grand total by the @GRANDTOTAL function

This adds together the subtotals in the range B8..L13 produced by the @SUBTOTAL function.

See Also @SUM, @SUMNEGATIVE, @SUMPOSITIVE

@SUM(list)

The @SUM function returns the sum of the values in *list*, where *list* can be the following in any combination, separated by separator characters:

► Numbers

► Numeric formulas

► Range addresses or range names containing numbers or numeric formulas

TIP The easiest way to add an @SUM function statement to a cell is to click on the Sum SmartIcon.

For example, to sum the values in the block A5..B13, you could use the following function statement:

    @SUM(A5..B13)

See Also   @DSUM, @GRANDTOTAL, @NSUM, @SUBTOTAL, @SUMNEGATIVE, @SUMPOSITIVE

@SUMPRODUCT(list)

The @SUMPRODUCT function multiplies the values in corresponding cells in a *list* of multiple ranges and then sums the products. *list* is any combination of ranges containing values, provided that the ranges are the same shape. If the ranges in *list* are not the same shape, @SUMPRODUCT will return ERR.

@SUMPRODUCT multiplies the values in corresponding cells either by rows or by columns, as follows:

▶ If the ranges in *list* are columns, @SUMPRODUCT multiplies by rows.

▶ If the ranges in *list* are rows, @SUMPRODUCT multiplies by columns.

▶ If the ranges in *list* are more than one column wide, @SUMPRODUCT multiplies by rows.

For example, if cells A1..A10 contained values and made up the named range ACELLS, and cells B1..B10 contained values and made up the named range BCELLS, you could use the following function statement to calculate the sum of their products:

    @SUMPRODUCT(ACELLS,BCELLS)

Since the ACELLS and BCELLS ranges are columns, @SUMPRODUCT will multiply by rows in this case and then calculate the sum of the products.

NOTE See Chapter 8 for another practical example of using this function.

See Also   @SUMSQ

@SUMSQ(list)

The @SUMSQ function returns the sum of the squares of the values in *list*, where *list* can be the following in any combination, separated by argument separators:

- Numbers
- Numeric formulas
- Range addresses or range names containing numbers or numeric formulas

For example, to calculate the sum of the squares of 3, 4, and 5, you could use the following function statement:

    @SUMSQ(3,4,5)

This returns 50, or 9 + 16 + 25.

See Also   @SUM, @SUMPRODUCT

@SUMXMY2

The @SUMXMY2 function subtracts the values in *range2* from the corresponding cells in *range1*, squares the differences, and then sums the results. For @SUMXMY2, *range1* and *range2* are ranges identical in size and shape that contain values. (If *range1* and *range2* are different in size or shape, @SUMX2MY2 will return ERR.)

@SUMXMY2 handles subtraction either by rows or by columns, depending on the shape of *range1* and *range2*:

- If *range1* and *range2* are single-column ranges, @SUMXMY2 subtracts by row.
- If *range1* and *range2* are multicolumn ranges, @SUMXMY2 subtracts by columns.

For example, to find the sum of the squared differences between two ranges named Week1 and Week2 that occupied cells B5..C10 and D5..E10, respectively, you could use the following function statement:

    @SUMXMY2(WEEK1,WEEK2)

Since Week1 and Week2 are multicolumn ranges, the subtraction in this case would be by columns.

See Also @SUMPRODUCT, @SUMSQ

@TAN(numeric-value)

The @TAN function returns the tangent of the angle represented by *numeric-value*, where *numeric-value* is an angle measured in radians and is any value from $-2^{32}*\pi$ through $2^{32}*\pi$. The tangent is the ratio of the side opposite an acute angle of a right triangle to the side adjacent the same acute angle.

For example, to calculate the tangent of an angle of 4 radians, you could use the following function statement:

    @TAN(4)

This returns 1.157821. To work out the tangent of an angle measured in degrees, use @TAN with @DEGTORAD, as in the following function statement, which returns the tangent of an angle of 31 degrees:

    @TAN(@DEGTORAD(31))

See Also @ATAN, @DEGTORAD, @TANH

@TANH(numeric-value)

The @TANH function returns the hyperbolic tangent of the angle represented by *numeric-value*, where *numeric-value* is a value between approximately –11355.1371 and approximately 11355.1371. The hyperbolic tangent is the ratio of the hyperbolic sine to the hyperbolic cosine. @TANH returns a value from –1 through 1.

For example, to calculate the hyperbolic tangent of an angle of 3, you could use the following function statement:

    @ATANH(3)

This returns 0.995054. To calculate the hyperbolic tangent of an angle measured in degrees, use @TANH together with @DEGTORAD, as in the following function statement, which calculates the hyperbolic tangent of an angle of 20 degrees:

    @TANH(@DEGTORAD(20))

See Also @ATANH, @DEGTORAD, @TAN

@TRUNC(numeric-value,[decimal])

The @TRUNC function returns *numeric-value* truncated to the number of decimal places indicated by *decimal*. The arguments for the @TRUNC function are as follows:

Argument	Description
numeric-value	A numeric value.
decimal	A value between –100 and 100, indicating how to truncate *numeric-value*, as follows: **Positive.** A positive value for *decimal* makes @TRUNC work on the decimal portion of the number, the portion to the right of the decimal point. For example, when *decimal* = 3, @TRUNC truncates *numeric-value* to the nearest thousandth. **Negative.** A negative value for *decimal* makes @TRUNC work on the integer portion of the number, the portion to the left of the decimal point. For example, when *decimal* = 3, @TRUNC truncates *numeric-value* to the nearest thousand. **Zero.** A value of 0 for *decimal* makes @TRUNC truncate *numeric-value* to the nearest integer. *decimal* is an optional value for this @TRUNC function; 0 is the default setting if you omit the *decimal* argument.

WARNING Use the @TRUNC function only when you need to change a number by truncating it. For all formatting purposes—for example, to reduce the display to three decimal places—format the style of the relevant cell.

For example, you could use the following function statement to truncate a number to one decimal place:

    @TRUNC(3.1415927)

This would return 3.1.

See Also @EVEN, @INT, @ODD, @ROUND, @ROUNDM, @ROUNDDOWN, @ROUNDUP

Overview of the Statistical Functions

1-2-3's statistical functions fall into five categories:

- **Forecasting functions.** For example, @REGRESSION, which performs multiple linear regression analysis.
- **General statistical functions.** For example, @GRANDTOTAL, which calculates the sum of all cells that contain a @SUBTOTAL function statement.
- **Probability functions.** For example, @POISSON, which calculates the Poisson distribution.
- **Ranking functions.** For example, @PRANK, which calculates percentile rank.
- **Significance-test functions.** For example, @ZTEST, which performs a z-test on the chosen population or populations.

For quick reference, the statistical functions are listed here in Table G.2.

Table G.2: **Statistical Functions Quick Reference**

Function	Returns
@AVEDEV	The average of the absolute deviations of the values in the given list
@AVG	The average of the values contained in the given list
@BINOMIAL	The binomial probability mass function or the cumulative binomial distribution
@CHIDIST	The one-tailed probability of the chi-square distribution
@CHITEST	The independence of the data in a given range or the goodness of fit for the data in two given ranges
@COMBIN	The binomial coefficient for two specified values
@CORREL	The correlation coefficient of the values for two given ranges
@COUNT	The number of nonblank cells in the given list

Table G.2: **Statistical Functions Quick Reference** (continued)

Function	Returns
@COV	Either the population or the sample covariance of the values in two given ranges
@CRITBINOMIAL	The largest integer for which the cumulative binomial distribution is less than or equal to alpha
@DEVSQ	The sum of squared deviations of the values in the given list from their mean (average)
@FDIST	The F-distribution of probability for the two given ranges (for determining the degree to which two samples vary)
@FORCAST	A forecast value
@FTEST	The associated probability of an F probability test for the two given ranges (to test if two samples have different variances)
@GEOMEAN	The geometric mean of the values in the given list
@GRAND-TOTAL	The sum of all the cells in the given list that contain the function @SUBTOTAL
@HARMEAN	The harmonic mean of the values in the given list
@KURTOSIS	The kurtosis of the values in the given range—the concentration of a distribution around the mean of a range of values
@MAX	The largest value in the given list
@MEDIAN	The median value in the given list
@MIN	The smallest value in the given list
@NORMAL	The normal distribution function for the specific mean (average) and standard deviation
@PERCENTILE	The xth sample percentile among the values in the given range

Table G.2:   **Statistical Functions Quick Reference (continued)**

Function	Returns
@PERMUT	The number of permutations (ordered sequences) of objects that can be selected from a given number of objects
@POISSON	The Poisson distribution (for predicting the number of events that will occur over a specific period of time)
@PRANK	The percentile of the given value among the values in the given range
@PRODUCT	The product of the values in the given list
@PUREAVG	The average of the values contained in the given list ignoring cells in the range that contain labels
@PURECOUNT	The number of nonblank cells in the given list, ignoring cells in the range that contain labels
@PUREMAX	The largest value
@PUREMEDIAN	The median value in the given list, ignoring cells that contain labels
@PUREMIN	The smallest value in the given list, ignoring cells that contain labels
@PURESTD	The population standard deviation of the values in the given list ignoring cells that contain labels
@PURESTDS	The sample standard deviation of the values in the given list, ignoring cells that contain labels
@PUREVAR	The population variance in the given list, ignoring cells that contain labels
@PUREVARS	The sample population variance in the given list, ignoring cells that contain labels
@RANK	The rank of the given value relative to other values in the range

Appendix G   Mathematical and Statistical Functions Reference

Table G.2:   Statistical Functions Quick Reference (continued)

Function	Returns
@REGRESSION	The statistic specified from a multiple linear regression
@SKEWNESS	The skewness of the values in the given range—the symmetry of a distribution around its mean (average)
@STD	The population standard deviation of the values in the given list
@STDS	The sample standard deviation of the values in the given list
@SUM-NEGATIVE	The sum of the negative values in the given list
@SUM-POSITIVE	The sum of the positive values in the given list
@TDIST	The Student's t-distribution (the distribution of the ratio of a standardized normal distribution to the square root of the quotient of a chi-square distribution by the number of its degrees of freedom)
@TTEST	The associated probability of a Student's t-test on the data in two given ranges (to establish whether two samples are likely to have come from the same two underlying populations)
@VAR	The population variance in the given list of values
@VARS	The sample population variance in the given list of values
@WEIGHTAVG	The weighted average of values in a data range
@ZTEST	The associated probability of a z-test on one or two populations (for judging the likelihood that a particular observation is drawn from a particular population)

Descriptions of the Statistical Functions

This section contains detailed descriptions of the statistical functions.

NOTE See "Statistical Functions" in Chapter 8 for a general description of these functions.

@AVEDEV(list)

The @AVEDEV function returns the average of the absolute deviations of the values in *list*, where *list* contains any combination of any of the following:

Item	Examples
Numbers	$362000
Numeric formulas	+D22/17
Addresses of ranges containing number or numeric formulas	DD3..DD24
names of ranges containing numbers or numeric formulas	HOUSES, MEN_LEFT

NOTE Separate the elements of your list with argument separators, such as semicolons (;).

See Also @DEVSQ, @PURESTD, @STD

@AVG(list)

The @AVG function returns the average of the values contained in the *list*, which can contain any combination of numbers, numeric formulas, and addresses or names of ranges that contain numbers or numeric formulas. For example, the following function statement returns 4, the average of the seven numbers:

    @AVG(5,2,2,1,4,6,8)

You can also use @AVG with addresses, with numeric formulas, with ranges, or with named ranges, as shown here:

    @AVG(A7, A44, B101)

    @AVG($1200/A47)

    @AVG(A7..A44, C11..C13)

    @AVG(TO_SELL)

You can also use @AVG with combinations of numbers, numeric formulas, addresses, and ranges:

    @AVG(4000, A12/5, B34..C56, AB80, UNPAID)

NOTE See @PUREAVG if you need to calculate the average of a list of values that includes labels; @PUREAVG ignores cells that have labels.

See Also   @DAVG, @GEOMEAN, @HARMEAN, @MEDIAN, @PUREAVG

@BINOMIAL(trials,successes,probability,[type])

The @BINOMIAL function calculates the binomial probability mass function or the cumulative binomial distribution, where the arguments are as follows:

Argument	Description
trials	The number of independent trials. The *trials* value must be a positive integer, but you can enter it as a decimal number. If *trials* is not an integer, 1-2-3 will automatically truncate it to an integer.
successes	The number of successes from the trials, a positive integer that must be less than or equal to *trials*. *successes* can be 0 but (needless to say) not less than 0. As with *trials*, if you enter *successes* as a number other than an integer, 1-2-3 will truncate it to an integer for you.

probability	A value from 0 through 1 expressing the probability of success on each trial. For example, a probability of 0.5 represents a 1 in 2 chance.
type	An optional argument that you can use to specify whether 1-2-3 calculates the probability mass function or the cumulative binomial distribution:

0 (the default setting if you omit the *type* argument) results in the probability of the trials producing exactly *successes* number of successes—that is, of the trials succeeding exactly the number of times you predict.

1 results in the probability of the trials producing at most *successes* number of successes—that is, of the trials succeeding the same number of times as or fewer than you predict.

2 results in the probability of the trials producing at least *successes* number of successes—that is, of the trials succeeding the same number of times as or more than you predict.

As an example of @BINOMIAL, say that you decide on a trip to Vegas to bolster your sagging fortunes following a disastrous decade on the stock market. Assuming that the dice may be loaded and that the table looks rigged, you decide that roulette will be your best bet. Assuming that the wheel isn't weighted and that the house hasn't yet managed to add a third zero to it, what are your chances of winning big by having the ball land on red seven times out of ten?

Well, pretty poor, as @BINOMIAL can tell you. The probability of the ball not landing on zero should be 36/38, and of it landing on red should be half that—18/38, or 0.4737. So you could use the following formula to determine the probability of red winning exactly 7 times out of 10:

```
@BINOMIAL(10,7,0.4737)
```

This produces a pathetic 0.09363. Still, you'd be more interested in the probability that you'd win *at least* 7 times out of 10:

```
@BINOMIAL(10,7,0.4737,2)
```

This produces 0.1321, which looks a fraction better but still isn't as good as your chance of throwing a 6 at dice straight off. Maybe craps would be a better choice? But really the most revealing @BINOMIAL figure for you is the probability that you would win *at most* 7 times out of 10:

    @BINOMIAL(10,7,0.4737,1)

This produces 0.9615—a high probability. And the probability of winning at most 5 times out of 10 is 0.6858—also uncomfortably high. Seeing this, you might consider the stock market instead...

See Also   @COMBIN, @CRITBINOMIAL, @PERMUT

@CHIDIST(numeric-value,degrees_freedom,[type])

The @CHIDIST function calculates the one-tailed probability of the chi-square distribution and can be used to test the validity of a hypothesis by comparing the observed values with the values expected.

The arguments for @CHIDIST are as follows:

numeric-value	The value at which to evaluate the chi-square distribution. *numeric-value* is affected by the value you enter for *type*:
	0 If *type* is 0, the critical value or upper bound for the value of the chi-square cumulative distribution random variable, expressed as a value greater than or equal to 0; this is the default if the argument is omitted.
	1 If type is 1, a probability (significance level), expressed as a value between 0 and 1.
degrees_freedom	The number of degrees of freedom for the sample, expressed as a positive integer (1-2-3 will truncate a value that is not an integer to an integer).
type	An optional argument that determines how 1-2-3 calculates @CHIDIST:
	0 If *type* is 0, the significance level corresponds to *numeric-value*; this is the default if *type* is omitted.
	1 If *type* is 1, the critical value corresponds to the significance level *numeric-value*.

For example, the following function statement returns 0.004995:

    @CHIDIST(40,20)

The following function statement returns 1.3863:

    @CHIDIST(0.5,2,1)

> **WARNING** 1-2-3's @CHIDIST approximates the chi-square cumulative distribution to within ±3*10^–7, but if it cannot approximate the result to within 0.0000001 after one hundred iterations, it will throw out an ERR—so if you receive an ERR when using @CHIDIST in a sequence, try adjusting your figures a little before concluding that your whole approach is flawed.

See Also   @CHITEST, @FDIST, @TDIST

@CHITEST(range1,[range2])

The @CHITEST function performs a chi-square test for independence on the data in *range1*, or a chi-square test for goodness of fit on the data in *range1* and *range2*, where *range1* and *range2* are ranges of the same size.

> **WARNING** *Range1* and *range2* must be the same size and must not contain labels, text formulas, or blank cells. (If they're different sizes, or contain any of the above, @CHITEST will return ERR.)

For example, Figure G.5 shows the results of a taste test for different colors of cola. Cell E7 contains the following function statement:

    @CHITEST(B5..C9)

This tests for independence, as does the function statement in cell E17:

    @CHITEST(B14..C18)

Cell E11 contains the following function statement to test for goodness of fit:

    @CHITEST(B5..C9,B14..C18)

See Also   @CHIDIST, @FTEST, @TTEST, @ZTEST

Appendix G Mathematical and Statistical Functions Reference

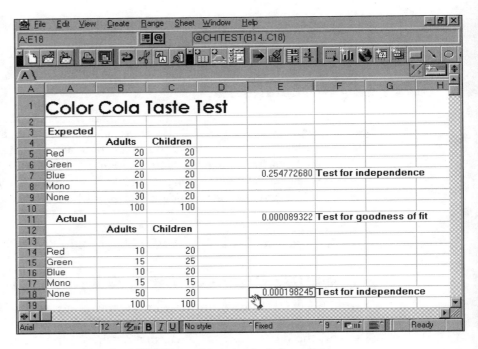

Figure G.5: *Using the @CHITEST function to test for independence*

@COMBIN(number,number_chosen)

The @COMBIN function calculates the binomial coefficient for *number* and *number_chosen*—the number of ways that *number_chosen* can be selected from *number*, without regard for order, where *number* is the total number of objects and *number_chosen* is the number of objects in each combination. *number* can be 0 or any positive integer; *number_chosen* can be 0 or any positive integer, but must be less than or equal to *number*. (If *number* and *number_chosen* are not integers, 1-2-3 will truncate them to integers.)

For example, if a Lucky Dip at a rodeo contains one bill of each of six denominations of U.S. currency—$1, $5, $10, $20, $50, and $100—you could use @COMBIN to work out the number of possible different combinations of bills pulled out in two dips like this:

    @COMBIN(6,2)

This returns 15.

See Also   @BINOMIAL, @CRITBINOMIAL, @PERMUT

@CORREL(range1,range2)

The @CORREL function returns the correlation coefficient of values in *range1* and *range2*, where *range1* and *range2* are range names or range addresses of ranges that are the same size. 1-2-3 orders ranges from top to bottom, left to right, first sheet through last. Correlation measures the relationship between two sets of data independently of the unit of measure; for measuring the relationship between two sets of data depending on the unit of measure, use @COV instead.

WARNING If *range1* and *range2* are not the same size, @CORREL will return ERR.

For example, if cells A2..A14 contained the named range MONTHS and cells B2..B14 contained the named range INCOME, you could compare the two by using either of the two following function statements:

    @CORREL(A2..A14,B2..B14)

    @CORREL(MONTHS,INCOME)

See Also @COV

@COUNT(list)

The @COUNT function returns the number of the nonblank cells in *list*, where *list* is any combination of range addresses or names separated by commas. @COUNT counts any kind of entry; @COUNT ignores only blank cells unless you enter a single cell address. For example, if cell A1 contains the label Plates of Shrimp, cell A2 contains the value 1, and cell A3 is blank, the following function statement returns 2, since cells A1 and A2 are not blank:

    @COUNT(A1..A3)

However, the following function statement returns 1, even though cell A3 is blank:

    @COUNT(A3)

To avoid returning a count of 1 for a single blank cell, refer to the cell as a block rather than as an individual cell and make part of the reference absolute:

    @COUNT($A3..A3)

This will return 0 rather than 1.

> **TIP** Use the @PURECOUNT function to exclude cells that contain labels. When using @COUNT, avoid including extra cells (for example, those containing separator lines) in your blocks, as they will be counted too.

Use @COUNT to stop or branch a macro that performs actions on a series of ranges when the cell pointer enters a range that contains no entries:

    {IF @COUNT(PROJECTIONS_97)=0}{QUIT}

If the range PROJECTIONS_97 does not yet contain any entries, the macro is instructed to stop.

See Also   @DCOUNT, @DPURECOUNT, @PURECOUNT

@COV(range1,range2,[type])

The @COV function returns either the population or sample covariance of the values in *range1* and *range2*, where *range1* and *range2* are names or addresses of ranges that are the same size. If *range1* and *range2* are different sizes, 1-2-3 will return ERR. 1-2-3 orders ranges from top to bottom, left to right, first sheet through last.

> **NOTE** Covariance is the average of the products of deviations of corresponding values in lists. For measuring the relationship between two sets of data independently of the unit of measure, use @CORREL instead of @COV.

type is an optional argument that determines whether @COV returns the population covariance or the sample covariance. If *type* is set at 0 (the default if *type* is omitted), @COV returns population covariance; if *type* is set to 1, @COV returns sample covariance.

For example, you could calculate the population covariance of the ranges A1..A5 and B1..B5 by using the following function statement:

    @COV(A1..A5,B1..B5)

(@COV(A1..A5,B1..B5,0) would produce the same result.) Or you could calculate the sample covariance by using the following function statement:

    @COV(A1..A5,B1..B5,1)

See Also   @CORREL, @PUREVAR, @PUREVARS, @VAR, @VARS

@CRITBINOMIAL(trials,probability,alpha)

The @CRITBINOMIAL function returns the largest integer for which the cumulative binomial distribution is less than or equal to alpha.

The arguments for @CRITBINOMIAL are as follows:

Argument	Description
trials	Any positive integer or 0 indicating the number of Bernoulli trials
probability	A value from 0 through 1 representing the probability of success for a single Bernoulli trial
alpha	A value from 0 through 1 representing the criterion probability

For example, say that your company manufactures ball bearings in consignments of 1,000. Four bearings out of every hundred are liable to have defects—a 96 percent chance that the bearings are free from defects. Your boss wants to be 99 percent sure that a certain number of bearings are not defective. To work this out, you would enter the following function statement:

    @CRITBINOMIAL(1000,0.94,0.1)

This would produce 930, the number of bearings free from defects in each batch.

> **WARNING** The @CRITBINOMIAL function is what's euphemistically known as "processor-intensive"—that is, running it involves spectacular amounts of chip-thrashing from your PC and thumb-twiddling from you. Before you assume that your computer has hung, look for the Calc indicator on the right side of the status bar to confirm that it's still working. Then go take an early lunch break or badger your boss for that Pentium you've long wanted but never been able to justify.

See Also   @BINOMIAL, @COMBIN, @PERMUT

@DEVSQ(list)

The @DEVSQ function calculates the sum of squared deviations of the values in *list* from their mean (average). *list* can contain any combination of numbers, numeric formulas, or addresses or names of ranges containing numbers or numeric formulas. As usual, multiple arguments need to be separated by commas or other separators (e.g., semicolons).

For example, the following function statement returns 166.875:

@DEVSQ(11,14,15,11,19,9,4,6)

Alternatively, you could use ranges or numeric formulas in *list*:

@DEVSQ(42,A11/B12,ENGINES,101)

In this example, ENGINES is a named range.

See Also @PURESTD, @STD

@FDIST(numeric-value,degrees-freedom1, degrees-freedom2,[type])

The @FDIST function calculates the F-distribution of probability. The F-distribution, used to determine the degree to which two samples vary, is a continuous distribution obtained from the ratio of two chi-square distributions, each divided by its number of degrees of freedom.

> **WARNING** @FDIST approximates the cumulative F probability distribution to within $\pm 3*10^{-7}$. If it cannot approximate the result to within 0.0000001 after 100 calculation iterations, the result is ERR.

The arguments for @FDIST are as follows:

Argument	Description
numeric-value	The value at which to evaluate the F-distribution. The *numeric-value* value depends on the value given for type as follows: 0 If *type* is 0, *numeric-value* is a value greater than or equal to 0 representing the critical value or upper bound for the value of the

	cumulative F-distribution. This is the default setting if you omit the argument *type*.
	1 If *type* is 1, *numeric-value* is a value from 0 to 1 that represents probability.
degrees-freedom1	A positive integer representing the first sample (the numerator degrees of freedom).
degrees-freedom2	A positive integer representing the second sample (the denominator degrees of freedom).
type	An optional argument used to specify how 1-2-3 calculates @FDIST:
	0 Calculates the significance level corresponding to the critical value *numeric-value*. This is the default setting if you omit the argument.
	1 Calculates the critical value that corresponds to the significance level *numeric-value*.

For example, the following function statement returns 0.465119:

```
@FDIST(1,5,10)
```

See Also   @CHIDIST, @FTEST, @TDIST

@FORCAST(a,range1,range2)

The @FORCAST returns a forecast value for *a* based on the linear trend between values in the *range1* and *range2* range.

For the following data:

YRANGE	XRANGE
250	3
545	5
550	5
450	6
605	6
615	7

@FORECAST(–1;YRANGE;XRANGE) returns –26.786.

@FORECAST(0;YRANGE;XRANGE) returns 56.786.

WARNING Note that if either *range1* or *range2* contains non-numeric data, @FORECAST will return ERR.

See Also @REGRESSION

@FTEST(range1,range2)

@FTEST returns the associated probability of an F probability test—to test if two samples have different variances—where *range1* and *range2* are ranges containing the data to be tested.

TIP *range1* and *range2* do not have to be the same size—they can be different sizes, as illustrated in the example in Figure G.6.

Figure G.6 illustrates the use of the @FTEST function. The spreadsheet contains the results of two tests, one in the range A5..A8 and the other in the range B5..B11. To calculate the variance, cell A15 contains the following function statement:

    @FTEST(A5..A8,B5..B11)

This returns 0.5299669.

See Also @CHITEST, @FDIST, @TTEST, @ZTEST

@GEOMEAN(list)

The @GEOMEAN function calculates the geometric mean of the values in *list*. The geometric mean is the nth root of the product of the values in *list*, where *number* is the number of values in *list*. *list* can include numbers, numeric formulas that result in numbers, and addresses or names of ranges containing numbers; or it can include numeric formulas that result in numbers. Note that all the values in *list* must be greater than zero.

For example, if cells B1, C1, D1, and E1 contain the values 100, 200, 300, and 400, respectively, the following function statement returns 221.3364.

    @GEOMEAN(A,B1,C1,D1)

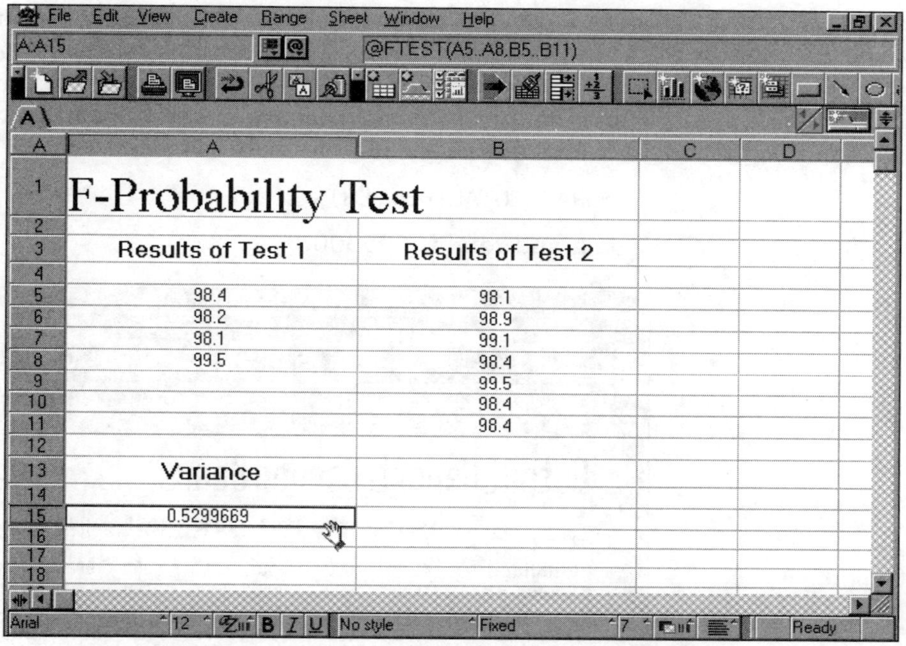

Figure G.6: Using the @FTEST function to return the associated probability of an f-test

TIP The difference between @GEOMEAN and @AVG is that @AVG returns the arithmetic mean rather than the geometric mean. The geometric mean returns a result less than the arithmetic mean unless all the values in *list* are the same, in which case the results of the geometric mean and the arithmetic mean are the same. For example, @AVG(100,200,300,400) returns 250, while @GEOMEAN(100,200,300,400) returns 221.3364; but @AVG(500,500,500, 500) and @GEOMEAN(500,500,500,500) both return 500.

See Also   @AVG, @HARMEAN, @MEDIAN, @PUREAVG

@GRANDTOTAL(list)

The @GRANDTOTAL function calculates the sum of all cells in *list* that contain the function @SUBTOTAL. *list* can be any combination of ranges.

For example, Figure G.7 shows an output report for five factories manufacturing carved bears, with subtotals for the group of three locations and for the group of two locations. In cell A16, the following function statement produces the grand total of all the cells in the range B8..L13 that contain the @SUBTOTAL function:

    @GRANDTOTAL(B8..L8)

The grand total is 295300.

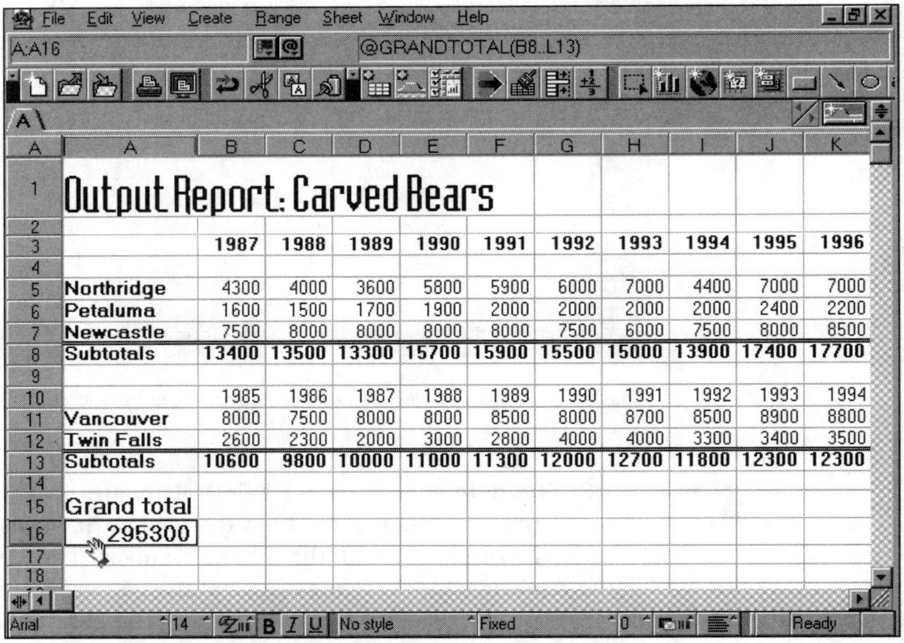

Figure G.7: Using the @GRANDTOTAL function to produce a grand total from all cells in a range that contain the @SUBTOTAL function

See Also   @DSUM, @SUM, @SUMNEGATIVE, @SUMPOSITIVE

@HARMEAN(list)

The @HARMEAN function calculates the harmonic mean of the values in *list*. The harmonic mean is the reciprocal of the arithmetic mean of the reciprocals of *list*. *list* can include numbers, numeric formulas that result in numbers, and addresses or names of ranges containing numbers, or numeric formulas that result in numbers. Note that all the values in *list* must be greater than zero.

For example, the following function statement produces 55.21405:

    @HARMEAN(25,99,78,105)

> **TIP** For the same *list*, the result of @HARMEAN is less than the result of @GEOMEAN (which in turn is less than the result of @AVG) unless all the values in *list* are equal. For example, @HARMEAN(100,200,300) produces 163.6363, @GEOMEAN(100,200,300) produces 181.7121, and @AVG (100,200,300) produces 200; @AVG(100,100,100), @GEOMEAN(100,100,100), and @HARMEAN (100,100,100) all produce 100.

See Also @AVG, @GEOMEAN, @MEDIAN, @PUREAVG

@KURTOSIS(range,[type])

The @KURTOSIS function calculates the kurtosis of the values in *range*, where *range* is the name or address of a range containing values. Kurtosis measures the concentration of a distribution around the mean of a range of values. A positive kurtosis indicates a relatively peaked distribution around the mean, while a negative kurtosis indicates a relatively flat distribution around the mean.

> **WARNING** Note that *range* must contain at least four values for the @KURTOSIS function to work. @KURTOSIS returns ERR if *range* contains fewer than four values.

type is either 0 (for a population kurtosis; this is the default if you omit the argument *type*) or 1 (for a sample kurtosis).

For example, if the range named RESULTS contains the values 1, 30, 1, and 1, the following function statement produces a population kurtosis of –0.66667:

    @KURTOSIS(RESULTS)

And this function statement produces a sample kurtosis of 4:

    @KURTOSIS(RESULTS,1)

See Also @SKEWNESS

@MAX(list)

The @MAX function finds and returns the largest value in *list*, where *list* can be the following in any combination, separated by argument separator characters:

- Numbers
- Numeric formulas
- Range addresses or range names containing numbers or numeric formulas

For example, in the worksheet in Figure G.8, cell C12 contains the following function statement to return the largest value from the range E4..E8:

    @MAX(E4..E8)

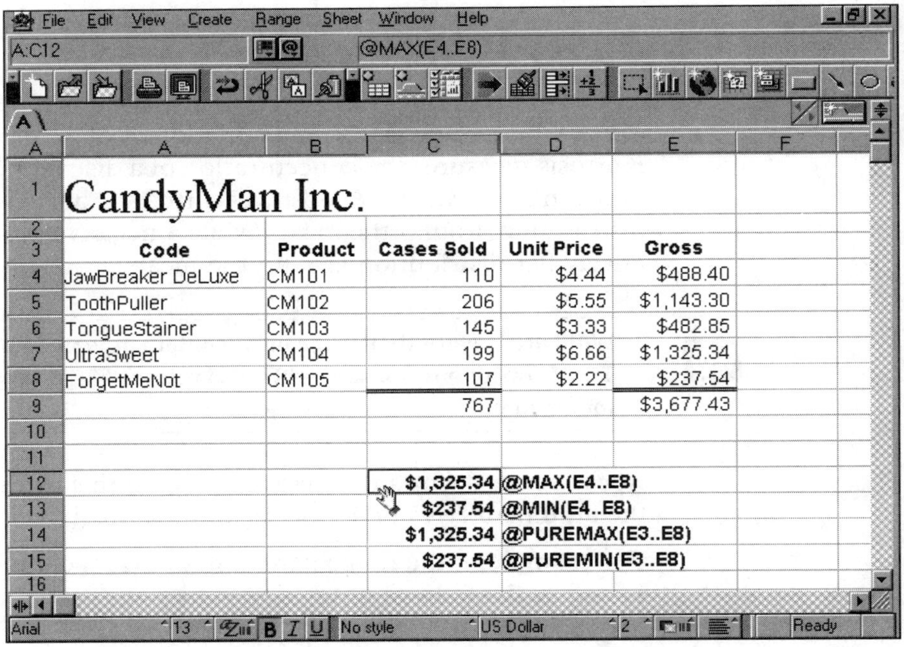

Figure G.8: **Using the @MAX function to return the largest value from a range that does not contain labels**

See Also   @DMAX, @LARGE, @MIN, @PUREMIN

Descriptions of the Statistical Functions

TIP If your range contains labels, use the @PUREMAX function instead of the @MAX function.

@MEDIAN(list)

The @MEDIAN function returns the median value in *list*, where *list* can be the following in any combination, separated by argument separator characters:

- Numbers
- Numeric formulas
- Range addresses or range names containing numbers or numeric formulas

For example, if the range MEDIATE contains the values 6, 5, 4, and 7, the following function statement returns 5.5:

    @MEDIAN(MEDIATE)

TIP @MEDIAN returns the middle value if *list* contains an odd number of values and the arithmetic average of the two middle values if *list* contains an even number of values.

See Also @AVG, @GEOMEAN, @HARMEAN, @PUREAVG

@MIN(list)

The @MIN function finds and returns the smallest value in *list*, where *list* can be the following in any combination, separated by argument separator characters:

- Numbers
- Numeric formulas
- Range addresses or range names containing numbers or numeric formulas

For example, in the worksheet in Figure G.9, cell C12 contains the following function statement to return the smallest value from the range E4..E8:

    @MIN(E4..E8)

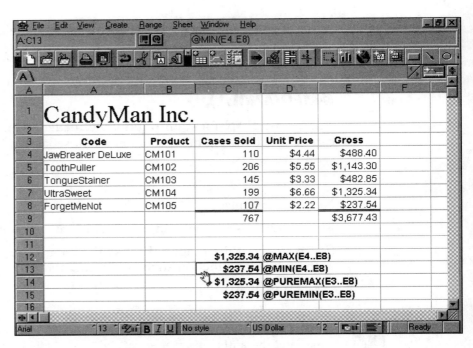

Figure G.9: Using the @MIN function to return the smallest value from a range that does not contain labels

TIP If your list contains labels, use @PUREMIN instead of @MIN; @PUREMIN ignores labels in *list*.

See Also @DMAX, @DMIN, @MAX, @PUREMAX

@NORMAL(numeric-value,[mean],[std],[type])

The @NORMAL function calculates the normal distribution function for the specific mean (average) and standard deviation. The arguments for the @NORMAL function are as follows:

Argument	Description
numeric-value	Any value indicating the upper boundary for the value of the cumulative normal distribution. *numeric-value* can be negative, but if it

Descriptions of the Statistical Functions

	is, @NORMAL converts it to its absolute (positive) value.
mean	Any positive value or 0 indicating the mean of the distribution. *mean* is an optional argument; if you omit *mean*, @NORMAL uses 0.
std	Any positive value or 0 indicating the standard deviation of the distribution. *std* is an optional argument; if you omit *std*, @NORMAL uses 1.
type	Zero, 1, or 2, indicating the function for @NORMAL to calculate, as per the following list: 0 If *type* = 0, @NORMAL calculates the cumulative function distribution. This is the default setting if you omit the *type* argument. 1 If *type* = 1, @NORMAL calculates the inverse cumulative distribution. 2 If *type* = 2, @NORMAL calculates the probability density function.

WARNING Note that you cannot use an optional argument unless you use those that precede it. For example, you cannot use *type* in @NORMAL if you do not specify *std*, and you cannot use *std* if you do not specify *mean*.

For example, to calculate the probability density function for 0.88, with a *mean* of 1 and a standard deviation of 0.5, you could use the following function statement:

    @NORMAL(0.88,1,0.5,2)

This returns 0.775233.

See Also   @CHIDIST, @FDIST, @POISSON, @TDIST

@PERMUT(number-object,number-chosen)

The @PERMUT function returns the number of permutations (ordered sequences) of objects that can be selected from *number-object*.

The arguments for the @PERMUT function are as follows:

Argument	Description
number-object	Zero or any positive integer indicating the number of objects. If *number-object* is not an integer, @PERMUT will truncate it to one.
number-chosen	Zero or any positive integer indicating the number of objects in each permutation. If *number-object* is not an integer, @PERMUT will truncate it to one. *number-chosen* cannot be greater than *number-object*; @PERMUT returns ERR if it is.

For example, suppose Lord Cardigan had had seven brigades at his command that fateful day in the Crimea and had been able to commit three of them to charging the wrong guns instead of just the poor old Light Brigade. Had he had 1-2-3 running on his OmniBook or Newton, he could have calculated the number of possible different ways of committing the brigades by using the following function statement:

    @PERMUT(7,3)

This returns 210 possible permutations. But you still have the feeling he'd have sent in the Light Brigade anyway...

See Also   @COMBIN

@PERCENTILE(numeric-value,range)

The @PERCENTILE function calculates the xth sample percentile among the values in *range*, where *numeric-value* (x) is a value between 0 and 1 indicating the percentile to find, and range is the name or address of a range containing values.

Figure G.10 illustrates the use of the @PERCENTILE function for establishing a threshold of acceptance. The Fourth Grade Test Results spreadsheet contains the following function statement in cell E12 to determine the score at the eighty-fifth percentile for the average scores (column G):

    @PERCENTILE(0.85,G5..G10)

This returns 91.25.

NOTE The @PERCENTILE function ignores any blank cells in *range* but includes any labels, to which it gives the value 0.

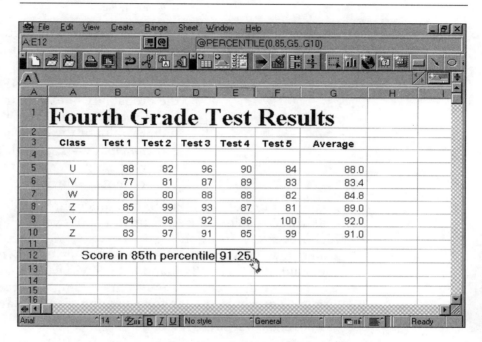

Figure G.10: Using the @PERCENTILE function to establish and determine the score at a percentile

See Also @PRANK, @DECILE, @QUARTILE

@POISSON(number,mean,[cumulative])

The @POISSON function calculates the Poisson distribution, which is mostly used for predicting the number of events that will occur over a specific period of time, using data collected from observation of similar events.

The arguments for the @POISSON function are as follows:

Argument	Description
number	Zero or an integer indicating the number of observed events. If you enter a number that is not an integer, @POISSON will truncate it to an integer.

mean	A positive integer indicating the number of expected events. If you enter a number that is not an integer, @POISSON will truncate it to an integer.
cumulative	Zero or 1, an optional argument to determine how 1-2-3 calculates @POISSON, as follows: 0 If *cumulative* = 0, @POISSON calculates the probability of exactly the predicted *number* of events occurring. 0 is the default setting if you omit the *cumulative* argument. 1 If *cumulative* = 1, @POISSON calculates the probability of *at most* the predicted number of events occurring.

As an example of the @POISSON function, consider a company with 100 workers, all of whose punctuality slips from an impressive Monday high—everyone in by the 8:30 A.M. starting time—to an acceptable Friday low. Last Friday morning you observed 40 employees entering the building between 8:30 and 8:45 A.M.; what is the probability that exactly 50 employees will enter the building between those times this Friday? You could use the following function statement to find out:

```
@POISSON(40,50)
```

This returns 0.0215. But a more realistic question might be how high the probability is that at most 50 employees will enter the building between 8:30 and 8:45 A.M. Use this function statement instead:

```
@POISSON(40,50,1)
```

This returns 0.08607, a much higher probability.

@PRANK(numeric-value,range,[places])

The @PRANK function returns the percentile of *numeric-value* among the values in *range*. The arguments for the @PRANK function are as follows:

Argument	Description
numeric-value	Any value indicating the percentile to find.
range	The name or address of a range containing values. *range* does not have to contain

	numeric-value, but if it does not, @PRANK assigns the 0th percentile position to the lowest value in *range*, assigns the 100th percentile position to the highest value in *range*, and then interpolates.
places	0 to 100, indicating the number of decimal places to which to round the result; the default setting is 2.

Figure G.11 illustrates the use of @PRANK. In this Second Grade Test Results worksheet, cell C12 contains the following function statement to calculate the percentile rank of the score 94 among the averages in column G:

```
@PRANK(94,G5..G10)
```

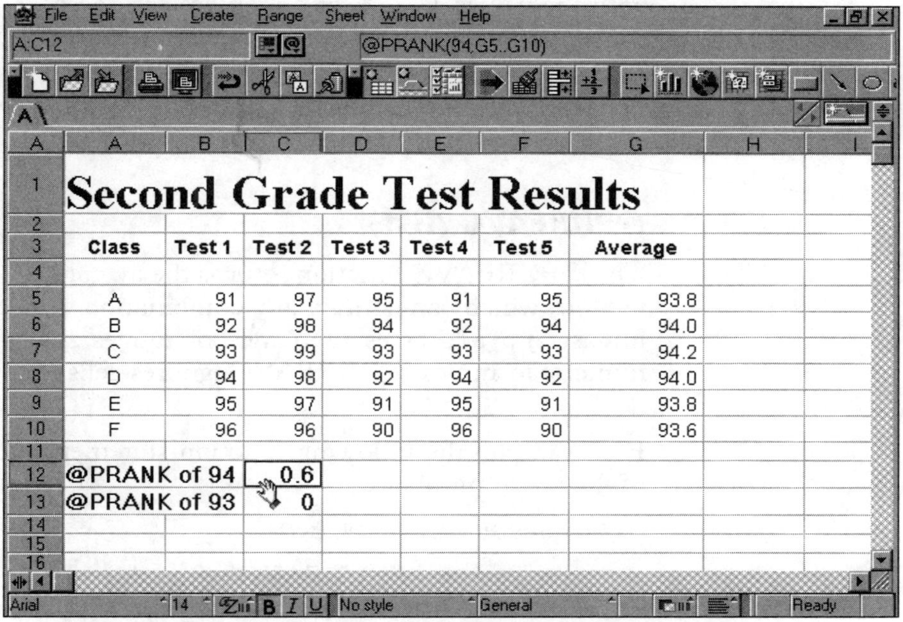

Second Grade Test Results

Class	Test 1	Test 2	Test 3	Test 4	Test 5	Average
A	91	97	95	91	95	93.8
B	92	98	94	92	94	94.0
C	93	99	93	93	93	94.2
D	94	98	92	94	92	94.0
E	95	97	91	95	91	93.8
F	96	96	90	96	90	93.6
@PRANK of 94		0.6				
@PRANK of 93		0				

Figure G.11: ***Using the @PRANK function to return the percentile rank of an item in a range***

This returns 0.6 (60 percent). Note the difference when you use @PRANK on a value that is not included in the *range*—cell C13 contains the following function statement:

```
@PRANK(93,G5..G10)
```

This returns 0, because the value 93 is not an item in the range.

See Also @PERCENTILE

@PRODUCT(list)

The @PRODUCT function multiplies the values in *list*, where *list* can be the following in any combination, separated by separator characters:

- Numbers
- Numeric formulas
- Range addresses or range names containing numbers or numeric formulas

For example, if a worksheet contains a range named ANTENNAE with the values 1, 2, 3, and 4 entered in the cells, the following function statement returns 24, the product of those four values:

    @PRODUCT(ANTENNAE)

See Also @FACT, @SUM, @SUMPRODUCT

@PUREAVG (list)

The @PUREAVG function returns the average of the values contained in a *list*, which can contain any combination of numbers, numeric formulas, and addresses or names of ranges that contain numbers or numeric formulas. @PUREAVG ignores cells in the range that contain labels.

For example, the following function statement returns 4, the average of the seven numbers:

    @PUREAVG(5,2,2,1,4,6,8)

You can also use @PUREAVG with addresses, with numeric formulas, with ranges, or with named ranges, not to mention with combinations of numbers, numeric formulas, addresses, and ranges:

    @PUREAVG(4000, A12/5, B34..C56, AB80, UNPAID)

See Also @DAVG, @GEOMEAN, @HARMEAN, @MEDIAN

@PURECOUNT(list)

The @PURECOUNT function returns the number of the nonblank cells in *list*, where *list* is any combination of range addresses or names separated by commas. @PURECOUNT ignores cells containing labels and does not include them in the number it returns. For example, if cell A1 contains the label Plate of Shrimp, cell A2 contains the value 1, and cell A3 is blank, the following function statement returns 1, since only one cell (cell A2) contains a value:

    @PURECOUNT(A1..A3)

You can use @PURECOUNT to stop or branch a macro that performs actions on a series of ranges when the cell pointer enters a range that contains no entries:

    {IF @PURECOUNT(PROJECTIONS_97)=0}{QUIT}

If the range PROJECTIONS_97 does not yet contain any entries, the macro is instructed to stop.

See Also   @COUNT, @DCOUNT, @DPURECOUNT

@PUREMAX(list)

The @PUREMAX function finds and returns the LARGEST value in a *list* that contains labels that you want to exclude from the calculation, where *list* can be the following in any combination, separated by argument separator characters:

▶ Numbers

▶ Numeric formulas

▶ Range addresses or range names containing numbers or numeric formulas

For example, in the worksheet in Figure G.12, cell C14 contains the following function statement to return the largest value from the range E3..E8:

    @PUREMAX(E3..E8)

See Also   @DMAX, @LARGE, @MIN, @PUREMIN

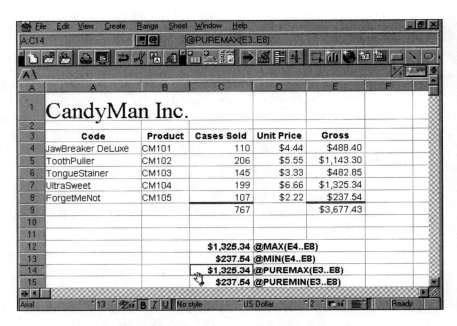

Figure G.12: **Using the @PUREMAX function to return the largest value from a range that contains labels**

@PUREMEDIAN(list)

The @PUREMEDIAN function returns the median value in *list*, ignoring blank cells, labels, and formulas that result in labels. *list* can be the following in any combination, separated by argument separator characters:

▶ Numbers

▶ Numeric formulas

▶ Range addresses or range names containing numbers or numeric formulas

For example, if the range PMEDIATE contains the values 6, 5, 4, and 7, the following function statement returns 5.5:

    @PUREMEDIAN(PMEDIATE)

See Also   @MEDIAN

TIP @PUREMEDIAN returns the middle value if *list* contains an odd number of values and the arithmetic average of the two middle values if *list* contains an even number of values.

@PUREMIN(list)

The @PUREMIN function finds and returns the smallest value in a *list* that contains labels that you want to exclude from the calculation, where *list* can be the following in any combination, separated by argument separator characters:

- Numbers
- Numeric formulas
- Range addresses or range names containing numbers or numeric formulas

For example, in the worksheet in Figure G.13, cell C15 contains the following function statement to return the smallest value from the range E3..E8:

    @PUREMIN(E3..E8)

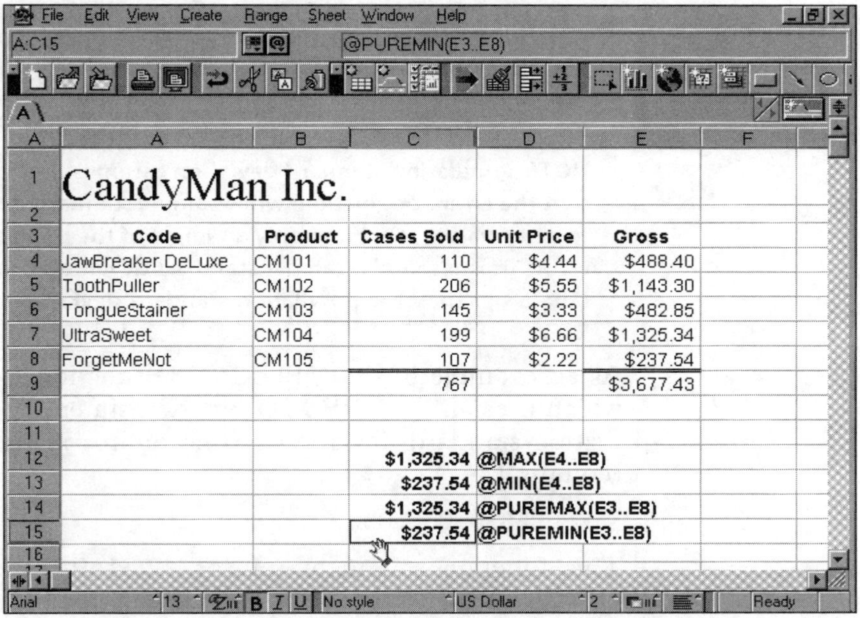

Figure G.13: **Using the @PUREMIN function to return the smallest value from a range that contains labels**

See Also   @MAX, @DMIN, @PUREMAX

@PURESTD(list)

The @PURESTD function returns the population standard deviation of the values in a *list* containing labels that you want to exclude from the calculation, where *list* can be the following in any combination, separated by separator characters:

- Numbers
- Numeric formulas
- Range addresses or range names containing numbers or numeric formulas

NOTE While the @STD, @STDS, @PURESTD, and @PURESTDS functions work in similar ways, they produce significantly different results. @STD calculates the population standard deviation, while @STDS calculates the sample standard deviation. @PURESTD calculates the population standard deviation, ignoring cells that contain labels that would throw off the @STD calculation; and @PURESTDS calculates the sample standard deviation, likewise ignoring cells with labels that would throw off the @STDS calculation.

NOTE Population standard deviation assumes that the selected values represent the entire population, while sample standard deviation assumes that the selected values represent only a sample of the population. To compensate for errors in the sample, sample standard deviation produces a standard deviation larger than the population standard deviation.

As an example of the @PURESTD function, consider Figure G.14, which uses an @PURESTD function statement to calculate the population standard deviation on the figures in the Cases Sold column (column C):

    @PURESTD(C3..C8)

This function statement returns 42.3159544. Note that the range C3..C8 includes the label in cell C3, since @PURESTD ignores labels included in the range, whereas @STD does not. While selecting the range without the label is no great chore in a small worksheet like this one, when you are working with larger worksheets that include many labels, the @PURESTD function can be very useful indeed.

See Also @DSTD, @DSTDS, @PUREVAR, @PUREVARS, @VAR, @VARS

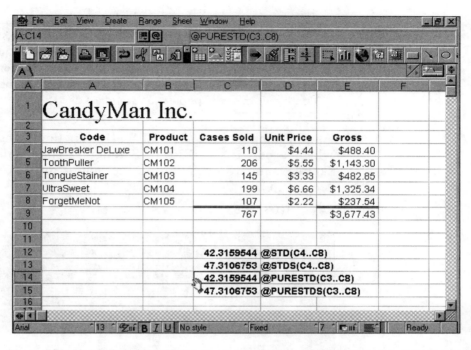

Figure G.14: *Using the @PURESTD function to return the population standard deviation from a range that includes labels*

@PURESTDS(list)

The @PURESTDS function returns the sample standard deviation of the values in a *list* containing labels that you want to exclude from the calculation, where *list* can be the following in any combination, separated by separator characters:

▶ Numbers

▶ Numeric formulas

▶ Range addresses or range names containing numbers or numeric formulas

NOTE While the @STD, @STDS, @PURESTD, and @PURESTDS functions work in similar ways, they produce significantly different results. @STD calculates the population standard deviation, while @STDS calculates the sample standard deviation. @PURESTD calculates the population standard deviation, ignoring cells that contain labels that would throw off the @STD calculation; and @PURESTDS calculates the sample standard deviation, likewise ignoring cells with labels that would throw off the @STDS calculation.

NOTE Population standard deviation assumes that the selected values represent the entire population, while sample standard deviation assumes that the selected values represent only a sample of the population. To compensate for errors in the sample, sample standard deviation produces a standard deviation larger than the population standard deviation.

As an example of the @PURESTDS function, consider Figure G.15, which uses an @PURESTDS function statement to calculate the sample standard deviation on the figures in the Cases Sold column (column C):

```
@STD(C3..C8)
```

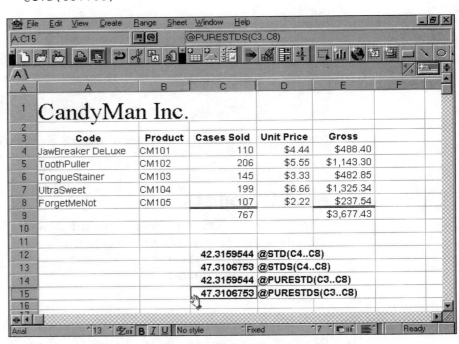

Figure G.15: Using the @PURESTDS function to return the sample standard deviation from a range that does not contain labels

This function statement returns 47.3106753. Note that the range C3..C8 includes the label in cell C3, which would interfere with the

@STDS calculation but which @PURESTDS ignores. In larger worksheets that contain multiple rows of labels among blocks of values, this function can prove handy.

See Also @DSTD, @DSTDS, @PUREVAR, @PUREVARS, @VAR, @VARS

@PUREVAR(list)

The @PUREVAR function calculates the population variance in a *list* of values, where *list* can be the following in any combination, separated by separator characters:

- Numbers
- Numeric formulas
- Range addresses or range names containing numbers or numeric formulas

> NOTE Population variance assumes that the selected values are the entire population, while sample variance assumes that the selected values represent only a sample of the population. To compensate for errors in the sample, sample variance produces a variance larger than the population variance.

Figure G.16 illustrates the @PUREVAR function. In this worksheet, cell C14 calculates the population variance of range C3..C8 by using the following function statement:

    @PUREVAR(C3..C8)

This function statement returns 1790.64. Note the difference between this function statement and that for @VAR: When using @PUREVAR, you do not have to exclude from the range any labels that would interfere with the @VAR calculation if included in the range. In this case, the difference between the ranges C3..C8 and C4..C8 is mostly academic; but in a more complicated worksheet, where rows of labels are interspersed in blocks of values, @PUREVAR can be most useful.

See Also @DVAR, @DVARS, @PUREVARS, @VAR, @VARS

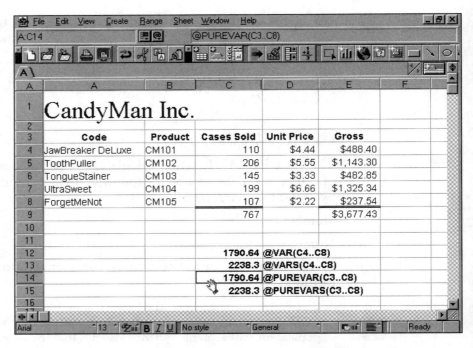

Figure G.16: Using the @PUREVAR function to calculate the population variance of a range that includes labels

TIP The functions @VAR, @VARS, @PUREVAR, and @PUREVARS all work in similar ways but produce substantially different results. While @VAR calculates population variance, @VARS calculates sample population variance. @PUREVAR calculates population variance but ignores cells that contain labels rather than values; and @PUREVARS calculates sample population variance ignoring cells that contain labels rather than values.

@PUREVARS(list)

The @PUREVARS function calculates the sample population variance in a *list* of values, where *list* can be the following in any combination, separated by separator characters:

- ▶ Numbers
- ▶ Numeric formulas
- ▶ Range addresses or range names containing numbers or numeric formulas

> **NOTE** Sample population variance assumes that the selected values represent only a sample of the population, while population variance assumes that the selected values comprise the entire population. To compensate for errors in the sample, sample variance produces a variance larger than the population variance.

Figure G.17 illustrates the @PUREVARS function. In this worksheet, cell C15 calculates the population variance of range C3..C8 by using the following function statement:

@PUREVARS(C3..C8)

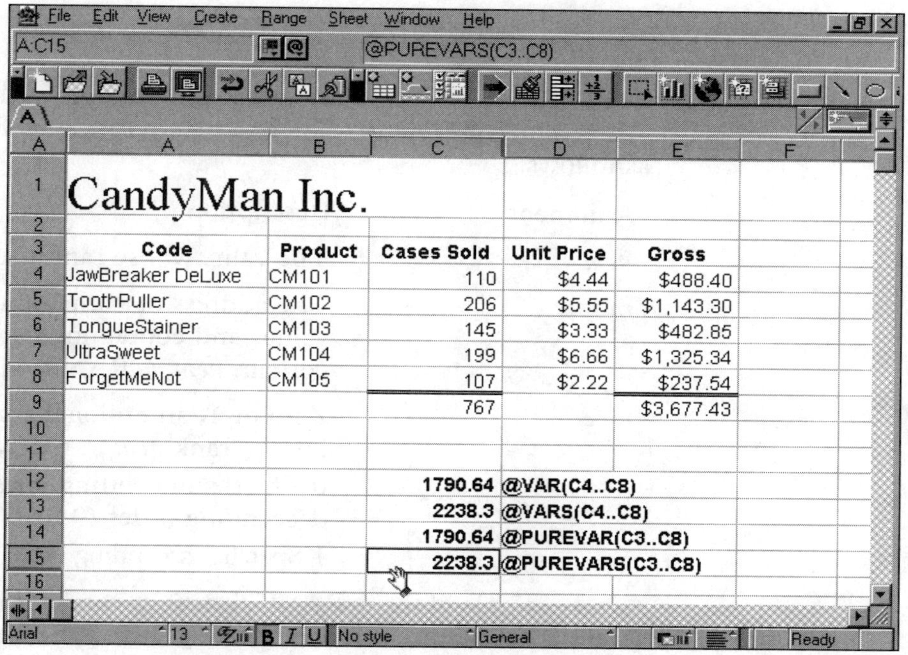

Figure G.17: *Using the @PUREVARS function to calculate the sample population variance of a range that includes labels*

This function statement returns 2238.3. Note the difference between this function statement and that for @VARS: When using @PUREVARS, you do not have to exclude from the range any labels that would interfere with the @VARS calculation. In this case, the difference between the ranges C3..C8 and C4..C8 is barely significant; but in a complex worksheet with many rows of labels identifying blocks of values, @PUREVAR really comes into its own.

TIP The functions @VAR, @VARS, @PUREVAR, and @PUREVARS all work in similar ways but produce substantially different results. While @VAR calculates population variance, @VARS calculates sample population variance. @PUREVAR calculates population variance but ignores cells that contain labels rather than values; and @PUREVARS calculates sample population variance ignoring cells that contain labels rather than values.

See Also   @DVAR, @DVARS, @PUREVAR, @VAR, @VARS

@RANK(item,range,[order])

The @RANK function calculates the rank of a value, *item*, relative to other values in a *range*. The arguments for the @RANK function are as follows:

Argument	Description
item	The value whose rank you want to establish.
range	The address or name of a range containing values and containing *item*; if *range* does not contain *item*, @RANK will return ERR.
order	Zero or 1, an optional argument indicating how to rank *item* in *range*, as follows: 0 The default setting for *order* and specifies descending order (9 to 1, z to a, etc.). 1 Specifies ascending order (1 to 9, a to z, etc.).

As an example of the @RANK function, consider Figure G.18, which shows a Frequently Accessed Newsgroups worksheet. Column E contains the range named TOTAL ACCESS, and column G contains function statements similar to the following one to establish the rank of the different newsgroups among those accessed:

    @RANK(E10,TOTAL ACCESS)

NOTE If *range* contains two items with the same value, @RANK assigns them the same rank. For example, in the Frequently Accessed Newsgroups worksheet, the newsgroups Control, Feminism, and Writing share eleventh place, and no twelfth or thirteenth place appears.

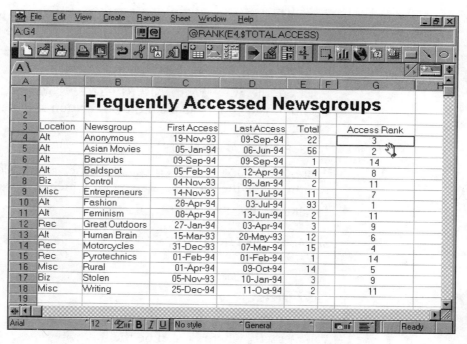

Figure G.18: Using the @RANK function to establish the rank of items within a range

@SKEWNESS(range,[type])

The @SKEWNESS function calculates the skewness of the values in *range*. Skewness measures the symmetry of a distribution around its mean (average). Positive skewness indicates a drawn-out tail to the left while negative skewness indicates a drawn-out tail to the right.

The arguments for the @SKEWNESS function are as follows:

Argument	Description
range	The name or address of a range containing at least three values. If *range* contains fewer than three values, @SKEWNESS will return ERR.
type	Zero or 1, indicating whether @SKEWNESS is to calculate population skewness or sample skewness, as follows:

0 If *type* = 0, @SKEWNESS calculates the population skewness. This is the

default setting if you omit the optional *type* argument.

1 If *type* = 1, @SKEWNESS calculates the sample skewness.

For example, if the range APPRECIATE contained the values 1, 2, 4, 6, and 8, you could calculate the population skewness by using the following function statement:

    @SKEWNESS(APPRECIATE)

This returns 0.205692. To calculate the sample skewness, you could use the following function statement, which returns 0.306628:

    @SKEWNESS(APPRECIATE,1)

See Also @KURTOSIS, @PURESTD, @PUREVAR, @STD, @VAR

@STD(list)

The @STD function returns the population standard deviation of the values in *list*, where *list* can be the following in any combination, separated by separator characters:

▶ Numbers

▶ Numeric formulas

▶ Range addresses or range names containing numbers or numeric formulas

NOTE While the @STD, @STDS, @PURESTD, and @PURESTDS functions work in similar ways, they produce significantly different results. @STD calculates the population standard deviation, while @STDS calculates the sample standard deviation. @PURESTD calculates the population standard deviation, ignoring cells that contain labels that would throw off the @STD calculation; and @PURESTDS calculates the sample standard deviation, likewise ignoring cells with labels that would throw off the @STD calculation.

NOTE Population standard deviation assumes that the selected values represent the entire population, while sample standard deviation assumes that the selected values represent only a sample of the population. To compensate for errors in the sample, sample standard deviation produces a standard deviation larger than the population standard deviation.

As an example of the @STD function, consider Figure G.19, which uses an @STD function statement to calculate the population standard deviation on the figures in the Cases Sold column (column C):

@STD(C4..C8)

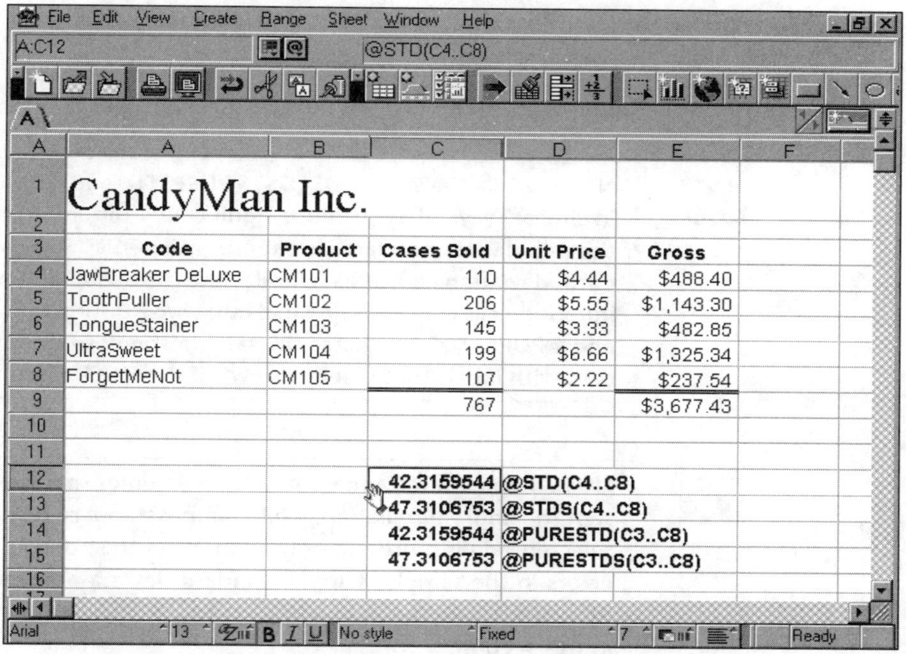

Figure G.19: Using the @STD function to return the population standard deviation from a range that does not contain labels

This function statement returns 42.3159544. Note that the range C4..C8 excludes the label in cell C3, which would interfere with the @STD calculation. If the range includes labels, use the @PURESTD function instead.

As an aside, if all the values in the @STD calculation are the same, the average will equal that value, and the standard deviation will be 0.

See Also @DSTD, @DSTDS, @PUREVAR, @PUREVARS, @STD, @VAR, @VARS

@STDS(list)

The @STDS function returns the sample standard deviation of the values in *list*, where *list* can be the following in any combination, separated by separator characters:

- Numbers
- Numeric formulas
- Range addresses or range names containing numbers or numeric formulas

> **NOTE** While the @STD, @STDS, @PURESTD, and @PURESTDS functions work in similar ways, they produce significantly different results. @STD calculates the population standard deviation, while @STDS calculates the sample standard deviation. @PURESTD calculates the population standard deviation, ignoring cells that contain labels that would throw off the @STD calculation; and @PURESTDS calculates the sample standard deviation, likewise ignoring cells with labels that would throw off the @STD calculation.

> **NOTE** Population standard deviation assumes that the selected values represent the entire population, while sample standard deviation assumes that the selected values represent only a sample of the population. To compensate for errors in the sample, sample standard deviation produces a standard deviation larger than the population standard deviation, as shown in the example in this section.

As an example of the @STDS function, consider Figure G.20, which uses an @STDS function statement to calculate the sample standard deviation on the figures in the Cases Sold column (column C):

    @STDS(C4..C8)

This function statement returns 47.3106753. Note that the range C4..C8 excludes the label in cell C3, which would interfere with the @STDS calculation. If the range includes labels, use the @PURESTDS function instead.

See Also @DSTD, @DSTDS, @PUREVAR, @PUREVARS, @STD, @VAR, @VARS

Descriptions of the Statistical Functions

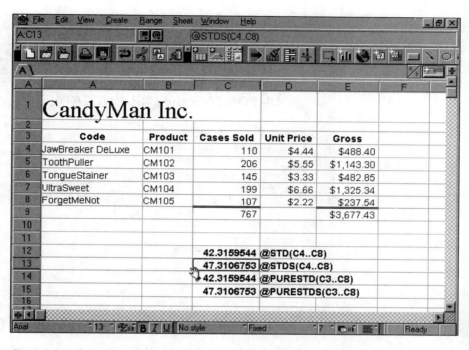

Figure G.20: Using the @STDS function to return the population standard deviation from a range that does not contain labels

@SUMNEGATIVE(list)

The @SUMNEGATIVE function sums only the negative values in *list*, where *list* can be the following in any combination, separated by argument separator characters:

▶ Numbers

▶ Numeric formulas

▶ Range addresses or range names containing numbers or numeric formulas

For example, if you keep track of your finances in an underdeveloped PDA and port them via the ether to your desktop PC and 1-2-3, you could use @SUMNEGATIVE as illustrated in Figure G.21 to calculate your total expenditure without having to divide the income and expenditure figures into separate ranges. In Figure G.21, cell D8 contains the following function statement to calculate total expenditure from the range CASHFLOWS:

```
@SUMNEGATIVE(CASHFLOWS)
```

Appendix G Mathematical and Statistical Functions Reference

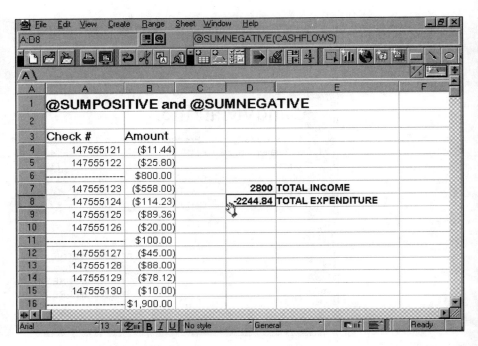

Figure G.21: *Using the @SUMNEGATIVE function to return only the negative values from a list*

See Also   @DSUM, @GRANDTOTAL, @SUBTOTAL, @SUM, @SUMPOSITIVE

@SUMPOSITIVE(list)

The @SUMPOSITIVE function sums only the positive values in *list*, where *list* can be the following in any combination, separated by argument separator characters:

- Numbers
- Numeric formulas
- Range addresses or range names containing numbers or numeric formulas

For example, if you keep track of your finances in an underdeveloped PDA and port them via the ether to your desktop PC and 1-2-3, you could use @SUMPOSITIVE as illustrated in Figure G.21 (in the previous entry) to calculate your total income without having to divide the income and expenditure figures into separate ranges. In Figure G.21, cell D7 contains the following function statement to calculate total income from the range CASHFLOWS:

    @SUMPOSITIVE(CASHFLOWS)

See Also   @DSUM, @GRANDTOTAL, @SUBTOTAL, @SUM, @SUMNEGATIVE

@TDIST(numeric-value,degrees-freedom, [type],[tails])

The @TDIST function calculates and returns the Student's *t*-distribution. The Student's *t*-distribution is the distribution of the ratio of a standardized normal distribution to the square root of the quotient of a chi-square distribution by the number of its degrees of freedom.

The arguments for the @TDIST function are as follows:

Argument	Description
numeric-value	The value at which to evaluate the *t*-distribution. *numeric-value* depends on the *type* argument, which can be 0 or 1, as follows: 0 If *type* = 0, *numeric-value* is the critical value (the upper bound) for the value of the cumulative t-distribution random variable. In this case, *numeric-value* can be any value. If you omit the *type* argument, @TDIST uses 0 as the default value. 1 If *type* = 1, *numeric-value* is a probability; enter *numeric-value* as a value from 0 to 1.
degrees-freedom1	Any positive integer indicating the number of degrees of freedom for the sample.
type	Zero or 1, an optional argument indicating the direction of the *t*-distribution, as follows: 0 If *type* = 0, @TDIST calculates the significance level that corresponds to the critical value, *numeric-value*. This is the default value if you omit the *type* argument. 1 If *type* = 1, @TDIST calculates the critical value that corresponds to the significance level, *numeric-value*.

tails	1 or 2, indicating the direction of the *t*-test, as follows: 1 If *tails* = 1, 1-2-3 performs a one-tailed *t*-test. 2 If *tails* = 2, 1-2-3 performs a two-tailed *t*-test. *tails* is an optional argument; 2 is the default setting if you omit *tails*.

WARNING You cannot use an optional argument unless you use those that precede it. For example, you cannot use *tails* in @TDIST if you do not specify *type*. Also be aware that @TDIST approximates the cumulative *t*-distribution to within ±3*10^–7; and if @TDIST cannot approximate the result to within 0.0000001 after 100 calculation iterations, it returns ERR.

Figure G.22 shows an example of calculating a *t*-distribution with the @TDIST function. Cell B4 contains 0.75 as *numeric-value*, and cell B5 contains 8 as *degrees-freedom1*. Cells B7 through B10 contain four @TDIST function statements, illustrating the different permutations possible. For example, cell B9 contains the following function statement, which returns ERR for these values because @TDIST cannot approximate the result to within 0.0000001 after 100 calculation iterations:

    @TDIST(B4,B5,1,1)

See Also @CHIDIST, @FDIST, @TTEST

@TTEST(range1,range2,[type],[tails])

The @TTEST function calculates the associated probability of a student's *t*-test on the data in *range1* and *range2*. The purpose of @TTEST is to establish whether two samples are likely to have come from the same two underlying populations.

The arguments for the @TTEST function are as follows:

Argument	Description
range1	The first data set, a range containing values.
range2	The second data set, a range containing values.

Descriptions of the Statistical Functions

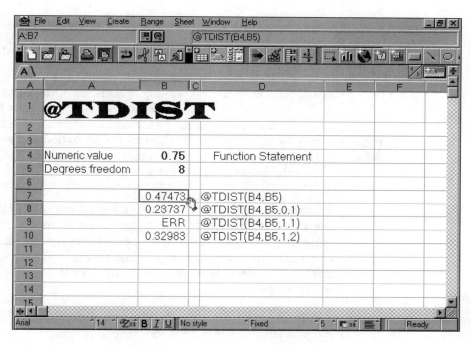

Figure G.22: **Using the @TDIST function to calculate a t-distribution**

type	0, 1, or 2, indicating what type of *t*-test to perform, as follows:
	0 If *type* = 0, 1-2-3 performs a *homoscedastic t*-test—a *t*-test for samples drawn from populations with the same variance. For a homoscedastic *t*-test, *range1* and *range2* do not have to contain the same number of cells. *type* is an optional argument; @TTEST uses 0 as the default if you omit *type*.
	1 If *type* = 1, 1-2-3 performs a *heteroscedastic t*-test—a *t*-test for samples drawn from populations with unequal variances. For a heteroscedastic test, *range1* and *range2* do not have to contain the same number of cells.
	2 If *type* = 2, 1-2-3 performs a *paired t*-test. For a paired *t*-test, *range1* and *range2* must contain the same number of cells.

tails   1 or 2, indicating the direction of the *t*-test, as follows:
1 If *tails* = 1, 1-2-3 performs a one-tailed *t*-test.
2 If *tails* = 2, 1-2-3 performs a two-tailed *t*-test. *tails* is an optional argument; 2 is the default setting if you omit *tails*.

WARNING Note that you cannot use an optional argument unless you use those that precede it. For example, you cannot use *tails* in an @TTEST function statement if you do not specify *type*.

Figure G.23 provides an illustration of the @TTEST function. Column A contains First Result, the result from the first test; column B contains Second Result, the result from the second test. Column C calculates the variance according to the different combinations that @TTEST offers; and column D contains the text of the function statements in column C.

Thus, cell C4 contains the following function statement to calculate a homoscedastic *t*-test with two tails:

@TTEST(A4..A11,B4..B11)

See Also   @CHITEST, @FTEST, @TDIST, @ZTEST

@VAR(list)

The @VAR function calculates the population variance in a *list* of values, where *list* can be the following in any combination, separated by separator characters:

▶ Numbers

▶ Numeric formulas

▶ Range addresses or range names containing numbers or numeric formulas

NOTE Population variance assumes that the selected values are the entire population, while sample variance assumes that the selected values represent only a sample of the population. To compensate for errors in the sample, sample variance produces a variance larger than the population variance.

Descriptions of the Statistical Functions

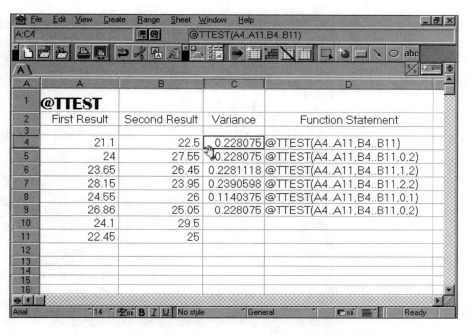

Figure G.23: **Using the @TTEST function to return the student's t-test probability**

Figure G.24 illustrates the @VAR function. In this worksheet, cell C12 calculates the population variance of range C4..C8 by using the following function statement:

    @VAR(C4..C8)

This function statement returns 1790.64. Note that the range used here is C4..C8, excluding the label in cell C3, which would interfere with the @VAR calculation if included in the range.

> **TIP** The functions @VAR, @VARS, @PUREVAR, and @PUREVARS all work in similar ways but produce substantially different results. While @VAR calculates population variance, @VARS calculates sample population variance. @PUREVAR calculates population variance but ignores cells that contain labels rather than values; and @PUREVARS calculates sample population variance ignoring cells that contain labels rather than values.

See Also   @DVAR, @DVARS

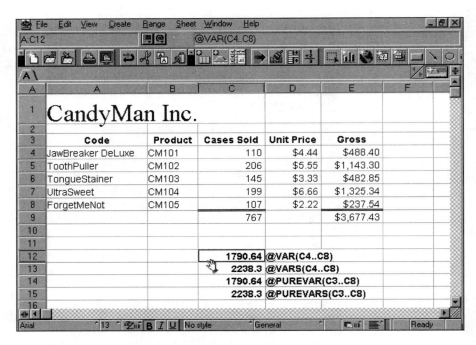

Figure G.24: *Using the @VAR function to calculate the population variance of a range*

@VARS(list)

The @VARS function calculates the sample population variance in a *list* of values, where *list* can be the following in any combination, separated by separator characters:

▶ Numbers

▶ Numeric formulas

▶ Range addresses or range names containing numbers or numeric formulas

 NOTE Sample population variance assumes that the selected values represent only a sample of the population, while population variance assumes that the selected values comprise the entire population. To compensate for errors in the sample, sample variance produces a variance larger than the population variance.

Descriptions of the Statistical Functions

Figure G.25 illustrates the @VARS function. In this worksheet, cell C13 calculates the sample population variance of range C4..C8 by using the following function statement:

@VARS(C4..C8)

This function statement returns 2238.3. Note that the range used here is C4..C8, excluding the label in cell C3, which would interfere with the @VARS calculation if included in the range.

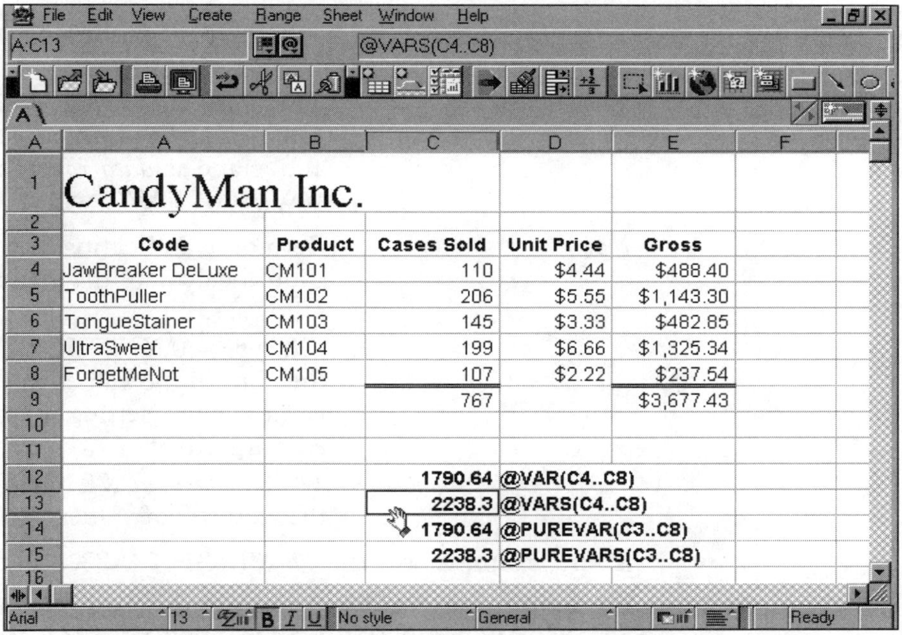

Figure G.25: Using the @VARS function to calculate the sample population variance of a range

TIP The functions @VAR, @VARS, @PUREVAR, and @PUREVARS all work in similar ways but produce substantially different results. While @VAR calculates population variance, @VARS calculates sample population variance. @PUREVAR calculates population variance but ignores cells that contain labels rather than values; and @PUREVARS calculates sample population variance ignoring cells that contain labels rather than values.

See Also @DVAR, @DVARS, @PUREVAR, @PUREVARS, @VAR

@WEIGHTAVG(data-range,weights-range,[type])

The @WEIGHTAVG function returns the weighted average of values in *data-range* by multiplying the values in corresponding cells of *data-range* and weight *r*, summing the products, and then dividing by the number of values in the list.

The arguments for the @WEIGHTAVG function are as follows:

Argument	Description
data-range	The name or address of a range containing values.
weights-range	The name or address of a range containing values. *weights-range* must be the same size and shape as *data-range*; otherwise, @WEIGHTAVG will return ERR.
type	Zero or 1, indicating how @WEIGHTAVG should calculate the weighted average, as follows: 0 If *type* = 0, @WEIGHTAVG divides by the sum of the values in *weights-range*. This is the default setting if you omit the optional *type* argument. 1 If *type* = 1, @WEIGHTAVG divides by the number of values in *data-range*.

As an example of the @WEIGHTAVG function, consider the AutoMates! car dealership worksheet shown in Figure G.26, in which cells C6..C8 contain the range named TOTAL SALES and cells E6..E8 contain the range named COMMISSION. To calculate the weighted average of sales and commission, cell D12 contains the following function statement:

    @WEIGHTAVG(TOTAL SALES,COMMISSION)

This function statement returns $69,277.78. Cell D13 contains the following function statement to return the weighted average by the number of values, which evaluates at $6,235.00:

    @WEIGHTAVG(TOTAL SALES,COMMISSION,1)

See Also   @SUMPRODUCT

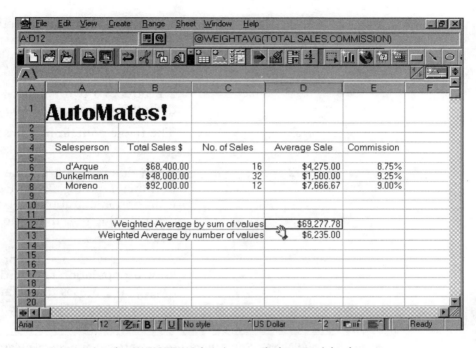

Figure G.26: *Using the @WEIGHTAVG function to calculate a weighted average*

@ZTEST(range1,mean1,std1,[tails],[range2], [mean2],[std2])

The @ZTEST function performs a *z*-test on one or two populations and returns the associated probability. A *z*-test is used to judge the likelihood that a particular observation is drawn from a particular population.

The arguments for the @ZTEST function are as follows:

Argument	Description
range1	The range containing the first (or only) set of data to be tested.
mean1	Any value representing the known population mean of *range1*.
std1	A value greater than 0 representing the known population standard deviation of *range1*.

tails	1 or 2, to specify the direction of the z-test. This is an optional argument; the values have the following effect: 1 Produces a one-tailed z-test. 2 Produces a two-tailed z-test (this is the default if you omit the *tails* argument).
range2	The range containing the second set of data to test.
mean2	Any value representing the known population mean of *range2*; can be any value. This is an optional argument; 1-2-3 uses the default value of 0 if you do not specify another.
std2	A value greater than 0 representing the known population standard deviation of *range2*; 1-2-3 uses the default value of 1 if you do not specify a value for *std2*.

WARNING You cannot use an optional argument unless you use those that precede it. For example, you cannot use *tails* in @ZTEST if you do not specify *range2*.

For example, suppose you have a range called SPECIMEN that contains the values 49, 47, 55, 48, 56, and 51; and the population mean of these values is 51; and the population standard deviation of these values is 3.41565. You could use this function statement to calculate the z-test for these values and return the associated probability:

```
@ZTEST(SPECIMEN,51,3.41565)
```

See Also @CHITEST, @FTEST, @TTEST

Appendix H
Text Functions Reference

THIS appendix examines 1-2-3's text functions, which fall into two categories:

- Functions that provide information about text in cells. For example, the @CHAR function returns the character of the Lotus Multibyte Character Set (LMBCS) that corresponds to a number code, and the @S function returns the entry in the first cell in a range as a label.

- Functions that perform operations on text. For example, the @CLEAN function removes nonprinting characters from text, and @LEFT function returns the specified number of leftmost characters in a text string.

Overview of the Text Functions

For quick reference, the text functions are listed here in Table H.1. They are discussed further in the next section of this appendix, "Descriptions of the Text Functions."

Table H.1: **Text Functions Quick Reference**

Function	Returns
@CHAR	The character of the Lotus Multibyte Character Set (LMBCS) that corresponds to the number code specified
@CLEAN	The specified text string with all nonprinting characters removed from it

Table H.1: **Text Functions Quick Reference (continued)**

Function	Returns
@CODE	The code for the Lotus Multibyte Character Set (LMBCS) code that corresponds to the first character in a text string
@EXACT	1 (True) if the two specified sets of characters match exactly; 0 (False) if the two sets do not match exactly
@FIND	The position in a given text string at which 1-2-3 finds the first occurrence of the specified search text, the search beginning at the given position
@FINDB	The byte position in a given text string at which 1-2-3 finds the first occurrence of the specified search text, the search beginning at the given position
@LEFT	The specified number of the first (leftmost) characters in a given text string
@LEFTB	The specified number of the first (leftmost) bytes in a given text string
@LENGTH	The number of characters in a string
@LENGTHB	The number of bytes in a string
@LOWER	The given string with all letters converted to lowercase
@MID	The specified number of characters from a text string, beginning with the character at the offset specified
@MIDB	The specified number of bytes from a text string, beginning with the byte at the offset specified

Table H.1: Text Functions Quick Reference (continued)

Function	Returns
@PROPER	The given string with all the letters converted to initial capital style (i.e., the first letter of each word in uppercase and the remaining letters all lowercase)
@REPEAT	The specified string repeated the specified number of times
@REPLACE	The specified text string with the given replacement text added or appended
@REPLACEB	The specified text string with the given replacement bytes added or appended
@RIGHT	The specified number of characters last (rightmost) in a text string
@RIGHTB	The specified number of bytes last (rightmost) in a text string
@S	The entry in the first cell of a given range as a label. If the entry is a value, @S returns a blank cell
@SETSTRING	A label the specified number of characters long consisting of the specified text string and enough blank spaces to align the text string with the chosen alignment
@STRING	The specified value converted to a label using the format specified
@TRIM	The specified text string with all leading, trailing, and consecutive space characters stripped from it
@UPPER	The specified string with all its letters converted to uppercase
@VALUE	The value corresponding to a number entered as a text string in one of the four formats 1-2-3 recognizes

For quick reference, the international text functions are listed in Table H.2.

Table H.2: *International Text Functions Quick Reference*

Function	Returns
@EDIGIT	The Thai number conversions from Arabic numbers
@FULLP	The Kanji double-byte character conversions from single-byte characters
@HALFP	The single-byte character conversions from Kanji double-byte characters
@NUMBERSTRING	The Kanji spelled-out text for a given number
@TDIGIT	The Arabic number conversions from Thai numbers
@TFIND	The Thai character position in a given text string at which 1-2-3 finds the first occurrence of the specified search text, the search beginning at the given position
@TLEFT	The specified number of the first (leftmost) characters in a given Thai text string
@TLENGTH	The number of characters in a Thai string
@TMID	The specified number of characters from a Thai text string, beginning with the character at the offset specified
@TNUMBERSTRING	The Thai spelled-out-text for a given number
@TREPLACE	The specified Thai text string with the given replacement characters added or appended
@TRIGHT	The specified number of characters last (rightmost) in a Thai text string

Descriptions of the Text Functions

This section explains all the text functions in alphabetical order.

NOTE See Chapter 8 for a general description of the text functions and how they work.

@CHAR(code)

The @CHAR function returns the character of the Lotus Multibyte Character Set (LMBCS) that corresponds to the number *code*. *code* must be an integer—if it is not, 1-2-3 will truncate it to an integer. *code* must also correspond to a character in the Lotus Multibyte Character Set; if it does not, @CHAR will return ERR.

WARNING Some of the LMCS characters are pretty weird. If your monitor can't display an LMCS character, 1-2-3 will do its best to display a similar character. Failing that, 1-2-3 will show a solid rectangle. Bear in mind that your printer also needs to be able to print the LMCS characters you use in your spreadsheets.

For example, to insert £ (the British pound sign), use this function statement:

 @CHAR(156)

To insert ¥ (the Japanese yen sign), use this one:

 @CHAR(190)

You can also refer to cell addresses. For example, to insert ® (the registered symbol) into cell A22, you could refer to the value in another cell:

 @CHAR(D45)

This would return ® in cell A22 if cell D45 contained 169, the LMCS code for ®.

See Also @CODE

@CLEAN("text")

The @CLEAN function removes nonprinting characters from *text*, where *text* can be text enclosed in quotation marks (""), the address or name of a cell containing a label, or a formula or function resulting in text. For example, this function statement would remove nonprinting characters from cell A34:

@CLEAN(A34)

> **WARNING** Consider using the @CLEAN function after importing data into 1-2-3 from another program—for example, a word-processing application may leave in-text codes that 1-2-3 cannot read and displays as gibberish.

See Also @CHAR, @TRIM

@CODE(text)

The function @CODE returns the code for the Lotus Multibyte Character Set (LMBCS) that corresponds to the first character in *text*, where *text* is

- text enclosed in double quotation marks (""),
- the address or name of a cell containing a label, or
- a formula or @ function statement resulting in text.

For example, if cell A1 contains the label "X-modem," the function statement

@CODE(A1)

would return 88, since 88 is the LMBCS code for *X*, the first character of the label "X-modem."

See Also @CHAR

@EXACT(text1,text2)

The @EXACT function compares two sets of characters, *text1* and *text2*. @EXACT returns 1 (True) if the two sets match exactly; if the two sets do not match exactly, @EXACT returns 0 (False). Enter *text1* and *text2* inside double quotation marks (""). Alternatively, you can enter formulas that result in text or the addresses or names of cells containing labels or formulas that result in labels.

> **WARNING** The main difference between @EXACT and = (the equals sign) is that @EXACT is case-sensitive and also distinguishes between letters with and without accent marks. This makes @EXACT much more suitable than = for testing user input for correct passwords (including upper- and lowercase letters) and other critical input.

For example, while the statement Life = life equates to True, the following statement equates to false because the difference in capitalization between the two strings means they are not exactly alike:

    @EXACT("Life","life")

Using @EXACT with @IF, you could set a password check like the following to check that the user had entered the words *Running Man* in cell A8:

    @IF(@EXACT("Running Man",A8),"Access granted. Perimeter
    deactivated.","Access denied. Perimeter activated.")

If users have entered the phrase with the correct spacing and capitalization, they get the *Access granted. . .* message; if they have entered the phrase incorrectly or have entered the wrong phrase, they'll see the *Access denied. . .* message instead. (If they haven't entered anything in cell A8, @IF will return ERR.)

@FIND(search-text,text,start-number)

The @FIND function returns the position in the string *text* at which 1-2-3 finds the first occurrence of the string *search-text*, the search beginning at the *start-number* position.

search-text and *text* should be entered as text enclosed in double quotation marks (""), as formulas that result in text, or the address or name of a cell that contains text or a formula that results in a label. *start-number* indicates the number of the character (offset from the beginning of the *text* string) at which to begin the search.

@FIND can be particularly useful to extract information from a spreadsheet entered into one column that you would normally enter into two columns for flexibility. For example, if one of your colleagues built a spreadsheet of employee names but put both first name and last name into the same field in column B, you could extract the last name from column B to column C by using the following function statement, as shown in Figure H.1:

```
@MID(B5,0,@FIND(" ",B5,0))
```

Similarly, the @FINDB function returns the byte position in the string *text* at which 1-2-3 finds the first occurrence of the string *search-text*, the search beginning at the *start-number* position.

WARNING You can generate an ERR in several ways by using @FIND. @FIND will return ERR if 1-2-3 does not find the *search-text* string in the *text* string, if *start-number* is a number larger than the number of characters in the *text* string, or if you enter a negative *start-number* (for example, by using a formula to produce the number without using @ABS to make sure it is positive). Note also that @FIND is case-sensitive—@FIND("p","Philadelphia",0) will return 9 rather than 1 because it will find the lowercase *p* rather than the uppercase *P*.

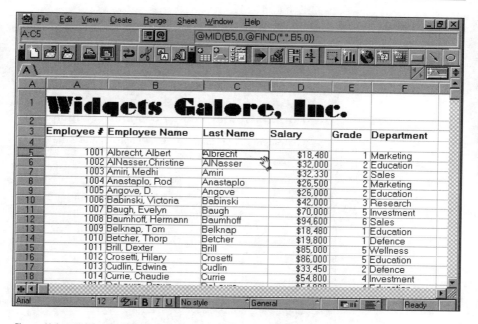

Figure H.1: Using the @FIND function to extract information from a text string in a spreadsheet

@LEFT(text,number)

The @LEFT function returns the first (leftmost) *number* of characters in *text*, where *text* is text enclosed in double quotation marks (""), a formula resulting in text, or the address or name of a cell containing a label or a formula resulting in a label. *number* indicates the number of characters to return and can be a positive integer or 0 (in which case @LEFT will return an empty string).

> **WARNING** Note that @LEFT will return all of *text* if *number* is greater than the length of the string *text*. If you run @LEFT on an empty cell, @LEFT returns an empty cell. Consider using the @ISEMPTY function before using @LEFT if it is important for you to retrieve a text string with at least some contents.

Use @LEFT when you need to copy part of a label into another cell—for example, to truncate phone numbers into area codes, as shown in the example in Figure H.2. In the figure, cell E4 contains this function statement to retrieve the first three characters from cell D4:

    @LEFT(D4,3)

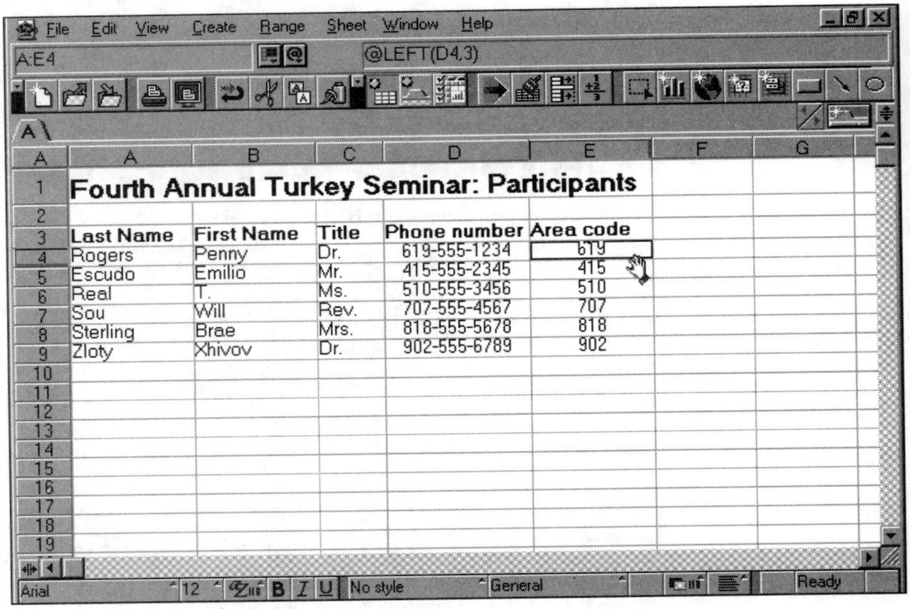

Figure H.2: Using the @LEFT function to copy part of a label from one cell to another

TIP When using @LEFT, bear in mind that it will count spaces and punctuation as one character each. Note also that in Figure H.2 the telephone numbers were entered as labels rather than as values—each is prefaced by a single quote (').

Similarly, the @LEFTB function returns the first (leftmost) *number* of bytes in *text*, where *text* is text enclosed in double quotation marks (""), a formula resulting in text, or the address or name of a cell containing a label or a formula resulting in a label. *number* indicates the number of bytes to return and can be a positive integer or 0 (in which case @LEFT will return an empty string).

TIP If you're not sure how many characters you need to extract from a string, you can use @LEFT in combination with @FIND. For example, if you wanted to return the first name from a cell named BOTHNAMES that contained a first name and a last name separated by a space (for example, Paulette Jones), you could use @LEFT(BOTHNAMES,@FIND("*",BOTHNAMES,0)) to return the first name, Paulette. (The * makes @FIND search for one space.)

See Also @MID, @RIGHT

@LENGTH(text)

The @LENGTH function returns the number of characters in a string, *text*, where *text* is text entered in double quotation marks (""), a formula resulting in text, or the address or name of a cell containing a label or a formula resulting in a label. When using @LENGTH, bear in mind that it will count spaces and punctuation as one character each.

For example, the following function statement returns 10, the number of characters in the string:

    @LENGTH("Appendix H")

TIP To strip unwanted spaces from a text string, use the @TRIM function in conjunction with the @LENGTH function.

A practical use for the @LENGTH function is to check that the entry for a particular cell is the right length. For example, if you divided telephone numbers into area codes and local numbers in a database, you could use @LENGTH to check that each area code was three digits long and that each local number was seven digits long, as illustrated in Figure H.3. In the figure, cell E4 contains the following function statement:

```
@IF(@LENGTH(D4)=3,"","ERROR!")
```

This returns nothing if the area code is three digits long, but returns ERROR! if it is not three digits long. Cell F4 contains a similar function statement.

Similarly, the @LENGTHB function returns the number of bytes in a string, *text*, where *text* is text entered in double quotation marks (""), a formula resulting in text, or the address or name of a cell containing a label or a formula resulting in a label.

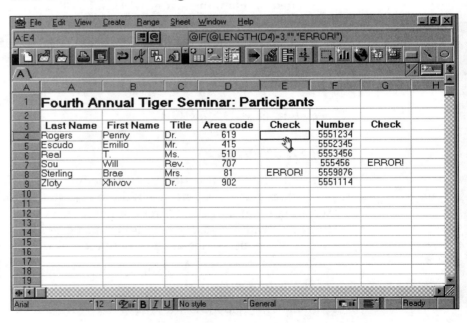

Figure H.3: *Using the @LENGTH function to check that area codes and local numbers each have the right number of digits*

@LOWER(text)

The @LOWER function converts all the letters in a string, *text*, to lowercase, where *text* is text entered in double quotation marks (""), a formula resulting in text, or the address or name of a cell containing a label or a formula resulting in a label.

For example, the following function statement returns the word *serpentine* in lowercase:

    @LOWER("SERPENTINE")

To return the first letter of a word or string as a lowercase letter—for example, if you wanted to extract the first letter of a word for alphabetical filing—you can combine the @LOWER function with the @LEFT function, as in the following function statement:

    @LOWER(@LEFT("Employee Policies",1))

This returns *e*, the first letter of Employee Policies.

If you run @LOWER on a number, 1-2-3 will return an error. For example, the following function statement will return ERR:

    @LOWER(987654)

But if you enclose the number in double quotation marks (""), @LOWER will return it as a label. For example, the following function statement returns 987654:

    @LOWER("987654")

Figure H.4 illustrates the use of the @LOWER function. In this worksheet containing customer occupations that were pulled unsatisfactorily in all uppercase from a database, cell E2 contains the following function statement to lowercase the occupation:

    @LOWER(B2)

 WARNING Because capitalization will affect the sort order of labels, it is often a good idea to use @LOWER (or @UPPER or @PROPER, whichever seems more appropriate) to establish consistent capitalization before using Range ➤ Sort or Query ➤ Sort.

See Also   @PROPER, @UPPER

Appendix H Text Functions Reference

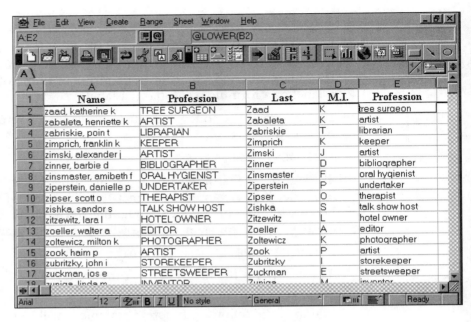

Figure H.4: Using the @LOWER function to lowercase labels

@MID(text,start-number,number)

The @MID function returns the specified *number* of characters from a *text* string, beginning with the character at the offset specified by *start-number*.

The arguments for the @ function are as follows:

Argument	Description
text	Text entered in double quotation marks (""), a formula resulting in text, or the address or name of a cell containing a label or a formula resulting in a label.
start-number	The offset number at which @MID is to start. @MID will return an empty string if *start-number* is larger than the length of *text*.
number	Any positive integer or 0, indicating the number of characters for @MID to return. @MID will return all the characters from

Descriptions of the Text Functions

start-number to the end of *text* if *number* is larger than the length of *text* from *start-number* to its end.

Figure H.5 illustrates the power of the @MID function. In this human resources worksheet for the MidString Corporation, the employee number, last name, and first name share a cell. To break the information out into its three component parts, the worksheet uses the following three @MID function statements:

```
@MID(A5,@FIND(" ",A5,1),20)
```

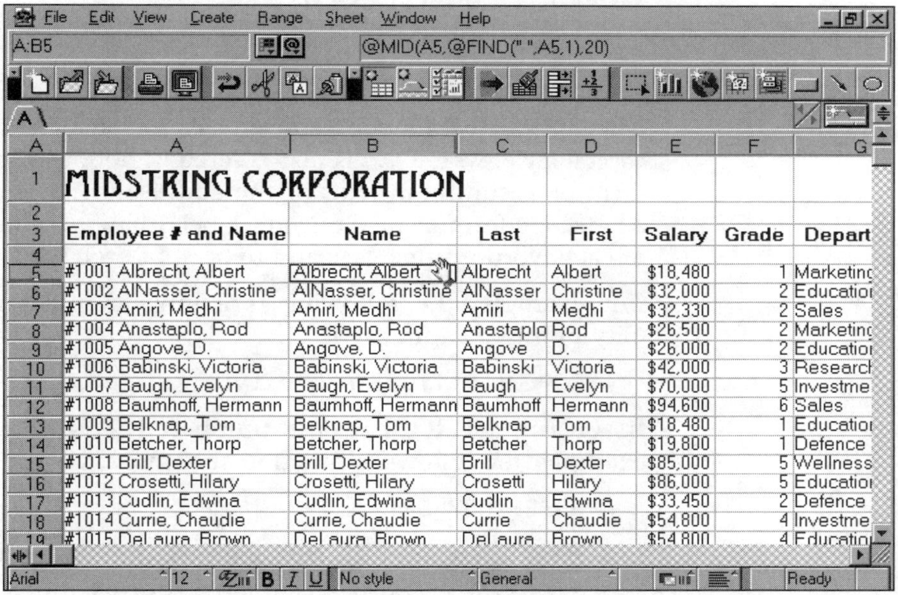

Figure H.5: Using the @MID function to extract information from strings

This first function statement (in cell B5) finds the space after the employee number in cell A5 and returns the remainder of the contents of cell A5. Then, in cell C5, the following function statement returns the contents of cell B5 up to the comma:

```
@MID(B5,0,@FIND(",",B5,0))
```

Finally, in cell D5, the following function statement returns the contents of cell B5 after the space:

```
@MID(B5,@FIND(" ",B5,2),20)
```

WARNING Remember that the @MID function counts punctuation and spaces as characters. If you're not sure how many characters you want to retrieve, enter a suitably large number to retrieve all of the *text* from *start-number* onward.

Similarly, the @MIDB function returns the specified *number* of bytes from a *text* string, beginning with the bytes at the offset specified by *start-number*.

See Also @LEFT, @RIGHT

@PROPER

The @PROPER function converts all the letters in a string, *text*, to initial capital style, where *text* is text entered in double quotation marks (""), a formula resulting in text, or the address or name of a cell containing a label or a formula resulting in a label. In initial capital style, the first case of each word is uppercase and the rest of each word is lowercase.

For example, the following function statement returns Rattlesnake City in initial capital style:

    @PROPER("RATTLESNAKE city")

If you run @PROPER on a number, 1-2-3 will return an error. For example, the following function statement will return ERR:

    @PROPER(987654)

But if you enclose the number in double quotation marks (""), @PROPER will return it as a label. For example, the following function statement returns 987654:

    @PROPER("987654")

Figure H.6 illustrates the use of the @PROPER function. In this worksheet containing customer occupations that were pulled unsatisfactorily in all uppercase from a database, cell C2 contains the following function statement to return the last name in initial capital style:

    @PROPER(@LEFT(A2,@FIND(" ",A2,1)))

For example, the label in cell A2 is returned as Zaad in cell C2 by this function statement.

Descriptions of the Text Functions

Figure H.6: Using the @PROPER function to return labels in initial-capital style

 WARNING Because capitalization will affect the sort order of labels, it is often a good idea to use @PROPER (or @UPPER or @LOWER, whichever seems more appropriate) to establish consistent capitalization before using Range ➤ Sort or Query ➤ Sort.

See Also @PROPER, @UPPER

@REPEAT(text,number)

The @REPEAT function repeats a string, *text*, the number of times specified by *number*, where *text* is text entered in double quotation marks (""), a formula resulting in text, or the address or name of a cell containing a label or a formula resulting in a label. *number* is any positive integer.

For example, the following function statement produces **INVALID RESULTS** stretching across the worksheet:

```
@REPEAT("**INVALID RESULTS**",20)
```

> **TIP** The main difference between the @REPEAT function and the repeating label-prefix character \ (the backslash) is that the @REPEAT function does not stop when the column is full but continues repeating the label up to the *number* specified. This can be handy if you need to fill in a row across a specific number of columns quickly—entering an @REPEAT function statement in the first cell can be quicker than entering \~- and then copying it across the row.

@REPLACE(original-text,start-number, number,new-text)

The @REPLACE function replaces the specified *number* of characters in the string *original-text* with the characters in *new-text*, starting at *start-number*.

The arguments for the @ function are as follows:

Argument	Description
original-text	The text to be replaced or added to, entered in double quotation marks (""), a formula resulting in text, or the address or name of a cell containing a label or a formula resulting in a label.
start-number	Any positive value or 0, indicating the offset number of the character in *original-text* for @REPLACE to start at. Note that @REPLACE will append *new-text* to *original-text* if *start-number* is greater than the length of *original-text*.
number	Any positive integer or 0, indicating the number of characters in *original-text* that @REPLACE is to replace with *new-text*. A value of 0 for *number* indicates that @REPLACE should insert *new-text* without replacing any characters of *original-text*.
new-text	The text for @REPLACE to insert at *start-number* in the *original-text* string, text entered in double quotation marks (""), a formula resulting in text, or the address or name of a cell containing a label or a formula resulting in a label.

TIP Remember that punctuation and spaces count as characters for text functions such as @REPLACE, and include them in your calculations.

For example, consider the worksheet shown in Figure H.7, which contains the Annual Crime Statistics for Anytown PD. For speed of assembly, column C contains @REPLACE function statements to change the labels in column A. For example, cell C3 contains the following function statement to replace the three letters of DUI in cell A3 with the word Assault:

```
@REPLACE(A3,5,3,"Assault")
```

The five-character offset takes care of the four characters of the year and the space following it.

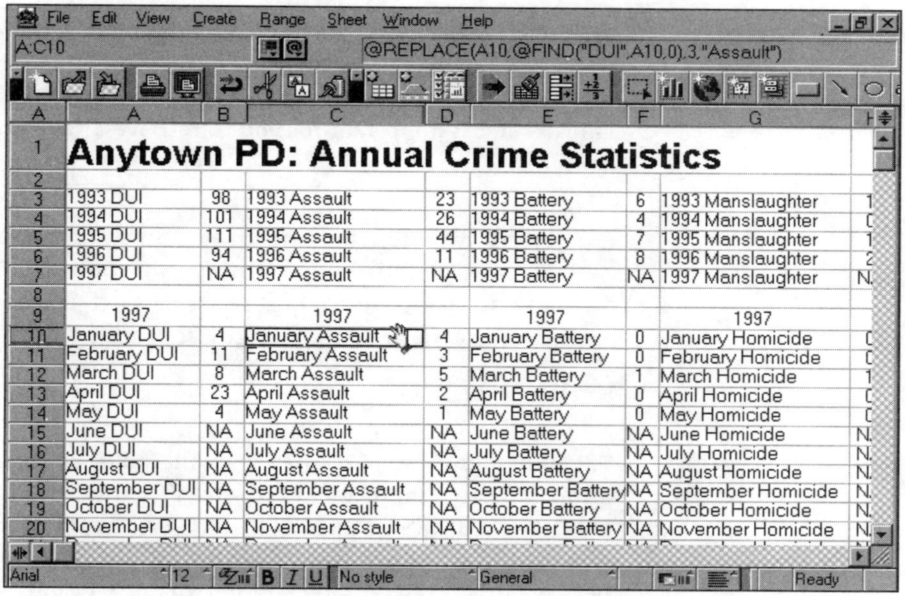

Figure H.7: **Using the @REPLACE function to replace a text string**

But in many cases, you won't know a consistent *start-number* to use with @REPLACE. In such cases, you can use the @FIND function to search for the relevant label, as in the following function statement contained in cell C10:

```
@REPLACE(A10,@FIND("DUI",A10,0),3,"Assault")
```

The @FIND function finds DUI, which is then replaced by Assault.

Similarly, the @REPLACEB function replaces the specified *number* of bytes in the string *original-text* with the bytes in *new-text*, starting at *start-number*.

@RIGHT(text, number)

The @RIGHT function returns the last (rightmost) *number* of characters in *text*, where *text* is text enclosed in double quotation marks (""), a formula resulting in text, or the address or name of a cell containing a label or a formula resulting in a label. *number* indicates the number of characters to return and can be a positive integer or 0 (in which case @RIGHT will return an empty string).

WARNING Note that @RIGHT will return all of *text* if *number* is greater than the length of the string *text*. If you run @RIGHT on an empty cell, @RIGHT returns an empty cell. Consider using the @ISEMPTY function before using @RIGHT if it is important for you to retrieve a text string with at least some contents.

Use @RIGHT when you need to copy part of a label into another cell—for example, to shear phone numbers of their area codes, as shown in the example in Figure H.8. Cell F4 contains this function statement to retrieve the last eight characters from cell D4:

```
@RIGHT(D4,8)
```

TIP When using @RIGHT, bear in mind that it will count spaces and punctuation as one character each—that's why the function statement is @RIGHT(D4,8) rather than @RIGHT(D4,7), as D4 contains hyphens to separate the groups of numbers. Note also that in Figure H.8 the telephone numbers were entered as labels rather than as values—each is prefaced by a single quotation mark (').

Similarly, the @RIGHTB function returns the last (rightmost) *number* of bytes in *text*, where *text* is text enclosed in double quotation marks (""), a formula resulting in text, or the address or name of a cell containing a label or a formula resulting in a label.

See Also   @LEFT, @MID

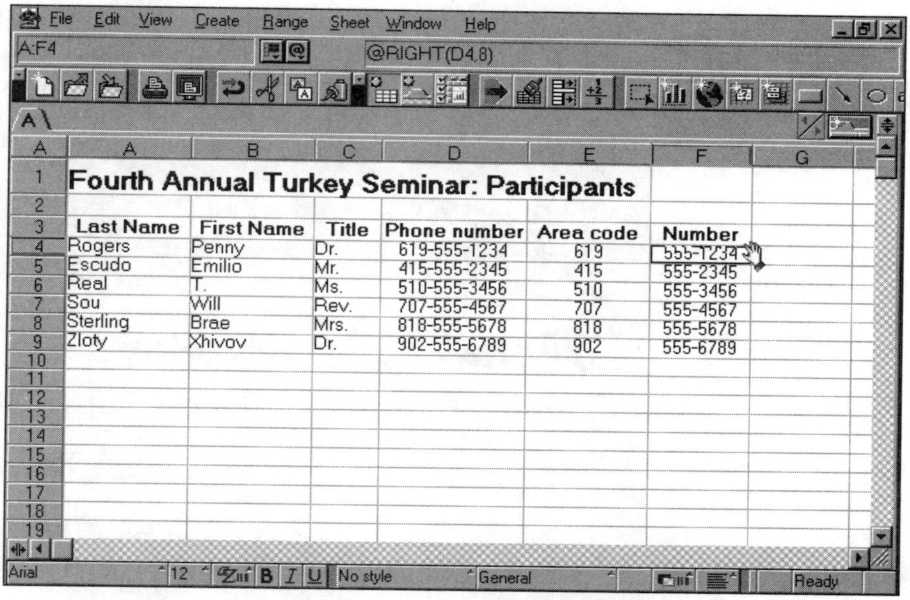

Descriptions of the Text Functions

Figure H.8: Using the @RIGHT function to copy part of a label from one cell to another

TIP If you're not sure how many characters you need to extract from a string, you can use @RIGHT in combination with @FIND. For example, if you wanted to return the last name from a cell named BOTHNAMES that contained a first name and a last name separated by a space (for example, Paulette Jones), you could use @RIGHT(BOTHNAMES,@FIND("*",BOTH-NAMES,0) to return the last name, Jones. (The * makes @FIND search for one space.)

@S(range)

The @S function returns the entry in the first cell in *range* as a label, where *range* is a cell address or a range name. If the entry in the first cell of the range is a value, @S returns a blank cell.

For example, consider the Pandora's Ponies worksheet shown in Figure H.9. Cell A12 contains the following function statement:

```
@S(A5..A8)
```

This returns Ponies, since Ponies is the label in the first cell of the range A5..A8. If the range were A3..A8, the function statement would return a blank cell because cell A3 contains a value (1997).

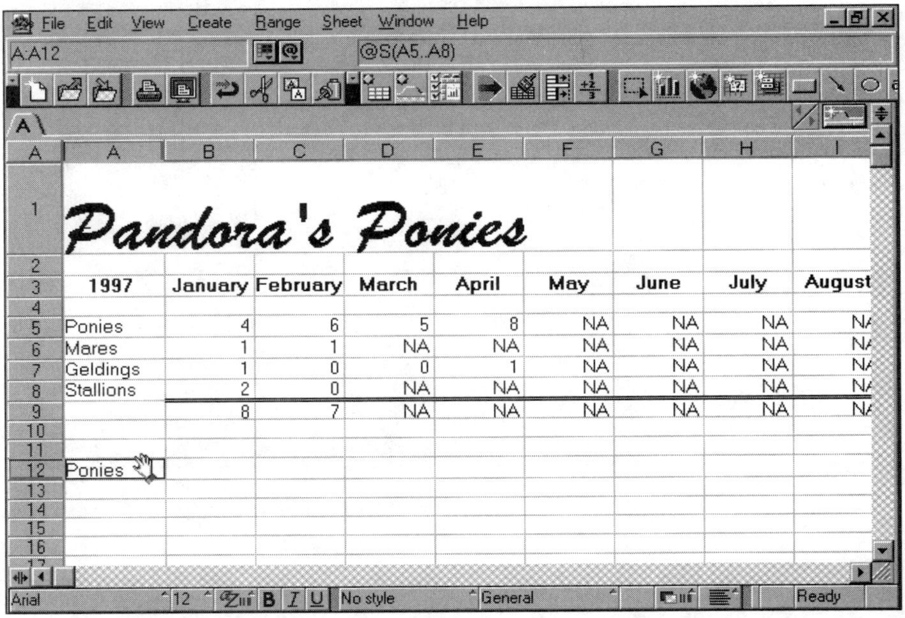

Figure H.9: Using the @S function to return the entry in the first cell of a range as a label

The @S function can be very useful in macros to check that a user enters a label where you need one. For example, you could use the following function statement:

    {IF @S(C1)=""}{BEEP}

This would cause a macro to beep if a user entered a value in cell C1 (because @S returns a blank cell for a value).

See Also   @ISSTRING, @N

@SETSTRING(text,length,[alignment])

The @SETSTRING function returns a label the number of characters specified in *length* long. The label consists of the *text* string and enough blank spaces to align *text* as specified by the *alignment* option.

The arguments for the @ function are as follows:

Argument	Description
text	Any text.
length	An integer between 1 and 512 indicating the length of the string to be returned. If *length* is smaller than the number of characters in *text*, 1-2-3 returns *text*.
alignment	0, 1, or 2, an optional argument specifying how to align *text*, as follows: 0 Specifies that *text* be aligned to the left of the extra spaces in *length*. 0 is the default setting if you omit the *alignment* argument. 1 Specifies that *text* be aligned in the center of the extra spaces in *length*. One leftover space is added to the left of *text* if there is an odd number of extra spaces. 2 Specifies that *text* be aligned to the right of the extra spaces in *length*.

Figure H.10 demonstrates the use of the @SETSTRING function to align text. Cell A3 contains a function statement that aligns the phrase at the left of the cell with the extra spaces to its right:

```
@SETSTRING("Understanding 1-2-3 '97 for Win 95 ",60)
```

This centers the phrase in the spaces:

```
@SETSTRING("Understanding 1-2-3 '97 for Win 95",60,1)
```

This aligns the phrase at the right of the cell with the extra spaces to its left:

```
@SETSTRING("Understanding 1-2-3 '97 for Win 95",60,2)
```

See Also   @TRIM

Appendix H Text Functions Reference

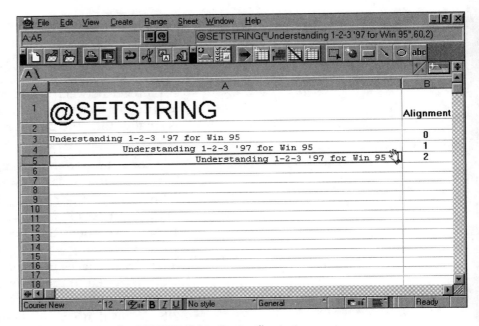

Figure H.10: *Using the @SETSTRING function to align text*

@STRING(numeric-value,decimal)

The @STRING function converts the value *numeric-value* and returns it as a label using the format specified by *decimal*.

The arguments for the @STRING function are as follows:

Argument	Description
numeric-value	Any value.
decimal	An integer from the following list that determines the format in which @STRING returns the label:
	0–116 Fixed format, with *decimal* decimal places
	1000–1116 Comma format, with *decimal* minus 1,000 decimal places
	–18–1 Scientific format, with @ABS(*decimal*) digits
	10001–10512 General format, up to *decimal* minus 10,000 characters

For example, the following function statement returns the label 1:

`@STRING(1.31415927,0)`

See Chapter 8 for another example of how to use @STRING.

> **WARNING** The @STRING function does not convert formatting characters used on a cell, whether you add them to a cell or whether 1-2-3 adds them as a result of your having applied formatting. For example, both 45.67% and $45.67 would be returned by @STRING as 45.67.

See Also @VALUE

@TRIM(text)

The @TRIM function strips leading, trailing, and consecutive space characters from a *text* string, where *text* is text entered in double quotation marks (""), a formula resulting in text, or the address or name of a cell containing a label or a formula resulting in a label.

For example, the following function statement strips extra spaces from the string and returns Wide-Eyed and Electric:

`@TRIM(" Wide-Eyed and Electric")`

The @TRIM function is especially useful for ensuring regular presentation and sorting of information imported from other formats.

See Also @SETSTRING

@UPPER(text)

The @UPPER function converts all the letters in a string, *text*, to uppercase, where *text* is text entered in double quotation marks (""), a formula resulting in text, or the address or name of a cell containing a label or a formula resulting in a label.

For example, the following function statement returns ANACONDA in uppercase:

`@UPPER("anaconda")`

To return the first letter of a word as an uppercase letter—for example, if you wanted to reduce a name to an initial—you can combine the

@UPPER function with the @LEFT function, as in the following function statement:

```
@UPPER(@LEFT("gordon shumway",1)
```

This returns G, the first letter of Gordon.

If you run @UPPER on a number, 1-2-3 will return an error. For example, the following function statement will return ERR:

```
@UPPER(123456)
```

But if you enclose the number in double quotation marks (""), @UPPER will return it as a label. For example, the following function statement returns 123456:

```
@UPPER("123456")
```

Figure H.11 illustrates the use of the @UPPER function. In this worksheet containing customer names that were pulled unsatisfactorily in all uppercase from a database with the last name, first name, and middle initial all in one cell, cell D2 contains the following function statement to pull out and change the middle initial to uppercase:

```
@UPPER(@RIGHT(A2,1))
```

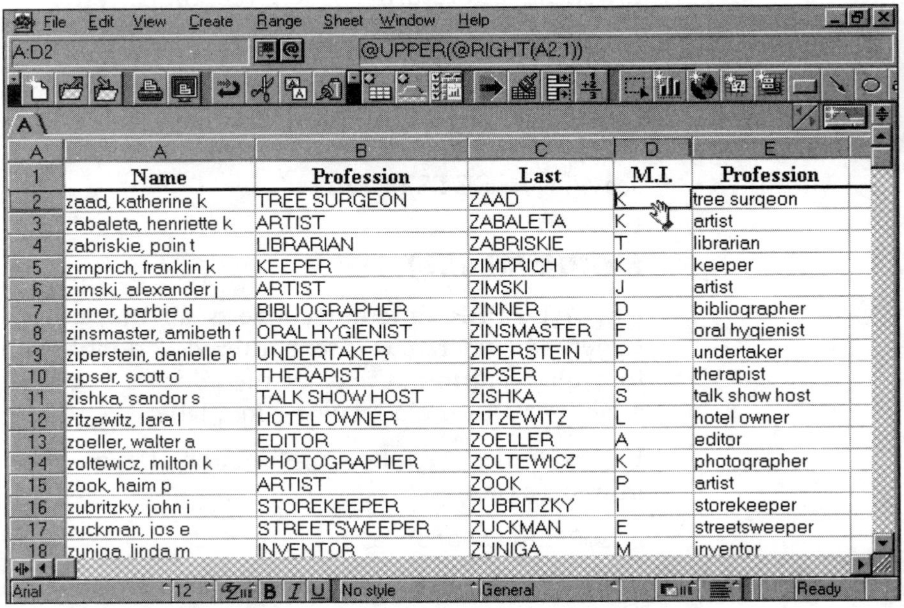

A	A	B	C	D	E
1	Name	Profession	Last	M.I.	Profession
2	zaad, katherine k	TREE SURGEON	ZAAD	K	tree surgeon
3	zabaleta, henriette k	ARTIST	ZABALETA	K	artist
4	zabriskie, poin t	LIBRARIAN	ZABRISKIE	T	librarian
5	zimprich, franklin k	KEEPER	ZIMPRICH	K	keeper
6	zimski, alexander j	ARTIST	ZIMSKI	J	artist
7	zinner, barbie d	BIBLIOGRAPHER	ZINNER	D	bibliographer
8	zinsmaster, amibeth f	ORAL HYGIENIST	ZINSMASTER	F	oral hygienist
9	ziperstein, danielle p	UNDERTAKER	ZIPERSTEIN	P	undertaker
10	zipser, scott o	THERAPIST	ZIPSER	O	therapist
11	zishka, sandor s	TALK SHOW HOST	ZISHKA	S	talk show host
12	zitzewitz, lara l	HOTEL OWNER	ZITZEWITZ	L	hotel owner
13	zoeller, walter a	EDITOR	ZOELLER	A	editor
14	zoltewicz, milton k	PHOTOGRAPHER	ZOLTEWICZ	K	photographer
15	zook, haim p	ARTIST	ZOOK	P	artist
16	zubritzky, john i	STOREKEEPER	ZUBRITZKY	I	storekeeper
17	zuckman, jos e	STREETSWEEPER	ZUCKMAN	E	streetsweeper
18	zuniga, linda m	INVENTOR	ZUNIGA	M	inventor

Figure H.11: ***Using the @UPPER function to uppercase labels***

Descriptions of the Text Functions

> **WARNING** Because capitalization will affect the sort order of labels, it is often a good idea to use @UPPER (or @PROPER, whichever seems more appropriate) to establish consistent capitalization before using Range ➤ Sort or Query ➤ Sort.

See Also   @LOWER, @PROPER

@VALUE(text)

The @VALUE function converts a number entered as a *text* string to its corresponding value, where *text* is text in double quotation marks ("") or a label that contains numbers only.

text must be in one of the four recognized formats:

- Fixed format: 111.99
- Scientific format: 1.11 E2
- Mixed number format: 1 1/4
- Formatted number: 11.99%

See Chapter 8 for more examples of using the @VALUE function.

For example, the following function statement returns the value .1199:

    @VALUE("11.99%")

> **WARNING** While the @VALUE function ignores leading and trailing spaces, it will return ERR if the *text* string contains spaces between symbols and numbers (e.g., 11.99 %) or if the *text* string contains any non-numeric characters. @VALUE returns 0 if *text* is a blank cell or an empty string.

> **TIP** You can replace a @VALUE function statement with the value it produces by pressing F2 and then F9 in the relevant cell. To assemble a formula using @VALUE, you need to repeat @VALUE. For example, @VALUE("100"+"500") is not valid and returns 0, but @VALUE("100")+@VALUE("500") returns 600.

See Also   @STRING

Index

NOTE: Page numbers in *italics* refer to tables or figures; page numbers in **bold** refer to primary discussions of the topic

Symbols & Numbers

$ (dollar-sign character), for absolute reference, 136–137
^ (caret)
  for center alignment, 93, 161, 163
  for exponentiation, 226
& (ampersand), for concatenation, 231
*** (asterisks), string in column, 157
+ (plus sign), to start formula, 132
; (semicolon)
  for comments, 222
  as standard argument separator, 215
<< >> (double angle brackets), for file names, 500
= (equal sign), to begin formula, 222
@@ function, *521*, *674*, **675**, *676*
@ character, for functions, 28, 214, 240
@ functions, *See* functions
\ (backslash prefix), for repeating characters, 165
, (comma), as argument separator, 215
" (double-quotation mark), for right alignment, 93, 126, 161
. (period), to anchor range, 100
' (single-quotation mark)
  for comments, 425
  for left alignment, 93, 161
  to designate labels, 97
/ (slash key), for 1-2-3 Classic Window, 20
1-2-3
  basics, 2–44
  date system, 181
  exiting, 3, **23**
  function to return version release number, 652
1-2-3 Classic window, 3, **20–21**, *21*

.123 file extension, 33, 114
1-2-3 Preferences dialog box
  General tab,
    Show New Workbook dialog, 463
    Update links when opening workbooks, 506
  Recalculation tab, *262*, 262
1-2-3 window, *6*, *7*, **48–54**
  control buttons, **49–50**
  Control menu, **51–53**
  edit line, **63–65**, *64*
    removing, 67
  sheet tabs, *73*, **73–75**
  sizing and moving, **50–51**, *51*
  SmartIcons, **67–72**
  title bar, **49–50**
360-day year, function based on, 276–277, **545–546**

A

abbreviations, in maps, 338
@ABS function, **268–269**, *635*, *689*, **692–693**
absolute cell references, 135, **136–139**
  in copied formula, 139
  function to return, 645
  function to return for cell containing largest value, 682
  function to return for cell containing smallest value, 682–683
absolute deviations, average of, **733**
absolute value of number, function for, **268–269**, **692–693**, 695
accelerated depreciation, *See* depreciation
@ACCRUED function, *521*, *594*, *596*, **598–599**, *600*

@ACCRUED2 function, *521*, *597*
@ACOS function, 258, *259*, *689*, **693**
@ACOSH function, *521*, *689*, *693*
@ACOT function, *521*, *689*, **694**
@ACOTH function, *521*, *689*, *694*
@ACSC function, *521*, *689*, *694*
@ACSCH function, *521*, *689*, **695**
Action menu
    creating, 413, **421–422**, *422*
    help text for command, 422
active worksheet, *13*, 13
Add Field dialog box, *373*, 373, 377, *381*, 381
add-in application for 1-2-3, testing for, **667**
add-in functions, testing for, 666
adding, worksheets to workbook, **13–15**, *13*
address, *See* cell references
address field, sorting database by, 362
alignment, **160–164**
    of labels, 92
    prefixes for, 93
    of range of cells, , 149
    @SETSTRING function for, 805
    on status bar, *19*, 19, 75, *76*, 161, 161, 186
alphabetic case functions, **282**
ampersand (&), for concatenation, 231
AM/PM formats, 188
AND, for database query, 372
#AND# operator, 229, 230, 278
    in @DGET function, 398
Annotate command (shortcut menu for Help), 81
annuities, functions for, *597*
applications
    minimized on taskbar, 51
    switching between, 46, **53–54**
    switching between Lotus 1-2-3 and other, 5
    for Windows 95, 48
approximation function to return error function, **588**
arc cosecant, function for, **694**
arc cosine, function for, **693**
arc cotangent, function for, **694**
arc hyperbolic cosecant, function for, **695**
arc hyperbolic cosine, function for, **693**
arc hyperbolic cotangent, function for, **694**
arc hyperbolic secant, function for, **695**
arc hyperbolic sine, function for, **696**
arc hyperbolic tangent, function for, **698**
arc secant, function for, **695**

arc sine, function for, **696**
arc tangent, function for, **696–697**
area charts, **316–322**, *319*
arguments
    for database functions, 394, **568–569**
    for depreciation functions, **248–249**
    for function, 215, 240, 520–521
arithmetic
    for dates, 180, **183–186**
    matrix, **483–485**, *484*
    operators in formulas, 28
    for time, **189–190**
arrow, adding to chart, 312
arrow keys, 96
Ascending sort, 355
@ASCH function, *522*
@ASEC function, *522*, *689*, **695**
@ASECH function, *522*, *689*, **695**
@ASIN function, 258, *259*, *522*, *689*, **696**
@ASINH function, *522*, *689*, **696**
asterisks (***), string in column, 157
@ATAN function, 258, *259*, *522*, *689*, **696–697**
@ATAN2 function, *259*, 259, *522*, *689*, **697–698**
@ATANH function, *522*, *689*, **698**
Attach Script dialog box, *427*, 427
automatic recalculation, 23–24, **34–36**, 112, 130
    @CELL function and, 647
    @CELLPOINTER function and, 647
    @INFO function to determine status, 652
    and @NOW function, 560
    @RAND function and, **261–264**
    and @TODAY function, 562
@AVEDEV function, *522*, *729*, **733**
average. *See also* mean
    @PUREAVG function to return, **756**
    of absolute deviations, **733**
    for field values in database table, **569–570**, *570*
    of values in list, **733–734**
    weighted, function to return, **780**, *781*
@AVG function, 245, *522*, *729*, **733–734**
    vs. @GEOMEAN function, 745

B

background color, 199
    on status bar, *19*, 19, 75, *76*

backslash prefix (\), for repeating characters, 165
Backsolver, 465, **474–475**, *476*
Backsolver dialog box, *475*
Bar can be displayed when context is option, 71
bar chart, 297–298, *298*
  horizontal, 310
base-10 logarithm, function to return, **708**
@BESSELI function, *522*, *582*, **584**
@BESSELJ function, *522*, *582*, **585**
@BESSELK function, *522*, *582*, **585**
@BESSELY function, *522*, *582*, **585–586**
best-fit width for column, 154, **157–158**
  mouse to size, 156
@BETA function, *522*, *582*, **586**
@BETAI function, *522*, *582*, **586**
binary operators, 229
binomial coefficient, function to calculate, **738**
@BINOMIAL function, *522*, *729*, **734–736**
bin range, 476, *477*
blank cells
  in crosstab, 405
  function to test for, **667–668**
  in @IF statement conditions, 664
  and @MIRR function, 616
  in sorting, 354, 362
Blank entry, in Available icons list, 71
bold style, using status bar, 32, 198, 201
bonds, functions for, *596*
border lines group, *201*
bottom-line, discovering input value to achieve, 465, **474–475**, *476*
Browse menu
  ▶ Delete Found Set, 374–375
  ▶ Find, 408
  ▶ Find Assistant, 371, 375
  ▶ Find Using Worksheet, 369, 374
  ▶ New Record, 385
bubble
  creating help message for, 427, *428*
  for InfoBox tabs, *59*, 59
  setting display, 71
  for SmartIcon description, 16, *17*
buttons. *See also* SmartIcons
  for script, on worksheet, **430–432**
byte position, function to return for search string, 791
bytes

function to return from string beginning at offset, 798
function to return number in string, 794

C

"Calc" on status bar, 262
calculated fields. *See also* database calculations; formulas
calculations. *See also* database calculations
calendar functions, **542–565**
  overview, **542–545**
  543–545
calling scripts, from within script, , 413
Canadian mortgage conventions, loan payment calculation and, **623–624**
Cancel button in edit line, 65, 65
capital-budgeting tools, functions for, *596*
caret (^)
  for center alignment, 93, 161, 163
  for exponentiation, 226
case sensitivity, of passwords, 117
cell, single as range, *101*
cell addresses, 7. *See also* cell references
cell contents
  deleting, 88, **94–95**
  display characteristics on status bar, 19
  editing, 46, 66
  fitting column width to, 154
  formula markers in, **224–225**, *225*
  function to retrieve, **675**, *676*
  function to return, 645
  function to return for cell at specific intersection, **686–687**, *687*
  function to return from specified column & row, **678–680**, *680*
  function to return if string, **803–804**, *804*
  function to return offset position of cell, **681–682**
  function to return for version, **660–661**
  multiline title within, 165
  text wrap for, **164–165**
@CELL function, *522*, *643*, **644–647**
cell pointer, 6, 7. *See also* mouse pointer
@CELLPOINTER function, *522*, *643*, **647–648**
cell references. *See also* file references
  absolute, 135, **136–139**. *See also* absolute cell references

@COORD function to return, **648–649**
elements of, 15
in formulas, 28, **221–222**
function to return, 645
mixed, 139
relative, 135, 139
in selection indicator, 63
in text formula, 232
types, 121, **136**
cells, 7. *See also* range of cells
 function to count those containing values in database table, **575–576**, *576*
 Infobox for, 19
 moving to named, , 148
 red dot in, 224, *225*
 selecting, 8
 selecting inside frozen range, 167
 shortcut menu for, *18*
 storing comments, , 213
center alignment, 162
 caret (^) for, 93, 161, 163
centering
 labels, 149, *163*, 163, *164*
 for printing, **208**
characters
 @CLEAN function to remove nonprinting, **789**
 function to compare sets, **789–790**
 repeating, **165**
@CHAR function, 284, *523*, **784**, **788**
Chart Assistant dialog box, 301
chart frame, viewing data table in, 310
Chart menu, *294*
 ➤ Axes and Grids, 304
 ➤ Chart Properties, 308
 ➤ Chart Style,
  ➤ Create, 330
  ➤ Set Default Chart, 330
 ➤ Chart Type, 319, 324, 328, 336
 context-sensitive change, 56
 ➤ Legend, 303
 ➤ Title, 303
 vs. Range menu, 39
Chart Properties SmartIcon, 295
charts, 4, **37–39**, 292–313
 changing elements, **303–307**
 creating, **38–39**, **299–301**

custom style definitions, 330
data series for, **297–299**, **307–310**
designing, **37–38**
displaying, 292
drawn objects on, 293, **311–312**
moving, 292, **301–302**, *303*
names for, 314, **320–322**
notes for, 326
revised data for, 293
selecting, 302
size of, 300
sizing, 292, **301–302**, *303*
steps to develop, **296**
subtitle of, 301
title of, 301
type changes, 293, **307–310**
 SmartIcons for, 320
types, 314–315, **316–337**
 area charts, **316–322**, *319*
 default, **329–330**
 HLCO charts, **334–336**, *335*
 line charts, **316–322**, *317*
 mixed charts, **332–334**, *333*
 pie charts, **322–329**, *323*
 radar charts, **336**, *337*
 XY charts, **331–332**, *332*
undoing changes to, 310
for what-if analysis, **310–311**
Chart SmartIcon, 39, 300
check boxes, 60
Check Spelling dialog box, *190*, 190–191
@CHIDIST function, *523*, *729*, **736–737**
chi-square distribution, one-tailed probability of, **736–737**
chi-square test for independence, **737**, *738*
@CHITEST function, *523*, *729*, **737**, *738*
@CHOOSE function, **286**, *523*, *674*, **676**, *677*
chronological values, *See* date; time
circular link, 650
@CLEAN function, *523*, **784**, **789**
Clear command (Edit menu), 94
Clear dialog box, *94*, 94
Clear Split command (View menu), 15
client in OLE, 510
Clipboard, 5, 94
 for OLE link creation, 510

Close button, *9*, 9
  for InfoBox, 59
Close command (Control menu), 52
closing
  shortcut menu, 18, 57
  windows, 15
@CODE function, 284, *523*, *785*, **789**
coefficient matrix, 483
collapsing details in outline, *491*, 493
collection, multiple ranges as, 101
color
  for sheet tabs, 75
  in stacked area chart, 320
  of text, status bar indicator, *19*, 19
  for worksheet tabs, 187
color box, 61
color palette, for background color, 199
@COLS function, *523*, *643*, **648**
column, function to return for cell, 645
column headings, field names as, 40
columns in worksheet, 7. *See also* range of columns
  centering label across multiple, *163*, 163, *164*
  copying data between range of rows and, 461, **487–488**
  function to return number in range, 648
  hiding, **158–160**
  inserting, 120, **127–130**
  moving to last, 10
  removing from data table for chart, 333
  restoring hidden, 160
column width
  best-fit, 154, **157–158**
  changing, 148
    with mouse, **155–156**
  formatting, **153–158**, *156*
  function to return, 647
Combine 1-2-3 File dialog box, 440, 509
@COMBIN function, *523*, *729*, **738**
combining workbooks, **508–510**
comma (,) as argument separator, 215
commands
  choosing from menus, **12–13**
  description on title bar, 11, 49–50
  dimmed, 52
  undoing last, 88, **95–96**
Comma number format, 172

comments
  for cells, 213
  deleting, 224
  in scripts, 425
  to document formulas, **222–225**
  viewing, 213
common logarithm, function to return, **708**
company address, script for, 420
complementary error function, 588
compounding periods, function to return number required for investment growth, **254–255**, **600–601**
concatenation, 231
  converting number into string for, 284
conference worksheet, final appearance, 90, *91*
Confirm button in edit line, *65*, 65
constant *e*, function to return value rasied to power, **704**
constant matrix, 483
Constant value, 480
contents box in edit line, 63, *64*
context-sensitive help, **79–80**, *80*
context-sensitive menus, 11, **56**
control buttons, **49–50**
Control menu, **51–53**
  of workbook, 8
controls, in Infoboxes, 60
@COORD function, *523*, *643*, **648–649**
Copy command (shortcut menu for Help), 81
Copy Down command, in shortcut menu, 227, 350, **503–504**
copying
  formulas, 30, 111–112, 121, **134–143**
    with drag and fill, **142–143**
    and relative references, 135
  query table to range in worksheet, 409
  range of cells, **110–114**
    copy and paste for, **112–113**
    copy and paste for, 89
    with drag and drop, 89
    keyboard shortcuts for, **113**
  selected database data to output range, **368–370**
copy mode, toggling out of, 189
Copy Right command, 138
Copy SmartIcon, 112
Copy Styles SmartIcon, *185*, 185, 186, 189, 201
correlation

mathematical analysis, 461
XY chart to show, 331
correlation coefficient, function to return, **739**
@CORREL function, *523*, *729*, **739**
cosecant, function to return, **701**
@COS function, 257, *258*, *523*, *689*, **698–699**
@COSH function, *523*, *689*, **699**
cosine, function for, **698–699**
cost, as depreciation function argument, 248
cotangent, function for, **699–700**
@COT function, *523*, *689*, **699–700**
@COTH function, *523*, *689*, **700**
count, of characters in text string, function for, **793–794**, *794*
@COUNT function, 244, *523*, *729*, **739–740**
covariance, function to return, **740**
@COV function, *523*, *730*, **740**
Create Button SmartIcon, 431
Create Form dialog box, *384*, 384
Create Mailing Label dialog box, *386*, 386
Create menu, 55
- ▶ Button, 430–431
- ▶ Chart, 296, 300, 336
- ▶ Create, 319
- ▶ Database, *344*, 344, *383*, 383
  - ▶ Dynamic Crosstab, 403, 404
  - ▶ Form, 384
  - ▶ Mailing Labels, 386
  - ▶ Query Table, 44, 367, 406
  - ▶ Report, 399, 400
- ▶ Drawing, ▶ Arrow, 312
- ▶ Join, 380
- ▶ Sheet, 74
- ▶ Text, 311
Create Report dialog box, *400*, 400
Create Sheet dialog box, *74*, 74
Create Style dialog box, *203*, 203, 204
Create Sub dialog box, *423*, 423
@CRITBINOMIAL function, *524*, *729*, **741**
criteria argument, for database arguments, *569*
criteria range, 396
cross-references, in help, 77, *79*
Crosstab Assistant dialog box, 404
crosstab objects, 391, **403–405**, *405*
@CSC function, *524*, *690*, **701**
@CSCH function, *524*, *690*, **701**

@CTERM function, **254–255**, *524*, *597*, **600–601**
Ctrl key
to copy range, 111
to select collection, 101
Ctrl+key shortcuts
for global scripts, 413, 421
cumulative binomial distribution
function for, **734–736**
function to return largest integer <= alpha, 741
current date
displaying, 243, 269
current time
displaying, 243, 269
custom keyboard shortcuts, vs. built-in, 423
custom SmartFill list, 212
creating, **218–220**
deleting, 220
Cut command (Edit menu), 94
cut and paste, to move ranges, **125**
cylindrical symmetry problems, 584

D

@D360 function, 272, 276, *524*, *544*, **545–546**, *546*
data. *See also* cell contents
changes in, **34–36**
database calculations, 342, **349–350**, 390–391, **392–410**
on numeric fields, **392–405**
database functions, **393–399**, **566–581**
arguments for, 394, **568–569**
join operations using, 394
database management, 4
database operations, **40–44**
database queries, **43–44**, 364–365, **366–389**
copying selected data to output range, **368–370**
creating, **367–368**
examples, 366
on external database, 391, **406–409**
with multiple criteria, **370–374**
name for, 408
selecting fields to display, 368
table for joining, 378
to delete records, **374–375**
database records

data entry, **41–42**, *42*
deleting from external database, 409
@DGET function to return field contents, 397–399
match for one criterion, 364
query to delete, 365, **374–375**
query to match complex criteria, 364
reading field entries, 390
revising, 365
databases. *See also* fields in database
combining information from multiple, 365
creating, **348**
creating complete, 342
defining, **41**
length of, 40
multiple tables in, **350–352**
objects, **383–388**
  forms, 383, **384–385**, *385*
  mailing labels, 383, **386–387**, *388*
selection criteria, **43–44**
sorting, **42–44**, *42*, *43*, **353–362**
database tables, 342–343, **344–363**, *348*
calculated fields in, **349–350**
creating, 342, **344–347**, *346*, *347*
defining range names for, **352–353**
editing query table to update, **375–378**, *378*
identifying, 342
joining, **378–382**
sorting, 343
sort results, *360*
data entry, **21–22**, **25–27**, **88–89**, **90–119**. *See also* database records
of formulas, **28–31**, 121, **131–134**, 212
for functions, **236–240**
for labels, **92–94**, 96–97
in temporary location, 92
testing for label, 804
for time value, **187–189**
to preselected range, 107
of values, **97–98**
DataLens message, function to return, 651
@DATALINK function, *524*, *643*, **649–650**
data series for charts, **297–299**
by row, 308
changing, **307–310**
redefining, 293
date

chronological information about, 243
displaying, 178
displaying current, 243
function to return earliest, 574
function to return most recent in database, 573
in header or footer, 209, 211
date arithmetic, 180, **183–186**
@DATECONVERT function, *524*, *544*
@DATEDIF function, 271, 274, 349, *524*, *544*, **548–550**, *550*
date formulas, **226–228**
@DATE function, 271, 275–276, *524*, *543*, 547, 548
date functions, **269–277**
@DATEINFO function, 270, *524*, *543*, **550–551**
date number. *See also* time value
in default sort, 354
function to return for date, 547
function to return for date falling specified workdays from specific date, **563–565**
function to return date label from, 551
function to return day of week for, **552–553**
function to return from date text, **551–552**
function to return month from, 556
function to return year from, 565
@NEXTMONTH function to return, **558–559**
@NOW function to return current based on computer clock, **560**
@TODAY function to calculate, **562–563**
dates, 22, **180–187**
calculating difference between two, 227
function to return number between dates, **548–550**, *550*
@DATESTRING function, 271, *524*, *543*, **551**, 559, 563
@DATEVALUE function, 271, 276, *524*, *543*, **551–552**, *553*
@DAVG function, 390, 393, 394–396, *524*, *567*, **569–570**, *570*
@DAY function, 269, 274, *275*, *524*, *543*, **552–553**
day of month, function to return for date number, **552–553**
@DAYS360 function, 271, 276, *525*, *543*, 545–546, *546*, **554–555**
days
calculating number between two dates, 213
function for calculating between dates, **545–546**, **553–554**

function for calculating between dates based on 360-day year, **554–555**
remaining in year, function to return, 550
@DAYS function, 272, *525*, *544*, 545–546, *546*, **553–554**
day of week
  filling cells with names, 217
  function to return, 550, **563**
  @MOD function to calculate, 708
@DB function, 248, 249, 250, *525*, *596*, **601–602**, *602*, 633
@DCOUNT function, 393, 394–396, *525*, *567*, **570–571**, *571*
@DDB function, 248, 249, 250, *525*, *596*, **602–604**, *604*, 633
Debug menu, context-sensitive change, 56
@DECILE function, *525*, *690*, **702–703**
@DECIMAL function, *525*, *582*, 583, **586–587**, *587*
Decimal Places button on status bar, *31*, *75*, *76*
decimal value, converting to hexadecimal, *591*, *592*
default settings
  alignment, 22
  for chart type, **329–330**
  resetting, 61–62
  restoring for number format, 172
  for sorting, 354
definition box, for terms in Help, 79
degrees
  function to convert radians to, **712**
  function to convert to radians, **703**
@DEGTORAD function, 257, *525*, *690*, 700, **703**
Delete Current Version command, in shortcut menu, 448
Delete Version command, 443
deleting
  cell comments, 224
  cell contents, 88, **94–95**
  custom SmartFill list, 220
  database records using query, **374–375**
  range of cells, 112
  records from external database, 409
  records in query result, 365
  scripts, 412, 418
  title from map, 339
  x-axis for chart, 308
dependent variable, in regression analysis, 479
depreciation, 242

arguments for functions, **248–249**
function for double-declining balance method, 248, 250, **602–604**, *604*
function for fixed-declining balance method, 248, 250, **601–602**, *602*
functions for, **248–251**, *250*, *596–597*
straight-line method, 248, 250, **631–632**
sum-of-the-years'-digits, 248, 250, **632–634**, *633*
variable-rate declining balance method, 248, 250, **636–638**, *638*
derivative of error function, **589–590**, *589*
descending sort, 355
description, of workbook file, 115
Designer frame, 199
Desktop interface, 4
destination file updating, 497
  automatic, 505
destination workbook, 498
@DEVSQ function, *525*, *730*, **742**
@DGET function, 390, **397–399**, *525*, *567*, **572–573**, *572*
dialog boxes
  Range Selector button in, **103–105**
  vs. InfoBoxes, 59
digits, *See* numbers
dimmed commands, 52
display formats, 25
Display Version command, 443
  in shortcut menu, 448
Display Version dialog box, 449–450, *450*
distribution, 465, **474–475**, *476*
  function to measure symmetry about mean, **767–768**
  kurtosis to measure concentration, 747
distribution document, tracking, 458
division, @QUOTIENT function for, **710–711**
division by zero, 233, 235
  avoiding, 665, 668
@DMAX function, 393, 394–396, *525*, *567*, **573**, *574*
@DMIN function, 393, 394–396, *525*, *567*, **574–575**, *575*
dollar-sign character ($), for absolute reference, 136–137
double angle brackets (<< >>), for file names, 500
double-declining balance depreciation method, 248, 250, **602–604**, *604*
double-quotation mark ("), for right alignment, 93, 126, 161
doughnut charts, **326–327**, *327*

@DPURECOUNT function, 393, 396, *525*, *567*, **575–576**, *576*
drag and drop, 10
   to copy range of values, 89, **110–112**
   SmartIcon to SmartIcon bar, *71*
   to change row height, 200
   to move range, **123–125**, *123*, *124*
drag and fill, 216–217, *218*
   for dates, 227
   for time, 228
   to copy formulas, **142–143**
Drawing menu
   context-sensitive change, 56
   ➤ Drawing Properties, 432
drawn objects, on charts, **311–312**
@DSTD function, 393, 394–396, *525*, *567*, **577–578**, *577*
@DSTDS function, 393, *526*, *567*, **578**
@DSUM function, 390, 393, 394–396, *526*, *567*, **578–579**, *579*
duration, 604, 614
@DURATION function, *526*, *596*, **604–605**
@DVAR function, 393, *526*, *567*, **579–581**, *580*
@DVARS function, 393, *526*, *567*, **581**
dynamic crosstab, 383
Dynamic Crosstab dialog box, *404*, 404

E

@EDIGIT function, *526*, *787*
edit line, 7, **63–65**, *64*, 76
   cell address display in, 7
   hiding, 301
   removing, 67
Edit menu, 54, 94–95, *95*
   ➤ Check Spelling, 190
   ➤ Clear, 224
   ➤ Copy, 510
   ➤ Copy Down, 429
   ➤ Copy Right, 429
   ➤ Cut, 125
   ➤ Go To, **150–152**, 321
   ➤ Manage Links, 507
   ➤ Open Into Full Window, 379
   ➤ Paste, 125, 510

➤ Paste Link, 510
➤ Paste Special, 264, 265
➤ Scripts & Macros,
   ➤ Global Script Options, 421
   ➤ Record Script, 414, 416, 420, 429
   ➤ Run, 419
   ➤ Show Script Editor, 418, 423
   ➤ Stop Recording, 417
➤ Undo Chart Edit, 310
Edit menu (WordPad), ➤ Links, 513
edit mode, 66, 76
Edit Script Options dialog box, *421*, 421
Edit SmartIcons dialog box, 427
editing
   frozen cells, 167
   in-cell, **65–67**, 162
e-mail, to send workbooks, 437
End Sub statement, in script, 417
engineering functions, *582–583*, **584–593**
equal sign (=), to begin formula, 222
@ERFC function, *526*, *583*, **588**, *589*
@ERFD function, *526*, *583*, *589*, **589–590**
@ERF function, *526*, *582*, **588**, *589*
ERR
   from @CHIDIST function, 737
   from @DECIMAL function, 587
   from @DGET function, 399, 572
   from @FACT function, 705
   from formulas, 233
   from @HLOOKUP function, 677
   from @IRATE function, 611
   from @IRR function, 612
   from @ISBETWEEN function, 667
   from @KURTOSIS function, 747
   from @LN function, 707
   from @MATCH function, 682
   from @RANGENAME function, 656
   function to test for, **668**, *669*
   in @IF statement conditions, 664
   as numeric value, 671
@ERR function, 521, *526*, *643*, **651**
   @CELL function and, 647
   using with @IF function, 666
error function
   complementary, 588
   derivative of, **589–590**, *589*

error function—Fit rows to page, as print option

@ERF function to return, 588
errors
  closed script workbook and, 428
  in formulas, **233–235**
errors in typing, correcting, 22
Escape (Esc) key
  to back out of menus, 13
  to close window control menu, 8
@EVEN function, *526*, *690*, **703**
@EXACT function, *281*, 283, *526*, *785*, **789–790**
exchanging data between applications, 5
exiting Lotus 1-2-3, 3, **23**, 52–53
@EXP2 function, *527*, *690*, **704**
expanding outlines, 493
@EXP function, 259–260, *526*, *690*, **704**
exploding, pie chart wedge, 315, **327–328**, *328*
exponential functions, **259–260**
exponentiation, 225–226
external database
  deleting records from, 409
  queries on, 391, **406–409**
  recalculation of functions referring to, 566

F

F probability test, **744**, *745*
@FACT function, *527*, *690*, **705**
@FACTLN function, *527*, *690*, **705**
factor argument, in @VDB function, 249
factorials, function for, **705**
false condition, logical formula to test, 228–229
@FALSE function, *527*, *662*, **664**
@FDIST function, *527*, *730*, **742–743**
F-distribution of probability, **742–743**
field argument, for database arguments, *568–569*
field names
  as column headings, 40
  in database, 345, *346*, 346
  and sorting, 355
fields in database, 40, 345
  adding to query table, 373–374
  calculations on numeric fields in, **392–405**
  selecting to display in query, 368
  structure for, 41
"File already exists" message, 116

File menu, *12*, 54
➤ Close Script Editor, 418, 424
➤ Exit 1-2-3, 53
file names in, 150
➤ Internet,
  ➤ Open, 84
  ➤ Publish, 84
  ➤ Save, 84
➤ New Workbook, 175, 415, 440, 463, 501
➤ Open, 122
➤ Preview and Page Setup, 204
➤ Print, 104, 204
➤ Save, 118, 130
➤ Save As, 33, 115, 456
➤ TeamConsolidate, 438
  ➤ Share Sheets, 459
➤ TeamReview, 438, 456–457
➤ User Setup,
  ➤ 1-2-3 Preferences, 262, 506
  ➤ SmartFill Setup, 218, 219
  ➤ SmartIcons Setup, 69, 425
➤ Workbook Properties, 62, 79
  View tab, *168*
File menu (Lotus Approach), ➤ Print Preview, 402
file names
  in File menu, 150
  in header or footer, 209
  long, 114
file references, **500–501**
  Range Names list box for, 496
files. *See also* workbooks
  function to test for existence of, **668–670**
Fill dialog box, 217
filling ranges, **216–217**
  with copied formulas, 121
  with labels, 212
  with number series, 212
financial functions, **248–256**, *594–597*, **594–640**
@FINDB function, *527*, *785*, **791**
@FIND function, *281*, 282, *527*, *785*, **790–791**, *791*
Find/Sort Assistant dialog box, 370, 371, 376–377
  Condition 1, *372*
  Find Type tab, *371*
Fit all to page option, when printing, 208
Fit columns to page, as print option, 209
Fit rows to page, as print option, 209

fixed-declining balance depreciation method, 248, 250, **601–602**, *602*
  vs. double-declining balance method, 603
Fixed number format, 172
fixed periodic payment, for loan payback, **253–254**
Font command (shortcut menu for Help), 82
fonts
  appearance, **198–201**
  for chart text, 305, 325
  for range of cells, 179
  on status bar, *19*, 19, 75, *76*
footers
  creating, **209**
  on printed output, 179
@FORCAST function, *527*, *730*, **743–744**
Form Assistant dialog box, 384
  Fields tab, 384, *385*
  Layout tab, 384
formatting, 148–149, **150–176**
  alignment of data, **160–164**
  column widths, **153–158**, *156*
  existing worksheet, **150–152**
  hiding columns, **158–160**
  numeric values, **170–176**
form letter, 384
forms, 383, **384–385**, *385*
formula markers, in cell contents, **224–225**, *225*
formulas, 23, **27–30**, *31*, **130–147**, 214, **220–235**
  adjustment after moving range, 124
  categories, **225–233**
    date and time, **226–228**
    logical, 213, **228–231**, *231*
    numeric, **225–226**
    text, **231–233**, *232*, *233*
  characters to begin, **220–222**
  comments to document, **222–225**
  converting to current value, 242
  copying, 30, 111–112, 121, **134–143**
  copying with drag and fill, **142–143**
  data entry of, **28–31**, 121, **131–134**, 212
    using Navigator, **133–134**
  elements in, 130
  errors in, **233–235**
  F9 to convert to value, 263–264, 272
  filling ranges with copied, 121
  input value to yield target result, 461

order of operations, **143–144**
  pointing technique to enter, **132**, 191–192
  for schedules using time values, **191–193**
  storing notes with, 213
  what-if scenarios, **145–146**
fraction, for time value, 188
frame for versions, hiding, 447
Freeze Titles dialog box, *166*, 166
freezing titles when scrolling, 149, **166–167**
frequency distribution, *See* distribution
Frequency Distribution dialog box, 477
@FTEST function, *527*, *730*, **744**, *745*
@FULLP function, *527*, *787*
function keys
  F1 for help, 79, 237
  F2 for edit mode, 66
  F3 for @Function List dialog box, 520
  F3 for Range Name dialog box, 356, 502
  F4 to switch to Point mode, 106
  F4 to toggle cell reference type, 137
  F5 for Go To, 151, 321
  F8 to recalculate what-if table, **470**
  F9 for recalculation, 262, 263
  F9 to convert function or formula to value, 263–264, 272
  F10 to activate menu bar, 12, 54
@Function List dialog box, **236**, *236*, *237*, 519
  Category list, *244*, 244
  to add to Function Selector list, 238–239, *239*
functions, 214, **235–240**
  arguments for, 215, 240, 520–521
  calendar, **542–565**
  categories, 242–243, 244
  database, **393–399**, **566–581**
  data entry of, **236–240**
  date and time, **269–277**
  elements of, **240**, 520–521
  engineering, **582–593**
  exponential, **259–260**
  F9 to convert to value, 263–264, 272
  financial, **248–256**, **594–640**
  help for, 213, **520**
  how they work, **214–216**
  information, 642, **644–662**
  list of, 64–65, *65*, 213
  logarithmic, **259–260**

logical, **277–279**, 642, **662–674**
lookup, **286–289**, 642, **674–687**
mathematical, **256–269**, **688–728**
overview, 518–541
quick reference, **521–541**
statistical, **244–247**, *246*, *247*, **729–782**
text, **280–286**, **784–807**
in text formula, 232
to begin formula, 222
trigonometric, **257–259**
using, **519–521**
Function selector in edit line, *64*, 64–65, *65*, *109*, 109, **236**, 519
customizing list, **238–239**, 520
future value
function for, **253**
number of periods required for payments to equal, **617–619**
future value of investment, **606–608**
@FV2 function, *528*, *597*
@FVAL function, *528*, *594*, **606–608**
@FVAMOUNT function, *528*, *594*
@FV function, **253**, *528*, *594*, **606**

G

@GAMMA function, *528*, *583*, **590**
@GAMMAI function, *528*, *583*, **590–591**
@GAMMALN function, *528*, *583*, **591**
General number format, 172
@GEOMEAN function, *528*, *730*, **744–745**, *747*
global column width, 153
Global Script Options dialog box, *421*, 421
global scripts, 413, 418
keyboard shortcuts for, 413, 421
goodness of fit, chi-square test for, **737**, *738*
Go To command, **150–152**
Go To dialog box, *151*, 151
for chart, 314
chart names in, 321
database name ranges in, 353
@GRANDTOTAL function, *528*, *730*, **745–746**, *746*
and @SUBTOTAL function, 723
grid lines, 27
removing display, 149
removing for workbook, *169*, 169

group message, when sending worksheet to team, 458
groups, in reports, **399–403**, *402*
groups of versions, 443, **451–453**, *454*

H

@HALFP function, *528*, *787*
hand, mouse pointer as, 72
@HARMEAN function, *528*, *730*, **746–747**
harmonic mean, **746–747**
headers, 179, **209**
help, **77–83**, *78*
context-sensitive, 47, **79–80**, *80*
for functions, 213, **236–237**, *238*, **520**
search by keyword, 47
text for Action menu command, 422
Help menu, 55
➤ Help Topics, 77, 82
➤ Lotus Internet Support, 83
➤ Lotus Home Page, 84
➤ Tour, 83
Help Topics window, 81
Help window
Contents tab, 77
features, **80–82**
shortcut menu for topic in, 81–82, *82*
hexadecimal value
converting decimal to, **591**, *592*
converting to decimal, **586–587**
hexadecimal values, 588
@HEX function, *528*, *583*, **583**, **591**, *592*
hiding
columns, **158–160**
details, outline and, 490, *491*
edit line, 301
frame for versions, 447
range of columns, 148
SmartIcons, 301
status bar, 301
high-low-close-open (HLCO) charts, **334–336**, *335*
@HLOOKUP function, 215, **287–289**, **677–678**, *679*, 680, 687
@COORD function and, *528*, *649*, *674*
holidays, excluding from working day calculation, 557, 564
Home key, 10

horizontal bar chart, 310
horizontal lines, **201–202**, *202*
horizontal lookup table, function to return cell contents from, **677–678**, *679*
horizontal scroll bar, 8
@HOUR function, 270, *528*, *543*, **555**
hyperbolic cosecant, function to return, **701**
hyperbolic cosine, function for, **699**
hyperbolic cotangent, function for, **700**
hyperbolic secant, function to return, **719–720**
hyperbolic sine, function to return, **721**
hyperbolic tangent, function to return, **727**

I

icons, *See* SmartIcons
IDE (integrated development environment), 414, 417
   opening, 423
identity matrix, 484
@IF function, 230, *529*, **662**, **664–666**, *665*
   @CELL function and, 243, 647
   nested, 279, 350
imported data, @DATEVALUE function and, 552
in-cell editing, **65–67**, 162
incomplete Beta function, **586**
incomplete gamma function, **590–591**
independent variable, in regression analysis, 479
indexed keywords, 77, 82
@INDEX function, 287, *529*, *674*, **678–680**, *680*, 687
   @COORD function and, 649
@INFO function, *529*, *643*, **651–653**, *654*
Infobox for cell, 19
InfoBox for chart properties, 293
   Basics tab, *321*, 321
   Ranges tab, *308*, 308
   Type tab, *295*, 295, *304*, 304, 310, *319*, *324*
   vs. SmartIcons, 320
InfoBox for Draw Object, *432*
InfoBoxes, 18–19, *19*, **58–62**, *58*
   collapsing, 319
   opening, 62, 152
   options in, **60–62**
   viewing results of, 59
   vs. dialog boxes, 59
InfoBox for Legend, *306*, 306
InfoBox for plot properties, Layout tab, 319
InfoBox for Preview & Page Setup Properties, *205*, 205
   Headers and Footers tab, *209*, 209, 211
   Include tab, *210*, 210
   Margins, orientation and placement tab, 211
   Named style tab, *206*
InfoBox for Query Table, *370*
InfoBox for range properties, *19*, 105, *152*
   Alignment tab,
      Align across columns, *161*, 163
      Wrap text in cell, 164
   Basics tab, 108
      column width controls, 154, 158, 164
      Height box, 200
      Hide column, 158, 160
   Cell Comments tab, *223*, 223
   Color, pattern and line style tab, *199*, 199
   Font tab, 200
   Named style tab, *203*, 203
   Number format tab, *171*, 171–172
      date formats, *181*, 181, *183*, 183
      Show in Frequently Used List, 173
      Time formats, 188
   Security tab, *194*
      protecting cells, 194
   Versions tab, *442*, 442
InfoBox for Series, 334
InfoBox for sheet, *59*, 59, *153*
   Basics tab, 60
      Default column width, 153
      Height, 164
      Lock contents of protected cells, 194, 195
      Tab color, 75, 187
   Number Format tab, *60*, 60, *171*, 171
      date formats, *181*, 181
   Outline tab, *61*, 61, *492*, 492
   View tab, *61*, 168
      Grid lines, 200
InfoBox for Title, *325*, 325
InfoBox for x-axis, 304–305, *305*
InfoBox for y-axis, Number format tab, *305*, 305
information functions, 642, *643–644*, **644–662**
input argument, for database arguments, *568*
input cells, and worksheet protection scheme, 193
input value

for formula to yield target result, 461, 465, **474–475**, *476*
inserting
  rows and columns, 120, **123–130**
insert mode, 66–67
Ins key, 66
integers
  formatting values as, 174
  function to return for numeric value, 705
integrated development environment (IDE), 414, 417
  opening, 423
interest payment of periodic loan payment, function to return, **608–609**
interest rate
  in functions, 251
  function to calculate, 255
  function to return to produce future value from annuity, **610**
  for investment of present value to increase to future value, **630–631**
internal rate of return
  function to return, **255–256**, **611–613**, *613*
  modified, **615–616**, *617*
international currency formats, 174
international financial functions, *597*
international text functions, *787*
Internet, **84**
Internet Explorer (Microsoft), 84
@INT function, 257, *529*, *690*, **705–706**
  with @RAND function, 260–261
inverse trigonometric functions, **258–259**, *259*
Invert Matrix, 465, **481–487**
Invert Matrix dialog box, *485*
@IPAYMT function, *529*, *594*, **608–609**
@IRATE function, *529*, *595*, **610–611**
@IRR function, **255–256**, *529*, *596*, **611–613**, *613*
@ISAAF function, *529*, *663*, **666**
@ISAPP function, *529*, *663*, **667**
@ISBETWEEN function, *529*, *663*, **667**
@ISEMPTY function, *529*, *663*, **667–668**, *802*
@ISERR function, *529*, *663*, **668**, *669*
@ISFILE function, *530*, *663*, **668–670**
@ISMACRO function, *530*, *663*, **670**
@ISNA function, *530*, *663*, **670**
@ISNUMBER function, **277–279**, *530*, *663*, **670–671**
@ISRANGE function, *530*, *663*, **671–672**

@ISSTRING function, *530*, *663*, **672**
Italics button, on status bar, 32, 198

J

Join dialog box, *380*, 380
joining strings, 213
join operation
  with @DGET function, 390, 398
  for related tables, 350, **378–382**, *382*
  using database functions, 394

K

Keep Help on Top command (shortcut menu for Help), 82
keyboard
  arrow keys, 96
  to preselect range, 106
  to select range, 89
keyboard shortcuts
  Alt+hyphen for Control menu, 8
  Alt+spacebar for Control menu, 52
  Alt+Tab to switch applications, 53
  for copy and paste, **113**
  Ctrl+Z for undo, 95
  custom vs. built-in, 423
  for cut and paste, 125
  for global scripts, 421
  for menus, 12
key fields, sorting by multiple, **357–359**, *360*
keys to sort, column for, 355
keywords
  help search by, 47
  indexed, 77, 82
@KURTOSIS function, *530*, *730*, *747*

L

Label format, 176
Label mode, 76, 92
label prefix, function to return, 646
labels, 21

alignment, 22, 160
  centering, 149
  in chart, 292
  creating range names from, 120
  data entry of, 3, **25–27**, **92–94**, 96–97
    testing for, 804
  for date entry, 181
  in default sort, 354
  displaying long, 92–94, *93*, *94*
  evening spacing in cell, 161
  filling ranges with, 212
  function to retrieve from database table, **572–573**
  function to return with specified length, **805–806**, *806*
  joining, 213
  on worksheet tabs, **186–187**, *187*
  wrapping long, 149
landscape print orientation, 207
@LARGE function, *530*, *690*, **706**, *707*
largest value, *See* maximum
leap year
  and date functions, 548
  function to determine, 550
left alignment, single-quotation mark (') for, 93, 161
@LEFTB function, *530*, *785*
@LEFT function, 280, *281*, *530*, *785*, **792–793**, *792*
left-justification, 22
legend for chart, 298, 299, 301
  position of, 306
@LENGTHB function, *530*, *785*, 794
length of database, 40
@LENGTH function, *281*, 283, *530*, *785*, **793–794**, *794*
life, as depreciation function argument, 248
linear trend, forecast value for alpha based on, **743–744**
line charts, **316–322**, *317*
  stacked vs. unstacked, 314
links between files, 496–497, **498–516**
  links to unopened files, 496
  with OLE, **510–513**, *515*
  source workbook revision, **504–505**
  updating files, **506–508**
Links dialog box (WordPad), *514*
list, function to return value or label from, **676**, *677*
List All option, in Function Selector, 236
list boxes, scrollable, 60

literal numeric values, in formulas, 28
literal strings, in text formula, 232
@LN function, 259–260, *530*, *690*, **707**
loan
  function to calculate payment, **620–623**
    and Canadian mortgage conventions, **623–624**
  interest payment on, **608–609**
  principal payment on, **624–626**
Loan Amortization SmartMaster, *464*, 464
logarithm. *See also* natural logarithm
logarithmic functions, **259–260**
@LOG function, 259–260, *531*, *690*, **708**
logical formulas, 213, **228–231**, *231*
logical functions, **277–279**, 642, **662–674**
logical operators, 229, 278
long file names, 114
Long International Date, 552
long labels, wrapping, 149
lookup functions, **286–289**, 642, *674*, **674–687**
lookup table, 243
  horizontal, function to return cell contents from, **677–678**, *679*
  lookup, function to return cell contents in specific cell, 684
Lotus Approach, 4, 366, 383
  Print Preview from, 402
  for query, 40
  switching to, 403
Lotus home page, 47, 84, *85*
Lotus Multibyte Character Set (LMBCS)
  function to return character based on number code, 284, **788**
  function to return number code for character, **789**
Lotus Notes, 459
LotusScript, 414, 415
  opening IDE, 423, 431
@LOWER function, *281*, 282, *531*, *785*, **795**, *796*

M

macro language, 415
macros, function to check for, **670**
Macro Trace window, @INFO function to determine status, 652
Mailing Label Assistant, 386, *387*
mailing labels, 383, **386–387**, *388*

preview, *388*
Manage Links dialog box, *507*, 507
manual recalculation, 242, 262–263
manual updating, of links between workbooks, 507
Map menu, context-sensitive change, 56
maps, 315, **337–340**, *338*
  abbreviations in, 338
  creating, **339–340**
  deleting title from, 339
margins, for printing, **208**
@MATCH function, *531*, *674*, **681–682**
mathematical correlation, analysis, 461
mathematical functions, **256–269**, *689–692*, **688–728**
matrix, 481
matrix arithmetic, **483–485**, *484*
@MAX function, 245, *531*, *730*, **748**, *748*
Maximize button, *9*, 9
  for window, 50, 51
Maximize command (Control menu), 52
maximum value
  function to return from database table, **573**, *574*
  @PUREMAX function to return, **757**, *758*
@MAXLOOKUP function, *531*, *674*, **682**
@MDURATION function, *531*, *596*, **614–615**
mean. *See also* average
  geometric, **744–745**
  harmonic, **746–747**
  normal distribution function for, **750–751**
median, @PUREMEDIAN function to return, **758**
@MEDIAN function, *531*, *730*, **749**
memory available, function to return, 653
menu bar, 7, **11–13**, 76
  activating,
    with Alt or F10 key, 2, 12
Menu mode, 76
menus, **54–56**. *See also* shortcut menus
  choosing commands, **12–13**
  command description on title bar, 49–50
  context-sensitive, **56**
  dimmed commands on, 52
messages
  "File already exists," 116
  "Protected cell," *196*
  when sending worksheet to team, 458
Microsoft Internet Explorer, 84
Microsoft Network, 84

@MIDB function, *531*, *785*, 798
@MID function, *281*, 281, 286, *531*, *785*, **796–798**, *797*
@MIN function, 245, *531*, *543*, *730*, **749–750**, *750*
Minimize button, *9*, 9
  for window, 51
minimum, @PUREMIN function to return, **759**, *759*
minimum value, function to return from database table, **574–575**, *575*
@MINLOOKUP function, *531*, *674*, **682–683**
@MINUTE function, 270, *531*, **556**
minutes, converting to decimal time value, 191
@MIRR function, *531*, *596*, **615–616**, *617*
mixed cell references, 139
mixed charts, 315, **332–334**, *333*
mode, @INFO function to determine, 652
mode indicator, on status bar, *22*, 22, *76*, 76
@MOD function, **267–268**, *531*, *690*, **708**
modified annual duration for security, **614–615**
modified internal rate of return, **615–616**, *617*
@MODULO function, *532*, *690*, **708**
@MONTH function, 270, 274, *275*, *532*, *543*, **556**
months
  filling cells with names, 216
  function to return, 550
  function to return number between dates, **548–550**, *550*
mouse
  for menu commands, 12–13
  to change column width, **155–156**
  to preselect range, 106
  to select range, 88
  to size window, 50
mouse pointer, *6*, 7, 8
  on chart item, 304
  as double-headed arrow icon, *155*, 155
  as hand, 72
  moving, 2, 9
    to named cell, 148
  as paintbrush icon, 186, 201
  when copying range, 111
Move command (Control menu), 52
moving
  1-2-3 window, **50–51**, *51*
  cell pointer, 2
  charts, 292, **301–302**, *303*
  range of cells, 120, **123–127**

to first cell, 10
to last column of worksheet, 10
to last row in worksheet, 10, *11*
to named cell, 148
multiple linear regression, **712–714**
multiple pie charts, **328–329**, *329*
multiplication, function for, **756**
Multiply Matrix, 465, **481–487**
Multiply Matrix dialog box, *486*

N

NA
  function to test value for, **670**
  in @IF statement conditions, 664
  as numeric value, 671
@NA function, 521, *532*, *643* **654–655**, *655*
Name dialog box, *107*, *129*, 129
named ranges, Navigator button to move to, 64
names
  for cell ranges, 89, **107–109**
  for charts, 314, **320–322**
  for sheet tab, 47, **74–75**, *74*
  of workbook files, 7
natural logarithm, **707**
  of gamma function, 591
Navigator button in edit line, *64*, 64, **108–109**
  database name ranges in, 353
  and Go To command, 151–152
  to enter formula, **133–134**
negative values
  function to sum, **771**, *772*
  function to test for, **720**
nested @IF functions, 279, 350
net present value, **619–620**
@NETWORKDAYS function, 272, *532*, *544*, **557–558**
New Sheet button, *13*, 13, 15, 73, 74, 348
New Version command, in shortcut menu, 448
New Version dialog box, *445*, 445
New Version Group dialog box, 451–452, *452*
New Workbook dialog box, 415
  SmartMaster list, 463
New Workbook SmartIcon, 175
@NEXTMONTH function, 272, *532*, *544*, **558–559**

@N function, *281*, 283, *532*, *674*, **683**
nonblank cells
  function to count, **739–740**, **757**
  in database table, **570–571**
nonprinting characters, @CLEAN function to remove, **789**
normal distribution function for mean, **750–751**
@NORMAL function, *532*, *730*, **750–751**
#NOT# operator, 229, 278
"not available," function to return, **654–655**, *655*
notes. *See also* comments
  for charts, 326
  storing with formulas, 213
@NOW function, 269, 272, *532*, *543*, **556**, **560**
@NPER function, *532*, *595*, **617–619**
@NPV function, 251–252, *532*, *596*, **619–620**, *621*
  and @IRATE function, 611
@NSUM function, *532*
number format, restoring default, 172
Number Format dialog box, for time format, 561
numbers. *See also* values
  in sort, 361, *362*
  to begin formulas, **221**
number series, filling range with, 212
@NUMBERSTRING function, *532*, *787*
numeric fields in database, calculations on, **392–405**
Numeric Format button on status bar, *19*, 19, 75, 76, 172–173, *173*
  options, *20*, *30*
  Percent format, 30
numeric formats
  examples of common, **172**
  function to return for cell, 645–646
numeric formulas, **225–226**
nutritional information, 25–27

O

objects
  printing, **210**
  properties, 46. *See also* InfoBoxes
@ODD function, *533*, *690*, **709**
OLE (Object Linking and Embedding), 5, 497, 498, **510–513**
  @DATALINK function to create links, **649–650**
  links, 497

one-tailed probablility of chi-square distribution, **736–737**
one-variable what-if table, 460, **467–469**, *468*
Open dialog box, *509*, 509
   Combine option, **508–510**
   for external database, 407
opening
   InfoBoxes, 62, 152
   workbooks, 122
Open SmartIcon, 122
operating system, function to return, 653
option buttons, 61
#OR# operator, 229, 230, 278
OR, for database query, 372
order of precedence, in formulas, **143–144**, 226
orientation of print, **207–208**
Original version, 446
outline frame, demoted rows on, *493*
outlines, 461, **489–494**
   collapsing details, *491*, 493–494
   expanding, 493
output range, copying selected data to, **368–370**

P

page count, in header or footer, 209, 211
page fit, for printed page, **208–209**
page number, in header or footer, 209, 211
paintbrush icon, mouse pointer as, 186, 201
panes, 36
   dividing workbooks into, 2, 14
parentheses
   in functions, 240
   to begin formulas, 222
   to override precedence rules, 143–144
password, 89
   assignment when saving workbook, **116–118**
   case sensitivity of, 117
   to lock workbook, 106
Paste SmartIcon, 112
Paste Special dialog box, *264*, *430*, 430, *512*
   Formulas as values, 264, 265
path, function to return, 651
payment argument, in @PV function, 252
@PAYMT function, *533*, *595*, **620–622**
   vs. @PMT function, 622

percentage, displaying ratio as, 30
percentile
   function to calculate for xth sample, **752–753**, *753*
   function to return for numeric value, **754–756**, *755*
@PERCENTILE function, *533*, *730*, **752–753**, *753*
Percent number format, 172
periodic loan payment, function to return interest payment of, **608–609**
period key (.), to anchor range, 100
periods
   as depreciation function argument, 248
   number required for payments to accumulate to future value, **617–619**, **634–635**
permutations, function to return number of, **751–752**
@PERMUT function, *533*, *731*, **751–752**
Picture editor, for SmartIcon, *426*
pie charts, 314, **322–329**, *323*
   exploding wedge, 315, **327–328**, *328*
   multiple, **328–329**, *329*
   three-dimensional, **326–327**
@PI function, 257, *691*, *709*
planning worksheets, **23–25**
plot, 319
plus sign (+), to start formula, 132
@PMT2 function, *533*, *597*
@PMTC function, *533*, *595*, **623–624**
@PMT function, 215, *533*, *595*, **622–623**
@PMTI function, *533*, *595*
pointing technique
   to create file reference, 501
   to enter formulas, **132**, 191–192
Point mode, 76, 99
point size, 200
   for chart text, 325–326
   for range of cells, 179
   on status bar, *19*, 19, **32–34**, *33*, 75, *76*, *198*, 198
@POISSON function, *533*, *731*, **753–754**
population covariance, function to return, *740*
populations, z-test to return associated probability, **781–782**
population standard deviation
   of database field values, **577–578**, *577*
   function to return, *760*, *761*, **768–769**, *769*
   vs. sample standard deviation, 762
population variance, 245
   function to calculate, **763–764**, *764*, **776–777**, *778*
   function to return for field of database table, **579–581**, *580*

portrait print orientation, 207
position of SmartIcon bar, 47
positive values
  function to sum, **772–773**, *772*
  function to test for, **720**
@PPAYMT function, *533*, *595*, *608*, **624–626**
@PRANK function, *533*, *731*, **754–755**, *755*
preferred chart type, 329
preselecting, range of cells, **105–107**
presentation of data, 178–179
presentations, worksheet preparation for, **32–34**
present value
  function for, 251–252
  of series of equal cash flows, **628–630**
Preview menu, context-sensitive change, 56
preview of printed page, 179, 204–205, *205*
@PRICE2 function, *534*, *597*
@PRICE function, *534*, *595*, *596*, **626–627**
principal payment on loan, **624–626**
Print dialog box, *206*, 206
printed page, adjusting worksheet size to, 179
Printer dialog box, *207*, 207
printing, 179, **204–211**
  Help topic, 81
  margins for, 208
  objects, **210**
  selecting settings, **207–210**
Print Topic command (shortcut menu for Help), 81
probability, F-distribution of, **742–743**
procedure call, 423
procedures, scripts as, **423–424**
processor-intensive function, 741
@PRODUCT function, *534*, *731*, **756**
@PROPER function, *281*, 282, *534*, *786*, **798–799**, *799*
properties of object, 46. *See also* InfoBoxes
"Protected cell" message, *196*
protection mode, deactivating, 196
protection scheme
  for worksheet, 178, 193
@PUREAVG function, *534*, *731*, **756**
@PURECOUNT function, *534*, *731*, **757**
@PUREMAX function, *534*, *731*, **757**, *758*
@PUREMEDIAN function, *534*, *731*, **758**
@PUREMIN function, *534*, *731*, **759**, *759*
@PURESTD function, *534*, *731*, **760**, *761*, 761
@PURESTDS function, *534*, *731*, **761–763**, *762*

@PUREVAR function, *534*, *731*, **731–764**, *764*
@PUREVARS function, *534*, *731*, **764–766**, *765*
@PV2 function, *535*, *597*
@PVAL function, *535*, *595*, **629–630**
@PVAMOUNT function, *535*, *595*
@PV function, **251–252**, *535*, *595*, **628–629**

Q

quarter, function to return, 550
@QUARTILE function, *535*, *691*, **709–710**
queries, 40, **43–44**
Query by Box tool, 365, *376*, 376–377, 408
Query menu, context-sensitive change, 56
query object, creation from database table, *369*
Query Table Assistant dialog box, *367*, 367
  external table in, *406*, 406
Query Table menu
  ➤ Edit, 371, 379
  ➤ Query Properties, 409
  ➤ Query Table Properties, 381
query tables, 364, 366
  adding field to, 373–374
  copying range, 409
  editing to change source table, **375–378**, *378*
  worksheet for, 367
"Quick key" for scripts, 422
quick menu, *See* shortcut menus
quick reference
  calendar functions, *543–545*
  engineering functions, *582–583*
  functions, **521–541**
  information functions, *643–644*
  international text functions, *787*
  logical functions, *662–663*
  mathematical functions, *689–692*
  statistical functions, *729–732*
  text functions, *784–787*
@QUOTIENT function, *535*, *691*, **710–711**

R

R Squared value, 481
radar charts, **336**, *337*
radians, 257

radians—recalculation

function to convert degrees to, 703
function to convert to degrees, 712
@RADTODEG function, 257, *535*, *691*, 693, 694, 695, 700, 712
@RAND function, 257, **260–265**, 429, *691*, 711
  and automatic recalculation, **261–264**
  converting entry to value, 263–264
random numbers. *See also* @RAND function
  script for, **429–430**
  sorting, *265*, 265
  using, **264–265**
random order, for record arrangement, 243
range of cells. *See also* filling ranges
  alignment, 149
  converting to current value, 242
  copying values, **110–114**
    with drag and drop, 89
  copy and paste, 89
  deleting, 112
  filling with copied formulas, 121, **142–143**
  filling with number series, 212, **216–219**
  font or type size, 179, **198–201**
  format applied to selected, 149
  function to return number of rows, **656–657**
  function to test for, **671–672**
  Infobox for, *19*, 19
  moving, 120, **123–127**
  name for, 89
  names for, **107–109**
  notation for, 101
  number format for, **173–174**
  period (.) to anchor, 100
  preselecting, **105–107**
  printing, 210
  selecting, 56, **100–107**
    with keyboard, 89
    with mouse, 88
range of columns
  hiding, 148
  selecting, 154
  width changes, **154–155**
Range menu, 55
  ▶ Analyze, **465–488**, *465*
    ▶ Backsolver, 465, **474–475**, *476*
    ▶ Distribution, 465, **474–475**, *476*
    ▶ Invert Matrix, 465, **481–487**

  ▶ Multiply Matrix, 465, **481–487**
  ▶ Regression, 465, **478–481**
  ▶ What-If Table, 465, **466–474**
vs. Chart menu, 39
context-sensitive change, 56
  ▶ Delete Columns, 333
  ▶ Fill, 217
  ▶ Insert, 127
  ▶ Insert Rows, 197
  ▶ Name, 107, 129, 250, 352
  ▶ Range Properties, 62, 105, 152
  ▶ Sort, 42, 265, 353, 354, 355, 357
  ▶ Transpose, **487–488**
  ▶ Version, 438, **441–443**, *441*
    ▶ Delete Version, 443
    ▶ Display Version, 443, 449
    ▶ New Version, 442, 445
    ▶ Report, 443, 454
    ▶ Version Groups, 443, 451
    ▶ Version Properties, 442, 448
@RANGENAME function, *535*, *643*, **655–656**
range names
  absolute reference from, 136
  creating from labels, 120
  defining for database tables, **352–353**
  in file references, 501
  in formulas, 132
  list in Navigator button, 64, 108
  selecting from list, 121
  undefined, and ERR, 233, 234–235
Range Names dialog box, *356*, 356
  for open file reference, 496
Range Options dialog box, *308*, 308
Range Properties command (shortcut menu), 18
Range Properties SmartIcon, 62, 105, 152, 199
Range Selector button
  in dialog boxes, **103–105**
  in Print dialog box, *104*, 104
Range Selector window, *106*, 106
Range SmartIcon bar, *68*
@RANK function, *535*, *731*, **766**, *767*
rate argument, in @PV function, 252
@RATE function, **255**, *535*, *597*, **630–631**
ratio, displaying as percentage, 30
Ready mode, 22, 76
recalculation

automatic, 23–24, **34–36**. *See also* automatic recalculation
manual, 242, 262–263
recording scripts, 412, **415–417**
Record Script dialog box, *416*, 416
records in database, 344. *See also* database records
red dot, in cells, 224, *225*
@REFCONVERT function, *535*, *644*, **656**
references, *See* cell references; file references
Region Check dialog box, 338
Regional Settings Properties dialog box (Windows 95), Number tab, List separator, 215
Regression, 465, **478–481**
Regression dialog box, *480*, 480
@REGRESSION function, *535*, *732*, **712–714**
relational operators, 229, 278
relative cell references, 135
  in copied formula, 139
remainder, after division, 708
remainder of division, function for, 267–268
@REPEAT function, *281*, 283, *535*, *786*, **799–800**
repeating characters, **165**
@REPLACEB function, *536*, *786*
@REPLACE function, *281*, 282, *536*, *786*, **800–802**, *801*
Report Assistant dialog box
  Fields tab, 400, *401*
  Groups tab, 400, *401*
  Layout tab, *400*, 400
  Totals tab, 401, *402*
reports, 383, 390–391
  with groups and totals, **399–403**, *402*
  revising, 391
  from versions, 443
    creating, **454–456**
Reset to Workbook Defaults option, 61–62
Restore button, 8, 50, 52
restoring hidden columns, 148, 160
revisions, preventing accidental, **193–197**
right alignment, 162
" (double-quotation mark) for, 93, 126, 161
@RIGHT function, *281*, 281, *536*, *786*, **802–803**, *803*
right mouse button, for shortcut menu, 18, 56–57, *57*
@RIGHTB function, *536*, *786*, 802
@ROUND function, 257, **266–267**, *267*, *536*, *691*, **714–715**
@ROUNDDOWN function, *536*, 555, *691*, **715–716**

rounding
  to nearest even integer, **703**
  to nearest odd integer, **709**
@ROUNDM function, *536*, *691*, **716–717**, *717*
@ROUNDUP function, *536*, 555, *691*, **718–719**
row range, *102*
@ROWS function, *536*, *644*, **656–657**
rows in worksheet, 7
  copying data between range of columns and, 461, **487–488**
  function to return for cell, 646
  inserting, 120, **123–130**, 197, *198*
  manually changing height, 200
  moving to final, 10, *11*
Run Scripts & Macros dialog box, *419*, 419
running scripts, 412, **419–420**

S

@S function, *281*, 283, *536*, *786*, **803–804**, *804*
salvage, as depreciation function argument, 248
sample, standard error of mean, **721**
sample covariance, function to return, **740**
sample population variance
  function to calculate, **764–766**, *765*, **778–779**, *779*
  function to return for field of database table, **581**
sample standard deviation
  of database field values, **578**
  function to return, **761–763**, *762*, **770**, *771*
  vs. population standard deviation, 762
sample variance, 245
Save As dialog box, 114, *115*, 115–116
Save SmartIcon, 118, 130
saving
  existing files, 89
  scripts with workbook, 418
  workbooks, **114–118**
    existing file, **118**
    first time, 89, **115**
    password assignment, **116–118**
scatter chart, 331
@SCENARIOINFO function, *536*, *644*, **657–658**
@SCENARIOLAST function, *536*, *644*, **658–659**
schedules
  adjustments to, 192–193, *193*

using formulas for time values, **191–193**
Scientific number format, 172, 221
screen display
  freezing titles when scrolling, **166–167**
  function to return size, 653
  removing grid lines, 149
Script menu, context-sensitive change, 56
script recorder, 414
scripts, **412–433**
  benefits of, 414
  for company address, 420
  creating button for, **430–432**
  creating SmartIcon for, **425–428**
  deleting, 418
  in editor, 430
  examining details, **417–419**
   412–413
  global, 418
  as procedures, **423–424**
  for random numbers, **429–430**
  recording, 412, **415–417**
  running, **419–420**
  writing from scratch, 425
scroll bars, 8
scroll box, 10
scrollable list boxes, 60
scrolling, freezing titles when, 149, **166–167**
search criteria, 40
searching text strings, function for, **790–791**, *791*
@SEC function, *536*, *560*, *691*, **719**
secant, function to return, **719**
@SECH function, *536*, *691*, **719–720**
@SECOND function, 270, *537*, *543*
securities
  accrued interest for, **598–599**, *600*
  annual duration for security paying periodic interest, **604**
  modified annual duration for, **614–615**
  price per $100 face value, **626–627**
  yield for, **639–640**
selecting
  cells, 8
  cells inside frozen range, 167
  charts, 302
  noncontiguous rows for pie chart, 323
  range of cells, 56, **100–107**

  range of columns, 154
  worksheet, 3
selection criteria, for database records, **43–44**
selection indicator in edit line, 63, *64*
  chart names on, 321
Selection keyword in script, 430
@SEMEAN function, *537*, *691*, **721**
semicolon (;)
  for comments, 222
  as standard argument separator, 215
@SERIESSUM function, *537*, *583*, **592–593**, *593*
server in OLE, 510
Set Default Chart dialog box, 329–330, *330*
Set Password dialog box, *117*, 117, 196
@SETSTRING function, *537*, *786*, **804–805**, *806*
shades, in stacked area chart, 320
Sheet menu, 55
  context-sensitive change, 56
  ▶ Outline, 489
    ▶ Clear Outline, 494
    ▶ Demote Columns, 492
    ▶ Demote Rows, 492
  ▶ Sheet Properties, 62, 152
Sheet Properties command (shortcut menu), 58
Sheet Properties SmartIcon, *62*, 62, 152, 187
sheets, *See* worksheets
@SHEETS function, *537*, *644*, **659**
Sheet SmartIcon bar, 68, *68*
sheet tabs, **73–75**, *73*
  color for, 75
  names on, 47, **74–75**, *74*, **186–187**, *187*
shortcut keys, *See* keyboard shortcuts
shortcut menu for column, *159*
  Fit Widest Entry, 158
  Fit Widest Number, 158
  Hide Columns, 158, *159*
  Unhide Columns, 160
shortcut menus, **17–19**, 46, **56–58**, *57*
  Cell Comment, *223*, 223
  for cells, *18*
  for charts, 304
  choosing command, 3
  closing, 18, 57
  Copy Down, 227, 350, 503–504
  copy and paste on, *113*, 113
  Copy Right command, 138

for Help, 81–82, *82*
for worksheet, *58*, 58
shortcut menu for version frame, *447*, 447–448
Short International Date, 552
"Show icon descriptions (bubble help)" option, 71
sideways printing, 207
@SIGN function, *537*, *691*, **720**
simultaneous equations, 461
   matrix command for, 482–483
   solving, **485–487**
@SIN function, 257, *258*, *537*, *691*, **720**
sine, function to return, **720**
single-quotation mark (')
   for comments, 425
   for left alignment, 93, 161
   to designate labels, 97
@SINH function, *537*, *691*, **721**
Size Columns SmartIcon, 158
Size command (Control menu), 52
sizing
   1-2-3 window, **50–51**, *51*
   charts, 292, 300, **301–302**, *303*
@SKEWNESS function, *537*, *732*, **767–768**
slash key (/), for 1-2-3 Classic Window, 20
@SLN function, 248, 249, 250, *537*, *596*, **631–632**
@SMALL function, *537*, *691*, **721–722**, *722*
smallest value, *See* minimum
SmartFill list
   creating custom, 218–220, *219*
   deleting custom, 220
SmartFill Setup dialog box, *218*, 218–220
SmartIcon bars, 77
   automatic display changes, 68
   changing contents, 47, **69–71**, *69*
   changing shape, 47, *72*, *73*
   for charts, *295*, 320
   customizing, 67
   displaying different, 47
   position of, 47, *72*, 72
   for recording scripts, *416*, 416
   viewing list, 17, 67–68, *68*
SmartIcon menu, ➤ SmartIcons Setup, 69
SmartIcons, 4, 7, **16–17**, 67–72
   creating for script, **425–428**
   description of, 3
   displaying, 415

hiding, 301
for scripts, 413
SmartIcons Setup dialog box, *68*, **69–71**, *69*, *70*, *71*, 425
   to add custom SmartIcon, *427*, 427
SmartMasters, 460, **462–464**
@SOLVER function, *644*
Sort command, for database, 41
Sort dialog box, *355*, 355, *356*, 356, *361*
   for multiple sort keys, *358*, 359
   for random numbers, *265*, 265
   for two-key sort, *42*, 42, *43*
sorting
   capitalization and, 795
   databases, **42–44**, *42*, *43*, 343, **353–362**
   default order, 343, **361–362**
   default settings for, 354
   by multiple key fields, **357–359**, *360*
   previous instructions saved, 359
source workbook, 498
space characters, function to strip, **807**
spelling, **190–191**
@SPI function, *537*, 595
Split dialog box, *14*, 14, 184
spreadsheets, 4
@SQRT function, 260, *537*, *691*, **722–723**
@SQRTPI function, *537*, *691*, **723**
squared deviations, function to calculate sum, **742**
square root, function to return, **722–723**
stacked charts, 316, *317*
   area chart, *318*, 320
   bar chart, 307
      three-dimensional, *309*, 309
   line charts, 314
standard argument separator, 215
standard deviation for population, 245
   of database field values, **577–578**, *577*
   function to return, **760**, *761*, **768–769**, *769*
standard deviation for sample, 245
   of database field values, **578**
   function to return, **761–763**, *762*, **770**, *771*
standard error of sample mean, **721**
Start menu, Lotus 1-2-3, 5
statistical functions, **244–247**, *246*, *247*, *729–732*, **729–782**
status bar, 3, 7, **19–20**, **75–76**, *76*, 77

status bar—text string

alignment on, *19*, 19, 75, *76*, *161*, 161, 186
buttons for charts, *295*
Calc on, 262
hiding, 301
Italics button on, 32, 198
Numeric Format button, *19*, 19, 75, *76*, 172–173, *173*
Style button on, *19*, 19, **32–34**, *33*, 75, *76*, 202, 204
Std Err of Coef, 481
Std Err of Y Est, 481
@STD function, 245, *537*, *732*, 761, **768–769**, *769*
@STDS function, 245, *537*, *732*, 761, **770**, *771*
Step mode, @INFO function to determine status, 652
stock market chart, **334–336**, *335*
Stop Recording SmartIcon, 417
straight-line depreciation method, 248, **631–632**
@STRING function, 284, *538*, *786*, **806–807**
strings
    converting case, 243
    converting digits to number value, 285
    converting number to, 243
    converting to dates, 271
    function to test for, 672
    joining, 213
Student's *t*-distribution, function to return, **773–774**, *775*
style names, **202–204**
styles, 25
    on status bar, *19*, 19, **32–34**, *33*, 75, *76*, 202, 204
sub, 417
substring functions, **280–282**
subtitle, of charts, 301
@SUBTOTAL function, *538*, *692*, **723–724**, *724*
    @GRANDTOTAL function and, **745–746**
sum
    of power series, **592–593**, *593*
    of values in field of database table, **578–579**, *579*
@SUM function, 28–29, 99–100, 244, *538*, *692*, **724–725**
summary reports, 391, 403
    from versions, 437
summary of versions, 443
@SUMNEGATIVE function, *538*, *732*, **771**, *772*
sum-of-the-years'-digits depreciation method, 248, 250, **632–634**, *633*
@SUMPOSITIVE function, *538*, *732*, **772–773**, *772*

@SUMPRODUCT function, 242, 245, 246–247, *247*, *538*, *692*, **725**
Sum SmartIcon, 98–99, *99*, 134
sum of squared deviations, **742**
sum of squares, **726**
@SUMSQ function, *538*, *692*, **726**
@SUMXMY2 function, *538*, *692*, **726**
switch argument, in @VDB function, 249
switching between applications, 46, **53–54**
@SYD function, 248, 249, 250, *538*, *597*, **632–634**, *633*
system information, function to return, **651–653**, *654*

T

tables, functions to select from, 286–289
tab line for workbook, 7, *13*, 13, 15, 77
Tab-scroll arrows, on tab line, 73
tabs, *See* sheet tabs
@TAN function, 257, *258*, *538*, *692*, **727**
tangent, function to return, **727**
@TANH function, *538*, *692*, **727**
@TDATESTRING function, *538*, *544*
@TDIGIT function, *538*, *787*
@TDIST function, *538*, *732*, **773–774**, *775*
@TDOW function, *538*, *545*
team development of versions, **456–459**
TeamMail dialog box, 457–458, *458*
TeamReview dialog box, *457*, 457
templates, *See* SmartMasters
@TERM function, **254–255**, *539*, *595*, **634–635**
@TERM2 function, *539*, *597*
text box, 60
text formulas, **231–233**, *232*, *233*
text functions, **280–286**, **784–787**, **784–807**
text properties, on status bar, *19*, 19
text string
    color of, 199
    converting to lowercase, **795**, *796*
    converting to value, **809**
    function to convert to initial caps, **798–799**, *799*
    function to convert to uppercase, **807–809**, *808*
    function to convert value to, **806–807**
    function to repeat, **799–800**
    function to replace characters in, **800–802**, *801*

text string—US Dollar number format 835

function to return cell contents if, **803–804**, *804*
function to return characters in middle, **796–798**, *797*
function to return first characters, **792–793**, *792*
function to return last characters, **802–803**, *803*
function to return number of characters, **793–794**, *794*
function to search, **790–791**, *791*
function to strip space characters from, **807**
function to test for, 672
text wrap, in cells, 93, 161, 163
@TFIND function, *539*, *787*
three-dimensional charts
  pie charts, **326–327**
  SmartIcons for, 320
  stacked bar chart, *309*, *309*
three-dimensional range, *103*
  selecting, 106
three-variable what-if table, **472–474**, *474*
time, 22
  arithmetic, **189–190**
  calculating elapsed, 561
  data entry for, **187–189**
  displaying current, 243
  formula for elapsed, 227
  formulas for, **226–228**
  in header or footer, 209
@TIME function, 271, *539*, *543*, **561**
  vs. @TIMEVALUE function, 562
time functions, **269–277**
@TIMEVALUE function, 271, 276, *539*, *544*, **561–562**
time values
  converting minutes to decimal, 191
  displaying, 178
  formats for, 188
  formulas in schedules for, **191–193**
  function to return, **561–562**
title bar, **49–50**, 76
  of Lotus 1-2-3, command description in, 11
  for window, 9
  worksheet name in, 49
titles
  in chart, 292, 301
  deleting from map, 339
  freezing when scrolling, 149, **166–167**
  for y-axis, deleting, 305

@TLDATESTRING function, *539*, *545*
@TLEFT function, *539*, *787*
@TLENGTH function, *539*, *787*
@TMID function, *539*, *787*
@TNUMBERSTRING function, *539*, *787*
@TODAY function, 269, *274*, 349, *539*, *543*, **562–563**
Total
  automatic formula creation for, 98
  in row or column, 28, *29*
totals, 88
  in reports, **399–403**, *402*
Totals workbook, **501–504**
tracking distribution document, 458
transpose command, **487–488**
Transpose dialog box, *488*
@TREPLACE function, *539*, *787*
@TRIGHT function, *540*, *787*
trigonometric functions, **257–259**
  inverse, **258–259**, *259*
@TRIM function, *281*, 283, *540*, 786, **807**
true condition, logical formula to test, 228–229
@TRUE function, *540*, 663, **672–674**, *673*
@TRUNC function, *540*, 692, **728**
@TTEST function, *540*, *732*, **774–776**, *777*
two-dimensional range, *102*
two variable what-if table, 460, **470–471**
type size, *See* point size
typeover mode, 66–67

U

unary operator, 229
Undo command (Edit menu), **95–96**
Undo SmartIcon, 95
undoing, last command, 88
Universal SmartIcon bar, *68*, 68
unopened files, links to, 496
unsaved workbooks, option to save when exiting, 53
unstacked charts, 316, *317*
unstacked line charts, 314
Untitled, 8
@UPPER function, *281*, 282, **807–809**, *808*
  quick reference, *540*, *786*
US Dollar number format, 172, 173

user name, function to return, 653
Use System Colors command (shortcut menu for Help), 82

V

@VALUE function, 284, *285*, *285*, *540*, *786*, **809**
Value mode, 76
  for formula entry, 132
Value mode indicator, 22
values, 22
  absolute, function for, **692–693**
  alignment, 160
    default, 22
  automatic formatting, **175**
  converting to dates, 271
  converting decimal to hexadecimal, **591**, *592*
  converting formula to, 242
  converting hexadecimal to decimal, **586–587**
  converting @RAND function entry to, 263–264
  converting to string, 243
  converting text string to, **809**
  data entry of, 3, **28–31**, **97–98**
  in default sort, 354
  entering dates as, 181
  factorial of, **705**
  formatting, **170–176**
  function to convert to string, **806–807**
  function to retrieve from database table, **572–573**
  function to test for, **670–671**
  global application of format, 149
  replaced with asterisk, 157
@VAR function, 245, *540*, *732*, 764, **776–777**, *778*
variable-rate declining balance depreciation method, 248, 250, **636–638**, *638*
variables, in simultaneous equations, 482–483
variance, 245, 580
variance of population
  function to calculate, **763–764**, *764*, **776–777**, *778*
  function to return for field of database table, **579–581**, *580*
variance of sample
  function to calculate, **764–766**, *765*, **778–779**, *779*
  function to return for field of database table, **581**
@VARS function, 245, *540*, *732*, 764, **778–779**, *779*

@VDB function, 248, 249, 250, *540*, *597*, **636–638**, *638*
Version Assistant, 442, *443*, 445
@VERSIONCURRENT function, *540*, *644*, **659**
@VERSIONDATA function, *540*, *644*, **660–661**
Version Groups dialog box, *453*, 453, *454*
@VERSIONINFO function, *540*, *644*, **661–662**
Version Report dialog box, 454–455, *455*
versions, 436–437, **441–459**
  defining, **444–446**
  defining additional, **448–449**
  sample worksheet preparation, **438–441**, *439*
  switching, **447–448**, *447*
  team development of, **456–459**
vertical lookup table, function to return cell contents in specific cell, 684
vertical scroll bar, 8
View menu, 54–55
  ▶ Clear Split, 15
  ▶ Hide Edit Line, 67, 301
  ▶ Hide SmartIcons, 301
  ▶ Hide Status Bar, 301
  ▶ Show Edit Line, 67
  ▶ Show SmartIcons, 415
  ▶ Split, 14
  ▶ Titles, 166, 167
  ▶ Zoom, 170
viewing, 1-2-3 Classic window, 3
@VLOOKUP function, **287–289**, *541*, *674*, 680, **684–685**, *685*, 687
  @COORD function and, 649

W

@WEEKDAY function, 269, 279, *541*, *543*, **563**
week of year, function to return, 550
@WEIGHTAVG function, *541*, *732*, **780**, *781*
Welcome to 1-2-3 window, 5, *6*, 48
what-if analysis, 24, 34, 122, **145–146**
  charts for, **310–311**
what-if table, 460, 465, **466–474**
  one-variable, **467–469**, *468*
  three-variable, **472–474**, *474*
  two-variable, 460, **470–471**
What-If Table dialog box, *468*, 468, *473*, 473
Window menu, New Window, 15

Windows 95 applications, common features, 48
Windows 95 Clipboard, 94
  copy and paste with, 112
Windows 95 taskbar, window reduced to button, 51
windows
  arranging, **8–11**
  closing, 15
  multiple open for same file, 15
  splitting to view multiple worksheets, 184
  for workbook, 48
Windows menu, 55
WordPad, 510–512, *512*, 515
Workbook Properties dialog box, 62, *63*, **168–170**
  Security tab, Lock workbook, 196
  View tab, *168*, *224*, 224
    Custom zoom, 169–170, *170*
    Grid lines option, 169
Workbook Properties SmartIcon, 62, 79
workbooks, 5
  adding worksheets to, **13–15**, *13*, 74
    fast tracks, 2, 47
  combining, **508–510**
  dividing into panes, 2, 14
  link for data within word processor, 510–513, *512*
  links between, 496
  locking, 196
  multiple windows for same file, 15
  name of, 7
  as OLE server, 497
  open files in Range Names list, *502*, 502
  opening, 122
  option to save when exiting, 53
  protection for, 178
  reducing size, 8
  removing grid lines, *169*, 169
  revising source for links, **504–505**
  saving, **114–118**
    for first time, **115**
  saving existing, 89, **118**
  saving scripts with, 418
  for scripts, 414–415, 416
  sending in e-mail, 437
  with sums of data from other workbooks, 497
  tabbed sheets in, 10
  for totals from other workbooks, **501–504**
  updating links when opening, 506

workbook windows, 48
  arranging, **8–11**
@WORKDAY function, 272, *541*, *544*, 547, **563–565**
working days, function to return number between 2
  dates, **557–558**
Worksheet Assistant dialog box, 368
  for external database, 407
Worksheet menu
  ➤ Add Field, 381
  ➤ Find, ➤ Find All, 379
Worksheet menu (Classic window), Window,
  Horizontal, 21
worksheets, 5, **7–11**. *See also* printing
  active, *13*, 13
  adding to workbook, 2, **13–15**, *13*, 47, 74
  button for script on, **430–432**
  changes in, **123–130**
    inserting rows and columns, **127–130**
    moving ranges, **123–127**
  column width changes on, 148
  creating chart from, 292
  creating from SmartMaster, **463–464**
  finishing touches, **197–204**
  formatting existing, **150–152**
  function to return for cell, 646
  function to return number in range, **659**
  last cell in, *11*
  moving to last column, 10
  name in title bar, 49
  number format for, **173–174**
  planning, **23–25**
  preparing for presentation, **32–34**
  preventing accidental revisions, **193–197**
  protection scheme for, 178
  publishing on World Wide Web, 5
  for query table, 367
  saving for first time, 89
  selecting, 3
  sending to team members, 457–458
  splitting window to view multiple, 184
  viewing or hiding features, 168
worksheet tabs, **73–75**, *73*
  color for, 75
  names on, 47, **74–75**, *74*, **186–187**, *187*
World Wide Web, 47
  1-2-3 to publish information on, 84

Lotus support on, 83
publishing worksheets on, 5
wrapping, long labels, 149

X

x-axis for chart, 298, 299
  changing title, 303
  deleting, 308, 319
  InfoBox for, 304–305, *305*
@XINDEX function, *541*, *674*, 680, **686–687**, *687*
@XIRR function, *541*, *596*
@XNPV function, *541*, *596*
XY charts, **331–332**, *332*
  and regression analysis, 479

Y

y-axis for chart, 298, 299
  changing title, 303
  deleting title, 305, 319

multiple on mixed chart, 334
number format for, 293
@YEAR function, 270, *541*, *543*, **565**
years
  data entry as labels, 318
  function to return number between dates, **548–550**, *550*
@YIELD function, *541*, *596*, **639–640**
@YIELD2 function, *541*, *597*
y-intercept, 480

Z

zero, division by, 233, 235
  preventing, 665, 668
zoom operation in map creation, 315, 339, *340*, 340
@ZTEST function, *541*, *732*, **781–782**

SYBEX BOOKS ON THE WEB!

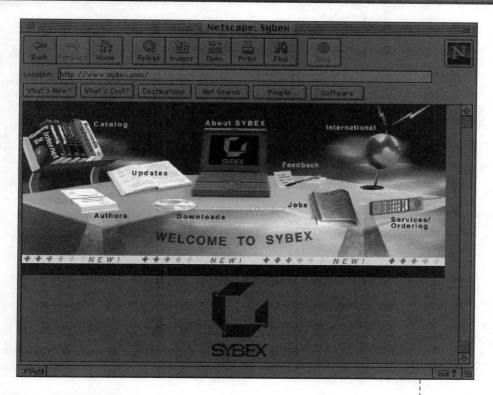

Presenting a truly dynamic environment that is both fun and informative.

- download useful code
- e-mail your favorite Sybex author
- preview a book you might want to own
- find a job
- order books
- learn about Sybex
- discover what's new in the computer industry

http://www.sybex.com

SYBEX Inc. • 1151 Marina Village Parkway • Alameda, CA 94501 • 510-523-8233